FAST TRACK TO A 5

Preparing for the **AP®**
World History
Examination

To Accompany
The Earth and Its Peoples
5th and 6th Editions
by Richard W. Bulliet, Pamela Kyle Crossley, Daniel R. Headrick, Steven W. Hirsch, Lyman L. Johnson, and David Northrup

Barbara Brun-Ozuna
Paschal High School, Fort Worth, Texas

Esther Adams
Walter Johnson High School, Bethesda, Maryland

Theisen Healey
Walter Johnson High School, Bethesda, Maryland

Nathan Schwartz
Walter Johnson High School, Bethesda, Maryland

Patrick Whelan
St Stephen's Episcopal School, Bradenton, Florida

David Uhler
Walter Johnson High School, Bethesda, Maryland

Michael Williams
Walter Johnson High School, Bethesda, Maryland

CENGAGE Learning®

Australia • Brazil • Japan • Korea • Mexico • Singapore • Spain • United Kingdom • United States

D1288505

National Geographic Learning/Cengage Learning is pleased to offer our college-level materials to high schools for Advanced Placement®, honors, and electives courses. To contact your National Geographic Learning representative, please call us toll-free at **1-888-915-3276** or visit us at **http://ngl.cengage.com.**

For permission to use material from this text or product, submit all requests online at **www.cengage.com/permissions** Further permissions questions can be emailed to **permissionrequest@cengage.com.**

ISBN-13: 978-1-285-76316-3
ISBN-10: 1-285-76316-5

Cengage Learning
200 First Stamford Place, 4th Floor
Stamford, CT 06902
USA

Cengage Learning is a leading provider of customized learning solutions with office locations around the globe, including Singapore, the United Kingdom, Australia, Mexico, Brazil, and Japan. Locate your local office at: **www.cengage.com/global**.

Cengage Learning products are represented in Canada by Nelson Education, Ltd.

To learn more about Cengage Learning Solutions, visit **www.cengage.com**.

To find online supplements and other instructional support, please visit **www.cengagebrain.com**.

AP® and Advanced Placement Program® are trademarks registered and/or owned by the College Board, which was not involved in the production of, and does not endorse, this product.

Printed in the United States of America
4 5 6 7 8 9 10 20 19 18 17 16

CONTENTS

ABOUT THE AUTHORS

This edition of *Fast Track to a 5* was revised by Barbara Brun-Ozuna and Patrick Whelan.

BARBARA BRUN-OZUNA holds a bachelor degree in history from Texas Christian University and a master's degree in history from the University of North Texas. She has taught AP European History, AP Human Geography, and Pre-AP World Geography at Paschal High School in Fort Worth, Texas. She began the AP World History program for the Fort Worth school district in 2001. She serves as a College Board consultant in world history and an AP World History reader and table leader.

PATRICK WHELAN earned a bachelor degree in history from Yale University. In addition to AP World History, he has taught AP U.S. History, AP European History, AP Art History, Humanities, Holocaust Studies, and English at Saint Stephen's Episcopal School in Bradenton, Florida. He has scored AP World and European History examinations since 1998 and has served as a College Board institute and workshop consultant for AP World History.

****

Walter Johnson High School, in Bethesda, Maryland, was recognized by the College Board for having a higher proportion of its students pass the 2005 AP World History Examination than any other high school of comparable size in the world. *Fast Track to a 5: Preparing for the AP World History Exam* was written by five teachers in the school's Social Studies Department:

ESTHER ADAMS earned a bachelor degree in history and a master of teaching from the University of Virginia. In addition to AP World History, she has taught AP U.S. History; Global History; Senior Project; U.S. National, State, and Local Government; Latin American Studies; and Model United Nations. She has graded AP World History examinations for four years, two as a reader and two as a table leader. In addition to writing the chapters for the period 600–1450, she served as coordinator for the writing of this book.

THEISEN HEALEY holds a bachelor degree in history from the University of Michigan and a master of education from George Washington University. Courses he has taught include AP U.S. History; U.S. National, State, and Local Government; AP European History; Philosophy; Peace Studies; and Model United Nations; as well as AP World History. He wrote the Foundations review chapters, covering the period ca. 8000 B.C.E.–600 C.E. He is chairman of the Social Studies Department at Walter Johnson High School.

NATHAN SCHWARTZ has a bachelor degree in Social Studies/History Education from the University of Maryland and a master of education from Bowie State University. Before joining the Walter Johnson faculty, he was chairman of the Social Studies Department at Surrattsville High School in Prince George's County, Maryland. He has taught both regular and honors sections of every core social studies course, and now teaches AP World History, AP U.S. History, and Model United Nations. His chapters review the period 1750–1914. He began as an AP World History examination reader in 2007.

DAVID UHLER has a bachelor degree in international affairs from George Washington University and graduate certification in secondary teaching from American University. A book editor before becoming a teacher, he has taught U.S. History, Modern World History, and Model United Nations, along with AP World History. Author of the chapters covering the period 1450–1750, he started reading AP World History examinations two years ago.

MICHAEL WILLIAMS, a professional soccer player for eight years, has taught for six years. He has a bachelor degree in political science from Howard University, a master's degree in history from Northwestern University, and a master in the art of teaching from Johns Hopkins University. He teaches both U.S. History and AP World History. He wrote Chapters 21–25, the review of the period from World War I to the present.

ACKNOWLEDGMENTS

This book is dedicated to our past, present, and future students and to students around the world who seek to use world history as a vehicle for understanding humankind.

We wish to thank our families and friends, who gave us so much encouragement and support throughout the writing process. We especially want to thank all the members of the Social Studies Department at Walter Johnson High School for fostering such a collegial and creative work environment. We are indebted to Angela Lee and Bill Strickland, outstanding AP World History teachers, who reviewed the entire manuscript and provided invaluable insights. Thanks to Margot Mabie, our editor, for her tireless work and organization and, finally, to Sharon Cohen, who introduced us to this great professional opportunity.

Esther Adams
Ty Healey
David Uhler
Nathan Schwartz
Mike Williams
Barbara Brun-Ozuna
Patrick Whelan

Part I

Preparing for the AP World History Exam

PREPARING FOR THE AP® EXAM

Advanced Placement is a challenging yet stimulating experience. Whether you are taking an AP course at your school or you are working on AP independently, the stage is set for a great intellectual journey. As the school year progresses and you burrow deeper and deeper into the coursework, you can see the broad concepts, events, conflicts, resolutions, and personalities that have shaped the history of our complex world. Examining the cultural, political, and economic developments that have brought great change while acknowledging the continuities that remain throughout world history is a thrilling task. Fleshing out those forces of change and continuity in world history is exciting. More exciting still is recognizing references to those forces in the media and how history has shaped current world events.

But as spring approaches and the College Board examination begins to loom on the horizon, Advanced Placement can seem quite intimidating, given the enormous scope and extent of the information you need to know. If you are intimidated by the College Board examination, you are certainly not alone.

The best way to approach an AP® examination is to master it, not let it master you. If you manage your time effectively, you will eliminate one major obstacle—learning a considerable amount of factual material along with the analytical skills needed to be a true world historian. In addition, if you can think of these tests as a way to show off how your mind works, you have a leg up: attitude *does* help. If you are not one of those students, there is still a lot you can do to sideline your anxiety. Focused review and practice time will help you master the examination so that you can walk in with confidence and get a 5.

BEFORE THE EXAM

By February, long before the exam, you need to make sure that you are registered to take the test. Many schools take care of the paperwork and handle the fees for their AP® students, but check with your teacher or the AP® coordinator to make sure that you are on the registration list. (This is especially important if you have a documented disability and need test accommodations.) If you are studying AP® independently, call AP® Services at the College Board for the name of the local AP® coordinator, who will help you through the registration process.

The evening before the exam is not a great time for partying. Nor is it a great time for cramming. If you like, look over class notes or drift through your textbook, but concentrate on the broad outlines, not the small details, of the course. You might also want to skim through this book and read the AP tips. Then relax. Get your things together for the next day. Sharpen a fistful of no. 2 pencils with good erasers for the multiple-choice section of the test, and set out several black or dark-blue ballpoint pens for the free-response questions. You should bring a watch in order to pace yourself since you will not be allowed to use the clock or timer functions on your smart phone. Get a piece of fruit or a snack bar and a bottle of water for the break. Depending on your testing site, you may need your Social Security number, photo identification, and an admission ticket. After you have set aside all of those items, put your mind at ease, go to bed, and get a good night's sleep. An extra hour of sleep is more valuable than an extra hour of study.

On the day of the examination, make certain to eat breakfast—fuel for the brain. Studies show that students who eat a hot breakfast before testing get higher grades. You will be given a ten-minute break between Section I and Section II; the World History exam lasts for over three hours, so be prepared for a long morning. You do not want to be distracted by a growling stomach or hunger pangs. Be sure to wear comfortable clothes, taking along a sweater in case the heating or air-conditioning is erratic. When you get to the testing location, make certain to comply with all security procedures. Cell phones are not allowed, so leave yours at home or in your locker if at all possible. Be careful not to drink a lot of liquids, necessitating trips to the bathroom, which take up valuable test time.

Remember, preparation is key! Best wishes on your journey to success—go out and get that 5.

TAKING THE AP® WORLD HISTORY EXAM

The AP® World History exam consists of two sections: Section I has seventy multiple-choice questions that make up half of your overall exam score. Section II has three parts. Section II, Part A, is the document-based question (DBQ); Section II, Part B, is the continuity and change over time question; Section II, Part C, is the comparative question. You will have 55 minutes for the multiple-choice portion of the test. Answer sheets for the multiple-choice questions are then collected, and you will be given a short break. You then have a total of 130 minutes for all three parts of Section II. There is a mandatory 10 minutes for reading the documents for the DBQ. The College Board recommends that you take 40 minutes to write the DBQ essay, then spend 40 minutes—5 minutes to plan and 35 minutes to write—on each of the two other essays. The essays are weighted equally, and together they make up the other half of your total exam score. Your proctor will monitor the time, but you need to keep an eye on your watch and pace yourself so you can do your best on all three essays. Remember that watch alarms and smart phones are not allowed.

Here is a chart to help you visualize the breakdown of the exam:

Section	Multiple Choice	Free Response (Essay)		
Weight	50% of Exam	50% of Exam		
		16.7% of Exam	16.7% of Exam	16.7% of Exam
# of Questions	70	DBQ Document-Based Question	Continuity and Change Over Time	Compare and Contrast
Time Allowed	55 minutes	10 minutes mandated for reading DBQ documents; 120 self-budgeted minutes to write 3 essays		
Suggested Pace	approx. 45 seconds per question	40 minutes to write	40 minutes to plan and write	40 minutes to plan and write

THE THEMES AND HISTORICAL THINKING SKILLS

In order to be successful on the exam, the AP® World History course requires you to use all of the historical thinking skills that you have worked all year in class to develop. These skills are essential for any historian, but they are particularly critical in world history because of the large amount of content in the course. The themes and historical thinking skills were created to provide a framework upon which you can hang all of the information you have learned throughout the year.

A practical exercise that should become a habit is to ask yourself, "What theme does this piece of historical information fall under?" "What historical thinking skill am I using right now to process this information and make meaning out of it?" This will help you to see the larger historical trends and global connections that twine through our past and present and into the future.

Below are the themes and historical thinking skills for the AP® World History course. Please examine them carefully and use them throughout this review book as an essential reference tool and guideline.

THEMES

1. Interaction between humans and the environment
   - Demography and disease
   - Migration
   - Patterns of settlement
   - Technology

2. Development and interaction of cultures
   - Religions
   - Belief systems, philosophies, and ideologies
   - Science and technology
   - The arts and architecture

3. State building, expansion, and conflict
   - Political structures and forms of governance
   - Empires
   - Nations and nationalism
   - Revolts and revolutions
   - Regional, transregional, and global structures and organizations

4. Creation, expansion, and interaction of economic systems
   - Agricultural and pastoral production
   - Trade and commerce
   - Labor systems
   - Industrialization
   - Capitalism and socialism

5. Development and transformation of social structures
   - Gender roles and relations
   - Family and kinship
   - Racial and ethnic constructions
   - Social and economic classes

These themes are constant topics throughout the course, and you should be working with them from the beginning of the year. Throughout the course keep asking yourself where you see elements of both continuity and change—in particular societies, across regions, and throughout time—as they relate to each of these themes.

HISTORICAL THINKING SKILLS

One of the broader goals of AP World History is to train you to think like an historian. That begs the question, "How do historians think?" The answer is found in the historical thinking skills. As a student in any rigorous history course, you should be able to do the following:

1. Crafting historical arguments from historical evidence
   - Historical argumentation: Answer a question by making a clear and persuasive argument.
   - Appropriate use of relevant historical evidence: Make conclusions about the past by using a variety of diverse sources.

2. Chronological Reasoning
   - Historical causation: Evaluate the causes and effects for what has occurred in the past.
   - Patterns of continuity and change: Analyze history through an investigation of what has stayed the same and what has changed.
   - Periodization: Describe the turning points in history and how they help historians categorize periods of history.

3. Comparison and Contextualization
   - Comparison: View the similarities and differences among societies or among developments within one society.
   - Contextualization: Connect large historical processes to individual situations in history.

4. Historical interpretation and synthesis
   - Historical interpretation: Analyze the perspectives and points of view involved in recording and describing history.
   - Synthesis: Understand the past by using multiple historical thinking skills and disciplines other than history.

To be successful on the AP® World History exam, you need to master these historical thinking skills as well as the content. The historical thinking skills are the tools you need to unlock the meaning from the content in the multiple-choice section as well as in the free-response portion of the exam. For example, on the DBQ you will use several different historical thinking skills, from analyzing primary documents to understanding diverse interpretations. Any time you write a thesis you are constructing an argument. Clearly the continuity and change over time essay requires you to demonstrate your ability to assess continuity and change, while the comparative essay requires you to compare societies in a variety of ways. In the multiple-choice section, you will apply the historical thinking skills when you examine graphs, maps, and primary source information and you will often deal with multiple-choice questions that require an understanding of diverse interpretations or ask you to address issues of continuity and change.

The historical thinking skills are also the tools you use in the classroom every day to think critically about the content of the course. These are the tools of historians that you train with all year; by the time of the exam you should be ready to demonstrate your understanding of these historical thinking skills as well as the content of the AP World History course.

STRATEGIES FOR THE MULTIPLE-CHOICE SECTION

As mentioned in the chart above, the multiple-choice section of the test makes up 50% of your total score. Thus, it is important that you spend time learning how to master this section—especially its timing. Here are some rules of thumb to help you work your way through the multiple-choice questions:

- **Read the question carefully** Pressured for time, many students make the mistake of reading the questions too quickly or merely skimming them. By reading a question carefully, you may already have some idea about the correct answer. You can then look for it in the responses. Careful reading is especially important in EXCEPT or NOT questions because, unlike the typical multiple-choice question, all the answers are right except for one.

- **Eliminate any answer you know is wrong** You can write on the multiple-choice questions in the test book. As you read through the responses, draw a line through any answer you know is wrong.

- **Read all of the possible answers, then choose the most accurate response** AP® exams are written to test your precise knowledge of a subject. Sometimes there are a few probable answers but one of them is more accurate.

- **Mark and skip tough questions** If you are hung up on a question, mark it in the margin of the question book. You can come back to it later if you have time. Make sure you skip that question on your answer sheet too.

- **Apply the historical thinking skills and the course themes to help you answer stimulus-based questions.** Many of the multiple-choice questions will ask you to use a primary source, a pair of documents, a map or graph or chart to help answer the question.

- **Watch your time carefully!** You can spend too much time pondering potential answers—especially when you have multiple sources to synthesize. Watch the time and don't get bogged down. Instead, mark the best answer and then flag the question for review should you have time remaining at the end.

EXAMPLES OF MULTIPLE-CHOICE QUESTIONS

There are various types of multiple-choice questions. Note the historical thinking skills and the course themes required for each question.

1. Confucianism first developed in
   (A) Japan.
   (B) India.
   (C) Russia.
   (D) China.

ANSWER: **D**. Confucianism originated in China before influencing areas such as Japan.

Historical Thinking Skill: Chronological reasoning

Theme: Development and interaction of cultures

2. All of the following were true about the Taiping Rebellion EXCEPT
   (A) it was a civil war that lasted over a decade.
   (B) it stemmed partly from continuing tension over the opium trade.
   (C) it occurred during the Mongol rule in China.
   (D) it revealed the ethnic tensions in China in the mid-nineteenth century.

ANSWER: **C**. Because the Taiping Rebellion occurred during the Qing Empire and revealed many of the difficult economic, social, and political issues of China in the nineteenth century, the only "wrong" statement is that it occurred during Mongol rule in China.

Historical Thinking Skills: Contextualization, Chronological reasoning

Themes: State building, expansion, and conflict; Creation, expansion, and interaction of economic systems

Image copyright © The Metropolitan Museum of Art. Image source: Art Resource, NY

3. Using the above illustration, what would be the best description of the interaction between Japan and the West in the nineteenth century?
    (A) Japanese society rejected Western technologies.
    (B) Japanese society embraced eighteenth-century traditions.
    (C) The West had significant influence on Japan after the Meiji Restoration.
    (D) Women were influenced by the West to seek more political rights for women in Japan.

ANSWER: C. This poster shows the types of items the Japanese brought in from the West after the Meiji Restoration of the mid-nineteenth century. Western clothing and sewing machines were in high demand. The people in these three panels are shown wearing Western-style clothing.

Historical Thinking Skills: Crafting historical arguments, Chronological reasoning, Synthesis

Theme: Development and interaction of cultures

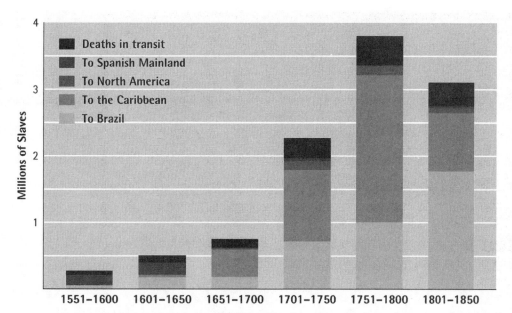

Source: Data from David Eltis, "The Volume and Structure of the Transatlantic Slave Trade: A Reassessment," *William and Mary Quarterly*, 3d Series, 58 (2001), tables II and III.

4. Which of the following statements does the above table best support?
   (A) The transatlantic slave trade remained at the same level from 1551 to 1850.
   (B) The period 1801–1850 witnessed the largest forced migration of African slaves.
   (C) Most slaves came from East Africa.
   (D) Beginning in 1651, the majority of slaves were brought to the Caribbean and Brazil.

ANSWER: **D**. After analyzing the table, option A can be eliminated because the measurement bars are not level in *any* period. Option B is incorrect because the total number of Africans in transit was highest in the period 1751–1800 and declined some in the period 1801–1850. Option C is incorrect in that there is no way to tell from the table what percentage of the slaves came from a specific region in Africa. Because the bars for transit of slaves to the Caribbean and Brazil are longest beginning in 1651, Option D is the correct answer.

Historical Thinking Skills: Appropriate use of historical evidence; Synthesis

Themes: Interaction between humans and the environment; Creation, expansion, and interaction of economic systems

Bettmann/CORBIS

5. What is the viewpoint expressed in the above cartoon?
   (A) The United States rejected the Roosevelt Corollary to the
       Monroe Doctrine.
   (B) Under Roosevelt the United States allowed European nations
       to take part in the colonization of South America.
   (C) Roosevelt brought the Caribbean under the control of the
       United States.
   (D) Roosevelt was protecting the Caribbean nations from U.S.
       intervention.

ANSWER: **C.** Roosevelt actually strengthened the Monroe Doctrine with
his Roosevelt Corollary. Therefore A and B are incorrect because one
of the primary purposes of the Monroe Doctrine and the Roosevelt
Corollary was to prevent European intervention in the Western
Hemisphere. Because the United States consistently intervened in
South American affairs, answer D is incorrect.

Historical Thinking Skills: Historical interpretation and synthesis;
Contextualization; Chronological reasoning; Use of appropriate
historical evidence

Theme: State building, expansion, and conflict

Code of Nesilim 8. If anyone blind a male or female slave or knock out their teeth, he shall give ten half-shekels of silver, he shall let it go to his home.

Hammurabi's code 17. If any one find runaway male or female slaves in the open country and bring them to their masters, the master of the slaves shall pay him two shekels of silver.

http://www.fordham.edu/halsall/ancient

6. It appears from the above excerpts of two ancient law codes that
    (A) slaves were considered property.
    (B) male and female slaves were considered equal in value.
    (C) slaves had legal rights.
    (D) silver was a common medium of exchange for slaves.

ANSWER: B. Although answers A, C, and D are also partially evident from the textual evidence, it is evident from the excerpts that both societies viewed the value of male and female slaves equally. Thus, B is the best answer.

Historical Thinking Skills: Crafting historical arguments from historical evidence; Comparison and contextualization; Historical interpretation and synthesis

Theme: Development and transformation of social structures

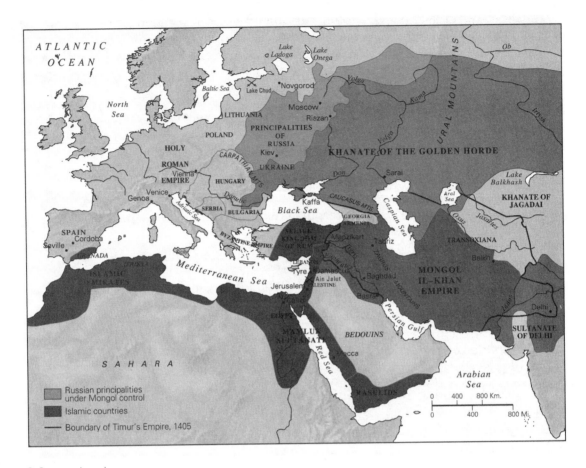

© Cengage Learning

7. This map of western Eurasia in the 1300s shows
    (A) the coexistence of Mongol domains and Islamic sultanates.
    (B) the khanate of the Great Khan, which Khubilai Khan ruled.
    (C) the Mongol takeover of all of western Eurasia.
    (D) the Mongol takeover of all of the Islamic world.

ANSWER: **A.** The map shows both Mongol khanates and Islamic kingdoms. The answer cannot be B because the domains of the Great Khan were in Central and East Asia. It cannot be C or D because we see other kingdoms that the Mongols did not control, including those of western Europe.

Historical Thinking Skills: Use of appropriate historical evidence; Historical interpretation and synthesis; Contextualization; Chronological reasoning

Theme: State building, expansion, and conflict

FREE-RESPONSE QUESTIONS

In Section II of the AP World History exam, you are required to write essays for three free-response questions. Part A presents the document-based question (DBQ). For the DBQ, you are given 10 minutes for reading the documents and organizing and outlining your material, and 40 minutes for writing the essay. Part B is the continuity and change over time essay, and Part C is the comparative essay. For Part B and Part C, you should allow 40 minutes each, 5 minutes to plan and outline and 35 minutes to write. You should carefully pace yourself during the 120 minute essay writing section so that you cover all three essay topics completely.

Each of the three essays is scored on a scale of nine, with nine the highest score. Each essay has its own rubric, with specific requirements for meeting seven basic core points. If and only if those seven basic core points are met can your essay be considered for expanded core. Expanded core can earn you one or two more points. The key to success on each of these essays is understanding and internalizing each rubric's components. That's what we will focus on here.

AP Tip

For each essay in Section II, the AP examination has built in time for you to develop an outline. Time spent on an outline is important for a number of reasons:

- It prevents you from writing an essay that is unorganized because you begin writing whatever comes into your head at the moment.
- It allows you to determine your analytical thesis after seeing the evidence you can gather to support your argument.
- It provides you with an opportunity to brainstorm before writing the essay.

Once you have outlined your essay, it is time to put pen to paper. Remember that examination readers are looking for a clear thesis backed up with specifics. Concentrate on setting out accurate information in straightforward, concise prose. You cannot mask vague information with elegant prose.

THE DOCUMENT-BASED QUESTION

As its name implies, the DBQ presents you with a wide variety of primary-source information in the form of four to ten documents. Primary sources are original material created during the time period under study, and they include everything from maps, photographs, and illustrations to excerpts of speeches, essays, books, and personal letters.

All free-response essays require you to utilize your knowledge of the topic, but with the DBQ your essay needs to be based on the documents. Your goal is to link each document to the question, and then use that information in an analytical and evaluative essay. Thus the following are necessary for a quality DBQ essay according to the AP World History rubric:

- ■ **Has an acceptable thesis (1 point)** An acceptable thesis is one that makes an analytical argument that responds specifically to what the prompt is calling for you to address in the DBQ.

- ■ **Addresses all of the documents and demonstrates understanding of all or all but one (1 point)** You need to use every document and show that you get the essential idea(s) of each one. You may misunderstand one but still get the point because you addressed it. Remember that ignoring one document is NOT the same as misinterpreting it.

- ■ **Supports thesis with appropriate evidence from all of the documents (2 points)** A thesis must be supported by good evidence drawn from each document to support the claims made in your thesis. (You can still get the two points if you misinterpret a document as long as you addressed all of the documents.) You need to demonstrate your ability to pull such evidence from each document and discuss the evidence in your own words in terms of how it relates to the thesis you have written in response to the DBQ prompt. Do not just quote the documents or summarize them in a list! You need to analyze them and show that you can make historical connections in your own words. You get only one point here if you support your thesis with evidence from all but two documents. But getting only one point here means you will not meet basic core, so make sure you use specific evidence from all of the documents!

- ■ **Analyzes point of view in at least TWO documents (1 point)** This is one of the hardest tasks on the DBQ for students to remember to do. It is very important that historians consider the author of a primary document—how class, gender, nationality, profession, and the like shaped a person's experience or interpretation of a particular historical event. Background information can help us understand why an individual might have a particular point of view or opinion or why a document might have a particular tone to it— for example, a tone of anger or a tone of respect. The type of document, the audience, and the timing of the document may also suggest point of view. You need to be able to show your ability to account for the point of view in at least two documents. It is not enough to just say what point of view you see presented in the documents; you must then account for why that point of view exists in the source. A good place to begin looking for clues to the point of view is the source line of the document. The source line gives the author or speaker in the document, the date of the document, which helps you place the document in a larger historical context, and it often has other important pieces of information about the document as well. Always read the source line carefully!

- ■ **Analyzes documents by grouping them in TWO or THREE ways, depending on the question (1 point)** Grouping documents is an important skill because it shows your ability to recognize the relationships that exist between documents. You can group documents several ways, but the answer to how you group them often lies in the prompt, which instructs you on how to approach the documents and analyze them. For example, if you are asked to analyze cause and effect, a reasonable way to organize the documents would be to group those that show causes and group those that show effect. You can also group documents by similarities and differences you see in them. Sometimes it is appropriate to group them chronologically. Again, the key is to look at what the prompt is telling you to do.

■ **Identifies and explains the need for ONE type of appropriate additional document or source (1 point)** As world historians, we are always trying to get as complete a picture as possible regarding the different points of view and experiences of individuals and societies. Therefore, the documents you are given are often not enough to get the fullest picture of a historical experience. You are asked to think about what other documents would add to your analysis of a historical situation. You should be thinking, "Whose voices am I missing?" "What particular document would help me understand this historical moment better?" You are not asked to come up with an actual primary source document that you know exists; rather <u>you are asked to come up with a realistic hypothetical source that would provide further insight in addressing the prompt.</u> For example, perhaps you are doing a DBQ on the French Revolution and you have no documents from women. A diary entry from a woman of the Second Estate in prerevolutionary France would add to your analysis of the causes of the French Revolution. The DBQ prompt gives some specifications for your additional document, so always begin with the prompt. This is another element of the DBQ that students often forget to address, so remember that you must provide an additional document AND explain WHY you need it. Be sure, too, to tie it back to the prompt.

If you meet all seven of the basic core requirements, there are many ways that you can earn up to two additional points—expanded core—on the DBQ. For example, you can offer additional groupings, analyze point of view in most or all documents, explain the need for more than just the one additional document, and bring in relevant outside historical content. You can also get expanded core if you do a particularly good job of shaping your thesis so that your argument is very clear, analyzing and covering all aspects of the prompt, analyzing the documents, or using the documents persuasively.

Take a look at this sample DBQ, one containing five documents. (You will find other DBQs in the Diagnostic Test and Practice Tests 1 and 2.)

1. Using the documents, analyze the role of ceremonial rituals in ancient Mesoamerican society. Identify an additional type of document and explain how it would help your analysis of the role of ceremonial rituals.

Document 1

Chrysler Museum of Art/Justin Kerr

Source: Illustration on a ceramic jar showing elaborately dressed Mayas involved in the ceremony of the ball game.

Document 2

Source: Modern photograph of a ceremonial center at the Maya city of Tikal.

Daniel Loncarevic/Shutterstock.com

Document 3

Source: Modern photograph of a ceremonial center at the Aztec city of Tenochtitlan.

G.Dagli Orti/The Art Archive

Document 4

Source: An Aztec elder's assessment of Toltec cultural accomplishments as recorded by a Spanish missionary.

In truth [the Toltecs] invented all the precious and marvelous things. . . . All that now exists was their discovery. . . . And these Toltecs were very wise; they were thinkers, for they originated the year count, the day count. All their discoveries formed the book for interpreting dreams. . . . And so wise were they [that] they understood the stars which were in the heavens.

Document 5

Source: Description of the Aztec ruler Moctezuma II by Bernal Diaz del Castillo, a Spaniard who participated in the conquest of the Aztec Empire.

. . . Many great lords walked before the great Montezuma, sweeping the ground on which he was to tread and laying down cloaks so that his feet should not touch the earth. Not one of these chieftains dared look him in the face.

Document 6

Source: Diego Duran, a Spanish priest writing over fifty years after the Spanish conquest of the Aztecs, excerpt from *Book of the Gods and Rites*.

I wish to give warning that even today there is a diabolical custom among the natives, especially in Cholula, where the god Quetzalcoatl was worshiped; peddlers will traffic for ten, twelve, and even twenty years, earning and saving up to two or three hundred pesos. And after all their toil, wretched eating and sleeping—without aim or reason—they offer a most lavish banquet. There they spend all their savings. What I most regret is that they follow the ancient custom of holding that memorial feast in order to celebrate their ancient titles and set themselves on high. This would not be wrong except that for their celebration they await the day on which the god Quetzalcoatl was honored.

The first step is an analysis of each document in order to come up with evidence in order to create your thesis. What is the meaning of the document? What or who is the source, and how does that affect their point of view? The source provides important clues in the position being put forth in the document. As you analyze the meaning or significance of the document, jot down margin notes—generalizations that relate to the document and the prompt. For example:

- **Margin note for Document 1** *An example of ritual permeating every area of life, including sport.*

- **Margin note for Document 2** *Shows the sophisticated architecture used to perform public ritual in ceremonial centers.*

- **Margin note for Document 3** *Similar to document two in showing the grandeur of buildings in ceremonial centers.*

- **Margin note for Document 4** *Astronomy and calendar work were very important parts of ritual life in Mesoamerican society.* This document is especially valuable for its point of view; the Aztec is praising the earlier Toltecs for their relationship to the cosmos. Questions to consider for analysis of point of view: Why would the tone be of respect? Would the fact that a Spanish missionary recorded this Aztec viewpoint influence what is said in the document?

- **Margin note for Document 5** *One of the conquerors comments on the godlike way the Aztec king is treated by the common person.* Because the source is a Spaniard, this document is interesting for its point of view. Think about why the Spaniard would comment on this public spectacle.

- **Margin note for Document 6** *A Spanish view of a ceremonial banquet honoring an Aztec god.* Would the fact that this document was written long after the Spanish conquest brought Christianity to Mesoamerica influence the reliability of the document?

Once you have done this, you should group the documents. One way to group them might be by documents specifically about the Aztecs versus those about other Mesoamerican societies. You could also group the documents that show architecture. Be thinking about what types of additional document(s) would help you answer the prompt. Also remember you need to analyze point of view for two documents. You want to account for the tone of respect that the Aztecs show the Toltecs in Document 4. You should also analyze why a Spaniard has his point of view about the behavior of the people toward Moctezuma II in Document 5 or about the banquet in Document 6. Give some thought to what you can add to reach expanded core. Finally, write your thesis, making sure it answers the prompt and shows your argument for how ritual was used in Mesoamerican society. <u>Make sure your thesis has an argument and does not just repeat the prompt.</u> With good planning at the beginning, your DBQ should be in great shape!

THE CONTINUITY AND CHANGE OVER TIME ESSAY

AP World History covers an enormous amount of time. The continuity and change over time essay is a unique essay because it asks you to step back and examine and analyze certain trends, characteristics, or patterns over a large span of time. You are often given a choice of region in which to discuss patterns of continuity and change.

One of the most challenging aspects of an essay like this is figuring out how to break down large time periods that might span hundreds or thousands of years. The most important thing is to take the reader of your essay through the entire period using key events of change and continuity. You need to be able to address continuities in history that span large time periods and account for why those continuities persist through periods of change. The following is the AP World History rubric for the continuity and change over time essay:

- **Has an acceptable thesis (1 point)** To have an acceptable thesis for the continuity and change over time essay, you need to address the entire time period in question. Take the reader through the main stages of change you will address as they pertain to the issue (for example, trade or cultural identity) that you are asked to discuss. Your thesis must also include the continuity you see present in the entire period and an overall statement of analysis. Continuity and change over time thesis statements are often hard to do in one sentence, so you want to write a well organized, clear and comprehensive thesis; if you need more than one sentence, make sure they are consecutive, flow together to make a clear thesis paragraph, and be mindful of your length.

- **Addresses all parts of the question (2 points)** The most important thing to remember here is that in order to address all parts of the question, you must discuss both change and continuity in your essay. You will only get one point for addressing the question if you address change but not continuity or vice versa.

- **Substantiates thesis with appropriate historical evidence (2 points)** Again, a thesis with no evidence to support it is unacceptable to historians. You need to cite specific examples of both change and continuity. You will get only one point if you partially substantiate your thesis with appropriate evidence. This can happen if you do not provide enough specific, relevant examples of evidence or if you do not have evidence for both change and continuity.

- **Uses relevant world historical context effectively to explain continuity and change over time (1 point)** Change does not happen in a vacuum. In world history change occurs for both short- and long-term reasons that often involve more than just one region or country. It is essential for you to place change in the larger context and identify global process, such as industrialization or imperialism, that bring about change.

- **Analyzes the process of continuity and change over time (1 point)** It is not enough to just say that something changed; you must also account for WHY the change occurred and how it impacted those in a particular region or country. You also should account for WHY continuity persisted. Remember, you always want to show your ability to analyze and do higher-level critical thinking.

If your essay meets these basic core requirements, it can be considered for up to two additional points in the expanded core. The continuity and change over time essay can receive those points for the following reasons: a clear thesis that is comprehensive while being analytical; addressing all parts of the question evenly—time periods, regions, and/or issues; providing ample evidence to support your argument; and analysis of all the issues that pertain to the time period.

THE COMPARATIVE ESSAY

The comparative essay is the third and final essay for the AP World History exam. Comparison is often thought to imply similarity, but for this essay you are expected to both compare and contrast particular characteristics in two regions. The AP World History rubric for the comparative essay is as follows:

- **Has an acceptable thesis (1 point)** Be sure your thesis makes a comparative argument that addresses the particular issues in the prompt. For example, if you are asked to compare the economic systems in China and Japan from 1750-1900, you need to be sure your thesis states how China and Japan were economically similar as well as different and why that was the case. Explaining why ensures that your thesis is analytical.

- **Addresses all parts of the question (2 points)** For the full two points, you need to address both similarities and differences. You get one point if you address only one or the other, which means you will not get basic core.

- **Substantiates thesis with appropriate historical evidence (2 points)** Appropriate means accurate. Be sure that the evidence you are using is accurate and works as a legitimate comparison. Appropriate also means that it addresses the characteristic or issue you are asked to compare. If you are asked to compare economic systems and you are providing evidence that compares social systems, that is not appropriate evidence for economic systems even if it is accurate. Work to have appropriate evidence for both similarities as well as differences. Minimal appropriate evidence will earn you one point, which means you will not get all seven basic core points.

- **Makes at least one relevant direct comparison between/among societies (1 point)** You are comparing two different regions and the societies among them. A direct comparison means that you are comparing those societies in a sophisticated and substantial manner. For instance, if you are asked to compare the political systems of the Byzantine Empire and feudal Europe, you should not discuss the Byzantine Empire in one paragraph and feudal Europe in another. You need to decide during your planning time what specific characteristics were similar and different about the two societies in terms of political structure and make sure that in each paragraph you discuss both regions. For example, if they had similar laws but different roles for kings, then one paragraph should be about law, in which you compare both societies, and one paragraph should be about the role of kings, in which you contrast both societies. Make sure that your comparisons are substantial comparisons in order to earn the point for a direct comparison.

- **Analyzes at least one reason for a similarity or difference identified in a direct comparison (1 point)** It is not enough to list the political similarities and differences between the Byzantine Empire and feudal Europe. You must also explain WHY those similarities and differences existed. Analysis flows from the direct comparison.

If you meet these basic core requirements, you can earn an additional one or two points in expanded core. Comparative essays are given those points for the following reasons: a clear thesis that is comprehensive while being analytical; addressing all parts of the question evenly—time periods, regions, and/or issues; providing ample evidence to support your argument; making several direct comparisons rather than the one or two required for basic core; and consistent analysis of the causes and effects of these direct comparisons rather than the one piece of analysis required for basic core.

To conclude, here are some tips for writing AP World History essays:

- **Thesis** Be sure that your thesis statement is at the very beginning of your essay. You need to present your main argument in the first paragraph so it is clear what you are proving in your essay.

■ **Grammar** You will not lose points for spelling or grammar errors, but it is important to write as coherently as possible. Remember, if the reader cannot understand what you are trying to say or cannot follow your arguments, it will be harder to get the necessary information across for points. It is also important to write as legibly as time permits so all of your good ideas can be understood!

■ **Dates** Do not panic if you cannot remember a specific date; try to use a broader description such as "early nineteenth century" or "around the sixth century" if you cannot remember the exact date.

■ **Quality over quantity** Remember: quality, not quantity. Writing a great deal does not mean you are writing what needs to be in your essay. Focus on making sure you are hitting all the rubric points rather than writing long introductions and conclusions. Make your argument, prove it with evidence, and wrap up. You want to have time to do all three essays well.

A DIAGNOSTIC TEST

The purpose of this diagnostic test is to provide you with an indication of how well you will perform on the AP World History examination. Keep in mind that the exam changes every year, so it is not possible to predict your score with certainty. The multiple-choice questions here are arranged so you can spot areas of weakness quickly. The multiple-choice questions are organized by the chronological units of the course. For each unit there are two questions for each region and at least four cross-regional comparative questions. For example, the first ten questions are for the periods before 600 C.E., with two questions each for Africa, the Middle East, Asia, Europe, and the Americas, followed by four comparative questions for the unit. The test follows this same format through the last chronological period. You can thus identify which periods and regions to concentrate on when preparing for the AP exam.

AP WORLD HISTORY EXAMINATION
SECTION I: Multiple-Choice Questions
Time—55 minutes
Number of questions—70

Directions Each of the questions or incomplete statements below is followed by four suggested answers or completions. For each question, select the best response in each case.

Note This examination uses the chronological designations B.C.E. (before the Common Era) and C.E. (Common Era). These correspond to B.C. (before Christ) and A.D. (anno Domini), which are used in some world history textbooks.

1. Which of the following was an effect of the Agricultural Revolution?
   (A) Early farmers lived shorter lives and had more diseases.
   (B) Early farmers worked less than hunter-gatherers.
   (C) Early farmers no longer worshipped animist religions.
   (D) Early farmers ate a more varied and nutritious diet.

2. Which of the following describes how the social structure of Mesopotamia differed from the social structures of ancient Egyptian and Indus River Valley civilizations?
   (A) Women had no property or inheritance rights.
   (B) Slavery existed only on a limited scale and included prisoners of war and debtors.

   (C) Little formal social hierarchy existed because of the disruptive nature of frequent invasion.
   (D) Priests were not very important or influential.

3. Which of the following was an important reason for the success of both the Persian Empire under Darius I and the Mauryan Empire under Ashoka?
   (A) Both allowed imperial subjects of various nationalities to follow their own traditions and culture.
   (B) Both imposed order through the widespread use of mercenary soldiers.
   (C) Both used road networks and standard coinage to promote trade and collect taxes more efficiently.
   (D) Both selected imperial officials based on successful completion of imperial examinations.

The Art Archive/Museum of Anatolian Civilisations Ankara/Gianni
Dagli Orti

4. The discovery of the figure above at
   Çatal Hüyük can be used to support
   which of the following theories about
   society in that city?
   (A) Hunting retained an important role in
       the city even as a reliance on
       agriculture increased.
   (B) There was a clear political structure
       and dominant social class in Çatal
       Hüyük.
   (C) The role of women was valued in
       Çatal Hüyük, and women may have
       played an important role in religious
       rituals.
   (D) Stone and metal work were far more
       advanced in Çatal Hüyük than in any
       other river-valley civilization.

5. Which of the following represents a
   long-lasting effect of the Arya migration
   into northwest India around 1500 B.C.E.?
   (A) They destroyed Harappa and
       Mohenjo-Daro, thus limiting our
       knowledge of these early Indus
       Valley civilizations.

(B) Their matrilineal system transformed
    the role and status of women in
    South Asia.
(C) They introduced the varna system,
    which served as the basis of the caste
    system.
(D) They brought Buddhism to South
    Asia and facilitated its spread
    through South and East Asia.

A woman's duties are to cook the five grains, heat
the wine, look after her parents-in-law, make
clothes, and that is all!.... She must follow the
"three submissions." When she is young, she
must submit to her parents. After her marriage,
she must submit to her husband. When she is
widowed, she must submit to her son.

biography of Mengzi, mother of
Confucian philosopher Mencius
(page 162)

Now examine the gentlemen of the present age.
They only know that wives must be controlled,
and that the husband's rules of conduct
manifesting his authority must be established....
But they do not in the least understand that
husbands and masters must also be served, and
that the proper relationship and the rites should
be maintained. Yet only to teach men and not to
teach women—is that not ignoring the essential
relation between them?

-Ban Zhao, "Lessons for Women"

6. The second passage qualifies the first
   passage by expanding the role of women
   to include.
   (A) education.
   (B) claiming that husbands should not
       control their wives.
   (C) denying the responsibility of
       widowed women to submit to their
       sons.
   (D) adding a fourth submission to the
       three mentioned by Mengzi.

7. Which of the following is true for both ancient Greece and Rome?
    (A) Women in ancient Greece were far less restrained politically and legally than women in Rome.
    (B) The rich soil of the Greek homeland was able to sustain a much larger population than was possible in the Roman homeland.
    (C) Romans extended citizenship to non-Romans, while the Greeks were hesitant to share such privileges with outsiders.
    (D) When they came into contact with the Romans, Greeks adopted their religious rituals and major deities as their own.

8. One of the primary reasons for Christianity's growth in the first two centuries after Jesus' crucifixion was
    (A) the efforts of missionaries and other converts to spread the religion.
    (B) the widespread acceptance of a single theological doctrine.
    (C) the appeal of Christianity to elite members of society.
    (D) the official sanction of the religion by Roman emperors.

9. The Olmec and Chavín civilizations both
    (A) developed in the Yucatan and the Valley of Mexico.
    (B) relied heavily on the llama for transportation, food, and wool.
    (C) incorporated collective labor systems that increased productivity.
    (D) developed self-sufficient economies that did not trade with other civilizations.

10. Which of the following helped enable the Chavín to become an influential civilization?
    (A) They were located at the crossroads of key trade routes, which gave them an economic advantage over their rivals.
    (B) They did not have strong religious beliefs, which helped them get along well with the diverse peoples of the neighboring areas.
    (C) Their decentralized political structure put all control at the local level, which appeased conquered peoples.

    (D) They were the first civilization in the Americas to effectively use the wheel, which gave them an economic and military advantage in the region.

11. Development of civilizations in the Americas differed from that in other regions because
    (A) the transition from nomadic, hunter-gatherer communities to settled, agricultural communities occurred much earlier in the Americas.
    (B) culture and technology in the Americas developed without the benefit of exchange and interaction with other regions.
    (C) early communities developed without the social stratification that arose in other regions.
    (D) early civilizations in the Americas did not interact with one another politically or economically.

12. Which of the following is true of the political organization of both Egypt and Mesopotamia?
    (A) Kings dominated the governing ruling structures.
    (B) Political legitimacy came from the belief that the leaders descended from the gods.
    (C) Immigration placed great strains on the culture of both societies.
    (D) Women in Egypt and Mesopotamia lacked physical freedom and legal protection.

13. Which of the following was true of the Roman and Han Empires?
    (A) The Roman Empire relied on agriculture as the main source of wealth while Han China was far more urban.
    (B) The Roman Empire had a professional military while Han leaders relied on peasants to serve as farmers and soldiers.
    (C) Opportunities for social mobility in China were far greater than in Rome.
    (D) Both empires built roads to provide military and economic advantages.

GO ON TO NEXT PAGE

14. Which of the following statements is true about Buddhism and Christianity?
    (A) Followers of both religions pray and make sacrifices to a variety of gods.
    (B) Each is tied closely to the teachings of an individual and rose from an established religion.
    (C) Most early Buddhist converts came from lower classes, while early Christians found most converts among upper classes.
    (D) Christianity experienced several divisions as time went on, while Buddhism remained a unified movement.

15. Which of the following represents a major difference between the empires of Ghana and Mali?
    (A) Unlike Ghana, Mali was a Muslim empire from the beginning.
    (B) Mali was a smaller empire than Ghana.
    (C) Ghana was not able to control the trans-Saharan trade routes, but Mali could.
    (D) Ghana controlled the trading area around the Niger, while Mali controlled the trading area around the Congo.

16. Great Zimbabwe and Calicut are both examples of
    (A) cities known for their monumental stone structures.
    (B) cities that prospered because of their location on long-distance trade routes.
    (C) walled cities that generated their wealth from agricultural production.
    (D) cities that declined and collapsed due to environmental degradation.

17. A historian describing the unity of Islam up to 1450 might use which of the following as evidence?
    (A) The formation of Shia Islam
    (B) The ethnic similarities among Muslims
    (C) The power of the caliph over all Muslim people
    (D) The dictate that the Quran be read and understood in Arabic

18. Which of the following describes changes in Muslim society in the period from 600 to 1450?
    (A) Movement away from identity-based on religion
    (B) Elimination of the political position of caliph
    (C) Increased women's rights as contact with Christian societies increased
    (D) Greater cross-cultural contacts and transfers of technologies

19. Which of the following statements helps explain the scientific and economic accomplishments of Song China?
    (A) The Song defeated the Mongol Empire in China and thus inherited all of its intellectual accomplishments.
    (B) The Song had a direct trading relationship with the Abbasid Caliphate.
    (C) The Song, not needing to defend their empire from northern rivals, focused on intellectual pursuits.
    (D) The Song inherited many of the advancements in science, technology, astronomy, and other academic fields from the cosmopolitan Tang dynasty.

20. Some historians argue that the inward-looking Ming Empire was less productive than the Mongol-ruled Yuan Empire. Which of the following pieces of evidence would refute this argument?
    (A) Ming rulers retained many aspects of Mongol rule, such as the provincial structure and the calendar.
    (B) Emperor Hongwu severely limited trade interactions with Central Asia and the Middle East.
    (C) Emperor Yongle funded the naval expeditions of Zheng He from 1405 to 1433.
    (D) Agricultural production remained level from the mid-1400s to the mid-1500s.

21. Which of the following describes a major change that occurred in the Byzantine Empire in the period 600–1450?
(A) Ties between the Eastern Orthodox and Roman Catholic Churches strengthened.
(B) A rural, family-based military aristocracy replaced rule by urban elites.
(C) Byzantine farmers used more efficient agricultural techniques.
(D) The plagues of Justinian depopulated rural areas.

22. Which of the following is a way that Kievan Russia differed from western Europe?
(A) Kievan Russia adopted Roman Catholicism rather than Orthodox Christianity.
(B) Power in Kievan Russia came from controlling trade rather than possession of land.
(C) Kievan Russia defeated the Mongols while the Mongols controlled western Europe for more than a century.
(D) Kievan Russia had weaker ties to the Byzantine Empire.

Daniel Loncarevic/Shutterstock.com

23. This photograph of the Great Plaza at Tikal, located in modern Guatemala, best exemplifies which of the following historical patterns?
(A) Environmental damage due to excessive mobilization of resources
(B) Conflict among competing city-states
(C) The development of cities as centers for religious rituals and political administration

(D) The building of fortifications to project military power over large areas

24. The Aztec and Inca Empires
(A) differed in that only the Inca established a strict social hierarchy.
(B) controlled populations made up of one ethnically homogeneous group.
(C) believed the ruler was the central political and religious authority.
(D) developed in Mesoamerica and fought against various Mayan kingdoms.

25. How did the role of tribute differ in the Tang Empire and the Aztec Empire?
(A) Unlike the Aztec Empire, the Tang Empire depended on the tribute of captured peoples to supply its food and other important material resources.
(B) The tribute system of the Tang Empire was more politically symbolic, while the tribute system of the Aztec Empire supplied a substantial percentage of the empire's material needs.
(C) Unlike the Tang Empire, the Aztec Empire required subject peoples to give tribute by sending a representative of the political elites to live at the capital.
(D) Tribute played only a minimal role for the Aztec Emmpire and was not in use by the end of the empire, but it grew in importance in the Tang Empire.

26. Which of the following is an accurate comparison of the effects of Mongol rule in the Middle East and Asia?
(A) Mongol leaders in China did not experiment with paper money after hearing of its failures from Mongol leaders in the Middle East.
(B) Mongol nobles distinguished themselves in the Middle East but were not able to penetrate the highest social rankings of Chinese society.
(C) The Mongols supported a tremendous exchange of ideas, people, technology, and culture in both the Middle East and China.

GO ON TO NEXT PAGE

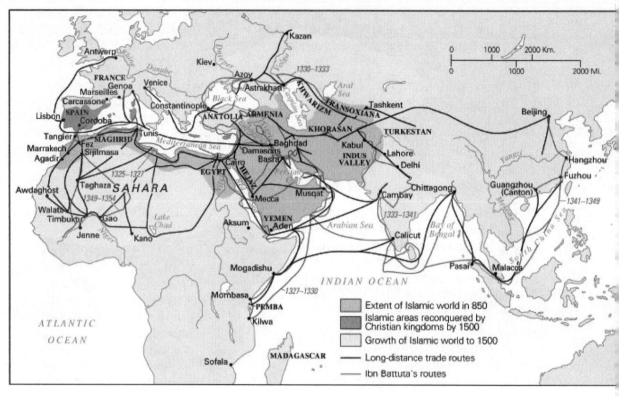

Cengage Learning

(D) The Mongols rejected both Islam and Confucianism and required conquered peoples to adopt traditional Mongolian religious practices.

27. Which of the following is an accurate comparison of the Mali Empire and the Delhi Sultanate?
   (A) Unlike Mali, the Delhi Sultanate relied on long-distance trade routes for wealth.
   (B) Mali's leaders were Arabs who invaded and established a caliphate, while the leaders of the Delhi Sultanate were originally Hindus who converted to Islam by choice.
   (C) Mali was a Muslim empire, while the Delhi Sultanate was a Hindu empire.
   (D) The rulers of the Delhi Sultanate invaded India, whereas the leaders of Mali were indigenous to the region and peacefully converted to Islam.

28. After looking at this map, what observations can be made about the growth of the Islamic world by 1500?
   (A) After the Mongol takeover, the Islamic world shrank considerably.

(B) Christian kingdoms reconquered most of the Muslim world by 1500.
(C) By 1500 the Islamic world stretched from Lisbon to Malacca.
(D) The spread of Islam coincides with the arteries of trade in Africa, South Asia, and Southeast Asia.

29. In North Africa, a continuing influence before, during, and after the period 1450–1750 was
   (A) trade of cash crops and slaves with the Americas.
   (B) unequal distribution of wealth gained from gold mining.
   (C) the Egyptian monarchy's dominance of neighboring tribute states.
   (D) the social, political, and economic practices of Islam.

30. The destruction of the West African empire of Songhai and the expansion of the slave trade in the central Sudanese kingdom of Bornu are both examples of
   (A) tribal conflict in the African interior.
   (B) the impact of European trading-post empires on states in interior West and Central Africa.
   (C) the impact of religious warfare in the African interior.

(D) the failure of powerful African rulers to defend against European military technology.

31. What is the significance of the Ottoman Empire's struggle to maintain cohesion and authority after 1585?
(A) It resulted in the empire's collapse, creating a power vacuum that led to World War I.
(B) It was caused mainly by Russia's efforts to capture Ottoman territory.
(C) It is an example of the difficulties faced by large land-based empires in an era dominated by European maritime powers.
(D) It contributed to the worldwide inflation of the sixteenth and seventeenth centuries.

32. Which of the following best explains why the Ottoman Empire made extensive use of Janissary soldiers?
(A) The Ottomans needed foot soldiers to carry guns that were too heavy for their Turkish cavalry archers.
(B) The Ottomans wished to diversify their army by incorporating soldiers with a Judeo-Christian background.
(C) Janissaries could serve as intermediaries in the sultan's peace talks with the Venetians and Portuguese.
(D) Their skills as mounted soldiers allowed them to incorporate easily into the existing military structure.

"Yesterday your Ambassador petitioned my Ministers to memorialize me regarding your trade with China, but his proposal is not consistent with our dynastic usage and cannot be entertained. Hitherto, all European nations, including your own country's barbarian merchants, have carried on their trade with our Celestial Empire at Guangzhou. Such has been the procedure for many years, although our Celestial Empire possesses all things in prolific abundance and lacks no product within its own borders."

(From "Emperor Qianlong, Edict on Trade with Great Britain," page 236.)

33. This quotation from an edict of the Chinese emperor to the king of Great Britain shows China's
(A) recognition of British naval supremacy.
(B) sense of national superiority.
(C) fear of Christian missionaries.
(D) concern over British imperialism.

34. The presence of European merchants and missionaries in Asia in the seventeenth century led to which of the following responses in Japan?
(A) a promotion of manufacturing and commerce
(B) a declaration of war following the arrival of the Portuguese
(C) a modernization of the military along European lines
(D) a banning of Christianity and the curtailing of foreign trade

35. What was an effect of Johann Gutenberg's printing press?
(A) It impressed Chinese officials, thus promoting diplomatic and trade relations between Europe and China.
(B) It provided access to the works of ancient scholars, political texts, and religious tracts, thus fueling the Renaissance and the Reformation.
(C) It enabled European monarchs to communicate more clearly and efficiently, thus stimulating the centralization of their authority and the end of feudalism.
(D) It made mass-produced, inexpensive books available for the first time, thus encouraging European officials to create a system of free public education.

GO ON TO NEXT PAGE

"The pretended power of suspending of laws or the execution of laws by regal authority without consent of Parliament is illegal; the pretended power of dispensing with laws or the execution of laws by regal authority, as it hath been assumed and exercised of late, is illegal; the levying money for or to the use of the Crown by pretense of prerogative, without grant of Parliament, for longer time, or in other manner than the same is or shall be granted, is illegal."

(From "English Bill of Rights," page 155.)

36. This quotation from the English Bill of Rights (1689) indicates that its major political concern was
    (A) between nobles and commoners over voting rights.
    (B) over the relationship between the Anglican and Catholic Churches.
    (C) between rival heirs to the British throne.
    (D) over the relative power of Parliament versus the monarchy.

akg-images

37. The image above of an Amerindian woman milking a cow illustrates
    (A) domestication of indigenous animals in the Americas prior to 1492.
    (B) high-status roles for women in Amerindian society.
    (C) the spread of European diseases to native Americans through cows' milk.
    (D) the introduction of European livestock to the Americas as part of the Columbian Exchange.

Slave Occupations on a Jamaican Sugar Plantation, 1788

Occupations and Conditions	Men	Women	Boys and Girls	Total
Field laborers	62	78		140
Tradesmen	29			29
Field drivers	4			4
Field cooks		4		4
Mule-, cattle-, and stablemen	12			12
Watchmen	18			18
Nurse		1		1
Midwife		1		1
Domestics and gardeners		5	3	8
Grass-gang			20	20
Total employed	125	89	23	237
Infants			23	23
Invalids (18 with yaws)				32
Absent on roads				5
Superannuated [elderly]				7
Overall total				304

Cengage Learning

38. Which of the following conclusions about slavery in the Caribbean is supported by the table above?
    (A) Female slaves outnumbered male slaves.
    (B) Field labor required the greatest number of workers.
    (C) Most female slaves worked in domestic jobs.
    (D) Elderly and invalid slaves were forced to work in the fields.

39. The political and social structure of the Mughal and Qing Empires were similar in that both
    (A) had a small foreign minority ruling as a strong central monarchy.
    (B) suffered agricultural shortages due to a lack of peasant farmers.
    (C) synthesized a variety of existing religious traditions to strengthen the ruler's claim to the throne.
    (D) faced few external threats and experienced generally peaceful conditions.

40. How did sub-Saharan Africans' contacts with Europeans compare with their contacts with the Islamic world from 1450 to 1750?
    (A) Muslim traders took much larger numbers of Africans as slaves than Europeans took.
    (B) English and other European languages began to replace knowledge of Arabic among traders and scholars throughout sub-Saharan Africa.
    (C) Islamic and European cultural influences were usually successfully rejected by indigenous peoples throughout sub-Saharan Africa.
    (D) Most African slaves sent to the Islamic world were women, while most taken by the Europeans were men.

41. Which region of the world experienced the least amount of change in gender and class roles between 1450 and 1750?
    (A) Africa
    (B) Europe
    (C) the Americas
    (D) the Middle East

42. Which of the following entries would you expect to see in a ship's cargo manifest for a voyage on the Atlantic Ocean between 1500 and 1800?
    (A) a ship traveling from Angola to Brazil: 100 slaves
    (B) a ship traveling from Brazil to Portugal: 10 cannon
    (C) a ship traveling from France to Nova Scotia: 10 beaver pelts
    (D) a ship traveling from the west coast of Africa to Spain: tobacco

43. Which of the following is an effect of the Berlin Conference (1885) for Africa?
    (A) West African trading empires grew.
    (B) Industrial factories opened in most of southern Africa.
    (C) The transatlantic slave trade ended.
    (D) European troops were sent to Africa to divide up the continent.

44. What was the primary goal of Muhammad Ali's program of modernization for Egypt in the early nineteenth century?
    (A) continued Egyptian imperial expansion into East Africa
    (B) the ending of British colonial rule of North Africa
    (C) the strengthening of Egypt to defend itself against foreign powers
    (D) the buildup of an industrial economy to export manufactured goods

45. In the early 1800s, the Janissary military corps revolted against state-sponsored military reform because
    (A) they resented their forced conversion to Islam.
    (B) they wanted to preserve special economic privileges associated with their status.
    (C) they wished to lead an independent Serbian state.
    (D) they wanted to avoid new taxes on tobacco and coffee.

46. One long-term reason for the collapse of both the Ottoman Empire and the Russian imperial government in the first quarter of the twentieth century was
    (A) the expense of maintaining colonial empires.
    (B) extraterritoriality for foreign residents.
    (C) the influence of socialist ideas on urban factory workers.
    (D) slow economic development and inconsistent attempts at top-down reform.

GO ON TO NEXT PAGE

Image copyright © The Metropolitan Museum of Art. Image source: Art Resource, NY

47. The Japanese print above showing the arrival of Matthew Perry's fleet in Edo Bay best demonstrates
    (A) Japanese military aggression.
    (B) Japanese feudal structure.
    (C) Japanese fascination with western technology.
    (D) Japanese advancements in manufacturing.

48. What event do Indian nationalists consider the beginning of their resistance to British colonialism and struggle for independence?
    (A) the creation of the Nawab of Bengal
    (B) the formation of the Indian Civil Service
    (C) the emergence of the British Raj
    (D) the Sepoy Rebellion

49. Nationalism in nineteenth-century Europe was most strongly centered around which of the following?
    (A) religion
    (B) social class
    (C) language
    (D) education

50. One significant change caused by industrialization in western Europe was
    (A) the end of social-class divisions.
    (B) rapid growth of urban centers.
    (C) widespread acceptance of socialism.
    (D) the growing power of religious institutions.

"It is harder, Montesquieu has written, to release a nation from servitude than to enslave a free nation. This truth is proven by the annals of all times, which reveal that most free nations have been put under the yoke, but very few enslaved nations have recovered their liberty. Despite the convictions of history, South Americans have made efforts to obtain liberal, even perfect, institutions, doubtless out of that instinct to aspire to the greatest possible happiness, which, common to all men, is bound to follow in civil societies founded on the principles of justice, liberty, and equality."

-Simón Bolívar, from the *Jamaica Letter*

51. The passage above indicates the influence of which of the following on nineteenth-century revolutionary movements in Latin America?
    (A) the rise of Napoleon in France
    (B) the abolition movement
    (C) the writings of Enlightenment thinkers
    (D) the defeat and occupation of Spain and Portugal

"The descendants of the Spanish conquerors, who knew nothing of labor or thrift, have incessantly resorted to fresh loans in order to fill the gaps in their budgets. Politicians knew of only one solution of the economic disorder—to borrow, so that little by little the Latin American countries became actually the financial colonies of Europe. Economic dependence has a necessary corollary—political servitude. French intervention in Mexico was originally caused by the mass of unsatisfied financial claims; foreigners, the creditors of the State, were in favor of intervention."

–Francisco Garcia Calderon, Latin American diplomat, 1912

52. Which of the following types of documents might be used to support Calderon's argument?
    (A) records of loans by Latin American countries
    (B) journals of Spanish conquistadors
    (C) maps of French military operations in Mexico
    (D) transcripts of United States congressional debates

53. Which of the following was a primary cause of the end of the transatlantic slave trade in the early years of the nineteenth century?
    (A) economic losses for Caribbean sugar plantations
    (B) the creation of the British Navy's antislave patrol

(C) the abolition of slavery in the United States and Brazil

(D) an edict from the Roman Catholic pope

54. Migration patterns changed dramatically throughout the period from 1750 to 1900 for all of the following reasons EXCEPT

(A) after the emancipation of slaves in British colonies, new laborers were recruited from India, China, and Africa.

(B) larger, faster shapes made transporting people over long distances more affordable.

(C) universal education made the average person more curious about the world and interested in travel.

(D) improved nutrition and medical care led to a significant population increase, creating a larger labor market.

55. Which of the following characterizes the responses to Western influence by China and Japan?

(A) Japan experienced reform from above, while China continued to support its traditional economic and social structure.

(B) China modernized its economy and military, while Japan drifted into social chaos.

(C) Japan fell victim to Chinese expansion after being weakened by European colonialism.

(D) China experienced reform from above, while Japan slowly drifted into civil war.

56. Which of following describes cultural diffusion during the period 1750–1900?

(A) Western European influence over Asia and Africa grew.

(B) Chinese influence over Central and South Asia grew.

(C) African influence over the Middle East grew.

(D) United States influence over western Europe and the Caribbean grew.

57. The African National Congress differed from the Indian National Congress in that

(A) the African National Congress was formed in response to emerging ideologies of anti-imperialism.

(B) the African National Congress was founded to defend the interests of underprivileged social groups.

(C) the African National Congress was a transnational movement designed to unite people across national boundaries.

(D) the African National Congress initially had little influence.

58. Which of the following best explains the spread of Islam in sub-Saharan Africa during the twentieth century?

(A) Islam was indigenous in Ethiopia, and began to spread with the improvement of transportation networks in Africa.

(B) Islam was an attractive option to Africans who viewed Christianity as the religion of the European oppressor.

(C) Islam emphasized literacy, and Africans preferred to learn to read in Arabic rather than in a European language.

(D) Muslim missionaries offered financial support and gifts to African converts.

59. The increased immigration of Jews to Palestine after World War I is one example of

(A) population resettlements resulting from the mandate system.

(B) attempts by religious minorities to escape persecution throughout Europe.

(C) the impact of British immigration policies on their colonies.

(D) the displacement of people resulting in refugee populations.

"An irrepressible conflict has arisen between two national communities within the narrow bounds of one small country. About 1,000,000 Arabs are in strife, open or latent, with some 400,000 Jews. There is no common ground between them. They differ in religion and in language. Their cultural and social life, their ways of thought and conduct are as incompatible as their national aspirations. The War and its sequel have inspired all Arabs

GO ON TO NEXT PAGE

with the hope of reviving in a free and united Arab world the traditions of the Arab golden age. The Jews similarly are inspired by their historic past. They mean to show what the Jewish nation can achieve when restored to the land of its birth."

60. This quotation from an official British report on Palestine (1937) would likely lead to what policy recommendation for British-controlled Palestine?
    (A) a return to the boundaries of the ancient Israeli kingdom
    (B) establishment of Turkish rule over the region
    (C) separate countries for Arab and Jewish populations
    (D) a single country for all ethnic and religious groups in the area

61. A major difference between the philosophy of Mao Zedong and Marxist-Leninist ideology was
    (A) Mao's belief that women should participate in a communist revolution.
    (B) Mao's belief that industrialization was not necessary for a successful communist state.
    (C) Mao's policy to distance society from social and cultural institutions of the past.
    (D) Mao's reliance on the peasantry as the driving force of revolution.

62. Japanese success in the 1970s and 1980s at exporting manufactured goods
    (A) resulted in huge Japanese trade surpluses, which caused the United States and other Western nations to attempt to force open Japanese markets.
    (B) resulted in great wealth and the remilitarization of Japan.
    (C) resulted in the global rejection of Japanese goods, especially automobiles.
    (D) resulted in the worldwide dominance of Japanese language and culture.

63. What role did World War I play in eroding European global dominance?
    (A) Spain lost all of its colonies because of the war, and civil war erupted in the Netherlands.

(B) The war caused the crumbling of the Austro-Hungarian Empire, and France and Great Britain were severely damaged economically.
(C) The war allowed the Asian nations of India and China to out-produce France, Great Britain, and Italy.
(D) Great Britain was forced to give up all of its colonies, while the Netherlands sold most of their colonies in order to pay for the war.

64. The Warsaw Pact was created in direct response to
    (A) Churchill's Iron Curtain speech.
    (B) the failure of the Soviet blockade of Berlin.
    (C) the establishment of NATO.
    (D) the signing of the Nuclear Non-Proliferation Treaty.

65. Which of the following is an accurate comparison of Mexico, Argentina, and Brazil during the early to mid-twentieth century?
    (A) All three nations implemented various forms of representative democracy.
    (B) Brazil resorted to a harsh dictatorship, while Argentina and Mexico established various forms of representative democracy.
    (C) Argentina was the most liberal and progressive of the three nations and as such was the first Latin American nation to establish complete gender equality.
    (D) Mexico underwent a profound social revolution, while Argentina and Brazil had conservative regimes devoted to the interests of wealthy landowners.

"Civilians will never understand the greatness of our ideal; we shall therefore have to eliminate them from the government and give them the only mission which corresponds to them: work and obedience."

66. This quotation from Argentina in 1943 is most likely from the point of view of a
    (A) military officer.
    (B) Marxist intellectual.
    (C) landless peasant.
    (D) Roman Catholic priest.

67. In what ways did the Depression affect Columbia and Malaya?
    (A) Both nations gained great wealth because of the increased demand for raw materials.
    (B) Colombia fell to a brutal communist dictator, while Malaya fell to a capitalist dictator.
    (C) Colombia was hit hard by the decline in coffee exports, while Malaya suffered from the decline of rubber exports.
    (D) Both nations were not severely affected by the Depression because they were societies isolated from the global market.

68. Which of the following is an accurate statement regarding globalization?
    (A) The spread of industrialization to different parts of the world requires the adoption of Western culture in every area of life.
    (B) Cultural imperialism has spread Western tastes and styles around the globe using political control and fear of military intervention.
    (C) Diverse cultural traditions have persisted despite the globalization of industrial society and the integration of economic markets.
    (D) Globalization, which spurs expansion of homegrown industries in small and poor nations, also allows for the reduction of government protectionism.

69. Based on the map below, which of the following statements most accurately reflects world population growth at the end of the twentieth century?
    (A) Because of declining mortality rates, India, Egypt, and the Philippines are experiencing the world's highest rate of population growth.
    (B) Population growth is highest in the United States and western Europe because of greater wealth and the abundance of health facilities.
    (C) While China has the largest population, its growth rate is slower than that of all other nations except the United States and Nigeria.
    (D) The highest rates of population growth are occurring in the world's poorest nations of Latin America, Africa, and Asia.

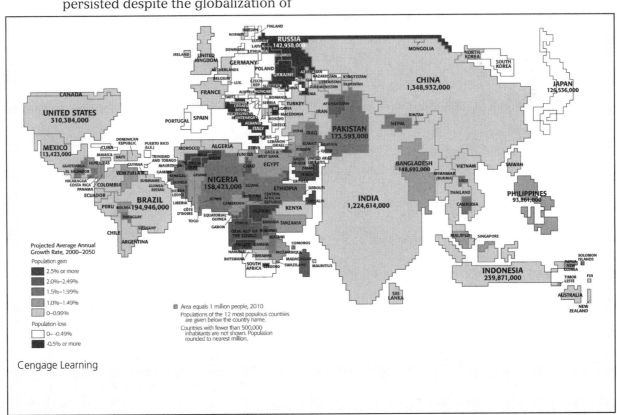

Cengage Learning

70. Which of the following is an example of the difference between women's rights movements in the Western and non-Western world?

    (A) Western women have led an international feminist movement, but non-Western women have generally been too oppressed to share their views and mobilize in any meaningful way.

    (B) Western feminists decried the oppression of women in other parts of the world, while non-Western feminists complained about the deterioration of morality and family life in the West.

    (C) American and Canadian women have led the international feminist movement with little input from or conflict with other women around the world.

    (D) British, French, and American women have been alone in their efforts to fight for fair government representation and other political rights.

STOP
END OF SECTION I
IF YOU FINISH BEFORE TIME IS CALLED, YOU MAY CHECK YOUR WORK ON THIS SECTION. DO NOT GO ON TO SECTION II UNTIL YOU ARE TOLD TO DO SO.

Section II: Free-Response Essays

NOTE This exam uses the chronological designations B.C.E. (before the Common Era) and C.E. (Common Era). These labels correspond to B.C. (before Christ) and A.D. (anno Domini), which are used in some world history textbooks.

Part A: Document-Based Question (DBQ)
Suggested writing time—40 minutes
Percent of Section II score—33⅓

DIRECTIONS The following question is based on the accompanying Documents 1–7. The documents have been edited for the purpose of this exercise. Write your answer on the lined pages of the Section II free-response booklet.

This question is designed to test your ability to work with and understand historical documents.

Write an essay that

- ▪ has a relevant thesis and supports that thesis with evidence from the documents.
- ▪ uses all or all but one of the documents.
- ▪ analyzes the documents by grouping them in as many appropriate ways as possible and does not simply summarize the documents individually.
- ▪ takes into account the sources of the documents and analyzes the authors' points of view.
- ▪ explains the need for at least one additional type of document.

You may refer to relevant historical information not mentioned in the documents.

1. Using the documents, evaluate the degree of success and failure of self-determination in the Middle East in the early twentieth century. Identify an additional document and explain how it would help your analysis of the success and failure of self-determination in the Middle East.

   Historical Background: World War I was fought from August 1914 to November 1918, and the defeat of the Central Powers dramatically changed the political landscape of the Middle East. When the war ended, Allied leaders met at Versailles to determine, among other things, the fate of the former Ottoman Empire.

GO ON TO NEXT PAGE

Document 1

Source: The Balfour Declaration, written by the British foreign minister to a prominent leader of the Jewish community in Europe.

November 2nd, 1917

Dear Lord Rothschild,

I have much pleasure in conveying to you, on behalf of His Majesty's Government, the following declaration of sympathy with Jewish Zionist aspirations which has been submitted to, and approved by, the Cabinet:

His Majesty's Government view with favour the establishment in Palestine of a national home for the Jewish people, and will use their best endeavours to facilitate the achievement of this object, it being clearly understood that nothing shall be done which may prejudice the civil and religious rights of existing non-Jewish communities in Palestine, or the rights and political status enjoyed by Jews in any other country.

I should be grateful if you would bring this declaration to the knowledge of the Zionist Federation.

Yours,

Arthur James Balfour

Document 2

Source: Woodrow Wilson, President of the United States, from his Fourteen Points, which listed his goals for US involvement in World War I, 1918.

V. A free, open-minded, and absolutely impartial adjustment of all colonial claims, based upon a strict observance of the principle that in determining all such questions of sovereignty the interests of the populations concerned must have equal weight with the equitable claims of the government whose title is to be determined.

XII. The Turkish portion of the present Ottoman Empire should be assured a secure sovereignty, but the other nationalities which are now under Turkish rule should be assured an undoubted security of life and an absolutely unmolested opportunity of autonomous development. . . .

Document 3

Source: The Covenant of the League of Nations, which established European control over non-Turkish parts of the former Ottoman Empire, 1919.

Article 22.

To those colonies and territories which as a consequence of the late war have ceased to be under the sovereignty of the States which formerly governed them and which are inhabited by peoples not yet able to stand by themselves under the strenuous conditions of the modern world, there should be applied the principle that the well-being and development of such peoples form a sacred trust of civilization. . . .

The best method of giving practical effect to this principle is that the tutelage of such peoples should be entrusted to advanced nations who by reason of their resources, their experience or their geographical position can best undertake this responsibility, and who are willing to accept it, and that this tutelage should be exercised by them as Mandatories on behalf of the League.

The character of the mandate must differ according to the stage of the development of the people, the geographical situation of the territory, its economic conditions and other similar circumstances.

Document 4

Source: Memorandum of the General Syrian Congress, 1919.

We the undersigned members of the General Syrian Congress . . . have agreed upon the following statement of the desires of the people of the country who have elected us. . . .

1. We ask absolutely complete political independence for Syria.

2. We ask that the government of this Syrian country should be a democratic civil constitutional Monarchy and that the King be the Emir Feisal, who carried on a glorious struggle in the cause of our liberation and merited our full confidence and entire reliance.

3. Considering the fact that the Arabs inhabiting the Syrian area are not naturally less gifted than other more advanced races . . . we protest against Article 22 of the Covenant of the League of Nations, placing us among the nations in their middle stage of development which stand in need of a mandatory power.

5. In the event of America not finding herself in a position to accept our desire for assistance, we will seek this assistance from Great Britain, also provided that such does not prejudice our complete independence and unity of our country.

6. We do not acknowledge any right claimed by the French Government in any part whatever of our Syrian country.

7. We opposed the pretensions of the Zionists to create a Jewish commonwealth in the southern part of Syria, known as Palestine, and oppose Zionist migration to any part of our country.

GO ON TO NEXT PAGE

Document 5

Source: Map of the mandate system established by the League of Nations, 1920

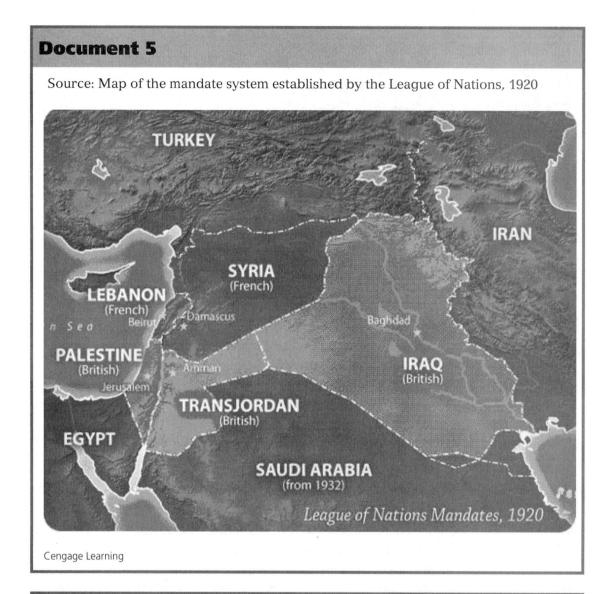

Cengage Learning

Document 6

Source: Mustafa Kemal Atatürk, first president of the Turkish republic, speech to the Turkish Congress of the People's Republican Party, 1927.

In order that our nation should be able to live a happy, strenuous, and permanent life, it is necessary that the State should pursue an exclusively national policy and that this policy should be in perfect agreement with our internal organization and be based on it. When I speak of national policy, I mean it in this sense: To work within our national boundaries for the real happiness and welfare of the nation and the country by, above all, relying on our own strength in order to retain our existence.

Document 7

Source: Photograph of Mustafa Kemal Atatürk teaching the new Turkish alphabet, which was based on the Latin script used in western Europe, 1928.

Fotosearch/Getty Images

End of Part A

Section II, Part B: Continuity and Change Over Time Essay
Suggested planning and writing time—40 minutes
Percent of Section II score—33 ⅓

DIRECTIONS You are to answer the following question. You should spend 5 minutes organizing or outlining your essay.

Write an essay that

■ has a relevant thesis and supports that thesis with appropriate historical evidence.
■ addresses all parts of the question.
■ uses world historical context to show continuities and changes over time.
■ analyzes the process of continuity and change over time.

2. Analyze continuities and changes in politics in Latin America from 1450 to 1900.

End of Part B

**Section II, Part C: Comparative Essay
Suggested planning and writing time—40 minutes
Percent of Section II score—33 ⅓**

DIRECTIONS You are to answer the following question. You should spend 5 minutes organizing and outlining your essay.

Write an essay that

■ has a relevant thesis and supports that thesis with appropriate historical evidence.
■ addresses all parts of the question.
■ makes direct, relevant comparisons.
■ analyzes relevant reasons for similarities and differences.

3. Compare the expansion of Islam to one of the following religions from their founding to 1450 C.E.
   ▧ Christianity
   ▧ Buddhism

END OF EXAMINATION

ANSWERS FOR SECTION I

MULTIPLE-CHOICE ANSWER KEY

1. A	15. A	29. D	43. D	57. C
2. B	16. B	30. B	44. C	58. B
3. C	17. D	31. C	45. B	59. A
4. C	18. D	32. A	46. D	60. C
5. C	19. D	33. B	47. C	61. D
6. A	20. C	34. D	48. D	62. A
7. C	21. B	35. B	49. C	63. B
8. A	22. B	36. D	50. B	64. C
9. C	23. C	37. D	51. C	65. D
10. A	24. C	38. B	52. A	66. A
11. B	25. B	39. C	53. B	67. C
12. A	26. C	40. D	54. C	68. C
13. D	27. D	41. D	55. A	69. D
14. B	28. D	42. A	56. A	70. B

SCORING The multiple-choice section counts for 50 percent of your examination grade.

EXPLANATIONS FOR THE MULTIPLE-CHOICE ANSWERS

Regional Coverage by Question Number

Africa 1, 2, 15, 16, 29, 30, 43, 44, 57, 58

The Middle East 3, 4, 17, 18, 31, 32, 45, 46, 59, 60

Asia 5, 6, 19, 20, 33, 34, 47, 48, 61, 62

Europe 7, 8, 21, 22, 35, 36, 49, 50, 63, 64

The Americas 9, 10, 23, 24, 37, 38, 51, 52, 65, 66

Comparative questions across units 11–14, 25–28, 39–42, 53–56, 67–70

Questions 1–14 cover Period One: Up to Circa 600 B.C.E. and Period Two: Circa 600 B.C.E. to Circa 600 C.E.

1. **ANSWER: A.** Farmers in settled communities had shorter lives than hunter-gathers because the density of the settlements and problems disposing of human waste often led to disease (Causation historical thinking skill; *The Earth and Its Peoples*, 5th ed., p. 12/6th ed., p. 12).

2. **ANSWER: B.** Because slavery existed on a limited scale in ancient Mesopotamia, it had little economic significance. Slaves were treated relatively humanely and debt slaves lived knowing that there was a possibility that they would be freed (Comparison historical thinking skill; *The Earth and Its Peoples*, 5th ed., p. 19/6th ed., p.19).

3. **ANSWER: C.** Both the Persian Empire under Darius and the Mauryan Empire under Ashoka used standard coinage, and both empires benefited from the availability of a network of roads (Comparison historical thinking skill; *The Earth and Its Peoples,* 5th ed., pp. 111–112, 183–184/6th ed., pp.109–110, 174–175).

4. **ANSWER: C.** The depiction of a pregnant female figure demonstrates the importance of the role of women in having and raising children, and the presence of many plump female deities suggests that inhabitants of Çatal Hüyük had a goddess as their main deity (Historical argumentation thinking skill; *The Earth and Its Peoples,* 5th ed., p. 15/6th ed., p. 14).

5. **ANSWER: C.** The Aryas pushed the native population into central and southern India and introduced the varna system, by which individuals were born into one of four classes: priests and scholars; warriors and officials; merchants, artisans, and landowners; or peasants and laborers (Causation historical thinking skill; *The Earth and Its Peoples,* 5th ed., pp. 175–176/6th ed., pp. 167–168).

6. **ANSWER: A.** Ban Zhao's "Lessons for Women" conform to traditional expectations such as obeying males and maintaining households, as indicated in the first passage. However, Ban Zhao suggests that these expectations are best realized when proper relationships are maintained and women are provided with at least a basic education (Use of evidence historical thinking skill; *The Earth and Its Peoples,* 5th ed., pp. 162–163/6th ed., pp. 156–157).

7. **ANSWER: C.** As Rome expanded its influence on the Italian peninsula and beyond, it granted political, legal, and economic privileges to conquered peoples. Additionally, it required its new subjects to serve as soldiers, which provided Rome with a vast supply of manpower (Comparison historical thinking skill; *The Earth and Its Peoples,* 5th ed., p. 146/6th ed., p. 142).

8. **ANSWER: A.** Missionaries, such as Paul of Tarsus, traveled throughout the Mediterranean world founding churches and converting individuals to Christianity. These efforts were helped by the appeal of the religion to the disenfranchised members of Roman society (Causation historical thinking skill; *The Earth and Its Peoples,* 5th ed., p. 152/6th ed., p. 147).

9. **ANSWER: C.** The Olmec elite required thousands of men and women to contribute to the construction of large-scale buildings. Similarly, the Chavín incorporated a reciprocal labor system that enabled them to construct and maintain infrastructure (Comparative historical thinking skill; *The Earth and Its Peoples,* 5th ed., pp. 60, 62/6th ed., pp. 192, 196).

10. **ANSWER: A.** The Chavín dominated large areas of the coastal plain and the Andean foothills because they were located along trade routes that connected these areas. As a result, Chavín rulers could control trade among different peoples and gain an economic advantage over

their neighbors (Causation historical thinking skill; *The Earth and Its Peoples*, 5th ed., pp. 61–62/6th ed., pp. 195–196).

11. **ANSWER: B.** Technological innovations were exchanged among the civilizations of Africa, the Middle East, Asia, and Europe, but the peoples of the Americas had to develop without such assistance and interaction (Comparative historical thinking skill; *The Earth and Its Peoples*, 5th ed., p. 331/6th ed., p. 214).

12. **ANSWER: A.** In both Egypt and Mesopotamia, kingship emerged as the dominant political form (Comparative historical thinking skill; *The Earth and Its Peoples*, 5th ed., pp. 17, 26/6th ed., pp. 17, 26).

13. **ANSWER: D.** Both empires built roads to ease military transportation and help maintain order. These routes also became important avenues for the spread of culture and commerce (Comparative historical thinking skill; *The Earth and Its Peoples*, 5th ed., p. 166/6th ed., p. 160).

14. **ANSWER: B.** Christianity and Buddhism are similar in that both are centered on the teachings of an individual (Jesus and Buddha) whose beliefs and actions were greatly influenced by the existing religious system of their time period (Comparative historical thinking skill; *The Earth and Its Peoples*, 5th ed., pp. 179, 212–213/6th ed., p. 170).

Questions 15–28 cover Period Three: Circa 600 C.E. to Circa 1450

15. **ANSWER: A.** Ghana and Mali developed in the same area, but Mali expanded to control more of the Niger and its surrounding areas. Therefore the tremendous wealth from the gold fields of the Niger as well as the trade of gold and other minerals was theirs. Both Ghana and Mali profited from control of the trans–Saharan trade routes. The key difference is that Mali was a Muslim empire from its origin while Ghana was not, and the leaders of Mali patronized one of the great centers of Muslim learning, Timbuktu (Comparative historical thinking skill; *The Earth and Its Peoples*, 5th ed., pp. 378–381/6th ed., pp. 380–382).

16. **ANSWER: B.** Great Zimbabwe, located on a plateau south of the Zambezi River, participated actively in gold mining and exporting between 1250 and 1450. Now abandoned, its monumental stone structures are a testament to its one-time prosperity. Calicut, a city on the Malabar Coast, prospered from trade in local products such as textiles and grains, as well as long-distance trade of the Indian Ocean (Comparison historical thinking skill; *The Earth and Its Peoples*, 5th ed., p. 388/6th ed., p. 389).

17. **ANSWER: D.** The concept of a single community united by the Muslim faith, common practices like the Five Pillars, cities where you could learn these practices, and the Arabic language all helped create a Muslim world that diverse cultures could feel a part of. The Islamic world was never unified politically, and different caliphates existed throughout the expanse of the Muslim world—from Spain to India and then beyond (Argumentation historical thinking skill; *The Earth and Its Peoples*, 5th ed., p. 244/6th ed., p. 264).

18. **ANSWER: D.** Conflicts between these societies resulted in frequent contact between individuals, who initiated technological and cultural transfers. Muslims, Mongols, and Christians shared scientific and mathematic discoveries, as well as artistic styles and other ideas (Continuity and change over time historical thinking skill; *The Earth and Its Peoples*, 5th ed., pp. 277, 352/6th ed., pp. 330–331).

19. **ANSWER: D.** The Song Dynasty was very concerned about protecting and defending their empire from northern rivals and had a large military. The Song, in power after the Tang Empire, benefited from the rich variety of intellectual pursuits under the Tang. The Mongols came after the Song (Causation historical thinking skill; *The Earth and Its Peoples*, 5th ed., pp. 292–293/6th ed., p. 305).

20. **ANSWER: C.** The Ming Dynasty experienced economic problems resulting from limitations on trade and elimination of paper money. They were also plagued by continued incursions by Mongol horsemen in the north. However, Ming influence expanded as a result of Zheng He's transoceanic maritime reconnaissance (Argumentation historical thinking skill; *The Earth and Its Peoples*, 5th ed., pp. 359–360/6th ed., pp. 337–338).

21. **ANSWER: B.** The decline of cities and shrinking of the urban elite class, possibly hastened by epidemics and military conflict, created a power vacuum that was filled by landowning families (Continuity and change over time historical thinking skill; *The Earth and Its Peoples*, 5th ed., p. 255/6th ed., p. 273).

22. **ANSWER: B.** Land was not scarce in Kievan Russia whereas trade relationships were the source of political power (Comparative historical thinking skill; *The Earth and Its Peoples*, 5th ed., pp. 268–272/6th ed., pp. 285–287).

23. **ANSWER: C.** The temple and residences pictured here exemplify the purpose of Tikal as a center for rituals and activities of the urban elite. There is no evidence in this image of walls or other kinds of fortifications (Contextualization historical thinking skill; *The Earth and Its Peoples*, 5th ed., pp. 312–313/6th ed., p. 199).

24. **ANSWER: C.** The political rulers of both the Aztec and Inca Empires participated in religious rituals and ceremonies that often included some form of sacrifice. This was a key tool for maintaining political authority (Comparison historical thinking skill; *The Earth and Its Peoples*, 5th ed., pp. 328–330/6th ed., pp. 393–397).

25. **ANSWER: B.** The Aztec required captured peoples to pay tribute in the form of food, textiles, and other supplies that were used for both religious ritual and basic economic needs. The Tangs' use of the tribute system was more symbolic, with independent tribute states acknowledging China's political supremacy through gift giving (Comparison historical thinking skill; *The Earth and Its Peoples*, 5th ed., pp. 318–319/6th ed., p. 395).

26. **ANSWER: C.** The conquest of the Eurasian land mass allowed for an unprecedented exchange of ideas between the Mongol domains in the East and the West. Many Mongol khans became converts of Islam and helped foster an incredible period of artistic and technological accomplishment under the Il-khan. The Yuan Empire adopted some Confucian practices in an effort to cement authority but placed Mongols on top of the social hierarchy by law (Comparison historical thinking skill; *The Earth and Its Peoples*, 5th ed., pp. 349, 356–357/6th ed., pp. 328, 334–335).

27. **ANSWER: D.** Although both empires were Muslim, large in size, and incredibly wealthy, Mali drew its wealth primarily from long-distance trade while the Delhi Sultanate did not. Mali's leaders converted to Islam, while the leaders of the Delhi Sultanate brought their religion with them when they invaded India (Comparison historical thinking skill; *The Earth and Its Peoples*, 5th ed., pp. 377–378/6th ed., p. 380).

28. **ANSWER: D.** Islam spread very easily along trade routes through missionary efforts of merchants and traders, intermarriage, and its easy adaptation to local cultures (Use of evidence historical thinking skill; *The Earth and Its Peoples*, 5th ed., p. 387/6th ed., p. 388).

Questions 29–42 cover Period Four: Circa 1450 to Circa 1750

29. **ANSWER: D.** With the exception of coastal Morocco, which was conquered by Portugal beginning in 1415, North Africa was dominated by Muslim empires before, during, and after the period 1450–1750.

    Islam first came to the region in the century following the death of Muhammad; later, the Mamluk Sultanate and Islamic Emirates controlled much of the region, followed by the Ottoman Empire. European influence in the region began to build in the nineteenth century, but by then Islam had long been established as a permanent element of North African culture and society (Continuity and change over time historical thinking skill; *The Earth and Its Peoples*, 5th ed., pp. 537–538/6th ed., pp. 512–513).

30. **ANSWER: B.** European trading-post empires were both profitable for and threatening to states in interior West and Central Africa. In Angola, Portugal controlled a significant amount of territory and directed much of the slave trade. Some powerful African leaders benefited from this trade as well. Songhai was destroyed when it attempted to expand into the Sahara from the south, prompting a swift and deadly military response from Morocco (Causation historical thinking skill; *The Earth and Its Peoples*, 5th ed., p. 537/6th ed., p. 512).

31. **ANSWER: C.** The ongoing decline of the Ottoman Empire would be a contributing factor to World War I. The inflationary crisis of the sixteenth and seventeenth centuries intensified the Ottoman rulers' problems; however, the gradual yet steady collapse of the empire was primarily a result of the sultans' inability to maintain authority over a diverse population stretched across a vast territory while facing new challenges from a modernizing Europe (Causation historical thinking skill; *The Earth and Its Peoples*, 5th ed., pp. 551–557/6th ed., pp. 527–531).

32. **ANSWER: A.** The Ottoman conquest of Christian territories in the Balkans in the late fourteenth century gave them easy access to male children, who were recruited and trained as foot soldiers. Starting early in the fifteenth century, these children were placed with Turkish families and instructed in the Turkish language and the Islamic religion (Causation historical thinking skill; *The Earth and Its Peoples*, 5th ed., p. 551/6th ed., p. 527).

33. **ANSWER: B.** This quotation refers to the idea that China does not need trade items from other countries and can dismiss European diplomatic outreach (Use of evidence historical thinking skill; *The Earth and Its Peoples*, 5th ed., p. 585/6th ed., p. 565).

34. **ANSWER: D.** The Tokugawa Shogunate reunified Japan in the early 1600s and viewed the Europeans as a destabilizing influence that could undermine the shogun's authority. While Japan never declared war on any European power in this era, the government did ban Christianity outright and strictly regulated trade with Europe and China. Not until the Meiji Restoration of the nineteenth century would the Japanese government actively promote modernization of the economy and military (Causation historical thinking skill; *The Earth and Its Peoples*, 5th ed., pp. 574–578/6th ed., pp. 555–556).

35. **ANSWER: B.** While books and other materials would eventually be put to many uses, since the printing press made them much less expensive and more widely available, the first to benefit were the humanist scholars and students of the Renaissance, as well as religious leaders such as Martin Luther, whose widely distributed criticisms of the Catholic Church launched the Reformation (Causation historical thinking skill; *The Earth and Its Peoples*, 5th ed., pp. 414–415/6th ed., p. 363).

36. **ANSWER: D.** Each of the issues addressed in the quotation reflects the notion that the authority of the monarch needs to be contained (Use of evidence historical thinking skill; *The Earth and Its Peoples*, 5th ed., p. 475/6th ed., p. 450).

37. **ANSWER: D.** Cows were introduced to the Americas through the Columbian Exchange. While Old World livestock provided native peoples with both food and leather, they also irrevocably altered the ecological balance in the New World (Contextualization historical thinking skill; *The Earth and Its Peoples*, 5th ed., p. 492/6th ed., pp. 467–468).

38. **ANSWER: B.** While most domestic occupations were assigned exclusively to female slaves, more women than men worked as field laborers on the typical Caribbean plantation, and field laborers formed the bulk of the slave population (Use of evidence historical thinking skill; *The Earth and Its Peoples*, 5th ed., pp. 524–525/6th ed., p. 498).

39. **ANSWER: A.** In the case of the Mughal Empire, a Muslim emperor descended from the Mongols ruled over a primarily Hindu population in India. The Qing Empire was headed by a Manchu family, though the

overwhelming majority of Qing peoples were ethnic Chinese (Comparison historical thinking skill; *The Earth and Its Peoples*, 5th ed., pp. 561, 581/6th ed., pp. 536, 552).

40. **ANSWER: D.** African slaves were traded across the Sahara, Red Sea, and Indian Ocean to the Islamic world in much smaller numbers than those taken across the Atlantic to the Americas. Of the approximately 2 million Africans enslaved in North Africa, the Middle East, or India, the majority were women who served wealthy Muslims as servants, entertainers, and concubines. Throughout the period, though, Islam, its accompanying cultural and political characteristics, and the Arabic language exerted a significant influence in sub-Saharan Africa, particularly in urban and coastal trading areas (Comparison historical thinking skill; *The Earth and Its Peoples*, 5th ed., pp. 538–539/6th ed., pp. 513–514).

41. **ANSWER: D.** As Europe emerged from the feudal system of the Middle Ages, the region underwent vast social, political, and economic changes that soon came to influence events in the Americas and Africa. During this period, only the Middle East remained relatively stable—a result of the regionally dominant Ottoman Empire's outright resistance to the changes that were transforming the new sea-based empires of Europe (Comparison historical thinking skill; *The Earth and Its Peoples*, 5th ed., p. 559/6th ed., p. 535).

42. **ANSWER: A.** The Atlantic Circuit was a clockwise network of sea routes exchanging raw materials and finished products. Angola was a large center for the African slave trade, and Brazil's sugar plantations required a constant supply of slave labor (Comparison and use of evidence historical thinking skills; *The Earth and Its Peoples*, 5th ed., pp. 530–531/6th ed., pp. 505–506).

Questions 43–56 cover Period Five: Circa 1750 to Circa 1900

43. **ANSWER: D.** At the Berlin Conference the western European powers agreed to the "effective occupation" of Africa, which led these powers to send troops and divide up Africa into colonial possessions (Causation historical thinking skill; *The Earth and Its Peoples*, 5th ed., p. 778/6th ed., pp. 698–699).

44. **ANSWER: C.** Muhammad Ali took control of Egypt after French troops had withdrawn in the early nineteenth century. Ali's central goal was to modernize Egypt so that it could prevent another military takeover by European troops. In doing this he skillfully used western technology and experts to reshape Egypt militarily, economically, and politically (Causation historical thinking skill; *The Earth and Its Peoples*, 5th ed., pp. 715–716/6th ed., p. 700).

45. **ANSWER: B.** The Ottoman reforms failed largely for political reasons. Janissary soldiers wanted to protect their status, and feared the loss of certain privileges should the military be reorganized. These revolts ultimately resulted in effective independence for Serbia and eventual destruction of the Janissary corps in 1826 (Causation historical

thinking skill; *The Earth and Its Peoples*, 5th ed., pp. 689–691/6th ed., p. 635).

46. **ANSWER: D.** Both the Ottoman Empire and Russia lacked a substantial middle class, and both were slow to develop industry. Some Ottoman rulers, notably Sultan Mahmud, imposed military and legal reforms, but many were suspended due to pressures of war. Similarly, Alexander I in Russia imposed some reforms, but many of these were reversed under his successor, Nicholas I (Causation and comparison historical thinking skills; *The Earth and Its Peoples*, 5th ed., pp. 691, 696/6th ed., pp. 636–637, 642).

47. **ANSWER: C.** This image of the arrival of United States ships led by Commodore Matthew Perry marked the beginning of increased Western pressure on the Tokugawa Shogunate to open up Japan. The Japanese vessels are coming up to the American warship because of their interest in the western technology (Contextualization historical thinking skill; *The Earth and Its Peoples*, 5th ed., p. 742/6th ed., p. 722).

48. **ANSWER: D.** Though British historians considered this uprising of Indian troops a rebellion, modern Indian historians have termed it the Revolution of 1857 and view it as the first steps toward Indian independence (Change over time historical thinking skill; *The Earth and Its Peoples*, 5th ed., p. 723/6th ed., pp. 703–704).

49. **ANSWER: C.** As nationalism grew in Europe during the nineteenth century, the most important element in creating a national identity was language (Causation historical thinking skill; *The Earth and Its Peoples*, 5th ed., p. 756/6th ed., p. 736).

50. **ANSWER: B.** Industrialism in western Europe had many dramatic effects, one of which was the rapid growth of urban centers (Change over time historical thinking skill; *The Earth and Its Peoples*, 5th ed., pp. 640–641/6th ed., p. 590).

51. **ANSWER: C.** In the passage, Simon Bolivar makes several references to Enlightenment ideals. Specifically, he expresses his belief in the idea that people should strive for an ideal government founded on natural rights such as justice, liberty, and equality. Although he does refer to freeing an enslaved nation, here he is not referring to slavery per se, but to political and perhaps economic servitude (Use of evidence historical thinking skill; *The Earth and Its Peoples*, 5th ed., pp. 656–658/6th ed., pp. 660–662).

52. **ANSWER: A.** According to Calderon a major cause of the involvement of Europe and the United States in the affairs of Latin America relates to the large national debts of Latin American countries. Records of loans might provide insight to the extent of the indebtedness and the nations that were involved (Use of evidence historical thinking skill; *The Earth and Its Peoples*, 5th ed., pp. 676–680/6th ed., pp. 681–683).

53. **ANSWER: B.** The British and abolitionist groups in a variety of nations pressured governments to end the slave trade, even going as far as having the British navy intercept slave ships (Causation historical thinking skill; *The Earth and Its Peoples*, 5th ed., pp. 718–719/6th ed., p. 701).

54. **ANSWER: C.** The end of slavery, new technology, and population pressures all contributed to changing migration patterns from 1750 to 1900. For the most part, people chose to relocate for better economic prospects in an increasingly competitive market (Causation historical thinking skill; *The Earth and Its Peoples*, 5th ed., pp. 732–733/6th ed., p. 717).

55. **ANSWER: A.** Though China and Japan shared several cultural characteristics, their responses to Western influence were markedly different. China rejected all Western influence and continued to support the traditional economic and social structure. Japan, after the Meiji restoration, began a program of reform from above that embraced Western technology and reshaped the country (Comparison historical thinking skill; *The Earth and Its Peoples*, 5th ed., p. 813/6th ed., pp. 765–766).

56. **ANSWER: A.** During the period 1750–1900 the political, economic, and cultural influence of western Europe over Africa and Asia had a profound impact and continued to grow (Periodization historical thinking skill; *The Earth and Its Peoples*, 5th ed., p. 791/6th ed., p. 715).

Questions 57–70 cover Period Six: Circa 1900 to the Present

57. **ANSWER: C.** Both the African National Congress and the Indian National Congress were formed in a time that anti-imperialist ideologies were gaining traction and Western-educated elites were aware of the need to defend the interests of underprivileged social groups, usually native populations. Typically, these organizations had little influence in their early years and gained traction as the twentieth century progressed. The African National Congress differed from the Indian National Congress in the sense that it was a transnational movement designed to defend the interests of all Africans, whereas the Indian National Congress was a domestic organization that addressed the needs of the Indian masses and sought to make a place for Indians in the Civil Service (Comparison historical thinking skill; *The Earth and Its Peoples*, 5th ed., pp. 727, 862, 870/6th ed., pp. 706, 791, 802).

58. **ANSWER: B.** Islam had been practiced for centuries in North Africa, parts of West Africa, and along the East African coast. During the European colonial period of the twentieth century, Islam was an attractive option. Like Christianity, it emphasized literacy, but it was less disruptive to the various African lifestyles. Moreover, Christianity, the religion of the European colonizer, was often seen as a symbol of colonization. Islam, therefore, was spread to many other parts of the continent by the influence and example of African and Arab merchants (Causation historical thinking skill; *The Earth and Its Peoples*, 5th ed., pp. 867–870/6th ed., pp. 801–802).

59. **ANSWER: A.** When Palestine became a British mandate, the Zionist movement gained new life, and large numbers of Jews came from Europe to settle in cities and on communal farms (Contextualization historical thinking skill; *The Earth and Its Peoples*, 5th ed., pp. 819–820/6th ed., p. 773).

60. **ANSWER: C.** This official report discusses what it calls the incompatibility of the Arab and the Jewish people of Palestine. A policy of separate countries for each group is the recommendation of the report (Argumentation historical thinking skill; *The Earth and Its Peoples*, 5th ed., pp. 819–820/6th ed., p. 773).

61. **ANSWER: D.** Marxist-Leninist ideology saw the peasants as backwards and believed that industrial workers were the key to a successful communist revolution. Mao, the son of a farmer in largely rural China, took a more pragmatic approach and aimed first to redistribute land among the peasantry in order to gain adherents among the rural population (Contextualization historical thinking skill; *The Earth and Its Peoples*, 5th ed., pp. 841–842/6th ed., p. 817).

62. **ANSWER: A.** Japan found such great success during the 1970s and 1980s at exporting manufactured goods that it built up a large trade surplus with Western nations such as the United States. The United States and the European Union conducted tough negotiations with Japan in an effort to force open Japanese markets, but the negotiations had only limited success (Causation historical thinking skill; *The Earth and Its Peoples*, 5th ed., p. 922/6th ed., p. 873).

63. **ANSWER: B.** World War I resulted in the crumbling of the Austro-Hungarian and Ottoman Empires, both of which were divided into many smaller independent nations. The war also weakened France and Great Britain, both of which suffered economically (Causation historical thinking skill; *The Earth and Its Peoples*, 5th ed., p. 809/6th ed., p. 762).

64. **ANSWER: C.** The United States and capitalist nations of western Europe established the North Atlantic Treaty Organization (NATO) in 1949. Still in the process of recovering from the devastation of World War II, Soviet leaders felt threatened by NATO. The Warsaw Pact, created in 1955, further intensified the distrust and suspicion between the two sides (Causation historical thinking skill; *The Earth and Its Peoples*, 5th ed., p. 888/6th ed., p. 840).

65. **ANSWER: D.** In their economic relations with European and North American countries, Mexico, Argentina, and Brazil had the weaker hand. In addition, all three had a vastly unequal distribution of wealth within their societies. Responding to the Depression, all three turned to state intervention. However, Mexico experienced an intense social revolution that sought to solve the problems of poverty and inequality. The conservative regimes of Argentina and Brazil maintained their devotion to protecting the interests of wealthy landowners (Comparison historical thinking skill; *The Earth and Its Peoples*, 5th ed., pp. 876–878/6th ed., pp. 797–799).

66. **ANSWER: A.** The idea that civilians should not have a voice and instead remain obedient to the government was proclaimed by the military officers who took control of Argentina in the 1940s (Interpretation historical thinking skill; *The Earth and Its Peoples*, 5th ed., p. 876/6th ed., p. 799).

67. **ANSWER: C.** Columbia and Malaya, like other countries dependent on the export of raw materials, were hit hard by the Depression (Comparison and causation historical thinking skills; *The Earth and Its Peoples*, 5th ed., p. 838/6th ed., p. 813).

68. **ANSWER: C.** Critics of globalization predicted it would result in the "Americanization" of the world. However, experience to date suggests that despite its vast spread, American culture has not displaced other traditions (Contextualization historical thinking skill; *The Earth and Its Peoples*, 5th ed., pp. 966–967/6th ed., pp. 918–919).

69. **ANSWER: D.** Industrialized nations of the West are experiencing a decline in fertility rates that is often ascribed to higher levels of female education, employment, and access to contraception. On the other hand, developing nations in Africa, Latin America, and Asia are experiencing rapid population growth. According to the map, 95 percent of the world's population growth will occur in these developing nations. Moreover, calculations suggest that every three years our world will see an increase in population equivalent to the population of the United States (Use of evidence historical thinking skill; *The Earth and Its Peoples*, 5th ed., pp. 930, 932/6th ed., p. 883).

70. **ANSWER: B.** The first and second International Women's Conferences (in Nairobi, Kenya, in 1985; in Beijing, China, in 1995) revealed a lack of global consensus on women's issues. Western feminists, who had often dictated the global women's agenda, were often accused of being domineering and condescending. Western feminists tended to focus on head coverings and practices of circumcision in non-Western nations. Non-Western feminists, however, considered poverty and disease the most urgent issues (Comparison historical thinking skill; *The Earth and Its Peoples*, 5th ed., p. 963/6th ed., pp. 915–916).

ANSWER FOR SECTION II, PART A: DOCUMENT-BASED QUESTION (DBQ)

THE DOCUMENTS

Below are short analyses of the documents. The italicized words suggest what your margin notes might include:

DOCUMENT 1 This map shows that during World War I Britain and France were already in agreement about areas that would either fall under their influence or direct control—years before the creation of the mandate system. *This document shows self-determination failing in the Middle East.*

DOCUMENT 2 This document is from the British perspective; it shows support for the Zionist movement while also promising to respect the rights of the Arab peoples already in Palestine. Why does the document promise both, and was that a realistic promise? *This document would seem to show self-determination as a possibility in the Middle East, with both groups co-existing.*

DOCUMENT 3 This excerpt from Wilson's Fourteen Points shows Wilson's idealist vision for the region and calls for self-determination for all people under the rule of the Ottoman Empire and an opportunity for them—and only them—to determine their future. *This document shows self-determination as a success and real possibility for the Middle East.*

DOCUMENT 4 Article 22 from the League of Nations calls for the creation of the mandate system and justifies it on the grounds that the Arab peoples were less developed and not ready to determine what their future nations needed. The language used in the document reflects Social Darwinism. *This document is very imperialistic and patronizing in its tone and is a failure for self-determination.*

DOCUMENT 5 This document, an explicit argument against Document 4, represents the voice of the Syrian people in protest against the mandate system, the French government, and the Zionist movement in Palestine. *This document shows the Syrians' demand for independence and thus shows strong support for the right of self-determination.*

DOCUMENT 6 By 1920, after the fall of the Ottoman Empire and four years after the map in Document 1, the Middle East is under the control of Europeans. *This document shows the success of the mandate system and the failure of self-determination in the region.*

DOCUMENT 7 After the fall of the Ottoman Empire, Atatürk led a passionate campaign to create a new national identity for the Turks, one that was secular and more reflective of European culture without falling under Europe's control. *This picture of Mustafa Kemal Atatürk shows the success of self-determination.*

The clearest ways to organize the documents is to group them—one group of those that seem to show the success of self-determination in the Middle East and one group of those that show the failure of selfdetermination there. Although there are documents that show elements of both success and failure, you need to determine which is more significant and group them accordingly.

Success Documents	Failure Documents
2, 3, 5, 7	1, 4, 6

A Sample Essay

There were strong attempts by Arab peoples in the Middle East to create their own political and national identities. However, the self-determination movement was largely a failure because of the imperialist mindset of Europeans who wanted to control the region for their own political and economic gain despite promises of autonomy made during World War I. Although some of the documents given show attempts at self-determination, in the end the movement was a failure and created many of the political issues in the region that have endured to this day.

There were opportunities for self-determination to be successful in the Middle East. Documents 2, 3, 5, and 7 show the potential success of self-determination in the region. Document 2, the famous Balfour Declaration, reflects the British desire to support the Zionist movement while not angering the Arabs. The British had this point of view because they did not want to alienate the Arabs entirely, in part because they promised the Arabs independence for fighting with them against the Ottoman Turks in World War I. Yet the British also courted the Zionist movement so as to garner Jewish-American support in World War I. This document can be interpreted as supporting the idea of self-determination for the Zionists while also respecting the rights of the Palestinians already there. In reality, the future would not be so rosy. Here it would be helpful to have a speech by the Zionist leader, Theodore Herzl, to hear his perspective on self-determination for Jews, why they needed to be in Palestine, and what British involvement in the Zionist movement would mean for its success. In Document 3, U.S. President Woodrow Wilson speaks directly, in Article XII of his idealistic Fourteen Points, about the opportunity for all of the nationalities under Turkish rule to be completely free to develop as nations on their own. This document, written while the war was still being fought and a full year before the Treaty of Versailles, reflects Wilson's lofty idealism in its promises that self-determination will be accomplished and that, after the fall of the Ottoman Empire, peoples of the region will finally be given political opportunities that ensure autonomy. Document 5 gives the perspective of the Syrians, whom the French wanted to control under the mandate system. The point of view of the General Syrian Congress reflects a tone of indignation that the Europeans are treating Syrians as inferior. The reasons for this point of view are disgust for the assumption that the French have a natural right to take Syrian land as well as distaste for the Zionist movement, which will also take Palestine, land that the Syrian Congress believed was in their country. Although Document 5 might be considered a failure for self-determination because it shows what was being done to Syria by the French, the document can also be interpreted as a success for self-determination because it presents the clear arguments and strong position that nations like Syria had about their belief in their right to self-determine and their willingness to fight for it. Another additional document that would be helpful in understanding the impact of the mandate system would be the personal journal of a common Syrian citizen; this would give a sense of how deeply Syrian citizens felt the impact of the European mandate system in their day-to-day lives. Finally, Document 7 shows the clear success of self-determination in Turkey, where Mustafa Kemal Atatürk created the new nation of Turkey out of the ashes of the Ottoman Empire and forged a new national identity for Turkey based on secularism and Westernization. This Westernization did not mean allowing Europeans to run the government; rather, Atatürk created a modern republic that was solely for the benefit of the Turks.

Ultimately, though, self-determination in the Middle East would fail, as Documents 1, 4, and 6 clearly show. Documents 1 and 6, maps, show that in the four years between the Sykes-Picot Agreement of 1916 for partitioning the Middle East and the establishment of the mandate system as supported by the League of Nations, the French and British got exactly what they wanted in continuing to carve up other regions of the world for their economic and political benefit; in other words, effective colonization. Document 4 gives their justification for doing it in Article 22 of the Covenant of the League of Nations. The tone of the document drips of Social Darwinist theory, which is an accurate portrayal of the imperializing nations of the world at that time, which believed they were superior in every way and therefore justified in drawing boundaries, breaking promises, and manipulating foreign policy for their own benefit. In Document 5, item 3, the Syrian National Congress refers directly to Document 4 to show how the League of Nations treated nations like Syria, even though the League of Nations claimed to champion self-determination.

The failure of self-determination in the Middle East set the stage for long-lasting conflict in the region that persisted throughout the twentieth century. Although the indigenous ethnic groups of the Middle East fought to be autonomous nations, it would be years before they achieved their goals.

COMMENT This essay uses each of the documents effectively and accurately to assess and analyze the success and failures of self-determination. The argument is clearly made that it was an overall failure, and each document is used and linked with the rest to show why this is an appropriate assessment.

SCORING 1 point for thesis in the opening line, 1 point for understanding the basic meaning of all documents, 2 points for using all of the documents as evidence that supported thesis, 1 point for analyzing the point of view in Documents 2 and 5, 1 point for groupings—Documents 1, 4, and 6; and Documents 2, 3, 5, and 7—and 1 point for an explanation of possible additional documents. This DBQ also got expanded core points for having relevant outside historical content, for persuasively using the documents as evidence, and for proposing—in addition to the one extra document required for basic core—a second extra document. This essay receives 9 out of 9 possible points. The DBQ counts for a third of the *total free-response grade*.

ANSWER FOR SECTION II, PART B: CONTINUITY AND CHANGE OVER TIME QUESTION

A SAMPLE ESSAY

Influenced by the global events between 1500 and 1900, political power in Latin America went through several stages of change, from indigenous empires and kingdoms, to European colonial rule to political independence and Western imperialism. Throughout these stages of change, power remained in the hands of a privileged few at the expense of the many, and foreign intervention forced political changes while furthering the continuity of political inequality for the majority of people in the region.

In 1500, there were several indigenous empires and kingdoms in Latin America, most notably the Aztecs and Maya in Mesoamerica and the Inca in the Andean region of South America. Both the Inca and Aztec were empires with male leaders who had both political and religious authority. Conquest of subject peoples was a key part of legitimizing rule, and both empires ruled from strong city centers that required tribute from subjects. In 1500, both the Aztec and Inca empires were thriving, but this success would be short-lived, as European maritime exploration brought conquistadors across the Atlantic and down into Mesoamerica and South America.

Because of European competition for wealth and glory, these conquistadors set up colonies in the name of Spain and placed the native populations under the immediate political control of the king of Spain, giving the Spanish and other European nations that followed direct political rule. From 1550 until approximately 1800, the Spanish imposed their political authority over the newly conquered Aztec, Inca, and other regions through royal bureaucracy. The king of Spain set up the Council of the Indies to rule from afar, but in order to keep a close eye on the colonies, the viceroyalties ruled the colonies. These governors ruled in the name of the king and thus had all the political power. For the first time, Latin America was subjugated under the laws of a foreign council and king who sat across the ocean. Peninsulares ruled the region in order to put the interests of the Spanish first. Despite these radical changes to the political structure, the viceroyalties believed they had a God-given right to rule—just as the indigenous empires had believed.

The period of 1800 to 1830 was a short yet powerful period in Latin America that saw the change from colonial rule to political independence in the form of republics. This movement was led by Creoles like Simón Bolívar, who demanded more political rights for themselves and took advantage of the weakening of Spain during the Napoleonic Wars to make their move for independence. Empowered by earlier political revolutions in the United States, France, and Haiti, as well as the Enlightenment ideals these revolutions embodied, men like Bolívar successfully fought to change Latin America from a political system of regional viceroyalties to one of newly independent nations, most of which became republics. One continuity was the enduring social and political inequalities endemic to Latin America; although Creoles had fought for political power for themselves, most of the indigenous peoples who were disenfranchised during the colonial period remained economically and politically subjugated after independence.

This continuity remained from 1830 until 1900 as Latin American elites now courted and welcomed a new foreign influence, the private businesses and corporations of countries such as the United States and Britain. By

1830, much of the West had industrialized and Latin America continued to possess many of the raw materials and foodstuffs that appealed to these Western nations. The United States and other European nations, through free-trade imperialism, encouraged Latin America's dependence on the industrialized world. The United States became heavily involved in influencing political decisions made in Central America and the Caribbean, beginning with the Monroe Doctrine. A key example of U.S political involvement in the region was the Spanish-American War, which allowed for the tremendous involvement of the United States in Cuba's political affairs.

For the entirety of the period 1500–1914, Latin America had to deal with foreign political intervention—intervention that looked out for the interests of foreign elites and those within Latin America who would benefit from such foreign political and economic involvement. This political inequality led to more cries for revolutionary change after 1914 that mirrored many of the changing global realities brought on by two world wars.

COMMENT This essay walks the reader through the entire period by means of a framework with a clear beginning, middle, and end. There is good historical evidence and detail that is focused on political changes and continuities, and it sets those changes in the global context of the period 1500–1914.

SCORING 1 point for a thesis in the opening line that addresses the whole time period, 2 points for fully addressing the question in terms of both change and continuity, 2 points for appropriate evidence to support the thesis, 1 point for the global context, and 1 point for analysis of change and continuity. The student received two expanded core points for addressing all parts of the questions evenly and providing good evidence rooted in a solid understanding of the global events that brought about change.

This essay receives 9 out of 9 possible points. The continuity and change over time essay counts for a third of the *total free-response grade*.

ANSWER FOR SECTION II, PART C: COMPARATIVE QUESTION

A SAMPLE ESSAY

Both of the great religions of Islam and Buddhism were spread from their points of origin though the trade routes that dominated the period from 100 B.C.E. to 1450 C.E.; however unlike Buddhism, which did not become the dominant religion in India, Islam continued to be the dominant religion in its place of origin. The political control of various empires was also an important factor in the spread of both religions because of the stability and relative peace brought by their regional control.

The development of trade routes facilitated interaction between cultures. The Silk Road, which connected Asia and the Middle East and allowed for the spread of ideas up into Europe by way of the Byzantine Empire, was one of the main overland trade routes by which first Buddhism, then later Islam, were spread. People of different cultures, ethnicities, and regions learned about these religions from the merchants, missionaries, and monks traveling along the Silk Road. This was particularly true for Buddhism, which reached East Asia via the Silk Road. Similarly, as Muslim merchants conducted business, intermarried, and shared their faith, the Indian Ocean trade network was another key trade route by which Islam spread to South and Southeast Asia as well as East Africa.

Both Islam and Buddhism spread under the rule of empires. Islam spread via the Abbasid Empire, which by 1000 was centered in Baghdad. Similarly, the Chinese Tang Empire, which was heavily influenced by Central Asian culture and was therefore exposed to Buddhism, served as a conduit to spread the religion throughout the empire, whose territory spread from Central to East Asia. Islam also spread across regions with the growth of the Muslim caliphates, which formed the central political organization for the Islamic Empire. Muslim caliphates spanned North Africa, into Spain, and extended as far as Iran, thus exposing different peoples on different continents to Muslim beliefs and practices. Islam also continued to be the dominant religion in its birthplace, the Arabian Peninsula. Although it maintained a strong presence in India, Buddhism did not become the dominant religion of India because of the cementing of Hinduism in the Gupta period. Still, it became highly influential in Central and East Asia. This was particularly true in Tibet and the Tang Empire, where Buddhism had a particularly strong political and social impact on Chinese society. When the Chinese started to absorb Buddhism into their culture, the religion spread through China and from there to Korea, then Japan, where the Japanese developed different sects of Buddhism.

The Mongols also impacted the spread of both religions. Their various khans took over the entire Eurasian landmass and traded all along the Silk Road. Their control of the intersections of Europe, Asia, and the Middle East exposed the Mongols to many faiths, including both Islam and

Buddhism. Some khans practiced Buddhism; some khans were Muslim. Islam would become the religion of the khans in both the Il-Khan region as well as the Golden Horde. The Mongols also became some of the greatest preservers of Islamic art and technology.

Because trade was a main factor that served to spread these two religions, Buddhism and Islam spread along flourishing trade routes. While Islam spread rapidly because of the territorial control of the Muslim Empire, Buddhism slowly grew to have a strong political and cultural influence in East Asian empires. Finally, Mongol conversion was another powerful force in supporting the spread of these faiths.

COMMENT This essay has a clear comparative thesis that addresses both similarities and differences that are then analyzed further in the body paragraphs. There are several direct comparisons that are woven consistently through the essay and are elaborated on and supported with specific evidence and detail.

SCORING 1 point for the thesis in the opening line, 2 points for addressing both similarities and differences, 2 points for using accurate evidence that supports the main ideas presented in the thesis, 1 point for making a number of specific direct comparisons, and 1 point for analysis. This essay earns basic core and, with consistent use of both evidence and direct comparison, 2 points for expanded core.

This essay receives 9 out of 9 possible points. The comparative essay counts for a third of the *total free-response grade*.

CALCULATING YOUR SCORE ON THE DIAGNOSTIC TEST

The following is based on the 2011 AP World History Examination, which is the only released examination at this time.

SCORING THE MULTIPLE-CHOICE SECTION

_____ × 0.8571 = _____
number   weighted Section I score
correct
(out of 70)

[Note: The guessing penalty has been eliminated for all AP exams starting with the 2011 exam.]

SCORING THE FREE-RESPONSE SECTION

Use the following formula to calculate your raw score on the free-response section of the exam:

Part A _____ × 2.2222 = _____
      (out of 9)   (do not round)

Part B _____ × 2.2222 = _____
      (out of 9)   (do not round)

Part C _____ × 2.2222 = _____
      (out of 9)   (do not round)

Sum = _____
weighted Section II score
(do not round)

YOUR COMPOSITE SCORE

_____ + _____ = _____
weighted   weighted   composite score
Section I   Section II   (round to nearest whole number)
score   score

Once you have calculated your composite score, see where it falls in the Composite Score Range below. *Remember that your composite score is only an estimate of your performance on the College Board exam.*

AP GRADES BY SCORE RANGE

Composite Score Range	AP Grade
78–120	5
64–77	4
48–63	3
32–47	2
0–31	1

Part II

A Review of AP World History

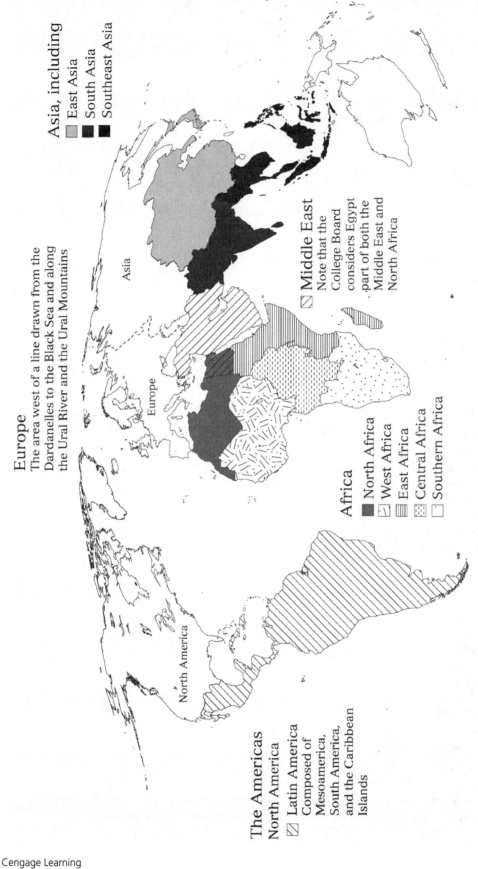

Asia, including
- ☐ East Asia
- ■ South Asia
- ■ Southeast Asia

Europe
The area west of a line drawn from the
Dardanelles to the Black Sea and along
the Ural River and the Ural Mountains

Asia

Europe

Middle East
Note that the
College Board
considers Egypt
part of both the
Middle East and
North Africa

North America

Africa
- ■ North Africa
- ⊠ West Africa
- ▥ East Africa
- ▦ Central Africa
- ☐ Southern Africa

The Americas
North America
- ⊠ Latin America
  Composed of
  Mesoamerica,
  South America,
  and the Caribbean
  Islands

Map of Regions for AP World History

1

AFRICA:
UP TO CIRCA 600 C.E.

KEY CONCEPTS

- The Agricultural Revolutions changed social and gender structures and paved the way for the emergence of civilizations.
- Ancient Egyptian civilization was shaped largely by geographic conditions.
- Ancient Egypt was a male-dominated society centered on the pharaoh.
- Sub-Saharan Africa was an isolated region with many separate societies, each with its own political and social characteristics, until the migration of the Bantu people provided cultural unity.

KEY TERMS

- Agricultural Revolutions
- Bantu
- foragers
- hieroglyphics
- Neolithic
- papyrus
- pastoralists
- pharaoh
- trans-Saharan trade

Life before and after the Agricultural Revolutions is discussed in *The Earth and Its Peoples*, fifth and sixth editions, Chapter 1. Ancient Egypt and Nubia is covered in fifth and sixth editions Chapters 1, 2, and 3. Sub-Saharan Africa and the trans-Saharan trade network are discussed in Chapter 7 of the fifth edition and Chapter 8 of the sixth edition.

THE EARLIEST HUMAN SOCIETIES

Anthropologists and historians theorize that human beings originated in Africa and migrated to other parts of the world over the course of thousands of years. Until approximately 8000 B.C.E., all humans lived in a similar manner: in small nomadic communities defined by marriage and kinship that relied on hunting and gathering in order to meet their needs. This **foraging** lifestyle did not support large numbers of people, and it required all members to participate in the food-gathering process—men were responsible for hunting and women for gathering fruits and plants. These early Paleolithic people migrated out of Africa to areas in Eurasia and eventually the Americas and Oceania.

Approximately 10,000 years ago the **Agricultural Revolution** ushered in dramatic changes. (These changes are also often referred as the **Neolithic** Revolution.) Over the course of generations, groups of people settled and developed techniques for plant and animal domestication. Because a smaller number of people could meet the nutritional needs of the entire community, this change allowed for specialization of labor and freed members of the community to make important technological and political advances. Those not engaged in food production were able to specialize in other trades and professions. Important technological developments centered on the use of metals—particularly bronze and, later, iron—for farm tools and weapons. The development of civilization also altered gender roles; women were now expected to bear and raise children and tend to the household. Though there are examples of women in prominent political positions, early civilizations were patriarchal systems that limited the rights and power of women.

AP Tip

For the AP exam you should be able to describe the development of the following foundational civilizations: Mesopotamia, Egypt, Indus Valley, Shang dynasty, Mesoamerica, and Andean South America. So pay careful attention to these details and practice making direct comparisons.

By 3000 B.C.E., major civilizations emerged in Mesopotamia and along the Nile. Later, civilizations emerged in the Indus River Valley, China, Mesoamerica, and South America. River valleys provided means of transportation as well as rich soil in the flood basins. Though farming provided an abundance of food, and thus greater stability from year to year, early civilizations suffered from disease brought on by living among animals and without adequate sewage facilities.

While civilizations emerged along river valleys, **pastoralism** developed in areas not well suited for agriculture. In arid regions, small societies dependent on herds of animals moved their livestock among grazing lands and watering places. Pastoralist communities were small compared with those of agriculturalists, with whom they sometimes came into conflict over land use.

Religion in Neolithic communities continued the pagan beliefs of the foragers. While their predecessors revered geographic features and animals that were no doubt important to their survival, agriculturalists worshiped Mother Earth and gods of the elements such as fire, wind, and rain.

EGYPT: 3100–1070 B.C.E.

Humans first transformed their settled communities into major civilizations in ancient Egypt. Over the course of two millennia, Egypt developed a complex social order and economy, attained scientific and artistic heights, and flexed its military muscle. These achievements, made possible by Egypt's geography, were accomplished through a centralized political system.

Early farming villages appeared in Egypt around 5500 B.C.E. as the people of the region domesticated plants and animals. Between 5000 and 3000 B.C.E., as Egypt's climate became drier, people migrated to the fertile land along the Nile River, which was surrounded by deserts. The geography of ancient Egypt provided the necessary resources for a powerful and self-sufficient empire. Flowing south to north, the river played a key role in agriculture, religion, and transportation. Annual fall flooding irrigated the surrounding land, leaving it fertile for farming. Though the Nile's flood patterns were more consistent than those of the Tigris and Euphrates in Mesopotamia, variations in the amount of water affected food levels—and therefore political stability. Large floods jeopardized residential areas; small floods decreased the amount of fertile land and thus food levels, which often led to regime change.

Migration and increased food production caused the population along the Nile to increase. Around 3100 B.C.E. the smaller communities along the Nile were unified into a single state led by a pharaoh. Dynasties were established within families and reflected which region along the Nile was most powerful. Egyptian history can also be broken into three kingdoms separated by periods of disunity and decline. The Old Kingdom was centered in Memphis; the Middle and New Kingdoms were based to the south, in Thebes.

Politically, Egypt centered on **pharaoh**, who was viewed as an earthly god. Charged with maintaining order and prosperity, pharaoh was the source of laws. Additionally, pharaoh controlled long-distance trade, which prevented the emergence of a merchant class. Though viewed as all-powerful, pharaoh was supported by a massive bureaucracy that kept records made possible by the development of **hieroglyphics** and the use of **papyrus** and collected taxes. Many pharaohs incorporated a merit-based system for awarding promotions or land grants. That said, pharaoh and his officials enjoyed the wealth and power associated with being at the top of the social hierarchy. Below them were low-level officials and local leaders, priests, and other professionals. At the bottom were peasants, who constituted the majority of the population. Though slavery existed on a limited scale, the prisoners of war, criminals, and others who were enslaved received better treatment and the promise of freedom that slaves in other societies lacked.

Ancient Egypt was a male-dominated society, but women enjoyed legal and economic rights denied to those in other ancient civilizations. For example, women could own and inherit property, and they were able to divorce and retain their dowry if the marriage failed. A few queens and queen mothers also held positions of political power.

The importance of the pharaohs is also apparent in the monumental architecture built in their honor after death. The pyramids at Giza, the most famous examples, demonstrate pharaoh's power to assemble workers who, with only simple tools, constructed massive structures. This monumental building spurred advances in mathematics, and the Egyptian fascination with the afterlife led to advances in chemistry that allowed for mummification. The Egyptians also used the stars to create an advanced calendar, and they developed efficient transportation methods along the Nile.

During the Old Kingdom (2575–2134 B.C.E.), Egypt was largely self-sufficient and self-interested. Physical isolation prevented mass migration or invasion, and the limited interaction with outsiders was only in the context of trade. During the Middle Kingdom (2040–1640 B.C.E.), Egypt's economic interests led it to invade Nubia to gain control of gold fields. Located along the Nile River south of Egypt, Nubia connected sub-Saharan Africa with North Africa. As a result of its location, Nubian leaders often served as middlemen in the trans-Saharan trade network that slowly developed—a role Egypt sought to destroy with its invasion. Egypt's expansionist tendencies increased during the New Kingdom (1532–1070 B.C.E.) as is evident with its move farther south into the kingdom of Kush. Egyptian control of Nubia and Kush would last over five hundred years and see the imposition of Egyptian culture on the conquered peoples. In addition to the cultural imprint, children from elite Nubian families were taken to Egypt—hostages to ensure cooperation among their new subjects.

In the last millennium B.C.E., powerful leaders emerged in Nubia and, later, farther south in Meroë. When control shifted south to Nubian kings, Egyptian culture, burial customs, and architecture were actually revitalized. Nubian rule ended with the invasion of the Assyrians in 660 B.C.E. Assyrian rule was broken, in the fourth century B.C.E., when power shifted still farther south, to Meroë, which replaced Egyptian customs with sub-Saharan ones.

SUB-SAHARAN AFRICA

Prior to the development of **trans-Saharan trade** and the rise of the Indian Ocean trade network, sub-Saharan Africa was an isolated region. Because of the scarcity of water, low population density, and the massive size of the Sahara Desert, sub-Saharan Africa was a complex mix of cultures having their own languages and political and social characteristics. Nonetheless, there were some common characteristics: all were monarchies with a clear social structure that grouped people according to age, kinship, gender, and occupation.

Though there had been some trade, only when the domesticated camel was introduced, in the first millennium B.C.E., did exchange expand significantly. Salt from the southern region of the desert was traded for palm oil and forest products from the forest zone near the equator. When the Roman Empire dominated North Africa, products from that region were incorporated into the Mediterranean until Rome's decline in the third century C.E.

> ## AP Tip
>
> When looking at a long period of time, you should be able to identify significant developments and explain how they initiated periods in regional or world history. For example, the development of settled agricultural communities, the use of bronze and iron, and the introduction of the domesticated camel to the Sahara Desert represent events that mark the beginning of new eras in history.

The **Bantu** people provided unity in sub-Saharan Africa in the first millennium C.E. when they slowly migrated from the equatorial region to southern Africa. As they migrated, they spread the Bantu family of languages—over three hundred languages of southern Africa belong to the Bantu family, the origins of which can be traced to the Niger-Congo region. The Bantu also spread the use of iron. Iron tools improved farming techniques and agricultural efficiency, and the greater food supply sparked economic development and population growth. The changes instigated by the Bantu migration increased the vitality of sub-Saharan Africa, which played a key role in the Indian Ocean's large and prosperous trade network.

Multiple-Choice Questions

1. Which of the following best explains life in communities prior to the Agricultural Revolutions?
   (A) The only role for women was to bear and raise children.
   (B) Groups were defined by the geographic region of origin.
   (C) The foraging lifestyle supported only small, nomadic groups of people.
   (D) Specialization of labor resulted in important technological advances.

2. Which one of the following reasons do most historians cite as the cause of the Agricultural Revolutions?
   (A) People migrated to regions that could finally support agriculture.
   (B) Climate change drove people to abandon foraging in favor of agriculture.
   (C) Foraging groups grew so large that they could no longer function as nomadic societies.
   (D) Major river valleys stopped flooding, which allowed people to settle along their banks.

3. Egypt benefited from its geographic location because
   (A) it was located at the crossroads of key trade routes.
   (B) isolated by desert, it was spared major invasions.
   (C) it sat atop some of Africa's richest gold mines.
   (D) its vast resources prevented it from ever having to engage in long-distance trade.

4. Women in ancient Egypt
   (A) never held any political power or influence.
   (B) were the main source of agricultural labor.
   (C) were empowered by the matrilineal nature of Egyptian civilization.
   (D) could inherit property and divorce their husbands.

5. The political system of ancient Egypt included all of the following EXCEPT
   (A) pharaoh as the source of all law.
   (B) a large bureaucracy that provided pharaoh with important support.
   (C) a large and powerful merchant class that facilitated long-distance trade.
   (D) the occasional presence of women in positions of influence.

6. Which two developments arose in Ancient Egypt?
   (A) hieroglyphics and papyrus
   (B) cuneiform and papyrus
   (C) monotheism and the concept of zero
   (D) a written law code and the calendar

7. Which of the following best describes sub-Saharan African societies prior to 1 C.E.?
   (A) Sub-Saharan Africa was tied to the rest of the world through the Indian Ocean trade network.
   (B) Most sub-Saharan African societies shared major cultural components such as language and religion.
   (C) Geographic isolation resulted in major cultural and technological developments coming from within the region.
   (D) Low population density and the massive size of the region prevented significant migration and interaction.

8. Archaeologists are able to trace the Bantu migration
   (A) through the written records of the people they conquered.
   (B) because of the distinct architectural style of their buildings.
   (C) through the spread of iron smelting and language.
   (D) through the adoption of its specific law code by societies across Africa.

9. Which of the following events had the greatest impact on trans-Saharan trade?
   (A) the domestication of the camel
   (B) the discovery of new water sources in the region
   (C) the Egyptian invasion of Nubia
   (D) the regular flood patterns of the Nile River

10. Which of the following is an accurate description of how Egypt changed from the Old Kingdom to the Middle Kingdom and New Kingdom?
    (A) Egypt's power and role in the region decreased dramatically.
    (B) Egypt undertook economically motivated expansion.
    (C) Nubians invaded Egypt, and thus later kingdoms were ruled exclusively by outsiders.
    (D) Egyptian civilization moved away from the Nile River.

11. Which of the following statements best describes the impact of the geography of Egypt?
    (A) Natural resources were widely available and enabled Egypt to be self-sufficient.
    (B) The arid climate of the region made survival a challenge for Egyptians.
    (C) The unpredictable nature of the Nile River made transportation, trade, and agriculture a challenge.
    (D) The harsh nature of the region prevented the establishment of an agricultural foundation.

12. The advent of hieroglyphics and cursive script in early Egypt resulted in all of the following EXCEPT
    (A) widespread use of inscriptions on monuments.
    (B) creation of written literature that told tales of adventure, love, and magic.
    (C) more efficient recordkeeping by the bureaucrats.
    (D) a dramatic increase in literacy among the working class.

13. Which of the following statements is true about religion in Egypt?
    (A) Nature had a minimal influence and role in religion.
    (B) Early Egypt was polytheistic before adopting monotheism from Nubia.
    (C) Female deities and priestesses reflected a level of respect for women.
    (D) There was no connection between religion and politics.

14. The social structure of ancient Egypt was
    (A) fluid, and status was based on one's skill and merit.
    (B) a tiered system dominated by the wealthy.
    (C) a caste system with no social mobility.
    (D) based on one's relationship and proximity to pharaoh.

EugenZ/Shutterstock.com

15. The temple shown in the photo above was most likely found in
    (A) ancient Egypt.
    (B) Mesopotamia.
    (C) Indus Valley.
    (D) sub-Saharan Africa.

Free-Response Questions

1. Compare life in foraging societies with life in agricultural societies after the Agricultural Revolutions.

2. Analyze the effects of two key transformations in African history before 600 C.E. Also describe continuities in Africa during the same time period.

Answers

MULTIPLE-CHOICE QUESTIONS

1. ANSWER: **C**. Though large enough to defend themselves, hunter-gatherer communities rarely exceeded around fifty people so as to not exhaust the food supply in their area (*The Earth and Its Peoples*, 5th ed., p. 6/6th ed., p. 8).

2. ANSWER: **B**. Global warming ended the last Ice Age around 9000 B.C.E. As the climate changed in different regions, people adapted to the environment. As a result, people created settled communities in those regions best suited for agriculture (*The Earth and Its Peoples*, 5th ed., p. 11/6th ed., p. 12).

3. ANSWER: **B**. Egypt was impacted greatly by its geographic environment; it was in essence an isolated land protected from invasion by deserts and a harborless coast along the Mediterranean (*The Earth and Its Peoples*, 5th ed., p. 24/6th ed., p. 23).

4. ANSWER: **D**. According to legal documents, Egyptian women could own and inherit property, and they had a role in deciding when to marry and when to dissolve the marriage (*The Earth and Its Peoples*, 5th ed., pp. 28–29/6th ed., pp. 29–30).

5. ANSWER: **C**. The government of Egypt controlled long-distance trade. As a result, the merchant class, which developed in other places that had less government involvement in the economy, did not take root in Egypt (*The Earth and Its Peoples*, 5th ed., p. 27/6th ed., pp. 27–28).

6. ANSWER: **A**. Hieroglyphics was the writing system of ancient Egypt, for which a unique writing material made from the stems of the papyrus plant was created (*The Earth and Its Peoples*, 5th ed., p. 27/6th ed., p. 28).

7. ANSWER: **C**. Many sub-Saharan African societies shared cultural characteristics that developed during the region's isolation from the rest of the world (*The Earth and Its Peoples*, 5th ed., p. 213/6th ed., p. 235).

8. ANSWER: **C**. Linguistic analysis of sub-Saharan Africans shows more than three hundred languages in the Bantu family. Additionally, as Bantu speakers migrated they transferred the use of iron, which greatly aided agricultural production (*The Earth and Its Peoples*, 5th ed., pp. 216–217/6th ed., p. 237).

9. ANSWER: A. Trans-Saharan trade was connected to the spread of camel domestication because these animals made it easier for people to cross the desert (*The Earth and Its Peoples*, 5th ed., p. 211/6th ed., p. 231).

10. ANSWER: B. During the Middle and New Kingdoms, Egypt extended its control to Nubia in an effort to control valuable natural resources such as the gold fields east of the Nile (*The Earth and Its Peoples*, 5th ed., pp. 52–53/6th ed., pp. 86–87).

11. ANSWER: A. The Nile River region provided Egypt with a wealth of natural resources, including papyrus reeds, clay, stone, and wild animals (*The Earth and Its Peoples*, 5th ed., p. 25/6th ed., p. 24).

12. ANSWER: D. An increase in literacy in Egypt caused by the development of writing in Egypt was limited mainly to a literate administrative class that carried out the functions of government (*The Earth and Its Peoples*, 5th ed., p. 27/6th ed., p. 28).

13. ANSWER: C. The presence of female gods and priestesses hints that women received a higher level of respect, rights, and social freedom in Egypt than in Mesopotamia (*The Earth and Its Peoples*, 5th ed., p. 29/6th ed., p. 30).

14. ANSWER: B. Though Egypt lacked the formal social structure seen elsewhere, Egyptians with more money and power enjoyed higher status, and the majority of the population were peasants (*The Earth and Its Peoples*, 5th ed., p. 28/6th ed., p. 29).

15. ANSWER: A. The Mortuary Temple of Queen Hatshepsut is located at Deir el-Bahri, Egypt (*The Earth and Its Peoples*, 5th ed., p. 74/6th ed., p. 58).

FREE-RESPONSE QUESTIONS

1. A good response would establish the criteria for the comparison— for example, political, economic, and/or social and gender structure. Politically, agricultural communities were much larger, and because of the specialization of labor that accompanied increased agricultural production, more formal government existed. Land took on great value in settled communities. In regions where pastoralists shared space with agriculturalists, tension and conflict arose over how to use land. Economically, fewer people were engaged in food production after the Agricultural Revolutions. This allowed for division of labor and technological advances, notably in metallurgy. Last, settled communities saw a more rigid social structure and changes in the role of women. When everyone was engaged in food collection in foraging societies, there was a greater sense of equality. Now that people had different roles in society, so too did people have different statuses. Women, in particular, saw their role shift from being important contributors to food gathering to a position in

which most of their influence was in raising children and tending the household.

2. A good start in approaching this essay is to think of the many major changes that occurred in early African history. You might choose the transition from the nomadic, foraging lifestyle to settled communities brought on by the Agricultural Revolutions. Or you could choose the transition from settled communities to the more established Egyptian civilization made possible by the clustering of communities along the Nile River. Other changes that were so significant as to spark a new period in African history include the introduction of the domesticated camel to the region, which greatly aided trade—of ideas and culture as well as goods—across the Sahara. You could also write about the Bantu migration and the transfer of language and technology that heightened cultural unity in the region and resulted in a population increase and a stronger economy, both of which enabled Africa to be an important participant in the Indian Ocean trade network. Continuities could include cultural aspects such as the presence of animist religions and the importance of the oral tradition.

2

THE MIDDLE EAST: UP TO CIRCA 600 C.E.

KEY CONCEPTS

- Civilizations emerged in Mesopotamia with their own distinctive culture and political and social structures.
- City-states and empires in the Middle East sat at the crossroads of major trade routes, such as the Silk Road and sea routes through the Mediterranean Sea and Indian Ocean, along which both products and culture traveled.
- The geographic, political, and economic characteristics of the Middle East gave rise to the first empires.
- Judaism and Christianity originated in the Middle East and had an impact on political events and social structure.

KEY TERMS

- Christianity
- city-state
- cuneiform
- Hellenism/Hellenistic Age
- Judaism
- Mesopotamia
- monotheism
- Neo-Assyrian Empire
- Persian Empire
- polytheism
- Zoroastrianism

Early Mesopotamian civilization is covered in the fifth edition of *The Earth and Its Peoples,* Chapters 1 and 3 and in the sixth edition, Chapters 1 and 2. The Persian Empire is covered in detail in fifth and sixth editions, Chapter 4. The Roman presence in the region and the rise of Christianity can be found in fifth and sixth editions, Chapter 5.

MESOPOTAMIA

The first domestication of plants and animals occurred in the Middle East around 8000 B.C.E. in the Fertile Crescent, which encompasses the area from the Persian Gulf through Iraq to the area around the border between Syria and Turkey. Jericho, located in present-day Palestine, was settled around 8000 B.C.E. It and the ruins of Çatal Hüyük (7000–5000 B.C.E.), located in present-day Turkey, provide archaeologists with evidence of early settled communities: mud-brick structures, pottery, metalworking, long-distance trade, religion, and an agriculture-based economy that allowed for division of labor.

By 5000 B.C.E. the Agricultural Revolution had reached **Mesopotamia**, the land between the Tigris and the Euphrates Rivers. The geography of the region allowed such development but offered many challenges. The rivers were important sources of irrigation and offered a means of transportation; however, their unpredictable flood pattern made farming difficult, and it occasionally isolated the fields, people, and towns. Techniques to maximize land use were incorporated beginning around 4000 B.C.E., first with the use of ox-drawn plows and then with the construction of irrigation canals to supply water to fields. Additionally, fields were left fallow every other year so that the soil retained nutrients.

Beginning around 3100 B.C.E., Mesopotamia gave rise to the first complex civilizations and empires, which over time would compete with one another and influence lands beyond the Middle East. The region also saw considerable cultural synthesis as customs, religion, and language were adopted and adapted over time.

Success in agriculture led to the emergence of the city-state—an urban center and the agricultural territory it controlled. Within a **city-state** many worked in the fields while others were craftspeople, religious leaders, or political leaders. Farmers produced food for the city, and city dwellers provided markets, as well as protection for farmers when conflict arose with neighboring city-states. Mesopotamian city-states were centered on two main focal points: the temple and the palace of the king. Religion in Mesopotamia, organized by the state, was a very public affair. Large temples constructed to gods of the elements reflected the geographic challenges of the region and the importance of agriculture. Temples were centrally located and tended by priests, who were important members of society. The importance of religion and the ownership of land—land being a source of wealth—put priests in a prominent political and economic role.

The importance of priests, however, was surpassed by that of the king. Viewed as the gods' representative on earth, he controlled the army, provided protection, built infrastructure, and maintained justice. A good example of strong political leadership is the Babylonian king Hammurabi, who ruled in the eighteenth century B.C.E. Through military campaigns he expanded Babylonian rule and implemented his famous Law Code over the region. Inscribed on a stone pillar, the Law Code established criteria for judicial decisions and clear, often severe punishment for criminals.

The rise of city-states supported long-distance trade by which regions exchanged natural resources native to their land. (The absence of money for most of its history meant that Mesopotamia had a barter economy.) The emergence of city-states also cemented social divisions within society. Rights and privileges differed according to wealth and profession. Hammurabi's Babylonia, with its three main classes, serves as a good example of the divisions within such a society. The highest class was the free landowning class consisting of royalty, high-ranking officials, warriors, priests, and some merchants. As trade flourished, merchants became more prominent members of society, and by the second millennium B.C.E. guilds—professional organizations—emerged. In the middle were farmers, who made up the agricultural workforce and were often attached to an estate owned privately or by the king or temple. The bottom of the social ladder was occupied by slaves, who worked mostly in a domestic capacity. Slaves were often prisoners of war or people who could not repay debts. Though a presence in society, slaves in Mesopotamia did not play a large role in the economy, unlike slaves in the classical or modern era.

Social distinctions also fell along gender lines. Women's status changed dramatically in the transition from the hunter-gatherer lifestyle to the agriculture-based settled communities. As families grew in size because of a stable food supply and an increased demand for labor, women's main role was bearing and raising children, which left little time for the acquisition of a skill or political influence. That said, women's legal and political rights varied from society to society. In Mesopotamia, women could own property, control their dowry, and engage in trade. Some women did work outside the home but in specific industries at the lower rungs of society. As the city-state emerged in Mesopotamia, women's status deteriorated further with the rise of the middle class. Marriage and divorce laws favored the husband, and marriage was often used as a way to create ties between families and bolster their economic standing. Women were often nothing more than economic objects.

AP Tip

Pay attention to the social and gender structures of a particular society. This is excellent information to include when making comparisons across time and place.

Writing developed in the Middle East prior to 3300 B.C.E. and likely evolved from a system for documenting property. The system of recording strokes and wedges on a damp clay tablet, which hardened as it dried, *cuneiform,* recorded first the Sumerian language and eventually other languages in the region. In spite of the expansion of cuneiform during the second millennium B.C.E., the number of people who could read and write remained small.

In addition to writing, Mesopotamians developed other important techniques and technologies that helped advance their civilizations. Beasts of burden such as cattle and donkeys were employed as important sources of power and transportation before the domestication of the camel in 1200 B.C.E. Horses, in use by 2000 B.C.E., provided another important mode of transportation. Like archers, horsemen and charioteers revolutionized military strategy. Bronze tools and weapons were made from imported ores, and the effective use of clay in making bricks and pottery was instrumental in constructing housing. Mesopotamians also developed the base-60 system in mathematics and studied astronomy.

Advances by city-states within Mesopotamia often spread through the Middle East. In the second millennium B.C.E., interaction with other regions increased, resulting in a cosmopolitan period. Diplomatic and economic interaction benefited the elite of the societies involved. The peasants, who continued to constitute the majority of the people, may also have seen some improvements in their lifestyles.

By 1500 B.C.E., Mesopotamia was essentially divided into two political and cultural zones. In the south, Babylonia continued in its position of dominance, gained under Hammurabi's leadership two hundred years earlier. In the north, Assyria, which for centuries had imported ore and textiles, appeared ready to conquer land and expand its economic interests. In contrast to the smaller city-states of the previous millennia, Babylonia and Assyria increased their interaction with Egypt and the Hittites in Anatolia, who provided copper, silver, and iron to much of the Middle East. The coexistence of these large states, however, did not last long. Around 1200 B.C.E., many of the economic and political centers in the region declined as a result of conflict in Anatolia and the subsequent economic collapse of their intertwined economies. For the next three hundred years, Mesopotamia experienced a period of isolation and poverty.

THE NEO-ASSYRIAN EMPIRE

The Assyrians rose again to establish what many historians consider the first empire, the **Neo-Assyrian Empire** (911–612 B.C.E.), by conquering and governing diverse peoples inhabiting far-off lands. The Assyrian homeland in northern Mesopotamia, with a more temperate climate and greater rainfall than areas to the south, enabled farmers to support a growing population and expansion. Additionally, experience in defending themselves from invaders to the north served many farmers well when they became foot soldiers for the empire.

The Assyrians succeeded because they had professional soldiers armed with iron weapons and aided by a cavalry and the machinery and techniques for besieging towns. Their expansion, because it followed trade routes, provided immediate economic rewards, and as neighboring kingdoms were conquered, a tribute system was put in place. The Assyrians treated the peoples they conquered harshly. Policies were designed to benefit the imperial center, and the use of terror and forced deportation effectively kept the conquered people in line and discouraged thoughts of rebellion. To administer the empire, regional officials who had sworn their obedience to the king oversaw payment of tribute, enforced laws, built infrastructure, and supplied the army in their region. Though this system proved effective at maintaining order and funneling the wealth of the region to the king, the Neo-Assyrian Empire extended economic prosperity to much of the region and expanded long-distance trade. Assyrian rule lasted until 612 B.C.E., when the empire eroded from the hatred of its conquered peoples and its own increasingly diverse—and less loyal—population.

ISRAEL

On the east coast of the Mediterranean, in about 2000 B.C.E., the Israelites were gathering into settled communities and transforming the nature of religion. The Israelites were a relatively small population inhabiting a small region poor in natural resources but strategically located at the crossroads of important trade routes. However, their contributions to history were large.

The story of the Israelites, as documented in the Hebrew Bible, begins with Abraham, who is considered the father of three **monotheistic** religions—**Judaism**, **Christianity**, and Islam. Abraham believed that there is only one god, Yahweh, who in a covenant with the Israelites agreed to make them his chosen people and promised them the land of Israel. In exchange, the Israelites would worship only Yahweh as specified by the Ten Commandments. These beliefs in many ways isolated Jews from others, but they also instilled a strong sense of community and identity.

The Israelites reached their political and economic peak in the tenth century B.C.E. under King Solomon. To solidify the position of the Israelites and their religion relative to others in the Middle East, Solomon constructed the First Temple. While the temple helped legitimize Judaism, it also heightened the importance of priests. With the expansion of the city of Jerusalem and the increased economic opportunities of this time, society became more stratified. Others joined the temple priests in setting themselves apart from the relatively homogeneous group that had made the initial transition to a settled community. Gaps between rich and poor emerged, and institutions like marriage took on an economic as well as social significance. Women were respected for the vital role they had played in the early history of Israel, but now they lacked the property and marriage rights of men. Women could not inherit property or initiate divorce, and while some women worked outside the home, most assumed duties in the home and in agriculture.

When the Neo-Assyrian Empire conquered the region around Israel in 721 B.C.E., much of the kingdom was destroyed and its people deported to the east. This destruction and deportation were repeated in 587 B.C.E. when the Neo-Babylonian Empire attacked Jerusalem. Despite these upheavals, Judaism survived the dispersal of Jews from their homeland, known as the Diaspora. The strength of Jewish rituals, rules, and beliefs sustained community and identity.

AP Tip

Be able to describe the basic features and origins of major religions, and note how they shape society through their rules and expectations for men and women.

THE PERSIAN EMPIRE

The Neo-Assyrian Empire was followed by the rise of the **Persian Empire**. Bound by language and culture, various groups that made their homeland in modern-day Iran joined to form the largest empire the world had yet seen. One group, the Medes, took the lead in challenging the Assyrian Empire and precipitating its collapse. Beginning about 550 B.C.E., the Persians, led by Cyrus, put together an empire of staggering size, stretching from Greece to India and from the Caucasus Mountains to North Africa. To administer such an expansive territory, Darius I created a unique organizational structure. He divided the empire into twenty provinces, each controlled by a *satrap*, or governor. Typically related to the royal family, satraps oversaw their territory and, most importantly, collected taxes and tribute to send to the king. Though roads were well maintained and patrolled, information traveled slowly, so satraps farther from the capital enjoyed some autonomy. Darius is also remembered as a lawgiver, and building on the decentralized nature of the provincial system, he allowed people within the empire to live according to their own traditions and rules. Darius and his followers also practiced **Zoroastrianism.** A unique religion that may have influenced Judaism, Zoroastrianism preached the belief in one supreme god, introduced the notions of Heaven and Hell, reward and punishment, and the Messiah—a savior sent by God.

After ongoing conflict with the Greeks in the fifth and fourth centuries B.C.E., the Persian Empire eventually succumbed to the armies of Alexander the Great in 330 B.C.E. The Greek Empire then controlled virtually the same territory as the Persians had and, after the death of Alexander, for the next three hundred years the region experienced the influence of Greek culture known as the **Hellenistic Age.**

The Hellenistic Age ended with the rise of the Roman Empire. Though centered more on the Mediterranean, Roman rule did extend through Anatolia, and by 6 C.E. had reached present-day Israel and Palestine. Occupying the eastern Mediterranean region, the Roman Empire sat at the end of the Silk Road, which brought goods from as far away as China.

The **polytheistic** and pagan nature of Roman religion did not blend well with the tenets of Judaism, and in this tense environment Jesus and Christianity emerged. That Judaism and Christianity emerged in the same geographic area and that Jesus was a Jew help explain many of the similarities between these two religions. Both are monotheistic; further, both believe in the same god. The Five Books of Moses that constitute the Hebrew Torah are the first five books of the Bible. The Ten Commandments apply to both religions. Christians, however, believe Jesus was the Messiah, and their Bible also contains the New Testament, which tells of the life and teachings of Jesus. After Jesus' crucifixion, Paul and other followers spread Christianity in spite of Roman opposition. In the face of hostility, many of the early converts were women, slaves, or the urban poor—groups oppressed by Roman rule.

The transition from settled communities to vast empires that took place in the Middle East also occurred in Africa, Asia, Europe, and the

Americas. All can be easily compared—in many respects the process was much the same, no matter the region. As these civilizations and empires emerged, they were bound together by the trade and interaction that traversed the Middle East.

Multiple-Choice Questions

1. Which of the following was the largest geographic challenge for the people settling in Mesopotamia?
   (A) the unpredictable nature of the Tigris and Euphrates Rivers
   (B) the absence of useful building materials
   (C) poor soil for agriculture
   (D) the absence of large animals that could be domesticated and employed in agriculture

2. All of the following were characteristic of city-states in Mesopotamia EXCEPT
   (A) clear social divisions.
   (B) provision of food for the city by farmers.
   (C) a diminished role of religion.
   (D) specialized labor.

3. Which of the following best describes women's roles in city-states in Mesopotamia?
   (A) The opportunity arose for women to occupy positions of political power.
   (B) Women no longer worked outside of the home.
   (C) Women could own property and engage in trade.
   (D) Fewer children were needed, so women had more time to work and acquire skills.

4. All of the following are true of slavery in Mesopotamia EXCEPT
   (A) slaves occupied the lowest class of society.
   (B) slaves in Mesopotamia played a more important role in society than those in Greece and Rome.
   (C) most slaves were prisoners of war.
   (D) slaves faced harsher punishment under law codes because of their position in society.

5. Which of the following best describes how the Assyrians treated the people they conquered?
   (A) Freedom and autonomy were granted to conquered people in an effort to win their allegiance.
   (B) Mass deportation and terror were used to keep people in line.
   (C) Wealth was channeled from the center to the outlying areas by the paternalistic ruler.
   (D) In an effort to control subjects, all long-distance trade was halted.

6. The Israelites were unique in the region because of their
   (A) location along the Mediterranean Sea and large involvement in trade.
   (B) continued existence as nomadic herdsmen while others formed settled communities.
   (C) wealth of natural resources.
   (D) belief in monotheism and a covenant with God.

7. To control the vast Persian Empire, Darius I
   (A) used terror and mass deportation to prevent uprisings.
   (B) instituted a limited democracy.
   (C) divided the empire into provinces run by governors.
   (D) controlled all aspects of life from his capital city.

8. Which of the following is an example of Hellenism?
   (A) Alexander the Great's military strategy for expansion
   (B) The presence of Greek architecture in the Middle East
   (C) The presence of pyramids in Egypt and ziggurats in Mesopotamia
   (D) The extensive roads of the Persian and Roman Empires

9. Which of the following is true of the Assyrian, Persian, Greek, and Roman Empires?
   (A) They all conquered major cities and trade routes of the region.
   (B) Each empire bordered the Mediterranean Sea.
   (C) They all instituted a centralized administration.
   (D) Each overlapped with the early river valley civilizations in Mesopotamia and Egypt.

10. All of the following are true of Judaism and Christianity EXCEPT
    (A) Jews received better treatment than Christians while under Roman rule.
    (B) both religions originated in present-day Israel and Palestine.
    (C) the Hebrew Torah is also part of the Christian Bible.
    (D) both Judaism and Christianity are monotheistic.

11. The Phoenicians were significant because
    (A) they developed the city-state model of governing.
    (B) they created an alphabetic system of writing.
    (C) they were the first empire in the region.
    (D) they dominated overland trade routes that crossed the region.

12. The Persian Empire imposed a tribute system in order to
    (A) share its wealth with neighboring regions.
    (B) promote conversion to Zoroastrianism.
    (C) fund all of the vast expenses of the empire.
    (D) hoard wealth and highlight its power over its neighbors.

13. Zoroastrianism was influential because
    (A) it promoted the rights of women and the idea that marriage was a partnership.
    (B) key ideas such as monotheism and the Messiah were later adopted by Judaism and Christianity.
    (C) it empowered the poor to rise up against the king and caused chaos within the empire.
    (D) it provided a rigid social structure in which one's life was dictated by gender, age, and occupation.

14. Which of the following statements best describes the condition of women in ancient Greece?
    (A) Women enjoyed freedom of movement and speech.
    (B) Women were equal participants in Greek democracy.
    (C) The condition of women varied depending on the community.
    (D) Women could own slaves and inherit property but had little say in marriage.

15. Which of the following is true of the empires of Alexander the Great and Darius I?
    (A) The leaders of both relied on loyal local officials, who could exercise some level of autonomy.
    (B) Both empires valued Greek culture and helped spread it from the Mediterranean to South Asia.
    (C) Both were democratic empires that gave a voice to all free, landowning males.
    (D) Both empires benefited from long-distance trade with Asia and sub-Saharan Africa.

Free-Response Questions

1. Analyze the political continuities and changes in the Middle East from circa 600 B.C.E. to circa 600 C.E.

2. Compare the basic features of TWO of the following religious systems prior to circa 600 C.E.
   ▪ Polytheism
   ▪ Judaism
   ▪ Christianity

Answers

MULTIPLE-CHOICE QUESTIONS

1. ANSWER: A. The flooding of the Tigris and Euphrates Rivers was unpredictable, and the rivers sometimes changed course, which isolated towns and fields (*The Earth and Its Peoples*, 5th ed., p. 16/6th ed., p. 15).

2. ANSWER: C. The two centers of power that anchored the city-state were the palace and the temple, the latter of which was centrally located in the town (*The Earth and Its Peoples*, 5th ed., p. 18/6th ed., p. 17).

3. ANSWER: C. Men monopolized political life, but women could own property, control their dowry, and engage in trade (*The Earth and Its Peoples*, 5th ed., p. 20/6th ed., p. 20).

4. ANSWER: B. Slaves in Mesopotamia played a lesser economic role than their counterparts in classical Greece and Rome (*The Earth and Its Peoples*, 5th ed., p. 19/6th ed., p. 19).

5. ANSWER: B. To prevent rebellion and break the spirit of the conquered people, the Assyrians employed terror tactics and forcibly uprooted entire communities (*The Earth and Its Peoples*, 5th ed., p. 82/6th ed., p. 53).

6. ANSWER: D. According to the Hebrew Bible, God made a covenant with the Israelites that made them his chosen people (*The Earth and Its Peoples*, 5th ed., p. 85/6th ed., p. 56).

7. ANSWER: C. Darius divided the empire into twenty provinces, each of which was run by a governor (satrap) who was often related to the royal family (*The Earth and Its Peoples*, 5th ed., p. 111/6th ed., p. 109).

8. ANSWER: B. After the conquests by Alexander the Great, the lands that came under Greek rule were influenced greatly by its culture (*The Earth and Its Peoples*, 5th ed., p. 130/6th ed., p. 128).

9. ANSWER: A. The four major empires of this region were located along key trade routes and benefited from this location (*The Earth and Its Peoples*, maps of empires, 5th ed., pp. 81, 108, 134, 144/6th ed., pp. 53, 106, 129, 140).

10. ANSWER: A. As monotheistic religions, both Judaism and Christianity did not fit well with the Romans, who worshipped many gods and also idolized the emperor (*The Earth and Its Peoples*, 5th ed., p. 153/6th ed., p. 148).

11. ANSWER: B. The Phoenicians developed an alphabet with about two dozen symbols, each representing a sound. The Greeks would add to this system by including vowels (*The Earth and Its Peoples*, 5th ed., p. 91/ 6th ed., p. 62).

12. **ANSWER: D.** The Persian Empire, like many others, imposed a tribute system so as to collect wealth from those it controlled. While some of these resources were used to pay for the empire's expenses, the king kept much of it. The system also reminded those in the region where power rested (*The Earth and Its Peoples*, 5th ed., p. 111/6th ed., p. 109).

13. **ANSWER: B.** Though relatively small today, Zoroastrianism was one of the great religions of the ancient world, and its ideas were a major influence on Judaism and subsequently Christianity (*The Earth and Its Peoples*, 5th ed., p. 116/6th ed., p. 111).

14. **ANSWER: C.** Gender roles varied across the Greek city-states. In Sparta, for example, women were expected to raise strong children, exercise, and be seen in public. In Athens, however, women were confined to the home and their rights suppressed (*The Earth and Its Peoples*, 5th ed., p. 127/6th ed., p. 124).

15. **ANSWER: A.** Alexander the Great maintained the Persian model for ruling over a large territory, but he replaced Persian officials with his supporters (*The Earth and Its Peoples*, 5th ed., p. 130/6th ed., p. 127).

FREE-RESPONSE QUESTIONS

1. A good response will begin with civilization in Mesopotamia. Though many civilizations dotted the region, generalizations about government can be made and then supported by using the specific details about the political structure and actions. The next key aspect of political change is the rise of empires; the political structure of the empires was much more extensive than the political structure of the city-states; empires expanded beyond their homeland, conquered other people, and needed a bureaucracy to rule over diverse people in distant lands. A good response would include analysis of the decentralized nature of the Persian Empire. Continuities would include the presence of geographically large empires organized as monarchies.

2. When comparing belief systems, it is important to frame the basis of the comparison. For example, belief systems could be compared according to the nature of god or gods, important texts, laws that govern behavior, or their impact on social and gender structures. In this case, choosing Judaism and Christianity would allow for analysis of similarities that stem from the fact that Christianity grew out of Judaism, as well as the differences that exist. Selecting polytheism and one of the others would allow for clear distinctions in the nature of god(s), who practiced each religion, and when they originated. The importance of religion in people's lives and the way religion influences behavior are similarities that could be explored.

3

ASIA:
UP TO CIRCA 600 C.E.

KEY CONCEPTS

- Both China and India experienced major political developments that gave rise to powerful empires.
- The Shang and Zhou dynasties established the political and social foundation for future Chinese dynasties.
- Buddhism, Confucianism, Hinduism, and Daoism are all important belief systems that impacted social and gender structures.
- Across Asia there emerged land and sea trade networks that fostered the transfer of goods and ideas.

KEY TERMS

- Buddhism
- caste
- Confucianism
- Daoism
- Hinduism
- karma
- Legalism
- Mandate of Heaven
- nirvana
- sati
- varna

Information on Asia up to circa 600 C.E. can be found in *The Earth and Its Peoples*, fifth edition, Chapters 1, 2, 5, and 6 and sixth edition, Chapters 1, 3, 5, and 6.

EAST ASIA

The transition to settled agricultural communities began along the Yellow River in China around 8000 B.C.E. By the second millennium B.C.E., the first Chinese dynasty emerged, and the foundation for two thousand years of Chinese history was established. Over that time, China became an economic and political force that was often the envy of peoples near and far.

Like river valley civilizations elsewhere, early Chinese settlements took advantage of the rich, fertile land along the Yellow and Yangzi Rivers. The geography of eastern Asia, however, kept Chinese civilizations isolated from those in the Middle East and the Indus River Valley. The climate of the southern region was well suited for growing rice, which produces a very high yield but requires substantial time and labor. As a result, the population and importance of the southern region eventually exceeded that of the northern region. Early civilizations in China exhibited many of the same characteristics as those elsewhere. Plants and animals were domesticated, stone and eventually bronze tools were used, and pottery was produced on a wheel and fired in a kiln. Labor was divided, and political and social structures took shape.

In 1750 B.C.E. the history of China truly began when the Shang clan rose to power. Originating in the Yellow River Valley, the Shang extended their control by means of their military strength and strategy. The Shang were ruled by a king, who was seen as an intermediary between the gods and the people. To expand and manage the land, the king was aided by an aristocracy that acted as generals, ambassadors, and public servants. Conquered territory was governed by members of the royal family, and far-off lands were left to native rulers who swore their allegiance to the king. Many of the conquered people were taken as prisoners of war and enslaved by the Shang rulers.

Shang cities grew into political and social centers. Surrounded by agricultural areas, cities were laid out on a grid and served as hubs for a far-reaching trade network. Jade, ivory, silk, and bronze weapons and vessels were prized by outsiders, who carried them perhaps as far as Mesopotamia. Writing developed under the Shang and facilitated administration, even though only a small number of the elite had time to master this skill.

In 1027 B.C.E. the last Shang king was defeated by the Zhou, who established the longest-lasting dynasty in Chinese history and introduced the concept of the Mandate of Heaven, the key to the dynastic cycle that would last nearly three thousand years. To justify the overthrow of the Shang king, Zhou rulers claimed that the new ruler had been chosen by "Heaven" and should be seen as the "Son of Heaven." As long as the king was a moral servant of the people, he would retain the Mandate of Heaven and China would prosper. If the king became corrupt, then he would lose the **Mandate of Heaven**, justifying his replacement. The end of the Shang was marked by corruption, violence, greed, and arrogance; therefore, according to the Zhou, the overthrow was justified.

The Zhou dynasty retained many of the traditions and rituals of the Shang and was similarly decentralized. The dynasty was divided into over one hundred territories, each ruled by allies or relations of the king. Government officials were expected to rule in a fair and moral fashion. This system worked well for a time, but around 800 B.C.E., territories began to compete with one another for power until 480 B.C.E, when China entered a two-hundred-year phase known as the Warring States Period. In many states, rulers imposed an authoritarian system known as Legalism in order to keep their subjects under control and promote the state above the individual. Legalism was based on the view that because human nature is evil, order is maintained with laws and punishment.

It was during the Zhou dynasty that the roots of another, more important philosophical and managerial approach were established. Though his influence would not be felt until after his death, Confucius (551–479 B.C.E.) established his teachings based on the culture and practices of the Zhou dynasty. Confucius drew parallels between the family and the state, with the king serving as a father figure to his people and ruling with their interests at heart. Coincidentally, social structure of the later Zhou period moved from the clan-based system to the smaller family model that included grandparents, parents, and children. With the help of its followers, **Confucianism** would eventually become the philosophy that future dynasties embraced as a means to establish clear social structure.

The Warring States Period inspired another important Chinese philosopher, Laozi (believed to have lived in the sixth century B.C.E.), who conceived **Daoism** as an alternative to the authoritarian nature of Legalism and the rigid hierarchy of Confucianism. Daoism promoted an end to conflict by teaching people to follow the path (Dao) and to accept the world instead of seeking to change it.

Throughout the Shang and Zhou dynasties, China's patriarchal nature resembled that of many other early civilizations and empires: the father was the head of the family, and women were expected to tend to the household. Marriage was often an economic and political tool to promote power among elite families. Any land the family owned belonged to the father and was divided among his sons upon his death.

The Warring States Period ended in the third century B.C.E. when the Qin, led by Shi Huangdi, defeated their rivals and created China's first empire. The Qin was a totalitarian regime that promoted **Legalism** and enacted laws to prevent the rise of a rival power that might challenge Shi Huangdi's authority. For example, upon the death of an owner, land was divided among several heirs, and slavery was abolished to create a free labor force that would pay taxes and provide labor and military service. Shi Huangdi standardized coinage and laws and built thousands of miles of roads, canals, and walls to secure China. Upon his death, people rose up against the oppressive rule; when the rebellion ended, the Han dynasty was established.

The Han dynasty (206 B.C.E.–220 C.E.) was the classical period in Chinese history, and its cultural and political characteristics greatly influenced all subsequent dynasties. Like previous dynasties, the Han dynasty was centered on the river valleys in the eastern portion of the country. This fertile region produced crops that supported the population and was the basis of the tax system. To build the infrastructure, the government required able-bodied men to donate one month's worth of labor each year for the construction of palaces, temples, and roads and required two years of military service.

As the Han expanded, Chinese culture and social structure spread. The tenets of Confucianism established a clear hierarchy in which individuals saw themselves as having a particular role in the family and society. Fathers were the head of the family; a woman was to submit to her parents while she was young, her husband while married, and her son if widowed. As in the Zhou, the emperor was the "Son of Heaven" who was to rule in a paternal fashion so as to retain the Mandate of Heaven. Throughout the empire, peasants, soldiers, and administrators had their own particular role under the rule of the emperor, and they followed his word as law.

To administer the vast empire, Han emperors relied on local leaders to collect taxes, organize labor, and defend the empire. In order to get a prestigious government position, young men attended universities located around the country. Theoretically, this was a meritocracy that provided an opportunity for anyone to rise through the hierarchy, but in reality it was the sons of the wealthy and privileged classes who had the time and resources to study the Confucian classics and attend the universities. In part because of this, a large number of peasants turned to Daoism, which questioned the hierarchy, rules, and rituals of Confucianism that kept most peasants on the bottom rung of the social ladder.

The Han dynasty achieved many advances in technology that sustained the empire and eventually reached Europe. The crossbow and the use of cavalry helped the Han withstand challenges from nomadic people of Central Asia. Military forces, people, and goods traveled the extensive road system begun under the Qin and expanded by Han rulers. The watermill harnessed the power of running water to turn a grindstone, and the Han developed a horse collar that improved the use of animals in agriculture. These developments, along with paper, eventually made their way to Europe and the Middle East. But China's most valuable innovation was the production of silk. Silk was in high demand elsewhere in the world, and China maintained a monopoly on its production for centuries.

AP Tip

When asked to make comparisons, you will often be given several items and asked to choose two to compare. Many times there will be natural pairs among the choices given. If you can identify those, you will have an easier time making direct comparisons. For example, if asked to compare the origins and tenets of early religions, Confucianism and Daoism have historical connections, as do Hinduism and Buddhism. While other combinations are certainly possible, these pairings allow for more substantial analysis.

Unable to maintain a large empire over vast territories, the Han dynasty ended in 220 C.E. The cost of maintaining a military presence on the frontier, coupled with corruption within the government, peasant rebellions, and the rise of regional warlords, returned China to a period of political, economic, and cultural fragmentation that lasted until the Sui unification of the late sixth century C.E.

SOUTH ASIA

The diversity and culture of the Indian subcontinent developed because of its geographic isolation from the rest of Asia, as well as a combination of political forces. India is separated from the rest of Asia by the Himalayas to the north and the Indian Ocean on the other three sides. The most accessible land route to India is to the northwest, but it requires passing over the Hindu Kush Mountains and traversing the Thar Desert. Despite its diversity and relative isolation, the region would achieve cultural and economic influence throughout Asia.

Civilization developed in South Asia along the Indus River shortly after it did in Mesopotamia and Egypt. While archaeologists have located hundreds of communities, the high water table in the region has limited excavation—and therefore knowledge—of these early civilizations. The extensive urban planning and construction of the cities of Harappa and Mohenjo-Daro, for example, suggest that a strong central authority ruled. A strong central authority combined with the use of technologies such as irrigation techniques, the potter's wheel, and metalworking lead us to believe that the people in the Indus River Valley had attained a high level of knowledge and skills. Long-distance trade existed, as evidenced by the presence of Indus River Valley artifacts in Mesopotamia. Cities in the valley were abandoned after 1900 B.C.E., perhaps because of political, economic, and social failures brought on by natural disasters such as earthquake or flood. Urban centers in the area were replaced by patriarchal villages that relied on herds of animals and limited farming.

AP Tip

Belief systems can profoundly affect a time and place because they often impact political, social, and gender structures. With that in mind, it is important to study not only the basic tenets of different belief systems but also the impact they have on government, social structure, and gender roles.

The next important phase in Indian history began in 1500 B.C.E. when nomadic warriors from the northwest migrated to India. The Vedic Age—so called because the Vedas, the religious texts, provide the main source of information—saw the rise to dominance of Indo-European groups. After 1000 B.C.E., the lighter-skinned Aryas, who spoke Indo-European languages, competed with the darker-skinned Dasas, who spoke Dravidian languages. Over time the Aryas pushed the Dasas south, and skin color became a basis for making sharp social divisions based on *varna*, the four major social classes: priests and scholars (Brahmin); warriors and government officials (Kshatriya);

merchants, artisans, and landowners (Vaishya); and peasants or workers (Shudra). Installed by the Aryas, the system naturally restricted the Dasas to the lowest class. Eventually a fifth group was added, the Untouchables, who were excluded from the system, isolated from the others, and given the most demeaning jobs such as leather-tanning, which required contact with dead animals. These classes within the varna system were further broken down into different jati, or castes. Born into a **caste**, a person was expected to live, marry, and interact with his caste members. The belief in reincarnation helped entrench people in their caste. It was thought that when the soul is separated from the body at death, it is reborn in another form according to the karma of the individual. If a person accepted his role and did his duty, then he built up good **karma** that would be rewarded in his next life. In this way, the varna and the belief in reincarnation cemented a rigid social hierarchy in India.

This rigid social system sparked opposing movements in the eighth century B.C.E. The most serious threats to the Vedic religion and the power of the Brahmin class were Jainism and Buddhism. Jainism emphasized the value of all living creatures and promoted self-denial and nonviolence, but its influence and impact paled in comparison to **Buddhism**, which was founded by Siddhartha, a prince from the Kshatriya class, who gave up his wealthy lifestyle to pursue spiritual insight. Eventually he settled on the Middle Path of moderation and identified the Four Noble Truths about life: life is suffering; suffering comes from desire; suffering will end if desire ends; the way to end desire is to follow the Eightfold Path that outlines proper conduct. Followers of the Buddha sought **nirvana**, which was the ultimate reward of tranquility at the end of the cycle of reincarnation.

Buddhism became more popular than Jainism and had much greater influence in India and throughout Asia. After the death of the Buddha in 483 B.C.E., Buddhism spread throughout India and, via trade routes, to much of Asia. Without clear instructions left by the Buddha, the religion evolved as it spread. Those who began to worship Buddha as a god and produced images of him became known as Mahayana Buddhists. Mahayana Buddhists also revered bodhisattvas, who were enlightened men and women who forsook nirvana in order to help others live the proper life. Conversely, those bound to the original teachings that prohibited worship of a divine Buddha and depictions of him were Theravada Buddhists.

The popularity of Buddhism in India forced the Vedic religion to evolve into what is known as **Hinduism.** Though Brahmins retained their lofty position, they adopted the accessibility of Buddhism and allowed for more individual and personal interaction with the gods. Hinduism emphasized one's personal relationship with one of the gods, all of whom manifest the same universal force. Adopting key aspects of Buddhism allowed Hinduism to sustain its popularity; in fact, it drove Buddhism from the land of its origin. Though it would have a resurgence under Ashoka during the Mauryan Empire, Buddhism's popularity in East and Southeast Asia would exceed its popularity in India.

The diversity, geography, and social structure of the subcontinent made political unification rare in its early history. Language and customs differed across India, as did the organization and economic nature of each region. A stronger deterrent to political unity was the complicated social hierarchy and its promotion of caste identification over loyalty to a centralized political power. In spite of these factors promoting decentralization, the Mauryan and Gupta Empires emerged and helped create a unified civilization in India.

In 324 B.C.E., the Mauryan Empire rose out of a landscape of competing kinship groups and independent states. Its reign would extend over the entire subcontinent save the southernmost tip. A quarter of agricultural production was paid to the king, who also controlled mines, issued coinage, and oversaw a large and powerful army. He also appointed relatives and allies in each district to tend to administrative affairs. The most famous Mauryan king was Ashoka, the founder's grandson. After extensive and brutal military campaigns to extend the borders of the empire, Ashoka converted to Buddhism and began preaching nonviolence and tolerance. He famously inscribed his moral codes on large pillars throughout the empire. The Mauryan Empire constructed roads and towns that increased their role in land and sea trade networks that connected East and Southeast Asia with the Middle East and Europe. This key role continued even after the Mauryan Empire, attacked by outsiders, collapsed in 184 B.C.E.

After some five hundred years of political rivalry within India, the Gupta Empire came to power in much the same way the Mauryan Empire had. Gupta leaders controlled both agriculture and mining and required that their subjects donate labor to construction projects. The Gupta Empire, however, was not as centralized as the Mauryan Empire. A strong army helped the Gupta retain control, but as distance from the center increased, so too did the autonomy of the local leaders. By sharing profits from trade with the local leaders, Gupta kings were able to provide those with greater autonomy with an incentive to remain part of the empire. In addition to maintaining an influential role in regional trade, Indians were interested in the arts and sciences; mathematicians invented the concept of zero and developed the "Arabic" numerals that are used in much of the world today.

The role of women in India changed as the economy of South Asia developed. Increased trade created an urban middle class that valued property and undermined women's rights to own or inherit it. Opportunities for influence outside of the home were limited, and women in India, like their counterparts in China under Confucianism, were expected to obey their fathers, husbands, and sons. In parts of India, a woman was expected to commit **sati**—throwing herself on her husband's funeral pyre—or else be shunned by the community. Buddhism and Jainism did provide women with some freedom from male domination in the Hindu empire. Additionally, upper-class women had access to education and enjoyed more freedom than the poor. The Gupta Empire collapsed in 550 C.E. when it was attacked by the Huns of Central Asia.

<u>SOUTHEAST ASIA</u>

Southeast Asia includes Indochina, Malaysia, and the many islands extending out into the Pacific Ocean. Vast amounts of fertile land and a climate that enables multiple growing seasons promoted population growth and produced plants and animals that would eventually be exported to other regions—among them wet rice, soybeans, sugar cane, chickens, and pigs. Periodic disruptions to overland trade across Asia increased the role and power of Southeast Asia as sea trade expanded to meet demand. Trade routes also brought Buddhism to the area as Indian missionaries and East Asian pilgrims passed through on their way to and from India.

Multiple-Choice Questions

1. Zhou leaders established their legitimacy by
   (A) instilling in the people feelings of terror and fear.
   (B) suggesting they were chosen to lead by Heaven.
   (C) erasing many of the traditions and rituals of the Shang.
   (D) installing a decentralized regime that respected the individual.

2. All of the following are true about Confucianism EXCEPT
   (A) Confucianism was more influential after the death of Confucius.
   (B) the state was modeled on the family.
   (C) people were given clear roles and expectations based on age and gender.
   (D) opportunities existed for social promotion and equality.

3. Which statement is most reflective of Legalism?
   (A) Human nature is evil, so rules and strict punishments are needed to maintain order.
   (B) The emperor should rule the land as the father heads the family.
   (C) When the emperor is corrupt, he loses the right to rule, and his overthrow is acceptable.
   (D) Conquered territories must follow Chinese laws and pay tribute to the emperor each year.

4. To help govern the Han dynasty, emperors relied on
   (A) a system that channeled wealth from the center to the periphery, thus winning the allegiance of locals.
   (B) local leaders who studied Confucianism at national universities.
   (C) advanced military weapons and techniques that came from Europe.
   (D) an ideology that effectively combined Legalism and Daoism.

5. Which of the following best explains the reason for the decline of the Han dynasty?
   (A) The Han dynasty declined because no suitable replacement emerged after the death of its prominent and powerful founder.
   (B) The Han dynasty was invaded by outsiders from Central Asia, who founded the next great Chinese dynasty.
   (C) Han China collapsed under the economic strain of having a negative balance of trade with Europe.
   (D) Han China declined due to the enormous expense and demands of maintaining a large empire.

6. Confucianism and Hinduism are similar in that
   (A) both are based on the teachings of an individual.
   (B) both were introduced by outsiders seeking to control the native population.
   (C) both promote gender equity.
   (D) both promote a rigid social hierarchy with limited social mobility.

7. All of the following are true about Buddhism EXCEPT
   (A) Buddhism began in China and spread to India.
   (B) Buddhism experienced a schism after the death of the Buddha.
   (C) Buddhists believe enlightenment comes from living according to clear rules.
   (D) Buddhists believe in reincarnation.

8. Which statement best describes the political nature of India prior to 400 B.C.E.?
   (A) The subcontinent was dominated by a large and powerful empire that rose shortly after the emergence of civilization along the Indus River.
   (B) Like China, India had periods of centralized authority separated by periods of conflict and disunity.
   (C) India consisted of many diverse societies whose organization and economies differed.
   (D) Aside from small cities along the Indus River, most people on the subcontinent were either pastoralists or foragers.

9. Which statement is true about the Mauryan and Gupta Empires?
   (A) They were both highly centralized regimes that relied on a strong army to retain control throughout each empire.
   (B) Mauryan and Gupta kings controlled the key economic aspects of society in order to construct a vast and effective infrastructure.
   (C) The Mauryan Empire rose from within India while the Gupta Empire was founded by an invading force that came through the Hindu Kush Mountains and across the Thar Desert.
   (D) The Gupta Empire was a Buddhist government ruling over a Hindu population while the Mauryan were Hindu as were their subjects.

10. Which of the following statements best describes the regional strength of Southeast Asia relative to South and East Asia?
    (A) Southeast Asia's economic and political importance increased whenever Silk Road trade was disrupted.
    (B) Southeast Asia's political strength grew when Buddhism was imported from India.
    (C) Southeast Asia was an economic equal to China but could never compete with the powerful Mauryan and Gupta Empires.
    (D) Southeast Asia lacked the natural resources to sustain a large enough population to compete economically with the rest of Asia.

11. Which of the following was true of Chinese society during the Han dynasty?
    (A) It was patriarchal and organized around the family.
    (B) Its commitment to gender equality made it unique in its time.
    (C) The popularity of Buddhism erased the strong, rigid social structure.
    (D) The majority of the population lived in an urban setting.

12. The Vedic Age in India was notable because
    (A) the subcontinent was isolated from other parts of the world.
    (B) it was one of the few times when great social mobility existed in India.
    (C) it was the period of greatest traffic along the Silk Road.
    (D) the foundations for much of Indian history were established.

13. Which of the following was true of the status of women during the Gupta Empire?
    (A) Women could own and inherit property.
    (B) Women began to marry later and had more say in who they wed.
    (C) Women of higher status enjoyed more freedom than poor women.
    (D) The Buddhist and Jainist communities increased their oppression of women.

14. Mauryan emperor Ashoka is known for all of the following EXCEPT
    (A) vast military expansion of the empire.
    (B) converting to Buddhism and preaching nonviolence.
    (C) publicizing decrees on sandstone pillars throughout the empire.
    (D) intolerance of others, most notably his harsh treatment of Hindus.

15. Which of the following best describes the Silk Road?
    (A) A trade route linking the Mediterranean region to East Asia
    (B) The Han system of roads that were used to move goods and soldiers within the empire
    (C) The route taken by tributary states of the Han dynasty as they made the annual trip to China to pay respect to the emperor
    (D) The circuit traveled by central Asian pastoral nomads as they moved their herds from one grazing area to the next

Free-Response Questions

1. Compare the origins and tenets of TWO of the following religious and philosophical systems.
■ Buddhism
■ Confucianism
■ Hinduism
■ Daoism

2. Analyze the continuities and changes in gender roles in India and China from circa 600 B.C.E. to circa 600 C.E.

Answers

MULTIPLE-CHOICE QUESTIONS

1. **ANSWER: B.** To justify the overthrow of the Shang king, the Zhou created the concept of the Mandate of Heaven, which would remain the source of legitimacy in China for thousands of years (*The Earth and Its Peoples*, 5th ed., p. 45/6th ed., pp. 78–79).

2. **ANSWER: D.** Confucianism imposed a rigid social hierarchy, and even when Confucian texts were used as the basis of civil service exams, only those with the time and means to study the classics excelled on the exams (*The Earth and Its Peoples*, 5th ed., p. 47/6th ed., p. 81).

3. **ANSWER: A.** Legalism was installed by the Qin dynasty in an effort to maintain order and prevent the rise of rival powers (*The Earth and Its Peoples*, 5th ed., p. 51/6th ed., p. 85).

4. **ANSWER: B.** Han leaders relied on local leaders to collect taxes, organize labor, and help defend the empire from attack. Young men obtained these desirable positions by studying the teachings of Confucius at national universities (*The Earth and Its Peoples*, 5th ed., p. 162/6th ed., p. 155).

5. **ANSWER: D.** The great expense of maintaining the large empire took its toll over time until peasant uprisings and regional fighting could no longer be suppressed (*The Earth and Its Peoples*, 5th ed., p. 165/6th ed., p. 159).

6. **ANSWER: D.** Both Hinduism and Confucianism are based on a rigid social structure in which people have clear roles and expectations depending on their family, gender, profession, etc. (*The Earth and Its Peoples*, 5th ed., pp. 47, 181–182/6th ed., pp. 81, 174).

7. **ANSWER: A.** Though it became much more popular in East and Southeast Asia, Buddhism began in India (*The Earth and Its Peoples*, 5th ed., p. 179/6th ed., p. 170).

8. **ANSWER: C.** Prior to the rise of the Mauryan Empire in 324 B.C.E., the cultural, linguistic, and economic diversity of the region made

political unification difficult (*The Earth and Its Peoples*, 5th ed., p. 183/6th ed., p. 174).

9. ANSWER: **B.** Both Mauryan and Gupta kings controlled agricultural production and the mining industry and used the income from this arrangement to build vast roads, cities, and ports (*The Earth and Its Peoples*, 5th ed., pp. 183–185/6th ed., pp. 175–176).

10. ANSWER: **A.** When overland trade routes between East Asia and the Mediterranean were disrupted, sea trade through Southeast Asia increased to meet the demand (*The Earth and Its Peoples*, 5th ed., p. 192/6th ed., p. 183).

11. ANSWER: **A.** The family was the basic unit of ancient China and served as a model for the state. While women's status varied depending on class, Han China remained a male-dominated society (*The Earth and Its Peoples*, 5th ed., pp. 162–163/6th ed., p. 156).

12. ANSWER: **D.** During the Vedic Age many key aspects of South Asian history were established, including the caste system and the core beliefs of Hinduism (*The Earth and Its Peoples*, 5th ed., p. 176/6th ed., p. 169).

13. ANSWER: **C.** During the Gupta Empire women's status declined. They married younger, could not inherit property, and sati, the ritual in which a widow threw herself on the fire when her husband was cremated, are all examples of this. Most women were treated as the lowest class, but women of higher status did enjoy more freedom and had some access to education (*The Earth and Its Peoples*, 5th ed., pp. 187–190/6th ed., pp. 178–179).

14. ANSWER: **D.** Ashoka expanded his grandfather's empire through violent military campaigns before he turned away from violence and converted to Buddhism. After his conversion he practiced nonviolence and religious tolerance (*The Earth and Its Peoples*, 5th ed., p. 183/6th ed., p. 175).

15. ANSWER: **A.** The Silk Road is a network of routes linking East Asia with the Mediterranean. The peak periods for the transfer of goods, technology, and religion occurred from approximately 100 B.C.E. to 900 C.E. and again under the Mongol rule in the thirteenth century C.E. (*The Earth and Its Peoples*, 5th ed., p. 202/6th ed., p. 224).

FREE-RESPONSE QUESTIONS

1. Key to writing a good response is making a good choice of the two religions to compare. For example, it is easy to compare Hinduism with Confucianism because of their similarities in cementing a social hierarchy. Other easy comparisons include Hinduism with Buddhism and Confucianism with Daoism because of their origins and relationship. Buddhism emerged in response to the Vedic religion. When Buddhism increased in popularity, the Vedic religion evolved into Hinduism with the adoption of some of the more popular aspects of Buddhism. Similarly, Daoism emerged in response to the rigid nature of Confucianism. As you can see, it is

worth taking a moment to consider the possible combinations because some pairs lend themselves more naturally to comparison.

2. To answer this question, consider the type of political systems in place in India and China over the time period. You could begin with a discussion of how the role of women changed with the emergence of complex civilization. Women's status in both regions deteriorated as their role shifted to raising children and caring for the family. You could then look at the emergence of Hinduism, Buddhism, and Confucianism in these regions and analyze how they impacted the role of women. Remember that most of your examples will address women's legal rights as they relate to marriage and property. It is also worth noting, where relevant, the role that status played, as upper-class women occasionally had more influence and rights. The continuities would include the pervasiveness of patriarchy and unequal legal rights.

4

EUROPE:
UP TO CIRCA 600 C.E.

KEY CONCEPTS

- The foundation of the Western world was established by the classical empires of Greece and Rome.
- The uneven collapse of the Roman Empire set Europe on two divergent paths for the following centuries.
- Christianity arose under Roman rule, and although initially reviled, it eventually flourished, in large part as a result of the policies of Emperor Constantine.

KEY TERMS

- Byzantine Empire
- Celtic Europe
- Hellenistic Age
- hoplite
- Linear B
- Minoans
- Mycenaeans
- Pax Romana
- polis
- Roman Republic
- Romanization
- third-century crisis

Information on Europe up to circa 600 C.E. can be found in *The Earth and Its Peoples,* fifth and sixth editions, Chapters 3, 4, and 5.

EARLY CIVILIZATIONS OF EUROPE AND THE MEDITERRANEAN

Farming communities emerged in southern Europe by 6000 B.C.E., years after similar developments in Africa, the Middle East, and East Asia. By 3500 B.C.E. agricultural communities existed throughout Europe, and the population density of the region increased as food sources became more reliable. Although European development of civilizations and empires was similarly delayed relative to its counterparts elsewhere in the world, when European civilizations did finally emerge a cultural and intellectual foundation was established for the Western world.

The first complex civilizations in Europe developed on the Mediterranean island of Crete and on the Greek peninsula. With natural resources such as arable land and metal deposits in short supply, the people of these lands took to the sea and created trade-based societies with close commercial and political ties to their neighbors. By 2000 B.C.E. the **Minoan** civilization had emerged on the island of Crete. Its centralized government, grand architecture, metal use, writing, and recordkeeping resembled the civilizations of Mesopotamia and Egypt. The similarities are best explained by the Minoans' proximity to western Asia and North Africa and a trade-based economy that allowed them to compensate for the geographic shortcomings of their homeland.

Around 1450 B.C.E. the **Mycenaean** Greeks destroyed much of the Minoan civilization and became the next significant civilization in the region. Borrowing the architectural, economic, and political components of their predecessors, the Mycenaeans were centered on the Greek peninsula and the islands in the Aegean Sea. They also used the Minoan writing system as the basis of their own, **Linear B**, which endured as an early form of Greek. Highly skilled sailors, the Mycenaeans built a trade-based economy, evidence of which is seen in the clay pots found throughout the Mediterranean and Middle East that once contained wine and olive oil and were traded for metals, grain, amber, and ivory. The accomplishments of the tough, warlike Mycenaeans were undone around 1200 B.C.E. by the economic and political collapse of their trading partners. Just one example of this is the destruction of the Hittite kingdom of Anatolia. The Middle East was destabilized, key relationships were lost, and soon the Mycenaean civilization declined. The cosmopolitan nature of the Middle East and the eastern Mediterranean that existed from approximately 1700 to 1100 B.C.E. gave way to a three-hundred-year period of poverty and isolation.

In this period of instability a group of small city-states arose on the east coast of the Mediterranean. While power shifted from one to another, as a group the Phoenician city-states prospered economically and politically by trading natural resources, food, and luxury items. Perhaps the most lasting contribution of the Phoenicians was their development of an alphabetic system of writing in which symbols represented sounds that could then be used to construct words. In the ninth century B.C.E., the Phoenicians established a trade network around the entire Mediterranean and colonized the region as their population grew. One of the most significant such colonies was Carthage. Located in present-day Tunisia, it was strategically positioned to control the middle portion of the Mediterranean. By 500 B.C.E., Carthage was one of the world's largest and most ethnically diverse cities. Though Carthage did not rule over a large territory, its strong navy and army of mercenaries protected its access to sea trade and made it influential in setting policies in the region until it was destroyed by the Romans in 202 B.C.E.

The geography, climate, and soil of continental Europe, as well as the rich natural resources, supported agriculture and herding animals. While humans lived in this region for thousands of years, little is known of the earliest societies because of a lack of writing. By 300 B.C.E., the Celts had significantly influenced the language and culture of Europe by migrating from central Europe and settling across much of the continent. This expansion across Europe was not a coherent movement or empire because, politically, the Celts were organized around kinship and it is unlikely there was a sense of a greater **Celtic** civilization. Socially, the Celts were divided into warriors, priests, and commoners. Wealth and power were concentrated among the land-owning warriors, while the priests performed religious rituals and supported education and the judiciary and the commoners worked the land. Women focused on domestic tasks like raising children, though they did possess marriage and property rights better than their counterparts' in Greece and Rome. Marriage was viewed as a partnership.

AP Tip

Pay attention to geographic characteristics of regions, which can help explain political and economic characteristics. Remembering whether an area is rich in natural resources or a certain people come from a land-locked homeland can help you recall political and economic characteristics of that region or people.

THE GREEK CITY-STATES AND EMPIRE

The first European empire grew out of the resource-poor region of Greece. The Dark Age that had settled in after the fall of the Mycenaean civilization lifted when Phoenician merchants helped reconnect the Greek peninsula to the regional trade network. By 800 B.C.E. Greek sailors were bringing goods and ideas home, and the Archaic period of Greek history had begun. A notable import was the Phoenician alphabet, to which the Greeks added symbols for vowels. The Greek alphabet was easier to learn than other forms of writing such as cuneiform or hieroglyphics and thus promoted more widespread literacy. However, Greek culture was still largely preserved through the oral tradition and the use of storytelling, theater, and philosophical dialogues.

Shortly into the Archaic period, Greece saw a population explosion likely caused by more effective farming and increased prosperity, thanks to its renewed role in the regional economy. As the population increased, villages expanded, and Greece became a collection of city-states. Each city-state, or **polis**, cherished its independence, and as a result, conflict among the heavily armed infantries of neighboring city-states was common. These infantrymen, known as **hoplites**, were not professional soldiers but rather citizens called upon in times of crisis. The military techniques employed by the Greeks did not require extensive training; the priorities were courage and strength to bear arms. Battles and campaigns were typically quick, which allowed the soldiers, most of whom were farmers, to return to their land.

While the population increase of the eighth century B.C.E. sparked urbanization and conflict, it also set off a period of colonization. From approximately 750 to 550 B.C.E., Greek people and culture spread around the Black Sea, across North Africa, and through southern Italy and Sicily. As they encountered new people and lands, the Greeks took on an air of superiority and reinforced their bonds among themselves. Their language and customs made them unique in these new lands. They referred to themselves as Hellenes, to non-Greeks as *barbaroi* (the root of the word "barbarian"). With a Greek presence throughout the region, the transfer of technology was facilitated. For example, the use of coins began in western Anatolia (modern-day Turkey) in the sixth century B.C.E. and quickly spread through the Greek world. Though hindered by the various weights and measures used by different states, coinage expedited trade and recordkeeping.

Greek society and politics evolved during the Archaic period and eventually resembled the democratic society for which ancient Greece is known. Early on, councils of nobles challenged and eventually surpassed Greek kings. Such nobles gained their wealth and status from owning large amounts of land. Peasants worked the land and kept only a portion of what they grew for themselves. Working alongside the peasants were debt slaves, who had defaulted on loans from the landowner and subsequently lost their freedom. Owners of small farms, merchants, and craftsmen made up a small middle class. In the mid-seventh and sixth centuries B.C.E., city-states saw the rise of tyrants. Typically ambitious and aggressive members of the nobility, these tyrants often seized control with the support of the middle class, which sought greater rights and power. While some tyrants were able to remain in power and even pass it on to an heir, eventually these leaders were removed, and communities reacted by installing an oligarchy (rule by a small group) or a democracy, in which all free adult males participated.

Greek culture saw important developments during this early time period and laid the foundation for the empire to come. Religion was based on a pantheon of anthropomorphic gods representing the power of nature. Altars and temples were constructed so that sacrifices could be made to these gods, and seers were employed to communicate with the gods and provide advice and insight. During the Archaic period, the role and value of the individual grew in importance. Colonists were valued for their efforts, and clearly the tyrants who assumed power believed in the strength and ability of the individual. The celebration of the individual became known as humanism, which remains a guiding principle in the Western world. In addition to rethinking the role and view of the individual, early Greeks challenged the traditional approach to knowledge. Pre-Socratic philosophers sought rational explanations for the origins and workings of the world. Later, Socrates (470–399 B.C.E.), his disciple Plato, and Plato's student Aristotle would lay the foundation of Western philosophy by asking probing questions about such topics as truth, knowledge, and ethics.

By the end of the Archaic period in 480 B.C.E., Athens and Sparta were the two dominant Greek city-states. Sparta's strength came from its army of highly trained and well-armed professional soldiers. The individual existed to support the state; in an effort to maintain internal peace, coinage and trade were banned for their potential to promote inequality. The Spartans formed cautious alliances with their neighbors and tried to remain as isolated as possible. Athens, on the other hand, had a clear social structure that made connections between wealth and power. Those in the top three classes could hold office; those with little or no property, who constituted the fourth class, could participate in meetings but not hold office. Although not the direct democracy that is often romantically associated with Athens, it broke the mold of rule by one or few that existed throughout much of the world at this time. In 450 B.C.E., Pericles altered the system so as to allow even those with little land to hold office and participate in government.

The rival city-states of Athens and Sparta each played a significant role in the next phase of Greek history, the fight against the Persian Empire in the fifth and fourth centuries B.C.E. Initially, Persian control of Greek city-states in western Anatolia was met with a revolt that the Persians eventually put down. These revolts inspired the Persian leader Darius to punish those city-states that supported the revolt, a group that included Athens. Many Greek city-states suffered harsh defeats in what is known as the Persian Wars, though Athens was able to fend off the Persians' initial attempts. Darius' son Xerxes would stage a larger invasion of Greece in 480 B.C.E. and succeed in attacking Athens. To halt this invasion, southern Greek communities aligned under Spartan rule, forming the Delian League, and though the first efforts failed, by the middle of the fifth century B.C.E., the Persians were expelled from Greek lands. The classical era of Greek history, which would last until 323 B.C.E., had begun.

During the classical age, Athens used its strong navy and economic strength to subjugate members of the Delian League. Neighboring city-states were required to make yearly payments to Athens, which funded further military spending and accomplishments in theater, philosophy, art, and science. Politically, classical Greece was a democracy limited to the 10–15 percent of the population that were free adult males. Foreign-born slaves made up 30 percent of the population; the typical Athenian family owned one or more. Most slaves served in a domestic capacity and developed relationships with their owners by working in close proximity to them. In spite of such relations, the Greeks viewed slaves as inferior beings who, unable to reason, were better off under Greek rule. Women's roles in the classical era varied depending on where they lived. In Sparta, they had the important role of raising strong children, and their presence and voices were welcomed in public. In Athens, however, women lacked access to education, had limited legal protection, and were confined to their homes, where they were expected to produce children. Women's treatment in Athens resembled that of slaves and was rationalized by males, who asserted that women were by nature promiscuous and that promiscuity could destabilize society.

In 431 B.C.E. the Peloponnesian War began between city-states aligned with Athens and those aligned with Sparta. After nearly thirty years, the Spartans, with financial help from Persia for their navy, defeated the Athenians and temporarily assumed a leadership role in Greece. Soon Greek city-states tired of strict Spartan rule, and unrest continued. While southern Greece endured the Peloponnesian War and Spartan rule, the kingdom of Macedonia in northern Greece was growing into a military power. Philip II (359–336 B.C.E.) had improved his military's technology and techniques with longer spears, catapults, and the use of calvary to support infantry. These changes proved effective in defeating southern Greek states and led to an all-Greek attack on the Persian Empire. Though Philip II did not live to see the outcome of the campaign against the Persians, his son Alexander (356–323 B.C.E.) avenged Persia's attacks on Greece by defeating the forces of King Darius III.

Alexander the Great's ambitious efforts resulted in Greek control of a territory similar in size and shape to the Persian Empire. To administer this vast empire, Alexander initially placed loyal Macedonian and Greek aides in charge of city-states. Later, he left Persian officials in place, allowed for Persian soldiers in his military, and adopted aspects of Persian culture. When Alexander died suddenly at the age of thirty-two, his empire fell into a period of chaos. Without a plan for succession, the empire was broken into three kingdoms ruled by Macedonians.

This next period in Greek history is known as the **Hellenistic Age** (323–30 B.C.E.). In this era, land from northern Egypt to nearly the Indus Valley was influenced by Greek culture. Long-distance trade and the growth of libraries, universities, literature, and art made Greek culture available; local populations accepted Greek culture because doing so brought political and economic advantages. The three Hellenistic kingdoms had the same difficulties defending a long frontier experienced by the Persians. In the face of this challenge, the Persian system of local control was maintained along with Alexander's policy of establishing city-states as administrative centers. The classical era in Greek history ushered in new intellectual and political approaches that would stand the test of time and, with the creation of a Hellenistic empire, would spread through a vast territory.

> ## AP Tip
>
> Having a sense of chronology (as opposed to memorizing specific dates) can be very helpful in answering multiple-choice and free-response questions on the AP exam. For example, in a continuity and change over time essay, the dates should give you an early clue about how you will start and end your essay. They often correspond to the beginning and/or end of a period in world or regional history. Knowing the order of events can help you see these.

ROME: REPUBLIC TO EMPIRE

While the Greeks established a foundation for the modern Western world, their legacy was cemented by their European successors, the Romans. Located in central Italy, Rome had many geographic advantages that the Greeks lacked. The fertile soil, long growing season, vast forests, and iron deposits on the Italian peninsula would be vital to their expansion through Europe and North Africa. The **Roman Republic** (507–31 B.C.E.) was largely a society of small, independent farms. In time some individuals acquired large portions of land, and as a group these wealthy men constituted the Senate, which dominated Roman politics. Although all male citizens were allowed to attend Senate meetings, votes of the wealthy were weighted more than those of the poor, and society was governed by the elite. Such inequality caused tensions in the Roman Republic, and periodic strikes by the working class were held in hopes of gaining more political rights.

In the fifth century B.C.E. Rome assumed a leadership position among central Italian cities that had formed a group for defense. By the third century B.C.E., Roman expansion accelerated as its highly trained and disciplined armies conquered new land in a never-ending effort to provide a buffer zone against enemies on the frontier. As Rome expanded its control, it granted citizenship to conquered peoples and required men from these lands to join the army. When the Romans finally defeated the Carthaginians in 202 B.C.E. they were the supreme power in the western Mediterranean region.

The vast Roman Republic was governed by senators, who served one-year posts as governors of the Roman provinces. Chosen for their connections rather than their ability, many governors were corrupt and ineffective. Local people cooperated with Roman rule because, as in the Hellenistic kingdoms, political and economic advantages came with adopting the customs of the ruling class. The adoption of the Roman lifestyle (**Romanization**) was a significant legacy of Roman expansion, although the eastern Mediterranean region continued to be dominated by the Greek language and culture. The expansion of the Roman Republic put strains on the system that would eventually lead to its failure. Italian peasant farmers, who constituted the backbone of the military, spent long periods away from their land. In their absence, land was purchased or obtained by wealthy individuals and consolidated into large tracts of land that were often used for the more profitable purpose of grazing than growing grain. These changes forced parts of

Italy to rely on imported grain and left a now landless population to compete against the cheap slave labor provided by war prisoners. The Republic had obligated landowning men to serve in the military; as the number of landowning men decreased, so too did the population of its soldiers. The poor, landless population had difficulty finding work on farms and in cities. Eventually they turned their allegiance from the Republic to ambitious military leaders who would battle one another for power.

By the dawn of the Common Era, Roman rule was transformed from a republic to an empire built on an agricultural foundation and controlled through a network of cities. Octavian Caesar emerged in 31 B.C.E. as a military dictator disguised in the trappings of a republican ruler. Adding Egypt, portions of the Middle East, and central Europe, Octavian became known by the title Augustus. He and his successors ruled with the approval of the Senate and ultimately became the source of laws and even viewed as gods after their death. In the cities, a large economic and physical gap existed between the rich and the poor. The wealth of the urban upper class came from a large and productive agricultural foundation or from manufacture and trade that prospered during the **Pax Romana** (Roman Peace). The poor in the cities inhabited crowded, low-lying slums; in rural areas they became tenant farmers as the source of slaves diminished when Roman expansion reached its limits.

Roman society was based on the family and the patron/client relationship. The oldest male headed the family and its slaves. The heads of wealthy families served as patrons for the dozens or hundreds of clients who worked and defended their land. In return for this service, clients received legal protection and financial aid from their patrons. Women in the Roman Republic could not own property or represent themselves in legal proceedings. That said, some upper-class women were able to influence their husbands or eldest sons. Religion was greatly influenced by the Romans' contact with the Greeks. Sacrifices were made to ensure protection of the gods, whose myths and identities were taken from the Greeks although given Roman names. When Christianity was born in Roman-controlled Palestine, early Christians were persecuted. In time, the Roman Empire's disenfranchised—the poor, women, slaves—were drawn to the teachings of Jesus.

Successful Roman control over a huge empire can be attributed in large part to technological innovations such as arches, aqueducts, roads, and concrete. But the empire endured a "**third-century crisis**" from 235 to 284 C.E. High turnover of rulers, economic problems, and the infiltration of the Germanic tribes in the central European frontier destabilized the empire. Trade declined to the point where a barter system replaced coinage, and the wealth of cities that served as administrative centers declined dramatically. Diocletian became emperor in 284 C.E. and, in an effort to stabilize the economy of the empire, fixed prices and forced workers in key industries to stay in their professions. Any stability that came about was offset by the resentment among the people at a government that became more intrusive and regimented.

Diocletian's successor, Constantine, is notable for his religious tolerance and his decision to move the capital of the Roman Empire east to Byzantium, which he renamed Constantinople. By the late third century C.E., Christian converts included educated and wealthy people, and the movement had a strong foothold in the Roman Empire. It would eventually become the religion of the empire. When Constantine had a vision of a cross prior to a military victory, he attributed his success to the Christian God and ended persecution of Christians, supported the church, and guaranteed freedom of religion for all others. Seeing the political and economic advantages of being Christian, more and more converted to the faith. The eastern portion of the Roman Empire, now centered in Constantinople, retained wealth better than the west during the third-century crisis and contained more educated people and Christians.

In 395 C.E. the Roman Empire officially split into an eastern and western portion. Rome was sacked in 410 C.E., and by 476 C.E. the western portion of the Roman Empire had disintegrated into a collection of kingdoms under Germanic rulers and entered the medieval era. No longer the political center of an empire, Rome nonetheless remained important because it was the home of the patriarch of Rome, the position that would eventually be called Pope. Culturally, the medieval era saw a decline in literacy and the emergence of local dialects that would evolve into modern Romance languages such as Portuguese, Spanish, French, Italian, and Romanian. Meanwhile, to the east, the Byzantine Empire continued the legacy of the Greek and Roman Empires. Tensions arose between the east and west over doctrinal disputes and eventually led to a division in Christianity. Under the rule (527–565 C.E.) of Justinian, the **Byzantine Empire** recaptured parts of North Africa and Italy. More important, Justinian established a collection of laws that would become the basis of European legal systems in the coming centuries.

Multiple-Choice Questions

1. Which of the following statements best describes the economic and political nature of the Minoan and Mycenaean civilizations?
   (A) Minoan and Mycenaean homelands had vast natural resources and could follow an isolationist foreign policy.
   (B) Minoan and Mycenaean societies relied heavily on trade and thus had close economic and political ties to their neighbors around the Mediterranean.
   (C) Because of the authoritarian nature of their government, Minoans were more aggressive economically and politically than the isolated Mycenaeans.
   (D) Minoan and Mycenaean civilizations frequently clashed as they competed for limited resources and trading partners.

2. The most lasting contribution of the Phoenicians was
   (A) a new approach to knowledge that challenged existing modes of thought and is the basis of Western philosophy.
   (B) developments in naval technology that enabled the Phoenicians to fend off Persian advances into the Mediterranean.
   (C) an alphabetic system of writing that used symbols for sounds instead of for whole words.
   (D) a democratic form of government that the Greeks used as a model for their system.

3. After the eighth century B.C.E. the Greek political system was based on the polis, or city-state. All of the following are aspects of the Greek polis system EXCEPT
   (A) each polis consisted of an urban center and the surrounding rural territory.
   (B) each polis used democratic elections to select their leadership.
   (C) each polis was fiercely independent, and as a result they often fought with one another to preserve their autonomy.
   (D) most urban centers were designed in similar fashion so as to meet the political and security needs of the people.

4. Which statement would most likely have come from a pre-Socratic Greek philosopher?
   (A) Earth, air, and fire are the key elements of the world and serve as building blocks for nature.
   (B) People have natural rights, and therefore it is immoral to enslave another human being.
   (C) For a democracy to function, the right to participate must be extended to all members of society.
   (D) The best way to understand issues like justice is to engage in a dialogue in which the questions and answers will lead to deeper understanding.

5. Which of the following best describes the position of women in ancient Athens?
   (A) They were encouraged to exercise and were allowed to be seen in public.
   (B) Husbands and wives were equals before the law and spent considerable time with each other.
   (C) Most women had some form of formal education and enjoyed opportunities to apply it outside the home.
   (D) Women were isolated in the homes and given very few legal rights.

6. Which of the following is an example of Hellenism?
   (A) excavation of Roman walls and roads in England
   (B) imitations of the Persian architecture at Persepolis found in present-day Turkey
   (C) the incorporation of Greek-style art into an Egyptian cameo piece
   (D) evidence of pottery from Han China reaching the Middle East

7. Which of the following statements best describes the relationship between the Greeks and Persians?
   (A) They were allied against the rising power of the Assyrians.
   (B) Their relationship was based exclusively on trade.
   (C) For over one hundred years the Greeks and Persians were at war.
   (D) The Greek city-states were absorbed into the Persian Empire and adopted that culture.

8. Which of the following accurately describes the political conditions of the Roman Republic?
   (A) Power rested in one, all-powerful leader whose legitimacy came from military success and conquest of new territory.
   (B) Power was shared among the people through direct democracy, although women and slaves had few rights.
   (C) Power was centered in the Senate, where select male citizens made foreign and domestic policies.
   (D) Wealth was divided equally among citizens, and political power resided in many assemblies where all voices in the decision-making process were equal.

9. One impact of the expansion of the Roman Empire was
   (A) efficient and profitable trade because of the safety and stability of Roman rule.
   (B) the spread of the Latin language and Roman customs around the entire Mediterranean region.
   (C) that land was divided more evenly among the people of the empire than in previous times.
   (D) a dramatic reduction in the gap between rich and poor.

10. All of the following contributed to the "third-century crisis" EXCEPT
    (A) frequent changes in rulers.
    (B) the invasion of Germanic tribes deep into the empire.
    (C) inflation and poor economic decisions by emperors.
    (D) large-scale conversion to Christianity.

11. Which statement best describes the reaction to the emergence of Christianity in the early Roman Empire?
    (A) Early converts were persecuted because their belief in monotheism did not fit with the prevailing expectation of emperor worship.
    (B) Early Christians were welcomed by Roman rulers, who saw them as an additional source of support for the fledgling Roman Empire.
    (C) Christians were persecuted by the Romans because upper-class Christians undermined the empire's economic strength as they abandoned their role in the bureaucracy for jobs as priests and bishops.
    (D) Christianity gained little notice in the Roman Empire because it emerged and spread largely in regions outside of Roman control.

Cengage Learning

12. The map above is of
    (A) the Greek Empire under Alexander the Great.
    (B) the Greek and Persian Empires.
    (C) the Roman Empire.
    (D) Phoenician city-states.

13. All of the following are true of women in the Roman Empire
    EXCEPT
    (A) women played very little role in public life.
    (B) women were not allowed to own property.
    (C) Roman women were more constrained than most of their Greek
        counterparts.
    (D) women lacked rights as they were viewed as children by the
        legal system.

14. Romanization most closely resembles
    (A) democracy.
    (B) Hellenism.
    (C) Christianity.
    (D) the Jewish diaspora.

15. Which of the following is true of the Roman Republic and Athenian
    democracy?
    (A) Both were dominated by wealthy males.
    (B) Slaves made up the majority of the population.
    (C) Both had a senate that advised kings and officials.
    (D) Outsiders were quickly granted citizenship and afforded
        respect.

Free-Response Questions

1. Compare the classical civilizations of Greece and Rome in terms of ONE of the following characteristics.
   - ▓ political developments
   - ▓ social and gender structures
   - ▓ art, science, and technology

2. Analyze the continuities and changes in European involvement in international trade from circa 2000 B.C.E. to circa 600 C.E.

Answers

MULTIPLE-CHOICE QUESTIONS

1. ANSWER: B. The Minoan homeland of Crete and the Mycenaean homeland on the Aegean Peninsula had few deposits of metals and little timber. As a result, these civilizations relied heavily on imports and were thus closely tied with those in the region (*The Earth and Its Peoples*, 5th ed., p. 76/6th ed., p. 48).

2. ANSWER: C. The Phoenicians developed an alphabet with symbols representing sounds. They did not have symbols for vowels, which were added by the Greeks (*The Earth and Its Peoples*, 5th ed., p. 91/6th ed., p. 62).

3. ANSWER: B. A population surge transformed small villages into an urban center and the surrounding territory it controlled. These city-states, which often fought with one another, had an acropolis to provide for the defense of the city and an agora where citizens came together to make decisions (*The Earth and Its Peoples*, 5th ed., p. 118/6th ed., pp. 115–116).

4. ANSWER: A. Pre-Socratic philosophers rejected traditional explanations for the workings of the world and instead sought out rational explanations (*The Earth and Its Peoples*, 5th ed., p. 122/6th ed., p. 119).

5. ANSWER: D. Women in Athens were not formally educated and were expected to serve as wives and mothers. They lacked political and legal rights and their husband or father was the complete authority in the home (*The Earth and Its Peoples*, 5th ed., p. 127/6th ed., p. 124).

6. ANSWER: C. During the Hellenistic Age (323–30 B.C.E.), the lands conquered by Alexander the Great were deeply influenced by Greek culture (*The Earth and Its Peoples*, 5th ed., p. 130/6th ed., pp. 125–126).

7. ANSWER: C. From the fifth to the fourth centuries B.C.E., wars between Greece and Persia were important historical events for the region (*The Earth and Its Peoples*, 5th ed., p. 124/6th ed., p. 121).

8. **ANSWER: C.** Political power in the Roman Republic (507–31 B.C.E.) was held by the Senate, a group of male officials who set policy and the leaders of which commanded the army (*The Earth and Its Peoples,* 5th ed., p. 142/6th ed., p. 138).

9. **ANSWER: A.** The Pax Romana (Roman peace) brought on a period of economic prosperity as goods traveled freely across great distances (*The Earth and Its Peoples,* 5th ed., p. 151/6th ed., p. 146).

10. **ANSWER: D.** Large numbers of people converted to Christianity after Constantine ended persecution of Christians and people saw the political and economic benefits of doing so. This demographic trend heightened tensions between the eastern and western portions of the Roman Empire, but it took place after the "third-century crisis" (*The Earth and Its Peoples,* 5th ed., p. 156/6th ed., p. 151).

11. **ANSWER: A.** As a monotheistic religion, Christianity did not permit worship of the Roman emperor. Christians were occasionally attacked by the government or other groups (*The Earth and Its Peoples,* 5th ed., pp. 152–153/6th ed., p. 148).

12. **ANSWER: C.** The map depicts the Roman Empire in 14 C.E. and the territory added by 138 C.E. (*The Earth and Its Peoples,* 5th ed., p. 144/6th ed., p. 140).

13. **ANSWER: C.** Despite the limitations on their rights and freedoms as well as the stringent expectations placed on them, Roman women enjoyed more freedom than the women of the Greek world (*The Earth and Its Peoples,* 5th ed., p. 145/6th ed., p. 139).

14. **ANSWER: B.** Romanization is the spread of Latin and the Roman lifestyle throughout the Roman Empire; Hellenism is the influence of Greek culture on lands conquered by Alexander the Great (*The Earth and Its Peoples,* 5th ed., pp. 130, 151/6th ed., pp. 128, 147).

15. **ANSWER: A.** Despite the romantic notion that modern democracy was born in the classical era of Greece and Rome, power in both the Roman Republic and Athenian democracy rested in the hands of wealthy men (*The Earth and Its Peoples,* 5th ed., pp. 126, 142/6th ed., pp. 124, 138).

FREE-RESPONSE QUESTIONS

1. A good response to this question would include many direct comparisons and stay focused on the selected criteria. When looking at political developments, there is ample opportunity to compare the organization of each empire and who had the power at various times. In Greece that could include describing the emergence of the city-state and the limited democracy that eventually came into being. For Rome, you could trace the rise of the republic and the transition to empire. Social and gender structure might overlap a bit with political developments as you could look at who had power in society and the treatment of those who did not. The difference in approaching these topics is that in choosing social and gender structure you should focus more on the social hierarchy and the relationships between and among men and

women. For the last selection, both civilizations made great advances in art, science, and technology that in many ways laid a foundation for the Western world. Specific examples for the Greek contributions could include philosophy and theater; for the Romans you could include the use of aqueducts and metalwork.

2. Think about the dates given and what you know about the region at that time. In the case of 2000 B.C.E., the Minoan civilization emerged and created a trade-based society in order to make up for the geographic shortcomings of their homeland. By 600 C.E., western Europe was headed into the medieval era, a period with little long-distance trade, while the eastern portion (Byzantine Empire) is strategically located at the crossroads of key trade routes. In between you need to decide what period helps illustrate the changes and continuities of the region's role in international trade. You might choose to look at the economic activity during the Hellenistic Age, and perhaps discuss long-distance trade and communication caused by the Pax Romana. In any case, choose information that matches the parameters established in your thesis, which must include both continuities and changes.

5

THE AMERICAS:
UP TO CIRCA 600 C.E.

A major focus of the first unit of the AP World History course is the development and characteristics of civilizations and empires. The development of complex civilizations in the Americas occurred later than in the Middle East, Indus Valley, and China. The first empires of the Americas do not arise until around 600 C.E. As a result of these curriculum choices and historical facts, this chapter is short, and it has fewer multiple-choice questions and no free-response questions (though you will find suggestions on how the information here can be used in some free-response essays). That said, key aspects of the early history of the Americas outlined in the AP World History course description are included.

KEY CONCEPTS

■ The development of civilization in the Western Hemisphere differed from that in the Eastern Hemisphere because of environmental factors and relative isolation.
■ Societies with complex political, economic, and social structures did emerge in the Western Hemisphere.

KEY TERMS

■ Olmec
■ Chavín
■ Mesoamerica

Information on the Americas from up to circa 600 C.E. can be found in *The Earth and Its Peoples*, fifth edition, Chapter 2 and sixth edition, Chapter 7.

THE WESTERN HEMISPHERE

Human beings had migrated to the Western Hemisphere from Asia by 13,000 B.C.E. and would remain isolated from the rest of the world for thousands of years. This isolation and the geographic characteristics of the Western Hemisphere resulted in different patterns of development among its early civilizations compared with those of the Eastern Hemisphere. The political and social structures of the Olmec and the Chavín societies, however, were similar to their counterparts in early Mesopotamia, Egypt, China, and the Indus Valley. These early American civilizations established a foundation for the classical age of the Maya, Aztecs, and the Inca.

By 3000 B.C.E. people in **Mesoamerica** (Mexico and northern Central America) had developed an agricultural system based on maize, tomatoes, peppers, squash, and potatoes. Similarly, by 1500 B.C.E. people of South America relied on manioc as the base of their agriculture. While the settling of farming societies may have begun later in the Americas, the domestication of dogs, which helped hunters find prey, likely began prior to the Neolithic age. In addition to dogs, people of the Americas eventually domesticated llamas, guinea pigs, and turkeys. The smaller number of species available for domestication and the absence of a true beast of burden (except for the llama) help explain some of the developmental differences in the Americas. While the Agricultural Revolution transformed much of the Americas, the Amerindians of the Great Plains hunted bison, and groups in the Pacific Northwest relied on fishing for sustenance. Following the Agricultural Revolution in the Americas came the emergence of the Olmecs and the Chavín, both of whom developed important and complex civilizations.

THE OLMEC

The **Olmec** flourished in Mesoamerica between 1200 and 400 B.C.E. and in that time greatly influenced much of modern-day Mexico. Though Mesoamerica was never unified politically, the civilizations there had clear similarities in their political and social characteristics. This can likely be accounted for by trade and cultural exchange. As agricultural production and efficiency increased, specialization allowed for the rise of religious and political figures. These people gained status from their role in religious and political rituals, and they used this status to organize the labor of the people. As a result, Olmec urban centers included large-scale religious and civic buildings, and irrigation and canal projects were completed. Historians speculate that the Olmec were led by a king who had religious and secular duties. It was perhaps these rulers and famous athletes and warriors who are commemorated in the famous large stone heads found in Olmec territory. In addition to efficient organization and direction of labor, the Olmec had elaborate religious rituals dedicated to their many deities, most of whom had a male and female nature. In addition to a political and religious foundation, the Olmec developed a writing system that influenced the Maya and a calendar based on astronomical observations, and they were probably the originators of a ritual ball game that became a fixture in Mesoamerican societies. Although the Olmec never physically dominated their neighbors, their cultural influence can be seen in a wide area and in succeeding civilizations.

THE CHAVÍN

In South America, the **Chavín** prospered between 900 and 250 B.C.E. Their society was built on the foundation of coastal societies, which relied on seafood to sustain their early cities, and the people of the foothills, who relied on corn and other foods. The Chavín emerged in part because of their strategic location between the coast and the Andes Mountains, and they preserved many of the cultural and economic characteristics of their predecessors, including irrigation networks, ceremonial plazas, and pyramids. Chavín growth was enabled by their location along trade routes and the increase in food production that came with the introduction of maize from Mesoamerica. As their society grew, the Chavín developed a reciprocal labor system that constructed the irrigation networks, roads, and bridges. The details of this system are not known, but the example would be adopted by later civilizations including the Inca. Also crucial to the Chavín success and development was the domestication of the llama. Llamas provided meat, wool, and transportation that increased the efficiency and effectiveness of trade. Chavín artifacts, like those of the Olmecs, were dispersed over a wide area and suggest cultural and economic influence rather than political control of neighbors. It is thought that regional wars disrupted this economic and cultural exchange, weakened the ruling class, and led to the collapse of Chavín society. Despite the society's collapse, Chavín architecture, urban planning, and culture, would influence people of the Andes for centuries.

Multiple-Choice Questions

1. Which modern-day territories constitute Mesoamerica?
   (A) Mexico and Central America
   (B) Central and South America
   (C) North and South America
   (D) Most of Mexico and the United States

2. Which of the following statements about early Amerindian peoples is true?
   (A) They relied heavily on the wheel and an impressive network of roads.
   (B) Seafaring knowledge allowed for extensive long-distance trade.
   (C) Though they were not politically united from North to South America, common language and culture existed.
   (D) They developed specialized technologies and domesticated plants and animals.

3. The successful completion of large building projects by the Olmec was in large part because of
   (A) the enormous wealth that came from the gold mines of the Olmec homeland.
   (B) the large population that lived in Olmec cities.
   (C) the ability of the Olmec elite to require and direct labor from its inhabitants.
   (D) the decentralized nature of their political system.

4. The dominance of the Chavín can be attributed to
   (A) early advancements in agriculture and trade.
   (B) being the first in the Americas to successfully domesticate horses.
   (C) superior military resources and strategy.
   (D) their strategic location at the center of Mesoamerican trade routes.

5. Which statement about the development of civilization in the Eastern and Western Hemispheres is true?
   (A) Civilizations in the Western Hemisphere were far more advanced than those in the Eastern Hemisphere.
   (B) The Western Hemisphere had large draft animals that could be domesticated, while the Eastern Hemisphere did not.
   (C) The development of civilization was influenced greatly by environment, and societies of both the Eastern and Western Hemispheres were sophisticated and complex.
   (D) The isolated and relatively peaceful nature of civilizations in the Western Hemisphere allowed them to emerge earlier and grow stronger than those of the Eastern Hemisphere.

A Note on Free-Response Questions

It is highly unlikely that you will find a free-response question on the AP World History exam that draws **only** on the information in this chapter. However, details about the Olmec and Chavín can be useful for both comparative and continuity and change over time essays. For example, you could be asked to compare the political and social structures of two early civilizations, and Mesoamerica and Andean South America could be included in the choices alongside Mesopotamia, Egypt, the Indus Valley, and China. It is also possible that a continuity and change over time essay might ask you to examine the transition from the Agricultural Revolution through the rise of empire in a region. Knowing how civilization rose in the Americas, the basic characteristics of the Olmec and Chavín, and details about the Maya, Aztec, and Inca (here, in Chapter 10) would enable you to effectively note such continuities and changes over the assigned time period.

Answers

MULTIPLE-CHOICE QUESTIONS

1. ANSWER: **A.** Mesoamerica, the homeland of the Olmec civilization, consists of modern-day Mexico and Central America (*The Earth and Its Peoples*, 5th ed., p. 59/6th ed., p. 192).

2. ANSWER: **D.** Within the diverse geographic region of the Americas many large civilizations emerged, thanks to technological advancements and the adoption of a more settled lifestyle based on farming and animal husbandry (*The Earth and Its Peoples*, 5th ed., p. 58/6th ed., p. 192).

3. ANSWER: **C.** Olmec urban centers were lightly populated but were surrounded by a large number of people in rural areas. The elite were able to require the labor of men and women from surrounding settlements to complete large projects (*The Earth and Its Peoples*, 5th ed., p. 60/6th ed., p. 194).

4. ANSWER: **A.** The Chavín came to dominate the area around modern-day Peru because of their superior economic strength and strategic location. Intersecting the trade routes connecting the coast with the mountains, the Chavín introduced maize to the region (*The Earth and Its Peoples*, 5th ed., p. 61/6th ed., p. 196).

5. ANSWER: **C.** Different geographic characteristics influenced the formation of civilization around the world. Although they did not develop in the same sequence, civilizations of both the Eastern and Western Hemispheres created complex political, economic, and social institutions (*The Earth and Its Peoples*, 5th ed., p. 64/6th ed., p. 214).

6

AFRICA: CIRCA 600 TO CIRCA 1450

KEY CONCEPTS

- The varied environments of different African regions had an important influence on the cultural and economic developments of societies.
- Regional and long-distance interactions among African societies and with outsiders helped create the cultural diversity that characterized the period.
- Various African societies played a major role in the larger networks of trade, including both the trans-Saharan and Indian Ocean trade networks.
- Islam's spread to Africa had a significant impact in terms of religious and economic influence in the period of circa 600–circa 1450.

KEY TERMS

- Ethiopia
- Ghana
- Great Zimbabwe
- ibn Battuta
- Mali
- Mansa Kankan Musa
- Swahili Coast
- Timbuktu

Africa is discussed in depth in *The Earth and Its Peoples*, Chapters 7 and 13 of the fifth edition and Chapters 8 and 14 of the sixth edition.

AFRICAN ENVIRONMENTS

The vast and diverse continent of Africa is home to many different cultures. During the period 600–1450 these cultures forged Africa's social, religious, and economic relationships with other cultures both within the continent and beyond. Africa cannot be looked at monolithically. Throughout the continent similarities and differences abound. Likewise, dramatic changes brought about by trade are as visible as the cultural continuities.

Building on generations of experience, the peoples of Africa used various techniques to adapt to the differing environments and climates of the continent, which produced incredible diversity among societies by 1200. Africa is almost entirely in the tropical zone of the earth, and its cycles are rainy and dry seasons rather than hot and cold seasons. Whether their environment was grassland, the dense tropical rain forests of West and Central Africa, or desert—the Sahara Desert in the north is the largest desert in the world—Africans could produce food. Because desert zones lie in both the north (Sahara) and southwest (Kalahari), most Africans lived in the moderate areas where some rainfall would be expected. (This is still the case today.) Some lived in settled agricultural societies; some formed pastoral societies; others hunted, gathered, and fished.

Africans also used irrigation. The importance of Africa's rivers cannot be overstated. The Nile, which flows from central Africa to the north; the Niger in West Africa; and the Zambezi in the south and the central African Congo are some of the crucial bodies of water that give life to trading cities and smaller communities. By 1200 agriculture had been the dominant enterprise for centuries. Regional exchange of plants, fruits, and crops occurred thanks in part to the Bantu migrations, which brought grains and other plants south from West Africa. A larger network of trade brought products like bananas and yams to Africa from Southeast Asia and carried African exports to other regions—for example, Ethiopian coffee to the Middle East.

Another great strength of the African tropical regions was the mining of precious metals. Skillful craftsmen worked metal into a variety of objects. Copper and gold were the most valuable metals, but iron, the most plentiful metal in tropical Africa, was especially important; iron was made into hoes, axes, and knives for farming, spears and arrows for hunting, needles and nails for day-to-day life. Copper, plentiful in southeastern Africa, was used to make copper wire and decorative objects. Some of the most famous art coming out of West Africa were the copper and brass statues of the period dating to 1500. Gold became incredibly profitable as an export, particularly to India. Important sources of gold were the Niger River and the hills south of the Zambezi River, where archaeologists have found thousands of mine shafts for the mining of gold.

NEW ISLAMIC EMPIRES IN AFRICA

The spread of Islam across North Africa and down into sub-Saharan Africa is one of the key developments of the period, both culturally and economically. North Africa was under Muslim rule by the eighth century. Only gradually did Islam spread to sub-Saharan Africa, the land south of the Sahara Desert known to the Arabs as *bilad al-sudan*, "land of the blacks." Muslim Berbers conquered **Ghana** in 1076; the subsequent empire of Mali, which flourished from 1200 to 1500, was one of the richest and largest Muslim states, rivaled only by the Delhi Sultanate in India.

Other religions had influence as well; in East Africa, Christianity maintained a stronghold in **Ethiopia** although the Christian Nubian kingdoms along the upper Nile were conquered in the name of Islam. However, throughout the whole sub-Saharan region, and the east coast of Africa in particular, most Africans were introduced to Islam peacefully. Economic interaction produced personal relationships that in turn provided opportunities for conversion. The teachings of Islam and Islamic methods of managing empires and cities appealed to African merchants and political leaders.

The first sub-Saharan place where Islam was adopted was Takrur, in 1030. By 1200, King Sumanguru had increased the status of Takrur, and in 1240, Sundiata of the Malinke people defeated Sumanguru. Both Sumanguru and Sundiata were Muslims who had peacefully converted to Islam before the empire was established. Sundiata's continued conquests brought about the birth of the **Mali** Empire.

Like many other earlier and contemporaneous Muslim empires, Mali's wealth derived largely from trade—not only from the sale of goods but also from the strategic control of the actual routes. As in Ghana, agriculture met basic needs; again, a river was the source of both physical and economic life. But Mali, with the trading area of the upper Niger as well as the gold fields of the Niger, controlled even more precious territory than Ghana did. Mali also had strong Muslim political and merchant classes that interacted well with North African Muslim traders. This combination of strategic control of key economic resources and established trading relationships brought astronomical wealth to the empire. **Mansa Kankan Musa**, who ruled Mali from 1312 to 1337, took so much gold with him on a pilgrimage to Mecca in 1324 that the value of gold in Cairo was reduced for years to come.

Mansa Kankan Musa's rule illustrates both Mali's wealth and the extent to which Islam permeated all aspects of administrative life, from law to military systems. Upon return from his pilgrimage, Musa sponsored the building of schools in many of the cities of the empire, and his successors ran a government that was praised for its effectiveness. One of the reasons historians know so much about Mali is because of the journals of **ibn Battuta** (1304–1369), a Muslim scholar from Morocco. He journeyed to Mecca to complete the hajj and went on to explore the Muslim world in the Middle East, Africa, and Asia, traveling 75,000 miles (120,000 kilometers) in twenty-nine years. His insights as the most traveled man of his time are invaluable in describing the Muslim world. When ibn Battuta visited Mali, he credited the leadership of Mansa Suleiman, Mansa Kankan Musa's successor, with the peace that permeated all the territories of the empire.

Unfortunately that peace did not last. The rule of Suleiman's successors opened the way for revolt by the various peoples who resented their domination by the Malinke. The Tuareg people took back the great city of Timbuktu in 1433, and by 1500 Mali was reduced to the home territory of the Malinke.

The spread of Islam continued into central Africa despite the end of Mali. For example, the leaders of the Hausa city-states in central Sudan converted and made Islam their official religion. Kanem-Bornu, also in central Sudan, was another huge empire that continued to spread Islam in the late fifteenth century.

AP Tip

The Islamic world expanded into the continents of Europe, Asia, and Africa during the period 600–1450. The ability to compare the nature of Islam on various continents is an important issue for AP World History and the exam. How could you analyze the similarities and differences in the cultures that spanned the Islamic world?

AFRICA AND INDIAN OCEAN TRADE

Between 1200 and 1500, the Indian Ocean trade network was the richest of the maritime trading routes. Much of this growth was spurred by the development of wealthy states in Europe, Asia, and Africa at the time. In addition, the Indian Ocean trade network grew in prominence with the end of the Mongol Empire. Once Mongol control was gone, and with it the guarantee of a smooth overland flow of goods, the maritime trade routes became more important. The Indian Ocean trade network connected Africa, Europe, Asia, and the Middle East in layers of communication that brought a large part of the world together on an unprecedented scale, and it fostered the spread of Islam.

Africa played a major role in this trade network. By 1500, between thirty and forty city-states—among them Kilwa, Mombasa, and Mogadishu—grew up along the east coast thanks to Indian Ocean trade. Ibn Battuta visited Kilwa and marveled at its beauty as well as the devotion to Islam. This thriving coast of trade became known as the **Swahili Coast**; Arabs and Persians called the people there "Swahili" after the Arabic *sawahil al-sudan*, which means "shores of the blacks." This name is a great example of the interaction among different peoples that occurred along the Indian Ocean basin.

Cities on the Swahili Coast prospered in part because of the trade in gold, which came from further inland, in southern portions of the continent. A state known as **Great Zimbabwe**, after the name of the capital city, relied on farming and cattle herding, but it also had considerable control of the gold trade south of the Zambezi River. Trade, first regional and then as part of the larger Indian Ocean trade network, brought real economic prosperity to Great Zimbabwe. Zimbabwe is known for massive stone structures built for the elite and to enclose the king's court. Zimbabwe declined in the fifteenth century.

SOCIAL AND CULTURAL CHANGE IN AFRICA FROM 1200 TO 1500

Although Islamic beliefs had a significant impact on society and culture in Africa, local cultures continued to thrive and sustain the diversity of dynamic sub-Saharan Africa. Local cultures also influenced the way outside religions were adapted in various regions and states. For example, mosques in Africa were based on Middle Eastern designs but used materials local to the region; a mosque in West Africa did not look like a mosque on the Swahili Coast. Christian churches also reflected diverse building styles. Mosques and churches were both houses of worship and centers of education. The spread of Islam in sub-Saharan Africa went hand in hand with an increase in literacy, first in Arabic and then in local languages written in Arabic characters. Islamic scholarship flourished in sub-Saharan Africa. In the West African city of **Timbuktu**, learning was so valued that books were among the hottest trading commodities.

With the increase in wealth came the growth of elite classes—and the demand for those to serve the elites. Mali, Bornu, and Ethiopia all participated in selling and transporting slaves across Africa and into the Middle East, India, and even China. It is estimated that some 2.5 million Africans crossed the Sahara and Red Sea as slaves between 1200 and 1500. The slavery that these Africans experienced was different from the slavery experienced under Europeans in later centuries. These slaves had some opportunities to advance. Although some slaves did work like mining, most were trained to specialize in a service. As a result, some slaves became powerful and wealthy because of their military ability or other skills—for example, a slave general took power in the Songhai Empire, which succeeded the Mali Empire. Female slaves were household servants or concubines and some male slaves became eunuchs.

Women in tropical Africa had many roles. They farmed, transported food, water, and other materials needed for cooking, made clay vessels for household purposes, and bought and sold food and crafts at markets. The impact of Islam on women in sub-Saharan Africa varied, reflecting the influence of local traditions and customs. Traveling in Mali, ibn Battuta was startled to see that women did not completely cover their bodies and veil their faces when in public and interacted with men who were not their husbands or family members.

AP Tip

The role of the trade networks in the period of 600–1450 was crucial in establishing a thriving, multifaceted Islamic world while allowing for the preservation of local cultures. Understanding the dynamics of the exchange of goods and ideas along these cross-regional trade routes is key to understanding this period.

Multiple-Choice Questions

1. From 600 to 1450, Muslims exerted influence in all of the following places EXCEPT
   (A) the Hausa city-states.
   (B) Ethiopia.
   (C) Mali.
   (D) the Nubian kingdoms.

2. Like Mali, Great Zimbabwe's wealth came from
   (A) regional and long-distance trade.
   (B) selling slaves to Europeans.
   (C) working as mercenaries for larger empires.
   (D) herding cattle and selling local goods at markets.

3. Which of the following best describes the spread of Islam in sub-Saharan Africa?
   (A) Immediate conquest of the entire region
   (B) The systematic takeover of port cities
   (C) The absence of indigenous religions
   (D) Gradual conversion in various parts of Africa

4. Examples of customary women's roles in various regions in Africa include all of the following EXCEPT
   (A) making pottery to use for practical purposes.
   (B) farm work.
   (C) serving as religious leaders.
   (D) selling goods at markets.

5. All of the following were encouraged by the spread of Islam in sub-Saharan Africa EXCEPT
   (A) literacy in both Arabic and local languages.
   (B) the Arabic language becoming the dominant language in sub-Saharan Africa.
   (C) literacy among children, particularly sons.
   (D) the study of law, science, and medicine.

6. By 1200, most Africans were making their living by
   (A) becoming regional traders.
   (B) herding cattle and other animals.
   (C) hunting and gathering.
   (D) farming and other agricultural activities.

7. Mali was founded by
   (A) North African Muslims who conquered Mali in the seventh and eighth centuries.
   (B) the Delhi Sultanate, which extended its rule across the Middle East and parts of Africa.
   (C) the Ethiopians, who introduced Christianity to the diverse peoples living in West Africa.
   (D) an indigenous African dynasty that had earlier converted to Islam through peaceful interaction with Muslims.

8. The increase of elites with wealth from commercial trading resulted in
   (A) the rise of slaves to serve the elites and the importance of slavery for commerce.
   (B) a decrease in the spread of Islam because the religion forbade slavery.
   (C) a decrease in the value placed on education because merchants did not need to study in order to become wealthy.
   (D) a decrease in the spread of Islam because the majority of Indian Ocean trading merchants practiced Hinduism.

9. Ghana was similar to Mali in that both
   (A) relied on hunting and gathering as the primary sources of food.
   (B) were approximately the same size.
   (C) controlled critical trans-Saharan trading routes.
   (D) were Christian states that rejected Muslim attempts at conversion.

10. All of the following are examples of the work performed by African slaves EXCEPT
    (A) serving as eunuchs or concubines in wealthy households.
    (B) mining for valuable minerals.
    (C) working as household servants.
    (D) working on European-owned plantations in colonized Africa.

11. Ibn Battuta and Mansa Musa were similar in that they both
    (A) enjoyed the wealth of Africa.
    (B) traveled throughout the extensive Muslim empire.
    (C) were African Muslim clerics.
    (D) wrote extensive legal treatises.

12. One reason for cultural similarities within Africa is that
    (A) the continent has a homogeneous ethnic group.
    (B) its early history centered around the Sahara.
    (C) the Roman and Egyptian empires lent a cultural homogeneity to the continent.
    (D) based on linguistic evidence, the Bantu migrated across sub-Saharan Africa.

13. Africa contributed to the Indian Ocean trade network by providing
    (A) batik cloth.
    (B) cinnamon.
    (C) vanilla.
    (D) ivory.

14. India and tropical Africa are climactically similar in that both have
    (A) definite temperature changes between winter and summer.
    (B) wet and dry seasons.
    (C) no seasonal changes because of their proximity to the equator.
    (D) coastal areas with abundant rainfall but very dry deserts in the interior.

15. Knowledge of ironworking diffused across Africa
    (A) with the migration of the Bantu.
    (B) through contact with early Minoan travelers.
    (C) through trade with the Roman Empire.
    (D) as a result of African conversion to Islam.

Free-Response Questions

1. Compare the political and economic characteristics of West and East African states from circa 600 to circa 1450.

2. Evaluate the cultural and religious continuities and changes resulting from Islam's presence in Africa during the period circa 600 to circa 1450.

Answers

Multiple-Choice Questions

1. **Answer: B.** Ethiopia was a Christian kingdom throughout this period and is one example of a religious continuity in East Africa (*The Earth and Its Peoples*, 5th ed., p. 378/6th ed., p. 381).

2. **Answer: A.** Both societies relied on agriculture to supply basic needs, but their wealth and prosperity were based on controlling and participating in trade (*The Earth and Its Peoples*, 5th ed., p. 388/6th ed., p. 389).

3. **Answer: D.** Sub-Saharan Africa was introduced to Islam primarily through merchants, missionaries, and marriage. Islam came to Africa over time. It was not the result of immediate conquest. Force was not the primary way the religion spread (*The Earth and Its Peoples*, 5th ed., p. 378/6th ed., p. 381).

4. **Answer: C.** Within patriarchal societies, women were rarely public leaders in the political and religious spheres, especially with the arrival of Islam. However, women had many other roles that required skill and training (*The Earth and Its Peoples*, 5th ed., p. 393/6th ed., p. 393).

5. **Answer: B.** Arabic characters were used initially to write some local languages. The many languages in sub-Saharan Africa suggest the extent of diversity in Africa (*The Earth and Its Peoples*, 5th ed., pp. 390–392/6th ed., p. 391).

6. **Answer: D.** Environmental conditions allowed most Africans to farm (*The Earth and Its Peoples*, 5th ed., p. 375/6th ed., p. 376–377).

7. **Answer: D.** Mali was founded by Africans who had converted to Islam in an earlier period. It was not conquered by outsiders (*The Earth and Its Peoples*, 5th ed., p. 378/6th ed., p. 380).

8. **ANSWER: A.** Slavery was a defining feature of societies that grew wealthy from regional and long-distance trade connected with the Indian Ocean trade network. Slavery was very common in wealthy Muslim households in Africa and other places such as India under the Delhi Sultanate (*The Earth and Its Peoples*, 5th ed., p. 393/6th ed., p. 392).

9. **ANSWER: C.** Ghana was smaller than Mali, which succeeded Ghana. Both relied on agriculture to provide food, and both controlled key trading routes, which brought great wealth. Mali was always an Islamic empire (*The Earth and Its Peoples*, 5th ed., p. 379/6th ed., p. 382).

10. **ANSWER: D.** African slaves in Africa, Asia, and the Middle East during this period performed a variety of functions. The type of slavery that Africans experienced under Europeans was to come later. The full colonization of Africa by Europeans was not complete until the early twentieth century (*The Earth and Its Peoples*, 5th ed., p. 393/6th ed., p. 392).

11. **ANSWER: B.** Both ibn Battuta and Mansa Musa traveled extensively. Mansa Musa went on pilgrimage to Mecca and dazzled the world with the opulent wealth his party displayed. Ibn Battuta was a Muslim scholar who traveled throughout the Muslim world and spent quite a bit of time in Mali (*The Earth and Its Peoples*, 5th ed., pp. 380–381/6th ed., pp. 382, 388).

12. **ANSWER: D.** Linguistic evidence indicates that the Bantu migrated south and east from the Congo River area in West Africa to the southeastern coast. This lent a linguistic and economic cohesion to a very diverse continent (*The Earth and Its Peoples,* 5th ed., pp. 216–217/6th ed., pp. 236–237).

13. **ANSWER: D.** Although Africa provided many types of natural products to the Indian Ocean trade network, its most important contribution was ivory (*The Earth and Its Peoples*, 5th ed., p. 209/6th ed., p. 230).

14. **ANSWER: B.** Both India and tropical Africa lie in the world's tropical zone, which is characterized by definite wet and dry seasons whose arrival depends upon shifting winds (*The Earth and Its Peoples*, 5th ed., p. 374/6th ed., p. 376).

15. **ANSWER: A.** Historians and archaeologists believe that the Bantu discovered how to make iron and then diffused that knowledge across Africa as they migrated (*The Earth and Its Peoples*, 5th edition, pp. 216–217/6th ed., p. 237).

FREE-RESPONSE QUESTIONS

1. For this essay you could compare the empires of Ghana and Mali with the Swahili Coast states. A comparison can be made in terms of the roles of regional and long-distance trade in both areas and in the wealth derived from the trade of precious minerals, gold in particular. One clear political contrast is political organization: Mali was an empire, while the Swahili Coast was made up of independent city-states, which grew and declined in power

depending on their commercial influence. You can also compare the effect of diversity on political stability. The Mali Empire controlled different peoples, who ultimately revolted against Malinke rule, hastening its decline. However, on the Swahili Coast the diversity that comes with long-distance trade helped the various city-states flourish.

2. Your essay should take up both change and continuity as they relate to Islam's impact on social interaction, social structure, language, and education. There are numerous examples of cultural changes; some topics include the role of Islam in increasing literacy in both Arabic and local languages, the rise of education centers in great cities like Timbuktu, the religious and social role of mosques, studies in science and medicine, and the increased use of books. Some key social changes occurred in the growth of elite classes and the subsequent increase in slavery. However, there are some social continuities in the roles that women played in various African societies while incorporating the changes brought by Islamic influence. An important continuity throughout the period is the adaptability of Islam to local cultures and traditions and the ability of peoples across Africa to become devout Muslims while maintaining their own cultural identities.

7

The Middle East: Circa 600 to circa 1450

Key Concepts

- The world of Islam represents peoples of different ethnicities, cultures, and languages throughout the Middle East, Africa, Asia, and parts of Europe who were unified through the religion of Islam while still maintaining regional diversity.
- The Islamic world made tremendous contributions to art, science, and technology that would have a huge impact on cultural and economic developments in Asia, Africa, and Europe.
- The Mongols had a significant impact on the spread of Islam and preserved and built upon Islamic intellectual discoveries.
- The Mongols affected the Middle East in both positive and negative ways in terms of social, political, and economic stability.

Key Terms

- Abbasid Caliphate
- bubonic plague
- caliphate
- Five Pillars
- hajj
- Il-khan
- Islam
- mamluks
- Mongols
- Ottomans
- Quran
- Seljuk Turks
- Shari'a
- Shi'ite

- Sufism
- Sunni
- ulama
- Umayyad Caliphate
- umma

Islam is discussed in depth in *The Earth and Its Peoples,* fifth edition, Chapter 8 and sixth edition, Chapter 9. The Crusades are discussed in Chapter 9 of the fifth edition, and Chapter 10 of the sixth edition; the Mongols are discussed in Chapter 12 of both the fifth and sixth editions. The Ottoman Turks are discussed in Chapter 19 of both the fifth edition and the sixth editions.

THE ORIGINS OF ISLAM

Islam, the youngest of the monotheistic religions, began on the Arabian Peninsula. The founding prophet of the faith, Muhammad, was born in the trading town of Mecca in 570. Mecca was important in pre-Islamic history not only as an economic center but also as a holy site. Pilgrims went to Mecca to visit the Ka'ba, a shrine believed to have been built by the patriarch Abraham. Muhammad was raised as an orphan by his uncle, chief of his clan, and grew up to be a successful trading merchant. About 610, Muhammad began to meditate and had visions in which he came to believe that God—Allah, in Arabic—was revealing himself. Sharing his revelations, he began to gather a following that embraced his belief that there is only one true god, who was responsible for all of creation, and that people must submit to the authority of God. The word *Islam* means submission; a Muslim is one who submits to the will of Allah.

AP Tip

The basic tenets of the Muslim faith, called the Five Pillars of Islam, are based on the practices of Muhammad and affirmed by the first caliph, Abu Bakr. The **Five Pillars** are

- the statement of faith in one God and Muhammad as his messenger,

- prayer five times a day,

- fasting during Ramadan,

- charity through giving to the poor,

- completion of a pilgrimage to Mecca, known in Arabic as the hajj.

The tribal leaders in Mecca came to fear that Muhammad's belief in one god threatened their power and security as well as the polytheistic traditions of their communities. Muhammad was therefore forced to flee to Medina in 622, a journey that is known as the Hijra, meaning the migration or flight of Muhammad from Mecca to Medina. This date, considered to be the beginning of the Islamic faith, marks the start of the Muslim calendar. It was in Medina that the Islamic community, or **umma**, solidified and ultimately was able to win over Mecca in 630. After completing a pilgrimage to the Ka'ba, a tradition that lives on as the **hajj**, Muhammad returned to Medina to manage both the political and religious affairs of this reinvigorated city-state, until his death two years later, in 632.

Muhammad's death immediately raised the question of who would be Muhammad's successor, or caliph, which provoked the first major split in the Islamic umma. This split ultimately divided Muslims into two major sects, the Sunnis and the Shi'ites. **Shi'ite** Muslims believe that succession should be traced through the bloodline of Muhammad; therefore, Muhammad's cousin Ali should have been the caliph and only Ali's descendants should be imams, or religious leaders of the Muslim community as a whole. To Shi'ites, the caliph is more of a secular leader. **Sunni** Muslims, believing that the caliph is to be chosen by the community, regard the first three caliphs who succeeded Muhammad as properly selected. Sunnis see the caliph as a secular and religious leader; therefore the caliph is an imam as well. While the concept of the **caliphate** was a unifying factor, in reality the caliphate was quite fragmented by the late ninth century.

ISLAMIC CALIPHATES

One of the first tasks of Abu Bakr, the first caliph, was to collect and organize Muhammad's revelations into a book. Muslims, like Jews and Christians, are considered to be people of the book; their holy book is the **Quran.** Unlike the Hebrew and Christian Bibles, the Quran is believed by Muslims to be the literal words of God as given to Muhammad, not a collection of writings by many authors over a long period of time. The Quran was revealed in Arabic, is written in Arabic, and is to be read in Arabic. As the Muslim world grew to non-Arabic-speaking regions, the need to read the Quran in Arabic encouraged the growth of schools to teach the language and to interpret the Quran. Out of this holy book and the traditions of Muhammad slowly came Muslim law, **Shari'a** in Arabic, as well as the practices and traditions that are essential to the religion.

As the dominant sect, Sunni Muslims established the **Umayyad Caliphate** in 661, with its capital in Damascus, Syria. The peoples living under the control of the Umayyad caliph were predominately Arab. By 732 Arab Muslims had conquered Syria, Palestine, and North Africa; they gained control of a part of southern Spain—referred to as al-Andalus—in the early eighth century. Under Muslim rule Spanish cities like Seville and Cordoba flourished as centers of government, where Muslims, Christians, and Jews created a unique culture known for its literature, art, architecture, and agricultural accomplishments.

After a period of increasing conflict, the **Abbasid Caliphate** was established in 750 and ruled until 1258 from its capital in Baghdad. Effective rule over such a large empire proved challenging for the Abbasids, particularly in terms of holding territory. The empire also became more diverse as more non-Arabs converted to Islam. Baghdad, the capital, became a thriving center for learning, culture, and technological advancements despite the political and territorial fragmentation of the ninth century and, later, the Crusades. Islam continued to spread despite territorial loss. Scholars from all over Eurasia came to Baghdad to learn about Islam and exchange information. Thanks to the transmission of papermaking from China, literature and books were much more available in the Middle East than in Europe. Unlike Christianity at this time, in particular the Catholic Church, Islam looked to many different sources for knowledge. Much of the great knowledge of antiquity, including the Greek classics, which would prove so important for the European Renaissance, as well as works from Persia and India, had been copied into Arabic, allowing the ideas to be shared across the Muslim world. Many of the works from the Hellenistic past helped Muslims to excel in science and technology. Astronomical observations, medicinal studies, and mathematics from the Greek past were reexamined, and Muslim scholars built on these studies.

Cities like Baghdad and Cordoba were essential for the Muslim empire, both as ways of spreading the faith and as governing centers. New converts, many of whom were not Arab, could count on the cities as places to learn the language and traditions of their new faith free of discrimination. The mosque, the Muslim house of worship, became a central architectural landmark that newcomers of the faith could recognize because of its distinctive features.

One social group that rose in cities was the **ulama,** an Arabic word for people with religious knowledge. As the Muslim empire grew in cultural diversity under the Abbasid Caliphate, the ulama sought to preserve central teachings and tenets of the faith. Two examples, both originating with Iranians, are the madrasa, or religious college; and **Sufi** brotherhoods, mystic religious groups, widespread in the Muslim world, that began to form in the early days of Islam.

Cities were also essential as places of trade. Since the time of the Umayyad Caliphate, a coinage system allowed for both local and long-distance trade that linked the more isolated portions of the Islamic empire and encouraged the burgeoning textile industry as well as other crafts. The Islamic world stood at the western end of the Silk Road, the most important overland trade route of the period 600–1450.

AP Tip

Women in the Islamic world had greater legal freedoms than Jewish or Christian women in post-classic times. Although seclusion of women and veiling are practices that are believed by many to have originated with Islam, they actually date to Byzantine and Sassanid times and later came to be a part of the Islamic tradition. Although Muslim women were not considered the equals of men, which was also true in the Byzantine Empire and western Europe, they were influential in family life, could own and inherit property, divorce, remarry, and testify in court.

The Islamic faith spread through Muslim merchants who traveled along the Silk Road, allowing the religion to spread from Spain to China, at the eastern end of the Silk Road.

By the middle of the ninth century several provinces had broken away and established their own caliphates, such as the Fatimid caliphate in Egypt. Another example was the Samanid caliphate, an Iranian dynasty that brought many Persian influences to the art and literature of the Islamic world. Because of territorial fragmentation, the Abbasid leaders came to rely on the **mamluks**, Turkish slaves from central Asia with exceptional skill in warfare. They became a powerful military presence in the Middle East during Islamic rule, and by the eleventh century, Turkish groups had significantly diminished the territory and political power of the Abbasid Caliphate. For example, in the early eleventh century the **Seljuk Turks** created a Turkish Muslim state that controlled territory from Baghdad up through Syria and into Anatolia and Byzantine areas. Christians viewed the Seljuk Turks as a tremendous threat, and they set out to take the Holy Land back from Turkish Muslims.

THE CRUSADES

The Crusades were a series of battles initiated by one monotheistic faith, Christianity, against another monotheistic faith, Islam. Study of the Crusades offers a wealth of fascinating ideas and details, but for AP students, the causes of the Crusades and their impact are of fundamental importance. The causes are discussed later, in Chapter 9, but the impact of the Crusades on the Middle East is discussed here.

By the eleventh century, Muslim leaders were in control of many cities that were considered sacred by Christians, among them Jerusalem, Antioch, and Alexandria. Christians had been allowed to make pilgrimage to these places, but as Muslims continued to eat away at the Byzantine Empire and conquer more territory deemed precious to Christendom, a campaign against the Muslims began to form in both western Europe and the Byzantine Empire.

Jerusalem, a city of particular significance to Christians, Muslims, and Jews, was in the hands of the Seljuk Turks, who at the time of the First Crusade were going through a period of internal dispute. Even though Christian crusaders had wrested Jerusalem from the Seljuk Turks in 1099, Islamic military forces under the dynamic leader Saladin were able to take back the city in 1187. The Islamic world in the Middle East continued to thrive despite the Crusaders' unsuccessful attempt to take land permanently, and the Crusades had very little long-term effects on Muslim territory.

The greatest impact of the Crusades was therefore not on the Muslims themselves. Instead, European life, which was far less sophisticated than Muslims', was dramatically improved. The incredible amount of information, ideas, goods, and resources that the Crusaders were exposed to in their encounter with the Muslim world was remarkable. Over time, the Crusaders brought back paper and sugar, and they learned how to make many of the goods they previously could only import. The establishment of trading ports in Italian cities like Venice and Genoa helped open Europe to the diverse Muslim world of the Middle East. Demand for goods from the Middle

East stimulated the markets of late medieval Europe and also encouraged trade between the Muslim world, western Europe, and the Byzantine Empire. Muslims also made enormous intellectual contributions to Europe in two ways: Their Arabic translations of works by ancient Greek scientists and philosophers such as Aristotle allowed for the restoration of ideas that had long been buried during the Middle Ages. Second, Arabs and Iranians, building on the work of the ancient philosophers, had added their own insights to give rise to new and innovative ideas. This double gift of knowledge by the Muslim world was essential in laying the groundwork for the Renaissance.

AP Tip

It is important to understand the similarities and differences between the monotheistic religions of Islam and Christianity as these two religions developed and grew into political and religious forces during the period 600–1450.

THE MONGOLS IN THE MIDDLE EAST

Migrating from the Central Asian steppes as a nomadic group, the **Mongols** were able to do what Europeans had failed to in the Crusades: they shattered what had once been the heart of the Muslim empire. The weakened and fragmented Abbasid Caliphate was destroyed when Baghdad was sacked in 1258. This event appalled the Islamic world, which did not expect a catastrophe of this magnitude. Rather than destroy all that Islam had contributed to the world, however, the Mongols became ardent patrons of Islamic culture, including art, literature, and architecture. Many of the Mongol leaders, known as khans, eventually converted to Islam and came to appreciate the urban infrastructure of the Islamic world. Still, tensions between Mongols and Muslims continued, much of it because of differences in cultural practices.

The Mongols set up four khanates in Eurasia. The **Il-khan** Empire in the Middle East was established in 1256 by the grandson of Genghis. Mongol nobles were placed in positions of power. Borrowing from an earlier Middle Eastern economic practice, the Mongols used tax farming—giving out private contracts to merchants to collect taxes by whatever means served them best. To foster the collection of as much money as possible, these merchants were allowed to keep any money above what was due to the government. Although this method was initially successful, tax farming coupled with an experiment using paper money from China eventually brought about an economic depression that outlived the Il-khan Empire.

The Islamic world had served as a major conduit for ideas and goods in its position at the western end of the Silk Road, and that continued under Mongol rule. Fine products from the East such as silk and porcelain flowed into the Middle East and from there to Europe.

Scholars, merchants, and missionaries traveled to the courts of the Mongols and recorded what they saw there. In addition, scholars such as Rashid al-Din were patronized by the Il-khans and wrote histories describing the greatness of the world controlled by the Mongols as well as histories of such faraway places as China and Europe. The Mongols were also fascinated by the scientific and mathematical innovations of the Muslim world. Algebra and trigonometry, as well as astronomical work that would one day be used by Europeans such as Copernicus, were all preserved and supplemented under both the Il-khans and their successors, the Timurids. This knowledge spread across the world of the Mongols and Turks and eventually through translation reached Europe. In addition, trade also brought disease, specifically the **bubonic plague,** which made its way through the Middle East and into Europe during Mongol rule. Far more than any attack or conquest, the plague would be the Mongols' most devastating impact.

By the fourteenth century, the Middle East was in the control of Turkish sultans and the Mongol khans. The Seljuk Turks still had a small kingdom that stood between the Byzantine Empire and the Mongols. The Mamluk Sultanate controlled Egypt and had successfully resisted a Mongol takeover to become a major player in shifting alliances with various khans to keep both Il-khan power at bay and the Crusaders from gaining any ground. The Il-khan Empire, which controlled territory from Syria to the Indus River, gave way to the Timurid Empire when the Central Asian Turkic leader Timur rose to take much of the Middle East before his death in 1405.

The Timurid Empire was short-lived. The **Ottoman** Empire would be the next great Turkish presence in the Middle East. Like the Seljuk Turks and the mamluks, the Ottomans were exceptionally skilled in warfare and conquest. As Mongol power began to decline, the Ottomans tightened their political organization and began their political ascent, establishing Turkic principalities in western Anatolia. Despite a defeat by Timur in 1402, the Ottoman sultans would take over the Byzantine Empire in 1453 and create a Muslim empire that would endure until the twentieth century.

Multiple-Choice Questions

1. The mamluks were
    (A) European mercenaries who traveled from the Byzantine Empire to Jerusalem.
    (B) Indo-Europeans who converted to Islam in the ninth century.
    (C) a subsect of Islam that developed shortly after Muhammad's death.
    (D) Turkic mercenaries in the Abbasid Caliphate who rose to control powerful Muslim states.

2. All of the following are characteristics of Islam EXCEPT
   (A) a monotheistic belief in one god that must be worshipped as the only god.
   (B) a belief in a community of believers unified by their faith above all else.
   (C) a tradition of passing down the central teachings of their faith orally.
   (D) a belief in the importance of prayer, fasting, and charity.

3. The caliph
   (A) always ruled over one extended area of land from Spain to India.
   (B) was a position that dissolved a short time after Muhammad's death.
   (C) was a position created by the Abbasid family to solidify their rule in Baghdad.
   (D) was considered to be the successor of Muhammad as well as a political leader.

4. The Sunni/Shi'ite split resulted from disagreement over
   (A) whether Muhammad was a god.
   (B) the role of the Ka'ba in Islam.
   (C) who should succeed Muhammad.
   (D) the validity of the Quran.

5. The word *Islam* means submission and refers to Muslims' obligation
   (A) to submit to the single authority of the caliph.
   (B) to submit to the teachers of the ulama.
   (C) to complete a pilgrimage to Mecca.
   (D) to submit to the will of God in all of life.

6. The group in control of Jerusalem at the time of the Crusades was the
   (A) Mongols.
   (B) Persians.
   (C) Sufi.
   (D) Seljuk Turks.

7. Cities were important in Islam for all of the following reasons EXCEPT
   (A) they were administrative centers for government.
   (B) they encouraged the exchange of new ideas.
   (C) they were the only places where women could travel freely.
   (D) they were central as places of trade.

8. The Mongols
   (A) destroyed all knowledge of the intellectual contributions of the Muslim world.
   (B) spread the bubonic plague through overland trade routes into Europe.
   (C) allied with Europeans to defeat the Abbasid Caliphate in 1258.
   (D) never converted to Islam because they disagreed with many Muslim cultural practices.

9. The Silk Road flourished under Mongol rule because
   (A) unlike the Muslims, who looked down on merchants, the Mongols encouraged trade.
   (B) the Mongols controlled all parts of the Silk Road, which allowed for relatively easy exchange.
   (C) the Turks hired Mongol armies to protect the Silk Road.
   (D) the Silk Road came into existence only during the period of Mongol rule in Eurasia.

10. Timur was notable for all the following reasons EXCEPT
    (A) helping to spread Muslim knowledge along the Silk Road.
    (B) patronizing Muslim art and learning in a variety of ways.
    (C) defeating the Ottomans in battle despite the sultan's growing power.
    (D) creating the concept of tax farming in the Middle East.

11. The Arabic Peninsula is characterized by
    (A) lush oases dotting the peninsula.
    (B) coastal cities and agricultural villages close to sources of water and a large empty quarter in the central areas.
    (C) a uniform arid climate, which can support only sparse nomadic populations throughout the peninsula.
    (D) agriculture in large portions of the southern area of the peninsula, but no other economic activity of significance in other areas of the peninsula.

12. The universal language of the Muslim empire was
    (A) Semitic, because it was the common language of Christians, Muslims, and Jews.
    (B) Persian, because scribes and other government officials considered it to be the most beautiful of languages.
    (C) Spanish, because most of the translators and philosophers studied in Andalucía, the Spanish area of the empire.
    (D) Arabic, because it was the language of the Quran.

13. The Muslim caliphate is significant in world history because
    (A) it is the first Afro-Eurasian empire.
    (B) it peacefully incorporated many different cultural groups.
    (C) it became the largest empire in history.
    (D) its beginnings as a nomadic culture made it remarkably egalitarian in its dealings between genders.

14. The Crusades are an important event in world history because
    (A) they were the first manifestation of belligerence between Muslims and Christians.
    (B) they proved clearly that Christians were technologically and tactically superior to the Muslims.
    (C) they provided an occasion for the Christian pope to prove to his detractors that he had secular power throughout Western Christendom.
    (D) they provided an opportunity for the diffusion of technology, ideas, and warfare tactics.

15. As a result of the forcible concentration of scholars initiated by Timur
    (A) most scholarship died because of the harsh conditions under which the scholars worked.
    (B) scholars made some advances in math and science, but because the Muslims and the Timurids were nomads, nothing was written down.
    (C) Greek scholarship in astronomy and mathematics continued.
    (D) scholars in Samarkand improved on Greek and Chinese ideas in astronomy and mathematics and also made many literary innovations.

Free-Response Questions

1. Compare the social and economic characteristics of the Muslim caliphates and the Mongols in the Middle East from circa 600 to circa 1450.

2. Evaluate the political continuities and changes over time in the Middle East from circa 600 to circa 1450.

Answers

Multiple-Choice Questions

1. **Answer: D.** The mamluks were originally purchased as slaves and eventually grew more powerful than the weakened Abbasid Caliphate and set up their own independent sultanates (*The Earth and Its Peoples*, 5th ed., p. 234/6th ed., p. 254).

2. **Answer: C.** The Quran is the holy book of Islam, believed to be the words of God, as given to Muhammad in Arabic, that were written down and organized formally by 650 (*The Earth and Its Peoples*, 5th ed., pp. 230–231/6th ed., p. 251).

3. **Answer: D.** The word *caliph* means successor. The caliph could lose political power if lacking military and political strength (*The Earth and Its Peoples*, 5th ed., p. 231/6th ed., p. 251).

4. **Answer: C.** Muhammad left no instructions for leadership after his death and did not specify a form of government for the umma. This left room for debate over who should be in power and the nature of their rule (*The Earth and Its Peoples*, 5th ed., p. 231/6th ed., p. 251).

5. **Answer: D.** The central tenet of Islam is submission to Allah and allowing his will to control all aspects of one's life. A Muslim is one who submits (*The Earth and Its Peoples*, 5th ed., p. 230/6th ed., p. 250).

6. **Answer: D.** The Seljuks were a nomadic Turkic group who gained power in the eleventh century after winning a battle against the

Byzantine army (*The Earth and Its Peoples,* 5th ed., pp. 237–238/6th ed., p. 256).

7. **ANSWER: C.** Women seldom traveled during this time period and were often secluded in their homes. They covered themselves when outside the home (*The Earth and Its Peoples,* 5th ed., pp. 241–243/6th ed., p. 262).

8. **ANSWER: B.** One of the most significant effects of Mongol rule was the spread of the bubonic plague along the trade routes supported and stabilized by the Mongols in the fourteenth century (*The Earth and Its Peoples,* 5th ed. p. 348/6th ed., p. 328).

9. **ANSWER: B.** The Mongol khanates were positioned at either end of the Silk Road, and for a time their khanate in Central Asia controlled the middle portion as well. After Timur's conquest, powerful kingdoms such as the Timurids controlled key cities along the trade route such as Samarkand (*The Earth and Its Peoples,* 5th ed., p. 351/6th ed., p. 329).

10. **ANSWER: D.** Timur was a Turk who wanted to be one of the great khans. Because he was not ethnically a Mongol he never became a khan, but he was able to take significant territory in the Middle East for a short period, and he encouraged the preservation and spread of Muslim knowledge and culture (*The Earth and Its Peoples,* 5th ed., p. 350/6th ed., p. 331).

11. **ANSWER: B.** Although the Arabian Peninsula is certainly arid in many places, there are many coastal cities, and agriculture is the dominant economic activity in the southern portion of the peninsula that is today called Yemen (*The Earth and Its Peoples,* 5th ed., p. 228/6th ed., p. 248).

12. **ANSWER: D.** Although its original speakers were relatively few in numbers, the fact that the Quran was written and recited in Arabic made this the universal language of the rapidly expanding empire. Other languages, like Persian, continued their regional importance (*The Earth and Its Peoples,* 5th ed., pp. 233–234/6th ed., p. 253).

13. **ANSWER: A.** The Muslim empire, also known as Dar-al-Islam, was the world's first Afro-Eurasian empire. It was large, very diverse, and quickly fragmented into multiple smaller areas nominally controlled by the caliph (*The Earth and Its Peoples,* 5th ed., pp. 232–233/6th ed., pp. 252–253).

14. **ANSWER: D.** Although Western Christians considered the Crusades a holy war and established a Christian presence in Jerusalem for about a century, the true significance of the series of wars was how exposure to new plants, technology, architecture, and medicine affected Europe (*The Earth and Its Peoples,* 5th ed., p. 277/6th ed., p. 291).

15. **ANSWER: D.** Like the Mongols and even the Arab Muslim conquerors before him, Timur promoted scholarship. In his capital, Isfahan, the concentrated scholars he accumulated made great strides in mathematics and astronomy, as well as history and

literature (*The Earth and Its Peoples,* 5th ed., pp. 351–352/6th ed., pp. 330–332).

FREE-RESPONSE QUESTIONS

1. For this essay you should include a comparison of treatment of conquered peoples, religious practices, and cultural contributions. Cultural contributions could also be considered in a comparative analysis of the role of trade and cities in both empires as part of economic characteristics. Another economic comparison could also be drawn between the unsuccessful attempts by the Mongol Il-khans to incorporate paper money and tax farming (an economic policy used earlier in the Middle East) and the Abbasid Caliphate's economic practices. The use of paper money by the Mongols is in contrast with the Abbasid Caliphate's continuation of coinage.

2. This essay calls for a discussion of both change and continuity as it relates to the caliphate and the khanate as political systems. The caliphate's inability to control a large territory effectively resulted in provinces breaking away and establishing their own caliphates. This changed when the Mongols came in and practiced varying degrees of local political autonomy while still maintaining overall political authority. The Mongols didn't attempt to rule the Middle East as part of one huge empire but established a separate political khanate under the Il-khans. Abbasid reliance on the mamluks to enforce their authority militarily became a continuity in the region because Mongol presence also forced Turkic groups such as the mamluks and the Ottomans to grow in political strength. The Ottomans would eventually come to dominate the Middle East entirely.

8

ASIA: CIRCA **600** TO CIRCA 1450

KEY CONCEPTS

- During the period 600–1450, China rose as the most influential state in East Asia in terms of economic and political dominance.
- Japan, Korea, and Vietnam accepted some aspects of Chinese culture and rejected others, carving out their own unique cultural and political identities.
- The impact of Mongol rule in Central, East, and Southeast Asia varied, depending on whether the Mongols had direct or peripheral control of a given area. Mongol presence in Asia had long-lasting consequences on the development of East Asia in particular.
- The Silk Road, an overland trade route, and the Indian Ocean trade network were the dominant trading networks of the period 600–1450 and allowed for important cultural and economic interactions among Africa, the Middle East, Europe, and Asia.
- Mahayana Buddhism exerted significant social, cultural, and political influence in China, Japan, Korea, and Vietnam during this period.
- While India experienced great political and religious turmoil as the Muslim Delhi Sultanate came to power, it also experienced economic prosperity because of its central location in the Indian Ocean trade network.

KEY TERMS

- bubonic plague
- Delhi Sultanate
- dhow
- footbinding

144

- Grand Canal
- Jagadai khanate
- junk
- Kamakura Shogunate
- Koryo
- Malacca
- movable type
- neo-Confucianism
- nomadism
- tributary system
- tribute state
- Yuan Empire

Asia is discussed in depth in *The Earth and Its Peoples*, fifth edition, Chapters 10, 12, and 13 and sixth edition, Chapters 11, 12, and 14.

CHINA

After a three-hundred-year period of disunity following the collapse of the Han dynasty in 220 C.E., the Sui family reunited China in a short forty years. The Sui dynasty was short-lived, but it set the stage for China's growth into a powerful society that dominated Asia up through the twentieth century and affected the evolving cultures of Korea, Japan, and Vietnam. The Sui laid the groundwork for many of the practices of the Tang Empire, which would come to power in 618. Under the Sui, Confucianism was reestablished as the philosophy of the state, and the examination system was revived. By the time of the Sui, Mahayana Buddhism had grown to be very influential in China and would be a defining characteristic of the Tang dynasty. The Sui placed their capital in Chang'an and built several canals to link the capital to the coast of southern China. The most important, the **Grand Canal**, linked the Yellow and Yangzi Rivers and would be a key part of the Tang's economic success.

THE TANG EMPIRE: 618–907

The Li family, whose roots were both Turkish and Chinese, established the Tang Empire in 618. The Tang established a large empire, giving a great deal of power to local nobility in order to ensure control. They expanded westward into Central Asia until Muslim Arabs and Turks stopped their advance. The Tang had ethnic ties to the areas of Central Asia where Buddhism had proved politically useful, and as they extended their empire into areas where Buddhism was popular among people of all classes, they continued to use it as a political tool. For this reason Tang princes rewarded Buddhist monasteries that supported their rule with monetary gifts, tax exemptions, and land grants. The Tang also reinstituted the **tributary system**, first used by the Han dynasty, by which independent states gave gifts to the Chinese emperor. Both Japan and Korea paid tribute to the Tang and in doing so acknowledged China's regional power.

The Tang Empire quickly attracted people from all over Asia, who flocked especially to the Tang capital at Chang'an, a trading center, where they could be found worshiping as Muslims, Christians, and Buddhists. With more than 1 million people in the city and its suburbs,

Chang'an was a center for cultural exchange in the arts, textiles, and music. This cultural exchange was possible in part because the Tang, with control of the coast of southern China, participated in Indian Ocean trade. Chinese maritime technology included the compass and the ability to make oceangoing vessels that could transport all kinds of goods up through the Grand Canal. The Chinese also began to master new kinds of skills such as cotton production, and increasing competition with the textile industry in western Asia spurred them to increase their expertise in silk production.

In the eighth century, the power of the Tang began to be threatened by rival states, including the Uighur and Tibetan Empires. These external threats, combined with internal rebellion and overexpansion, signaled the decline and eventual destruction of the Tang Empire. Buddhism, because it had come to China from India, became a scapegoat for many of the problems the Tang faced. Buddhist monasteries were accused of being a foreign evil that drained money from the state because they were tax-exempt. They were also blamed for causing the breakdown of the family because elite sons and daughters were entering monasteries rather than getting married and producing heirs.

THE SONG EMPIRE: 960–1279

After the fall of the Tang dynasty, three smaller empires controlled territory in China. The Song Empire, based in central China, had a large army but never grew as large as the Tang, primarily because of the strength of the rival Tanggut and Liao Empires in northern China. These three empires had different religious and ethnic identities and competed for resources. The Song fought against these "barbarians" in the north and focused on advancing their maritime expertise in order to build relationships with other states by sea. The Jin, who defeated the Liao in 1115, captured the Song emperor two years later in the capital city of Kaifeng and forced the Song south of the Yellow River, where they established a new capital at Hangzhou. From this point on, historians refer to the Song Empire as the Southern Song.

Although never as large as the Tang, the Song made outstanding scientific and technological contributions by building on the mathematical and engineering skills that had come to the far-flung Tang Empire. For example, they used their knowledge of astronomy to build a mechanical celestial clock and to improve the compass and the junk, the main Chinese seafaring ship. The **junk** navigated the oceans with ease and had special features such as watertight compartments that allowed it to preserve all kinds of goods. Military technologies were also essential because the Song military commanded more than 1 million men. Improvements in iron and steel production and experiments with gunpowder produced innovative and effective weapons.

The Song also had many economic accomplishments. Paper money, possibly thanks to printing techniques such as **movable type**, was a tremendous technological contribution that would spread across Asia, into Europe, and beyond. Printing also allowed for the dissemination of agricultural techniques, educational resources, and public-health materials in cities and villages across China, improving production and health conditions in areas by combating malaria and the plague.

Another economic tool was credit, which could be used across the region.

Although the religious influence of Buddhism remained strong, Confucianism reemerged as the philosophical and ethical basis for Song society. **Neo-Confucianism**—Confucian ideas that emerged in the Song period and thereafter—reflected Buddhist influence and incorporated new understandings of Confucian teachings. Mastery of the Confucian classics was required under the scholar examination system, and merit-based appointments gave new prominence to the role of the scholar-official in Chinese society. Confucianism's patriarchal tradition, coupled with the backlash against Buddhism dating from the end of the Tang period, meant that expectations for women were closely regulated in China and subsequently in all East Asian states. In China, women did not have property rights or the ability to remarry and rarely had educational opportunities comparable to those of men. **Footbinding,** a practice unique to China, came to embody the restrictions on women in Song China. Their feet were tightly wrapped and they subsequently broke, then healed in a way to make the feet appear smaller—making a woman unable to work. Footbinding became a status symbol among the elite in China.

AP Tip

The cities of Song China, such as Chang'an, Kaifeng, and Hangzhou, were thriving economic and cultural centers and were among the largest cities in the world at this time. You should be able to make comparisons between these cities and other city centers in the world during this period. For example, the AP exam could ask you to compare the economic role of cities in China with the economic role of the cities of the Islamic empires or the cities of the Americas.

THE MONGOLS

The Mongols, a **nomadic** group that originated in Central Asia in what is now Mongolia, were self-sufficient pastoralists; families moved quickly, and from the earliest ages, children learned the skills necessary to thrive in the steppes of Central Asia. The Mongols had many traditional practices and beliefs centered on shamanism. A shaman could move between the physical and spiritual worlds and influence events in both worlds. The Mongols often adopted other faiths that spread along the Silk Road, such as Buddhism, Islam, and Christianity, but still maintained their shamanistic traditions. They believed the tribal leader, or khan, and his shamans could speak for the god of the universe, known as Sky or Heaven. The most powerful families could voice their opinions to the khan, and they grew even more powerful through intermarriage and warfare.

Genghis Khan rose to power as the supreme leader of the Mongols, a title known as the Great Khan. In 1206, he set out to conquer Eurasia and force rival kingdoms to pay tribute. By 1215, he had captured Beijing, then the capital of the Jin Empire. By 1221, he had control of Iran, and his first attacks on Russia had begun. Genghis Khan died in 1227, but conquest of the north of China continued with his son, the Great Khan Ögödei. By 1234, the Mongols were positioned to take the Southern Song Empire in China. The Middle East came under Mongol control in 1258 with the sacking of Baghdad, the capital of the Abbasid Caliphate.

What made the Mongols able to conquer Eurasia relatively quickly? Much of their success was a result of the military techniques these steppe nomads had practiced for centuries. Mongol expertise in horsemanship and use of the Central Asian bow, which could shoot one-third farther than the bows of their enemies, made them nearly unstoppable. The only true military rivals to the Mongols were the mamluks, who shared many of the same cultural traditions and were therefore familiar with Mongol weaponry and tactics. The Mongols also adapted the iron weaponry and tactics they encountered in China, and they absorbed many captured peoples into their army, including Iranians, Turks, Chinese, and even Europeans.

From 1240 until 1260 the capital of the Mongol Empire was Karakorum, a flourishing city that attracted merchants, missionaries, and scholars from all over Eurasia. During this period, the Great Khan remained in Mongolia and ruled over the khanate of the Golden Horde in Russia, the Jagadai khanate in Central Asia, and the Il-khan in Iran. After 1265, the Jagadai khanate continued to control Central Asia and developed and thrived independently from the domain of the Great Khan in the East. Both Turkish nomads and Muslims had a tremendous influence on developments in the Central Asian khanate.

THE GOLDEN HORDE AND THE JAGADAI KHANATE

The Golden Horde, established under Genghis' grandson Batu in 1223, began as a unified khanate but broke apart into smaller khanates, the longest-lasting one surviving up until the eighteenth century. The Mongols ruled Russia from a distance; their capital was just north of the Caspian Sea. This allowed Russia to avoid direct subjugation and kept Russia's principalities in place. Much of the credit for this was due to Prince Alexander Nevskii, who convinced his peers that their best strategy was to cooperate with the Mongols. In appreciation for his help, the Mongols favored Nevskii's territory of Novgorod. Moscow, the town his son ruled, eventually became the most important political hub in Russia. The Mongols also recognized and patronized the Orthodox Church, a shrewd political move to win the hearts of the Russian people. Islam was also very influential and became a source of tension among the Mongols of the Golden Horde. Batu's successor declared himself a Muslim, which sparked conflict between Golden Horde leaders and those of the Il-khan that culminated in war in 1260. In 1295, the Il-khan leader declared himself a Muslim, which shifted alliances again.

In securing and controlling Eurasia, the Mongols allowed missionaries, merchants, and diplomats to move freely and exchange ideas and goods. However, the Mongols also unknowingly spread disease, in particular the **bubonic plague**. It began in China under the Tang dynasty. As Mongol troops moved from their stations in China, rats in their cargo spread the disease across Central Asia into Russia and port cities like Kaffa on the Black Sea, and from there eventually to western Europe. In addition, influenza, typhus, and smallpox were spread. The death and devastation caused by the plague is one of the greatest legacies of the Mongols; peaceful trade allowed for an unforeseeable pandemic. The Mongols brought demographic change in other ways as well. The heavy burden they placed on western Eurasia in terms of taxes and resources led to population loss, drained the local economy, and destroyed rural areas.

As the Il-Khan khanate was declining in the Middle East, new leadership rose in the **Jagadai khanate** under Timur (also known as Tamerlane in the West, he ruled from 1370 to 1405). Although he was an ambitious military leader, Timur could never be khan because he was not born a Mongol; he was a Turk who had married into the Mongol dynasty. This did not stop him from having incredible success in attacking the Delhi Sultanate and the Ottoman Empire and bringing the Middle East under his control. He then set his sights on East Asia but died before he could attack China. Timur's legacy lived on through his descendants, the Timurids, in the Mughal Empire of the sixteenth century.

Placed strategically between Iran and China, the ends of the Silk Road, Timur's capital at Samarkand, became a key trading point on the Silk Road. Timur also patronized great scholars, painters, and historians, helping to preserve and build on the significant contributions of the Muslim world. Astronomy was another field that flourished during this time. Timur's own grandson built an observatory in Samarkand and studied astronomy with great precision and dedication.

THE YUAN EMPIRE

The death of Ögödei caused conflict over who would be the next Great Khan. When Genghis' grandson Khubilai Khan took the title of Great Khan in 1265, Jagadai's descendants refused to recognize Khubilai as the supreme leader. The fighting that ensued destroyed Karakorum, and as a result, Khubilai began to rule from Beijing, where he created an incredible city that was linked to the Grand Canal. In 1271, he created the **Yuan** Empire in China, the new domain of the Great Khan.

One of Khubilai's greatest contributions to Chinese regional identity was his ability to unify the area after the Song's fragmentation. He destroyed the Tanggut and Jin Empires in northern China and conquered the Southern Song dynasty in 1279, thereby laying out the territory of modern China. Eager to establish himself as the rightful ruler of China, he worked to bring together Mongol and Chinese traditions. To that end, Khubilai adopted many of the successful political and cultural practices of the previous dynasties—with a few striking exceptions: he did away with the scholar examination system and placed Mongols in the highest positions of authority in his court. Chinese scholar officials kept their positions but were subordinate to the Mongols. The Confucians were at odds with many of the practices of the Yuan Empire, including the rising status of merchants, whom Confucians did not respect.

Mongol control of the entire Eurasian landmass revitalized the Silk Road. The Yuan Empire stood at one end and the Il-khan at the other, which allowed for the Pax Mongolica, or the Mongol peace. The flow of ideas, religion, technological innovations, and resources brought tremendous wealth and grandeur to the Yuan Empire. Khubilai financed the building of canals and roads to bring the tribute and wealth right to his glorious palace in Beijing. Because Khubilai valued this exchange so much, he welcomed to his court important men from all parts of the world, including Marco Polo. Polo was a Venetian merchant whose record of his alleged years at the court of Khubilai has given tremendous insight into life in the Yuan dynasty. Muslims furthered astronomical studies, brought new medicinal practices, and left their imprint on language—Mandarin Chinese, a dominant language in China today, has many Mongolian influences that date back to this time.

The Mongols significantly affected Chinese demographics. For various reasons—including warfare, flooding, migration, and bubonic plague—the population under the Mongols declined significantly, perhaps up to 40 percent. By the 1340s, feuding among Mongol princes led to mass rebellion and the eventual rise of a new empire that focused on reestablishing Chinese traditions. The Mongols did not disappear; some were absorbed into Chinese society and others returned to the Mongol homeland. The Ming would never rule over all the Mongols, who continued to be a serious concern on the northern edge of the Ming Empire.

THE MING EMPIRE

In response to the foreign threat represented by the Mongol's Yuan dynasty, a priority of the first Ming emperor, Hongwu, was to reassert Chinese authority and indigenous cultural practices. He moved the capital from Beijing to Nanjing, on the Yangzi River, and reinstituted the Confucian examination system. The Ming also made many social and economic changes to reflect their desire to take back control from the Mongols. Communication with the rest of Central Asia and the Middle East was scaled back tremendously, and silver replaced paper money as the main currency. Growing staple crops became more important than growing commercial crops because of the large population increase under the Ming. They also completed the Great Wall, which stood as a tangible symbol of imperial desire to keep foreigners out. Despite these efforts, many of the influences of the Mongols remained, including the Mongol calendar.

The second Ming emperor, Yongle, was quite different from Hongwu. He increased ties to the previous empire by moving the capital back to Beijing and added onto Khubilai's royal complex, the Forbidden City. Yongle also reopened trade with the Indian Ocean trade network and reestablished economic relations with the Middle East. To avoid conflicts with the remaining Mongol presence in Central Asia, he sent the eunuch naval admiral Zheng He on maritime voyages to Indian Ocean ports. In the course of seven expeditions between 1405 and 1433, Zheng established trading, mercantile, and diplomatic relationships and added fifty new **tribute states** to China's realm. During this time, Ming cultural achievements blossomed in the areas of literature and painting, and Ming porcelain, known as Ming ware, became the most famous Chinese product throughout Eurasia. The Ming Empire would endure until the mid-seventeenth century.

KOREA

The first written records of Korean history come from Chinese sources, which make clear that the Chinese heavily influenced Korea but that Korea also maintained its own identity. Both Confucianism and Buddhism had a tremendous impact on Korean culture, but political roles were not determined by a civil service examination system as in China. Instead, Korea's landed aristocracy created ruling families who were in power for centuries, and wealth was based on agriculture. One of these families, the Silla, conquered the Korean peninsula with the support of the Tang. The Silla fell in the tenth century, and the **Koryo** family, from which the name Korea derives, took over. Like the Southern Song in China, the Koryo also feared the Liao and Jin Empires, and they established a diplomatic relationship with the Song in light of this threat. The Koryo also had a tense relationship with the Mongols that climaxed when the Mongols attacked in 1231. In 1258, the same year that they sacked Baghdad, the Mongols finally defeated the Koryo and brought Korea under their control. The Mongols demanded economic tribute from the Koreans, and the Koryo family married into the Mongols, which resulted in further exposure to the Yuan culture.

After the Yuan fell, the Yi family rose to power and established a new kingdom focused on reasserting Korean identity. The Yi remained in power until the Japanese takeover in 1910; part of their ability to remain independent as a tributary state to the Qing Empire was their strong naval power—gunpowder technology taken from the Chinese allowed them to mount cannon on ships.

One of the greatest contributions of the Koreans was in printing. Although the earliest woodblock print dates back to Han China and movable type was in place in Korea by the 1300s, it was the invention of metal movable type by the Koreans in the 1400s that allowed for increased accuracy and readability.

JAPAN

The first written records of Japan, like those of Korea, come from the Chinese. Many Chinese influences reached Japan through Korea, among them Confucianism and Buddhism. Indeed, Japan became a center for Mahayana Buddhism in the eighth century. Like Korea, Japan adopted some practices from China but had some key differences in political organization. There was no concept of a Mandate of Heaven in Japan; instead, emperors descended from one continuous lineage. The Fujiwara family assumed protection of the emperor and was in power from 794 to 1185, although civil war plagued the last thirty years. The **Kamakura** family took power in 1185 and established a shogunate that controlled Japan through the military. Japan became a decentralized feudal state that recognized the emperor and shogun but was not unified.

It was the threat of a Mongol invasion that unified feuding Japanese lords and helped create a national identity out of a politically decentralized environment. Every effort went into protecting Japan's economic resources and preparing for attack. Japan's ability to resist a Mongol invasion twice was partly because of weather; both times storms undermined the Mongols' attempts. This fact helped cement the view that Japan was a unique state among her East Asian neighbors. Defending Japan successfully strengthened the power of the warrior elite, or samurai, who developed a culture centered on Zen Buddhism during the period of the Ashikaga Shogunate, established in 1338.

AP Tip

An important comparison in AP World History is between Japanese feudalism and European feudalism. These two feudal systems had strikingly similar characteristics.

VIETNAM

During the period 600–1450, Vietnam was divided into two rival kingdoms—Annam, in the north, and Champa, in the south. Sharing an environment similar to southern China's and agriculturally based like its East Asian neighbors, Annam was culturally, politically, and economically tied to China beginning in the Tang period. Because it was part of the Indian Ocean trade network, Champa was heavily influenced by India and Malaya. Both Annam and Champa were tributary states to the Song, and the Champa made a significant tribute gift of Champa rice, which grows fast and allowed Chinese farmers in the Song period to produce more of this staple crop. When the Mongols came, they made both Annam and Champa tribute states. This continued under the Ming, who occupied Annam for a time. Annam regained tribute status, then took Champa, uniting the two kingdoms into one state named Annam by 1500. Annam continued to have Confucian political structures, including the examination system, but women retained property rights.

SOUTH ASIA AND THE INDIAN OCEAN TRADE NETWORK

Since the decline of the Gupta Empire, India was divided into separate states that often fought one another. In the twelfth century, Turkish invaders from Central Asia poured into northern India and established the **Delhi Sultanate**. From 1206 to 1526, this Muslim empire ruled almost the entire subcontinent of India except the south, which Hindu princes held, and did much to centralize India under a strict government bureaucracy. The Turks destroyed temples and massacred thousands. Once the initial conquest was over, the Delhi Sultanate required Hindus to pay a special tax in exchange for protection. This created an ongoing tension between Hindus and Muslims that would ultimately weaken the Delhi Sultanate significantly—in fact, this tension between Hindus and Muslims still goes on today and causes much conflict in the region. The sultanate received a fatal blow in 1398 when Timur sacked and captured Delhi, a defeat that signaled the end of the prominence of Delhi. Despite its difficulty in controlling all of

India, the Delhi Sultanate profited tremendously from the Indian Ocean trade network because it held many of the key port cities and regions along the trade routes.

The key to Indian Ocean trade was mastering the monsoon winds and navigating their currents. The typical ship of the Indian Ocean was the **dhow**, a boat fitted with a lateen sail—a triangular sail that caught the winds beautifully. The Chinese junk became known in the Indian Ocean as the best vessel for travel and large transport. The Indian Ocean trade network grew to be the richest trade network during the period 600–1450 and was at its height from 1200 to 1500. So precious was this trade network that gaining control of it would become the quest of European explorers like Christopher Columbus by the end of the period.

The complex trading patterns of the Indian Ocean were not controlled by one central political authority but worked through a series of smaller economic relationships. Gold from Africa flowed through the East African city-states. Goods from the Mediterranean, the Middle East, and Europe were transported across the Arabian Peninsula. Port cities like **Malacca** stood as a gateway between Southeast Asia, China, and the Indian Ocean. Islam was the dominant religion of the network and facilitated trading relationships between peoples of all languages and ethnicities who shared this faith, among them ibn Battuta (1304–1369), a Moroccan Muslim, who chronicled his extensive travels to many of the prominent locations along the Indian Ocean trade route.

Multiple-Choice Questions

1. Which statement best defines the Mongols' political relationship to Russia?
   (A) Russia was immediately plundered and pillaged when the Mongols arrived.
   (B) Russians were the only group other than the mamluks to defeat the Mongols in battle.
   (C) Russian princes were persuaded to cooperate with Mongol khans and thereby maintained some local autonomy.
   (D) Russia was united under one tsar, who descended from the Mongols.

2. What was the tributary system?
   (A) A labor system that required each family member to send the oldest son to serve in the court of the Chinese emperor
   (B) A requirement that each family in China pay one-tenth of its income to the Chinese emperor
   (C) Gifts given by independent states in East and Southeast Asia to acknowledge the supremacy of China
   (D) A system of waterways that flowed from the center of the Grand Canal to bring water to all parts of China

3. The Tang elite blamed Buddhism for the social upheaval occurring at the end of their empire because
   (A) Buddhism taught that the emperor was inherently evil.
   (B) Buddhist followers were required to rebel against the government to prove their loyalty.
   (C) Buddhist monks convinced the emperor to adopt Buddhism rather than Confucianism as the model for the state government.
   (D) Buddhism had come to China from India and therefore was a foreign influence that went against traditional Confucianist ideals.

4. The Song Empire contributed to science and technology by
   (A) creating a new form of gunpowder.
   (B) improving maritime expertise by improving the compass and the junk.
   (C) borrowing military techniques with gunpowder from the Europeans.
   (D) being the first to use iron and steel weapons.

5. The Yuan dynasty was significant for many reasons, including
   (A) establishing the Koryo dynasty in Japan as a puppet government.
   (B) playing a significant role in decreasing the Chinese population.
   (C) marrying into the Delhi Sultanate in order to dominate the Indian Ocean trade network.
   (D) creating an empire with Genghis Khan as the emperor of China.

6. The use of paper money began with the
   (A) Persian Empire.
   (B) Tang Empire.
   (C) Abbasid Caliphate.
   (D) Song Empire.

7. The innovation of metal movable type began in
   (A) Korea.
   (B) Japan.
   (C) Annam.
   (D) Russia.

8. Both the Mongols and Yongle's Ming Empire
   (A) based all political appointments on the Confucian examination system.
   (B) made Beijing the capital of their empires.
   (C) expanded the Great Wall to keep foreigners out.
   (D) were wary of establishing close trade relations with South and Southeast Asia.

9. One result of the Mongols' attempted invasions of Japan was
   (A) the death of the Japanese emperor.
   (B) a civil war in Japan.
   (C) the unification of Korea and Japan in order to fight the Mongols.
   (D) protection of Japanese resources and temporary unification of Japanese lords.

10. The Indian Ocean trade network
    (A) was a significant trade route but brought wealth only to the coast of East Africa.
    (B) brought wealth to the Delhi Sultanate and furthered its interest in economic growth.
    (C) was primarily used by Christians from eastern Europe and the Mediterranean regions.
    (D) was controlled by the Mongols beginning with Khubilai Khan in the thirteenth century.

11. Cities in the Middle East and in China were similar in that they
    (A) were much smaller than comparable cities in Europe and the Americas.
    (B) served as areas of administrative, commercial, and cultural interactions.
    (C) were surrounded by fortress-like walls to ward off strangers.
    (D) served as trade centers.

12. Zhenge He and Ibn Battuta were similar in that both were
    (A) eunuchs.
    (B) travelers.
    (C) published authors.
    (D) pilgrims.

13. After the Ming dynasty gained power from the Mongols, it
    (A) tried to continue Mongol traditions such as a focus on trade.
    (B) gradually turned away from the commercial nature of the Song and the Yuan dynasties by emphasizing food crops over commercial crops.
    (C) outlawed Buddhism.
    (D) invited foreigners to help them trade and rule.

14. The Japanese feudal system
    (A) was remarkably similar to the European feudal system.
    (B) was invented in response to the Mongol threat.
    (C) worked because it gave the emperor significant power.
    (D) ended when the Ming dynasty took over.

15. Vietnam's greatest contribution to Tang China was
    (A) iron smelting.
    (B) the exam-system bureaucracy.
    (C) the domestication of draft animals.
    (D) wet rice cultivation.

Free-Response Questions

1. Compare the political systems of TWO of the following civilizations from circa 600 to circa 1450.
   - Japan
   - China
   - Korea

2. Evaluate the continuities and changes in the role of religion in Chinese society from circa 600 to circa 1450.

Answers

MULTIPLE-CHOICE QUESTIONS

1. **ANSWER: C.** Thanks to Alexander Nevskii, Russian princes were convinced to cooperate with Mongol khans, who then left local government in place (*The Earth and Its Peoples*, 5th ed., p. 354/6th ed., p. 332).

2. **ANSWER: C.** This system, dating back to the Han dynasty, is an example of Chinese political dominance in East and Southeast Asia (*The Earth and Its Peoples*, 5th ed., p. 287/6th ed., p. 298).

3. **ANSWER: D.** The Confucian elite believed Buddhism undermined Chinese social structure, including women's roles, marriage, and family responsibilities (*The Earth and Its Peoples*, 5th ed., pp. 287–288/6th ed., p. 300).

4. **ANSWER: B.** Although the Song successfully used gunpowder and had a huge military, they were not the first to use iron and steel weapons. They improved upon the compass and perfected shipbuilding techniques (*The Earth and Its Peoples*, 5th ed., p. 293/6th ed., p. 305).

5. **ANSWER: B.** Khubilai Khan created the Yuan Empire as the domain of the Great Khan in 1271, and under the Mongols the population declined dramatically (*The Earth and Its Peoples*, 5th ed., p. 358/6th ed., p. 336).

6. **ANSWER: D.** The Song dynasty is responsible for the innovation of paper money in large part because of their use of printing (*The Earth and Its Peoples*, 5th ed., p. 296/6th ed., p. 308).

7. **ANSWER: A.** Movable metal type was invented on the Korean peninsula and was quickly adopted by neighboring East Asians (*The Earth and Its Peoples*, 5th ed., p. 295/6th ed., p. 307).

8. **ANSWER: B.** The second Ming emperor continued many of the practices of the Yuan Empire, including the location of the capital in Beijing (*The Earth and Its Peoples*, 5th ed., p. 359/6th ed., p. 337).

9. **ANSWER: D.** Japan was decentralized at the time of the Mongol invasions, but rival lords worked together to defend the country from multiple Mongol attacks (*The Earth and Its Peoples*, 5th ed., p. 365/6th ed., p. 343).

10. **ANSWER: B.** The Indian Ocean trade routes formed a peaceful network that linked goods and peoples from Asia, Europe, and Africa for hundreds of years. It was never controlled by one political entity, although the Delhi Sultanate did benefit economically. Islam was the major religion that fostered communication and trade (*The Earth and Its Peoples*, 5th ed., pp. 385–387/6th ed., pp. 384–386).

11. **ANSWER: B.** Cities all over the world, whether large or small, functioned as administrative, trade, and cultural centers (*The Earth and Its Peoples*, 5th ed., pp. 240, 295 /6th ed., pp. 259–260, 308).

12. **ANSWER: B.** Ibn Battuta was a Muslim cleric who traveled throughout the Indian Ocean Basin. Zheng He, the admiral in charge of China's treasure fleet during the early Ming dynasty, also traveled extensively (*The Earth and Its Peoples*, 5th ed., pp. 372, 431/6th ed., pp. 375, 405).

13. **ANSWER: B.** The Ming made a gradual transition from Mongol rule to Chinese traditions. One way this was done was by encouraging the production of staples over commercial crops (*The Earth and Its Peoples*, 5th ed., p. 361/6th ed., p. 339).

14. **ANSWER: A.** Although both the Europeans and the Japanese developed a decentralized, feudal governing system, they did so completely independently (*The Earth and Its Peoples*, 5th ed., p. 365/6th ed., p. 344).

15. **ANSWER: D.** Wet rice cultivation, which was developed in Champa (thus the name Champa rice), allowed for the rapid population growth that China experienced during the Tang dynasty (*The Earth and Its Peoples*, 5th ed., p. 302/6th ed., p. 314).

FREE-RESPONSE QUESTIONS

1. For this essay you should include a comparison of characteristics such as the Confucian examination system and its role in shaping Chinese bureaucracy; Japan's unique blend of centralized imperial rule and the feudal shogunate system; and Korea's aristocracy, which, like Japan's, based its wealth on the ownership of land.

2. You should begin this change over time essay with an explanation of the characteristics of Buddhism and Confucianism in China in 600. Then address the role that each religion played in Chinese society as the dynastic cycle progressed through the Tang and Song Empires—Buddhism's early appeal in the Tang dynasty and its subsequent rejection by the Confucian elites. This was followed by the birth of neo-Confucianism as the Song rulers synthesized Confucian and Buddhist beliefs. When the Mongols conquered Chinese territory and established the Yuan Empire, they did not reject Confucianism outright; however, they significantly reduced the status of Confucian officials in Chinese society while welcoming other religions such as Islam. Finally, the Ming rulers reasserted Chinese authority by drawing upon traditional Confucian values.

9

EUROPE: CIRCA 600 TO CIRCA 1450

KEY CONCEPTS

- After the fall of the Roman Empire, the western part of the empire became a decentralized feudal system while the eastern part of the empire continued under imperial rule as the Byzantine Empire.
- Christianity had both a political and a religious impact as the power of the church grew in both western and eastern Europe, and the concept of Christendom took on a territorial context. In particular, the Catholic Church competed for political authority and influence.
- The Crusades sowed the seeds for economic and intellectual changes in late-medieval Europe that would culminate in the Renaissance.
- The Black Death, a horrific pandemic for Europe, was also a major factor in ending feudalism and awakening urban life in western Europe.

KEY TERMS

- Black Death
- Byzantine Empire
- The Crusades
- feudalism
- gothic cathedral
- Great Western Schism
- Hanseatic League
- Holy Roman Empire
- investiture controversy
- Kievan Russia
- Latin West

- manor
- medieval
- monasticism
- pilgrimage
- schism
- scholasticism
- serf
- vassal

Western Europe and the Byzantine Empire are discussed in depth in *The Earth and Its Peoples* fifth edition, Chapters 9 and 14 and sixth edition, Chapters 10 and 13.

EARLY MEDIEVAL WESTERN EUROPE: 600–1000

The period from the fall of the Romans until the beginning of the Renaissance is known as the medieval period, or the Middle Ages, chiefly because it is bracketed by periods of cultural, economic, and political ascendancy—the once-great Roman Empire and the Renaissance. The fall of the Roman Empire, in the fifth century, brought drastic changes to western Europe, which entered a period of economic decline and subsistence living. Local lords and chieftains replaced Roman imperial rule, and the laws of the Roman Empire were supplanted by the Germanic traditions and practices of the tribes in the area. With the absence of centralized imperial authority, safety became the primary concern, and peasants turned to local lords rather than faraway kings to provide safety. This need for protection was the political and cultural context out of which the feudal system emerged in the seventh century.

One exception to the weak kings of the early medieval period was Charlemagne, whose grandfather, Charles Martel, had prevented the Muslims from taking over France (Gaul at the time) at the Battle of Tours in 732. By that time Muslims controlled all of the Iberian Peninsula, having taken over the Visigoth kingdom and pushed the Christians back. By then, Charlemagne's family, the Carolingians, had created an empire that included all of Gaul and parts of Germany and Italy. Charlemagne brought about a brief period of intellectual revival, but with the death of his son Louis the Pious, the Treaty of Verdun split the empire into three parts, one part for each of Louis's sons, and this brief period of empire in medieval Europe came to an end.

While the Roman Empire had focused on urban life, exemplified by the city of Rome itself, western European cities declined and in some cases became smaller villages. Roman roads also fell into disrepair, as did the great buildings of Rome. The Roman coin became a thing of the past, and local trade was by barter. Contact with the larger world through long-distance trade around the Mediterranean severely declined. With less communication with the larger world and no strong central government, most Europeans relied on their own local resources for both political control and economic survival.

Organization of medieval life thus settled around the institution of the **manor**, which became the primary source of local agricultural production in both northern and southern Europe. The manor was far more than a single fortified dwelling; life behind its walls sustained a small community of people and included a mill, church, workshops, and a village where serfs lived. **Serfs**, both men and women, worked the lands of the manor in exchange for protection and were under the complete control of the lord of the manor, the noble whose armed men provided for their safety. Serfs were tied to the land and could not leave. Most peasants across France, England, and western Germany in the tenth and eleventh centuries were serfs.

The rigid system of serfdom did not allow for much personal or political advancement. However, for the noble class, opportunities for political and economic advancement centered on warfare to protect lands from distant enemies like the Vikings as well as other competing lords. This centuries-long tradition of linking land rights to military service was termed **feudalism**. The feudal society was based on the vassal relationship, in which kings and lords gave land to vassals in exchange for sworn military allegiance. This **vassal** relationship looked different from region to region, but by the eleventh century the key person in the medieval military was the knight. Land given to a knight by his lord or king allowed him to afford armor and horses, and the land, known as a fief, could be passed down through generations. This allowed knights themselves to become wealthy lords, who could then enter into vassal relationships with other knights. Knights could also be in a vassal relationship with more than one lord at a time.

Noblewomen were also an important part of this system of land ownership and inheritance and were carefully and strategically married. Marriage became a tool to make military alliances or gain more lands, and noble children had very little choice in whom to marry. Likewise, kings used marriage alliances to increase their territorial and political control. Women could own land, however, and while husbands were away on military service, women could manage the estate.

The Church in the West

The other central institution of medieval Europe was the Catholic Church, the strongest unifying force in medieval Europe. The church created the moral framework for society, a task it took very seriously. The church also owned and controlled extensive lands throughout medieval Europe on which it placed its monasteries and convents. The Catholic Church wrestled with secular lords and kings to be the dominant authority over all matters, ecclesiastical or not. This tension was not present in the Byzantine Empire; because he appointed the patriarch of Constantinople, the emperor had both political and religious supremacy.

The head of the western Church was the pope, whose authority continued to grow stronger and stronger in the early medieval period. The pope was based in Rome and controlled territory in Rome and central Italy. He exercised authority over all clergy and, through his councils of bishops, drew up the rules and doctrines that priests communicated to lay people—Catholics who were not part of the clergy. He also demanded that secular leadership honor and respect his authority.

Needing political allies, the pope crowned the first Holy Roman Emperor in 962 to serve as the defender of Christendom. The **Holy**

Roman Empire started out as a basic alliance of German princes and held more symbolic than practical power. The creation of the Holy Roman emperor did little to prevent the struggle for control between secular authority and the church from climaxing into what is known as the **investiture controversy**. Kings and lords had grown used to investing, or handing over authority to, the bishops in their territories. Technically, canon, or church, law assigned responsibility for appointing bishops to the church. But many bishops were also in a vassal relationship to a lord or king. Lords and kings argued that they should be the ones to appoint the bishops in their lands in order to make sure bishops fulfilled their feudal duties. Exacerbated by the proclamations of Pope Gregory VII in 1073, which declared the Catholic Church infallible, capable of removing emperors, and solely responsible for appointing bishops, the controversy came to symbolize the general struggle over who had more political control. The Concordat of Worms finally eased tensions in 1122: the Holy Roman emperor and the pope agreed that the emperor could invest papally appointed bishops with their secular responsibilities and rights.

The tensions between the church and secular monarchs in England, Germany, and France boiled down to competing legal systems. Feudal law, based on Germanic traditions, gave all power to the king; canon law, based on Roman traditions, held that one legal system should govern all of Western Christendom. The Catholic Church would continue to come into conflict with royal control, but as the feudal system and the status of knights declined because of changes in weaponry like the crossbow and firearms, kings began to tighten their control over their territory and the church. In 1302 Pope Boniface asserted papal supremacy, which the French king, Philip, challenged by orchestrating the election of a French pope. The papal seat was moved to Avignon, giving rise to a period of competing papal claimants, which in turn precipitated the **Great Western Schism** (1378–1415). The papacy was eventually returned to Rome, but these events showed how far monarchs could go in challenging papal authority.

One other unique aspect of medieval European Christian life was **monasticism**. Monks and nuns separated themselves from daily life and lived in gender-specific communities focused on a celibate life of devotion, religious work, and simple living. Nuns provided a refuge for women who were widowed or sought a spiritual life instead of their traditional obligations to marry. Monks served as missionaries, produced food on their lands, and made their monasteries resting places for weary pilgrims and other travelers. Monks were also the essential link between the past and the future; they were the keepers of literacy and learning. In addition to writing their own books on religious matters, monks conserved the works of the **Latin world** by painstakingly copying them.

LATE MEDIEVAL WESTERN EUROPE: 1000–1450

Important changes occurred in late **medieval** Europe between 1000 and 1200. Increases in population and agricultural production allowed for a surplus, which created more opportunities for trade in towns. A surplus of food freed people to focus on other industries in artistry and construction. These changes resulted from technological advances in agriculture. A new plow, the use of the horse collar, and the use of horses instead of oxen all contributed to an increase in the food supply, which in turn helped population growth.

The most dramatic shift in population—a reversal—came to medieval Europe in the fourteenth century because of the bubonic plague. Known as the **Black Death**, it ravaged Europe from 1347 to 1351, killing one in three Europeans. The plague first hit Mongol armies stationed in Kaffa, a port on the Black Sea; Italian traders brought the disease from Kaffa to Italy, and from there it traveled across the continent and to England. Not until 1500 did Europe's population rebound to its level before the plague.

The Black Death left an impact far more significant than just demographic change. In many ways, the Black Death killed serfdom as well. With so many dead, laborers could charge more for their services, and they rebelled against nobles who initially refused to comply. A demand for the end of serfdom sparked uprisings across Europe. Production rose as free laborers bought land for themselves or became urban workers and could demand higher wages. For those still working the land, technological improvements such as the water wheel and windmill—technologies that had long been in use in the Muslim world—increasingly came into use in western Europe. These devices improved efficiency by powering a number of necessary tasks, from the grinding of grain to papermaking. These technologies were also used for iron production, which brought about the expansion of iron mining.

AP Tip

In addition to the Muslims, the Scandinavian Vikings were a formidable presence in medieval Europe. The Vikings, who were excellent shipbuilders, raided towns along the coasts of England and France and eventually settled in Normandy. From there they conquered parts of England and took Sicily permanently from the Muslims. The Vikings were among the earliest European explorers, also settling Iceland and Greenland. Around 1000, almost five hundred years before Columbus, they made it to the North American continent without the use of maritime technologies such as the compass and established Vinland, on Newfoundland.

Another important change was a revival of trade, propelled by the politically independent cities in Italy and Flanders that were exclusively focused on seaborne trade. These cities sprang up when individuals banded together to demand freedom from their lord. A lord who allowed this independence was sure to benefit from the economic prosperity the city brought to the region. Laws were passed so that serfs who made their way to these cities were guaranteed their freedom and were able to engage in other forms of industry. These laws would be very important after the Black Death. Walled cities like

Pisa, Florence, and Siena had to keep expanding as their population increased. Other Italian cities that rose to tremendous economic importance were Genoa, with its access to the western Mediterranean, and Venice, which would become a trading powerhouse on the Adriatic Sea. Venice engaged in trade with the Muslim ports of North Africa and the Mediterranean. In this way, western Europe was slowly exposed to the wealth of goods traveling along the Silk Road and circulating in the Indian Ocean trading system. Mongol control of the entire Eurasian landmass further opened trade between Italian ports and the great ports of the East.

Two other vibrant centers of sea trade in Europe were the **Hanseatic League**, a network of trading cities centered in the Baltic, and the Flanders network, which included cities around the North Sea like Ghent and Bruges that focused on the fishing industry and the growing trade in wool and other textiles. With the increase in trade came increased demand for coined money. Most coinage in the ninth and tenth centuries came from the Muslim world and Byzantium, but with trade reviving in the Mediterranean, gold and silver coinage was no longer a luxury.

As the autonomous trading cities began to flourish, they offered more opportunities for social mobility and individual opportunity. Most of Europe's Jews lived in cities, where they experienced periods of great tolerance, as in Muslim Spain, but also periods of horrific persecution, most often during times of uncertainty and disaster like the Black Death. Cities also became centers of learning as universities specializing in fields such as education, law, and theology sprang up across Europe. Universities allowed for new questions about the relationship between reason and faith, a pursuit that came to be known as **scholasticism**. Scholars like Thomas Aquinas and other pre-Renaissance thinkers tried to reconcile the Bible with rediscovered Greek works from philosophers like Aristotle. Architecture also flourished; the best example of this is the **Gothic cathedral**, which first appeared in France in the twelfth century. By trial and error, European architects mastered the mathematical and engineering skills required to construct these huge, soaring buildings.

All of the changes in the late medieval period set the stage for the Renaissance. A rebirth of classical learning and artistry stimulated by urban revival, a growing merchant class, renewed economic contact with the Muslim world, and the rise of new scholarship and artistry in the cities of Europe, the Renaissance began in Italy and spread to northern Europe over the coming centuries.

THE CRUSADES

Economic revival in western Europe occurred alongside of, and contributed to, **the Crusades**, which had a profound effect on Europe as a whole and on western Europe in particular. The series of military expeditions, spanning more than a hundred years, began with Pope Urban II's call in 1095 for Frankish (a broad term synonymous with *western European*) princes to take back the Holy Land from Muslim control.

Many elements of European culture contributed to the Crusades. In an effort to calm the constant warring characteristic of the feudal system, the church had introduced truces—limits to times of fighting. These truces redirected warring from Christian versus Christian to Christian versus the enemies of Christendom. Because land was inherited only by eldest sons, the Crusades also provided an opportunity for younger sons to gain new lands and titles for themselves. Italian merchants, having reestablished a foothold in Mediterranean trade, encouraged crusades as a way to gain access to ports under the control of Muslims.

By the eleventh century, Muslim leaders had long been in control of the Holy Land; territory sacred to Christians included cities like Jerusalem, Antioch, and Alexandria. Christians had been able to make **pilgrimages** to these cities, but as Islamic control continued to expand into Byzantine—and therefore Christian—territory, the calls for a crusade quickened. Despite the differences between the Latin church and the Orthodox church, the Byzantine emperor requested help—both secular and religious—in securing the land in the name of Christendom. Pope Urban II raised the call to fight in 1095, and the First Crusade resulted in the capture of Jerusalem in 1099 and the establishment of four Crusader kingdoms. The following two Crusades focused on holding these territories, but in 1187 Muslim armies took back Jerusalem. The Fourth Crusade had completely new goals; the capture of Constantinople was driven by economic incentives; it was encouraged by Venetians, who wanted to expand their trading to ports formally under Byzantine and Muslim control.

The Crusades failed in their attempts to take the Holy Land, but they had a tremendous, long-lasting impact on European life. Exposure to the Muslim world sparked the flow of an enormous amount of information, ideas, goods, and resources to Europe. In addition, crusaders brought back discoveries and manufacturing techniques that allowed Europeans to make many of the goods they originally could only import. Demand for these goods from the Middle East stimulated the markets of late medieval Europe and also expanded trade between the Muslim world, western Europe, and the Byzantine Empire. The incredible intellectual contributions of Muslims made their way to Europe in two forms: first, the knowledge of the ancient Greeks, preserved by Muslims; second, scientific and technological understanding, which were more advanced in the Muslim world. Together, they served as the intellectual underpinnings for western Europe's transition from the Middle Ages to the Renaissance.

THE BYZANTINE EMPIRE

After the fall of the Roman Empire, the eastern portion continued as the **Byzantine Empire**, with Constantinople as its great capital, and the empire would endure until its defeat by the Ottoman Turks in 1453. Geographically centered in Greek and Anatolian areas, the Byzantine Empire, or Byzantium, used Greek as its language, and the empire maintained and built upon many of the traditions of the Roman Empire in terms of both law and economics. Economically, the Byzantine emperors continued to regulate prices, the trading of luxury goods, and grain shipments, which may have slowed technological and economic advancements. Constantinople received the most economic attention, to the detriment of other Byzantine cities and the countryside, where farm tools and practices lagged in efficiency when compared with those used in western Europe. Part of Constantinople's appeal was its ideal location between the Black Sea and the Mediterranean, which made it an ideal center for trade and travel, attracting merchants, aristocrats, and journeying pilgrims. For hundreds of years, this port city—one of the five great patriarchal seats of Europe—would be envied by many. Constantinople's glory hid the reality that the Byzantine Empire was on a slow and steady decline.

The Byzantine Empire enjoyed many cultural and artistic achievements, all reflecting the Greek Orthodox interpretations of Christianity as opposed to the Latin interpretations used in western Europe. The empire reached its height under the emperor Justinian, who ruled from 527 until 565 and built the Hagia Sophia, the greatest example of Byzantine architecture. Byzantine sacred art had a great influence on pre-Renaissance painting in western Europe.

The Byzantine Empire also had a tremendous impact on the religious and cultural traditions of Slavic Christians. Followers of two Byzantine missionaries sent in the ninth century to preach to the Slavs in their local language developed the Cyrillic writing system, which became the written language of Slavic and Russian Orthodox Christians.

Socially, the Byzantine Empire gradually moved from an urban way of life to a more rural one, although cities, particularly Constantinople, remained important. Local urban elites holding power up through the seventh century gave way to an increase in the power of rural landowners and imperial court aristocrats. This change could in part be the result of the demographic impact of the bubonic plague, which hit the Byzantine Empire in the sixth century—much earlier than in western Europe—as well as the loss of territory to Muslims. Byzantine women also saw a change in their position, moving from a freer status in the public arena during the Roman period to a more secluded existence in the home, marked by wearing the veil in public. Social interactions with men were limited to family members. Despite this, there are strong examples of women ruling with their husbands in the eleventh century. The increasing seclusion of women in the Byzantine Empire can be compared with the seclusion of women in the neighboring Muslim empires.

The rising strength of the Muslim empire always proved to be a formidable challenge for the Byzantine Empire, despite the growing importance of the military, which was the basis of the aristocratic class by the eleventh century. Arab Muslims quickly took territory away from the Byzantine Empire in the seventh century. At the same time, the patriarchal cities Alexandria, Antioch, and Jerusalem came under Muslim control. Other groups, such as the Slavic and Turkic peoples, would also serve as threats to the borders of the Byzantine Empire. The Seljuk Turks in particular would establish a Turkish Muslim state in the early eleventh century; it became the main enemy of the crusaders. The Fourth Crusade in 1204 was a mortal blow for the empire because western European crusaders sacked and destroyed much of Constantinople. After 1200, the Byzantine Empire declined, largely because of a weak military. For the next two hundred years the empire continued to lose territory. It would limp along until 1453, when Sultan Mehmed II captured Constantinople and ended the Byzantine Empire's reign of over eleven hundred years.

AP Tip

Not only did the Roman Empire split politically into East and West; the Christian Church would eventually split as well. A series of doctrinal disputes over issues such as the humanity and divinity of Jesus, the place of icons, and the role of Mary weakened the relationship between the Eastern Orthodox Church and the Roman Catholic Church. At one point, the patriarch in Constantinople also challenged the territorial control that the western church enjoyed. These disagreements eventually resulted in **schism** in 1054, a formal split in Christendom that has endured through the centuries. This split produced two different cultural expressions of Christianity in the period 600–1450.

KIEVAN RUSSIA

To the north of the Byzantine Empire, a unique society developed in Russia that also followed the traditions of the Orthodox Church. The word *Rus,* from which *Russia* derives, came to refer to Slavic-speaking peoples who were ruled by the Varangians, Swedish Vikings who sailed down into Russia from the Baltic. Varangian princes lived in cities and focused on trade while the Slavs worked the lands. Kiev was one of the key cities for trade with the Byzantine Empire. In 980, Vladimir I made himself grand prince of Russia. He chose Orthodox Christianity as the religion of the region, married an Orthodox princess of the Byzantine imperial family, and let in Orthodox missionaries. Until the arrival of the Mongols in the thirteenth century, **Kievan Russia** stood as an independent state that spread Orthodox Christianity to eastern Slavs and prevented the spread of Latin Christianity from the west.

Economic prominence in Kiev came from trade, which provided the money to pay soldiers, and artisans were valued above peasants. Churches were built in the Byzantine style, and slowly Christianity obliterated the polytheistic traditions of the Slavs. By the twelfth century, the church had taken over some economic roles such as tax collection and had also assumed political responsibilities. Nonetheless, the large cities of Kiev and Novgorod never matched the population levels or cosmopolitan life found in cities like Constantinople and Baghdad.

Multiple-Choice Questions

1. Which of the following is an accurate depiction of the experiences of women in Christendom in the period 600–1450?
    (A) Byzantine women continued to have the same freedoms that they had experienced in the Roman Empire.
    (B) Arranged marriages disappeared as courtly love became valued in western European culture.
    (C) The Catholic Church refused to allow women to enter the monastic life after reaching childbearing age.
    (D) Noblewomen in particular were closely monitored in terms of behavior and personal relationships, and the majority of women were expected to marry.

2. The investiture controversy primarily concerned conflicts
    (A) between the eastern and western churches regarding territorial rights.
    (B) between the pope and the patriarch of Constantinople over the sacking of Constantinople in the Fourth Crusade.
    (C) between the pope and the kings of western Europe over who had the authority to appoint bishops.
    (D) between the Byzantine emperor and the kings of western Europe over territorial boundaries.

3. The Orthodox Church and the Latin Church
    (A) were united under the pope, who appointed the patriarch of Constantinople to rule as his representative.
    (B) met in a series of council meetings to decide what parts of Europe would be Orthodox and what parts would be Catholic in order to avoid competition.
    (C) worked closely with the Muslim empire to fight against the Mongol invasions of the thirteenth century.
    (D) formally split over doctrinal disputes in the eleventh century but still united to fight together in the Crusades.

4. The vassal relationship
    (A) was a complex system of sworn military alliances in exchange for fiefs.
    (B) required a knight to swear allegiance to a lord or king in return for money and titles.
    (C) never became a central part of the feudal system and did not last beyond the eleventh century.
    (D) required lords to send their eldest sons to the courts of the kings for military service.

5. Manor life
   (A) was similar to the labor systems of the Roman Empire in that free laborers received land in exchange for their service.
   (B) created a localized, basic, and self-sufficient agricultural economy that kept serfs protected.
   (C) was based on a system of free labor in exchange for protection and allowed peasants to move freely between the town and the manor.
   (D) was a way of life that first began in the Byzantine Empire and then spread to western Europe.

6. The Byzantine Empire
   (A) was cut off from trading opportunities with the Silk Road and the Indian Ocean trade network.
   (B) became a feudal and agricultural society like its European neighbors to the west.
   (C) built on the Roman imperial model but followed Greek cultural and religious traditions.
   (D) joined forces with the Muslim empires to destroy Kievan Russia.

7. All of the following were causes of the Crusades EXCEPT
   (A) the conquest of Byzantine lands by Muslim empires.
   (B) the belief that Muslim rulers were defiling the Holy Land.
   (C) the economic motives of burgeoning trading cities like Venice to gain more ports.
   (D) Muslim anger over the Norman conquest of Sicily and the defeat of the Muslims at the Battle of Tours.

8. Western Europe and the Byzantine Empire differed politically because
   (A) western Europe maintained more of the political traditions of the Roman Empire.
   (B) the Byzantine Empire maintained more of the political traditions of the Germanic peoples.
   (C) the Byzantine Empire gave political and religious authority to a patriarch while western Europe gave it to the pope.
   (D) the Byzantine Empire maintained a centralized government while western Europe broke apart into localized political entities.

9. Economics in western Europe changed in the later medieval period by
   (A) allowing for more social mobility because of the end of serfdom and the rise of urban job opportunities.
   (B) allowing women to own property for the first time and participate in long-distance trade.
   (C) gaining control of the Indian Ocean trade network by sending out Viking explorers.
   (D) refusing to accept trading goods from the Muslim world after the Crusades.

10. Kievan Russia
    (A) adopted the manor system from the Byzantine Empire and the feudal system from western Europe.
    (B) based its economic wealth on trade and traded extensively with the Byzantine Empire.
    (C) conquered Muslim territories around the Baltic Sea to extend its regional control.
    (D) accepted Roman Catholicism as the faith of the region and welcomed Catholic missionaries.

11. One of Byzantine emperor Justinian's biggest accomplishments was
    (A) codification of a thousand years of Roman legal tradition in the *Corpus Juris Civilis*.
    (B) the creation of the Eastern Orthodox church.
    (C) the creation of a large bureaucratic system with which to run the Byzantine Empire.
    (D) determining the location of Constantinople.

12. Cyril and Methodius are significant in world history because they
    (A) helped bring silk technology to the Byzantine Empire.
    (B) traveled the complete stretch of the Silk Road.
    (C) traveled to Rome and influenced musical styles such as Gregorian chant.
    (D) traveled to Moravia, where they helped introduce a new writing system to the Slavic peoples.

13. Vikings were similar to Arabs in that both
    (A) were Muslim.
    (B) came from very arid territories.
    (C) looked to western Europe as an area for expansion.
    (D) raided and traded, Vikings using ships and Arabs using horses and camels.

14. Vladimir I, ruler of Kievan Russia, imposed the following religion on his subjects.
    (A) Islam
    (B) Judaism
    (C) Roman Christianity
    (D) Orthodox Christianity

15. The impact of the Crusades included all of the following EXCEPT
    (A) the sanctioning of annulments and remarriage.
    (B) the discovery of Greek philosophical works.
    (C) the making of pasta.
    (D) the development of troubador music and of poetry.

Free-Response Questions

1. Compare the social and economic characteristics of western and eastern Europe from circa 600 to circa 1450.

2. Evaluate the political continuities and changes over time in western and eastern Europe from circa 600 to circa 1450.

Answers

MULTIPLE-CHOICE QUESTIONS

1. ANSWER: D. Marriage alliances continued to be an important political tool for lords and kings in terms of solidifying their power and territorial control. Thus noblewomen were carefully controlled and given in marriage to meet those ends. Women were also closely monitored in the Byzantine Empire and were supposed to interact only with males who were family members (*The Earth and Its Peoples*, 5th ed., p. 263/6th ed., p. 279).

2. ANSWER: C. The investiture controversy stemmed from disputes between the pope and kings and lords in western Europe over who had more authority; the appointment of bishops was the topic that brought this larger issue to a head (*The Earth and Its Peoples*, 5th ed., p. 266/6th ed., p. 281).

3. ANSWER: D. The Orthodox Church and the Latin Church permanently split in a schism in 1054 over doctrinal issues but did band together to try and take the Holy Land from the Muslims in the First Crusade (*The Earth and Its Peoples*, 5th ed., p. 254/6th ed., p. 273).

4. ANSWER: A. The vassal relationship was complex partly because knights, lords, and kings could be in vassal relationships with more than one person. A central institution of feudal life, it was centered on military service and allegiance in exchange for land, the main measure of wealth in feudal Europe (*The Earth and Its Peoples*, 5th ed., pp. 261–263/6th ed., p. 278).

5. ANSWER: B. The manor system met the basic needs for protection and food for the majority of people living in western Europe but kept them tied to the land. The Black Death shook Europe out of this way of life (*The Earth and Its Peoples*, 5th ed., p. 260/6th ed., p. 277).

6. ANSWER: C. The Byzantine Empire reached its height in the sixth and seventh centuries and was in decline by the eleventh century. Its culture and religious practices were based more on those of the Greeks than on the Latin tradition of the West (*The Earth and Its Peoples*, 5th ed., pp. 253–254/6th ed., pp. 271–272).

7. ANSWER: **D.** The causes of the Crusades were multifaceted, reflecting a combination of economic, political, and religious motives. It was Christians, not Muslims, who initiated the Crusades (*The Earth and Its Peoples,* 5th ed., pp. 274–275/6th ed., pp. 289–290).

8. ANSWER: **D.** The Byzantine Empire was unified under one emperor, who had both political authority and a religious role because he appointed the patriarch of Constantinople. This is in contrast with western Europe, which was politically fragmented under the feudal system (*The Earth and Its Peoples,* 5th ed., pp. 253–254/6th ed., pp. 271–272).

9. ANSWER: **A.** The Black Death precipitated a huge economic shift in western Europe because former serfs could demand more for their labor, move to the towns, and apprentice in other areas. Opportunities for social mobility increased as regional trade and independent trading cities flourished (*The Earth and Its Peoples,* 5th ed., pp. 401–402/6th ed., p. 351).

10. ANSWER: **B.** Kievan Russia was allied much more closely with the Byzantine Empire and adopted the Orthodox faith as well as engaged in trade with the empire (*The Earth and Its Peoples,* 5th ed., pp. 268–269/6th ed., p. 285).

11. ANSWER: **A.** Although Justinian can tout many accomplishments, including the building of the Hagia Sophia, his biggest cultural contribution is the codification of Roman law in the *Corpus Juris Civilis* (*The Earth and Its Peoples,* 5th ed., p. 156/6th ed., p. 144).

12. ANSWER: **D.** As Orthodox missionaries, Cyril and Methodius traveled far and wide. Their most lasting contribution, however, was the development of the Cyrillic alphabet, which is still used in most eastern Slavic countries, including Russia (*The Earth and Its Peoples,* 5th ed., pp. 256–257/6th ed., p. 274).

13. ANSWER: **D.** Vikings need to be seen as nomads who used boats as other nomads used horses. The boats allowed easy access to many areas and gave Vikings the advantage of the element of surprise (*The Earth and Its Peoples,* 5th ed., p. 259/6th ed., p. 276).

14. ANSWER: **D.** Legend indicates that Vladimir I researched all of the major religions and decided that Greek Orthodox would fit best in Kiev. This set up a long-term trade and cultural relationship with the Byzantine Empire that would eventually lead Russia to see itself as the third Rome (*The Earth and Its Peoples,* 5th ed., p. 269/6th ed., p. 285).

15. ANSWER: **A.** Although Eleanor of Aquitaine divorced the king of France to marry the King of England after she went on crusade, this was not a tradition followed by many. The other innovations were brought to western Europe as a result of the Crusades (*The Earth and Its Peoples,* 5th ed., p. 277/6th ed., p. 291).

FREE-RESPONSE QUESTIONS

1. For this essay you should include a comparison of the role of the church in the East and the West as it relates to social impact in both regions of Europe. You should also contrast the localized economies of western Europe, which did not take part in long-distance trade until late in the period, with the economy of the Byzantine Empire, which continued to be part of the larger trade network of Eurasia via the Silk Road. Be sure to discuss its capital city, Constantinople, which was a key trading center because of its location. You could also discuss the impact of the Crusades and the end of serfdom that came with the Black Death. Finally, a comparison of women's roles could contrast Byzantine seclusion with women's roles in western Europe.

2. This essay should include a discussion of aspects of both change and continuity as they relate to the change from decentralized feudal systems to stronger monarchies. The political roles of the Catholic Church can also be analyzed to show how the church and secular authority vied for more political authority. What changes allowed for the rise of stronger monarchies in western Europe? Continuity in political authority would be seen in eastern Europe, where the Byzantine Empire continued under a succession of emperors who served as both emperors and appointers of patriarchs to the Eastern Orthodox Church. The Byzantine Empire's political power waned with its loss of territorial control, but the empire did continue as one fairly stable political organization until the end of this period.

10

THE AMERICAS: CIRCA 600 TO CIRCA 1450

KEY CONCEPTS

- Mesoamerica was never a single politically unified region, but its civilizations shared important cultural and religious characteristics and traditions that are continuities throughout the period 600–1450.
- The Aztec and the Maya of Mesoamerica and the Inca of the Andean region developed complex, sophisticated civilizations with defined social, economic, cultural, and political characteristics that represent important aspects of Amerindian life in the Americas.
- The environment of each society had an important influence on its technological and agricultural development.
- Religion was a central aspect of Amerindian life and shaped many of the cultural rituals and political practices of the Americas.
- The civilizations and empires of the Maya, Aztec, and Inca built on the earlier civilizations in their respective geographic regions.

KEY TERMS

- Anasazi
- ayllu
- Aztecs
- chinampas
- Inca
- khipus
- Maya
- mit'a
- Moche
- Tenochtitlan
- Teotihuacan

- Tiwanaku
- Toltecs
- tribute system
- vertical integration
- Wari

The history of the Americas in the period from circa 600 to circa 1450 is discussed in depth in *The Earth and Its Peoples,* fifth edition, Chapter 11 and sixth edition, Chapters 7 and 17.

CLASSIC-ERA CULTURE AND SOCIETY IN MESOAMERICA: 600–900

Although never under one central rule, the peoples of Mesoamerica developed similar religious, social, and cultural practices. Mesoamericans also made strides in agriculture, astronomy, math, and political organization, building on the work of earlier civilizations like the Olmec. Population growth and the rise of long-distance trade led to the development of large urban centers with both religious and political significance. These cities had many architectural features, including pyramid structures, designed for elaborate religious ceremony. Thousand-year-old agricultural practices like terraced farming and irrigation continued to serve as the economic foundation for Mesoamerican society in the classic period; the distinctive feature of the classic period in Mesoamerican society was not agricultural advances but rather social changes. These changes created a new political elite that controlled larger numbers of laborers and soldiers, grew in power, and extended its political reach over larger areas of Mesoamerica. Two civilizations that exemplify the classic period are the people of Teotihuacan in Mexico and the Maya in the Yucatan peninsula.

TEOTIHUACAN

Located just north of modern-day Mexico City, the city of **Teotihuacan** reached its zenith in 600. The largest city in the Americas at the time, it had well over 100,000 inhabitants, perhaps as many as 200,000, and was one of the largest cities in the world as well. Teotihuacan was also a religious center that drew people from neighboring areas; priests were highly regarded and played a central role in society. The elite status of priests was common in other Mesoamerican societies as well. The people of Teotihuacan were polytheistic, and much of their religious architecture focused on pyramid-like structures dedicated to worshiping the sun, moon, and the god Quetzalcoatl, who was believed to be the source of agriculture and the arts. The people of Teotihuacan practiced human sacrifice, which they considered a sacred duty necessary for the maintenance of human society.

As the city grew, the governing elite developed the surrounding lands for agricultural production. In addition to irrigation and terraced farming on hillsides, the use of chinampas increased. **Chinampas**, manmade islands constructed out of materials found in the lake environment, allowed for agricultural production year-round, which provided a constant food supply for the growing population. A reliable food supply permitted specialization of labor in architecture as well as trade and art pottery and obsidian tools were key goods in long-distance trade.

Other Mesoamerican societies had one central ruler. Historical evidence suggests that in Teotihuacan, an alliance of aristocratic families had political authority. Scholars also debate the role of Teotihuacan's military; archaeological evidence suggests that soldiers were used both to secure long-distance trade and to ensure that agricultural surpluses were used to the city's benefit. Why Teotihuacan was destroyed is not clear, but there is evidence that the final decades were violent and that disagreements among the elites as well as mishandling of resources led to disorder and mass conflict, resulting in the destruction of much of the city by 650.

THE CLASSIC PERIOD OF THE MAYA: 600–900

The **Maya** civilization covered modern-day Guatemala, Honduras, Belize, and southern Mexico. The Maya were never politically unified but shared a single culture. Rulers of the various city-states competed with one another for territorial supremacy. As in Teotihuacan, feeding the large populations in Maya urban centers necessitated planned agricultural strategies like terraced farming and irrigation. Strong Maya cities featured elaborately decorated and colorful religious palaces, pyramids, and temples—all designed to express the political and religious authority of the king. Pyramids like Tikal in Guatemala, which rose above the trees, represented the access point to both the heavens and the underworld, and they were visible from large plazas where people gathered to witness the elaborate ceremonies of sacrifice and ritual that awed them. Amazingly, the Maya and other Amerindian societies were able to construct such incredible buildings without the use of the wheel or metal tools; stone tools and levers were the only technology used by the thousands of men and women who built these structures.

The role of religious ritual cannot be overstated. The elite had both secular and religious responsibilities and acted as intermediaries between the spirit world and the material world. Both bloodletting and sacrifice were considered essential to success in life and in war. Kings and other members of the elite led their soldiers in war, and their captives were sacrificed. Women of the ruling families also had important religious and political roles and participated in ritual bloodletting ceremonies. Two kingdoms are known to have been ruled by women. Although less is known about lower-class women, scholars believe women played important religious roles in their homes, wove cloth, managed their households, and directed family life.

Some of the most important intellectual contributions of the Maya were in the areas of astronomical observation, hieroglyphic writing, and math, which included a concept of zero. These intellectual accomplishments allowed for the development of elaborate calendars that represent the best of Mesoamerican culture. The Maya had three calendars: one tracked a ritual cycle of 260 days; one was a solar calendar of 365 days; the third, a long-count calendar, began on a set date in 3114 B.C.E., the Maya date of creation, and was continual.

There is much speculation about how the classic period of the Maya ended. Although a few Maya urban centers lasted far beyond the classic period, it is clear that between 800 and 900 many centers were destroyed or abandoned. Of the many reasons suggested, the strongest is that the combination of expansion and lack of agricultural productivity caused social tension that degenerated into warfare.

THE POSTCLASSIC PERIOD IN MESOAMERICA: 900–1500

The postclassic period had many continuities with the Mesoamerican classic period in social structure, art, and culture, including religious practices, architecture, and the role of cities. Population growth demanded the management of agricultural resources, and military and political control of various peoples became a priority for the two strongest societies of the postclassic period, the Toltecs and the Aztecs.

THE TOLTECS

A migrating people who eventually settled in central Mexico, the **Toltecs** built on many of the cultural practices of the people of Teotihuacan to create a sophisticated civilization. Their innovative contributions were mainly political and were based on military conquest that allowed them to create a state reaching from north of Mexico City to Central America. The Toltec capital of Tula, though never as populous as Teotihuacan, was an elaborate architectural achievement in central Mexico. Toltec art depicted and glorified the militaristic aspects of its culture, including scenes of human sacrifice. Political organization was based on two kings who ruled together; at some point after 1000, a struggle between political elites resulted in the expulsion of one of the kings. This was the beginning of the end for the Toltecs, culminating in the destruction of the capital around 1156 when invaders from the north overtook it. As new peoples came into the Toltec region, they built on the ancient Mesoamerican traditions combined with the new Toltec military and political strategies. The strongest group that emerged from the migrating northern peoples in the centuries following the Toltecs were the Mexica, or Aztec people.

THE AZTECS

Organized by clan, the Mexica people, known as the **Aztecs**, were originally serfs and mercenaries for the more powerful groups in the area. As they grew in power, the Aztecs moved to islands off the shore of Lake Texcoco and in 1325 began building the two cities that would become the foundation of modern Mexico City, the twin capitals of **Tenochtitlan** and Tlatelolco.

Aztec society was based on military conquest and looked to the Toltec as models. Continual military success allowed the Aztecs to take good agricultural lands and establish a monarchy in the region. The monarch did not have absolute authority. Selected by a council of aristocrats from among all the males of the ruling family, a new king had to complete a new round of military conquests to validate his rule and the warring class. As these practices continued, social hierarchy tightened. The highest status was assigned to the warrior elite, who enjoyed huge estates that relied on the labor of peasants, who had little say in decision making. Clan-based organization continued to be important in the twin capitals, serving as the method for dividing agricultural labor and civic duties and also for creating military units.

Agricultural laborers provided the food for the Aztecs' large urban population of approximately 150,000. The Aztecs, like the people of Teotihuacan before them, used the chinampa system to grow maize and various fruits and vegetables. They also built an impressive dike to separate freshwater from the salt water in Lake Texcoco so that the land could be used for cultivation. Another vital resource for the Aztecs was the **tribute system**, which allowed the Aztecs to draw on the labor and resources of conquered peoples. This tribute system provided a quarter of the food supplies for the Aztec Empire and also brought a variety of other practical items and luxury goods to the Aztecs. These tribute goods, along with products from long-distance trade, diversified the rich markets of Tenochtitlan.

By 1500, the population of the twin cities and the surrounding lakeshore areas was approximately half a million people. Aztec society was very stratified, and there was great division based on wealth. The rich ate, dressed, and lived well, while commoners had a very basic diet and lived simply. Commoners could have only one spouse, while the elite could have a number. One distinct Aztec social group was the merchant class, who managed long-distance trade and also served as valuable sources of political and military information for the elites. Trade, based on barter instead of money or credit, was carried out without the use of beasts of burden or wheels, so the goods needed to be light enough to carry. Merchants grew wealthy as the empire grew, but they could not achieve the same status as the nobility, who watched them with a jealous eye.

Like many other Mesoamerican cultures, religious rule and ceremony were key components of the king's political success and authority. The Aztecs were polytheistic; their most famous religious cult centered on the worship of Huitzilopochtli, a hummingbird from the south. This god was first associated with war, then with the sun. Worship of the sun was a religious continuity throughout Mesoamerican history. The Aztecs believed that Huitzilopochtli needed human hearts to keep the sun shining, thereby sustaining life. As a result, the temple of Tenochtitlan, devoted to Huitzilopochtli and Tlaloc, the rain god, was the site of large-scale rituals involving human sacrifice. This is another continuity from previous Mesoamerican societies, but the Aztecs expanded the ritual significantly, sacrificing war captives, criminals, slaves, and people who were given as tribute. Thousands were sacrificed each year; the very violent and public aspect of the ritual sent a clear message to subject peoples that they must submit to the authority of the empire. The Aztec Empire continued until the arrival of the conquistador Cortés, who captured Tenochtitlan in 1521 before going on to conquer the rest of Mexico.

AP Tip

The Aztecs created an empire based on tribute and maintained a vibrant urban life. Both of these characteristics can be compared with contemporaneous empires in China. Making this comparison on the AP exam requires an understanding of the movement of the Aztecs from a nomadic group to a settled people able to create an empire. What other peoples could you compare the Aztecs with in terms of this transition from a migrating group to a settled empire?

THE PEOPLES OF NORTH AMERICA

Around 900, the southwestern desert and the Mississippi River Valley were two areas of high cultural achievement in North America. Building on the economic benefits from long-distance trade, including the introduction of key staples like maize, beans, and squash from Mesoamerica, the peoples of these areas developed societies with defined social structures and political roles unique to each region.

SOUTHWESTERN DESERT CULTURES

The Hohokam people, who lived in what is today Arizona, were heavily influenced by Mesoamerican cultures, particularly Mexican, as is reflected in their architecture, pottery, and ceramics. They in turn influenced other societies in the region, who built on the agricultural technology and the artistic techniques of the Hohokam.

The second group that exemplifies southwestern desert culture is the **Anasazi,** a Navajo word used by archaeologists meaning "ancient ones" to refer to the various desert cultures located in what is now the southwestern United States. By 600, the Anasazi also had an economy based on maize, beans, and squash. They specialized in decorative pottery as well as cotton weaving. Underground buildings called kivas were community centers used for both religious ritual and craftwork. After 900, the Anasazi constructed larger multilevel buildings, which were prominent features in the larger towns.

Chaco Canyon is the site of one of the largest Anasazi societies. Of the eight towns in the canyon, the largest was Pueblo Bonito, which contained large kivas and other residential buildings. Archaeological research of its infrastructure suggests that Pueblo Bonito held religious or political dominance over the region. Merchants engaged in long-distance trade in northern Mexico. Because men hunted, cared for the irrigation works, and traded, they often had to be away. Women specialized in various crafts as well as helped with agriculture and other domestic duties. Chaco Canyon was abandoned in the twelfth century because of drought, but the Anasazi continued to dwell in the larger region of the southwest.

MISSISSIPPIAN CULTURES: 700–1500

The first Amerindians along the Mississippi River were primarily hunter-gatherers. As maize, beans, and squash were introduced, most likely by intermediaries who had contacts with Mesoamerica, a more settled and urban lifestyle emerged. They too built mounds for ceremonial and religious use and as dwellings for chiefs. The chief had both religious and political roles and also oversaw long-distance trade, which supplemented food supplies and brought access to luxury goods. Urban communities developed as the food supply became more constant, the bow and arrow was introduced, and trade expanded. With a larger population and larger towns, which served as centers for bartering, class distinctions increased.

Cahokia, the best example of the apogee of Mississippian culture, contained the largest mound—one hundred feet high—in North America. In 1200, with about 20,000 inhabitants, Cahokia was equal in size to many postclassic Maya cities. Cahokia had political dominance over the surrounding agricultural territories and towns, and its long-distance trade, by canoe, brought in tools and goods used for rituals. Cahokia declined after 1250 because of climate changes and population increase, which in turn put pressure on the food supply. Cahokia was eventually abandoned, but other mound cultures continued to thrive in the southeast until the arrival of the Europeans.

Andean Civilizations: 600–1500

At the same time that highly sophisticated societies were developing in Mesoamerica, they were also developing in the Andean region. The ability to create and maintain complex civilizations in the difficult environment of the Andes mountains is amazing, and geography played a huge role in how those communities and then larger states were constructed. Andean peoples had to cope with three ecological zones: the high altitudes and harsh weather of the mountainous zone; the arid zone of the coastal region by the Pacific Ocean; and the hot, humid Amazonian tropical zone. Sustaining life in these zones required various technologies, among them terraced hillside farming, irrigation systems, road networks for long-distance exchange, accurate calendars, and plant domestication. In addition, animals like the llama and the alpaca were used as beasts of burden as well as sources of meat and wool. **Khipus**, knotted colored cords that could be used for recordkeeping, were a unique technology that served as an important administrative tool as well.

Productive and efficient use of human labor was also essential in managing the environment. The basic unit that allowed for such labor was the **ayllu**, a clan that worked a piece of land. Families within the ayllu were expected to work together on everyday jobs and were also obligated to supply food and labor to the chief of the ayllu. When larger political organization was placed under the authority of a hereditary king, the **mit'a** system was created. Every ayllu rotated in and out of the mit'a system, which required the ayllu to contribute a specific number of workers every year to do maintenance work for the state—building projects, road maintenance, textile production, and irrigation work. They also cared for the herds and fields that belonged to the royal family, the religious elite, and the aristocracy. The mit'a system was used by Andean societies for more than a thousand years.

Because so many smaller ecological zones existed in the Andean region and each zone produced different goods that were necessary resources, vertical integration was necessary. **Vertical integration** is a term coined by historians to describe the practices of the Andean peoples who purposely exchanged the goods from these differing ecological zones in order to have everything they needed. Colonists were sent out by different ayllus in order to gain access to these goods and the economic benefit they provided.

PRE-INCA SOCIETIES

Although the Inca created an empire that represented the height of Andean civilization, several earlier societies exhibited many of the cultural, social, and political continuities of the Andean peoples.

By 600, the **Moche** were dominant in the northern coastal area of Peru. They relied on the mit'a system to supply laborers for irrigation and depended on the llama and alpaca for trade. The wool of these animals allowed the Moche to create a strong textile industry, and women of all classes had special roles as weavers. The Moche excelled in ceramic work, creating pottery that included vases with detailed portraits, religious imagery, and depictions of daily life. The Moche also developed metal tools for agriculture and military use. A rigid social structure allowed for the clear division of labor, and religion was a central component of society. Priests and military leaders held political control, and their clothing and elaborate gold jewelry demonstrated their wealth and set them apart. The bulk of people, both men and women, focused on agricultural production and other labor requirements. Because we have no written records about the Moche, archaeological evidence alone provides the clues for their decline. Repeated natural disasters seem to be the cause for the weakening of both the economy and the authority of religious and political leaders, who drew their power from the belief that they could control the natural world.

The peoples of **Tiwanaku** and **Wari,** Moche contemporaries, lived in the highlands. Tiwanaku was an urban center located in modern Bolivia next to Lake Titicaca. Once drained, the marshes around the lake provided thousands of acres of land. The lake fish provided protein, as did llamas, which were also used for transport in long-distance trade that brought in a variety of foodstuffs and agricultural goods. Tiwanaku was a grand ceremonial and religious center built out of stone, which was cut and moved many miles to build pyramids and other buildings as well as huge human statues. With limited tools, the labor used to complete the projects was extensive, making the achievement all the more impressive and demonstrating the ability of the people of Tiwanaku to manage a large labor system. Military conquest allowed the Tiwanaku people to establish colonies to ensure food supplies from the different ecological zones of the Andean region. Wari was larger than Tiwanaku, but the relationship between the two centers is unclear even though their peoples had some cultural similarities. Wari contained a walled city that included a huge temple as well as urban and suburban housing. By 1000 both the Wari and Tiwanaku had declined significantly. The stage was set for the Inca, the next great Andean society.

THE INCA

The **Inca** created an amazing empire that stretched up and down the coast of South America and had more than six million people under its control by 1525. Their rise to power began in the 1430s when strong political leaders joined together and began an age of military conquest.

Many of the Andean traditions were fundamental to the life of the Incas. They were pastoralists who depended on the llama and the alpaca for food, clothing, and transport. Caring for these animals was the job of both men and women and was a representation of the obligations of the gods and the ruler to the people. The mit'a system continued as the fundamental building block of the empire. Each ayllu contributed one-seventh of its males for labor to create a food surplus for the elderly and sick. Laborers also built thirteen thousand miles of road, which linked the empire economically and militarily.

In order to rule effectively, local chiefs were kept in place and handled local administrative duties and judicial matters. However, to minimize the risk of rebellion, heirs of defeated territories had to live at the Inca royal court, and images of local deities also had to be brought to Cuzco, the center of government. Inca society was highly stratified; the imperial elite of Cuzco and other urban centers could live a life very removed from the lower class—so much so that a commoner who looked the ruler in the face could be executed. To cement its authority, the royal family also claimed a divine link to the sun, one of the primary gods worshiped by the Inca. Finally, all those who made up the royal bureaucracy had to be kinsmen. As in other American societies, religious ritual reaffirmed the power of the king. Like the Aztec kings, each new Inca king was expected to extend the empire through conquest.

Cuzco was located near the center of the empire and was connected to other cities by the intricate network of Inca roads. Although Cuzco was never as populated as the Aztecs' Tenochtitlan, it was a true imperial city, with massive, detailed stonework as well as elaborate palaces and temples reflecting each ruler's glory. The Temple of the Sun was the most glorious, with gold adorning its inner walls. Sacrifices to the sun included animals, textiles, and, infrequently, humans. As in Mesoamerica, calendars based on astronomical observation were important for religious ritual. Inca textile weaving and metallurgy—continuities handed down from earlier Andean societies—surpassed the Mesoamericans'. Copper and bronze weapons were decorated with gold and silver. Khipus continued to be used for communication and recordkeeping and were especially important because the Inca multiplied their production and economic output with the conquest of peoples in different environments.

The Inca ruled for a century, but in 1525, when the Inca ruler Huayna Capac died, the empire spiraled into a bloody conflict over which son should succeed him. The conflict escalated into a civil war that allowed disgruntled conquered peoples of varying ethnicities and regions to rise up as well. This was the state of the Inca Empire when Europeans arrived in the Andean region in the beginning of the sixteenth century.

Multiple-Choice Questions

1. Cities in Mesoamerican and Andean societies
   (A) did not contain large architectural structures because of the lack of technologies such as the wheel.
   (B) usually stood on the outskirts of the empire because of their role as centers for religious ritual.
   (C) were able to provide the food to feed all of their inhabitants and therefore did not need outside land for agriculture.
   (D) were richly decorated political centers that also played central religious and economic roles.

2. Characteristics of Mesoamerican societies included
   (A) one unified political authority that ruled over the whole region.
   (B) long-distance trade networks that allowed for trade across the Atlantic Ocean.
   (C) the use of khipus for recordkeeping and other administrative uses.
   (D) shared cultural and social characteristics as well as religious rituals.

3. Religion influenced societies in the Americas because
   (A) it caused constant conflict between the priestly class and the political elites over who had more authority in society.
   (B) it undermined the stability of societies because each clan worshiped different gods.
   (C) its monotheistic characteristics allowed for all societies in the Americas to worship the same god.
   (D) it created societies with complex rituals of worship that included sacrifice and were often designed to validate the political authority of rulers.

4. Women's roles in Amerindian societies included all of the following EXCEPT
   (A) making crafts, including textiles and pottery.
   (B) domestic household duties and child rearing.
   (C) participating in religious ritual both privately and publicly, depending on class.
   (D) serving as the sole determinant of family lineage.

5. Andean and Mesoamerican civilizations differed because
   (A) Andean societies had no form of writing.
   (B) Inca priests did not make astronomical observations.
   (C) the Andean region could not engage in long-distance trade because of the harsh climate.
   (D) Cuzco was much larger than Tenochtitlan in terms of population.

6. The geography and environment of the Andean region
   (A) required societies to use a variety of innovative methods including terraced farming, animal domestication, and long-distance trade to meet all their needs.
   (B) allowed societies to do very little because the climate was naturally suited to produce ideal agricultural conditions Aztec.
   (C) formed one type of ecological zone that was challenging because of the dominance of the Andes mountains.
   (D) had little influence on those living there in comparison to the impact of the environment on those living in Mesoamerica.

7. Which of the following similarities did the Aztec and Inca NOT share?
   (A) Both relied on public displays of large-scale human sacrifice of war captives.
   (B) Both believed military conquest was a requirement for an incoming political leader.
   (C) Both relied on tribute extracted from conquered regions and peoples.
   (D) Both relied on military control that required large, well-trained armies.

8. Northern peoples in the Americas
   (A) used maize, beans, and squash as dietary staples, as did Mesoamerican peoples.
   (B) left archaeological evidence of empires as large as the Incas'.
   (C) were subject peoples of the Aztecs during the height of the Aztec Empire.
   (D) were not able to engage in long-distance trade.

9. The Aztecs
   (A) had a loose social structure that allowed for the lower classes to influence political decisions.
   (B) placed the merchant class above the military in terms of their importance to society.
   (C) originated as nomadic mercenaries and later founded a settled empire.
   (D) conquered the Toltec and adapted many of their political practices.

10. The Maya
  (A) created one politically unified territory of hereditary rulers that defeated rival kingdoms and lasted until European conquest.
  (B) were unable to develop successful irrigation techniques needed to farm land and therefore relied on long-distance trade for food.
  (C) made valuable intellectual contributions in the areas of math and astronomy that improved Mesoamerican calendar systems.
  (D) did not practice human sacrifice and rarely participated in bloodletting rituals.

11. The Aztecs were similar to the Chinese or the Mongols in that they
  (A) were nomads.
  (B) created tribute-based empires.
  (C) sacrificed warriors.
  (D) had a very negative view of women.

12. Aztecs perceived the _____ as the Romans perceived the _____.
  (A) Maya/Israelites
  (B) Toltecs/Greeks
  (C) Moche/Carthagenians
  (D) Inca/Han Chinese

13. Maya culture was
  (A) a unified political empire ruled by a divine king.
  (B) a series of rival kingdoms that competed with one another for regional dominance.
  (C) influenced by the Inca to the south, with whom it had intensive trade relationships.
  (D) the only Mesoamerican society with a system of writing.

14. The process by which maize, beans, and squash became domesticated in North America is known as
  (A) diffusion.
  (B) transcendence.
  (C) coercive tribute.
  (D) mit'a.

15. The ayllu was important to the Inca for all the following reasons EXCEPT
  (A) it held land communally and facilitated cooperation.
  (B) it served as the source of tribute labor.
  (C) it helped to undermine the state's authority.
  (D) it provided labor and goods to the hereditary chief.

Free-Response Questions

1. Compare the social and economic characteristics of the Mesoamerican societies with those of the Andean region from circa 600 to circa 1450, focusing on the Aztec and Inca Empires in particular.

2. Evaluate the cultural continuities and changes over time in Mesoamerican society from circa 600 to circa 1450.

Answers

MULTIPLE-CHOICE QUESTIONS

1. **ANSWER: D.** Mesoamerican and Andean cities rivaled their contemporaries around the world in both their architecture and sophistication. They contained multilevel, complex building structures including private dwellings and temples. Teotihuacan, Tenochtitlan, and Cuzco are all examples of some of the great cities of the region in the period 600–1450 (*The Earth and Its Peoples*, 5th ed., pp. 312, 328–330/6th ed., pp. 198, 213).

2. **ANSWER: D.** Mesoamerican societies were made up of kingdoms that competed for political authority but did share cultural characteristics (*The Earth and Its Peoples*, 5th ed., pp. 309–310/6th ed., pp. 191–192).

3. **ANSWER: D.** Society in the Americas placed tremendous significance on religious ritual and worship, and believed honoring the many gods of their cultures was essential for the well-being of mankind. In addition, religious rituals were shaped to support the political authority of rulers (*The Earth and Its Peoples*, 5th ed., pp. 312–314, 328–330/6th ed., pp. 198–200).

4. **ANSWER: D.** In a number of Mesoamerican and Andean societies women performed all of the roles except for serving as sole determinants of family lineage (*The Earth and Its Peoples*, 5th ed., p. 314/6th ed., p. 200).

5. **ANSWER: A.** Andean and Mesoamerican civilizations had a lot of similarities including astronomical observation, calendar production, and examples of long-distance trade. Other than oral communication, the khipu was the main means of communication for the Inca (*The Earth and Its Peoples*, 5th ed., pp. 328–330/6th ed., p. 395).

6. **ANSWER: A.** The Andean region was a very complex environment that included different ecological zones and required domestication of the llama and alpaca, innovative ways of farming, irrigation, and the use of the ayllu and mit'a labor systems (*The Earth and Its Peoples*, 5th ed., pp. 322–324/6th ed., pp. 207–208).

7. **ANSWER: A.** There is evidence that the Inca practiced textile and animal sacrifice but did not practice human sacrifice on the large scale that the Aztecs did (*The Earth and Its Peoples*, 5th ed., pp. 328–330/6th ed., p. 395).

8. **ANSWER: A.** Northern peoples used these crops, and the desire to grow maize encouraged irrigation projects. Their political traditions differed from Mesoamericans', but they did have some cultural similarities. The mound builders did engage in long-

distance trade (*The Earth and Its Peoples,* 5th ed., pp. 319–322/6th ed., pp. 205–208).

9. ANSWER: **C.** Like other successful empires of the period 600–1450, the Aztecs were initially a nomadic group that migrated to fill the power vacuum left after the decline of the Toltec. They quickly rose to power in the region and built on much of the legacy of the Toltecs, who had declined centuries before (*The Earth and Its Peoples,* 5th ed., pp. 316–317/6th ed., pp. 393–396).

10. ANSWER: **C** The Maya built on the work of the Olmec civilization and created two different calendars that reflected their interest in the cyclical nature of the cosmos. A patrilineal society, the Maya were successful with irrigation. They were never the rulers of a unified Mesoamerican territory (*The Earth and Its Peoples,* 5th ed., pp. 312–314/6th ed., pp. 198–200).

11. ANSWER: **B.** The Aztecs were much like many other conquerors in that they did not try to control the entire area they conquered. Instead, they subjugated the people and expected tribute—whether labor, agricultural goods, or luxury items (*The Earth and Its Peoples,* 5th ed., p. 319/6th ed., p. 395).

12. ANSWER: **B.** Like the Romans, who considered the Greeks to be the source of advanced culture, the Aztecs considered the Toltecs to be the source of all great cultural achievements (*The Earth and Its Peoples,* 5th ed., p. 316/6th ed., p. 201).

13. ANSWER: **B.** The Maya, much like the Greeks, were united culturally but never politically. They were rival kingdoms who struggled with one another for regional dominance (*The Earth and Its Peoples,* 5th ed., p. 312/6th ed., p. 198).

14. ANSWER: **A.** The introduction of anything new, in this case food crops and agriculture from Mesoamerica into North America, is known as diffusion (*The Earth and Its Peoples,* 5th ed., p. 320/6th ed., p. 204).

15. ANSWER: **C.** The Ayllu provided for collectivism. Workloads, tribute labor, agricultural products, and trade were shared by the entire population of an Ayllu (*The Earth and Its Peoples,* 5th ed., p. 324/6th ed., p. 208).

FREE-RESPONSE QUESTIONS

1. For this essay you should contrast the environmental conditions that each empire had to contend with in order to have economic success. The aspects of long-distance trade, the role of cities, and the reliance on tribute should be discussed as similarities. A key similarity in social characteristics is the role of religion in shaping societal values as well as affirming the elite status of the military and priestly classes. You should include an analysis of why those two classes were so highly valued. In both empires the grandeur of public ceremonial architecture and elaborate public rituals helped cement the dual role of the king as a political and religious leader.

2. Your essay should include a discussion of aspects of both change and continuity as they relate to the cultural continuities between the people of Teotihuacan and the Maya and between the Toltec and the Aztecs in their respective regions of Mesoamerica. The continuity in the role of ritual, religion, urban centers, and architecture can all be discussed. For change, you can address the value placed on military conquest as the Toltec and Aztec came into power. The continuity in cultural and religious traditions is very apparent from 600 to 1450.

11

AFRICA: CIRCA 1450 TO CIRCA 1750

KEY CONCEPTS

- While Africa had long been linked to the Islamic world through trade (and the Muslims' conquest of North Africa), this period saw the first significant European contact with the continent.
- European involvement in Africa began with the Portuguese and initially included a variety of religious, economic, and political motivations. As the period continued, other European powers initiated contact with Africa as well, drawn mainly by the prospect of acquiring slaves to be put to work on New World plantations.
- In general, African interactions with European powers were fairly static, as the Europeans became preoccupied with New World colonization, and were interested in Africa primarily to maintain the slave trade. Most major conflicts that occurred—with the exception of the Portuguese destruction of the East African trading cities in 1505—were among rival groups within Africa itself, such as the Moroccan invasion of the Songhai Empire in 1591.
- The slave trade led to the depopulation of certain areas of sub-Saharan Africa, and forced millions of Africans into lives of grueling labor in other parts of the world. However, the economic, political, and social structures of the continent remained largely intact during this period; not until the nineteenth century would European involvement in Africa widen from a focus on the slave trade to true imperialist domination.

KEY TERMS

- Benin
- Cape Colony
- cassava
- Dahomey
- Gold Coast
- Hausa
- Kongo
- maize
- manikongo
- Oyo
- Slave Coast
- Songhai Empire
- Swahili Coast
- trans-Saharan trade
- Whydah

Chapters 15 and 18 of the fifth edition of *The Earth and Its Peoples*, and Chapters 15 and 18 of the sixth edition, describe the impact of the European maritime revolution on coastal sub-Saharan Africa, the subsequent rise of the Atlantic System, and the effects of Africa's slave trade with Europe and the Islamic world.

WEST AND EAST AFRICA: THE EUROPEANS' FIRST CONTACTS

Prince Henry the Navigator of Portugal sowed the seeds of tremendous change for Africa in the early to mid-1400s, as he and his men cautiously explored farther and farther south along Africa's west coast. Following their conquest of the Moroccan city of Ceuta in 1415, the Portuguese became intensely curious to discover the origins of the gold and slaves that were brought to North Africa via well-established trade routes from the continent's sub-Saharan interior. They also sought to spread Christianity to any lands they might discover, and counteract the expansion of the rising Ottoman Empire. These economic, religious, and political motives combined with European advances in maritime technology during the fifteenth century to spur the Portuguese to reach the southern tip of Africa before the century's end. Along the way, they found many West Africans who were experienced in trade and ready for new contacts that would expand their volume of exports and imports. In 1482, the African king, Caramansa, allowed the Portuguese to open a trading post on what the Europeans would call the **Gold Coast** of West Africa, where vast amounts of African gold were soon traded for goods from Europe, Asia, and other parts of Africa that arrived on Portuguese ships. Soon after, monarchs such as the oba of Benin and the **manikongo** of Kongo sent delegates to Portugal to gather information on the homeland of these foreign men. Satisfied with what they learned, the traders of **Benin** continued to provide the Portuguese with pepper, ivory, and textiles. They also allowed the Portuguese to purchase prisoners of war, who would be taken as slaves to work on the sugar plantations of the previously uninhabited island of São Tomé off the African coast. Africa would soon be forever transformed, and the effects of the European slave trade would be felt in nearly every corner of the world.

The leaders of Benin chose to restrict their contact with the Portuguese by the 1530s, but by then the king of **Kongo** had made Catholicism the official faith of his land, and had begun providing the Portuguese with more and more slaves. The Kongolese slave trade soon got out of control, however, with unauthorized traders resorting to kidnapping to meet the growing demand for slaves. The king's plea for help from the Portuguese was met with no response; the Portuguese had already begun to turn their attention to finding a sea route to link with the Indian Ocean trade. The manikongo faced rebellion, and by the 1540s the center of the slave trade moved farther south, to what was dubbed the **Slave Coast**. Sudden social, political, and economic changes such as these would later become the norm for Africa, as the Europeans continued their exploration—and eventual exploitation—of the continent.

Meanwhile, by the end of the fifteenth century, the **Swahili Coast** of East Africa featured a number of prosperous Muslim-ruled trading states. In 1505, nearly all of them were attacked and plundered by the Portuguese, who had just recently rounded the southern tip of Africa in their continuing quest for a sea route to India. Only Ethiopia was spared Portuguese aggression in East Africa—under attack from the Muslim state of Adal, the Christian queen of Ethiopia pleaded for Portuguese aid. The Muslims were held off, but Ethiopian hopes for a permanent alliance with Portugal went unfulfilled as a result of the Ethiopian rulers' refusal to affiliate their church with the pope in Rome rather than the patriarch of Alexandria. More significantly, by the mid-1500s, Portuguese attention had shifted to the Indian Ocean trade as well as to their colonial conquests in the New World. European involvement in Africa would level off temporarily, but as the seventeenth century unfolded, the seeds of change planted by Henry the Navigator would begin to burst forth with dramatic consequences.

THE TRANSATLANTIC SLAVE TRADE EXPLODES

Portugal led the way in bringing change to the Americas as well as to Africa; by the late 1500s, the Portuguese had copied the plantation-style sugar production of their western Atlantic islands, such as Madeira and São Tomé, in their New World colony of Brazil. Initially the Portuguese planters relied on Amerindian slaves to produce their crops, but as epidemics of Old World diseases ravaged the indigenous American population, African slaves were taken across the Atlantic in ever-increasing numbers by the Portuguese, Spanish, British, and other European colonists. By the seventeenth century, the European ships of the so-called Atlantic System were transporting large numbers of young African adults (more males than females) to a life of slavery in the Americas, in exchange for European manufactured goods (including guns) and Indian textiles. African gold, timber, and other products also found their way into the expanding global economic network. It must be noted that the European traders were not the only ones to profit from these transactions: European guidebooks provided detailed information on the preferred trade items of different areas of Africa's Atlantic coast, as African traders were often found to be shrewd bargainers. Indeed, over the eighteenth century, the price demanded for a slave on the Gold Coast more than doubled. The Africans' bargaining advantages resulted in part from their exploitation of the rivalry among several European nations that had established trading "castles" along the West African coast. Traders from the Dutch East India Company and other European concerns found themselves forced to supply the Africans with more and more guns and gunpowder (thus increasing African military strength and preventing European takeover of African territory) in order to compete in trade. The Europeans were also forced to follow African trading rituals and pay customs duties to African leaders.

The European fervor for African slaves fueled the growth of a number of West African kingdoms. The small kingdom of **Whydah**, an early Gold Coast center for the slave trade, was overtaken in 1727 by the neighboring kingdom of **Dahomey,** which had been able to supply its army (of males and females) with firearms furnished in exchange for slaves by European traders. Dahomey was in turn dominated by the inland kingdom of **Oyo** in 1730, and forced to pay tribute to Oyo to remain independent. For Oyo and the adjacent kingdom of Asante, the Atlantic slave trade was merely one element of a thriving economy that also included extensive commercial activity within West Africa and across the Sahara Desert.

AP Tip

In writing an essay discussing aspects of slavery in this period, it may be useful to mention the varying sources of African slaves. Contrary to the belief of many in Europe at that time, only rarely did parents sell their children into slavery. Instead, prior to the eighteenth century slaves sold to the Europeans by West African traders were usually prisoners of war; however, historical debate continues over just how frequently wars were initiated solely for the purpose of capturing slaves for export. Current theory (bolstered by eighteenth- and nineteenth-century European and African accounts) holds that most wars in the region were fought over territory and other political disputes, and the capture and sale of enemy prisoners was simply a side endeavor. Later, the Europeans moved farther south and east to the Bight of Biafra in search of new sources of slaves. Here there were no large kingdoms, and hence few large-scale wars, so slave traders turned to kidnapping to maintain their supply, which was supplemented by debtors and convicted criminals.

ANGOLA AND THE CAPE COLONY

For the most part, outright European colonization of Africa would not take place until well after 1750. Two exceptions occurred before that time, however. Both the Portuguese and Dutch established African colonies after 1500. The Dutch East India Company's **Cape Colony**, located at the far southern tip of Africa, played a very minor role in African affairs during this period, as the company's economic activities were oriented almost entirely to the Indian Ocean trade and focused very little on commercial ventures within Africa. Even the Cape Colony's slaves were imported primarily from places outside of Africa such as South Asia and the East Indies.

Angola was a somewhat different story. As the African slave trade moved steadily south and east during the sixteenth century, the Portuguese realized they could profit from maintaining a permanent settlement along Africa's Atlantic coast. Centered on the ports of Luanda and Benguela, the colony of Angola soon became the primary supplier of African slaves for the Americas. Portuguese settlers in these cities found profitable employment acting as middlemen, transferring slaves brought by caravan from Africa's far interior to ships bound for Brazil. The ships had brought goods from Europe and the Americas, which were taken back to the interior for exchange at huge markets and fairs for more slaves, thus continuing the internal cycle of commerce that fed into the larger Atlantic Circuit.

The Portuguese presence on the Angolan coast was maintained via relationships—partnerships, even—with inland African leaders, many of whom were loosely allied in an enormous federation of kingdoms. Environmental crises in the region actually aided these leaders in boosting their subject populations and maintaining a steady supply of young adults for the slave trade. Severe droughts in Africa's southern grasslands forced refugees to flee to less arid areas. After providing the refugees with food and water, African leaders would then assimilate the children and women of reproductive age (who were also valued as the region's primary food producers), while selling most of the adult males into slavery. The Angolan leaders were thus able to consolidate an ever-growing population (with little threat of rebellion, since few adult males remained); stabilize the land, sometimes by planting new high-yield crops such as **maize** and **cassava** from the Americas; repopulate drought-ravaged territory; and reap substantial profits from the European slave trade. The strong African states that emerged from this process were able to discourage further encroachment and territorial takeover by the Europeans, who—preoccupied with the Indian Ocean trade and colonization in the Americas—remained basically content to trade textiles, metals, and weapons for African slaves until the nineteenth century, when a combination of humanitarian and economic pressures would bring an end to the slave trade and drive the Europeans to formal colonization of African territory.

AFRICA AND ISLAM: NORTH AFRICA, THE SUDAN, AND THE SWAHILI COAST

While the fifteenth century marked the beginning of significant European contact with Africa, the Islamic world had of course long since developed strong ties with the continent, beginning in the century after Muhammad's death. Muslim beliefs and practices had spread from North Africa to the sub-Saharan region via overland trade, and to the Swahili Coast of East Africa through the trade ships that plied the Red Sea and Indian Ocean. By the time Henry the Navigator's men were beginning their exploration of West Africa, Islamic legal and governmental structures—as well as the Arabic language—had become firmly entrenched in the African trading cities south of the Sahara and on the southeastern coast. Indeed, the Islamic world would maintain a much stronger influence than Europe over African culture and politics throughout the period of 1450–1750. But while nearly all of North Africa had been engulfed by the Ottoman Empire by the sixteenth century, the kingdoms and states of sub-Saharan Africa remained independent from both Middle Easterners and Europeans, as a result of the region's protective geography and the military skills of its leaders.

One such kingdom was the **Songhai Empire**, which had succeeded Mali as the leading center of **trans-Saharan trade.** As Songhai grew from its base in the western Sudan, its indigenous Muslim leaders began to expand northward into the Sahara. Perhaps fearing an impending territorial rivalry, the kingdom of Morocco sent an expedition of several thousand men and camels across the desert in 1590. Half the men died on the journey, but the remaining two thousand mounted an attack on Songhai's massive military in 1591. Despite a size advantage of nearly twenty times, the Songhai army was no match for the twenty-five hundred muskets of the Moroccans. For the next two hundred years the Moroccans maintained a tributary dominance over the people of the western Sudan, demanding slaves and goods from them and charging tolls to merchants crossing the territory. Following this decline of the Songhai Empire, those involved in the trans-Saharan trade soon shifted their operations from the western Sudan to the central Sudan, where the **Hausa** trading cities began to provide merchants from North Africa with gold and slaves in exchange for textiles, weapons, and hardware.

AP Tip

Understanding the impact of religion on various aspects of society can be useful for both multiple-choice and free-response questions. For example, the tenets of Islam played a significant role in many areas of African life, even economics. While the Atlantic Circuit trade brought rum and other alcoholic beverages to coastal Africa, the Muslim merchants of the Hausa trading cities were forbidden by their religion to use alcohol. Conversely, Muslims (as well as Christians) of this period felt free to engage in the trade of slaves—and in fact, Muslims viewed the enslavement of "pagans" to be an act of virtue, as it would bring new followers to their faith.

While the slave trade with the Islamic north played an important role in the economy of the Sudan, what little historical evidence remains indicates that the size of the trans-Saharan slave trade was smaller than that of the transatlantic trade. From the seventeenth to nineteenth centuries, some 1.7 million Africans were marched across the Sahara or shipped over the Red Sea or Indian Ocean to lives of slavery in the Middle East and India. In contrast, between 1550 and 1800 nearly 8 million slaves crossed the Atlantic to the Americas.

Their final destination determined the type of work that African slaves were forced to do. Most slaves sent to the Americas ended up performing grueling physical labor on sugar, tobacco, or cotton plantations. Those who wound up in the Islamic world were debatably more fortunate, as they were often placed in employment as soldiers or household servants. The gender balance was different as well: while most African slaves sent to the Americas were men, the majority of African slaves sent to the Middle East or India were women, forced into service as concubines, domestic servants, and entertainers. Many more children were taken to the Islamic world, too—including boys who would have to endure dangerous (often fatal) castrations to be transformed into eunuchs, and thus considered suitable for serving as harem guards.

By the beginning of the nineteenth century, the slave trade had brought considerable profit to certain African leaders and merchants (and a great deal more, of course, to Europe, the Americas, and the Islamic world). It also decimated the population of young, healthy adults in some parts of sub-Saharan Africa, particularly the inland territory of the Slave Coast. However, the overall population of the region was still quite substantial, and the African artisans and traders who persevered in this era of increasing change were for the most part able to maintain their production and sale of textiles and metal goods, despite the volume of competing products flowing in from Europe and the Islamic world. Thus, a very generalized examination of the slave trade might conclude that, within Africa, its impact was far from devastating. Indeed, it is rather ironic that it was late-nineteenth-century imperialism, initiated after the end of the slave trade, rather than the slave trade itself, that would bring changes of unimaginable consequence to the continent.

Multiple-Choice Questions

1. Initial Portuguese contact with West Africa was spurred in part by
   (A) the Portuguese desire to halt the expansion of the Ottoman Empire.
   (B) Ethiopia's initiation of a Christianity-based alliance with Portugal.
   (C) Portugal's quest for new sources of tea and sugar to trade with England.
   (D) the Portuguese need to block Spain from controlling all transatlantic trade routes.

2. Early Portuguese activities in exploring Africa's Atlantic coast included all of the following EXCEPT
   (A) spreading Christianity.
   (B) purchasing slaves.
   (C) acquiring gold.
   (D) eradicating Islam.

3. Which of the following was the LEAST common source of African slaves taken to the Americas or the Islamic world?
   (A) kidnap victims
   (B) convicted criminals
   (C) children sold by their parents
   (D) prisoners of war

4. What was the impact of the rivalry among European powers in the West African trade in the period 1450–1750?
   (A) The long-established trade networks of West Africa were destroyed.
   (B) The price demanded for African slaves rose sharply.
   (C) Fearing European warfare in their territory, African leaders forged a military alliance.
   (D) African leaders were able to institute a ban on undesired imports of rum and tobacco from the Americas.

5. Angola is an example of
   (A) a territory that banned the slave trade.
   (B) an African territorial conquest of the Ottoman Empire.
   (C) a trading "castle" of the Dutch East India Company.
   (D) an early European colony in Africa.

6. What was one significant impact of environmental crises such as droughts in sub-Saharan Africa during this period?
   (A) European attempts at sugar cultivation failed, thus fueling colonization of the Americas.
   (B) African leaders became dependent on European agricultural imports, which drove the price of slaves downward.
   (C) New crops brought to Africa from the Americas such as corn and potatoes failed to thrive.
   (D) Many of those who fled stricken areas were given refuge by neighboring leaders, then forced into resettlement or sold into the slave trade.

7. Except for Morocco, North Africa was under the control of which power by the sixteenth century?
   (A) Egypt
   (B) The Ottoman Empire
   (C) Portugal
   (D) Ethiopia

8. The Moroccan defeat of the Songhai Empire was attributable to
   (A) Morocco's powerful alliance with the Ottoman Empire.
   (B) the Songhai military's inability to fight in the Sahara Desert.
   (C) the Songhai Empire's depopulation as a consequence of the European slave trade.
   (D) the spread of new military technologies to the Moroccan kingdom.

9. How did the European slave trade with Africa compare with the African slave trade with the Islamic world?
   (A) More women than men were taken as slaves by Europeans, to repopulate the Americas, than were taken to the Islamic world.
   (B) The European slave trade was driven more by religious motivation, as European Christians planned to convert enslaved Africans to Christianity.
   (C) More women than men were transported to the Islamic world; therefore they placed African slaves in less grueling types of labor.
   (D) A much higher percentage of African slaves died on the harsh journey across the Sahara Desert than crossing the Atlantic by ship.

10. How did the Columbian Exchange affect Africa during this period?
    (A) New World crops such as maize, potatoes, and cassava brought a new source of food to famine-stricken areas of Africa.
    (B) The demographics of Africa included significant numbers of Europeans and Americans by the end of the period.
    (C) Large numbers of Africans succumbed to New World diseases to which they had never before been exposed.
    (D) Livestock from the Americas such as cattle and horses transformed African pastoral practices.

11. African slavery in the Americas increased dramatically when
    (A) gold was discovered in Peru.
    (B) silver was discovered in Peru and Mexico.
    (C) sugar plantations were expanded in the West Indies.
    (D) cassava was introduced to Africa, thus significantly increasing the population.

12. Factors that fueled the growing dependence of African slaves included all of the following EXCEPT
    (A) mortality rates in the tropics due to diseases—both native and imported.
    (B) Africans were relatively cheaper to purchase than Europeans or Asians.
    (C) African slaves would serve their masters longer than European indentured servants.
    (D) racial prejudice favored the use of Africans over other ethnic groups.

13. The term *Atlantic System* refers to
    (A) the triangular trade network.
    (B) the trading of slaves for sugar.
    (C) the entire trading network that the Europeans developed in the Atlantic.
    (D) the Middle Passage.

14. In exchange for slaves, African merchants
    (A) were very discriminating in what they purchased and would often refuse European merchandise that did not meet their needs.
    (B) accepted pretty much anything because they were so happy to have an opportunity to trade.
    (C) accepted only rum or guns because these were items that could not be produced in Africa.
    (D) accepted only specialty textiles with unique patterns.

15. African kingdoms benefited from the slave trade through all the following reasons EXCEPT
    (A) becoming very wealthy by collecting substantial customs duties.
    (B) annexing other kingdoms with the profits from the slave trade.
    (C) increasing their relative strength through the acquisition of firearms.
    (D) controlling the arrival of Europeans by selling slaves only in the spring.

Free-Response Questions

1. Analyze the continuities and changes in ONE of the following areas.
   - social
   - political
   - economic

2. Compare political and economic aspects in North Africa and political and economic aspects in West Africa between circa 1450 and circa 1750.

Answers

MULTIPLE-CHOICE QUESTIONS

1. **ANSWER: A.** While competition with Spain, coupled with the desire for a sea route to India, would later play a role in Portugal's continuing exploration of the West African coast, it was Henry the Navigator's desire to spread Christianity and launch crusades against the Ottomans that led to the earliest Portuguese voyages to Africa (*The Earth and Its Peoples*, 5th ed., p. 434/6th ed., p. 410).

2. **ANSWER: D.** Despite Henry the Navigator's desire to defeat the growing Ottoman Empire, there were no significant religious conflicts that occurred between the European explorers and the peoples of Africa—even those who had already converted to Islam (*The Earth and Its Peoples*, 5th ed., pp. 434, 437, 534/6th ed., pp. 408, 410, 509).

3. **ANSWER: C.** It was a common notion within Europe at the time—perhaps developed to bolster the image of the African people as "uncivilized" and thus fair targets of European exploitation—but in reality very few African children were ever sold into slavery by their parents, and then only under extreme circumstances (*The Earth and Its Peoples*, 5th ed., pp. 535–537/6th ed., pp. 510–511).

4. **ANSWER: B.** In general, West African leaders and merchants welcomed the European trade, and the ensuing rivalry among competing European powers—coupled with their growing desire for slaves to work the plantations in the Europeans' new American colonies—created a surge in demand for African slaves that was accompanied by significant price increases (*The Earth and Its Peoples*, 5th ed., p. 534/6th ed., p. 509).

5. **ANSWER: D.** Significant European colonization of Africa would not occur until the late nineteenth century, following the end of the slave trade, but the Portuguese and Dutch did come to control certain territories—Angola and the Cape Colony, respectively—in Africa during the period 1450–1750 (*The Earth and Its Peoples*, 5th ed., pp. 536–537/6th ed., p. 511).

6. **ANSWER: D.** Droughts drove refugees to Angola in particular, where leaders would provide them with food and water, then retain control over most of the women and children while selling the adult males into slavery (*The Earth and Its Peoples*, 5th ed., pp. 536–537/6th ed., p. 511).

7. **ANSWER: B.** As the last in a series of Islamic empires that dominated much of the Mediterranean region, the Ottoman Empire gained control of much of North Africa by the 1500s—only Morocco maintained its independent status throughout this period (*The Earth and Its Peoples*, 5th ed., p. 537/6th ed., p. 512).

8. **ANSWER: D.** The Songhai Empire had a strong central government and a large, well-trained military. However, the Empire's troops were unable to hold off the invading Moroccans, whose much

smaller army was equipped with muskets and gunpowder, and thus able to quickly overpower the Songhai military, which lacked such technology (*The Earth and Its Peoples*, 5th ed., pp. 537–538/6th ed., pp. 512–513).

9. ANSWER: **C.** As more female slaves than male were taken to the Islamic world, most of them were put to work as entertainers, domestic servants, and concubines, while those taken across the Atlantic to the Americas (mostly men) were usually forced into arduous agricultural labor on large plantations (*The Earth and Its Peoples*, 5th ed., pp. 538–539/6th ed., p. 516).

10. ANSWER: **A.** New World crops were brought to Africa by the Columbian Exchange, and Central African rulers soon directed the predominantly female farmers of their territories to cultivate them, providing a new source of sustenance in drought-prone areas— and perhaps fueling a population increase that partly counterbalanced those lost to the slave trade (*The Earth and Its Peoples*, 5th ed., pp. 524–525, 536–537/6th ed., pp. 498, 511).

11. ANSWER: **C.** Expansion of sugar plantations in the West Indies required a sharp increase in the volume of the slave trade from Africa (*The Earth and Its Peoples*, 5th ed., p. 521/6th ed., p. 496).

12. ANSWER: **D.** There are many factors, including increased death rates due to tropical diseases, the relative cheapness of African slaves when indentured servants began to prefer to go to North America where land was cheaper, and the fact that slaves worked on average seven years whereas indentured servants only worked four. Prejudice was not one of the factors that lead to the choosing of African slaves (*The Earth and Its Peoples*, 5th ed., pp. 520–522/6th ed., pp. 494–496).

13. ANSWER: **D.** The Atlantic System is the totality of the trade that occurred in the Atlantic, most of it dominated by European nations (*The Earth and Its Peoples*, 5th ed., p. 519/6th ed., p. 493).

14. ANSWER: **A.** African merchants were very selective and had strong bargaining power because of the high demand for slaves (*The Earth and Its Peoples*, 5th ed., pp. 534–536/6th ed., pp. 510–512).

15. ANSWER: **D.** African kingdoms profited from increased trade in firearms, increased customs duties, and the ability to annex other kingdoms through warfare. They were not able to control the arrival of the Europeans (*The Earth and Its Peoples*, 5th ed., pp. 534–537/6th ed., pp. 510–513).

FREE-RESPONSE QUESTIONS

1. Change over time during this period in Africa should be analyzed through the framework of growing European influence in the region. The predominant economic change that occurred was, of course, the sharp increase in European demand for slaves after 1500 or so, which brought great wealth to African political leaders and merchants. Socially, the growing slave trade initiated demographic shifts within the continent (regional depopulation, gender imbalances in certain areas), and introduced aspects of

European culture (languages, the Christian religion) to coastal cities. Politically, changes included the Ottoman Empire's takeover of North Africa; the Portuguese destruction of key Swahili Coast trading cities; the establishment of the colonies of Angola and the Cape Colony; and territorial disputes and transfers between indigenous Africans—such as the clashes between Adal and Ethiopia, Oyo and Dahomey, and Morocco and the Songhai Empire. Major continuities to highlight include the ongoing influence of Islamic religious, legal, and educational practices, particularly in North Africa; the persistence of African weavers and metalworkers, who maintained their production even as competing goods arrived from Europe and the Americas; and the fact that, unlike the indigenous peoples of the Americas during this period, Africans maintained political control of nearly all of their continent.

2. Africa between 1450 and 1750 was influenced by both Europe and the Islamic world. Thus, a comparative essay in response to this prompt should draw analysis from the larger global context. The Islamic world's influence on Africa was much stronger than Europe's during this period, particularly in North Africa. Politically, of course, nearly all of North Africa was unified under the Muslim-ruled Ottoman Empire in the 1500s, while West Africa remained more independent (due to protective geography and skilled leaders) but less politically cohesive, with various regional kingdoms and empires (such as Benin, Kongo, and Oyo) rising and falling. West Africa also saw the beginnings of European imperialism, with the establishment of the Portuguese colony of Angola, but in general, Islam continued to play a larger role in African affairs in West Africa, too—the Songhai Empire is one example of a Muslim-ruled West African dynasty. Economically, the trans-Saharan gold trade continued to bring wealth to both North and West Africa, with indigenous artisans also producing textiles and metalwork for local consumption and export. West African merchants also began to profit from the transatlantic slave trade, however, which allowed certain regional leaders to acquire European firearms, boost their military strength, and maintain territorial control throughout this period of increased contact with the growing global trade network.

12

THE MIDDLE EAST: CIRCA 1450 TO CIRCA 1750

KEY CONCEPTS

- The central event marking the Ottoman Empire's dominance of the Middle East during this period was its capture of Constantinople from the vanishing Byzantine Empire in 1453.
- Once established, the Ottoman Empire faced growing challenges from the emerging European powers of the period, which had far-ranging (and ultimately detrimental) effects on the empire's social structure, economic prosperity, and political stability.
- Like the Ottoman Empire, the Safavid Empire of Iran emerged during this period as something of a throwback, a land-based empire in an era when power and wealth came increasingly from naval might and sea trade.
- The global inflation caused by the sudden glut of New World silver in the world economy brought crisis to both the Ottomans and the Safavids by the 1700s. The Ottoman Empire would continue struggling to survive—until the early twentieth century—while the Safavid Empire had crumbled completely by 1750.

KEY TERMS

- anderun
- askeri
- devshirme system
- fatwa
- harem
- Isfahan
- Ismail
- Janissary
- mufti

- qizilbash
- raya
- Shari'a
- Sufi

The Ottoman and Safavid Empires are covered in Chapter 19 of *The Earth and Its Peoples,* fifth and sixth editions.

THE OTTOMAN EMPIRE

Although the Turkic warrior Timur had briefly seized power in the region in the early 1400s, his death signaled the dawning of a new era in the Middle East: the formerly nomadic Turks who established the Ottoman Empire would come to dominate territory previously under Mongol and Timurid control, and they would build the largest Islamic empire since the Abbasid Caliphate. And when the Ottomans captured Constantinople in 1453, their influence was extended even farther, toward Europe, in an area once dominated by the Byzantine Empire. This victory was achieved by Sultan Mehmed II, known as "the Conqueror," who combined the strong military skills of Turkish warrior tradition with more innovative tactics. For example, he put gunpowder to use in huge cannon that broke through the walls that ringed Constantinople, hauled his warships over land to circumvent the Byzantine sea forces and reach the vulnerable inner harbor, and then unleashed his troops on the nearly defenseless city. The takeover of Constantinople, soon renamed Istanbul, was crucial for the Ottomans in more ways than one—not only did it solidify Ottoman control over the vital trade link between the Mediterranean and Black Seas (and hence between Europe and Asia), but it also brought about the final demise of the Byzantine Empire and clearly marked the ascendancy of a new regional power.

Having conquered most of southeastern Europe, including Greece, Serbia, and Albania, prior to seizing Constantinople, the Ottomans turned their attention to the east. In the Battle of Chaldiran in 1514, Ottoman ruler Selim I held firm against the expanding Safavid Empire of Iran, establishing a boundary between the two powers that stands more or less intact to this day. A few years later Selim added Egypt and Syria to the Ottoman domain by conquering the Mamluk Sultanate, then continued his expansion when the Muslim rulers of Algeria and Tunisia joined the empire voluntarily.

When Selim's son Suleiman (known to Europeans as "the Magnificent" and to his own people as "the Lawgiver") set his sights on Christian Europe, however, the seemingly invincible Ottoman forces faced a rare setback. Initially victorious—conquering Belgrade and the island of Rhodes in the early 1520s—Suleiman assaulted Vienna in 1529 but was forced to turn back before winter set in. Meanwhile, Ottoman attempts to capture control of the Mediterranean also met with unexpected challenges. From the mid-fifteenth to the mid-seventeenth centuries, various sultans battled the Italian city-state of Venice, which had dominated Mediterranean commerce through control of key territories such as the islands of Crete and Cyprus and certain Greek port cities. The Ottomans never managed to vanquish their Venetian rivals completely; they settled instead for a tribute relationship and allowed the Venetians and other foreign traders to conduct business in Ottoman ports. Indeed, while Mediterranean trade was seen as an important source of revenue, the Ottomans—perhaps because of their Turkish warrior heritage and lack of any maritime history—always viewed theirs as a land-based, rather than sea-based, empire. They found themselves in control of the Red Sea after their takeover of Egypt, coastal Ethiopia, and the Muslim homeland surrounding Mecca and Medina in Arabia. But they tended to leave the lucrative Indian Ocean trade to the Portuguese and other Europeans, despite controlling outposts at Aden and Oman on the southern Arabian Peninsula.

MILITARY, POLITICAL, AND ECONOMIC STRUCTURES

Ottoman military traditions and practices played a key role in the development of the empire's character. After the Ottoman takeover of the Balkans in eastern Europe, Christian prisoners of war were used to create a corps of new troops called **Janissaries**; supplementing the traditional Turkish archers on horseback, these military slaves fought on foot with guns. After 1400 or so, the Janissary corps began to be replenished through the **devshirme system**, in which young Christian boys from the Balkans (and sometimes other Ottoman-controlled territories) were taught to speak Turkish and given military training. Some were selected to study Islam, liberal arts, and military strategy at the sultan's palace in Istanbul, in effect being groomed to become high-ranking military commanders and government officials. The Ottoman navy, meanwhile, was composed of Greek, Turkish, Algerian, and Tunisian sailors who patrolled the Mediterranean in galleys.

> ## AP Tip
>
> You should be able to compare characteristics of the Ottoman system of slavery, which allowed non-Muslims to rise to high-ranking positions in the Ottoman military and political systems, with slavery in the European colonies of the New World, which forced Africans into lives of grueling, menial agricultural labor in most cases. Other forms of forced labor also demonstrate characteristics that contrast significantly with Ottoman slavery—for example, Russian serfdom, which tied peasant farmers to land they did not own.

Such calculated incorporation of outsiders into the Ottoman military was typical of an empire that was becoming a virtual mosaic of cultural influences. The court language, Osmanli, blended Turkish with Arabic and Persian; speaking this language was one mark of membership in the **askeri** (military and government bureaucrat) class, whose close ties with the sultan exempted them from paying taxes. The **raya** ("flock of sheep") was the name given to the rest of the population, which combined Muslims, Christians, and the Jews who fled to Ottoman territory following their expulsion from Spain in 1492. While Islam—and **Shari'a**, Islamic law—spread steadily into the urban areas of conquered territories in the Balkans, local customs and non-Muslim practices persisted as well, particularly in more rural areas. Most Ottoman subjects, in fact, were influenced more by local officials and religious leaders than by imperial administrators, who were usually Turkish cavalrymen given land grants by the sultan. These provincial officials collected taxes from their subjects and provided order in the region when not off on military campaigns in the summer, but otherwise they maintained a fairly limited involvement in the day-to-day activities of the raya.

URBAN LIFE DURING THE EMPIRE'S PEAK

Istanbul, the Ottoman capital, was also a major crossroads, bridging the European and Asian components of the empire, and it rivaled other major port cities of the time in size, wealth, and cosmopolitan character. The city itself was hilly and crowded, with a mazelike network of narrow streets centered on a busy harbor where Jewish, Hindu, and Christian merchants from Europe and Asia carried out their trading. Dominating the city's skyline was the former Byzantine cathedral Hagia Sophia, converted to a mosque and renamed Aya Sofya after the Ottoman conquest of Constantinople in 1453.

While male citizens frequented the shops and markets run by the guilds of merchants and artisans, most Ottoman women spent their days confined to the **harem**, or "forbidden area," of their homes. Despite such restrictions, women in the Ottoman Empire wielded great influence. Wives were joined in the harem by children, female servants, and in some cases eunuchs (castrated male servants). In addition to running the household, some Ottoman women, taking advantage of the fact that Islamic law allowed females to retain their property after marriage, involved themselves in managing inheritances from their fathers and buying and selling real estate. Because Muslim court systems did not include attorneys, women were also permitted to appear in court and testify on their own behalf on legal matters.

Much of the tone of Ottoman life was set by **fatwas**, or legal opinions issued by urban religious scholars known as **muftis**. A mufti's interpretations of Shari'a theoretically overruled any conflicting policies issued by the sultan, but in practice the muftis seemed to tailor their opinions to match the views of the sultan, who had appointed them. The fatwas demonstrated not only the religious motivation behind matters as mundane as the ban on drinking coffee, but also the Ottoman justification for military campaigns intended to annex territory the empire considered to be under the control of "infidels."

MILITARY REFORMS BRING CRISIS

Such military campaigns gradually became more taxing for the empire to carry out. As the use of gunpowder expanded throughout Asia and Europe, the Ottoman military increased its reliance on the Janissary corps. At the same time, the number of landholding cavalrymen was reduced in order to balance the military budget. The late sixteenth century then saw a period of inflation caused by the influx of New World silver into the economy, which hampered the ability of many of the remaining landholding elites to collect taxes and purchase their military supplies. The sultan's government took this opportunity to further reduce the cavalry, reclaim their lands, expand the Janissary corps, and hire temporary soldiers—but in order to fund such military expansion, emergency taxes were levied on much of the population.

By 1590, a crisis had developed; displaced landholders, unemployed temporary soldiers, peasants overwhelmed by taxes, and other frustrated citizens joined together in periodic revolts throughout Anatolia and other parts of the empire. The Janissaries emerged from this period with increased leverage, demanding the right to pass corps membership along to their sons. The devshirme system (along with its thorough training) was thus abolished, the size of the corps grew steadily, and the Janissaries' superior military skills began to deteriorate. As a result, Ottoman officials of the early seventeenth century faced serious challenges in maintaining the strength and unity of their empire.

OTTOMAN DECLINE BEGINS

During this period of crisis, one official response had been to confine the sultan's male relatives to the palace in Istanbul to thwart any possible coup attempts. Such confinement bred a new type of Ottoman sultan, no longer a military leader in touch with all corners of his empire, but rather a figurehead remote from involvement in the day-to-day activities of running the government. Grand viziers, or chief administrators, took over the duties of maintaining control in an increasingly fractured empire by the early 1600s. For example, the old system of land grants for high-ranking cavalrymen was finally phased out entirely, replaced with a new program of tax farming that allowed absentee landlords to profit from the taxes they levied on individual farmers, who often resented the arrangement. The sultan was thus forced to shift some of his power to provincial governors to maintain order in many rural areas. Meanwhile, the Janissaries continued to exercise their newfound influence to gain the right to participate in manufacturing and trade activities, further weakening their military skills. Such interest in commerce reflected the global changes of the era, and parts of the empire saw great transformation. Port cities such as Izmir (known in Europe as Smyrna) experienced rapid population growth, in part because of the influx of migrants seeking refuge from the upheaval in other parts of the empire, along with the arrival of European merchants and settlers of Armenian, Greek, and Jewish background. By the late 1500s, the region comprising western Anatolia, the Balkans, and the Mediterranean coast became a key component in the growing world trade network, as farmers there switched from growing grain for subsistence to producing cash crops such as cotton and tobacco.

Tobacco, in fact, was prohibited by the imperial government; its continued cultivation and trade were indicative of the growing weakness of the sultan's central bureaucracy. By the 1700s, European traders had forced the Ottomans to grant them capitulations, or special trade agreements with low duties and fees, in their largely successful quest to dominate the Indian Ocean trade network. The Ottoman economy thus was becoming more and more dependent on Europe at a time when the once-great Ottoman military was steadily weakening—more and more of the Janissaries lacked necessary training, and many of them began sending substitutes on seasonal campaigns. The sultans turned to the provincial governors for assistance in raising temporary armies, yet another step toward a shift in power away from the central government. As the sultan's inner circle in Istanbul distracted itself by throwing lavish parties and indulging in a craze for growing outlandishly expensive tulips, provincial governors, wealthy landowners, and others took advantage of the opportunity to seize power for themselves. As a result, various groups came to wrest control—practical if not official—of different parts of the empire from the sultan: mamluks in Egypt, Janissaries in Baghdad, conservative Sunni Muslims in Arabia. In 1730, the power struggle came to Istanbul itself when a conservative Janissary revolt forced Sultan Ahmed III to abdicate. The rebellion itself was short-lived—imperial power was restored after several months—but the fact that the Ottoman Empire had slipped into serious disarray could no longer be ignored.

THE SAFAVIDS OF IRAN

Following the death of Timur in 1405, several tribal chiefs and military leaders battled for dominance in Central and western Asia. In Iran, the eventual victor was **Ismail,** a young boy who was heir to the leadership of a Sufi brotherhood known as the Safaviya; he declared himself shah of Iran in 1502 and ordered that Shi'ite Islam would be the religion of the realm. A tumultuous century of war and persecution followed, as many Iranians resisted abandoning their Sunni beliefs. By the early 1600s, however, Iran had been transformed into a land that was majority Shi'ite, surrounded by Sunni neighbors. Its isolation was heightened by cultural differences as well—centuries of scholarship and writing in Persian rather than Arabic had produced a distinctive Iranian library of legal and theological texts; epic, lyric, and mystic poems; historical volumes; and drama and fiction. Other unique aspects of Safavid society were shaped by mystical **Sufi** traditions and rituals that merged with militant politics aimed at spreading Islam, by force if necessary.

AN INLAND EMPIRE

Under the reign of Shah Abbas I, who ruled from 1587 to 1629, **Isfahan** became the capital of Iran. Located near the center of the realm to give the shah ready access to any frontiers under attack, Isfahan had an economy founded on the trade of silk fabrics and intricately designed wool carpets, facilitated by its location in the centuries-old zone of transport by camel caravan. In many aspects, Isfahan resembled the Ottoman capital of Istanbul: small, crowded streets; houses with interior courtyards and separate women's quarters (known as **anderun,** or "interior," in Iran); a main bazaar filled with the guild-run shops of artisans and merchants. Its citizens even shared similar styles of dress, with women veiling themselves outside the home, and both sexes covering their hair (scarves for women, turbans for men) and wearing flowing dresses or caftans to conceal their arms and legs. Unlike Istanbul, though, Isfahan could not be described as truly cosmopolitan—colonies of Jews, Hindus, and Armenian Christians were involved in trade ventures, but lacking a harbor, Isfahan rarely received the variety of European, Middle Eastern, and Asian visitors and immigrants that Istanbul did, and its volume of trade was correspondingly lower as well.

> ## AP Tip
>
> The Ottoman harem and Safavid anderun exemplify the complex, sometimes bewildering role of women in Muslim societies: while women were largely sequestered from the outside world and confined to their separate household quarters, they were allowed to participate in certain business activities independent of their husbands and appear in court to attend to legal matters if necessary. In some ways, this is the direct opposite of the contemporaneous status of European women, who faced fewer restrictions on their participation in public activities but were usually forced to turn over any wages or inheritances to their fathers or husbands.

ECONOMIC CRISIS AND THE SAFAVID DOWNFALL

The manufacture and trade of rugs and silks did not provide Iran with a vital economy. Subsistence farming and herding occupied most of the shah's subjects, and nomadic groups known as **qizilbash** ("red-heads," because of their red turbans) were given large sections of land by the shah in exchange for providing mounted soldiers for the military. The chieftains of these groups did not subdivide the land to promote agricultural development, and they often ruled according to their own whims. Thus, the Safavid shah lacked both a solid economy and a firm rule over his territory.

In the late 1500s, pressure from Sunni neighbors such as the Ottomans and the Uzbeks of Central Asia drove Shah Abbas to create a corps of slave soldiers who agreed without resistance to employ modern firearms, unlike the nomadic warriors who insisted on fighting with traditional bows and arrows. Like the Ottoman Janissaries, this new corps (mostly former Christian converts to Islam who had been taken as prisoners of war from the Caucasus region) began to rival the nomadic chiefs for power in the Safavid political and military structure. Shah Abbas's less capable successors faced serious difficulty in keeping these factions under control.

These successors also lacked skill in managing the overland silk trade that had been contributing to the Safavid economy; at the same time, the global inflation caused by the influx of American silver into the world trade market brought on a crisis similar to that faced by the Ottoman Empire: finding the funding to maintain the military and the government. Attempts to force the nomads from their lands in order to increase tax revenues proved futile; the nomads still maintained military capabilities of their own and could successfully elude the shah's forces. Support for the regime dwindled rapidly, and in 1722 invading Afghans seized Isfahan and brought a fairly abrupt end to Safavid rule.

The expense of maintaining a military large and versatile enough to defend a land-based empire such as the Ottoman or Safavid was rapidly becoming untenable. Taxes from agricultural production would fail to generate the wealth necessary to compete with the growing economic might of the European powers. While cultural achievements in poetry, arts, and craft production remained a source of justifiable pride, the Muslim rulers of the Ottoman and Safavid Empires simply did not foresee the vast change that the world economy was about to undergo. Their centuries-old traditions of territorial conquest and expansion as a means of amassing—and displaying—power would become relics in the new era of sea-based trade empires that was set to begin.

Multiple-Choice Questions

1. How did the Ottoman Empire compare with other Islamic empires?
   (A) It was the first to clash with the Christian Byzantine Empire.
   (B) It rose much more slowly than any previous empire.
   (C) It was the largest Islamic empire since the Abbasid Caliphate.
   (D) It was the only Muslim empire to allow certain freedoms to followers of other faiths.

2. Why was Constantinople such a prize for the Ottomans?
   (A) Its capture signified the final eradication of Christianity in Ottoman territory.
   (B) Following their takeover of the city, the Ottomans were able to unite with the remnants of the Byzantine Empire.
   (C) The Ottomans' capture of the city prevented its takeover by their rivals, the Safavids of Iran, and ended further competition between the two powers.
   (D) Constantinople would allow Ottoman participation in the growing sea-based trade economy of the next several centuries.

3. Why did the devshirme system play such an important role in Ottoman military and political matters?
   (A) It created a loyal corps of commanders and advisers among the Ottoman Christian population.
   (B) It perpetuated the traditions of the Turkish archers who had helped to establish the empire.
   (C) It created a network for espionage activities in the eastern European holdings of the empire.
   (D) It enabled the development of a strong Ottoman navy that would transform the empire from land-based to sea-based.

4. What did the harem represent in Ottoman society?
   (A) The semi-isolation of Ottoman women from public life
   (B) The system of land grants given to Turkish cavalrymen by the sultan
   (C) The use of military slaves to fight with guns rather than traditional bows and arrows
   (D) The tax-exempt upper class of military and government officials

5. Which of the following was NOT a factor in the Ottoman crisis of the late sixteenth century?
   (A) The growing influence of the Janissary corps
   (B) The flood of New World silver into the global trade economy
   (C) The rise of the rival Mughal Empire of India
   (D) The sultan's decision to reclaim the land holdings of elite Turkish cavalrymen

6. What does the Ottoman passion for growing expensive tulips in the 1720s signify?
   (A) The growing detachment of the Ottoman sultan from unrest within the empire
   (B) An attempt to beautify Istanbul at the expense of taxpayers in rural areas
   (C) Ottoman interest in scientific advancement, including botany and horticulture
   (D) The efforts of Istanbul's elites to outdo their European rivals

7. Which of the following contributed the most to the unique character of Safavid Iran?
   (A) A religious and political mix of militant Shi'ite and mystical Sufi traditions.
   (B) A reliance on European Christian advisers in forming a strong central monarchy
   (C) A renunciation of all elements of Iran's Persian legacy
   (D) Strong diplomatic ties to both the Ottoman and Mughal Empires

8. What was the most significant feature of the Safavid capital of Isfahan?
   (A) Its complete isolation from the rest of the empire
   (B) Its use of European city-planning techniques
   (C) Its citizens' resistance to the spread of Shi'ite Islam
   (D) Its location at the center of the empire

9. Which of the following served as the foundation of the economy of the Safavid Empire?
   (A) Exports of cash crops such as cotton
   (B) The manufacture and trade of textiles and firearms
   (C) Subsistence farming and herding
   (D) Taxes on trade in the empire's ports on the Arabian Sea

10. What brought about the end of the Safavid Empire?
    (A) A lack of support for the shah's central government
    (B) An agricultural crisis leading to economic collapse
    (C) Civil war between rival Shi'ite and Sunni factions
    (D) A voluntary merger with the growing Mughal Empire

11. The Venetians and Ottomans battled for two centuries because
    (A) the Crusades proved very profitable for the Venetian city-state.
    (B) the Muslim Ottomans and the Christian Venetians were natural enemies.
    (C) Venice saw itself as the natural protector of the Byzantine Empire.
    (D) trade through the Mediterranean was lucrative, and both regions wanted control.

12. The raya of the Ottoman Empire was known as the "flock of sheep" because it
    (A) referred to the Christian majority.
    (B) referred to tax-paying citizens of Jewish descent.
    (C) included the Muslim, Christian, and Jewish tax-paying population of the Ottoman Empire.
    (D) was composed of members of the military upper class.

13. Why did cheap silver cause such a crisis in the Ottoman Empire?
    (A) Europeans suddenly had more buying power than comparable Ottoman subjects. This caused inflation.
    (B) Peasants were given cheap silver, which they used to buy muskets.
    (C) Religious schools spent much of the cheap silver on missionary work.
    (D) The Janissaries lost power as the landowners and cavalry gained power.

14. The major religious difference between the Ottomans and the Safavids was that
    (A) the Ottomans were Muslim while the Safavids were Nestorian.
    (B) the Ottomans were Sunni while the Safavids were Shi'ia.
    (C) the Ottomans had a large number of non-Muslim subjects while the Safavids were completely homogenous.
    (D) religion was imposed from the sultan in the Ottoman Empire, but each person had freedom of religion in the Safavid Empire.

15. Isfahan and Istanbul were similar in that both
    (A) were capitals of empires.
    (B) allowed for a public role for upper-class women.
    (C) were located in rather hilly areas.
    (D) were located on important bodies of water.

Free-Response Questions

1. Compare the impact of the global inflation of the late sixteenth century on the Ottoman and Safavid Empires.

2. Describe the continuities and changes in the political structure of the Middle East from circa 1450 to circa 1750.

Answers

MULTIPLE-CHOICE QUESTIONS

1. **ANSWER: C.** Previous Islamic empires had stretched around the Mediterranean as far as southern Spain, and the Crusades were fought by Roman Catholic and Byzantine Christians to recapture the Holy Land from Muslim control. The Ottoman Empire rose very quickly, in part because of policies of religious tolerance comparable to those practiced in the Mughal Empire of India, and soon became the largest Muslim empire in centuries, stretching around the eastern Mediterranean to encompass parts of the Middle East, North Africa, and eastern Europe (*The Earth and Its Peoples*, 5th ed., pp. 547–548/6th ed., p. 524).

2. **ANSWER: D.** As a link between the Mediterranean and Black Seas, Constantinople (or Istanbul, as the Ottomans renamed it) was a vital connection between Europe and Asia in the growing global trade network of the sixteenth century onward (*The Earth and Its Peoples*, 5th ed., pp. 548, 558–560/6th ed., pp. 524, 534–536).

3. **ANSWER: A.** The prestigious devshirme system took young Christian boys from Ottoman-controlled territories (mainly in the Balkan region of eastern Europe) and trained them for military and government service from a young age onward. The Ottoman sultan thus had a valuable link to the empire's sizable Christian population, who were otherwise allowed to continue their own religious practices (*The Earth and Its Peoples*, 5th ed., pp. 548, 551/6th ed., pp. 524, 527).

4. **ANSWER: A.** While Ottoman women were mostly forbidden from appearing in public, the harem, or "forbidden area," of their home saw much activity, including female participation in business activities, through male intermediaries (*The Earth and Its Peoples*, 5th ed., p. 559/6th ed., p. 535).

5. **ANSWER: C.** The global inflation of the late 1500s, caused by the influx of silver mined in the New World territories of Spain and Portugal, had a devastating effect on the Ottoman Empire, particularly its military structure—starting a period of internal revolt and decline in Ottoman military superiority. The rise of the Mughal Empire, although concurrent, had no effect of note on the

Ottomans (*The Earth and Its Peoples,* 5th ed., pp. 551, 554–555/6th ed., pp. 527, 530–531).

6. ANSWER: **A.** The early 1700s saw an Ottoman sultan far removed from, even unaware of, events in outlying territories of his realm. Instead, he and his inner circle busied themselves with growing high-priced tulips and throwing lavish parties in Istanbul while unrest grew in other parts of the empire (*The Earth and Its Peoples,* 5th ed., pp. 555, 557/6th ed., p. 531).

7. ANSWER: **A.** Safavid founder Ismail insisted on establishing Shi'ite Islam as the dominant religion of his empire, while also respecting the traditions of his Sufi ancestry. This combination isolated the Safavid Empire from its Sunni neighbors (*The Earth and Its Peoples,* 5th ed., p. 557/6th ed., pp. 532–533).

8. ANSWER: **D.** Although home to a small number of Jews, Hindus, and Christians, and superficially similar in character to Istanbul, Isfahan's inland location marks Safavid Iran as a true land-based empire in an era when the sea-based empires of Europe were rising to dominance in global economics and politics (*The Earth and Its Peoples,* 5th ed., p. 560/6th ed., p. 535).

9. ANSWER: **C.** Nearly all of the empire's citizens were farmers or herders; the Safavids' failure to modernize their economy would contribute to their eventual downfall (*The Earth and Its Peoples,* 5th ed., pp. 560–561/6th ed., p. 536).

10. ANSWER: **A.** Global inflation in the late sixteenth century led the Safavid shah to pursue unpopular policies of taxation and military reorganization. The leaders of various nomadic groups within the empire refused to heed the shah's dictates and withdrew to their homelands, weakening the influence of the central government and enabling a band of Afghans to take control of the capital and end the Safavid rule of Iran (*The Earth and Its Peoples,* 5th ed., pp. 560–561/6th ed., p. 536).

11. ANSWER: **D.** The Venetians battled the Ottomans over control of the Mediterranean Sea trade. Venice lost and eventually had to pay tribute to the Ottomans in exchange for continued trading rights (*The Earth and Its Peoples,* 5th ed., p. 548/6th ed., p. 524).

12. ANSWER: **C.** The raya is the majority of the population of the Ottoman Empire (*The Earth and Its Peoples,* 5th ed., p. 551/6th ed., p. 527).

13. ANSWER: **A.** Cheap silver caused inflation and forced taxes to increase, which led to riots among the peasants, landowners, temporary cavalrymen, and religious students (*The Earth and Its Peoples,* 5th ed., p. 551/6th ed., p. 527).

14. ANSWER: **B.** The biggest difference between the two empires is that the Ottomans were Sunni and the Safavids were Shi'ia. This split along the border between modern day Iran and Iraq continues to this day (*The Earth and Its Peoples,* 5th ed., pp. 557–558/6th ed., pp. 532–533).

15. **ANSWER: A.** Both cities served as the capital of their respective empires. Istanbul was located on seven hills on the coast, while Isfahan was located in the desert. Shah Abbas deliberately located Isfahan in the center of his empire, whereas Istanbul was located along the water for trade purposes (*The Earth and Its Peoples*, 5th ed., pp. 558–559/6th ed., pp. 534–535).

FREE-RESPONSE QUESTIONS

1. A good response to this comparative question would note that, overall, the influx of silver from Spain's New World colonies into the world economy had a very similar impact in the Ottoman and Safavid Empires of the Middle East. In both territories, the inflationary crisis came at a time of transition, when the rising sea-based empires of Europe began to wield power that the Middle Eastern Muslims found threatening. In response, the Ottomans and Safavids attempted to reform their militaries, which necessitated far-ranging changes in their social and economic structures as well—reducing the power of the traditional landholding cavalrymen, boosting the numbers of foot soldiers using guns and other modern weapons and tactics, and levying new taxes to fund their militaries and imperial governments. However, the internal unrest fostered by these changes played out differently in the two empires: the Safavid Empire was torn apart fairly abruptly by the resistance of nomadic chieftains followed by the overthrow of the shah by a group of Afghans; the Ottoman Empire remained nominally intact until the twentieth century, but it was forced to grant more and more autonomy to various religious and ethnic groups within its borders.

2. Change over time in the Middle East during this period begins with the death of Timur, whose forces had interrupted the consolidation of the Ottoman Empire. By the mid-1400s, the Ottomans had eliminated the once-mighty Byzantine Empire by capturing its capital of Constantinople, and they continued to add territory around the Mediterranean to their domain for decades to come. Meanwhile, to the east, Timur's death spurred a battle for power among a number of would-be successors; a young Sufi leader named Ismail emerged to establish himself as shah of Iran in 1502. Unlike the Ottomans, the Safavids of Iran battled not to expand beyond their territorial boundaries, but to establish militant Shi'ism as the religion of the realm. The Safavid Empire endured as a regional rival to the larger Ottoman Empire until the mid-1700s, when an economic crisis led to an overthrow of the shah and a period of instability in Iran that would last until the twentieth century. Both the Ottoman Empire and Iran would face growing challenges for control of their territory by the rising powers of Europe as this period came to an end. One continuity of note during this period is the influence of Islam as a source of law and unity in both the Ottoman and Safavid Empires; while the Sunni Ottomans and Shi'ite Safavids were sworn enemies, the leaders of both followed the Shari'a and interpretive fatwas issued by ulama (Muslim scholars) in governing their lands.

13

ASIA: CIRCA 1450 TO CIRCA 1750

KEY CONCEPTS

- In China, the return of indigenous rule following the Mongol conquest brought about a resurgence of traditional Chinese social, political, and economic practices. However, without the unifying Mongol presence, China retreated from contact with lands to the east and west during the Ming Empire.
- Following the Ming Empire's collapse, the Manchu-ruled Qing Empire expanded China's borders while continuing careful regulation of outside trade and other influences.
- The Tokugawa Shogunate, which emerged after a long period of civil war in Japan, centralized authority over the entire archipelago; like China's emperors, Japan's shoguns maintained strict control over contact with European merchants and missionaries to minimize destabilizing influences in their society.
- While Islam continued to spread around the Indian Ocean, the age of Muslim-dominated trade in the region gave way to European control, with Portuguese, Dutch, British, and French commercial ventures laying the foundation for a coming era of colonial domination.
- On the Indian subcontinent, the Mughal Empire emerged. Under its greatest ruler, Akbar, policies of religious toleration supported the empire's expansion, but his successors would fail to maintain the centralized authority necessary to withstand European involvement in India.

KEY TERMS

- Canton system
- daimyo

214

■ Dutch East India Company
■ Jesuit
■ kabuki theater
■ Little Ice Age
■ Manchu
■ Rajputs
■ samurai
■ shogun
■ Sikhs

Asia in this period is discussed in depth in *The Earth and Its Peoples*, fifth and sixth editions, Chapters 12, 19, and 20.

CHINA DURING THE MING EMPIRE

Shortly after seizing power and ending the Mongol-ruled Yuan Empire in 1368, the first Ming emperor, Hongwu, moved to isolate China from outside influence and shake off the "foreign" practices of the Mongols. These extreme reactionary policies did not stand very long. Hongwu's successor, Yongle, revived the Yuan provincial government structure, hereditary professions, and the use of the Mongols' Muslim calendar and moved the capital back to Beijing. There, Yongle expanded the Forbidden City begun under Khubilai Khan.

But the Ming Empire retreated from any plans of expansion or increased global contact following Yongle's death in 1424, when China faced growing pressure to defend its borders against Japanese pirate attacks from the east and Mongol raids in the north and west. In fact, the Ming Empire entered a period of stagnation or even decline by the mid-1400s, with shrinking agricultural yields, a lack of innovation in bronze and steel weapons production, and few steps forward in shipbuilding and printing. The return to Confucianism—and its civil-service examination system—begun by Hongwu attracted the most talented young Chinese men to intensive scholarship, pulling them away from commercial ventures. Meanwhile, the pressures of feeding a growing population forced many farmers to focus on staple crops such as wheat and rice; this also reduced the commercial progress associated with crops such as cotton, which had stimulated earlier economic and technological growth in related areas. Population pressures were particularly acute in southern and central China, where heavy deforestation occurred as more and more fields were cleared for growing crops.

The need to defend China's borders led Ming officials to restrict access to technology they feared would get into enemy hands. This had the converse effect of actually stimulating new steelmaking processes in Japan, while Korea emerged as a regional leader in printing, shipbuilding, firearms production, weather prediction, and calendar making. Nevertheless, the bustling cities of Ming China continued to produce masterpieces of literature, opera, poetry, painting, and other artistic pursuits. Novels such as *Romance of the Three Kingdoms* reflected the resurgent Chinese national pride following the overthrow of Mongol rule. A similar source of pride was the strong demand for Ming products such as furniture, silk, and especially blue-and-white "Ming ware" porcelain throughout Asia,

India, the Middle East, and East Africa. By the mid-1500s, Ming China was awash in silver from Japan and the Spanish and Portuguese colonies in Latin America, thanks to its high volume of exports. This fueled rapid economic expansion as the Ming Empire progressed, but the government's poor monetary policies, along with corruption and mismanagement in the huge government-run ceramics factories, led to inflation and strikes in China's urban areas. Meanwhile, the **Little Ice Age** of the seventeenth century, along with epidemics of disease and stagnant agricultural productivity, led to unrest in the countryside.

THE QING EMPIRE EMERGES

By the late 1500s, the Ming Empire faced both serious internal disorder and a number of external threats. In the southeast, repeated raids by Japanese pirates led many Chinese to migrate to Southeast Asia, where they found opportunities to participate in the growing Indian Ocean trade network. To the north, the Mongols, bonded by their Tibetan Buddhism faith, retained a firm hold on their homeland; Mongolia regained its status as a regional military power by 1600 and competed with China for control of territory along their mutual border. Meanwhile, a group known as the **Manchu** was consolidating power in its homeland northwest of Korea and would soon emerge as a dominant force in the region. For Ming China, a crisis developed in 1592 when the Japanese warlord Hideyoshi attacked Korea, then advanced through Manchuria and into China with a force of 160,000 men. The resulting upheaval created an opportunity for the Manchu, who first allied with Ming troops but then—after Hideyoshi's death in 1598 and the subsequent Japanese withdrawal—proceeded to conquer Korea and set their sights on China itself.

The cost of defending the empire through this period created a severe economic crisis in China; internal rebellions erupted by the 1630s, and a rebel army captured Beijing in 1644. The Ming emperor hanged himself, and in desperation a Ming general turned to the Manchu for aid in retaking the capital. They did so, but instead of returning control of the empire to Ming officials, the Manchu held on to Beijing and soon established an empire of their own—the Qing—capturing all of China, the island of Taiwan, and even parts of Mongolia and Central Asia.

The Manchu-ruled Qing Empire would retain control of the Chinese government and military until the twentieth century, but most bureaucratic officials, soldiers, merchants, and farmers were ethnic Chinese. As a small minority ruling China, Manchu leaders quickly realized that they would have to adopt many of the practices, customs, and institutions of the land they had conquered. At the same time, an ever-growing European interest in Asian trade brought additional influences into the region.

TRADE AND EXPANSION IN THE MING AND QING ERAS

Ming rulers initially were cautious about regulating contact with European voyagers, who were drawn to China in the sixteenth century by the promise of trade and access to technological information. The

Portuguese and Spanish were forced to establish trade outposts in Macao and the Philippines, respectively, thus limiting the volume of commerce they could conduct with the empire. The Dutch, through the Dutch East India Company, were somewhat more successful in gaining the trust of imperial officials, as the company's representatives were willing to perform the rituals of respect and submission asked of them by the emperor himself. The **Dutch East India Company** came to dominate European trade with East Asia for nearly a century. Meanwhile, the Spanish and Portuguese traders who did gain access to China were accompanied by Catholic missionaries; by sharing European scientific and technological advances, **Jesuit** missionaries in particular were able to gain more and more status in the late Ming and early Qing periods. In fact, when the Qing emperor Kangxi, who ruled from 1662 to 1722, contracted malaria in the 1690s, quinine supplied by the Jesuits helped to bring about his recovery—and bolstered the status of Christianity among imperial officials in China at that time.

Kangxi recruited Jesuit advisers to fill key positions in the imperial government; among their duties was the creation of European-style maps of the newly conquered territories of the Qing Empire. Kangxi's Qing predecessors had pursued the restoration of internal order and progress following the chaotic end of the Ming Empire by repairing infrastructure; lowering taxes, rents, and interest rates; and resettling areas disturbed during the peasant rebellions. Upon assuming control of the empire at the age of sixteen, Kangxi found China entering an age of remarkable peace and prosperity, which allowed him to focus much of his attention on continued expansion. China's northern border remained an area of concern, with both the Russians and the Mongols vying for control in the Amur River region. Following several clashes, Russia and the Qing Empire (with the help of Jesuit interpreters) signed the Treaty of Nerchinsk in 1689, which established a firm border and regulated trade between the two empires. Turning his attention to Mongolia, Kangxi himself led troops in defeating the Mongol leader Galdan, adding Inner Mongolia to the Qing Empire in 1691.

To maintain continued economic growth through this period of territorial expansion, the Qing happily accepted European silver in exchange for Chinese silk, porcelain, tea, jewelry, and furniture, while continuing to restrict European trade to the port of Canton and placing severe restrictions on the import of European goods. By the late 1700s, however, the British (having displaced the Dutch East India Company as China's dominant trade partner) faced an enormous deficit. Hoping to create a market among China's enormous population and thus restore a balance of trade, Britain would soon lead the other European powers in forcing an end to the Qing Empire's "**Canton system**" of restricting international commerce. The late eighteenth and nineteenth centuries would bring an end to the era of remarkable growth, wealth, and peace of the early Qing era.

Throughout this period, Confucianism endured as the basis of China's social, political, and economic systems. Having previously spread beyond China's borders, Confucian values could also be found throughout much of East Asia during this time. The arrival of European merchants and Christian missionaries, however, forced leaders, particularly in China and Japan, to reevaluate the low status of merchants—by tradition, agriculture was the basis of Confucianism in China—and to decide whether to allow Christian beliefs as an alternative to Confucianism in their empires. An understanding of Confucianism's impact on various Asian societies can be valuable for answering multiple-choice questions or writing free-response essays.

JAPAN: CHAOS AND CONTROL

Following the failure of the Mongol invasion and the rise of the Ashikaga Shogunate in 1338, Japan entered a period of decentralized feudalism that lasted for well over two centuries. Elite warlords known as **daimyo**—perhaps forgetting the precepts of peace and simplicity of their Zen Buddhist faith—began competing for territory and power. They soon destroyed themselves, the city of Kyoto, and any real authority the Ashikaga Shogunate may once have had. (Japan's emperor also remained merely a figurehead, the symbolic leader of the native Shinto religion.) New warlords emerged, often basing their wealth on partnerships with local merchants, who traded raw materials, folding fans, and swords for Chinese books and porcelain. Some warlords also affiliated themselves with pirates who plundered trade ships headed to and from China. By the late 1500s, rivalries among the daimyo and their armies of warriors, known as **samurai**, had heated into a civil war. The conflict was resolved only gradually as the most powerful warlords expanded their territorial control to unite the various islands of the Japanese archipelago. Ultimately, one warlord, Hideyoshi, rose above the rest, even attempting to expand beyond Japan and into Korea, Manchuria, and China. Hideyoshi died in 1598, and his successors chose to withdraw their forces from the Asian mainland and focus their energies on stabilizing and centralizing the Japanese government.

The warlord who accomplished this task was Tokugawa Ieyasu, who assumed the title of **shogun**, or supreme military leader, in 1603. The Tokugawa Shogunate, in power until the nineteenth century, saw Japan through that era by balancing the central authority of the shogun with the regional autonomy of the daimyo. The Tokugawa shoguns maintained their power largely through fostering significant economic growth in Japan—they established an administrative capital at Edo (present-day Tokyo) and linked it to the imperial capital of Kyoto with a road that became a key route in the rice trade that sustained the Japanese economy. By 1700, Edo's population had grown to nearly one million, and Japan's urban centers saw major progress in manufacturing and trade, particularly in steel making, pottery, lacquer, and porcelain.

JAPANESE ISOLATION DEVELOPS

The Portuguese first arrived in Japan in 1543. The firearms they brought with them were studied with great interest, and by the 1570s Japanese-made copies were in the hands of the daimyo fighting for control in the civil war. Trade with the Portuguese, Spanish, and Dutch was carefully controlled once the Tokugawa Shogunate assumed power. Porcelain was Japan's chief export, and few European-made goods were of interest to the Japanese.

Christianity, however, was received with great interest by many Japanese, who learned of the religion from the Jesuit missionaries who accompanied the European traders. By the early 1600s three hundred thousand Christian converts were spread throughout Japan. Fear of a destabilizing foreign influence motivated the shogun to issue an edict forbidding the practice of Christianity in 1614. The threat of harsh punishments—including crucifixion and beheading—for those who disobeyed the edict brought an end to the religion's practice as the century progressed. In fact, the government began forcing citizens to acquire certificates from their temples as proof of their adherence to Buddhism and their obedience to the shogunate.

Strict new cutbacks on trade accompanied the Japanese elimination of Christianity. All Europeans except the Dutch were forbidden from trading in Japan in the 1630s; Chinese trade was also curtailed sharply, although some daimyo in remote northern and southern regions ignored official policy and encouraged piracy and trade to promote economic growth in their territories. By the 1700s, it was in these provinces, far from central Japan, where economic progress and innovation were at their highest.

In central Japan, near the imperial and administrative capitals, rapid population growth and economic imbalance began to create problems for the Tokugawa government. In a period of relative peace and centralization, many of the daimyo and especially the samurai found themselves with little function in a society that, despite Confucianism's veneration of agriculture, was moving rapidly toward a basis in manufacturing and trade. In Japan's urban centers, and even in more rural areas, a new merchant class was pushing the nation forward into a period of growth and cultural innovation, with new household conveniences, the rise of **kabuki theater**, artistic experimentation with woodblock prints and silk-screened fabrics, and the opening of new shops and restaurants. These merchants also provided lines of credit to the daimyo and samurai, whose fortunes, based largely on income from the production of rice, were steadily dwindling. As the eighteenth and nineteenth centuries progressed, the Tokugawa Shogunate found itself in the difficult position of having to protect the traditional samurai values that had allowed its rise to power, while upholding the civil laws and policies necessary for continued stability and growth. Not until Westerners renewed their efforts to open the Japanese market to trade in the mid-nineteenth century would this stalemate of tradition versus progress be broken.

European Domination of Indian Ocean Trade

While their efforts to establish strong trading relationships with China and Japan met with heavy resistance, the Europeans were much more successful in establishing dominance over the Indian Ocean trade network, which had become the most lucrative in the world by the fifteenth century. Initially, of course, this network was controlled largely by Muslim traders, and their presence continued to grow even after European expansion into much of the region. Muslim communities all around the Indian Ocean, such as the Brunei Sultanate of Borneo and the Acheh Sultanate of Sumatra, expanded as many local non-Muslims joined the faith through intermarriage or to facilitate their participation in commercial activities. Muslims from Southeast Asia began making pilgrimages to Mecca, and their more scholarly understanding of the religion's orthodox practices resulted in the end of a series of women rulers in Acheh in the late 1600s. Shari'a, Muslim religious law, displaced adat, or custom, in most of the urban centers in the region. The growth of Islam also encouraged the spread of literacy around the Indian Ocean. The Muslims and Europeans would come to clash over trade and territory in Southeast Asia, and in some cases the Muslims prevailed—despite Spain's takeover of most of the Philippines starting in 1565, Muslims in the southern islands held out through several wars to establish the Sulu Empire there. Ultimately, though, the Europeans would transform the Indian Ocean region and its trade network in the centuries to come.

The Portuguese fleets took the lead in displacing many of the local rulers of the Indian Ocean's coastal city-states, establishing control of major trading routes from West Africa to East Asia in the 1500s. The valuable ports of Gujarat, Goa, and Calicut on western India's Malabar Coast fell to Portuguese control in the early part of the century. Malacca, on the Malay Peninsula in the eastern end of the ocean, was seized by a Portuguese force in 1511; this gateway between East Asia and India had become a major distribution center for goods from China, Japan, and India—as well as a cosmopolitan blend of various cultural influences—and was thus seen as a major prize for Portugal.

AP Tip

It is important to understand the impact of European technological developments on the Indian Ocean trade. The Portuguese took control of the network from Muslim traders because of the Portuguese pursuit of new techniques in shipbuilding, navigation, and the use of firearms. Ironically, many of these innovations were adapted from earlier Muslim technologies that the Portuguese first encountered in the Mediterranean. Two important AP World History themes—the effects of technology and cultural interactions among societies—are at work here.

Having linked the major port cities of the Indian Ocean, the Portuguese were able to establish a trading monopoly on spices and other goods transported on their routes between Goa and Macao (their outpost in southern China) by forcing merchants to ship their goods on Portuguese vessels. Also, any foreign merchant ships using one of their ports had to maintain a Portuguese license and pay customs fees. Traders and local officials who attempted to defy Portuguese authority faced serious consequences—confiscated cargoes, crews enslaved or put to death, and local economies devastated. Those who agreed to Portuguese terms continued to prosper from the growing European demand for luxury goods from China, Japan, India, and Africa.

Eventually, the Portuguese domination of the Indian Ocean trade was challenged by other European powers. The Dutch, with their well-organized, privately owned Dutch East India Company, finally displaced the Portuguese stronghold in the region by capturing Malacca in 1641. The Dutch also consolidated power by fighting a number of wars against Acheh and other kingdoms, establishing a regional capital at Batavia (now Jakarta) on the island of Java. British, French, Portuguese, and Spanish competition continued, though, as those nations developed their own trading links to Southeast Asia throughout this period. Thus, during the eighteenth century, Dutch economic activity in the region was transformed from the shipping and trade of foreign-produced goods to the production and sale of crops—such as coffee and teak—in the territory they had conquered. It was in essence a transition to true colonial rule, which would set an example for Britain and other European countries in the region during the late eighteenth and nineteenth centuries.

THE MUGHAL EMPIRE OF INDIA

While the Europeans were attempting to gain control of the Indian Ocean, a different group—the Mughals—began establishing their authority over the Indian subcontinent, where centralized rule had not been seen for nearly a thousand years. The Timurids had gravely weakened the Delhi Sultanate of northern India in the late 1300s. A Timurid, Babur, swept into India from Central Asia, displaced the last sultan of Delhi in 1526, founding the Mughal Empire. (While *Mughal* means *Mongol* in Persian, the Timurids, and hence Babur, were primarily of Turkic rather than Mongol descent.) However, it was Babur's grandson Akbar who would establish truly centralized rule over the growing empire. He and his three successors would unite all of India (save the southernmost tip) before the end of the seventeenth century.

Akbar maintained economic growth by trading cotton cloth with European merchants, and promoted cultural blending and innovation in the arts, but he demonstrated true genius in creating a well-organized central bureaucracy and strong military. The loyalty of these officials was ensured through the reward of lifetime (but nonhereditary) land grants. Akbar's greatest challenge was in dealing with various Hindu kings, who resented centuries of Muslim domination of their homeland. By incorporating **Rajputs**, Hindu warriors from the north, into the Mughal military and government,

Akbar set a tone of religious tolerance that largely freed him and his initial successors from enduring conflict with the Hindus. In fact, Akbar went on to create a new "Divine Faith" that mixed Muslim, Hindu, Christian, and other beliefs. Another, more enduring religion that blended Muslim and Hindu elements also emerged during the Mughal period: the **Sikhs**, of the Punjab region in northwest India, initially focused on the peaceful attainment of enlightenment, but transformed dramatically into a militant group opposing Mughal rule after Akbar's great-grandson Aurangzeb beheaded their guru for refusing to convert to Islam. Aurangzeb also broke the Mughal policy of religious tolerance by imposing a number of limitations on Hindu rights in the late 1600s. As the 1700s began, the Mughals faced challenges to their authority from both the Sikhs and the now-resentful Hindus. This internal strife combined with the invasion of Nadir Shah of Iran to bring an end to centralized Mughal rule in 1739. The empire disintegrated into a number of regional powers, just as the French, Dutch, and British began turning their attention away from the coastal Indian Ocean trade to seek new opportunities on the subcontinent itself.

Multiple-Choice Questions

1. Which of the following is NOT a reflection of Hongwu's embrace of nativism in China?
   (A) He revived the Confucian civil-service examination system.
   (B) He limited imports and foreign visitors.
   (C) He established a decentralized provincial government.
   (D) He moved China away from the use of paper currency.

2. Which of the following was NOT a contributing factor in the fall of the Ming Empire in China?
   (A) Climate changes
   (B) Disease epidemics in the countryside
   (C) Reliance on European imports
   (D) Labor unrest in urban areas

3. How did the Ming and Qing Empires respond to the presence of Christian missionaries in China?
   (A) Christians were persecuted from the start and were never able to convert a significant segment of the Chinese population.
   (B) Certain missionaries were encouraged to share European advances in science and technology with imperial officials.
   (C) Christians in China attempted to eradicate ancestor worship and thus met with little interest from the Chinese population.
   (D) Ming officials unsuccessfully attempted to expel the Christians, who allied with the Manchus to help establish the Qing Empire.

4. What caused the period of civil war in Japan in the late 1500s?
   - (A) Rivalries among landowning daimyo hoping to gain more power and territory
   - (B) Disagreements among government officials over whether to allow trade with Europe
   - (C) The collapse of the Tokugawa Shogunate because of the destabilizing introduction of Christianity
   - (D) Runaway inflation from the trade of goods for European silver

5. How did the Chinese and Japanese responses to Christianity compare?
   - (A) Both Chinese and Japanese peasants embraced Christianity as a welcome alternative to the hierarchical nature of Confucianism.
   - (B) Chinese peasants rejected the religion while the Japanese emperor forced it on the lower classes.
   - (C) The influence of Christianity was limited to the Chinese and Japanese middle classes, introduced to the religion through merchants.
   - (D) Chinese elites welcomed Christian missionaries who accepted Confucian ancestor worship, but Japanese elites opposed Christianity's disruptive influence.

6. Which group faced the most significant challenges in maintaining its economic status in Tokugawa Japan?
   - (A) Shoguns
   - (B) Samurai
   - (C) Merchants
   - (D) Farmers

7. Which of the following is NOT a result of the growth of the Indian Ocean trade network in the fifteenth century?
   - (A) The spread of centralized rule into India
   - (B) Rising literacy rates in the region
   - (C) Increased conversion to Islam
   - (D) Cultural blending in trade centers such as Malacca

8. What is the significance of the rivalry among European nations for dominance of the Indian Ocean trade in the sixteenth, seventeenth, and eighteenth centuries?
   - (A) Warfare periodically broke out among the European powers for control of Indian Ocean islands.
   - (B) Price wars led to economic recession in most European countries.
   - (C) The Dutch, followed by other European powers, moved from controlling trade to the production of goods, setting the stage for a transition to colonial control in the region.
   - (D) Finding the conflict draining on its resources, Britain abandoned trade activity in Asia to concentrate on developing its North American colonies.

9. What key factor allowed Babur to establish the Mughal Empire in India?
   (A) He ascended the throne peacefully as a descendant of Timur.
   (B) He defeated the Delhi Sultanate after invading from Central Asia in 1526.
   (C) He first took control of the key port of Calicut, then used wealth gained from trade to develop a powerful army and take the rest of India.
   (D) He gained the military support of India's Hindu majority by promising rights and freedoms denied them by previous Muslim rulers in the region.

10. Which of the following is NOT an example of Akbar's genius in ruling the Mughal Empire?
   (A) He developed a large but well-organized government structure.
   (B) He built a strong military that incorporated Hindu warriors as well as Muslims.
   (C) He provided land grants to ensure the loyalty of government and military officials.
   (D) He encouraged the Sikhs to abandon their militant ways and focus on peaceful coexistence with India's other religious groups.

11. Islam spread throughout Southeast Asia through all of the following EXCEPT
   (A) Sufi missionaries.
   (B) merchants coming to Southeast Asia to trade.
   (C) intermarriage.
   (D) forced conversion through jihad.

12. The Dutch managed to wrestle Indian Ocean trade dominance from the Portuguese by
   (A) creating joint-stock companies which allowed for easier financing of economic expeditions.
   (B) missionaries taking positions in the local power structure that gave them control of supply.
   (C) developing new and secret navigation techniques that allowed them unrivaled domination for the next century.
   (D) creating well-armed castles from which they controlled the choke points off the island of Sumatra.

13. One method that the Tokugawa used to achieve Japanese unity was to
   (A) force commercial integration by having daimyos take rice to the capital.
   (B) officially facilitate sake and porcelain exchanges.
   (C) foster economic integration, which happened naturally as daimyos frequently moved to Edo and traded their rice allotment at rice exchanges there.
   (D) elevate merchants over samurai to neutralize the power of the daimyos.

14. The port of Nagasaki became the only area where
    (A) samurai could take refuge.
    (B) Japanese could learn about European innovations after the edicts forcing the expulsion of the Europeans.
    (C) daimyos had free rein.
    (D) the ronin could feel safe.

15. The Macartney mission tried to change the dynamics between the Qing and the British by
    (A) offering to buy tea, porcelain, and silk in exchange for silver.
    (B) willingly performing the kowtow in order to show that the British government was a tributary state to the Qing.
    (C) suggesting that the Russians, French, and Dutch share trading forts close to Beijing.
    (D) suggesting that new ports be opened and that goods other than silver be traded.

Free-Response Questions

1. Analyze the continuities and changes in the roles that Confucianism played in both the Ming and Qing Empires of China from circa 1450 until circa 1750.

2. Compare and contrast the methods used to consolidate political authority in TWO of the following empires during the period from circa 1450 to circa 1750.
   - Tokugawa Shogunate
   - Qing Empire
   - Mughal Empire

Answers

MULTIPLE-CHOICE QUESTIONS

1. ANSWER: C. Hongwu began the Ming Empire by establishing a highly centralized government, based on the Confucian principles that regarded the emperor as defender of the Chinese people and their values. However, later Ming officials returned to the less-centralized provincial government of the Mongol-ruled Yuan Empire (*The Earth and Its Peoples,* 5th ed., pp. 358–359/6th ed., pp. 336–337).

2. ANSWER: C. While experiencing various crises in both rural and urban areas and continued Mongol threats even after the collapse of Mongol rule, China during the late Ming Empire maintained a high volume of exports to Europe in exchange for silver currency but few imported goods (*The Earth and Its Peoples*, 5th ed., pp. 579–580/6th ed., pp. 560–562).

3. ANSWER: **B.** Christian missionaries (particularly Jesuits) gained the interest and trust of Chinese elites by sharing various European accomplishments in medicine, astronomy, and other areas (*The Earth and Its Peoples*, 5th ed., p. 581/6th ed., pp. 552–553).

4. ANSWER: **A.** Japan lacked unified rule from the twelfth through the sixteenth centuries, during which time powerful warlords known as daimyo emerged and began to consolidate their territories through armed conflict with one another (*The Earth and Its Peoples*, 5th ed., pp. 573–574/6th ed., pp. 551–552).

5. ANSWER: **D.** Having centralized its control over Japan only recently, the Tokugawa Shogunate took severe measures to maintain its authority, and banned the religion by decree in 1614 (*The Earth and Its Peoples*, 5th ed., pp. 576–578/6th ed., p. 554).

6. ANSWER: **B.** While merchants faced the official disapproval of Japan's Confucian-based society, they continued to profit from increased contact with the world trade network. Meanwhile, the samurai warriors faced a growing economic crisis as their traditional function declined in an era of centralization (*The Earth and Its Peoples*, 5th ed., pp. 578–579/6th ed., pp. 558–559).

7. ANSWER: **A.** Centralized rule in India had collapsed in the seventh century. It would reemerge as a result not of the Indian Ocean trade but of the successful establishment of the Mughal Empire by invaders from Central Asia in the 1500s (*The Earth and Its Peoples*, 5th ed., pp. 388–389, 561–564/6th ed., pp. 536-537).

8. ANSWER: **C.** Facing continued rivalry from the Spanish, Portuguese, and other European powers, the Dutch began transforming their holdings in Java into a lucrative source of teak, coffee, and other export crops in the eighteenth century (*The Earth and Its Peoples*, 5th ed., p. 567/6th ed., p. 545).

9. ANSWER: **B.** A descendant of Timur, Babur defeated the Delhi Sultanate at the Battle of Panipat in 1526, which allowed him to found the Mughal Empire (*The Earth and Its Peoples*, 5th ed., p. 561/6th ed., p. 536).

10. ANSWER: **D.** The Sikhs had emerged shortly before Akbar's reign began. They initially devoted themselves to the attainment of enlightenment through a blend of Muslim and Hindu practices. Akbar's great-grandson Aurangzeb, however, attempted to force the Sikhs to convert to Islam, thus provoking their ire and pushing them into a much more militant stance (*The Earth and Its Peoples*, 5th ed., p. 562/6th ed., p. 537).

11. ANSWER: **D.** The religion of Islam spread in many ways, including contact with merchants, the Sufi missionary movement, the return of pilgrims from Mecca, and intermarriage between local women and Muslim traders. Forced conversion was not one of them (*The Earth and Its Peoples*, 5th ed., p. 392/6th ed., pp. 389–390).

12. ANSWER: **A.** The Dutch tried several methods, one of which was to neutralize Portuguese power by taking over their territories and

creating more efficient joint-stock companies (The *Earth and Its Peoples*, 5th ed., p. 469/6th ed., p. 446).

13. ANSWER: D. The Tokugawa Shogunate tried to facilitate the political integration of Japan, but the economic integration happened more quickly and more informally (*The Earth and Its Peoples*, 5th ed., p. 574/6th ed., p. 557).

14. ANSWER: B. Such learning took place on Nagasaki, the only port where interaction between Japanese and Europeans could take place (*The Earth and Its Peoples*, 5th ed., p. 578/6th ed., p. 555).

15. ANSWER: D. The British desperately wanted to change the Canton system, but the Qing, not understanding the relative power of the Europeans refused. This caused European admiration of the Chinese to fade (*The Earth and Its Peoples*, 5th ed., p. 585/6th ed., pp. 565–566).

FREE-RESPONSE QUESTIONS

1. This continuity and change over time essay first invites a discussion of the Ming ruler Hongwu's use of a return to Confucian values in reestablishing indigenous control in China following the Mongol rule of the Yuan dynasty. Because Confucianism stressed the value of agriculture as the basis of a strong society, commercial activity in the Ming Empire was somewhat hindered. On the other hand, pride in native Chinese styles in art and literature led to an era of great achievement in poetry, painting, and the production of blue-and-white Ming porcelain that became immensely popular in the Indian Ocean trade. Hongwu's successor, Yongle, broke with the isolationist aspects of Confucian tradition somewhat, reestablishing commercial links with the Middle East and sending the Muslim voyager Zheng He on several voyages of exploration to India, Arabia, and East Africa. When the Manchus invaded and established the Qing Empire, they recognized the enduring importance of Confucianism in Chinese society and realized that they must embrace its values in order to maintain minority rule over the Chinese people. Confucianism thus remained the basis of the Qing government's civil-service examination system. At the same time, however, persistent European merchants and missionaries started to bring outside commercial and religious influences that would begin to weaken the established dictates of Confucian society in China by the middle of the 1700s.

2. A good response to this comparison essay could note that the Qing and Mughal Empires were established with the forceful defeat of an earlier regime by outside invaders. In contrast, the Tokugawa Shogunate accomplished the unification of Japan from within when the Japanese shoguns centralized their authority. Other comparisons include the restrictions on the outside influence of European traders and missionaries by both the Tokugawa Shogunate and the Qing Empire. The Mughal Empire, meanwhile, found its greatest success, stability, and expansion under Akbar's reign, when policies of religious tolerance and inclusion allowed a Muslim minority to rule over a predominantly Hindu population.

The Manchu rulers of the Qing Empire adopted China's traditional Confucian beliefs as the basis of their government, a similar method of gaining support for minority rule. Tokugawa Japan found structure in Confucianism as well and, like the Qing rulers, struggled with the role merchants should be permitted to play in their society. Finally, leaders in all three empires gained legitimacy by providing improvements in infrastructure—building roads, bridges, canals, and other means of facilitating transportation and communication—thus fostering economic growth.

14

EUROPE: CIRCA 1450 TO CIRCA 1750

KEY CONCEPTS

- Following the Crusades and the Black Death, major changes began to sweep through Europe and bring about the end of the Middle Ages. Towns and cities revived, driven by a growing European interest in trade. This led to important economic changes that soon went hand in hand with an era of world exploration and colonization.
- The humanist worldview of the Renaissance continued to spread throughout Europe. The perfection of the printing press allowed for increasing literacy and a rapid exchange of ideas and technologies; the Scientific Revolution and the Enlightenment emerged as two major results.
- Numerous challenges to the power and influence of the Catholic Church also opened the door to new attitudes regarding science, politics, and society in general.
- Meanwhile, European monarchs began centralizing their authority to create absolutist regimes, which in some cases planted the seeds for their citizens to push for democratic reforms.

KEY TERMS

- Atlantic System
- bourgeoisie
- capitalism
- caravel
- Catholic Counter Reformation
- Columbian Exchange
- Enlightenment
- guild

- humanist
- indulgence
- joint-stock company
- mercantilism
- Middle Passage
- papacy
- printing press
- Protestant Reformation
- Renaissance
- Scientific Revolution
- serf
- stock exchange
- vernacular

Europe in the period from circa 1450 to circa 1750 is discussed in detail in *The Earth and Its Peoples*, fifth edition, Chapters 14, 15, 16, and 18 and sixth edition, Chapters 13, 15, 16, and 18.

THE END OF THE HUNDRED YEARS WAR AND THE RISE OF EUROPEAN MONARCHS

Several factors drove the changes Europe underwent as the Middle Ages came to a conclusion. The end of the Hundred Years War served as one catalyst for the steadily increasing power of the European monarchs between 1450 and 1750. This in turn allowed for increased European involvement in world exploration and colonization and for the beginnings of a European-dominated world economy. To finance the Hundred Years War (1337–1453), a conflict between the monarchs of England and France over control of the French throne, these monarchs were forced to levy taxes on their vassal subjects' landholdings and merchants' transactions. This had the important effect of elevating the power and status of the English and French monarchies while also nurturing a growing sense of "national" unity among their citizens. While generally supporting their kings in the war, these citizens also began to recognize the collective power of the representative institutions of Parliament in England and the Estates General in France. Throughout this period and beyond—particularly in France—as the monarchs wielded more and more authority, their subjects' sense of nationalist unity would grow at a similar pace. Eventually, these monarchs would be forced to limit their absolutism in favor of more democratic governments.

Meanwhile, other European territories also witnessed important steps toward unification. Spain as it exists geographically today came into being following the marriage of Isabella of Castile and Ferdinand of Aragon in 1469. This led to the merger of their respective kingdoms and the retaking of Granada from Muslim control in 1492. Ferdinand and Isabella, of course, would heighten the prestige of their new nation by financing the exploratory voyage of Christopher Columbus. And challenges to the authority of the Catholic Church led to the crumbling of the Holy Roman Empire, as German princes waged war against the empire beginning in 1546. This religious conflict gave the princes an opportunity to reclaim church-held lands in their territories; they also demanded—and won, via the Peace of Augsburg in 1555—the right to choose Catholicism or Lutheranism as the religion of their individual realms. A unified Germany would not emerge until the late nineteenth century, but the Peace of Augsburg was a key early step in the process toward a secular political authority in the region.

THE PROTESTANT REFORMATION, THE CATHOLIC COUNTER REFORMATION, AND EUROPEAN SOCIETY

While Christianity served as a major source of unity and hope for European peasants in the Middle Ages, most Roman Catholics were unaware of the growing abuses of power that church leaders were committing in Rome. For centuries the church had supported itself by collecting taxes from its members, renting out church-held lands for farming, and operating businesses such as breweries in its monasteries. Much of this income went toward maintaining the lavish lifestyles of the pope and other high church officials, many of whom had given their lives to church service not out of a sense of devotion to the faith but, rather, out of a desire for wealth and power. By the early 1500s, the church had created a showplace of **Renaissance** art and architecture in Rome, and Pope Leo X began using the sale of **indulgences**—forgiveness of punishment in purgatory for past sins in exchange for a financial donation to the church—to further support church projects. A young German monk, Martin Luther, spoke out against such actions as contrary to the Christian idea of atoning for one's sins through true faith, not unfeeling action. He held that Christianity should involve a true belief in God's word rather than a blind following of church doctrine or **papal** edicts. After posting a stinging protest, known as the 95 Theses, against the sale of indulgences, Luther was excommunicated by the Catholic Church in 1521, and subsequently broke away from the church entirely. His actions paved the way for other reformers such as John Calvin in France and John Knox in Scotland to join in what became known as the **Protestant Reformation**, which established new branches of Christianity throughout western Europe.

By the mid-1500s, the unified Latin Christendom of the Middle Ages no longer existed; weakened by the challenges to its authority and the loss of followers to Lutheranism and other new Protestant churches, Catholic leaders met at the Council of Trent (1545–1563) to address church abuses. The so-called Catholic Reformation also saw the establishment of a new order, the Jesuits, who would aid in the church's attempts to rebuild its membership by opening educational institutions throughout Europe and, eventually, in the European colonies that were then being established in the Americas.

While both the Protestant and Catholic Reformations had great impact in curbing abuses of religious power and would be linked to key political and economic developments in this time period, gender roles in Europe remained largely unchanged. Both Protestants and Catholics continued to promote a male-dominated order in religious leadership, secular authority, and family relationships. For the typical woman, the most common means of preserving her social status upon reaching adulthood was through an advantageous marriage. Noble families frequently arranged marriages among their children to maintain a privileged position in society, while the new and growing bourgeoisie (middle-class townspeople) often created marriage alliances that yielded benefits in business. Marriage in Europe occurred later than in other regions during this period; young adults of the lower classes needed time to save money to live independently from their parents, while bourgeois men delayed marriage to complete vocational training or a professional education. Such delayed marriages played a role in reducing European birthrates and family size in comparison with other regions, where most people married before reaching the age of twenty and thus had more time to have children. Few women were allowed to pursue an advanced education, but bourgeois women often received informal training as bookkeepers to assist their husbands in business. Some European lands allowed women to inherit the throne in royal families that lacked a male heir, but such cases were exceptions to the rule of a social structure dominated by males at every level.

AP Tip

In spite of the tremendous amount of social change occurring throughout this period, European women remained lower in status than men, but the social status of a woman's family was a critical factor in her life.

THE LATER RENAISSANCE AND THE HUMANIST WORLDVIEW

The spread of Protestant ideas was aided by the movable-type **printing press,** which had been perfected by Johann Gutenberg in the 1450s. Initially used to produce Bibles and other religious materials, the printing press soon proved invaluable in the development of a more secular-oriented **humanist** worldview throughout western Europe. As Europe's feudal system collapsed and the Catholic Church lost its dominance over everyday life, Renaissance writers returned to the works of the ancient Greeks and Romans, translating and printing them in **vernacular** languages for widespread distribution. The increased access to such printed materials was accompanied by a rise in literacy. Exposure to such texts provided inspiration for a new generation of scholars in fields such as history and ethics, who emphasized human potential and achievement. The cumulative effect of this rise of humanism was to move more and more Europeans away from lives dominated by church doctrine; as education spread and literacy rates rose, so too did new, more reason-based ideas in science, technology, and politics. Painting and sculpture of the later Renaissance also reflected the humanist worldview—Biblical figures and scenes no longer dominated European art as they had in the Middle Ages. In addition, artists depicted scenes of everyday life, painted portraits of themselves and their contemporaries, and created works inspired by the history and mythology of classical Greece and Rome.

MERCHANTS, BANKERS, TRADE, AND CAPITALISM

Many renowned Renaissance artists were supported by patrons, men who had amassed great wealth by tapping into the economic revival of Europe's towns and cities. After the Crusades, European interest in long-distance trading with the Middle East and Asia had continued to grow; the Black Death then cleared the way for lower-class Europeans who had survived the epidemic to move to urban areas to work in manufacturing and commerce, where they could demand higher wages. These factors blended to bring about the decline of the agriculturally based feudal system of the Middle Ages and the rise of a new economic system known as **capitalism.** This in turn allowed for the development of a new social order in which the **bourgeoisie** and the upper class were no longer dominated by hereditary nobles.

In the cities, most craftsmen or merchants joined **guilds,** professional associations that promoted good business practices, set prices, and protected their members' interests in interactions with local government leaders. Although some women were allowed to join guilds (occasionally as professionals in their own right, but more often only if they had a family connection to a male member), most guilds excluded women to maintain male control over positions of skilled labor. As a result, Europe's lower-class women remained underpaid, usually working in nonguild jobs in textiles or the food and beverage trade. Jews were also excluded from guild membership; however, because Christianity considered usury—the charging of interest—to be a sin, many Jews found a niche in the banking trade, which grew along with the rest of the European economy during this period.

A strong banking system allowed for more crucial developments in the move toward a capitalist economy. Standardized currencies soon appeared, and enterprising businessmen took advantage of bankers' offers of credit and opportunities to join in shareholding companies. As the era of European exploration and colonization was getting underway at the same time, colonial settlements in the Americas and chartered trading companies such as the Dutch East India Company were often financed by groups of private investors in **joint-stock companies.** Soon, Europe's economy came to be dominated by large banks, chartered companies, and **stock exchanges** that allowed the growing middle and upper classes of the towns and cities to engage in private enterprise. European governments often adopted policies of **mercantilism** to promote such activities for national benefit. Using force if necessary to protect their overseas colonies, the British, French, Portuguese, and Spanish began bringing the natural resources of the Americas back to Europe; manufacturing them into finished goods; and selling many of the goods back to the American colonists, who, to maintain European monopolies, were usually prohibited from manufacturing such products of their own.

WORLD EXPLORATION AND THE COLUMBIAN EXCHANGE

The Europeans' lucrative colonial empires were, of course, the result of one of history's greatest mistakes: Columbus's westward voyage across the Atlantic Ocean in search of a more direct trade route to India. In the Middle Ages, while the world economy was dominated by the Muslim empires of the Middle East, Italian traders had taken advantage of their Mediterranean location to establish a trade link between northern Europe, the Middle East, Africa, India, and China. By the fifteenth century, Spain and Portugal were determined to break the Italian city-states' virtual monopoly on long-distance trading by finding new, Atlantic-based trade routes to Africa and India. Employing the newly devised **caravel**, a small, maneuverable vessel, along with navigational technologies such as the compass and the astrolabe—brought to Europe via trading contact with the Middle East and China—Prince Henry the Navigator of Portugal explored the west coast of Africa during the mid-1400s. By 1488 Bartolomeu Dias rounded Africa's Cape of Good Hope and reached the Indian Ocean. Ten years later, Vasco da Gama voyaged all the way to India.

Determined not to allow Portugal to monopolize overseas exploration and trade, Ferdinand and Isabella of Spain turned to an Italian named Christopher Columbus, who believed he could sail to India faster than the Portuguese by heading west across the Atlantic— virtually unknown in Europe at the time was the fact that two continents lay in between. Soon, the monarchs of western Europe realized that North and South America were a literal goldmine of opportunity because overpowering the natives and stripping their land of its resources posed little challenge. In what was known as the **Atlantic System**, European ships laden with manufactured goods landed first in Africa, where some of the goods were traded for slaves. The slaves and remaining goods next crossed the Atlantic in what was known as the **Middle Passage**; they were then distributed throughout the Americas. The African slaves were put to work in the fields and mines of the Americas, replacing the Amerindians, who had died in record numbers following exposure to European diseases such as smallpox. Meanwhile, the ships were restocked with American products, most of which served as raw materials for manufacturers back in Europe, and were sent back across the Atlantic to complete the circuit.

This continuous loop of people and products traveling around the Atlantic was an important conduit for the **Columbian Exchange**: the transfer of foods, animals, diseases, technologies, and of course people (accompanied by important elements of their cultures) between the Old World (Europe, Asia, and Africa) and the New (the Americas). In Europe, unlike Africa and the Americas, the impact of the Columbian Exchange was largely positive; in addition to reaping the economic benefits detailed above, Europeans found their diet enriched by such exotic additions as tomatoes, peanuts, chilies, and chocolate. More significantly, New World starches such as maize and potatoes began to provide a dependable source of calories that fueled a worldwide population boom after 1700.

AP Tip

By the end of this period, the various European nations had created a more unified world economy in comparison with the fragmented trading networks such as the Silk Road or the Inca network of roads in previous centuries. With European colonial empires in North and South America, a growing European trade presence in Africa (at least along the coasts, where Europeans linked with overland trade networks of goods and slaves), and European ships sailing the Indian and Pacific Oceans to acquire goods in India and China, an era of European domination of the world economy was set to begin.

THE SCIENTIFIC REVOLUTION AND THE ENLIGHTENMENT

The post-1700 population boom was also a result (in Europe, at least) of contemporaneous advances in science and medicine. The humanist worldview of the early Renaissance inspired not just writers and artists, but astronomers and mathematicians such as Copernicus, who determined that the universe was not centered upon the earth (the official doctrine of the Catholic Church) but that the sun was the center of a system of planets, of which the earth was merely one. Kepler and Galileo then built upon his work. Despite condemnation by Catholics and Protestants alike, the publication of such theories soon inspired other scientists, such as Isaac Newton, to adopt and expand upon the new scientific method of careful experimentation developed by these pioneering astronomers. Continuing the period's trend away from an unquestioning worldview dictated by the doctrines of the Catholic Church, logic- and reason-based natural laws and theories in chemistry, physics, mathematics, anatomy, and medicine began to develop.

Rational new theories about political, social, and economic life soon emerged as well, in a movement that became known as the **Enlightenment**. Inspired by the **Scientific Revolution**—along with captivating accounts of lifestyles and governmental structures in the Americas and China—Voltaire, John Locke, and other philosophers promoted religious tolerance, economic opportunity, and political institutions based on the consent and involvement of the governed. This last element of the Enlightenment developed in direct response to the rise of absolute monarchs that had begun after the end of the Hundred Years War. While Germany remained decentralized for another three hundred years, the monarchs of Spain, France, and England steadily increased their nations' unity at the expense of the authority of the church and nobility. Religion remained influential in various ways, however: Philip II of Spain used the Spanish Inquisition to develop a Catholic-based nationalism that promoted his absolute authority, while the Bourbon kings of France reduced the rights of Protestants to appeal to their predominantly Catholic citizenry and created a powerful monarchy that was supported by the church. In England, though, the Catholic Church suffered another blow when Henry VIII convinced Parliament to name the English monarch, not the pope, as the head of the Church of England. Over the ensuing decades, English monarchs attempted to extend their authority even further; but those attempts sparked the English Civil War when members of Parliament insisted that their rights be respected. By the end of the seventeenth century the English Bill of Rights and other laws upheld the power of Parliament, transforming England into a constitutional monarchy offering protection of certain political rights and religious freedoms.

RUSSIA

The English, French, and other western and central European monarchs gained power in part by investing in new technologies (mobile cannon, hand-held guns) and ever-growing, well-trained armies (or, in England's case, a navy). By the early eighteenth century a balance of power emerged among England, France, Austria, and the small German kingdom of Prussia. Alliances among these nations (and others of lesser status, such as Sweden, Spain, the Netherlands, and Poland) shifted constantly, preventing any one of them from emerging as dominant. None was particularly large in territory, but their success in world trade allowed their monarchs to increase taxes to finance such military expansion.

In eastern Europe, a different history prevailed. By the late 1400s, the Mongol-ruled Golden Horde had long been in decline; the prince of Moscow, Ivan III, then seized the opportunity to declare himself tsar ("Caesar"), and ushered in a return of native Russian rule to the region. Ivan IV soon expanded Russia's borders to the south and east, and by the early 1700s the vast northern region of Siberia had been added to the empire as well. Siberia's wealth of natural resources, particularly animal pelts, provided a link with the vigorous trade economy of western Europe, but otherwise, much of Russia languished in an agriculturally based economy until the reign of Peter the Great, from 1689 to 1725. As tsar, Peter concerned himself with Westernizing Russia by developing industry and trade, reducing the influence of noble boyars in government, modernizing the Russian army and navy, and forcing European fashions and social traditions on the Russian elite. By 1712, his new capital on the Baltic Sea, St. Petersburg, served as a valuable link between Russia and the West, but Peter's vast empire still struggled with issues of religious and ethnic diversity, and its population was dominated by **serfs**, peasant farmers tied almost as slaves to land belonging to a tiny group of landowners. In a sense, much of Russia's land and population retained the feudal structure Europe had shrugged off after the Middle Ages. Not until the early twentieth century would this land-based empire be dramatically transformed.

Multiple-Choice Questions

1. Which of the following was NOT a major factor permitting the rise of secular European monarchs and their centralization of power?
   (A) The Hundred Years War
   (B) The Peace of Augsburg
   (C) The signing of the English Bill of Rights
   (D) The revocation of the Edict of Nantes

2. The Protestant Reformation
   (A) began with the pope trying to rid the Catholic Church of corrupt practices.
   (B) sparked wars of religion throughout Europe for more than a hundred years.
   (C) pushed most European monarchs to reject Catholicism outright.
   (D) resulted in the eradication of Catholicism in most of Europe.

3. Which of the following most accurately describes the humanist worldview that developed in Europe following the Middle Ages?
   (A) Catholic doctrine should be rejected in favor of a new Protestant focus on an individual relationship with God.
   (B) Writers and artists should take inspiration in the scholarly and aesthetic accomplishments of the ancient Greeks and Romans.
   (C) Human foibles can be eradicated by a disciplined, scientific approach to life.
   (D) The feudal system should be abolished to allow individuals the freedom to take advantage of opportunities in the growing towns and cities.

4. Early European capitalism
   (A) was thwarted by the revival of chaotic urban life.
   (B) saw a reduction in tariffs to promote economic interdependence.
   (C) depended on trade agreements among the major nations.
   (D) allowed private investors to participate in large-scale economic projects.

5. Which of the following most frequently provided the opportunity to rise in social status in Europe during the period 1450–1750?
   (A) New business ventures or jobs in manufacturing and trade
   (B) A university education
   (C) Marriage to someone from a higher class
   (D) Moving from urban to rural areas

6. All of the following are true of the Columbian Exchange EXCEPT
   (A) Amerindians were exposed to diseases to which Europeans, Africans, and Asians had already developed immunities.
   (B) Old World livestock such as cattle and horses devastated the Amerindian cultures into which they were introduced.
   (C) the social structure of the Americas became much more complex.
   (D) yellow fever killed a significant percentage of the European population of the tropical Americas.

7. Theories of heliocentrism
   (A) upheld the beliefs of the ancient Greeks regarding the structure of the universe.
   (B) provided the impetus for Martin Luther and others to begin the Protestant Reformation.
   (C) changed prevailing views on the orbits and composition of the planets.
   (D) were initially proposed by Isaac Newton and fully developed by Galileo Galilei.

8. Which of the following was NOT an important influence on the development of Enlightenment thought?
   (A) Missionary activity in China
   (B) European colonization in the Americas
   (C) The Protestant Reformation
   (D) The Hundred Years War

9. Peter the Great is best known for
   (A) promoting Westernization in the Russian government, society, and economy.
   (B) restoring native Russian rule after the period of Mongol domination.
   (C) initiating Russian control over Siberia.
   (D) reducing legal restrictions on Russian serfs.

10. By 1750, the world economy could best be described as
    (A) consisting of fragmented regional trading networks.
    (B) centered on the agricultural output of the Columbian Exchange.
    (C) driven by trade centered on the Mediterranean Sea.
    (D) moving toward unification based on European maritime dominance.

11. Peasants in Italy and Ireland
    (A) produced wheat for large European cities while eating potatoes and maize.
    (B) drank lots of wine and beer produced on the estates that they worked.
    (C) lived a better life than they had lived before because they could sell potatoes for cash.
    (D) exported wheat because it was seen as inferior to the new American crops such as maize and potatoes.

12. One of the most visible environmental disasters of eighteenth-century Europe was
    (A) air pollution caused by the burning of coal, which created a black fog in cities such as London.
    (B) deforestation caused by the new iron industry's sudden need for wood and a period of colder temperatures.
    (C) soil depletion and eventually famine caused by the emphasis on new crops such as potatoes.
    (D) famines caused by intense periods of either rain or drought.

13. Which of the following true about the roles of women in Europe?
    (A) Although sometimes inferior to those of men, most women were seen as completely equal economically and politically.
    (B) Women were more likely to become nuns, a result of the Protestant Reformation's emphasis on keeping women single.
    (C) Women were largely dependent on one's social class.
    (D) Women's roles changed completely.

14. Political developments in France and England
    (A) can be contrasted in the high war debts France accumulated while England fought few wars between 1450 and 1750.
    (B) can be compared in the similar opulence of Versailles and Buckingham palaces.
    (C) can be contrasted in the relative powers of the French Estates General and the British Parliament.
    (D) can be compared in the powerlessness of the monarchy that both areas shared as a result of inept governance.

15. The Protestant Reformation changed Europe
    (A) by contributing to violent wars in areas outside of Europe.
    (B) by curtailing the power of the Catholic pope in Europe.
    (C) by limiting the power of the women in the church.
    (D) by making Europe more tolerant of other religions such as Judaism and Islam.

Free-Response Questions

1. Evaluate cultural and intellectual continuities and changes in Europe in the period from circa 1450 to circa 1750.

2. Compare sea-based western European empires and Russia in the period from circa 1450 to circa 1750.

Answers

MULTIPLE-CHOICE QUESTIONS

1. ANSWER: C. The English Bill of Rights of 1689 was a setback for absolute monarchy in England; it provided for an active Parliament with specific legal and military powers (*The Earth and Its Peoples,* 5th ed., p. 475/6th ed., p. 450).

2. ANSWER: B. While Henry VIII of England rejected papal authority several years after Martin Luther began the Reformation, many European monarchs actively promoted Catholicism in their lands in the ensuing years. This led to many years of warfare (*The Earth and Its Peoples,* 5th ed., p. 475/6th ed., p. 438).

3. ANSWER: B. The humanist movement began in the mid-1300s and flourished first in Italy, then throughout western Europe, as the Renaissance spread. Humanism was marked by an emphasis on

human potential and achievement that could be inspired by an examination of the literature of the classical civilizations of Greece and Rome (*The Earth and Its Peoples,* 5th ed., pp. 412–415/6th ed., pp. 364–365).

4. ANSWER: **D.** Individual investors could now choose to place their money in banks, the stock market, or joint-stock companies, where they could reduce their financial risk by pooling resources with other investors in overseas trading ventures or colonial settlements (*The Earth and Its Peoples,* 5th ed. p. 469/6th ed., p. 444).

5. ANSWER: **A.** While other opportunities for social advancement occasionally arose, taking advantage of the wealth of opportunities in the growing trade-centered urban areas provided the best chances of creating positive social change for European males (*The Earth and Its Peoples,* 5th ed., pp. 468–469/6th ed., pp. 443–444).

6. ANSWER: **B.** Old World livestock did have a destructive impact in the Americas in some cases, but many Amerindians were provided with a new source of food and clothing, and the horse was incorporated into the cultures of many native peoples of North and South America (*The Earth and Its Peoples,* 5th ed., p. 492/6th ed., pp. 467–468).

7. ANSWER: **C.** The geocentric theories of Aristotle and other ancient Greeks held that the earth was at the center of the universe and was the only planet made of heavy matter. Medieval Europeans accepted these ideas because they fit well with the Bible's story of creation. Not until the sixteenth century did Copernicus, Kepler, and Galileo publish observations that contradicted geocentrism and described a sun-centered planetary system, in which the earth and other heavenly bodies were composed of heavy matter and orbited the sun in elliptical, not circular, paths (*The Earth and Its Peoples,* 5th ed., pp. 465–467/6th ed., pp. 442–443).

8. ANSWER: **D.** The Enlightenment developed after the Scientific Revolution and was in part inspired by reports of social and political life in the Americas and China. The Reformation also played an important role in encouraging Enlightenment thinkers to promote religious tolerance as an element of a just society. The Hundred Years War was an important early catalyst of the events of this period, but it had no direct connection to the Enlightenment (*The Earth and Its Peoples,* 5th ed., pp. 467–468/6th ed., pp. 441–442).

9. ANSWER: **A.** Peter the Great actually increased restrictions on the Russian serfs, as the Russian economic system still depended on their agricultural output, but consciously promoted changes modeled after postfeudal Europe in many other areas: he built the modern new capital of St. Petersburg in the French baroque style, forced Russian nobles to adopt Western fashions, reshaped his government following the Prussian style of organization, and developed a merit-based system of military promotion (*The Earth and Its Peoples,* 5th ed., pp. 590–591/6th ed., p. 541).

10. ANSWER: **D.** The sixteenth and seventeenth centuries saw remarkable changes in the world economy, as various European nations aggressively pursued innovations in maritime technology; explored territories previously unknown to them; established sea-based trade networks with Africa, India, and China; and claimed territory throughout North and South America for lucrative colonial settlements. The end result was a world economy centered in large part on the manufacturing and trading activities of the nations of western Europe (*The Earth and Its Peoples,* 5th ed., pp. 482, 529–530/6th ed., pp. 457, 504–509).

11. ANSWER: **A.** Peasants produced wheat for the world market because the new American crops were seen as inferior foods. Most peasants could not afford the wheat that they were forced to grow on their masters' estates (*The Earth and Its Peoples,* 5th ed., p. 471/6th ed., p. 446).

12. ANSWER: **B.** Driven by the new iron industry and the colder temperatures of the Little Ice Age, deforestation caused huge problems for the poor, who were accustomed to using the forests as a source of free lumber as well as food (*The Earth and Its Peoples,* 5th ed., pp. 471–472/6th ed., pp. 446–448).

13. ANSWER: **C.** Women's roles continued to be inferior to men, but in some areas they could become merchants, could become queens, and could choose their own spouse. In general, the power of a woman was very dependent on her family's social status (The *Earth and Its Peoples,* 5th ed., p. 472/6th ed., p. 449).

14. ANSWER: **B.** Britain's Parliament was a lot stronger than France's Estates General, which ceased to function once the Bourbon kings came to the throne (*The Earth and Its Peoples,* 5th ed., p. 475/6th ed., p. 452).

15. ANSWER: **B.** The weakening of the pope's power was the only direct result of the Protestant Reformation (*The Earth and Its Peoples,* 5th ed., pp. 460–463/6th ed., pp. 436–438).

FREE-RESPONSE QUESTIONS

1. This continuity and change over time essay should begin by addressing the decline of the medieval worldview, which was dominated by an unquestioning, unchallenging faith in church doctrine. Repeated challenges to the authority of the Catholic Church form a thread of continuity throughout this time period and can provide a focal point for a good response. The humanist worldview, with its inspiration from the writings of classical Greek and Roman scholars and its emphasis on human potential and achievement, begins to replace the medieval worldview and inspires a variety of cultural and intellectual developments: the art, architecture, and literature of the Renaissance; Martin Luther's Protestant Reformation, with its criticism of corruption in the Catholic Church and an insistence on an individualized relationship with God; the Scientific Revolution, which drew inspiration from Greek theories on astronomy and medicine

and rejected the church's vision of a geocentric universe; and the Enlightenment, whose philosophers promoted a social and political order favoring religious toleration and democracy over the divine right of kings.

2. A good response to this comparative essay will review the rise of a capitalist economy in western Europe, with its emphasis on mercantilist policies: gaining wealth by maintaining a favorable balance of trade, taking possession of other territories, and using their natural resources in the manufacture of trade goods. By 1650, the western European economy had moved away from a dependence on the agricultural output of the feudal system and revolved around the Atlantic System—raw materials from the Americas, slaves from Africa, and trade goods from Europe were circulating in the Atlantic Ocean to generate wealth for European monarchs and their growing bourgeois classes. An important similarity is that after finally shrugging off the rule of the Mongols' Golden Horde, which had drained the region of any wealth it had previously had, Russia also set out to transform its economy in an attempt to link with the wealth of western Europe's manufacturing-based capitalist system. Under Peter the Great, Russia too gained control of new lands—but the annexation of Siberia and other territory to the east created a land-based empire that was forced to struggle with issues of economic stagnation and ethnic and religious diversity. Peter was able to build a modern new capital in St. Petersburg and begin using his newly gained natural resources to move western Russia toward a manufacturing-based economy similar to those of the countries of western Europe, but he and his successors remained saddled with a vast eastern territory that continued to be dominated by a dependence on agricultural output. While Russia also relied on a system of forced labor, Russian serfdom actually resulted in an economy that had more in common with the feudal system of Europe's Middle Ages than with the contemporaneous sea-based empires of western Europe.

15

THE AMERICAS: CIRCA 1450 TO CIRCA 1750

KEY CONCEPTS

- Prior to European contact, civilizations throughout the Americas continued to rise and fall in relative isolation from one another.
- Once Columbus made Europeans aware of the existence of the "New World," explorers from Spain, Portugal, England, France, the Netherlands, and other European lands rapidly settled throughout the Western Hemisphere.
- Via the Columbian Exchange, European settlement in the Americas drastically reduced Amerindian populations and significantly altered—or even destroyed—indigenous cultures.
- Following the Europeans' economic takeover of the Americas, African slaves were introduced throughout the region, with far-ranging economic, social, and political consequences.
- By 1750, Spain and Portugal remained firmly in control in Mesoamerica and South America; North American territory was shared by several European colonial powers, but the British settlements would soon begin to press for independence from monarchical control.

KEY TERMS

- Algonquin
- Arawak
- Atlantic System
- Aztec
- Carib
- chartered company
- Columbian Exchange
- conquistador

- Dutch West India Company
- encomienda
- Huron
- Iroquois Confederacy
- Inca Empire
- indentured servant
- mit'a
- plantocracy
- Treaty of Tordesillas
- viceroyalty

The Americas in the period from circa 1450 to circa 1750 are discussed in detail in *The Earth and Its Peoples*, fifth edition, Chapters 11, 15, 17, and 18 and sixth edition, Chapters 7, 15, and 18.

THE ARRIVAL OF THE SPANISH

For the Americas, the period 1450–1750 was one of profound change. Christopher Columbus's encounter of the Western Hemisphere, a dramatic leap in globalization, sparked intense competition among European powers for dominance in the Americas. By the end of this era, however, the stage was set for a revolt against European hegemony in the region.

In October 1492, Christopher Columbus's ships landed in the Caribbean; within the decade European explorers realized that he had encountered a "New World," territory previously unknown in what became known as the Old World—Europe, Asia, and Africa. In fact, a mere two years after Columbus's first voyage to the Americas, Spain and Portugal negotiated the **Treaty of Tordesillas**. The agreement divided the world's uncharted territory between the two nations, allowing them to claim lands without competition. The lack of involvement of any indigenous inhabitant of the New World in treaty negotiations set the tone for an era of European domination in the Western Hemisphere; Spain and Portugal were followed by England and France in establishing major colonial settlements in the Americas, in some cases through diplomatic negotiations with the Amerindians, but often through conflict and force.

Early on, the Spanish established a precedent for using force against the Amerindians. When Columbus returned to the Caribbean in 1493, he brought with him hundreds of Spanish settlers hoping either to gain wealth or to convert the natives to Christianity (motives similar to those of the Spanish who had retaken Spain from Muslim control in the preceding centuries). With licenses from the Spanish monarch, **conquistadors**, or conquerors, such as Hernán Cortés soon made their way from the islands of the Caribbean to the Mesoamerican mainland in search of gold, slaves, and converts. Cortés and his men made their way to the **Aztec** capital of Tenochtitlan in 1519, used cavalry charges and steel swords to easily defeat their opponents, and imprisoned the Aztec emperor, Moctezuma II. Many of the Aztecs' subjects willingly assisted the Spanish in hopes of regaining their independence. Instead, the conquistadors swiftly laid claim to much of modern-day Mexico, then set their sights on the **Inca Empire**, which controlled almost three thousand miles of territory along the Pacific coast of South America. With just two cannon, Francisco Pizarro and his small band of 180 men overpowered the Inca, helped themselves to a wealth of gold, silver, and emeralds, and captured the Inca capital of Cuzco in 1533. They also forced the emperor, Atahualpa, to convert to Christianity, then executed him anyway. Their conquest of the entire Inca Empire proceeded quickly, and it encouraged other conquistadors to seek their own fortunes in the Americas as the sixteenth century progressed; by 1600, Spain's colonial empire encompassed much of the Caribbean and a vast expanse of land from southern North America through central South America and territories beyond.

THE COLUMBIAN EXCHANGE

One unforeseen advantage the Spanish had in their rapid takeover of New World territory was the lack of Amerindian resistance to Old World diseases. Centuries of isolation from Europe, Asia, and Africa meant that the indigenous peoples were extraordinarily susceptible to diseases—smallpox, in particular—that the Spanish brought with them. In Mesoamerica, the most conservative estimate puts native population loss at well over 50 percent; the same occurred as the Spanish moved farther into South America. Soon the Portuguese, claiming the territory that became Brazil, devastated the indigenous population there as well. With a few isolated exceptions, those who survived such epidemics found themselves in no position to fight off European control.

As significant as their impact was, however, these diseases were merely one aspect of a much greater phenomenon, called the **Columbian Exchange,** in which plants, animals, technology, religion, and other elements of culture began to make their way across the Atlantic Ocean from the Old World to the New, and vice versa. Very soon after European contact, Old World crops such as wheat, grapes, rice, bananas, citrus fruits, and sugar cane were being successfully cultivated in the Americas and were introduced to the diets of many Amerindians. At the same time, American crops, especially corn and potatoes, found their way to Europe, Africa, and Asia, where they soon provided a steady source of calories that may well have contributed to a boom in world population after 1700. Other New World products such as tomatoes, chocolate, and tobacco became staples in the Eastern Hemisphere as well. The Europeans also introduced livestock such as cattle, horses, and pigs to the Western Hemisphere, causing important changes in the Amerindians' environment and culture. In some areas, grazing cattle and sheep damaged wild grasslands; in others, such as the plains of South America, Mexico, and Texas, herding cattle and sheep provided Amerindians with new sources of food and clothing. Horses also had a great impact, providing indigenous warriors and hunters throughout the Americas with an important new resource.

From the beginning of their conquest of American lands, the Spanish and Portuguese had used a coercive labor system, the **encomienda**, to force the Amerindians to work without pay in the fields and mines taken over by the Europeans. Reforms in the 1500s led to new systems of labor, such as the **mit'a** in Peru, by which adult males worked on a rotating basis producing silver or textiles for the Spanish, receiving only token wages in return. However, waves of disease continued to decimate native populations, forcing the Europeans to turn elsewhere for exploitable labor.

It was in the Portuguese colony of Brazil that African slavery first began to take hold. The Portuguese, having profited from slave labor on their sugar plantations on Atlantic islands such as the Azores, recognized that Brazil would be an excellent place to expand their cultivation of the lucrative crop, for which they needed African slaves. The Spanish and, later, the English followed suit, and the trade of European manufactured goods in Africa in exchange for slaves to transport to the Americas soon exploded. Between 1600 and 1750, more than 3 million Africans were brought to the Americas and forced into slavery (mainly on sugar and tobacco plantations, but also in domestic service) in the **Atlantic System**.

AP Tip

One of the important cultural legacies of this period is the influence of Africans on American society. African traditions in art, music, and storytelling served as a source of strength and unity through the era of slavery and eventually would be recognized as a vital part of American culture, particularly after the civil rights movement of the twentieth century. Cultural and social history of this kind can be recognized as a reason for continuities and changes within a society.

LATIN AMERICAN GOVERNMENT, SOCIETY, AND ECONOMY

By 1600, Spanish and Portuguese settlement had created a complex new social structure in the New World. The Catholic Church, the colonial governments (or **viceroyalties**, administrative extensions of the Spanish and Brazilian monarchies), and business enterprises in Latin America were usually headed by peninsulares, or native-born Europeans who had immigrated to the Americas. Creoles—whites of Spanish or Portuguese background born in the New World—often oversaw farming and mining activities; intermarriage between Europeans and creoles was not uncommon. Amerindian elites (descended from Aztec and Inca nobles) and mestizos, or those with a mix of European and Amerindian ancestry, formed a third level of society in certain areas, often functioning as administrators who oversaw the tax and labor obligations of the Amerindians. Indigenous peoples of many cultural and linguistic backgrounds were simply lumped together near the bottom of the social structure as "Indians" by the colonists; those who survived the devastation wrought by the Columbian Exchange faced special taxes and enforced labor, not to mention the significant alteration or destruction of their cultures. Finally, an ever-growing population of African slaves formed the lowest rung of the colonial social ladder in Latin America. (Eventually,

European and African cultures would blend in individuals known as mulattos, who held a social status similar to that of the mestizos.) In Brazil, much the same social structure as that of the Spanish colonies developed, although the Portuguese settlement lacked a class of elite Amerindians. In fact, Brazilian colonial society ultimately would be influenced much more by the culture of its African slaves than by that of its indigenous peoples.

One link, although tenuous, among the various social classes of Latin America was religion. Catholic missionaries had arrived in the New World with some of the first conquistadors. By the middle of the sixteenth century, the Society of Jesus, or Jesuits, had been established by the church in response to the challenges of the Protestant Reformation. Jesuit priests began to open missions, schools, and universities throughout the region to spread Catholicism among the Amerindians, and Christian beliefs and Catholic rituals sometimes blended with the native religious practices of both the Amerindians and the African slaves. But the church soon looked beyond its missionary role and came to dominate colonial Latin America, with powerful interests in banking and the plantation economy.

Despite church involvement in lucrative business ventures, the Spanish and Portuguese governments continued to maintain strict control over economic activity in Latin America. The monarchs of Spain and Portugal granted monopoly trade rights to certain merchants in their colonies and forced the colonists to buy goods from them. Meanwhile, warships from the royal navies of the two colonial powers protected trading vessels crossing the Atlantic between Europe and Latin America. This system allowed for the safe shipment of goods and the efficient collection of taxes, but it also fostered the growth of a black market for products smuggled into Latin America from England, France, and the Netherlands.

THE WEST INDIAN PLANTATIONS

In the 1500s, the Spanish and Portuguese shifted the focus of much of their colonization to Mesoamerica and South America. As a result, their older colonies, in the Caribbean islands that became known as the West Indies, were largely abandoned. In the next century, however, England and France began to see in these islands an opportunity for the profitable export of tobacco and then—as more tobacco cultivation moved to the North American mainland—sugar. Many of the English and French colonies in the West Indies began as **chartered companies**, in which private investors paid the government a fee for exclusive rights to trade. This system, copied from the **Dutch West India Company's** activities in the Caribbean, allowed European governments to maintain a presence in the region without incurring the administrative costs of direct control that Spain and Portugal faced in Latin America. Chartered companies soon became a key component of European mercantilism, which dictated that nations could gain wealth by extracting gold, silver, and valuable agricultural products from other lands.

The production of sugar in the West Indies was at first dependent on the use of **indentured servants**, poor Europeans who were given free passage to the colonies in exchange for several years of unpaid labor. By the 1700s, though, West Indian land had become very expensive, leading most indentured servants to choose to go to North America, where inexpensive land remained available for their purchase after the completion of their labor period. Needing another form of coercive labor, European planters began to bring more and more African slaves to the West Indies, even though the cost of purchasing slaves outright was more expensive than the cost of transatlantic passage for indentured servants.

Gradually, large sugar plantations emerged in the West Indies as investors took steps to maximize their economic returns. These investors formed a **plantocracy**, a small class of rich Europeans who owned large amounts of land and large numbers of slaves; profits depended on the planters getting as much as possible out of both. For slaves of all ages, this meant long days of work in labor gangs, high production quotas, and severe physical punishments for those who fell behind. A very high mortality rate from overwork and disease soon developed among the slaves, which served only to increase the volume of the Atlantic slave trade. Meanwhile, the land itself began to suffer from deforestation and soil depletion, and the transfer of Old World plants and animals to the Caribbean islands added to the environmental transformation of the region. It was also in the West Indies that European colonization led to the most thorough devastation of the indigenous population—the **Arawak** and **Carib** peoples were driven nearly out of existence as colonial settlement progressed throughout the sixteenth, seventeenth, and eighteenth centuries.

AP Tip

During this period silver mined by the Spanish in the Americas played a crucial role in the development of a European-dominated world economy. Mexican and Peruvian silver boosted the supply of money in Europe, which allowed for continued economic expansion there, setting the stage for the Industrial Revolution. In addition, Spanish merchants also took silver to the Philippines (their Pacific island colony) to trade for Asian goods such as tea, silk, and porcelain that were then in high demand in Europe. This flood of American silver also generated severe inflation in Europe in the sixteenth and seventeenth centuries, an economic crisis that spread eastward to the Ottoman Empire—further evidence of the development of a truly global economic system. These important shifts can be emphasized in any essay that asks for analysis of economic changes during this era.

THE COLONIAL SETTLEMENTS OF NORTH AMERICA

Initially, North America's European settlers came mostly from England and France. Their colonies developed differently from those of Spain and Portugal in that neither England nor France chose to institute strong governmental control over their North American territories. Instead, they allowed chartered companies and enterprising individuals to settle and develop their lands independently. The result was a region of much greater political, economic, and cultural diversity than in the Spanish colonies or Brazil.

The earliest English settlements in the New World—in Newfoundland, Canada, and on Roanoke Island off the coast of the Carolinas—met with failure, but in 1607 nearly 150 settlers representing the privately funded Virginia Company established the colony of Jamestown in the Chesapeake Bay region. Facing far greater challenges than they expected in dealing with the Amerindians and in finding wealth in mining, trade, or agriculture, the few colonists who survived began to spread out around the bay and into the interior. Soon these Virginians developed a sustainable economy based on the export of furs, lumber, and tobacco and dependent on the use of indentured servants. Remaining rural in character—again in contrast to the Spanish and Portuguese colonies, which were developing sizable cities and towns through the seventeenth century—Virginia was under the control of a governor appointed by the English monarch. Representatives of the colonists themselves, however, soon began meeting outside of the Crown-approved House of Burgesses and set the English colony on a path towards representative democracy. Meanwhile, English settlement continued to spread into present-day Maryland and North and South Carolina. So too did the population of African slaves, brought to the region by plantation owners who began to consider them a better long-term investment than indentured servants. Many Amerindians initially profited by supplying the English settlers with skins for their fur trade, but the long-term effects of this new opportunity were highly damaging to the environment of the region—and to indigenous cultures. Trade conflicts among the Amerindians and between the Amerindians and the English settlers soon followed; in most cases the Europeans prevailed and took control of more and more Amerindian land.

To the north, the settlement of New England was directed more by religious influences than economic ones. Following the Reformation in Europe, two groups of English Protestants—the Pilgrims and the Puritans—journeyed to the New World rather than face continued confrontation with the Church of England over religious issues. There they formed what became known as the Massachusetts Bay Colony. The company charter of the colony, granted by the English monarch, dictated the development of political institutions in the region: an elected governor and representatives from each town set the colony on a course of local control with increasingly limited involvement by the Crown. (The indigenous population, meanwhile, was nearly driven out of existence by Old World diseases and military conflicts with the European settlers.) With its harsh climate and relatively poor soil, the region provided limited agricultural opportunities. New England instead became more urbanized than the southern colonies, with an economy based on manufacture, commerce, and shipping services that linked North America and the Caribbean with the Old World. Because it did not rely on large numbers of slaves and indentured servants, New England lacked the rigid, unbalanced social structure of the plantation-based southern colonies; class and economic differences were thus much less pronounced in the northern English colonies.

In between, the so-called Middle Atlantic region developed into a culturally diverse, economically prosperous territory with Dutch—German in Pennsylvania—influences in addition to English ones. For example, New York, founded by the Dutch West India Company as the colony of New Netherland, capitalized on profitable agreements with the Iroquois Confederacy, creating a large fur-trade network stretching north toward French-controlled Canada. After capturing the colony and renaming it New York in 1664, the English continued to exploit its strategic location between the Atlantic Ocean and the Hudson River to provide a shipping link from the New World to the Old. Pennsylvania, meanwhile, was founded with near-total autonomy when England's king, Charles II, gave an enormous land grant to repay a debt to the Penn family. The Penns, peace-loving Quakers who had come to the New World to escape religious persecution in England, relied more on negotiation than armed conflict in dealing with the region's Amerindians. This factor, in combination with a fairly mild climate and good land, allowed Pennsylvania to prosper rapidly. Its capital, Philadelphia, soon became the largest British colonial city, and it would play a key role when England's North American colonies began to push for independence as the eighteenth century wore on.

NEW FRANCE

Following several sixteenth-century exploratory voyages to Canada, France established its first North American colony at Quebec in 1608. New France's economic development relied heavily on fur-trading alliances with the indigenous **Huron** and **Algonquin** peoples, which in turn drew the French settlers into conflict with the opposing **Iroquois Confederacy** and its allies, the Dutch and English. The widespread use of firearms in these seventeenth-century battles altered the way of life of most Amerindian groups in the region, who adopted the technology for their own hunting and military practices and thus hampered the European takeover of western North America for more than two hundred years. Further, the Amerindians of Canada, recognizing their economic importance to the French, were able to resist much of the territorial loss and cultural destruction brought by earlier European settlers to other parts of the Americas—even the Jesuit missionaries of New France had abandoned most of their conversion efforts by the eighteenth century.

Continuing their quest for territorial expansion in the New World, the French established the territory of Louisiana (which covered much of the middle of the present-day United States) in 1699. French settlement throughout North America remained relatively sparse, however, and France's colonies faced frequent military threats from the wealthier and more populous colonies of English North America. Eventually losing control of Canada and Louisiana to England and

Spain, France restricted its New World activities to the Caribbean after the mid-eighteenth century.

Multiple-Choice Questions

1. Which of the following statements correctly links the Aztec religious and political systems?
   (A) The Aztecs used divination techniques to choose new kings.
   (B) Aztec leaders continually demanded tribute items and human sacrifices from conquered peoples.
   (C) Members of the Aztec ruling council were chosen from the priestly class.
   (D) The Aztecs considered Huitzilopochtli their only true king.

2. Which of the following characteristics is NOT shared by the Aztecs and Inca?
   (A) A society based on the achievements of earlier peoples
   (B) An emphasis on territorial expansion through warfare
   (C) Impressive engineering projects completed without the use of the wheel
   (D) A reliance on pastoralism to support an ever-growing population

3. The Treaty of Tordesillas
   (A) is an example of the diplomatic tactics Europeans used in negotiating with Amerindians.
   (B) was the name of the charter given by the king of Spain to Cortés, allowing for the conquest of the Aztecs.
   (C) brought about a peaceful conclusion to the Spanish takeover of the Inca.
   (D) established territorial borders for Spanish and Portuguese colonization of the Americas.

4. Which of the following did NOT contribute to the sharp increase in African slaves shipped to the Americas between 1600 and 1750?
   (A) The high cost of land in the West Indies
   (B) Outbreaks of smallpox and other diseases among Amerindians
   (C) European colonial takeover of African territory
   (D) Mercantilist policies designed to maximize European profits in the American colonies

5. Social structure in Latin America
   (A) was based on the social structure of the Amerindians, with the Europeans simply imposing themselves at the top.
   (B) lacked uniform characteristics and varied significantly within the region.
   (C) quickly obliterated all aspects of native culture.
   (D) evolved into a complex, yet hierarchical, mixture of European, Amerindian, and African cultures.

6. How did mercantilist policies affect the economic system of colonial Latin America?
   (A) Spain and Portugal actively promoted private enterprise in their colonies.
   (B) The colonies were used as a market for manufactured goods shipped from Spain and Portugal.
   (C) Mercantilism fostered the growth of open trading throughout the Western Hemisphere.
   (D) Industrial exports from Latin America rose steadily throughout the colonial period.

7. What is a key difference between the British and French colonial settlements in the West Indies and those of the Spanish and Portuguese elsewhere in the Americas?
   (A) Spanish and Portuguese settlements developed a more complex social structure than that of the British and French settlements in the West Indies.
   (B) British and French settlements relied far more on government involvement in the economy.
   (C) British and French settlements were more heavily influenced by the indigenous peoples there.
   (D) Spanish and Portuguese settlements caused much more physical damage than the environmentally friendly sugar plantations of the Caribbean.

8. The English and French colonies in the New World were characterized by
   (A) a dependence on slave labor similar to that found in the colonies of Spain and Portugal.
   (B) less hostile relations with the indigenous peoples of the Americas than the Spanish and Portuguese had.
   (C) the earlier development of urban commercial centers than the Spanish and Portuguese colonies.
   (D) a greater reliance on private investment for settlement and development than the Spanish and Portuguese colonies.

9. Why did the planters of colonial Virginia switch from using indentured servants to using African slaves?
   (A) Slaves represented a lower up-front cost than indentured servants.
   (B) Most indentured servants had begun pursuing opportunities in the Caribbean rather than North America.
   (C) Slaves were easier to train.
   (D) Slaves served as a better long-term investment than indentured servants.

10. Which of the following best describes France's colonial settlements in North America?
    (A) They failed to thrive because of ongoing conflicts with indigenous peoples and other European settlers.
    (B) They were agriculturally productive, but the French abandoned them because of their lack of exploitable mineral wealth.
    (C) They were more urban in character than neighboring English settlements.
    (D) They were dismantled as a result of the Jesuits' lack of success in converting the indigenous peoples to Christianity.

11. The economy of the English North American colonies was based on all of the following EXCEPT
    (A) indigo.
    (B) rice.
    (C) shipping.
    (D) silver.

12. The castas system
    (A) was a social hierarchy based on religion, ethnicity, and native ancestry.
    (B) was a distinction of which every member of society was aware.
    (C) placed only the creoles at the top.
    (D) allowed natives to maintain control of their native lands.

13. Reform in Spanish America meant that
    (A) Creoles' rights diminished.
    (B) Amerindian populations gained more rights.
    (C) silver output decreased as priests clamored for more humane mining reforms.
    (D) the economies of Cuba, Venezuela, and Chile expanded as agricultural products became more important.

14. Britain attempted to control its North American colonies by
    (A) increasing the elected assemblies' power so as to give the colonists the false illusion that they had the power to govern.
    (B) passing the Navigation Acts, which sought to control colonial production of manufactures that competed with British manufactures.
    (C) fighting wars with the Spanish and French in order to reduce the revolts in overcrowded New World cities.
    (D) replacing British governors with native-born governors.

15. The Columbian Exchange
    (A) brought epidemics to Africa.
    (B) brought better life expectancy to the Americas.
    (C) brought new plants to the Andes.
    (D) brought new crops to marginal areas of the world.

Free-Response Questions

1. Analyze the continuities and changes in the political system of ONE of the following areas during the period from circa 1450 to circa 1750.
    - North America
    - Mesoamerica
    - the Caribbean
    - South America

2. Compare the economic systems of the American colonies of TWO of the following European powers in the period from circa 1450 to circa 1750.
   - England
   - France
   - Portugal
   - Spain

Answers

MULTIPLE-CHOICE QUESTIONS

1. ANSWER: **B.** Aztec leaders subjugated other Amerindian groups for political and economic purposes, but also to ensure a constant supply of human sacrifices to please their god Huitzilopochtli (*The Earth and Its Peoples,* 5th ed., p. 319/6th ed., p. 393).

2. ANSWER: **D.** While the Inca were pastoralists, relying on llamas and alpacas for food, clothing, and commercial and military transportation, the Aztecs lacked draft animals and instead focused their agricultural efforts on the cultivation of crops (*The Earth and Its Peoples,* 5th ed., pp. 317, 328–330/6th ed., pp. 393–396).

3. ANSWER: **D.** The Treaty of Tordesillas, negotiated in 1494 between Spain and Portugal, was intended to prevent conflict between the two powers by splitting the world into two regions, one open to colonization by the Spanish, the other to colonization by the Portuguese (*The Earth and Its Peoples,* 5th ed., pp. 438–439/6th ed., pp. 414–415).

4. ANSWER: **C.** All of the other factors played a role in diminishing the use of indentured servants and increasing colonial reliance on African slaves in the Americas, but European colonization of Africa did not occur until the late nineteenth century (*The Earth and Its Peoples,* 5th ed., pp. 520–522/6th ed., pp. 494–496).

5. ANSWER: **D.** While individuals of pure European descent remained at the top of the Latin American social ladder, a blending of cultures soon occurred at lower levels (*The Earth and Its Peoples,* 5th ed., p. 503/6th ed., p. 479).

6. ANSWER: **B.** The governments of Spain and Portugal controlled the trade of their American colonies by granting monopoly trading rights to industries in the home countries (*The Earth and Its Peoples,* 5th ed., p. 499/6th ed., p. 475).

7. ANSWER: **A.** British and French West Indian colonial settlements generally developed a very simple social structure known as a plantocracy, in which a small class of wealthy European land-owners ruled over huge numbers of African slaves (*The Earth and Its Peoples,* 5th ed., p. 524/6th ed., p. 498).

8. ANSWER: **D.** England and France, settling the New World a century later than Spain and Portugal, chose not to create costly

administrative bureaucracies in their colonies. Instead, private chartered companies and individual settlers were given much more autonomy in the English and French territories (*The Earth and Its Peoples,* 5th ed., p. 504/6th ed., p. 479).

9. ANSWER: **D.** By the eighteenth century, Virginia's planters had begun to realize that a slave owned for life, although initially expensive to purchase, would provide a much higher rate of return than an indentured servant whose contract would run for only four to seven years (*The Earth and Its Peoples,* 5th ed., pp. 504–505/6th ed., p. 480).

10. ANSWER: **B.** While the French often treated indigenous peoples as valued trading partners, they faced constant struggles against the English settlers of North America and their Amerindian allies (*The Earth and Its Peoples,* 5th ed., p. 508/6th ed., pp. 483–484).

11. ANSWER: **D.** The economies of the British North American colonies centered around diverse products. Silver was not an important export in the British or French colonies (*The Earth and Its Peoples,* 5th ed., pp. 504–508/6th ed., pp. 479–483).

12. ANSWER: **B.** The castas system was a race-based system that placed Europeans on top and peoples of African descent or natives on bottom. It denied the natives their traditional rights. Everyone was very aware of their place in the hierarchy with the help of prominently placed castas paintings (*The Earth and Its Peoples,* 5th ed., p. 503/6th ed., p. 479).

13. ANSWER: **A.** The Spanish and Portuguese increased restrictions on Creoles while imposing changes such as new silver quotas and the expulsion of Jesuits, who were deemed too independent of the government (*The Earth and Its Peoples,* 5th ed., pp. 511–512/6th ed., pp. 486–487).

14. ANSWER: **B.** In an effort to maximize control, the British instituted the Navigation Acts to restrict colonial trade (*The Earth and Its Peoples,* 5th ed., p. 513/6th ed., p. 488).

15. ANSWER: **D.** The Columbian Exchange refers to the wholesale exchange of disease, animals, and plants from the Old World to the New and from the New World to the Old. New crops allowed people in Afro-Eurasia to move to areas that had not previously been able to sustain large populations (*The Earth and Its People,* 5th ed., p. 490/6th ed., p. 466).

FREE-RESPONSE QUESTIONS

1. A good response to this continuity and change over time question would have to include a discussion of the indigenous political practices of the region chosen, followed by details on the colonial government imposed by the European power that seized control of the territory. In North America, the indigenous political tradition of chiefdom generally gave way to governors appointed by the European powers, although various forms of colonist-led representative government began to develop in the English settlements. The Caribbean islands had seen settlement by the

Arawak and Carib peoples, but their small communities were fairly decentralized and focused mainly on subsistence farming. The Dutch, English, and French eventually established plantation-based colonies throughout the West Indies, with governors who were generally in league with the plantocracy, the small class of wealthy Europeans who owned most of the land and privately governed large populations of African slaves engaged in sugar production. In Mesoamerica and South America, both the Aztec and Inca monarchs had ruled a large and diverse territory, controlling conquered peoples and extracting tribute from them through the threat of invasion; the Spanish and Portuguese then imposed the most elaborate form of colonial government found in the Americas, establishing several viceroyalties that exerted day-to-day administrative control over the economic activities and complex social structure of New Spain, Peru, La Plata, and Brazil. In all regions, the political changes far outweighed the continuities, although hierarchical societies with government oversight of a trade-based economy remained a constant throughout most of the region.

2. This comparative essay question focuses on a key development during this time period: the growing European domination of the world economy. Within the Americas, colonial economic systems generally fell into one of two categories—government control or private control. Both England and France allowed their colonies throughout North America and the Caribbean to develop with little government involvement; in fact, their colonies began as chartered companies whose private investors hoped to profit through agricultural and trading ventures. Settlers in French Canada and Louisiana faced challenges in building a fur trade by allying with Amerindian groups, while colonists in New England—which, like Canada, was not ideal for agriculture—prospered by developing urban commercial centers with links to the lucrative Atlantic System of trade between the New World and the Old. In English Virginia and the Caribbean settlements of England and France, a plantation-based agricultural economy evolved, similar in some ways to the Spanish and Portuguese settlements in Mesoamerica and South America. All of these colonies displayed a hierarchical social structure dominated by wealthy white landowners profiting from the labors of a large class of African slaves growing sugar or tobacco. The Spanish and Portuguese governments, however, maintained much stricter control over their colonists' economic activities.

16

AFRICA: CIRCA 1750 TO CIRCA 1900

KEY CONCEPTS

- African trading empires continued to control most parts of eastern and western Africa before the 1850s.
- Moral pressure and changes in the global economy led to the end of the transatlantic slave trade by 1867.
- Industrialism and nationalism fed the desire of European nations for increased influence in Africa by the 1870s.
- New Imperialism reshaped the continent of Africa as European countries began exerting political, economic, and cultural control over their African colonies.
- In the "scramble" for Africa, European nations carved up the continent into colonial possessions, with only Ethiopia and Liberia remaining independent.
- European imperialism altered Africans' political, economic, and cultural way of life.

KEY TERMS

- Afrikaners
- Battle of Adowa
- Berlin Conference
- colonialism
- Industrial Revolution
- modernization
- nationalism
- New Imperialism
- palm oil
- "scramble" for Africa
- Sokoto Caliphate

- South African War
- Suez Canal
- transatlantic slave trade
- Zulu

Africa is discussed in depth in *The Earth and Its Peoples,* fifth edition, Chapters 25 and 27 and sixth edition, Chapter 25.

THE RISE OF AFRICAN EMPIRES

In the early nineteenth century, changes in trading patterns and population growth, familiar to other parts of Africa, came to the Nguni people of southern Africa. In addition, a severe drought led to increased conflict over grazing and farmlands. The Nguni had traditionally organized themselves in small independent clan groups, but with their society in crisis, a military visionary came forward to reshape southern Africa. In 1818 Shaka created the **Zulu** kingdom. The Zulu were successful because of their powerful military, which included disciplined drills, hand-to-hand combat, and new, advanced technologies—notably the stabbing spear and oxhide shield. In less than a decade Shaka and the Zulu became a feared force as they seized neighboring grazing and agricultural lands. Areas that were raided lost cattle, and many women and children were enslaved or made homeless, thus creating a large refugee population in southern Africa. Similar to the Mongols' approach, conquered men were integrated into the Zulu army and became fiercely loyal to Shaka. The Zulu did more than any other group in moving central and southern Africa away from clan-based political organization to strong centralized monarchies. In response to the growing Zulu threat many other clans and displaced people united behind charismatic leaders and adopted Zulu military tactics to control growing populations.

In West Africa Islam had been an important religion for hundreds of years, though rural people often resisted conversion and continued their traditional religious practices. Because of this, earlier Islamic empires had tolerated local religion. In 1804 Muslim reformers who wanted a more traditional adherence to Islam called for a jihad, or holy war, to enforce shari'a, Islamic religious law, in western Africa. This call for reform was most strongly accepted in the Hausa states (northern Nigeria). The Islamic reformers challenged the Hausa kings, helped to unite Hausa peasants and devout Muslims against traditional West African elites, and established a caliphate based in the city of Sokoto. The **Sokoto Caliphate,** as it came to be known, was the largest Islamic empire in West Africa since the Songhai Empire in the late sixteenth century. Sokoto became a center for Islamic learning, with schools and libraries attracting Muslim scholars from all over West Africa. Non-Muslims were allowed to remain in the caliphate if they paid a tax, but traditional religious ceremonies and festivals were suppressed. Those who resisted were killed or enslaved; many of those slaves were sold through the trans-Saharan slave network. Once power had been consolidated, the Sokoto Caliphate controlled much of western Africa for the remainder of the nineteenth century.

AFRICA AND THE SLAVE TRADE

The effect of the **transatlantic slave trade** on Africa was staggering. It is estimated that over 10 million Africans were enslaved between 1550 and 1800. Eight million of these enslaved African men, women, and children were sent to the Western Hemisphere, while another 2 million lived in bondage in the Middle East and North Africa. Scholars generally agree that this displacement of people from Africa did not have a dramatic effect on the overall population of sub-Saharan Africa but that some regions, such as parts of western Africa, were greatly affected by the large population losses over many years. They theorize that the ability of some regions to recover from depopulation was directly related to the proportion of women of childbearing age that were enslaved.

In the late eighteenth century the institution of slavery and the slave trade came under attack. Successful slave revolts in St. Domingue (present-day Haiti) were initially met with brutal repression by European colonial leaders, but the revolts provoked some to question the moral legitimacy of slavery. Several nations banned the international slave trade: Denmark in 1803, Britain in 1807, and the United States in 1808. Abolitionists groups, particularly in Britain, lobbied their governments to outlaw slavery and enforce a ban on slave trading.

By the 1840s, with slavery and the international slave trade having been declared illegal in most of Europe, the British navy began policing the West African coast. Having taken control of Sierra Leone in 1808, the British made that area a colony for liberated slaves. The Royal Navy's aggressive antislavery patrols resulted in the capture of over 1,600 ships and the rescue of 160,000 Africans headed for the slave markets in the Caribbean and South America. As it became more difficult to obtain slaves in West Africa, the slave trade moved farther south and then to East Africa. The transatlantic slave trade joined an already well-established East African slave trade that had existed for decades. A third of the slaves from East Africa were sent to the Americas; the remainder went to North Africa and the Middle East. Because of the high demand for slaves in Cuba and Brazil, the transatlantic slave trade was not completely ended until 1867.

AP Tip

The end of the transatlantic slave trade did not mean that all slavery or slave trade ended. After 1867 thousands of Africans, many from East Africa, would be enslaved over the next several decades. These slaves were shipped to Brazil and Cuba, as well as parts of the Middle East. Ironically, the end of the transatlantic slave trade signaled the growth of slavery in Africa itself. African-led trading companies in West Africa and clove plantations in East Africa enslaved thousands of Africans throughout the nineteenth century. Slavery in Africa increasingly took on the features of the oppressive slave societies that had developed in the Western Hemisphere. Ethiopia did not finally abolish slavery until 1932. This often-overlooked final chapter of slavery and the slave trade provides interesting background information for a free-response essay that deals with slavery or the slave trade.

The slave trade accounted for much of the trade with Africa before 1825, but after that, exports like gold, ivory, and palm oil became dominant. The palm oil trade reshaped the Niger River delta of western Africa. **Palm oil,** used in Europe and the United States for industrial machines, soap, and candle making, was in high demand during the nineteenth century. Palm oil companies used many slaves to harvest the oil from the interior of West Africa and transport it to the coast. Leaders of these trading companies were like merchant princes, politically and economically controlling port cities and interior lands as well as thousands of slaves. Slaves owned by these trading companies could work and buy their own freedom, though that rarely happened. King Jaja of Opobo, one slave who purchased his freedom, established an independent trading state from the port of Opobo in 1869. By shifting their trade from slaves to raw materials, Africans were able to keep their access to Western industrial imports.

EGYPT AND ETHIOPIA: MODERNIZATION AND WESTERNIZATION

During the nineteenth century both Egypt and Ethiopia began efforts to adopt European technology in order to compete with and defend themselves from Western power. As **modernization** began, ideas of **nationalism,** which had been on the rise in Europe, arrived in Africa. Egypt was the first African empire to be reshaped by the modernizing influence of western Europe. The power vacuum created when Napoleon's troops were pushed out of Egypt in 1801 was filled by Muhammad Ali. Ali initially led Albanian soldiers to restore Ottoman imperial control in Egypt. Once in control, Ali began a decades-long process to modernize and Westernize Egypt. Shocked by the ease with which Napoleon had taken control of Egypt in 1798, Ali moved quickly to begin a political, economic, and military restructuring program.

European experts were brought in to train and reorganize the Egyptian military, new weapons were imported, and a European-style military training college was opened. Promising young officers were sent to Europe to be trained in the latest techniques of warfare. Additionally, schools were opened to train both army surgeons and military bandleaders. Ali's new army would be built by the conscription of Egyptian peasants. To pay for his modern military, Ali revoked traditional mamluk land privileges and forced Egyptian peasants to grow cotton for export. In other areas Ali attempted to blend Islamic culture with modernization by starting an Islamic newspaper and printing Islamic classics in Arabic. Though an industrial economy was never fully realized, Ali and his family, who retained control after his death, continued to experiment with modernizing the nation. Egypt was linked by railroads, new irrigation canals increased agricultural production, and a postal service was formed. Ali's grandson Ismail Ali continued Egyptian modernization and Westernization efforts in the second half of the nineteenth century, proclaiming, "My country is no longer in Africa, it is in Europe." Egypt's goal of becoming a Western-style power was cut short when the cotton market collapsed after 1870, which led to increasing Egyptian debt and control by European investors.

The ancient kingdom of Ethiopia also began modernizing in the nineteenth century. Partial imperial control was reestablished in the 1830s by Emperor Téwodros II, who began his modernization program with the purchase of European weapons, which he then attempted to manufacture locally, in an effort to update the kingdom's military. When Menelik became emperor in 1889, the integration of his Shoa kingdom created what would constitute modern-day Ethiopia. Under Menelik's rule, Ethiopia continued to industrialize its military and defend against the growing threat of European imperialism. By continually shifting alliances with European powers, Ethiopia was able to import the latest modern weaponry. In 1896 at the **Battle of Adowa**, Menelik and his army routed Italian troops. Ethiopia was one of only two independent African nations at the end of the nineteenth century.

AP Tip

When students see the term *nationalism,* they often think only about how it affected Western nations. But the building of national identity can also be seen in the actions taken by African nations like Egypt and Ethiopia during the nineteenth century. The construction of the Suez Canal in Egypt in the 1860s and the military defeat of Italian troops by Ethiopia in the 1890s helped foster nationalistic sentiments among their citizens. If a free-response essay deals with nationalism, mention its importance in Africa.

OLD IMPERIALISM VERSUS NEW IMPERIALISM

As the **Industrial Revolution** emerged in Europe and the United States, Western nations continued expanding their political, economic, and cultural reach. European powers had imperial aspirations before the nineteenth century, and nations like Spain, France, and Britain had built colonial empires in the Americas and Asia over several hundred years. Their goal was to obtain from their colonies the resources for their industries back home.

In the late nineteenth and early twentieth centuries this **colonialism** was replaced by what historians refer to as **New Imperialism**, by which Europeans used their economic and technological power to reshape Africa politically and culturally. New Imperialism sought to bring Africa more fully into the global economy as both a supplier of raw materials and a purchaser of manufactured goods. To accomplish this, Europeans, who until the 1850s were in Africa primarily as traders on the coasts, invaded and set up colonial governments. These governments reorganized Africa to tap the natural resources of various African regions. A variety of motives pushed Europeans to build new imperialistic empires in Africa. Politically, with nationalism on the rise, creating an empire became important to newly industrial powers. When Britain claimed territory in Africa, its rival France followed suit. By the end of the nineteenth century, even smaller European powers like Belgium had staked claims to parts of Africa. Economically, industrialized countries needed to secure a constant source of raw materials—gold, diamonds, copper, and cotton were among the most significant. Culturally, Europeans wanted to Westernize the parts of Africa they had influence over. Thousands of Christian missionaries came to Africa in the late nineteenth and early twentieth centuries to transfer both religious and cultural ideas. Westerners had begun to equate their advances in technology with the superiority of their cultures. Given this fact, African values were increasingly viewed as a barrier to the development of modern society. As the poet Rudyard Kipling exhorted, Europeans had to embrace the "white man's burden" and "civilize" Africa, assuming political, economic, and cultural control.

Before the 1870s Europeans had only a few colonial settlements, such as Britain's Sierra Leone and France's Algeria. But in the last quarter of the nineteenth century, several western European nations invaded and quickly divided up Africa, an example of New Imperialism commonly referred to as the **"scramble" for Africa**.

NORTH AFRICA

Egypt seemed an unlikely victim to be swept up in the quest to control Africa. In 1869 the nation completed the **Suez Canal**, shortening the distance between Europe and Asia and ushering in an age of increased global trade. To many Egyptian elites the canal symbolized the modernization of Egypt and a source of national pride. But projects like the canal, funded by cotton exports and international loans, increased Egypt's foreign debt. By 1876 over a third of all export earnings went to pay the debt, and Egypt was forced to sell its shares in the Suez Canal to European investors. As Europeans became more involved in financing the debt, they pressured their governments to protect their investment. In the late 1870s both Britain and France used their influence to install Europeans as the minister of public works and minister of finance. In 1882 the Ottoman sultan deposed Ismail Ali, setting off a series of revolts. Britain feared the loss of access to India through the canal and stepped in to "stabilize" the country. The British army arrived in Egypt and began a seventy-year occupation, ruling indirectly through a puppet Egyptian government. Development projects—for example, damming the Nile River—did increase agricultural production in the country, but this primarily benefited the traditional elite at the expense of the peasants. European control brought Western customs that challenged traditional Islam. This was the hallmark of the New Imperialism in Egypt.

WESTERN AND EQUATORIAL AFRICA

European nationalism stimulated the competition for colonial territory and exacerbated a potential for armed conflict. In the 1870s France wanted to increase its access to raw materials in the interior of western Africa by building a railroad. During the same period in equatorial Africa, Belgium's king Leopold II, convinced by explorers that great wealth could be obtained, began his expansion into the Congo River basin. The French were also interested in the vast territory of the Congo.

To avoid increased tension, German chancellor Otto Von Bismarck called together European diplomats to help redefine their role in Africa. At the **Berlin Conference** (1884–1885) the nations of Europe agreed to divide up Africa peacefully. The new rules in the "scramble" for Africa, as it was later called, included no slave trading and, most important, no interference in the territory of other European occupiers. From 1885 to 1900, Britain, France, Germany, Italy, Portugal, Belgium, and Spain consolidated their colonial territory in Africa. By the end of the nineteenth century Ethiopia and Liberia remained the only two independent nations in Africa.

King Leopold II created the Congo Free State after the Berlin Conference, while France and Portugal took control of the remaining territory in equatorial Africa. Unlike western Africa, the Congo region did not have a long history of trade in desirable raw materials. Instead of directly ruling the region, France, Portugal, and Belgium hired private companies to administer their territory and obtain resources that would be profitable. Many of these areas did not have cash crops that could be sold, so Africans were forced to develop new crops to pay the taxes demanded by the private companies. In territories like the Congo Free State, Africans were forced to harvest rubber and transport it out of the jungle themselves. Methods used to coerce people into these new economic activities led to atrocities committed by the private companies to maximize profit. Press coverage of the horrors in the Congo Free State led to the Belgium government taking over King Leopold's private company in 1908.

SOUTHERN AFRICA

Europeans had long been active on the coast of southern Africa. The Dutch East India Company established the Cape Colony in 1652. The

British came to control the trading outpost in 1795. **Afrikaners**, descendents of Dutch settlers on the Cape of Good Hope, moved into the interior throughout the next century. The discovery of diamonds in the 1860s brought other European settlers to the region in search of riches. Seeking to control the diamond territory, British troops launched campaigns into the interior of southern Africa. After defeating the Xhosa in 1878, British troops faced off against the most powerful kingdom in southern Africa, the Zulu, led by King Cetshwayo. The large, well-disciplined Zulu military was initially able to hold its own against the outsiders, but in the end superior European weapons led to British victory and the exile of King Cetshwayo. Zulu land was parceled into farms for white ranchers as Britain expanded its imperial rule, founding Southern Rhodesia (now Zimbabwe) and Northern Rhodesia (now Zambia.) The British then turned their eyes toward the Afrikaner republics, Transvaal and Orange Free State. **The South African War** (1899–1902) pitted these two early European colonizers, the Afrikaners and the British, against each other. With over 450,000 troops the British were able to defeat the Afrikaners and extend their colonial control in southern Africa. Concerned by the increasing costs of their overseas commitments in Africa as well as other parts of the world, the British created the Union of South Africa, which gave European colonial settlers greater control in administering the empire. Ironically, the recently defeated Afrikaners emerged as the dominant force within the new Union of South Africa. To increase their own power and isolate the indigenous African population, the white South African parliament passed the Native Land Act in 1913. The law placed Africans on reservations and did not allow them to own land in other parts of the nation. Segregation and racial division increasingly became a part of South Africa in the early twentieth century.

THE EFFECTS OF NEW IMPERIALISM ON AFRICA

In the nineteenth and early twentieth centuries New Imperialism affected all regions of Africa, but not always in the same way. Responses to colonialism took many forms. Some Africans seized on the opportunity to supplant traditional ruling African elites and found jobs in colonial governments or as soldiers in newly developed colonial armies. Others tried desperately to retain their status and their traditional way of life. Groups such as the Zulu in the south and the Asante in the west continued to challenge imperial control. Most Africans tried living the same way they had before colonial power came, but they found this increasingly difficult. Colonial powers disrupted long-established societies by replacing local leaders with new, professional bureaucrats. Challenges to long-held landowning patterns drastically altered the lives of many rural Africans; in parts of Africa where land was held communally, Western ideas of private property reshaped communities. As they put more territory into agricultural production, European powers held that local ideas on land use inhibited progress. The need to pay taxes to colonial governments forced many Africans into new occupations as miners, construction workers, and field hands. Families were split up as men took work in areas away from their homes. Thousands of Christian missionaries came to Africa during this period to open schools and teach Christian doctrine. In southern and central Africa, Christianity found converts, though for many Africans Christianity was tainted by its connection to the European colonial masters who had brought the religion with them. Missionaries had much less success in areas such as northern and eastern Africa, where Islam had a long tradition. Muslims also expanded their reach into sub-Saharan Africa, appealing to Africans in part because they were unburdened by the New Imperialism.

Multiple-Choice Questions

1. The Ethiopian victory over the Italian invasion in 1896
   (A) showed that an African military force could resist Europeans.
   (B) was made possible because Italians succumbed to malaria and smallpox.
   (C) convinced other African leaders to resist with traditional weapons.
   (D) was based on the Ethiopian alliance with Sudan and France.

2. Europeans controlled equatorial Africa by all of the following methods EXCEPT
   (A) creating colonial governments staffed solely by Europeans.
   (B) controlling native trade at key port cities.
   (C) offering incentives to local rulers to collect taxes and raise armies.
   (D) insisting that taxes be paid in cash crops or European currencies.

3. The major effect of the Berlin Conference of 1884–1885 on Africa was
   (A) Europeans could not colonize the eastern region of Africa.
   (B) Africa's industrial capacity would be developed through European grants and loans.
   (C) Africa would be colonized through "effective occupation."
   (D) treaties would be created to develop new African nations.

4. Nineteenth-century modernization in Egypt and Ethiopia began with
   (A) creating schools for peasants.
   (B) building modern militaries with European weapons.
   (C) creating state-owned farm cooperatives.
   (D) growing staple crops for agricultural export.

5. All of the following are examples of modernization in Egypt EXCEPT
   (A) European-style military training schools.
   (B) construction of the Suez Canal.
   (C) construction of railroads to link parts of the country.
   (D) increasing political democracy.

6. The leading force for modernization in Egypt during the nineteenth century was
   (A) Muhammad Ali.
   (B) Shaka Zulu.
   (C) Menelik.
   (D) King Leopold II.

7. All of the following were characteristics of New Imperialism EXCEPT
   (A) the need for raw materials.
   (B) the belief that Europeans were culturally superior.
   (C) the desire to increase the slave trade.
   (D) the desire to bring Christianity to Africans.

8. Which of the following is the best explanation for the ending of the transatlantic slave trade in the nineteenth century?
   (A) Africans refused to supply slaves for the transatlantic slave trade.
   (B) Ideas of European superiority increased.
   (C) Moral opposition to slavery grew in industrialized nations, particularly Britain.
   (D) Sugar prices on the global market fell.

9. Which African nations were able to remain independent at the end of the nineteenth century?
   (A) Egypt and Liberia
   (B) Congo Free State and Ethiopia
   (C) Union of South Africa and Sierra Leone
   (D) Ethiopia and Liberia

10. The South African War (1899–1902) was different from other imperialist struggles for which of the following reasons?
    (A) European colonizers fought one another.
    (B) Democratic reform came to southern Africa.
    (C) Africans defeated modern European armies.
    (D) African elites used Europeans to consolidate political power.

11. Which of the following resulted from the rapid growth of Islam in West Africa during the late 1700s?
    (A) Cultural connections with Ethiopians
    (B) Closer ties with Spain
    (C) Decreased tribal warfare
    (D) Increased enslavement

12. Which of the following was an important cause for the rise of the Zulu kingdom of Southern Africa?
    (A) Islamic conversion
    (B) The Atlantic slave trade
    (C) Drought and warfare
    (D) The Indian Ocean trade system

13. Most of the slaves held by West Africans in the late 1800s were
    (A) trained for military purposes.
    (B) forced into domestic service.
    (C) sold to the Middle East.
    (D) used to grow food crops.

14. French conquest of Algeria began as a direct result of
    (A) naval blockages by Algerian warships.
    (B) Algerian mistreatment of French diplomats.
    (C) attacks on French settlements by Algerians.
    (D) discovery of gold in Algeria by merchants.

15. "The Europeans said that there were to be no more slaves; if someone said 'Slave!' you could complain to the *alkali* who would punish the master who said it, the judge said, 'That is what the Europeans have decreed.'"

    This recollection, by Baba of Karo, a Nigerian woman, suggests that Europeans
    (A) mistreated Nigerian women.
    (B) enslaved Nigerians.
    (C) ended slavery in Nigeria.
    (D) altered Nigerian religious practices.

Free-Response Questions

1. Analyze the demographic and economic continuities and changes that occurred in Africa as a result of the African slave trade from 1550 to 1890.

2. Compare the causes, goals, and effects of "old imperialism" and New Imperialism in Africa.

Answers

MULTIPLE-CHOICE QUESTIONS

1. ANSWER: **A.** Ethiopian forces had modernized their military with Western weapons and finally stopped the Italian invasion at the Battle of Adowa. Ethiopia and Liberia were the only two independent African nations at the turn of the nineteenth century (*The Earth and Its Peoples,* 5th ed., pp. 780-781/6th ed., p. 701).

2. ANSWER: **C.** European nations did not use local rulers to administer their new colonial territories in equatorial Africa, nor would they have supported their raising of local military forces (*The Earth and Its Peoples,* 5th ed., p. 778/6th ed., pp. 697-698).

3. ANSWER: **C.** The Berlin Conference brought together European nations to divide up territory in Africa in what the conference termed "effective occupation." By the end of the nineteenth century all but two nations in Africa had fallen under the control of European colonial powers (*The Earth and Its Peoples,* 5th ed., pp. 777-778/6th ed., p. 699).

4. ANSWER: **B.** Egypt and Ethiopia, which understood the potential threat of European military power, began modernization programs by purchasing weapons and using European military

training methods (*The Earth and Its Peoples,* 5th ed., p. 716/6th ed., p. 700).

5. ANSWER: **D.** Throughout the mid-nineteenth century Egypt's modernization program focused on economic measures and did not include any elements of increased political democracy (*The Earth and Its Peoples,* 5th ed., p. 716/6th ed., pp. 634-635).

6. ANSWER: **A.** Muhammad Ali stepped into the power vacuum left by the French in 1801 and ruled Egypt until 1848. Ali attempted to remake the nation militarily and economically so that it could compete with the growing power of Europe (*The Earth and Its Peoples,* 5th ed., pp. 715-716/6th ed., p. 634).

7. ANSWER: **C.** European nations that participated in the New Imperialism in the nineteenth century sought to include Africa as part of a global economy; it would supply raw materials and purchase industrial goods made in Europe. This type of imperialism did not require slave labor (*The Earth and Its Peoples,* 5th ed., pp. 772-774/6th ed., p. 717).

8. ANSWER: **C.** The rise of the antislavery movement in western Europe brought increasing pressure to end the transatlantic slave trade. Britain led in ending the slave trade by stationing its navy off the coast of West Africa and enforcing international agreements that prohibited the slave trade (*The Earth and Its Peoples,* 5th ed., pp. 718-719/6th ed., p. 701).

9. ANSWER: **D.** The "scramble" for Africa left only Ethiopia and Liberia independent at the end of the nineteenth century (*The Earth and Its Peoples,* 5th ed., p. 776/6th ed., p. 700).

10. ANSWER: **A.** The British and Afrikaners (descendents of the Dutch), two European groups that had colonized southern Africa, battled each other in the South African War. The victorious British reorganized the territory several years later as the Union of South Africa, in which the defeated Afrikaners played a leading political role (*The Earth and Its Peoples,* 5th ed., pp. 779-780/6th ed., p. 697).

11. ANSWER: **D.** A dramatic movement toward centralization and reform based on Islamic law resulted in the establishment of new political states in West Africa. As political centralization increased, so did the internal system of slavery in West Africa (*The Earth and Its Peoples,* 5th ed., pp. 715-716/6th ed., p. 697).

12. ANSWER: **C.** Southeast Africa was hit hard by a drought in the early 1800s. In 1818 Shaka created the Zulu kingdom out of the conflicts for cattle and grazing lands caused by the drought (*The Earth and Its Peoples,* 5th ed., pp. 713-714/6th ed., p. 694).

13. ANSWER: **D.** Slaves in West Africa, such as those in the Sokoto Kingdom, were mostly used for raising food. By 1865 more slaves were held by West Africans just in the Sokoto Kingdom than in any slave state in the Western Hemisphere (*The Earth and Its Peoples,* 5th ed., pp. 715-716/6th ed., p. 697).

14. ANSWER: **B.** When France would not repay a trade debt to the Algerians, an Algerian official struck a French diplomat. France

invaded Algeria because it wanted to avenge the insult (*The Earth and Its Peoples,* 5th ed., pp. 717-718/6th ed., p. 693).

15. ANSWER: **C.** The quotation (for Baba of Karo's full account, see the Diversity and Dominance section in Chapter 27) describes how the British put an end to the institution of slavery in Nigeria (*The Earth and Its Peoples,* 5th ed., p. 782/6th ed., p. 698).

FREE-RESPONSE QUESTIONS

1. In this continuity and change over time question, dates are significant. At the beginning of the period the African slave trade was just beginning; by the end it was effectively over in the Atlantic. In the sixteenth century the growing desire for slave labor for sugar plantations in the Caribbean was increasing. You should point out that some regions of Africa were severely affected by the loss in population, while others were relatively untouched; western Africa was the area hardest hit, and the demographic and economic structure of this region greatly changed. The desire for European manufactured goods and hardware encouraged strong West African empires to meet the growing demand by expanding the taking of prisoners of war to sell to slave traders. As the supply of slaves became more difficult to obtain in western Africa, the slave trade moved down the coast to Angola. In the nineteenth century increasing industrialism, rising moral objections, and the increase in legitimate trade goods, such as palm oil, led to the decrease of the overall number of people enslaved. In a continuity and change over time question, don't forget to address what may remain the same. Throughout the period, both Africans and Europeans worked together to obtain victims who were sold into slavery. By 1890 the slave trade supplying the Americas had ended, but slavery in Africa and the Middle East still remained.

2. For this comparison question, make certain you clearly state the difference between "old" and New Imperialism. Originally, imperialism looked to obtain the resources of Africa, such as slaves and gold, but did not feel the need to control the continent politically or culturally. By contrast, New Imperialism was driven not just by economic motives but by a desire to take greater control of Africa itself. This shift from old to new can be tied to changes primarily in Europe, such as nationalism, industrialism, and the aspiration to "civilize" Africans. Unlike the earlier form of imperialism, which left most Africans untouched by the European presence, New Imperialism would drastically affect all. Traditional political, economic, and social structures were reshaped as Europeans took the decision-making role, which often viewed Africans as second-class citizens and economically marginalized them.

17

THE MIDDLE EAST: CIRCA 1750 TO CIRCA 1900

KEY CONCEPTS

- During the nineteenth century the Ottoman Empire was faced with a series of political, economic, and social setbacks that led to a decline in its power.
- Throughout the nineteenth century attempts at modernization, such as the Tanzimat ("reorganization") and Young Ottoman reforms, sought to strengthen the empire.
- Reform did not include women, who were unable to increase their work or educational opportunities, and certain reforms caused them to lose economic powers they previously held.
- Despite these widespread reforms, the Ottomans still lagged behind other more developed nations.
- As the twentieth century approached, the Ottoman Empire was labeled the "sick man of Europe," and European leaders posed the Eastern Question: Should the Ottoman Empire continue to exist; if not, who should take over its territory?
- Nationalistic Turkish reformers called the Young Turks gained increasing influence in the empire. They supported a crackdown on ethnic minorities and closer alignment with Germany.

KEY TERMS

- Crimean War
- Eastern Question
- extraterritoriality
- Greek independence
- Janissaries
- "sick man of Europe"
- Tanzimat

- ulama
- Young Ottomans
- Young Turks

The Middle East is discussed in depth in *The Earth and Its Peoples,* fifth edition, Chapters 24 and 28 and sixth edition, Chapter 23.

THE OTTOMAN EMPIRE AT THE START OF THE NINETEENTH CENTURY

As the nineteenth century began, the Ottoman Empire, which had controlled much of the Middle East since the 1450s, was faced with a series of serious political, economic, and social issues. Economic and technological changes taking place in both Europe and the United States began to have a profound impact on the Middle East. As Western powers continued to modernize, adopting new technology and successfully industrializing, the Ottoman Empire lagged behind. The Ottomans' stagnant economy, lack of financial reserves, and weak governing elites initially made Western-style modernization difficult. In addition, the empire was steeped in centuries of tradition, and powerful political groups within the empire had much to lose if reform was undertaken. Much of the period from 1800 to the start of World War I would be dominated by the Ottomans' struggle to adapt to the powerful changes taking place around them.

By the late eighteenth and early nineteenth centuries the Ottoman central government had grown weak, and it was increasingly difficult to control an empire that included most of the Middle East and North Africa. Regional power bases had arisen in both Egypt and Arabia, where local ruling elites often ignored the imperial government in Constantinople (modern Istanbul). In Arabia, the Islamic fundamentalist Saud family took control of the sacred cities of Mecca and Medina. This was an embarrassing loss of control for the Ottoman sultan Selim III (1789–1807), who was unable to lead Muslims in the traditional pilgrimage to Mecca, one of the Five Pillars of Islam. In Egypt Napoleon's French troops had invaded and controlled the region before they were finally forced out in 1801. The Ottomans were unable to reinstate imperial control, which led to the rise of Muhammad Ali. Though Ali did not openly separate himself from the Ottoman Empire in the early part of the nineteenth century, his independence would serve as a constant reminder of the difficulty the Ottomans had in controlling distant territories.

Political divisions in the heart of the empire became more apparent at the start of the nineteenth century. The **Janissaries**—originally young Christian boys taken primarily from the Balkans, converted to Islam, and trained to be the elite military guard of the sultan—resisted the adoption of new, Western ideas. Economic privileges that had been given to these troops strengthened their influence in the empire. Change was viewed as an attack on traditional values and the power of the Janissaries. In addition, the **ulama**, Muslim religious scholars, controlled the Islamic courts within the empire and had great influence over political and cultural policy. Talk of modernization was seen by the ulama as an attack on Islam. Regardless of these opposition forces,

Sultan Selim III would be the first of many Ottoman rulers who would try to restore the power of the empire with a program of reform.

MODERNIZATION IN THE OTTOMAN EMPIRE

Sultan Selim III was interested in the technological and military changes that were taking place in western Europe. To strengthen the empire, he devised a modernization plan that included a European-style military, standardized taxation, and reinstitution of Ottoman control over provincial governors. To fund this reform agenda, the Sultan used excise taxes on goods such as tobacco and coffee. These reforms met with strong opposition from both the Janissaries and the ulama. In Serbia, an Ottoman province in which the Janissaries acted as provincial governors, military forces vented their frustration with the reforms on the local Serbian Orthodox Christian population. Unable to put down the military uprising, the Ottoman sultan was forced to seek help from the ruler of Bosnia, and together they were able to defeat the Janissaries. But because of the threat of Russian intervention, the Ottomans were unable to limit future Bosnian influence in the region, and they could not disarm Serbia's Orthodox Christians. Serbia became effectively independent, another piece of the decaying empire lost from Ottoman control. The resistance of the Janissaries and the ulama forced Sultan Selim III to end his reform program in 1806, but that did not stop a looming rebellion. In a demonstration of the powers arrayed against change, an uprising by traditionalist forces took control of Istanbul; Selim was imprisoned and later killed.

Mahmud II (r. 1808–1839), Selim's cousin, gained the support of the ulama and Janissary forces in Istanbul and became sultan, calming the uprising. Mahmud supported limited reforms but understood that change needed to occur slowly if he hoped to solidify his power. It would be events at the far edge of the empire that would enable him to embark on drastic reform. In Greece, local groups were organizing against Ottoman control throughout the 1820s. European nations, eager to reclaim the Greek and Roman traditions that had been identified as the source of Western civilization, aided **Greek independence** fighters. Volunteers from all over western Europe, among them the English poet Lord Byron, fought and died to liberate Greece from Ottoman control. Mahmud looked to Muhammad Ali's Egyptian forces to help defend the empire from attack. The modernized Egyptian army greatly impressed the sultan as they fought to continue Ottoman control over the region. Still, Egypt's help would not be enough; at the Battle of Navarino, in 1829, the bulk of the Ottoman naval fleet was destroyed by European powers that were determined to see an independent Greece.

After witnessing the effectiveness of the Egyptian troops, Mahmud began an aggressive push to modernize the Ottoman military. In 1830 the sultan's argument to modernize was given added support when his former Egyptian ally attacked Syria and looked to supplant the Ottomans as the dominant power in the Middle East. In response, the sultan reorganized both the empire's military and its financial institutions. A new artillery unit was created, which once again led to revolts by the Janissary forces. Taking more dramatic steps, Mahmud officially dissolved the Janissary corps and turned his new artillery on them to crush the uprising. Mahmud also wanted to limit the power of the ulama, which he saw as a barrier to modernization. Even with these changes, Egyptian troops continued their assault on Ottoman territory. The sultan had trouble retaining the loyalty of his own armed forces, which shocked the empire in 1839 when the rebuilt Ottoman naval force sided with Egyptian troops. In this period of crisis, Mahmud died and was replaced by his sixteen-year-old son, Abdul Mejid (r. 1839–1861). Sensing an opportunity, Egyptian troops attacked in Anatolia (modern Turkey) and headed toward the Ottoman capital, Istanbul. With few alternatives, the new sultan was forced to turn to the British and French, who helped defend the capital and used financial threats to force Egyptian withdrawal from Ottoman territory. Thereafter, the survival of the empire depended on European aid.

The modernizing spirit of Mahmud II would be continued by Abdul Mejid, who announced a series of reforms that would become known as the **Tanzimat** ("reorganization"). These guaranteed political rights for men—for example, free public trials, a limited right of privacy, and more equitable methods of tax collection. The reforms also attempted to modernize the Ottoman Empire and were supported strongly by its European allies. Military training schools modeled on western European methods were opened. Adopting Muhammad Ali's approach for Egypt, young officers would be trained in Europe, and Westerners were brought in to educate the Ottoman elite. Later, a system of national preparatory schools was established to funnel graduates into military colleges and universities. Increasingly, French became the language of instruction, though most students still learned to read and write using the Quran. Young men educated in these new schools took on the style and fashions of modern Europeans and slowly replaced traditional bureaucratic elites. In Istanbul, a small though prominent elite embraced the Westernization of Ottoman society. They read newspapers in French, traveled to Europe, and supported the importation of military, industrial, and communications technology.

European governments were especially pleased to see reforms concerning religious minorities within the empire. The tax on non-Muslims was abolished, and codes specifying equal legal protection for Muslim, Jewish, and Christian subjects were passed. European powers were increasingly interested in the status of Christians in the empire, and missionaries flowed into Ottoman territories in the second half of the nineteenth century. New tax collection practices ended tax farming, a source of much hardship for the rural population. More secular legal codes began replacing shari'a, Islamic law. As a consequence, the power of the ulama declined, as did the lure of religious education, and fewer students entered religious schools.

Reform dealt exclusively with men. In some ways it further restricted Ottoman women. Women were not given increased political participation or educational opportunities. Industrial labor and professional occupations, hallmarks of the new process of modernization, were not open to women, who lost more ground as industrialism gripped Ottoman cities and a competitive cash-based economy developed. The Westernization of the court system also led to a loss of power for women, as secularization shifted property and inheritance issues from Islamic courts to state courts, where women had no standing. Despite these widespread reforms, the Ottomans still lagged behind other more developed European nations, a fact that would threaten the empire repeatedly in the second half of the nineteenth century.

AP Tip

Do industrialism and Westernization give women more rights and opportunities? When students first examine this idea, they think of western Europe and the United States and quickly think yes; more factory jobs open up, women leave home and demand equal treatment and pay, as well as increased access to the political process. Though this did happen in some societies, the process of Westernization narrowed the role of some women in the Ottoman Empire. Industrialization did not lead to new opportunities in either the factories or the professions, which were the exclusive domain of men. In addition, the Westernization of the court system led to women's loss of power over inheritance and property. In Islamic courts women could continue to control property and wealth by establishing trusts in the name of their sons and acting as executors. But with no standing in the new secular courts established by the Tanzimat reforms, women lost this power.

THE CRIMEAN WAR: 1853–1856

Throughout the nineteenth century, Russia, looking to expand, had laid claim to Ottoman territory in the northern part of the empire. The tsar had taken over the Georgian region of the Caucasus and supported Serbian independence. The Ottomans' northern neighbors viewed themselves as the protectors of Orthodox Christianity in both Europe and the Middle East. When Egyptian forces invaded Syria, the tsar and his troops came to the defense of the Ottoman sultan, successfully pushing back Muhammad Ali's forces. The treaty that followed officially recognized Russia as "defender of the Orthodox faith" within the Ottoman Empire. But the sultan viewed Russia as a territorial threat in the north, and in the 1840s and 1850s Britain and France were the Ottomans' primary European allies. In 1852 France was named protector of the Holy Sepulcher in Jerusalem, a Christian religious site. Considering this a violation of earlier treaty rights, Russia invaded Ottoman territories in modern-day Romania in 1853, thus beginning the **Crimean War.**

Britain and France quickly came to the aid of their Ottoman allies. Both European nations distrusted Russia and saw its expansion as a threat to their overland access to trade through Central Asia. For the next three years, the Ottoman Empire, Britain, France, and the Italian Kingdom of Sardinia-Piedmont battled the Russians in Romania, the

Black Sea, and the Crimean peninsula. The war was fought on both land and sea, with Ottoman troops effectively resisting in Romania, despite reports of incompetence delivered by French and British commanders. In a dramatic naval confrontation on the Black Sea, Tsar Nicholas (r. 1825–1855) was forced to sink the entire Russian naval fleet to protect the approaches to the port city of Sevastopol. The city was placed under siege and finally taken in 1856. The death of Nicholas in 1855 and repeated military setbacks for Russian troops forced the new tsar, Alexander II (r. 1855–1881), to sue for peace. The peace terms ended Russian expansion and balanced France's and Britain's territorial ambitions in the Ottoman Empire, with both countries agreeing that Ottoman land would not be taken exclusively for their own use. The Crimean War was a clash between traditional and modern methods of warfare, and it altered the world's perception of the Ottoman Empire. Highly trained cavalry troops, the elite of the Ottoman forces, were decimated by new infantry with modern artillery and breech-loading rifles. Ottoman military strength was clearly declining. European powers began to question the legitimacy of its continued existence.

THE "SICK MAN OF EUROPE" AND THE EASTERN QUESTION

Tsar Nicholas had called the Ottoman Empire the **"sick man of Europe."** As the twentieth century approached, it continued to fall behind the European nations militarily, economically, and technologically. As a result, many Western powers asked if the Ottoman Empire should continue to exist, and if not, who should take control of its territory. This idea, known as the **Eastern Question**, was hotly debated during the second part of the nineteenth century.

The Ottomans had serious economic problems that continued to worsen. Declining agricultural revenues, large debts to foreign nations, inflation, widespread corruption—all made reform difficult. Ottoman elites held that the only solution to these systemic problems was to continue reform and tie the empire more closely to Europe. An Ottoman imperial bank was created, the gold coin currency was tied to the British pound, and factories began opening in urban areas. During the period 1860–1880 a large demographic shift of people from rural villages to large urban areas began to occur in many parts of the empire. Cities such as Istanbul, Damascus, Beirut, and Cairo expanded as an urban professional class was created and industrial wage laborers found work. In addition, Russian expansion in Central Asia, which they would invade and gain control of Azerbaijan, Dagestan, and Chechnya, released a flood of Muslim refugees making their way to the Ottoman Empire and Iran. These new immigrants fueled the growth of cities, and competition for wage labor jobs was intense. Imports into Anatolia far exceeded exports, causing inflation that hit the new arriving urban poor hardest.

Communities of Europeans had increased their presence in the empire, particularly in cities. Bankers, merchants, missionaries, technical experts, and diplomats were just some of these new residents. Europeans lived apart from the rest of Ottoman society, housed in Western enclaves not subject to Ottoman laws. **Extraterritorially**, the exemption from the legal jurisdiction of the country of residence, was granted by some nations to foreign diplomats, but in the Ottoman Empire all Europeans were exempted. For many young reformers this violation of Ottoman sovereignty was unacceptable and demanded action.

AP Tip

One of the most important skills in AP World History is the ability to recognize global patterns and processes, such as industrialization, and analyze their effects in various regions. In many ways, attempts at reform and industrialization in the Ottoman Empire were similar to comparable efforts in the Americas, Africa, and Asia. All of these regions were forced to grapple with the issues of modernization and industrialization in the nineteenth century. Western European nations were the first to use the new technology to change and retool their economic system and military power. The Ottoman Empire and other less developed areas were especially interested in gaining new military technology. The creation of a global industrial market turned nations into either manufacturers of consumer goods or suppliers of raw materials for those goods. As suppliers of raw materials, the Ottomans were unable to generate enough wealth to become fully industrialized. Attempts at further industrialism had to be funded from Europe and the United States, leaving many underdeveloped nations in debt and with unwelcome European and American interests managing parts of their economy. The Ottoman Empire's inability to industrialize and the causes of that failure can be compared with the experience of many other areas that went through this global process in the nineteenth and twentieth centuries.

A reform group known as **Young Ottomans** demanded change in the 1860s and 1870s. They were looking to assert Ottoman authority over Europeans living in the empire, who, they held, had been allowed to ignore Ottoman laws and traditions. To that end, they wanted to Westernize the empire and thereby make extraterritorially obsolete. These reformers saw universal male suffrage and the creation of a constitutional monarchy as steps in that direction. A constitution was drafted and accepted by Sultan Abdul Hamid II (r. 1876–1909) in 1876. After that, the Young Ottoman movement lost much of its momentum when the threat of war with Russia arose in 1877, but limited reform continued under the Tanzimat programs.

Multiple-Choice Questions

1. Attempts to modernize and industrialize the Ottoman Empire affected women by
   (A) opening up new job opportunities but decreasing political participation.
   (B) limiting new job opportunities but increasing political participation.
   (C) limiting new job opportunities and political participation.
   (D) keeping their status as it had been before reform began.

2. Because of declining military power, internal rebellion, and widespread corruption, this empire in the late nineteenth century was referred to as the "sick man of Europe."
   (A) Portuguese
   (B) Spanish
   (C) Ottoman
   (D) Russian

3. The Ottoman Empire began a reform campaign to modernize its military after its defeat in this war.
   (A) Crimean War
   (B) World War I
   (C) Macedonian Independence Movement
   (D) Greek War for Independence

4. Which of the following characterizes European influence in the Ottoman Empire at the end of the nineteenth century?
   (A) Europeans funded Ottoman attempts at industrialization and used the increasing debt to exert control over Ottoman policies.
   (B) European nations occupied large portions of the Ottoman Empire during the late nineteenth century.
   (C) Europeans fought several wars over parts of the declining Ottoman Empire, creating colonies that supplied raw materials for industrialization.
   (D) Europeans aided in the creation of a secular and industrialized Ottoman Empire.

5. Land-based empires like the Ottoman Empire dealt with which of the following problems during the nineteenth century?
   (A) A lack of financial resources, a stagnant economy, and weak governing elites
   (B) Internal rebellion, colonization, and hyperinflation
   (C) Military modernization, industrialization, and constant warfare
   (D) A stagnant economy, industrialization, and constant warfare

6. The Tanzimat reforms begun in the 1830s included restructuring and limiting
   (A) the power of the religious elite.
   (B) the role of the sultan.
   (C) ownership of land.
   (D) secular legal codes.

7. All of the following were efforts at reforming the Ottoman Empire
   EXCEPT
   (A) standardizing the tax system.
   (B) ending tax farming.
   (C) creating a more effective military.
   (D) connecting to Russian markets.

8. The language used in Ottoman military schools and universities in
   the second half of the nineteenth century was
   (A) Turkish.
   (B) Russian.
   (C) French.
   (D) Arabic.

9. Extraterritoriality in the Ottoman Empire was
   (A) the practice of granting special trading privileges to Asians
       and Europeans.
   (B) exemption from Ottoman laws given to European residents.
   (C) debt restrictions placed by European financiers.
   (D) use of a European monetary system within the empire.

10. The major reason Janissaries resisted modernization of the
    military was because
    (A) they did not support the sultan's reforms.
    (B) they had weak leadership within the corps.
    (C) they saw it as a threat to their special privileges.
    (D) Egyptian troops had not had success with a modernized
        military.

11. The major exports of the Ottoman Empire were
    (A) silk and spices.
    (B) slaves and textiles.
    (C) opium and tobacco.
    (D) gold and ivory.

12. The Young Turks promoted
    (A) nationalism and modernization.
    (B) extraterritoriality.
    (C) fundamentalist Islam.
    (D) landowners and elites.

13. By the late 1800s the population of the Ottoman Empire was
    (A) declining because of epidemic diseases.
    (B) shifting to areas outside of the empire.
    (C) moving to urban areas.
    (D) expanding into desert and mountain regions.

14. Which of the following was an effect of the Westernization of the
    Ottoman Empire on women's lives?
    (A) Expanded educational opportunities
    (B) Greater legal restrictions
    (C) More participation in religious institutions
    (D) Larger economic roles

15. Muhammad Ali's transformation of Egyptian society in the early
     1800s included the use of
     (A) Ottoman governmental organization.
     (B) British naval strategies.
     (C) ancient Egyptian cultural references.
     (D) French military practices.

Free-Response Questions

1. Compare the effects of nationalism on the Ottoman Empire to the
    effects of nationalism on Europe from circa 1750 through circa
    1900.

2. Trace the continuities and changes in the effects of Islam on the
    political structures of the Ottoman Empire from circa 1750 to circa
    1900.

Answers

MULTIPLE-CHOICE QUESTIONS

1. ANSWER: C. Women were unable to work in either the new
    industrial or professional jobs that development brought, and
    political participation by women was not an element of reform
    (*The Earth and Its Peoples,* 5th ed., pp. 693–694/6th ed., pp. 638–
    639).

2. ANSWER: B. The Ottoman Empire had a number of serious
    problems in the second half of the nineteenth century, such as an
    outdated military force, internal revolts in outlying provinces, and
    widespread corruption in its imperial government (*The Earth and
    Its Peoples,* 5th ed., pp. 799–800/6th ed., p. 634).

3. ANSWER: D. The Ottoman Empire was impressed by the effective-
    ness of Muhammad Ali's Egyptian forces, which had adopted
    Western weapons and training techniques. The Ottomans saw
    these new methods up close when Egyptians aided the empire in
    its effort to retain control of Greece (*The Earth and Its Peoples,* 5th
    ed., pp. 688–689/6th ed., p. 634).

4. ANSWER: A. European nations and financial institutions supported
    Ottoman attempts at industrialism, but as these attempts failed, the
    Ottomans increasingly fell into debt. This debt gave western
    European nations the opportunity to have a say in internal
    Ottoman affairs (*The Earth and Its Peoples,* 5th ed., p. 694/6th ed.,
    p. 640).

5. ANSWER: A. The Ottoman Empire, like Russia and China, struggled
    with a lack of financial resources, a stagnant economy, and weak
    governing elites (*The Earth and Its Peoples,* 5th ed., pp. 687–688/6th
    ed., p. 640).

6. **ANSWER: A.** The Tanzimat reforms attempted to reshape Ottoman society for its push to modernize and industrialize. Among these reforms were the attempts to restructure and limit the power of the ulama, the Islamic religious elite (*The Earth and Its Peoples,* 5th ed., pp. 691–692/6th ed., p. 637).

7. **ANSWER: D.** The early Ottoman reform efforts addressed a number of problems, such as the practice of tax farming, an inequitable tax system, a weak military, and rebellion in the provinces (*The Earth and Its Peoples,* 5th ed., pp. 689–690/6th ed., p. 634).

8. **ANSWER: C.** The Ottoman education system embraced Western ideas and materials, with French becoming the dominant language in both military schools and universities (*The Earth and Its Peoples,* 5th ed., pp. 691–692/6th ed., p. 637).

9. **ANSWER: B.** Europeans who lived in Ottoman cities created separate enclaves apart from the rest of Ottoman society. In these communities extraterritoriality made Europeans exempt from the empire's laws (*The Earth and Its Peoples,* 5th ed., p. 694/6th ed., p. 640).

10. **ANSWER: C.** The Janissaries rejected Western military technology because they saw it as a rejection of their traditional horse-based warrior culture (*The Earth and Its Peoples,* 5th ed., pp. 689–690/6th ed., p. 635).

11. **ANSWER: C.** Ottoman export trade was limited. Trade items mostly included tobacco and opium sent to the Chinese market by merchants from the United States (*The Earth and Its Peoples,* 5th ed., p. 694/6th ed., p. 640).

12. **ANSWER: A.** The Young Ottomans advanced an agenda of liberal European ideas, national pride, and religious reform (*The Earth and Its Peoples,* 5th ed., pp. 694, 696/6th ed., p. 640).

13. **ANSWER: C.** As the Ottoman Empire became more Westernized, an increasing percentage of the population lived in its big cities of Istanbul, Cairo, Damascus, Beirut, and Alexandria (*The Earth and Its Peoples,* 5th ed., p. 694/6th ed., p. 640).

14. **ANSWER: B.** The Tanzimat reforms in education and greater opportunity applied to men. Women had less legal rights since many of their rights of inheritance were not recognized by the new secular laws (*The Earth and Its Peoples,* 5th ed., pp. 692–693/6th ed., p. 636).

15. **ANSWER: D.** The French use of conscription and schools for European-style military skills were used by Muhammad Ali to strengthen his army (*The Earth and Its Peoples,* 5th ed., pp. 688–689/6th ed., p. 634).

FREE-RESPONSE QUESTIONS

1. Begin this comparison essay with a definition of nationalism—the identification of people with a nation, often centered on language or religion. The effects of nationalism and the creation of the

nation-state were seen first in Europe. Unlike the Ottoman Empire, Europe—the western areas in particular—formed political states often based around a common language or shared culture. Leaders of these new nations used nationalistic sentiment to rally citizens to compete economically, politically, and militarily, fueling the industrial growth of Europe during this period. The European states that suffered the most from nationalism were those that contained many ethnic and religious minorities, such as the Austro-Hungarian Empire, and were not able to create one effective national identity. This was also an issue for the Ottoman Empire. With multiple ethnic, religious, and linguistic minorities in Ottoman territory, creating a shared national identity was difficult, if not impossible. As nationalism grew stronger in the nineteenth century, Ottoman elites worried that outlying provinces would not be loyal to the empire and instead would support a separate state based on local identity. Instead of increasing industrial development to compete with other strong nations, the Ottoman Empire slowly broke apart. By the start of the twentieth century, the reforming Young Turks would begin to give the Ottomans a national identity that was based on ethnic Turks, further alienating minority groups in the empire.

2. In 1750 the Ottoman Empire had used shari'a to define many aspects of society, such as the roles of men and women. Religious minorities were welcome in the empire, but they had to pay a tax for their refusal to accept Islam. The Ottoman Empire had a divided power structure; the sultan and imperial bureaucracy dealt with political, economic, and diplomatic affairs, while the ulama controlled many daily issues of Ottoman life, such as the Islamic courts. Finally, the elite troops known as the Janissary corps wielded significant power, particularly in outlying provinces. Leading Janissaries were often appointed imperial governors for parts of the empire.

    By the 1850s the Ottomans had undergone significant change and reform. Western influences and efforts to industrialize had lessened the power of Islam in several different ways. The Tanzimat reforms had created equal-protection laws for religious minorities and ended the practice of taxing non-Muslims. The ulama had lost power under the reforms when many legal issues were transferred to state courts. Finally, the Janissary corps, which had resisted change—particularly the modernization of the military—was shown to be ineffective during the Greek War of Independence. To protect their power, Janissaries rebelled in some provinces. The corps would finally be disbanded.

    By the turn of the twentieth century, groups like the Young Turks began attacking European influence. But these new reform groups were secular in nature and did not support a reemergence of traditional Islamic rule under the ulama. Islam had lost a significant amount of its control over the political and social structure in the empire. Though the majority of Ottoman citizens continued to be Muslim and locally the ulama still had strong influence throughout this period, Western values had reshaped much of Ottoman society.

18

ASIA: CIRCA 1750 TO CIRCA 1900

KEY CONCEPTS

- European colonialism directly and indirectly affected most of Asia during the nineteenth and early twentieth centuries, as nations such as Britain and France enlarged their imperial possessions in the region.
- India came under Great Britain's complete colonial control by the mid-nineteenth century as a large and efficient British bureaucracy reshaped the nation politically, economically, and socially.
- Throughout the nineteenth century the Qing dynasty's control of much of China was threatened by internal economic crisis and rebellion and by increasing pressure to open up the nation to European colonial powers.
- Unlike most other parts of Asia, Japan was able to limit the influence of the colonial powers and become a strong imperial power as it modernized and industrialized using new ideas and technology from the West.
- By the end of the nineteenth century nationalist movements that questioned European colonial control began to attract supporters, especially among the educated class.

KEY TERMS

- Aborigines
- Bannermen
- British East India Company (EIC)
- clipper ships
- durbars
- extraterritoriality
- Indian Civil Service

- Maori
- Meiji Restoration
- most-favored-nation status
- nawab
- Opium War
- raj
- Russo-Japanese War
- sepoys
- Sepoy Rebellion
- Sino-Japanese War
- Taiping Rebellion
- Treaty of Nanking

Asia is discussed in depth in *The Earth and Its Peoples,* fifth edition, Chapters 24–27 and sixth edition, Chapters 21, 23, 25, and 26.

THE BRITISH EMPIRE IN INDIA

By the late eighteenth century the Mughal Empire was disintegrating. The Maratha Confederation, a group of aligned states in central India, ruled over more territory than the Mughals, and Muslim princes, known as **nawabs**, created powerful states all over India. The Mughals had become just one of the many groups competing for power in South Asia.

South Asia came under the influence of Europeans earlier and more completely than did East Asia or Africa. British, Dutch, and French trading companies pursued access to profitable trade goods, but by the late eighteenth century Britain was the dominant European power, supplanting the French and Dutch while slowly gaining power over local groups. The British made alliances with various regional powers to strengthen their access to trade and established trading bases in port cities, which they hired Indian troops, known as **sepoys**, to protect. By 1818, the East India Company had regional power bases in Bengal, Madras, and Bombay. In some states—such as Bengal—the EIC took complete control of the area, but in others they ruled through local princes.

THE RAJ

In 1818 the British Empire's presence in India dwarfed its other colonial possessions, containing more people than all of western Europe. The British **raj** (reign) set out to transform India administratively and economically using a Western model. Like the Mughals before them, the British had to moderate their cultural interference, and long-standing, diverse Indian customs made formulating consistent policies difficult. The British focused on creating a powerful, efficient government that, relying heavily on military power, primarily sepoy regiments, set out to disarm the over two million local warriors. The raj also emphasized private property and attempted to reshape the varied and complex system of land ownership in India. With military control and simplified property ownership, the British maximized taxes to pay for further economic and administrative reform.

While attempting to modernize, the British also supported some Indian traditions, and in the process often increased the power of local princes and religious leaders. Indian and British elites had periods of conflict and harmony, but the common Indian citizens often suffered throughout. Women, members of lower castes, and the poor experienced little benefit from reform or tradition.

British control of the Indian economy spurred trade both within India and with other nations. Opium from Bengal, coffee from Ceylon, and tea from Assam brought needed revenue into South Asia. But increased competition from British textile mills turned India, once a world leader in textile exports, into an exporter of raw cotton. The new economic order did not provide any protection for the poor or needy, and rebellion was common in the first half of the nineteenth century. Though many of these uprisings were easily suppressed, the EIC was concerned with the loyalty of Indian sepoys, who by the 1850s were well armed and made up over 80 percent of the British military force in India.

Discontent was growing among the sepoys. Most initially came from the Bengal region, but as the force grew with recruits from other ethnic groups, the Bengali sepoys felt threatened. Hindu and Muslim sepoys encountered service requirements that conflicted with their religious obligations. The British soon changed the requirements, but in 1857 the early protests grew into widespread rebellion by sepoys, peasants, and discontented elites, all joining to challenge the authority of the British. The **Sepoy Rebellion** was put down the next year, but it called for reevaluation of British rule in India.

Political change began immediately with the final removal of Mughal and EIC control. A British viceroy, much like a Mughal emperor, now ruled India from Delhi. Queen Victoria decreed that all Indians would receive equal protection of the law and freedom to practice their religion and traditional customs. Though reform was speeded up, tradition still had its place in a modernizing India. Viceroys continued to grant privileges to local Indian princes as long as they were loyal to the queen, and nurtured that loyalty by inviting the princes to **durbars**, elaborate celebrations similar to the pageants Indian princes had held during the Mughal reign.

India under British control was most notable for an efficient bureaucracy that governed the huge South Asian region. The **Indian Civil Service** (ICS) was open to all applicants, but only those who could afford an elite university education in Britain were eligible for the senior posts. Beyond educational qualifications, the negative racial views of the British kept the number of Indians in the ICS low. The British also spent millions of pounds to modernize Indian infrastructure—harbors, irrigation canals, and other public works—with increased trade in mind. Public and private money poured in as staple crops such as tea and cotton became central to the Indian economy. Railroads, begun in the 1840s, crossed most parts of the country by the 1870s, giving India the fifth-largest railroad network in the world. By 1900 over 188 million people used the vast Indian railroad network for business and religious pilgrimage, and to search for work. With the increase in travel came the growth of cities, which, lacking clean water supplies and adequate sewer systems, led to the spread of cholera. In 1869, Calcutta had new water-filtration and sewer systems, which dramatically reduced the number of cholera deaths. Other big cities followed suit, but in small villages, which could not afford the new systems, cholera deaths remained high.

By the end of the nineteenth century India had become a provider of raw materials and a purchaser of manufactured goods, and through technological change it was becoming economically more profitable. Still, the majority of Indians remained impoverished.

INDIAN NATIONALISM

Indian nationalism had begun to develop in the early part of the nineteenth century. Rammohun Roy, educated in the West and employed by the EIC as an administrator, urged greater Indian control of the nation and argued for Pan-Indian nationalism that would reduce social, economic, and ethnic divisions. Through the Brahmo Samaj (Divine Society), founded in 1818, he attempted to meld both Western nationalism and religious tradition and led an effort to abolish customs such as child marriage, sati (widow burning), and slavery.

AP Tip

Nationalism, which reshaped much of Europe in the late nineteenth century, was not limited to Europe. As Britain, France, and other colonial powers gained control of parts of Asia and Africa, they introduced a variety of political, economic, and cultural ideas, including nationalism. In India, British control of the education system meant that a new, rising upper-middle class was shaped by many of these European values. As you consider comparative, change over time, or document-based essay questions, expand your discussion of rising nationalism to regions beyond Europe. Many nations and groups in Asia and Africa did not become independent in the late nineteenth century, but the dream of nationalism was providing the basis for movements that would confront colonialism in the twentieth century.

After the Sepoy Rebellion, the Brahmo Samaj became less influential. As Western education spread, Indian intellectuals became more interested in Western secular ideas and nationalism. Many of the new nationalists, members of the rising middle class who sent their children to Western-style schools, felt politically and economically excluded. To push forward new initiatives, the Indian National Congress was founded in 1885. It called for reduced military spending and more government assistance for the poor and needy, and it promoted Pan-Indian unity across the many social, religious, and economic divisions in India. But because the Indian National Congress presented the views of Indian elites, it lacked the widespread popular support needed to challenge the British Empire's control.

THE DECLINE OF THE QING EMPIRE

By the late eighteenth century, the Qing dynasty in China was experiencing many of the problems common to other Asian land empires—rebellion within the empire among the poor and displaced, corruption of local officials, and failure to recognize the growing threat of European powers. Europeans were starting to complain about China's restrictive trade policy, which allowed Europeans to trade only in Canton. Initially, the Canton system, as Europeans called it, benefited both the Europeans and the Chinese, but by the 1790s Britain was increasingly concerned about its trade deficit with China. Britain had been importing tea from China for centuries, but could find no goods that the Chinese would purchase in return. British silver had to be used to purchase tea. As the **British East India Company** drifted closer to bankruptcy, it used its connections in Parliament to press for a diplomatic mission to open the Chinese market. In 1792 Lord George Macartney was sent to meet with the Qing Emperor, but his mission failed; the Chinese were not interested in changing the system. Other Europeans had the same experience with the Qing. Many European leaders concluded that the Chinese were a barrier to modern industrial growth.

China also began to deal with an economic decline that would continue into the next century. Some historians have estimated that the population had exploded to 350 million people by the late 1700s. With more people, the demand for food increased as land available for farming decreased. The need for wood for heat and construction led to the deforestation of large parts of China, and the government's inability to maintain dams and dikes led to flooding. Portions of the Grand Canal became impassable, devastating communities that depended on it to transport their crops. Rebellion became common and severe. The Qing, whose empire was twice the size of the Ming Empire, relied on local elites to govern, and corruption became widespread as decline continued. Further, many Han Chinese viewed the Qing as foreign Manchurian conquerors in league with Europeans. The White Lotus Rebellion (1794–1804), a messianic attempt to restore the Ming dynasty and see the return of Buddha to China, set the stage for uprisings throughout the early nineteenth century.

THE OPIUM WAR

During the early 1800s the Chinese still had little appreciation for the growing power and threat of Europeans. British and American traders were making large profits by importing opium into China as early as the seventeenth century. The first Qing law restricting its importation was enacted in 1729, but opium continued to be smuggled in. Both importers and Chinese merchants benefited as supply rose and addiction increased. By the 1830s people from all parts of Qing society were using opium, and the government met with European diplomats in Canton to demand a ban on the drug. The British saw any attempt to restrict the importation of opium as a threat to their continued economic success; when negotiations broke off, British naval forces moved into the south China coast and the **Opium War** (1839–1842) began.

The Chinese, like the Ottomans, relied on hereditary soldiers known as the **Bannermen**, many of whom went into battle with swords and knives—no match for British artillery. With no navy, the Chinese could not counter naval bombardments of their ports, and they could not quickly move troops to protect inland cities when the British began sending naval vessels up the Yangzi River. When Nanjing was threatened, the Qing negotiated for peace. The resulting treaty ended the Canton system. Four more cities were open to foreign traders; the island of Hong Kong became a permanent British colony; the tariff on imports was lowered; **extraterritoriality**—exemption from Qing laws—was given to British citizens living in China; an indemnity of 21 million ounces of silver was paid to Britain, which was granted **most-favored-nation status**—any privileges the Qing granted to other nations would also be granted to Britain. Most-favored-nation status would prevent colonization of China because land given to one European power would have to be given to Britain as well.

Future treaties would give Europeans more freedom within China, and in 1860 the import of opium would be legalized. By 1900 the number of treaty ports open to Westerners had grown to more than ninety. The treaty ports and extraterritoriality created small, insulated communities of Europeans with little concern for the economic and political conflicts playing out in China. Christian missionaries were moving into rural China to preach the gospel while opening hospitals and social service organizations. Many Chinese saw this new religion as a subversion of traditional Confucian values. Foreigners, who were growing in numbers and privileges, were increasingly resented by the Chinese, who were sinking deeper into poverty.

THE TAIPING REBELLION

The mix of economic crisis, rebellion, and declining Qing power erupted in a civil war. In the southern province of Guangxi, weak agricultural harvests, class conflict, and ethnic divisions gave rise to the Taiping movement. Led by Hong Xiuquan, a Hakka (an ethnic minority long at the bottom of Chinese society), the Taiping ideology was based on the teaching of Christian missionaries. Hong saw himself as the younger brother of Jesus, told by God to build a new kingdom on earth and bring peace by driving the Manchu out of China. As the Taiping movement grew, Hong emphasized the anti-Manchu aspects of his ideology, rallying ethnic Chinese to the movement. As the rebellion expanded, Chinese villages were captured and forced to join the movement, men and women were segregated, and the practice of foot binding was ended because women were required to participate fully in farming and become soldiers. By 1853 the Taiping had taken Nanjing and made it their capital.

This widespread threat forced the Qing to begin to modernize their military under the leadership of provincial governors. With greater knowledge of their terrain and local self-defense forces, provincial governors convinced many Bannermen to serve under civilian military leadership.

In 1856, the Qing were confronted with the **Taiping Rebellion**, the Nian rebellion in northern China, and a renewed threat from European powers, who claimed that all of the provisions of the **Treaty of Nanking** had not been fulfilled. The Arrow War (1856–1860), a series of coastal attacks by French and British forces, culminated in the 1860 invasion of Beijing and the destruction of the Summer Palace. The Qing were forced to agree to a new set of treaties to satisfy European powers; in return, they received European money and weapons, which enabled them to defeat both the Nian and Taiping Rebellions in the 1860s.

The Taiping Rebellion was devastating. Deaths were estimated at twenty to thirty million. Disease became widespread as bubonic plague, which had been around for centuries, began to infect large numbers again and to spread beyond China. Land lay waste. The government had declining revenue from land taxes.

Recovery took place at the local level as the provincial governors who had come to prominence during the Taiping Rebellion continued to increase their power. Governors began to levy and collect taxes, raise armies, and develop their own bureaucracies. Men like Zeng Guofan instituted reform programs to rebuild agriculture, communications, and the military. An alliance of provincial governors and high-ranking aristocrats, like Cixi, later known as the "Empress Dowager," often supplanted Qing officials by controlling domestic and foreign policy decision making.

THE BOXER REBELLION

The Qing dynasty was a shell of its former self. This was confirmed in 1894 when China went to war against the rising Asian power of Japan over its encroachment into Korea. The **Sino-Japanese War** lasted only six months and would force China to leave Korea, cede Taiwan and the Liaodong Peninsula, and pay a large indemnity. European powers stepped in to help the Qing keep Liaodong, but the dynasty was clearly nearing collapse. China's population had grown to 400 million. Food production was not keeping pace. Most Chinese peasants survived on a diet of grain and vegetables. Landlords lived off the rents of their tenants, while officials, still chosen by the exam system, had become increasingly corrupt. Young men living in port cities, with few opportunities to get ahead, resented the European elite.

In 1898 the Empress Dowager Cixi seized power in a palace coup. Two years later, she started supporting a secret society known as the Righteous Fists, or Boxers, who attacked foreigners with the goal of forcing them from the country. After attacks on Western missionaries throughout the country, the Boxers turned their sights on the foreign legations in Beijing. Western powers and Japan mobilized a military force and captured the city, ending the Boxer Rebellion and forcing the Chinese to pay reparations.

JAPAN AND MODERNIZATION

Like China, Japan was forced to deal with Western powers in the nineteenth century. But unlike China, Japan used Western industrial and military technology to become an important global power. In the late eighteenth and early nineteenth centuries the emperor of Japan was revered but had no real power; the country was governed by the Tokugawa Shogunate, headed by a military leader in Edo (present-day Tokyo). Regional lords, or daimyos, controlled large parts of the country with little intervention from the shogunate. The shogunate feared Western influence and in the 1600s had outlawed foreigners from entering Japan. When Russian and British ships were spotted off the Japanese coast in 1792, leading daimyos understood the potential threat and began enlarging their armies.

When American Commodore Matthew C. Perry sailed into Japanese waters in 1853, the potential foreign threat became real. Perry demanded that his steam-powered warships—and U.S. vessels arriving in Japan in the future—be able to enter ports to trade and resupply. Looking to China's defeat in the Opium War and fearing a similar fate, the shogunate accepted the Treaty of Kanagawa, which was modeled on the unequal treaties signed by China and the West. Disappointed with that decision, some provincial governors began secretly plotting the overthrow of the Tokugawa regime. When British and French ships shelled the southwestern coast of Japan in 1864 to protest Japan's treatment of foreigners, provincial leaders—particularly those in Choshu and Satsuma, which had prospered from black-market foreign trade—united against what they viewed as a weak and ineffective shogunate.

THE MEIJI RESTORATION

The civil war that followed was short, but it drastically reshaped Japan. The Tokugawa Shogunate was removed; Emperor Mutsuhito (1868–1912) was declared restored. The new government was referred to as the **"Meiji Restoration,"** after the emperor's reign name. The emperor remained a figurehead. Real power was held by a small group known as "Meiji oligarchs," who wanted to transform the nation into "a rich country with a strong army." To that end, they began a widespread program of modernization and industrialization that would take knowledge from anywhere in the world as long as it would strengthen Japan. Foreign technical help was brought in but always carefully controlled by the state. Reform was funded with deficit financing so as to avoid the debt that suffocated other developing nations. Meiji leaders modeled their redesigned government on imperial Germany's and their military on Britain's navy and Prussia's army. The new educational system included vocational, technical, and agricultural schools, and a system of universities. State-run industries were started up to produce consumer goods, then later sold off to repay governmental debts to large Japanese investors. Private enterprise and innovation were strongly encouraged.

Japan modernized to protect itself from Western powers, but as it grew stronger, it too turned its eyes to becoming a colonial power. Meiji leaders like Yamagata Aritomo urged that Japan create a sphere of influence that would include Korea, Manchuria, and a portion of China; if Japan did not actively control these areas, others would—a threat to Japan's security. Japan first went to war with China in 1894. The six-month conflict forced China to cede control of Taiwan to Japan and leave Korea. Having sent forces to help China put down the Boxer Rebellion in 1900, Japan pressed for control of the mineral-rich Chinese province of Manchuria. In 1905, to the shock of many around the world, Japan defeated Russia in the **Russo-Japanese War**. By 1910, with control over Korea and southern Manchuria, Japan matched the world's colonial powers.

AP Tip

Comparing how India, China, and Japan reacted to foreign influence can help you understand the growing impact of the West on this region in the nineteenth and early twentieth centuries. By the early 1800s, India had several regional powers struggling for control, among them the British East India Company, which controlled a large part of the country by the 1850s. After the Sepoy Rebellion, the British Empire took control. India did receive benefits from British colonial rule, but like other colonial possessions India was shaped to benefit Britain commercially, and all significant decisions were made in the mother country. China openly resisted Western influence and first attempted to control European access and trade. But by closing themselves off, the Qing prevented themselves from learning about and adopting new technology and were ultimately unable to resist repeated demands from Western nations. Only Japan was able to control and shape Western influence. Japan had the luxury of being at the far edge of European influence. With few resources, it was not as desirable as India or China. Using Western ideas and technology, Japan was able to develop an industrial economy and a modern military with which to protect itself—and even defeat Russia, an important European power.

WESTERN DOMINANCE IN SOUTHEAST ASIA AND THE PACIFIC

Britain, France, and Holland competed to become the dominant global power in Asia. By the 1850s, it was becoming clear that Britain was surpassing the others. Several factors resulted in the increasing British presence in Southeast Asia and the Pacific. The aggressive attempts by the British East India Company both to secure new trade routes and centers and to protect its position in India led to its expansion into Singapore in 1824, Burma in 1826, and the port of Rangoon and the remainder of coastal Burma in 1852. But the EIC was attempting to create a mercantilist network of trade to match the one it had created a century earlier. Tied to the needs of its growing industrial economy, Britain wanted to trade freely with Asia from protected port cities. Raw materials in Asia and other regions were necessary for factories back in Great Britain. Those raw materials would come back to Asia as low-priced manufactured goods for Asian consumers. Both sides benefited, but industrialized nations like Britain dictated the terms of the new trading system. Another major factor propelling British expansion in Southeast Asia was the larger and faster clipper ship. After 1850, **clipper ships** made up the majority of the British commercial fleet. Able to transport more cargo in less time, they further increased Great Britain's commercial dominance.

Captain James Cook mapped and explored New Zealand and the eastern coast of Australia from 1769 to 1778. Increased trade and advanced ship design would lead the British to once-remote parts of the South Pacific. Unlike India, where a limited number of Englishmen controlled a large indigenous population, the South Pacific saw the arrival of many British migrants, who displaced the native residents. Having had few contacts with the outside world, the 650,000 indigenous people in Australia and 250,000 **Maori** in New Zealand had little resistance to diseases brought by the British settlers. The British migration to Australia, originally founded as a penal colony in 1788, proceeded slowly until the discovery of gold in 1851. This brought thousands of European and Chinese migrants to the growing colony. After the gold rush waned, the British pursued an active policy of colonization, which resulted in over a million settlers by 1860. The colonization of New Zealand moved more slowly. The first settlers came to hunt seals and whales. By the late nineteenth century, with the defeat of the Maori resistance, migrants looked to the frontier for profitable agricultural lands. As they had earlier in colonial Canada, the British supported increasing self-government for both Australia and New Zealand. In 1901 six separate colonies united to form a self-governing Australia, and in 1907 New Zealand did the same. These increasingly independent nations did not extend equal rights to the indigenous peoples within their borders. In 1897, Australia legally segregated **Aborigines** onto reservations where they had very few legal rights or protections. A New Zealand law that required that voters be able to read and write English disenfranchised most Maori. On a more progressive note both Australia and New Zealand were among the first nations to allow women the right to vote as early as 1894.

Pressure for new markets and resources led Western powers further into Southeast Asia in the late nineteenth century. Indochina was occupied and finally controlled by the French in 1895. Britain annexed the last piece of Burma (today Myanmar) in 1885 and extended its control into Malaya (today Malaysia) in waves throughout the 1870s and 1880s. In Southeast Asia, only Siam (today Thailand) would remain independent, although significantly reduced in size. Most of the region contained fertile land and had a history of intensive agriculture. In places where the population was sparse, Europeans imported labor and began profitable agricultural enterprises, growing crops from other parts of the world such as tobacco, manioc, and maize. These political and economic changes reshaped many social elements of Southeast Asian society. As new land was brought under cultivation, people who had traditionally been hunters and gatherers were displaced. Large-scale migration changed the ethnic makeup of many Southeast Asian nations as people from China and India migrated to places like the Malay Peninsula. European missionaries attempted to convert Southeast Asian residents, but it was Islam, which had been in the region for hundreds of years, that became increasingly accepted because it had no ties to foreign occupiers. By the beginning of the twentieth century, nationalist political movements in places like India were starting to have an impact on Southeast Asia's views on colonial occupation. Young people were beginning to question the motives and nature of European imperialism.

Still, Asians recognized the power of industrialism and the increasingly global economy. Beginning in the mid-nineteenth century, thousands of Indians, Chinese, and Pacific Islanders migrated for work overseas. The end of the slave trade and the emancipation of slaves in the British colonial plantation societies created a labor shortage, as many agricultural workers, who were no longer bound to the land, left to seek other opportunities. British plantation owners targeted high poverty areas to recruit field workers. These migrants, initially from India, signed contracts of indenture that bound them to work for a specified amount of time in return for free passage—faster, larger ships made transporting migrants easier and more economical—as well as a salary, housing, clothing and medical care. As other nations like France and Holland outlawed slavery, the migration of Indians, Chinese, and Japanese to the Caribbean plantations swelled. By the turn of the century, thousands of migrants had left their homes in Asia in search of economic opportunity and a new start.

Multiple-Choice Questions

1. To protect their trading empire in India, the British East India Company used
   (A) British troops trained in India.
   (B) British troops trained in Britain.
   (C) Indian troops led by British officers.
   (D) British troops led by company officials.

2. In the late eighteenth century the Mughal Empire in India
   (A) strengthened its hold over most of South Asia.
   (B) began to disintegrate as it was challenged for power by new Indian states and Europeans.
   (C) created a power-sharing system with France and Britain.
   (D) disappeared after its defeat at the hands of British troops.

3. Which of the following were the most important causes of Britain's growing nineteenth-century dominance in Southeast Asia and the Pacific?
   (A) Military victories, free-trade polices, and changes in shipbuilding technology
   (B) Military victories, mercantile policy, and industrial technology
   (C) Free-trade polices, treaty making, and changes in shipbuilding technology
   (D) Mercantile policy, changes in shipbuilding technology, and forced migration

4. By the end of the nineteenth century Southeast Asia
   (A) remained independent of European influence.
   (B) was completely under the political and economic control of European powers.
   (C) worked cooperatively to organize new independent autonomous nations.
   (D) had been colonized by European powers with the exception of Siam (Thailand).

5. Which of the following characterizes the relations of the Asian powers with European influence during the nineteenth century?
   (A) Japan and China strictly limited European influence.
   (B) India and Japan were militarily controlled by European powers.
   (C) Japan was able to limit European influence, but China was not.
   (D) India and China both became part of the British empire by 1900.

6. All of the following reasons were causes that led to the migration of increasing numbers of indentured servants from Asia in the nineteenth century EXCEPT
   (A) the end of the transatlantic slave trade.
   (B) the abolition of slavery in European countries.
   (C) the increase in the number of slaves brought from East Africa.
   (D) poverty in Asian regions such as India and China.

7. Which of the following was a consequence for China of the Treaty of Nanking ending the Opium War?
   (A) Trade in opium was abolished.
   (B) New territories were annexed to the Chinese Empire.
   (C) Europeans opened new trading ports.
   (D) The position of Qing Manchu elites was strengthened.

8. All of the following were results of the Taiping Rebellion EXCEPT
   (A) over twenty million people were killed.
   (B) disease epidemics spread.
   (C) refugees flooded into cities looking for safety and food.
   (D) the Qing reestablished their authority over regional warlords.

9. Japan's modernization was successful primarily because of
   (A) the adoption of Western technology and ideas and the limitation of foreign influence.
   (B) limits on individual rights and a strong centralized state.
   (C) overseas conquest and the creation of an imperial army and navy.
   (D) the decentralization of the Meiji Restoration.

10. Which of the following are examples of Japanese military success and the growth of their colonial empire?
    (A) Sino-Japanese War, Boxer Rebellion, and the Russo-Japanese War
    (B) Taiping Rebellion, Sino-Japanese War, and the Sepoy Rebellion
    (C) Sepoy Rebellion, Sino-Japanese War and the Arrow War
    (D) Russo-Japanese War, Sepoy Rebellion, and the Boxer Rebellion

11. Which of the following countries had the greatest political and economic influence on both Hawaii and the Philippines at the end of the 1800s?
    (A) China
    (B) Japan
    (C) United States
    (D) Spain

12. What was a major transformation in Central Asian areas, such as Kazakhstan, during the late 1800s?
    (A) The introduction of Islam
    (B) The drive for political independence
    (C) The expansion of the Qing Empire
    (D) The settlement of Russian farmers

13. "Our nation's emphasis on civil service examinations has sunk deep into people's minds for a long time. Intelligent and brilliant scholars have exhausted their time and energy in such useless things as the stereotyped examination essays, examination papers, and formal calligraphy. . . . We should now order one-half of them to apply themselves to the manufacturing of instruments and weapons and to the promotion of physical studies."

    What aspect of Chinese society is reflected in this 1861 quotation from Feng Guifen, a Chinese official?
    (A) The adoption of a legalist governing philosophy by the Chinese
    (B) The weakness of China as a result of the Taiping Rebellion
    (C) The increasing importance of Confucianism in maintaining Chinese stability
    (D) The willingness of China to accommodate European domination

14. Which of the following British introductions changed Indian society the most during the 1800s?
    (A) Opium
    (B) Railroads
    (C) Cotton agriculture
    (D) Parliamentary government

15. What was the founding idea of the Indian National Congress when it was formed in 1885?
    (A) Modernize the Indian military
    (B) Promote gender and caste equality
    (C) Link India more closely with Britain
    (D) Expand the role of Indians in the colonial government

Free-Response Questions

1. Compare the rise of nationalism in China and India from circa 1850 until circa 1900.

2. Analyze the continuities and changes in British colonialism in Asia from circa 1750 to circa 1900.

Answers

1. **ANSWER: C.** The EIC trained many Indians to protect its interests. These troops known as sepoys were led by British officers (*The Earth and Its Peoples*, 5th ed., p. 721/6th ed., p. 703).

2. **ANSWER: B.** The Mughal Empire lost much of its power at the end of the 1700s as smaller regional powers and Europeans began carving up its possessions (*The Earth and Its Peoples*, 5th ed., pp. 720–721/6th ed., p. 703).

3. **ANSWER: A.** The growth of the British Empire in Southeast Asia and the Pacific was the result primarily of several military victories along the Southeast Asia coast, the pursuit of free-trade policies in the region, and faster and larger clipper ships (*The Earth and Its Peoples*, 5th ed., pp. 729, 731/6th ed., p. 707).

4. **ANSWER: D.** As the nineteenth century came to a close, the majority of Southeast Asia had been colonized by European powers. Only Siam (Thailand) remained an independent power (*The Earth and Its Peoples*, 5th ed., pp. 785, 787–788/6th ed., p. 707).

5. **ANSWER: C.** Japan did seek technical assistance from Western nations, but strictly limited the amount of political and economic influence Europeans had on the nation. China, on the other hand, was unable to limit European influence as China was forced to make numerous concessions to various Western nations (*The Earth and Its Peoples*, 5th ed., pp. 765–766/6th ed., p. 746).

6. **ANSWER: C.** The increase in the number of Asian indentured servants going to work on plantations, primarily in the Americas, was the result of the end of the slave trade and the abolition of slavery by most European countries. In addition, people from India, China, and Japan who lived in extreme poverty saw the system of indenture as an opportunity. (*The Earth and Its Peoples*, 5th ed., pp. 732–734/6th ed., p. 717).

7. **ANSWER: C.** The Treaty of Nanking, which ended the Opium War, forced the Qing to open China to more European trading influence. The number of treaty ports would continue to rise throughout the nineteenth century (*The Earth and Its Peoples*, 5th ed., pp. 700–701/6th ed., p. 646).

8. **ANSWER: D.** The Taiping Rebellion was the most destructive civil war before the twentieth century. Estimates range from twenty to thirty million dead, and serious outbreaks of disease occurred because of the difficulty in burying the dead. Many refugees from the country poured into cities looking for help. The Qing was unable to fully reestablish control over the growing power of regional warlords (*The Earth and Its Peoples*, 5th ed., pp. 704–705/6th ed., p. 648).

9. ANSWER: A. Japan used Western ideas and technology to modernize the nation, but it was careful to limit the amount of Western presence in Japan itself (*The Earth and Its Peoples*, 5th ed., pp. 762–763/6th ed., p. 747).

10. ANSWER: A. The Japanese imperial empire developed as a result of the Sino-Japanese War, by which Japan gained Taiwan and forced China to leave Korea; the Boxer Rebellion in which Japan began to stake a claim on Manchuria; and the Russo-Japanese War, in which Japan received the island of Karafutu (*The Earth and Its Peoples*, 5th ed., p. 765/6th ed., p. 747).

11. ANSWER: C. U.S. settlers had large economic and political interests in Hawaii. In 1898 the United States annexed the country. The United States acquired the Philippines after the Spanish-American War (*The Earth and Its Peoples*, 5th ed., p. 788/6th ed., p. 714).

12. ANSWER: D. During the 1860s and 1870s the Russian Empire expanded into Central Asia. Russian people moved to the area in large numbers to grow cotton and other agricultural goods (*The Earth and Its Peoples*, 5th ed., pp. 784–785/6th ed., p. 643).

13. ANSWER: B. This quotation in the *Diversity and Dominance* special section concerns Chinese responses to imperialism. Feng Guifen's quotation was written to advocate strengthening China through modernization. It was written as Feng was escaping Taiping violence (*The Earth and Its Peoples*, 5th ed., p. 706/6th ed., p. 652).

14. ANSWER: B. By the 1840s India had a railroad network controlled by British interests. The railroad linked the diverse subcontinent, spread diseases like cholera, and mixed castes and sexes (*The Earth and Its Peoples*, 5th ed., pp. 725–726/6th ed., pp. 705–706).

15. ANSWER: D. The Indian National Congress was comprised of mostly Western-educated, elite Indians. They sought to reform Indian society and expand their influence by having more native participation in the Indian colonial government (*The Earth and Its Peoples*, 5th ed., pp. 727–728/6th ed., p. 706).

FREE-RESPONSE QUESTIONS

1. India's colonial experience was vastly different from China's, and this difference affected the political and ideological growth of nationalism in each. India was under full British control by the mid-nineteenth century. British colonial policy led to the growth of an elite educated class, many of whose members would be employed by the Indian Civil Service. These Western-educated elites picked up the ideas of nationalism and organized political organizations like the Indian National Congress. Early nationalists in India supported many of the secular ideas brought by the British and also pushed for religious and social unity. Late nineteenth-century nationalism did not reflect the views of common Indians, and as World War I approached the Indian people had made few real gains toward the ultimate goal of independence.

   Unlike India, China was not under direct European colonial control. As the Qing dynasty declined, nationalists in China characterized the Manchu-led government as a foreign power.

Nationalists did not want to prop up the Qing against increasing European control and influence, but instead wanted a new Chinese government that would modernize the nation. Like Indian nationalists, Chinese nationalists were often Western-educated men, such as Sun Yat-sen.

2. Britain was a colonial presence in Asia by 1750, with trading settlements led by the British East India Company. Between 1750 and 1900 Britain would greatly increase its colonial empire in Asia adding many possessions throughout this period. The competition with France for power and influence in Asia in the early nineteenth century saw Britain expand into India, Southeast Asia, and the Pacific islands. Most of these possessions initially had indirect British rule through the EIC. But after the Sepoy Rebellion in India, Britain began to administer its South Asian possessions more directly. Large numbers of British residents emigrated to places like Australia and New Zealand, and by the twentieth century these colonies were encouraged to begin governing themselves. Other parts of the empire, most notably India, were still strongly controlled by the mother country at the start of World War I, though nationalism was on the rise.

19

Europe: Circa 1750 to circa 1900

Key Concepts

- Revolutionary ideas based on Enlightenment philosophy, dealing with individual liberty and a citizen's right to question the government, swept across Europe in the late eighteenth and early nineteenth centuries.
- The French Revolution produced a conservative reaction throughout Europe, leading traditional elites to actively suppress radical movements.
- The Industrial Revolution transformed European nations in the late eighteenth and nineteenth centuries, as innovation in technology led to massive increases in productivity, creating a new industrial society.
- The Industrial Revolution and Enlightenment ideas combined to create new ideologies that addressed the problems that came with an industrial society.
- By the end of the nineteenth century European industrialization had linked the global economy as never before, as trade in raw materials and manufactured goods increased in all parts of the world.
- The rise of nationalism in the nineteenth century led to the birth of several new nations in Europe, based on shared language and culture.

Key Terms

- Congress of Vienna
- Crimean War
- Declaration of the Rights of Man
- division of labor

- Enlightenment
- Estates General
- Industrial Revolution
- Jacobins
- labor unions
- laissez-faire
- liberalism
- mass production
- mechanization
- National Assembly
- nationalism
- Pan-Slavism
- positivism
- Revolutions of 1848
- "separate spheres"
- Slavophile
- socialism
- steam engine
- Victorian Age

Europe in this period is discussed in depth in *The Earth and Its Peoples,* fifth edition, Chapters 21, 22, 24, 25, and 26 and sixth edition, Chapters 21, 22, 23, and 26.

REVOLUTIONARY IDEAS

In the eighteenth century the battle over colonial possessions and trade routes to the Americas and Asia would lead to revolutionary changes for much of Europe. The growing sea powers of Great Britain and France had supplanted Spain and Portugal, and Great Britain and France would do battle for dominance over North American colonies and trade outlets. The French and Indian War, part of the Seven Years War in Europe, pitted the French with their Amerindian allies against the British. Britain won, forcing France to relinquish its holdings on the North American continent and withdraw from territory in India. The financial cost of these battles was enormous; traditional tax collections would not cover the war debt.

In addition, **Enlightenment** ideas that attempted to apply scientific method to the study of human society had many intellectuals questioning the actions of their government. Europe's growing middle class read about the new Enlightenment ideas in books and newspapers and were familiar with the ideas of social philosophers like John Locke, who argued that government was created to protect life, liberty, and property, and Jean-Jacques Rousseau, who argued that the power of monarchs depended on the consent of the governed. At the same time, these ideas found their way across the Atlantic and would spark protest against the colonial governments in Europe.

Great Britain was the first to learn the power of new Enlightenment ideas when its demands that its colonial subjects help pay for the French and Indian War sparked popular protest in Britain's North American colonies. New taxes and the Proclamation Line of 1763, which placed limits on colonial expansion, led urban and rural poor to join with colonial leaders in questioning the legitimacy of British rule.

Throughout the 1760s repeated British attempts to tax the colonies led to colonists boycotting English goods and attacking royal officials and property. In 1773 the British responded to the Boston Tea Party by closing that port and placing the military in charge of local government. With that, an already active revolutionary leadership was galvanized to break with the colonial master. After an eight-year war, the 1783 Treaty of Paris formalized independence for the new United States of America and a continuing English presence in Canada.

THE FRENCH REVOLUTION

The impact of the American Revolution was deeply felt in France, which had helped the rebelling colonists. An ally of the new United States during the war, France was grappling with its own political and social tensions. French society was made up of three groups, called estates. The First Estate, members of the clergy, accounted for less than 1 percent of the French population; however, the church owned over 10 percent of all land in France and through ecclesiastical fees and tithes controlled a large amount of the country's wealth. The First Estate was organized from the top down, with most of the powerful positions controlled by hereditary nobility. The Second Estate was made up of nobles—about 300,000 people—who controlled over 30 percent of the nation's land and held most of the nation's important political, economic and judicial positions. The rest of French society made up the Third Estate. Peasants made up 80 percent of the Third Estate, but this estate included everyone from the rising middle class, known as the bourgeoisie, to the poorest residents of Paris.

During this period France, under King Louis XVI, was facing severe economic difficulties. Repeated borrowing to fund military action and support for the colonists during the American Revolution had put the nation deep in debt. France was spending more than half of its national budget to service the debt. In 1788, to deal with this crisis, Louis XVI drew up a series of reforms, which he called on a group of nobles to approve. Instead of rubber-stamping them, the nobles questioned the king's leadership. Unable to gain added tax revenue from the elite, Louis XVI called for a meeting of the **Estates General**, the French national legislature, which had not met since 1614. All three estates came together in 1788 and 1789 to discuss ways to solve the economic crisis, but, deeply divided over which direction reform should take, they made little headway. During the stalemate a new union between members of the First and Third Estates began to form. Called the **National Assembly**, it wanted to create a form of constitutional monarchy. To quash this, the king and his advisers locked the Third Estate out of their meeting place, whereupon the members gathered in an indoor tennis court and vowed to write a constitution. Before Louis had organized military forces for an attack on the National Assembly, the urban poor of Paris rose up on July 14, 1789, and attacked the Bastille, a prison that had come to symbolize the old regime. During the Paris revolt, peasants in the countryside began to attack nobles, seizing land, refusing to pay taxes, and destroying documents that recorded their traditional obligations.

These revolts strengthened the National Assembly and emboldened it to issue the Declaration of the Rights of Man. Modeled in some ways on the American Declaration of Independence, the **Declaration of the Rights of Man** went further in listing the natural rights of man, among them "liberty, property, security, and resistance to oppression." While debate in the National Assembly continued, the economic crisis worsened in Paris. Food became an increasingly volatile issue, as it became more difficult for the poor to feed their families. In October thousands marched to Versailles to demand action from the National Assembly, and they searched for the royal family, particularly Queen Marie Antoinette, who had become a symbol of the nobility's disregard of the people. Louis XVI and his family were forced back to Paris, and over the next two years the National Assembly, renamed the Legislative Assembly, radically reshaped France. The new constitution limited the power of the king and abolished the nobility. Strong economic reforms were enacted. Church lands were taken to fund a new paper currency, and priests were made employees of the state and had to be elected to their positions.

Neighboring European countries that at first had favored the weakening of the French monarchy began to reconsider. Austria and Prussia threatened to come to the aid of the monarchy; in response, the Legislative Assembly declared war. The threat of foreign intervention stirred French national identity, and large numbers of citizens joined a new volunteer army, which would battle foreign forces to a standstill by 1792. When Louis XVI attempted to escape Paris and find foreign support, he was arrested and sentenced to death by the newly elected National Convention. (Louis XVI was executed by one of the new symbols of the French Revolution, the guillotine.) The National Convention was made up primarily of middle-class people, and most of these members, including the faction known as **Jacobins**, had strongly held democratic values. Within the Jacobins factions arose. The radicals, led by a young lawyer, Maximilien Robespierre, focused in particular on the needs of the Parisian poor and working class. With support in the streets, Robespierre began using the Committee of Public Safety, established to identify domestic threats to the nation, to purge his enemies in the National Convention. Parisian women who had ardently supported the Revolution, at times arming themselves to battle conservative forces, now became targets of the Reign of Terror. This bloodiest period of the French Revolution saw Robespierre and his allies execute 40,000 people and imprison another 300,000. Additional attacks on the church led to forcing priests to marry and changing the calendar to eliminate Sundays. As the threat from outside powers diminished, the Terror continued as Robespierre began to attack former supporters. In July 1794 conservatives in the National Convention took advantage of French military victories to consolidate their power and voted to arrest Robespierre. On July 27 after a two-day trial Robespierre was executed by the guillotine.

After the fall of Robespierre, the Convention began to abandon many of the Revolution's most radical reforms. Violent uprisings by working-class Parisians were put down, and a more conservative constitution was enacted. A new executive power was created. Named the Directory, it refused to step aside when it lost a popular election in 1797. The republicanism of the French Revolution was being swept away. When the young general Napoleon Bonaparte took control of the nation, a new period in its history had begun.

CONSERVATIVE REACTION IN EUROPE

Napoleon's success had much to do with French society's exhaustion after ten years of revolutionary change. Napoleon became Europe's first popular dictator. He did not turn his back on all of the Revolution's reforms—equality under the law and the protection of personal property were retained and expanded. At the same time while the Napoleonic system was committed to personal security, it often restricted individual rights in the name of national security. Napoleon's run of military victories had stalled by 1812. Looking to boost the French economy, he decided to invade Russia in 1812. His army of 600,000 invaded Russia and occupied Moscow, but was forced back by residents who set fire to the city. After more defeats and a difficult winter, only 30,000 troops returned to France. The defeat spurred several European powers to band together to attack France. Unable to defend Paris against the combined forces of Russia, Prussia, Austria, and England, Napoleon was finally forced to abdicate and was sent to exile off the coast of Italy in 1814. In 1815 he escaped and attempted to reestablish his power, but the monarchy had been restored and the age of Napoleon had passed.

The effect of the French Revolution was widely felt throughout Europe. The Revolution had stirred up ideas of nationalism and liberalism that challenged the old aristocratic order and the power of the church. In 1814 and 1815 diplomats from Britain, Russia, Austria, and Prussia met at the **Congress of Vienna**. Counseled by Austrian foreign minister Klemens von Metternich to help reestablish the monarchy in France, these nations desired to create a peaceful Europe that would protect the conservative order. All of the great nations of Europe received some sort of territorial gains as the "Holy Alliance" of Russia, Austria, and Prussia worked to defeat liberal revolutions in Spain and Italy. Through conservative retrenchment, these traditional powers sought to prevent revolutionary ideas from spreading in Europe.

Throughout the next three decades nationalist and revolutionary movements arose, but they were more often than not put down, as the conservative order continued in control. In Greece, nationalists attempting to throw off Ottoman control appealed to Europeans for help. Although many conservative leaders like Metternich did not support the idea of a nationalist democratic government in Greece, many intellectuals and artists believed that the cradle of Western culture should be liberated from Ottoman oppression. In 1830 Britain, Russia, and France pressured the Ottoman Empire to grant Greek independence. The Greek example was not typical in this period. In a series of uprisings in Europe known as the **Revolutions of 1848**, urban workers in France, Italy, Austria, and Prussia demanded more democratic rights and economic opportunities. But the conflicts of 1848 brought little real change, as monarchs continued to retain the support of aristocrats and the military.

THE RISE OF THE WEST: THE INDUSTRIAL REVOLUTION

The economic and social change wrought by the **Industrial Revolution** reshaped every aspect of society from the eighteenth century on. Innovations in manufacturing, transportation, and communication brought massive increases in productivity. New technologies coupled with changing economic and social relationships transformed all regions of the world by the twentieth century. This change was first seen in Britain. Soon after, other parts of western Europe scrambled to create an industrial economy.

Scholars have identified a set of preconditions that explain why Europe was the first region to undergo the Industrial Revolution: population growth, an agricultural revolution, technological experimentation and innovation, and the growth of trade. In the late eighteenth and early nineteenth centuries Europe experienced a population explosion as people developed more resistance to disease and new crops from the Americas provided a stable food supply. At the same time, an agricultural revolution resulted from the introduction of crops, like the potato, that doubled or tripled the per-acre yield. In addition, new methods of agriculture such as crop rotation and selective livestock breeding enabled wealthy landowners to "enclose" their land and push many tenant farmers and sharecroppers off the land and into the urban areas to look for work.

An increase in population led to an increase in demand for products. It was in Great Britain that a variety of technological innovations and social conditions came together to push forward the first industrial economy. As demand increased, roads and canals were improved. With transportation strengthened, first local trade but increasingly national and international trade grew. Britain increased its overseas trading networks and soon became the world's leading exporter of manufactured goods. The British were quick to experiment with innovative methods of manufacturing. Continental Europeans were aware of the increasingly industrial British economy, but high transportation costs and governmental regulation delayed their ability to industrialize until the early part of the nineteenth century.

AP Tip

Although industrialization occurred first in Europe, its impact in the nineteenth century was global. How industrialism affected the relationships among various regions of the world has been a popular topic of both multiple-choice and free-response questions on the AP World History exam. For example, did the vast wealth and the technological innovation that resulted from the Industrial Revolution alter how industrialized nations viewed nonindustrialized nations? Being able to make global comparisons is an essential skill for this course, and the impact of industrialism makes for an interesting global comparison.

THE TECHNOLOGICAL REVOLUTION

Industrial innovation did not first occur during the Industrial Revolution. Centuries earlier, the Song dynasty in China had used mass production, mechanization, and manufacturing. What made this age of industrial development so remarkable were innovations in the use of energy—steam power and electricity for transportation and communication.

In the eighteenth century European industries began to use techniques of **mass production**. Men like Josiah Wedgwood divided the process of production—in his case, of pottery—into many small tasks. With the **division of labor** and close monitoring of workers, less time was wasted and the production process was speeded up. This changed age-old methods of craftsmanship but also provided consumers low-cost manufactured goods of high quality.

The growth in **mechanization** was another hallmark of the industrial change. The British textile industry used mechanization to spin thread and weave thread into cloth in a fraction of the time it took a worker. By 1830, cotton that took a worker in India five hundred hours to spin took a machine in England eighty minutes to spin. The economist Adam Smith, who described in glowing terms the increased productivity that mechanization and the division of labor brought, disagreed with the old view that a nation's wealth could be measured in the amount of gold and silver it possessed. Instead, Smith held that a nation's economic health should be measured in the amount of goods and services it created. To Smith, Britain's increase in productivity marked an increase in the country's wealth. What Smith failed to address was the fact that only owners could afford the large amounts of capital needed to innovate and expand. Industrialization was replacing the self-employed craftsman with the wealthy. The other early beneficiaries of the Industrial Revolution were members of the middle class, who formed a new group of entrepreneurs able to invest in the new industrial technology and acquire wealth and influence out of reach to nonaristocratic Europeans in early periods.

Industrialism was advanced by the increasing use of iron. British innovations in iron making during the eighteenth century brought its cost down, and with a greater supply of iron available, the use of interchangeable parts, called the "American system of manufactures," became dominant. Interchangeable parts speeded up the manufacturing process while lowering the price of goods.

The ability to transform fossil fuels into energy distinguished the Industrial Revolution from earlier periods of economic growth and expansion. In 1764 British inventor James Watts developed a **steam engine** powered by coal. In the next decades, the steam engine replaced waterpower and made its way into cotton mills and factories. With a seemingly unlimited supply of coal, innovators looked for every possible use of the new engine. Steamboats that traveled on rivers and canals were built in Europe and the United States, and by 1819 steam engines were powering ships across the Atlantic. By the end of the 1820s, Great Britain and the United States had railroad networks linking cities and factories. The construction of railroads sparked industrialization on the European continent as Belgium, Germany, and France linked regions with rich deposits of coal to urban areas.

Experiments in the use of electrical current in the early nineteenth century culminated in the invention of the electric telegraph in 1837. With the introduction of Samuel Morse's Morse code, the telegraph made instant communication possible. The railroad companies were the first to use the new system to track departures and arrivals and improve safety. By the mid-nineteenth century, telegraph lines were strung over all of western Europe and the United States, and in 1851 the first submarine telegraph cable, placed across the English Channel, linked Britain and France. Unlike other periods of technological growth, in which progress was halted by invasion or natural disaster, the Industrial Revolution never slowed but continued to grow, one technological innovation after another.

THE IMPACT OF THE INDUSTRIAL REVOLUTION

The impact of the Industrial Revolution was not just economic. Daily life was drastically altered as a society industrialized. This was especially true in urban areas. The growth of cities in the eighteenth and nineteenth centuries was unprecedented. In only a century London doubled in size, and smaller towns, like Manchester, witnessed a twenty-fold increase between the mid-eighteenth and nineteenth centuries. Cities were redrawn. The winners in the new industrial age built large homes and funded new churches, museums, and theaters. The poorer sections of cities lacked adequate housing and basic services, which, combined with severe overcrowding, made them breeding grounds for smallpox, dysentery, and tuberculosis.

Most factory jobs were controlled by the clock. Workers performed simple repetitive tasks for long hours under the constant watch of overseers. Unlike the agricultural life that most had left behind, neither the work nor the hours changed over the seasons. Though some more-skilled workers were able to get ahead, most workers toiled day after day, year after year doing physically difficult work. Family life was also changed as women and men rarely worked in the same place and were apart from each other for most of the day. Women who worked in factories generally received significantly less pay than men and, if married, faced difficult decisions concerning their children—public schools and day care did not exist. Most women chose to work either in domestic service or at home, taking in laundry, sewing, and embroidery. When Europe was beginning to industrialize, children often worked to add to the family income. Many factory owners wanted children as workers because they were inexpensive and easy to manage. Children made up the majority of workers at some textile mills, working between fourteen and sixteen hours a day. The British government enacted laws to restrict child labor in the mid-nineteenth century.

The new industrial era was hardest for traditional workers who did not change their skill-set to keep up. Most workers did not experience the drastic changes that traditional craft workers did, but instead were victims of a new industrial phenomenon: the business cycle. Economic growth and good times could change quickly and without warning into business contraction and bad times. Few workers had savings, and the governments of Europe had yet to adopt the idea of a safety net for their citizens. Downturns in the business cycle were scary for workers. Only after the 1850s were the benefits of industrialization felt by larger numbers of working-class Europeans.

NEW ECONOMIC AND POLITICAL IDEAS

The sweeping changes brought on by the Industrial Revolution led to new political tensions and ideological clashes. As the rich grew richer and the working classes struggled with the new conditions, ideas that both justified and reviled the economic system arose. **Laissez-faire** economics, developed by Adam Smith in his influential book *The Wealth of Nations* (1776), argued that if people were allowed to seek their fortunes unimpeded by government regulation, all of society would benefit. Directly attacking mercantilism, which supported regulation of trade to protect and build up the nation's supply of gold and silver, Smith theorized that free-market capitalism between nations would increase the wealth of all nations. The British government adopted Smith's laissez-faire principles and lowered import taxes though other European nations retained restrictive tariffs on import goods. German economist Friedrich List argued that free-trade policies kept Britain in a position of power over other less industrialized European nations, which could not compete with well-developed English manufacturers. List proposed that the German states trade freely with one another while raising tariffs against other countries to protect their newly developing industries.

Other political thinkers were more immediately concerned with the plight of the working poor. Two in France were the Count de Saint-Simon and Auguste Comte, who developed a new ideology called **positivism**. Positivists argued that by using the scientific method, enlightened business leaders and artists could come together and fix the problems of industrialism for the working poor. Positivism proved popular with bankers and entrepreneurs, who used it to press for the construction of railroads and canals, which were viewed as symbols of a bright future for workers and owners. Others such as the Frenchman Charles Fourier argued that the workers needed to be protected from industrialists. An ideal worker society would be one where all lived and worked together, sharing the hardships and benefits of their labor. These new ideas, known as utopian socialism, never gained many followers among workers, who viewed them as too dreamy and unrealistic.

The most significant reform ideology of the nineteenth century was known as **socialism**, which questioned the rights of individuals to own private property and supported increased power for industrial workers. The German socialist Karl Marx was one of the earliest and best-known socialists. Working with Friedrich Engels, Marx brought together ideas from German philosophy, the French Revolution, and industrial conditions that workers were living under to create a grand theory about historical and economic development. Marx argued that all through history there had been conflicts among social classes. In the industrial age, the conflict was between workers (the proletariat) and owners (the bourgeoisie). What Marx called capitalist exploitation was producing a society composed of a few extremely rich owners and large numbers of increasingly impoverished workers. Ultimately, Marx predicted, workers would rise up against owners and create a new classless communistic society. Marx's ideas resonated with both intellectuals and workers and can be seen most clearly in the creation and development of labor unions.

In the early nineteenth century workers often ignored the ideas of middle-class thinkers and developed benevolent societies to protect them from the worst conditions of industrial life. Later transformed into trade unions demanding shorter hours and better working conditions, these early labor movements were unsuccessful, but they set the stage for future organizing. In continental Europe, workers erupted violently during the Revolutions of 1848, which led to more acceptance of the idea that trade unions would represent workers' interests.

In the second half of the nineteenth century, **labor unions** linked improved conditions for workers with increased participation in electoral politics. Unlike Marx, who saw revolt by workers as the only way to change the system, labor unions worked to gain influence within the political system. By 1885, universal male suffrage was achieved in France, Germany, and Britain. Labor leaders used their members' voting power to gain additional concessions, and union members began joining socialist-leaning political parties throughout Europe.

WOMEN IN THE INDUSTRIAL AGE

As countries like France, Britain, and Germany become more industrialized, **Victorian** morality, named for Queen Victoria, advanced a new view of the roles of males and females in society. A man's nature was brave, strong, and courageous, while a woman was beautiful, peaceful, and kind. It followed that because men and women were so different, they should be in **"separate spheres,"** men out in the tough world of business and politics, and women at home raising children and building a supportive home environment. This idea of different roles for men and women fit the lifestyles of the growing industrial middle and upper class. It was acceptable for unmarried women to work, but once married, they should leave work and start a family. These women were not encouraged to start careers, and except in education, there were few women professionals before 1914. Education first opened up to women in large part because it fit women's traditional role of working with children. In the mid-nineteenth century running a household was increasingly time-consuming. Elite women were expected to entertain frequently, and coordinating the activities of many servants could be difficult. Not all middle-class women were content to stay at home; some joined reform organizations fighting prostitution, child labor, or alcohol consumption. At the beginning of the twentieth century, others began to question women's exclusion from the political process. In Britain, Emmeline Pankhurst protested women's lack of voting rights, though not until 1918 would British women finally receive the vote.

Working-class women, toiling long hours for low wages in factories and domestic service, found the new industrial age even more difficult. Sexual abuse was common for women in domestic service. Leadership opportunities were limited, and women were usually paid less than their male counterparts. Married working-class women, pressured by Victorian ideals to stay at home, had to find ways to make money at home if a second income was necessary. Many took in boarders, did sewing piecework, or did laundry.

> ## AP Tip
>
> Industrialism had a number of effects on European women in the nineteenth century. Creating separate spheres for men and women, at work and home, and limiting women's economic and political rights are two of the most significant. What was the status of women in other regions during this period? The change in the status of women in Europe over time is another interesting topic. We sometimes assume that because industrialism brought more modern conveniences, the status of women must have improved. Is that true?

NEW WORLD ECONOMY

From about 1850 until the beginning of World War I, global trade increased tenfold. Industrialized economies like Britain's needed trade connections to supply the raw materials for manufactured goods. The increased speed of transportation cut the cost of shipping drastically. This new global trade pattern affected both industrialized and nonindustrialized nations. Countries that were becoming more industrialized saw their economies diversify, producing a wide range of consumer products, many at low prices, but they were often victims of the business cycle, which could lead to recession and depression. Suppliers of raw materials, nonindustrial regions were more connected to the world economy than before, but they too could be hurt in an economic downturn. Throughout this period Great Britain, the dominant economic power of the new global market, controlled over half of the world's shipping and invested heavily in building harbors and railroads in other nations. Nine-tenths of global trade was done in the British pound sterling, which, unlike other national currencies, rarely fluctuated.

THE RUSSIAN EMPIRE

Although Peter the Great had attempted to integrate the massive Russian Empire into the western European economic and cultural orbit, most European powers viewed Russia as backward and underdeveloped. Indeed, Russia in the nineteenth century had almost no middle class and was primarily an agricultural society in which serf labor was controlled by elites. Europe begrudgingly began to notice Russia after its victory over Napoleon in 1812. Tsar Alexander I began to align with other conservative European powers working to keep the old order in power. Alexander I did attempt to begin reform in Russia, but his absolute power remained unchallenged. When his more conservative and anti-Western brother Nicholas I became tsar in 1825, modernization took a backseat to retrenchment.

Russia's limited attempts at industrialization in the nineteenth century were always under the watchful eye of the tsar. Some railroads were built, but a road system linking the immense nation got off to a slow start. Most industrial goods that came to Russia were purchased from the West with profits from agricultural sales.

This lack of interest in modernizing became apparent when Russia entered the **Crimean War** in 1853. Attempting to gain territory from the decaying Ottoman Empire, Russia invaded the Balkan region. Battling the Ottomans' British and French allies, Russians found their weapons no match for their enemies'. Even in defeat, Russia was seen as a power that had to be diplomatically addressed. But Western values and ideals did not appeal to some Russian elites like the **Slavophiles**, who ascribed the nation's strength to its traditions, such as the Orthodox Church, quiet peasant life, and the power of the tsar. After the Crimean defeat, this conservative intellectual group promoted **Pan-Slavism**, the unity of all Slavic peoples, including Slavs living under the Ottoman and Austrian regimes. This view of Russia as a protector of Slavs would shape Russia's relations with western Europe until World War I.

Even though conservative ideology dominated Russia throughout the nineteenth century, reform and change did make headway. The most significant was the emancipation of serfs in 1861. In addition to ending the centuries-old system of forced labor, Tsar Alexander II gave peasants property rights to portions of the land they worked. The practice of monitoring the liberal teachings at Russian universities was continued, but new ideas were increasingly finding their way into Russian society. Writing in the late nineteenth century, Feodor Dostoyevsky and Leo Tolstoy made the growing debate over reform central to their storytelling. Though not yet industrialized and grappling with reform ideas, Russia remained tied to its authoritarian agricultural past.

NATIONALISM, EMPIRE, AND UNIFICATION

The idea that had the greatest effect on Europe in the nineteenth century was nationalism, which was increasingly viewed as the creation of a national identity through a common language and culture. New nationalistic political leaders attempted to rally people around shared values. In nations like France, where the borders coincided with the use of the French language, nationalism was easily accepted. But in states with a number of linguistic and ethnic groups, this new concept of **nationalism** was problematic. German speakers, for example, were spread over many nations and empires, each with its own wide variety of languages. Nationalism before 1869 was also associated with **liberalism**, an outgrowth of the French Revolution holding that people should direct their own nations through constitutional governments that protected individual freedoms. Many of the unsuccessful revolutionary movements of 1848 were linked to both nationalism and its supporting liberal ideology. After 1860, many conservative European leaders, sensing the need for some concessions to citizens demanding more say in their governments, used nationalistic ideology to strengthen conservative regimes and maintain the traditional power structure. This can be seen in the unifications of both Italy and Germany.

By mid-century, popular support was growing in Italy for unification. In 1858, Count Camillo Benso di Cavour, Prime Minister of the Kingdom of Piedmont-Sardinia, led a movement, joined by Italian-speaking provinces to the north, that put down a liberal revolutionary movement in the south, and laid the ground for Italy's unification as a constitutional monarchy under King Victor Emmanuel. In Italy, nationalism shifted from a liberal revolutionary movement to a conservative process, which built support for a strong centralized government controlled by a monarch and aristocrats.

German was the most widely spoken language in Europe in the nineteenth century, and political leaders like the authoritarian aristocrat Prussian chancellor Otto von Bismarck looked to unite German-speakers into a nation. After declaring war and defeating Austria, Bismarck created the North German confederation in 1867. Then in 1870 he again went to war, this time with France. The Franco-Prussian War led to territorial gains from France. The new German empire acquired the region of Alsace-Lorraine, which Germans saw as rightly theirs because most people there spoke German. The French, on the other hand, viewed Alsace-Lorraine as theirs because it was part of the nation when it was formed in the revolution. These two different ideas of nationalism would continue to lead to tension between the nations until World War I.

The close of the nineteenth century and beginning of the twentieth century saw a Europe increasingly divided over ideology, borders, trade routes, and colonial ambitions. With its large military force and a powerful, industrialized economy, Germany had become the dominant power on the European continent. When Wilhelm II replaced his father in 1888 and removed Bismarck, Germany also set out to build a colonial empire.

Multiple-Choice Questions

1. All of the following were changes brought about by the French Revolution EXCEPT
   (A) seizure of church lands.
   (B) eliminating noble titles.
   (C) creating a representative democracy.
   (D) establishing a socialist society.

2. Napoleon restricted all of the following reforms of the French Revolution EXCEPT
   (A) representative democracy.
   (B) protection of private property.
   (C) freedom of speech and free expression.
   (D) political rights of women.

3. Which of the following was a peace settlement that safeguarded Europe's conservative political order in the early nineteenth century?
   (A) Treaty of Paris
   (B) Congress of Vienna
   (C) Declaration of the Rights of Man
   (D) Berlin Conference

4. Why did the Industrial Revolution occur first in Britain in the late 1700s?
   (A) Britain had a rising population, good water transportation, and a fluid social structure allowing for contacts between aristocrats and merchants.
   (B) Britain had a slowly growing population, vast amounts of energy resources, and a strong monarchy.
   (C) Britain had widespread railroad connections and large cities.
   (D) Britain had a decentralized political system, a small merchant class, and limited access to raw materials.

5. Which of the following was NOT an innovation that spurred the Industrial Revolution?
   (A) Mass production of goods through the division of labor
   (B) An increase in the manufacture of iron
   (C) The use of the steam engine
   (D) The expansion of trade unions

6. The most dramatic environmental change that took place in industrializing European nations was
   (A) the expansion of family farms.
   (B) the growth of large cities.
   (C) the damming of navigable rivers.
   (D) the depletion of oil resources.

7. Beginning in the nineteenth century, this movement argued against private property and in support of the workers and their demands.
   (A) Laissez-faire capitalism
   (B) Liberalism
   (C) Socialism
   (D) Democracy

8. Nineteenth-century Victorian morality viewed men and women as
   (A) equals both at home and work.
   (B) having separate spheres, men's outside the home and women's within it.
   (C) equals in the work world but men dominant within the home.
   (D) equals in the home but men dominant at work.

9. Which of the following best characterizes Russia's attitude toward western Europe during the nineteenth century?
   (A) Slowly recognized the importance of industrialization and modernization, but monitored Western ideas closely
   (B) Ignored industrial advances and closely monitored Western influence
   (C) Embraced industrialization and opened Western-style schools and universities throughout the nation
   (D) Reformed major industries using Western models and competed with other industrial powers by the end of the century

10. The best example of the emergence of nineteenth-century nationalism based on language was
    (A) the French Revolution.
    (B) the unification of Germany.
    (C) the expansion of the Austro-Hungarian Empire.
    (D) the growth of Pan-Slavism.

11. "If the spring of popular government in time of peace is virtue, the springs of popular government in revolution are at once virtue and terror: virtue, without which terror is fatal; terror, without which virtue is powerless. Terror is nothing other than justice, prompt, severe, inflexible; it is therefore an emanation of virtue...."

    This quotation from Maximilien Robespierre in 1794 is used to support
    (A) violence against French counter-revolutionaries.
    (B) the re-enslavement of Haitian revolutionaries.
    (C) the overthrow of Louis XVI's monarchy.
    (D) the creation of new French colonies.

12. The revolutions that occurred in Europe in 1848 were
    (A) modeled on South American revolutionary movements.
    (B) promoted by business owners and other economic elites.
    (C) inspired by Marx's Communist Manifesto.
    (D) seeking democratic reform and nationalism.

13. Which of the following is a result of the European Agricultural Revolution and the Enclosure Movement?
    (A) The elevation of the peasant class to more middle-class standards of living
    (B) The migration of colonial farm laborers to the British Isles
    (C) The decrease in population growth rates
    (D) The movement of underemployed people from rural to urban areas

14. What was a social change for working-class European women that resulted from industrial labor?
    (A) Factories provided pay equity for women.
    (B) Women's labor was more removed from the household.
    (C) Wives were more likely to work together with their husbands in the factory.
    (D) Women had more opportunity to become managers.

15. Which European social group was most attracted to Adam Smith's philosophy of laissez-faire?
(A) Businesspeople
(B) Peasants
(C) Nobility
(D) Workers

Free-Response Questions

1. Compare the effects of nationalism during the nineteenth century in TWO of the following European nations.
   - Russia
   - France
   - Germany
   - Austro-Hungarian Empire

2. Analyze the impact of industrial change in western Europe from circa 1750 until circa 1900.

Answers

MULTIPLE-CHOICE QUESTIONS

1. **ANSWER: D.** During the French Revolution church lands were seized, a representative democracy was created, and titles of nobility were abolished. Many of these changes would be abandoned during the rise of Napoleon. Socialism would not be developed until the nineteenth century (*The Earth and Its Peoples*, 5th ed., pp. 612–614/6th ed., p. 615).

2. **ANSWER: B.** Napoleon rolled back many of the reforms that the French Revolution had created, such as freedom of speech, representative democracy, and the political power of women. One reform he continued was the protection of private property (*The Earth and Its Peoples,* 5th ed., p. 618/6th ed., p. 622).

3. **ANSWER: B.** Under the leadership of Austrian Foreign Minister Prince Klemens von Metternich, in 1815 the major powers of Europe sought to create a balance of power on the continent and limit the liberal revolutionary impulse that the French Revolution had stirred up (*The Earth and Its Peoples,* 5th ed., pp. 621–622/6th ed., p. 626).

4. **ANSWER: A.** There were several important factors that made Britain the first nation to begin to fully industrialize, among them a rising population, good water transportation, and a fluid social structure (*The Earth and Its Peoples,* 5th ed., pp. 631–633/6th ed., p. 582).

5. ANSWER: **D.** Mass production through the division of labor, the increase in the production of iron, and the creation of the steam engine were all innovations that spurred the Industrial Revolution (*The Earth and Its Peoples,* 5th ed., pp. 634–635/6th ed., p. 582).

6. ANSWER: **B.** The greatest environmental impact of the Industrial Revolution on European nations was the rapid growth of large cities (*The Earth and Its Peoples,* 5th ed., pp. 640–641/6th ed., p. 590).

7. ANSWER: **C.** The revolutionary ideals of the Enlightenment thinkers together with the effects of industrialism on the working class gave rise to socialism, which attacked private property and looked to curb the power of industrialists (*The Earth and Its Peoples,* 5th ed., pp. 751, 753/6th ed., p. 596).

8. ANSWER: **B.** During the Victorian period the concept of separate spheres was commonly accepted, particularly by middle- and upper-class people. The man's world was outside the home at work and in public life, while the woman's role was at home raising children and running the household (*The Earth and Its Peoples,* 5th ed., p. 750/6th ed., p. 731).

9. ANSWER: **A.** During the nineteenth century, as Russia viewed the economic success of western Europe, it slowly began a program to modernize. At the same time, ideas of liberal democracy and nationalism were closely monitored and revolutionary movements quickly suppressed (*The Earth and Its Peoples,* 5th ed., pp. 698–699/6th ed., p. 642).

10. ANSWER: **B.** Nationalism based on shared language as opposed to a shared leader became increasingly important in the nineteenth century. German nationalism united German-speakers in the mid-nineteenth century and led to the unification of Germany in 1871 (*The Earth and Its Peoples,* 5th ed., pp. 762–763/6th ed., p. 737).

11. ANSWER: **A.** By 1794 Robespierre was head of the Committee of Public Safety, which was responsible for the revolutionary government's purge of those opposed to the new French government (*The Earth and Its Peoples,* 5th ed., pp. 727–728/6th ed., p. 618).

12. ANSWER: **D.** The 1848 revolutions that started in Paris and spread across much of Europe were propelled by workers, students, and other reformers who wanted changes to the old conservative order (*The Earth and Its Peoples,* 5th ed., pp. 622–623/6th ed., p. 627).

13. ANSWER: **D.** The Agricultural Revolution and Enclosure Movements led to a dramatic increase in productivity and a dramatic decrease in the need for farm labor. Many rural British people moved to urban areas to seek wage labor employment (*The Earth and Its Peoples,* 5th ed., pp. 630–633/6th ed., p. 578).

14. **ANSWER: B.** Women's lives changed dramatically as a result of industrialization. Factory work meant that for the first time large numbers of women worked away from the home. Pay was much less for women than men, and health conditions were worse (*The Earth and Its Peoples,* 5th ed., pp. 644–645/6th ed., p. 592).

15. **ANSWER: A.** The Scottish economist Adam Smith advocated free market capitalism in his 1776 book *Wealth of Nations.* Business-people were especially attracted to his ideas about lower government involvement (*The Earth and Its Peoples,* 5th ed., pp. 646–647/6th ed., p. 596).

FREE-RESPONSE QUESTIONS

1. For this comparison question you should be able to define nationalism as the creation of a national identity based on language, shared culture, and geography. Both the Austro-Hungarian Empire and the Russian Empire contained a variety of different ethnic minorities. In the Austro-Hungarian Empire, nineteenth-century nationalism led to growing dissent and division among groups that wanted independence from the weakening multi-ethnic empire. Russia also had to deal with many groups that were not ethnically Russian as it expanded during the nineteenth century, though Russia was more successful in stifling ethnic nationalistic dissent. France and Germany were primarily made up of people who spoke the same language and shared common cultural bonds. Germany became a unified nation during the nineteenth century, and France strengthened its citizens' allegiance during the period.

2. In this continuity and change over time question, make sure to identify specific nations that the Industrial Revolution impacted; Britain, France, Germany, and Belgium are possible choices. In the first period only Britain had begun to industrialize. Changes in trading patterns, the growth of urban areas, environmental impacts, and an increase in factory production are some possible topics. In the second period, around 1840, most of western Europe had gone through drastic industrial change. Technological innovation such as railroads, steam engines, and telegraph lines increasingly linked Europe with the rest of the world in a global trading system. Great income gaps began to develop between the very rich and poor, as families were separated by the demands of the factory and radical political ideas like socialism gained supporters. By 1900, nations like Britain, France, and Germany had begun to see many of the benefits of the Industrial Revolution because the middle class had grown stronger with increased standards of living. Throughout the period the everyday lives of ordinary citizens were often subject to the boom and bust of the business cycle, and life in a new industrial society could bring great benefits or great hardships.

20

THE AMERICAS:
CIRCA 1750 TO CIRCA 1900

KEY CONCEPTS

- Enlightenment political ideas were adopted by revolutionary thinkers in the Americas and would serve as the ideological basis for their independence movements.
- The American Revolution created the first constitutional democracy and influenced revolutionary movements throughout the world.
- Revolutions in the Americas created limited political democracies in which only a minority of the population participated.
- Independence came to Latin American nations in the nineteenth century, but the creation of stable, successful governments was difficult.
- The process of industrialism transformed the Americas, creating an economically developed North America that produced manufactured goods and an underdeveloped Latin America that supplied raw materials for those consumer goods.
- The impact of industrialism created new economic and social challenges that led to a series of social reform movements during the nineteenth century.
- The United States became the dominant economic and political force in the Americas and began building an empire after its victory in the Spanish-American War.

KEY TERMS

- abolitionists
- American Revolution
- Confederate States of America
- Constitutional Convention

- ■ creole
- ■ Declaration of Independence
- ■ Empire of Brazil
- ■ Enlightenment
- ■ free-trade imperialism
- ■ *gens de couleur*
- ■ Gran Colombia
- ■ Haitian Revolution
- ■ industrialism
- ■ Monroe Doctrine
- ■ Platt Amendment
- ■ Transatlantic slave trade

The Americas are discussed in depth in *The Earth and Its Peoples,* fifth edition, Chapters 21, 23, and 27 and sixth edition, Chapters 22, 24, and 25.

REVOLUTION AND CHANGE

The emergence of revolutionary ideas and action had caused dramatic political, economic, and social changes in the Americas by 1750, which would continue through the end of the nineteenth century. The traditions of Europe's old order, the control of absolute monarchs, widespread church influence, and powerful large landowners were attacked. Hallmarks of this change were new ideas such as increased political participation, a questioning of faith while embracing scientific inquiry, and changes in traditional society as more economic competition gave rise to individual pursuit of wealth.

During the eighteenth century European powers were involved in several imperial conflicts that would prove costly, as empires battled each other for more power in both Europe and the Americas. Extended conflicts like the War of Spanish Succession (1701–1714), the War of Austrian Succession (1740–1748), and the Seven Years War (1756–1763) left empires in debt and looking for new ways to pay their heavy war expenses. Mercantilism, the dominant imperial economic philosophy, held that wealth equaled power and that colonies existed to benefit the mother country by increasing its wealth. Colonial subjects were asked to share the economic burden of a growing empire. What European powers did not count on was the reaction of their subjects to these economic demands.

Enlightenment ideas had a great impact on colonial elites in the Americas. Thinkers like John Locke and Jean-Jacques Rousseau challenged the political and social order of Europe. Locke argued that government needed to protect citizens' "life, liberty, and property" and that if these natural rights were not protected, people could rebel against their government. Rousseau declared that a social contract existed between a monarch and his people and that a monarch's rule depended on the consent of his people. These Enlightenment ideas were widely accepted and discussed by American intellectuals in the mid-eighteenth century.

THE AMERICAN REVOLUTION

Revolution would first take shape in Great Britain's North American colonies. In 1763, at the conclusion of the Seven Years War (also known as the French and Indian War), the British reigned supreme; they had defeated the French and removed them as an imperial power in North America. But the British had incurred a large war debt. To deal with it, they called on their colonial subjects to help with repayment of the debt and for the first time directly taxed the colonies. Fueled by Enlightenment ideas and resentment of imperial control, colonial leaders such as Benjamin Franklin began to speak out against the mother country. When the British enacted the Proclamation of 1763 in an attempt to calm frontier conflict with Amerindians by limiting colonial expansion, colonists increasingly questioned whose interests the British government was serving.

Tension rose throughout the 1760s as Great Britain continued to misjudge the colonists' level of dissatisfaction. Groups like the Sons of Liberty responded to what they perceived as attacks on their liberties by organizing boycotts of British goods and intimidating royal officials. In the early 1770s incidents like the Boston Massacre and legislation like the Tea Act of 1773 further convinced colonists that imperial oppression was increasing. Many colonists saw no choice but open rebellion against Great Britain.

By the time colonial leaders met in Philadelphia in 1775 at the Continental Congress, colonists and British troops had already clashed in Massachusetts. The Congress set up a new government and created an army, to be led by George Washington, a veteran of the French and Indian War. Thomas Jefferson's **Declaration of Independence**, summing up the philosophical principles of the new revolutionary age, was approved by Congress on July 4, 1776. Restating the Enlightenment ideals of popular sovereignty and personal liberty, the document would influence revolutionaries throughout the world over the next hundred years.

The underfunded and marginally trained colonial forces found success because of a number of external developments. Military assistance came from France, Britain's traditional enemy. Having focused on the French threat to its more profitable Caribbean colonies, the British government did not commit sufficient forces to the battle for the North American colonies. With the support of French land and naval forces, the colonists defeated the British, who surrendered at Yorktown in 1781. The resulting Treaty of Paris, signed in 1783, gave recognition to American independence. Amerindian tribes, which had fought on both sides, saw their territory ceded to the new United States of America. The Enlightenment ideals of individual freedom and political participation that the new nation was founded on were not applied to the original residents of North America.

Before the war, individual colonies had written constitutions that limited executive power and protected personal liberties. The Articles of Confederation, the nation's postwar government system, was also designed to limit central power. Leaders soon realized that the Articles of Confederation were inadequate for effective government and would have to be revised; the national government needed more power for functions such as public safety, taxation, and payment of postwar debt. Delegates to the **Constitutional Convention**, held in Philadelphia in

1787, determined what powers would be given to the central government, what powers to local governments. They then devised a new form of federal government made up of three branches— executive, legislative, and judicial. The Constitution of the United States laid out the most democratic government of its time, and to this day it serves as a model for codified constitutional governments. Still, only a minority of white males were able participate in it; women and African-Americans, whose help had been crucial to the victory over the British, did not have a voice in the new American constitution.

THE HAITIAN REVOLUTION

News of the revolutionary activity in France in the late 1780s made its way to France's colonial possessions in the Americas. The colony of Saint Domingue (present-day Haiti) was France's richest possession in the Americas. Haiti's large cotton, indigo, coffee, and sugar plantations, which depended on a brutally repressive slave system, accounted for a third of French foreign trade in the eighteenth century. The early stages of the French Revolution had a strong impact on Haiti's mixed-race population, the **gens de couleur**, who pressed their demands for increased political equality. Neither the *gens de couleur*—some of whom owned slaves—nor their white opponents aimed to end slavery. But as their conflict turned into open warfare, the colony's slaves seized the opportunity to begin their own revolt. Afro-Haitians turned to a former domestic slave, François Dominique Toussaint L'Ouverture, who assumed leadership of the revolution, creating a well-organized, effective military force. When France's radical National Convention in Paris abolished slavery in all colonial possessions, Toussaint and his followers identified their efforts as part of the struggle for individual freedom for all, begun by the French Revolution.

During the 1790s Haitian rebels were able to defeat both white slave holders and invading British troops while liberating slaves in both Haiti and Spanish-held Santo Domingo. Toussaint continually pledged allegiance to France but did not allow the French to play an active role in governing their former colony. As conservative reaction replaced revolution in France, Napoleon consolidated his power and looked to bring Haiti back under French control. In 1802 French troops initially found success with the capture of Toussaint, who would die in a French prison, but they soon met stiff resistance from the Haitian forces, which included armed women. In 1804, after two years of costly struggle, France withdrew, and the free republic of Haiti was established. The toll of the first successful slave rebellion in the Americas was great: tens of thousands dead, a ruined economy, and political violence that would continue throughout the century.

LATIN AMERICAN INDEPENDENCE MOVEMENTS

Spain's and Portugal's Latin American colonies did not ignore the revolutions in the United States and France, but it was the French attack on the Spanish monarchy that spurred change. When Napoleon invaded Spain and Portugal in the early nineteenth century, the Spanish resistance organized a new political body, the Junta Central.

Most colonial subjects in the Americas supported the Junta, but a vocal minority, led by Latin American elites, began to challenge royal authority. The early challenges in Venezuela, Mexico, and Alto Peru (now Bolivia) were put down by violent repression, which only strengthened the support for change. In Venezuela a revolutionary group of **creoles** (colonial-born whites) declared independence in 1811. The group supported the Enlightenment values of political democracy and individual liberty, but it comprised large landowners, who saw little need to liberate slaves or give additional rights to the majority mixed-race population. Loyalists used these facts to rally those groups to defend the crown.

The creoles turned to Simón Bolívar, one of their own, to lead the revolutionary movement. The charismatic Bolívar, a student of the Enlightenment, was able to inspire his troops while building coalitions with other segments of society. To bring additional numbers to his cause, he agreed to support emancipation for slaves. From 1813 through 1820 the battle raged between loyalists and Bolívar's revolutionary army.

Events in Europe again spurred revolutionary changes in the Americas. A military revolt in Spain in 1820 forced King Ferdinand VII to accept new restrictions on his power, which emboldened Bolívar's army to press for definitive military victories. By 1824 revolutionary troops had liberated what today are the nations of Venezuela, Columbia, Ecuador, Peru, and Bolivia, named after the "great liberator" himself. Bolívar and his supporters attempted to build a political confederation from the newly independent regions. Venezuela, Colombia, and Ecuador united to form **Gran Colombia**, and efforts were made to link Peru and Bolivia, but by 1830 unity had failed and several smaller nations were formed.

A second area of revolutionary activity centered around Buenos Aires, the capital city of Argentina. When news of Ferdinand VII's forced abdication reached Buenos Aires, local elites, military commanders, and ranchers formed a new junta to resist the power of colonial officials. The Argentine Junta claimed loyalty to the ousted monarch, but when Ferdinand regained power the junta refused to give up control and in 1816 announced the independence of the United Provinces of Rio de la Plata.

Mexico, Spain's richest colony, contained large numbers of Spanish immigrants and owed much of its wealth to the exploitation of the rural poor and Amerindian population. This oppression of the peasants, as well as increasing political conflict and instability in Spain, gave rise to revolutionary action. In 1810 Miguel Hidalgo y Costilla, a priest in the small town of Dolores, urged peasants to rise up and fight oppression from Spanish colonial officials. A disorganized armed force began to attack mines and ranches, striking at both Spanish and creole elites. Though Hidalgo at first appealed to some wealthy Mexicans, the threat of a peasant-led revolution caused them to turn on Hidalgo, who was captured and executed in 1811. The uprising continued throughout the rest of the decade, by the end of which colonial rule seemed to be reestablished. But the crisis in Spain in 1820 greatly affected Mexico, which declared its independence in 1821. Creole elites replaced their colonial counterparts, demonstrating the conservative nature of the Mexican independence struggle.

The presence of the Portuguese royal family in Brazil, forced to flee Portugal after their defeat by Napoleon in 1808, shaped the colony's independence movement. When King John VI returned to Portugal to protect his power in 1820, he left his son Pedro to act as regent. Pedro, a student of the Enlightenment, supported the independence movement, and in 1822 he separated from Portugal, creating the **Empire of Brazil**. Unlike other newly liberated colonies that established constitutional republics, Brazil had a constitutional monarchy with Pedro as emperor. Often more liberal than Brazil's elites, Pedro advocated the abolition of slavery even though the nation was controlled by a wealthy slaveholding class. Conflict between Brazilians and Portuguese immigrants, whom Pedro protected and supported, led to his abdication in 1831 and the transfer of power to his five-year-old son, Pedro II. After a period of regency, Pedro II ruled Brazil until 1889, when he was finally overthrown and the constitutional monarchy ended.

The newly independent Latin American nations strongly supported constitutional government—even Brazil placed constitutional limits on the emperor's power. But throughout the nineteenth century political factionalism and threats to constitutional democracy arose. Difficulty in defining the role of the Catholic Church and trouble keeping the military from overthrowing weak constitutional leaders were common problems during this period.

THE INDUSTRIAL REVOLUTION: IMPACT AND CHANGE

The Industrial Revolution transformed economic and social relationships over the late eighteenth and nineteenth centuries. Innovations in manufacturing, mining, transportation, and communications led to changes in both the economic relations of nations and the everyday life of their citizens. Industrializing countries, like the United States, were able to increase production and productivity as they learned to tap the wealth provided by natural resources such as coal, iron ore, and oil. In the Americas there were both winners and losers; nations that industrialized became rich, while those that did not grew poor.

The development and use of railroads powered by steam engines became the mark of a nation attempting to industrialize in the nineteenth century. By the end of the century Canada and the United States had developed giant railroad networks that transported raw materials to manufacturing centers and cities. In the early twentieth century the United States had over 390,000 miles of track. In non-industrial regions of the Americas, imperial powers and international corporations invested large sums in rail transportation to connect previously isolated areas containing raw materials and agricultural products to densely populated urban areas. Even the railroads in Europe had an impact on the Americas, which experienced a dramatic increase in immigration during this era; as railroads spread deeper into eastern and southern Europe, more people used them to leave their homeland and start a new life in the United States, Argentina, and Canada.

Sea travel became quicker with ships made with steel and the availability of coaling stations throughout the world, making refueling of steam-powered vessels increasingly convenient. Submarine telegraph cables allowed for instant communication between the Western and Eastern Hemispheres. Electricity had a more direct effect on people's lives than any other industrial innovation. With the invention of the incandescent lamp by Thomas Edison and the growth of electrical distribution systems, the rhythm of people's lives was altered. With electric lighting, people got up earlier and stayed up later. **Industrialism** connected the Americas to one another and to the global economy as never before.

While regions like North America became fully industrial, with a diversified economy producing consumer goods for their growing middle class, the nonindustrial nations in Central and South America provided raw materials and a market for manufactured goods. Attempts to industrialize in Latin America were often unsuccessful because of the difficulty in funding these changes from within. Latin American countries that took outside loans for industrial development incurred large debts that impeded additional economic modernization. The need for labor led to large-scale immigration in both North America and South America. In the United States immigrants from eastern and southern Europe came to work in factories. In Brazil and Argentina immigrants came to work on coffee plantations.

AP Tip

Economic and demographic changes are often linked in history. As industrialism occurred in the Americas during the nineteenth and early twentieth centuries, the proliferation of manufacturing centers increased demand for more raw materials—and additional labor—for manufacturing. Immigrants numbering in the millions came to nations like the United States, Canada, Argentina, Chile, and Brazil. Coming primarily from Europe, though a minority were from Asia, immigrants would continue the expansion of industrialism, which led to growing urbanization as they settled in cities. Though immigration brought enormous economic benefits, many immigrants met with hostility from nativists, who believed that foreigners could not be integrated into their new culture. In free-response essays and document-based questions, look for the links between economic change and demographic movements.

SOCIAL AND ECONOMIC CHALLENGES

Newly independent nations faced social and economic challenges, some left to them by colonialism, others created by industrialism. Slavery and the slave trade, calls for increased political participation, and the economic and social effects of industrialism—all sparked reform movements in the nineteenth century. Though many elites resisted change, by the end of the nineteenth century these reform movements would become popular and produce rapid change.

Under colonial control, Amerindian populations had been both exploited and feared by imperialists. To limit the potential for armed conflict between settlers and indigenous peoples, Spanish, Portuguese, and British colonial governments restricted the areas that settlers could move into. With independence, new nations wanted to expand, which often meant confronting powerful native groups. Conflicts with still-independent indigenous populations often resulted in setbacks for frontier settlements and initially hindered expansion. But throughout the nineteenth century Amerindians were faced with the choice of adapting to the expanding culture or attempting to resist. Resistance inevitably proved futile; by the early twentieth century indigenous peoples had been defeated.

SLAVERY AND THE SLAVE TRADE

Slavery and the slave trade were discussed as colonies went through their independence struggles. Many revolutionaries in the Americas saw the irony of calling for liberty while denying it to millions of slaves. Slavery as an institution was strongest in places that grew export staple crops such as sugar and coffee on large plantations. These products were in high demand and created large profits for slave owners. People in places like the United States, Brazil, and Cuba who opposed slavery were called **abolitionists.** Using moral pressure, abolitionist groups were able to slow the slave trade when the United States agreed in 1808 to end its importation of slaves. Many slaves were freed during the Latin American revolutions of the 1810s and 1820s as they fought for the cause of independence.

The slave trade was dealt a serious blow in 1807 when the British outlawed slave trading and became more active in ending what was seen as a moral evil. With slavery abolished in Great Britain in 1833, that nation turned the world's most powerful navy toward stopping the transport of slaves from western Africa to the Americas. That, along with diplomatic pressure, enabled Britain to slow—and in 1867 finally stop—the **transatlantic slave trade.**

In the United States the struggle to end slavery divided the nation. Northern states increasingly saw slavery as both morally objectionable and a barrier to economic progress. With the 1860 election of Abraham Lincoln, who had pledged to limit the spread of slavery, the country was torn apart when southern states claimed the right to leave the union and formed the **Confederate States of America.** The American Civil War, begun in 1861, saw thousands of slaves flee the South to join Northern troops and fight for their freedom. The Northern victory in 1865 ended slavery, but it was replaced by a system of economic and social segregation that limited African-American liberty over the next century.

In Brazil slavery would continue for twenty years after the American Civil War. In an 1830 treaty with Britain, Brazil pledged to end its involvement in the slave trade. But the great demand for slave labor on Brazilian plantations led to the illegal importation of over more than 500,000 slaves over the next twenty years. Though Pedro II supported abolition, the powerful slaveholding elite made ending slavery in Brazil difficult. During the 1860s and 1870s educated Brazilians began to warn that slavery was impeding Brazilian progress, and laws of gradual emancipation were passed. Slavery in Brazil was abolished in 1888.

Cuba and Puerto Rico, Spanish-held Caribbean colonies with valuable sugar plantations, worried about the successful slave revolt in Haiti. Colonial elites expressed little interest in the independence movements that were sweeping the Americas; instead they counted on the Spanish government to protect their slaveholding property rights. Not until the 1870s did colonial elites begin to question Spanish imperial control and challenge the institution of slavery. Puerto Rican reformers worked to achieve the abolition of slavery in 1873. Cuba waged a decade-long war for independence; though unsuccessful, Cuban pressure forced Spain to end slavery there in 1886. By the end of the century slavery had been abolished throughout the Americas.

WOMEN'S RIGHTS AND RACIAL EQUALITY

Women were key players in the reform movements of the nineteenth century, particularly in the abolition movement. But women in the Americas faced limits on their own rights and opportunities. At the Women's Rights Convention at Seneca Falls, New York, in 1848, women who had been excluded from an antislavery conference gathered to discuss their treatment as second-class citizens. They demanded the right to vote and greater economic opportunities. During the nineteenth century women's suffrage (voting rights) was the central demand of the women's rights movement. In South America, women demanded educational opportunities similar to those for men. Argentina and Uruguay were among the first nations in Latin America to educate men and women together. In Chile and Brazil, professional careers in medicine and law opened up to women. In industrialized countries women also protested the dangerous conditions in factories where many women and children were forced to work. Even with these gains, most women did not attain political equality in the nineteenth century.

Racial inequality and discrimination were also widespread in the Americas. In the southern region of the United States, African-Americans were denied the right to vote, and segregation laws created separate and unequal schools and public accommodations. Those who tried to fight these limits on liberty often found themselves victims of violence; thousands of African-Americans were lynched during the last three decades of the nineteenth century. Though racial discrimination was not codified by law in Latin America, people of color still struggled for equal rights. In all parts of the Americas groups began organizing to fight the racial stereotypes of the era. In Brazil, Argentina, and the United States, newspapers and magazines publicized the achievements of people of color, and universities were founded to meet the growing demand for advanced education. At the turn of the century racial discrimination could be seen in all parts of the Americas, but opportunities for people of mixed race were generally greater in Latin America than in the United States.

INDUSTRIAL AND NONINDUSTRIAL REGIONS

By the end of the nineteenth century in the Americas, only North American nations had fully industrialized, but their need for raw materials had linked most of the Americas. Individual income levels rose for everyone during this period, but only in Argentina, Canada, and the United States did individual incomes match those in western Europe. Demand for raw materials such as copper, zinc, and tin led to mining booms in both North and South America, but the expense of mining equipment forced nonindustrialized nations to cede control of these valuable natural resources to foreign corporations. International business interests often intimidated governments that needed their investment capital. Other new forms of industrial technology—for example, railroads and telegraph lines—also needed to be funded by companies from North America and western Europe, increasing their power in Latin America. By 1900 nations had either begun to develop industrial economies or become dependent on those economies, primarily exporting raw materials and creating low-wage jobs. These structural differences would have a long-term impact on economies throughout the Americas.

AP Tip

Old imperialism, by which European powers played an indirect role, primarily as traders in Africa and Asia, began to change in the late nineteenth century. The industrial nations of Europe began to take political, economic, and cultural control of vast regions in Africa and Asia in what is called New Imperialism or neocolonialism. What about New Imperialism in the Americas? A form of New Imperialism first began in the Americas when Spain and Portugal defeated Amerindian empires such as the Aztec and Inca. These societies were reshaped politically, economically, and culturally, but in the sixteenth and seventeenth centuries technology had not linked the global market as it would during the growth of industrialism. Though these colonies were profitable, their raw materials would not be essential for industrial production in Europe. By the time industrialism gave nations an economic motive for New Imperialism, the colonies in the Americas had achieved independence, and European imperialists did not have the same opportunity to occupy them as they had in parts of Africa and Asia. At the same time, you could argue that both the United States and international corporations did exert powerful political and economic influence without actually occupying nations. For an essay question that deals with New Imperialism, consider contrasting it with the earlier forms of colonialism in the Americas.

THE UNITED STATES AND NEW IMPERIALISM IN LATIN AMERICA

In 1823 the United States issued the Monroe Doctrine warning European nations, which exerted strong political and economic power over Latin America, to refrain from further expansion in the Americas. The **Monroe Doctrine,** however, did not stop the United States from intervening in the region. In 1846 the United States used a questionable border attack to declare war against Mexico. The short struggle that followed ended when United States troops took the capital, Mexico City; in the Treaty of Guadalupe Hidalgo, a third of Mexico was ceded to the United States. The United States also had long been interested in Cuba, the wealthiest Spanish colony. A revolution led by Cuban nationalist José Martí that erupted in 1895 was supported by the American popular press. When the U.S. battleship *Maine* accidentally exploded in the Havana harbor, the United States was quick to implicate Spain. The war that followed brought an end to four hundred years of Spanish colonial rule in the Americas. The Treaty of Paris (1898) liberated Cuba (though the 1901 **Platt Amendment** granted the United States the right to intervene there if necessary) and gave the United States possession of Puerto Rico, Guam, and the Philippines. The United States had become an imperial power.

By 1900 the United States had the largest economy in the world. Unlike European nations, which had used their economic and technological power to reshape Africa and Asia, the United States was not interested in occupying large parts of the Americas. Instead, New Imperialism was modified to **free-trade imperialism**—though the United States did use military force in the Americas in the early twentieth century when the supply of raw materials needed for their industrial economy was threatened.

Multiple-Choice Questions

1. The Enlightenment idea that had the greatest impact on revolutionary thinkers in the Americas advocated
   (A) abolition of slavery.
   (B) equality of all people.
   (C) government protection of individual rights.
   (D) centralized government.

2. At the conclusion of the Seven Years War, the British North American colonies
   (A) expanded west into Amerindian territory.
   (B) opened trade with Caribbean colonies.
   (C) were prohibited from expanding westward.
   (D) declared independence.

3. The major reason colonial elites chose to replace the Articles of Confederation with the United States Constitution was
   (A) the need to limit the power of local governments.
   (B) the overbearing power of the central government.
   (C) the threat of war between northern and southern regions.
   (D) the inability of the central government to put down rebellion and settle disputes between states.

4. The Haitian Revolution was the first successful revolution in the Americas to be instigated by
   (A) slaves.
   (B) creoles.
   (C) peninsulares.
   (D) mestizos.

5. Simón Bolívar's goal was
   (A) to form smaller, stable South American states.
   (B) to form a union of North America and South America.
   (C) to create a confederation of South American Spanish colonies.
   (D) to form a creole-led monarchy in South America.

6. Latin American revolutions were most closely caused by
   (A) the French Revolution.
   (B) the United States Constitution.
   (C) Haitian independence.
   (D) Napoleon's invasion of Spain and Portugal.

7. Brazil's independence movement was unique in South America because it
   (A) created a constitutional monarchy.
   (B) gave women the right to vote.
   (C) nationalized slave plantations.
   (D) gave Amerindians full citizenship rights.

8. The last nation in the Americas to abolish slavery, in 1888, was
   (A) Mexico.
   (B) Peru.
   (C) Cuba.
   (D) Brazil.

9. All of the following were demands of women's rights movements in the Americas during the nineteenth century EXCEPT
   (A) voting rights.
   (B) educational opportunity.
   (C) safer working conditions for women.
   (D) limits on industrial development.

10. Victory in this conflict turned the United States into an imperial power as it gained Puerto Rico, Guam, and the Philippines.
    (A) Mexican-American War
    (B) Spanish-American War
    (C) Boxer Rebellion
    (D) Cuban Revolution

11. Which group in the French colony of Saint Domingue had the most in common with French radicals during the French Revolution?
    (A) Wealthy planters
    (B) *Gens de couleur* (people of mixed race)
    (C) Urban merchants
    (D) Enslaved Africans

12. After Haiti gained independence from France in 1804,
    (A) Europeans still controlled the top political positions.
    (B) voting rights were extended to all males.
    (C) Toussaint L'Ouverture established a monarchy.
    (D) military dictatorship and corruption dominated politics.

13. Which of the following groups formed the leadership of the independence movements of Spanish South America?
    (A) Former slaves and people of mixed race
    (B) Creole landowners
    (C) Middle-class intellectuals
    (D) Peasant farmers

14. In which of the following ways did Mexican independence differ from independence movements in Spanish South America?
    (A) Mexico achieved independence without violence.
    (B) Mexican independence was focused on the issue of slave emancipation.
    (C) Mexican revolutionaries were motivated by the grievances of the poor.
    (D) Mexico had a constitutional democracy as a result of independence.

15. The creation of the new Dominion of Canada was motivated by
    (A) growing trade ties with Britain.
    (B) growing economic connections between provinces.
    (C) potential expansion of the Russian Empire in the far west.
    (D) French-language separatists in Quebec.

Free-Response Questions

1. Analyze the continuities and changes for different labor systems on the social and economic structures of the Americas between 1550 and circa 1900.

2. Compare the effects of industrialism on North America with the effects of industrialism on Latin America.

Answers

MULTIPLE-CHOICE QUESTIONS

1. ANSWER: **C.** Enlightenment thinkers like John Locke argued that governments were created to protect life, liberty, and property—natural rights of every individual (*The Earth and Its Peoples,* 5th ed., p. 604/6th ed., p. 606).

2. ANSWER: **C.** The conclusion of the Seven Years War saw increased conflict with Amerindian tribes on the western frontier, and in response, Britain passed the Proclamation of 1763, which limited colonial expansion (*The Earth and Its Peoples,* 5th ed., pp. 606–607/6th ed., p. 606).

3. ANSWER: **D.** Under the Articles of Confederation, the decentralized political structure of the United States led to many disputes between states. In addition, the government was seriously threatened by a rebellion of former Revolutionary Army soldiers led by Daniel Shays (*The Earth and Its Peoples,* 5th ed., p. 610/6th ed., p. 614).

4. ANSWER: **A.** The Haitian Revolution was the first successful slave-led rebellion in the Americas (*The Earth and Its Peoples,* 5th ed., p. 619/6th ed., p. 628).

5. ANSWER: **C.** Simón Bolívar, known as the "greater liberator," wanted to create a confederation of South American Spanish colonies (*The Earth and Its Peoples,* 5th ed., pp. 656–658/6th ed., p. 660).

6. ANSWER: **D.** When Napoleon's armies invaded Spain and Portugal, Latin American elites felt empowered to begin the struggle for independence (*The Earth and Its Peoples,* 5th ed., pp. 656–657/6th ed., p. 660).

7. ANSWER: **A.** The Brazilian independence movement was shaped by the fact that the Portuguese royal family had been forced to live in Brazil for a decade. When Brazil declared independence in 1822, it was with the support of the Portuguese royal family. Pedro, the son of the king, became the nation's constitutional monarch (*The Earth and Its Peoples,* 5th ed., pp. 660–661/6th ed., p. 660).

8. ANSWER: **D.** The Brazilian parliament and emperor passed legislation to abolish slavery in 1888 (*The Earth and Its Peoples,* 5th ed., pp. 671–672/6th ed., p. 674).

9. ANSWER: **D.** The women's rights movements in the nineteenth century demanded equal access to political and educational opportunities, as well as protection of women in the workplace. However, they did not expect to turn back industrial development and growth to achieve their goals (*The Earth and Its Peoples,* 5th ed., pp. 675–676/6th ed., p. 678).

10. **ANSWER: B.** The United States victory in the Spanish-American War brought the nation a set of imperial possessions in the Caribbean and Pacific (*The Earth and Its Peoples,* 5th ed., pp. 790–791/6th ed., p. 710).

11. **ANSWER: B.** The freed people of mixed race on Saint Domingue identified strongly with the calls for freedom and liberty that the French radicals demanded. They too wanted to end privilege based on birth. Wealthy planters sided with the nobility. Enslaved Africans formed the bulk of the Haitian Revolutionary force, but their revolutionary agenda was to end the system of slavery itself (*The Earth and Its Peoples,* 5th ed., p. 619/6th ed., p. 623).

12. **ANSWER: D.** After Haitian independence a succession of military dictators controlled the devastated and depopulated new nation. Toussaint L'Ouverture had been killed during the revolutionary struggle, and Europeans political domination was over (*The Earth and Its Peoples,* 5th ed., pp. 621–622/6th ed., p. 626).

13. **ANSWER: B.** The leadership of the independence movements in South America was much like that in the United States. American-born wealthy landowners wanted to establish political dominance over European-born officials (*The Earth and Its Peoples,* 5th ed., pp. 656–658/6th ed., p. 665).

14. **ANSWER: C.** The Mexican struggle for independence from Spain was long and violent. Miguel Hidalgo and others called on peasant farmers and other poor people to rise up against Spanish rule (*The Earth and Its Peoples,* 5th ed., pp. 658, 660–661/6th ed., p. 662).

15. **ANSWER: B.** The Dominion of Canada, which was created in 1867, linked the various provinces together. The railroads in particular provided economic connections that favored a desire to unite. The United States, which had just emerged from bloody civil war, and Mexico were poor examples of stable political units. The Dominion represented a movement away from British rule (*The Earth and Its Peoples,* 5th ed., pp. 661–663/6th ed., p. 665).

FREE-RESPONSE QUESTIONS

1. Begin by identifying the systems of labor used. Slavery, indentured servitude, the encomienda system used in many Spanish colonies, as well as free wage labor—all can be discussed. The English colonies of North America could be used as an effective example, because three different systems of labor were used (slavery, indentured servitude, and wage labor) and played a role in shaping the social and economic structures. In the British-held southern colonies, the great demand for labor to work on plantations led to a large population of indentured servants and slaves. This region developed a hierarchal social structure in which economic decisions were most often made by elites who could afford to buy slaves and servants. Great Britain's northern colonies saw a more limited use of indentured servants and slaves with free wage labor dominant. This made for more equitable social and economic structures, though class differences based on wealth still existed.

You could also compare a Latin American colony that used the encomienda system, a system of forced labor for a predetermined number of days, with one that used slaves. By 1900, slavery, indentured servitude, and the encomienda system had been abolished, but the legacy of these labor systems had strongly influenced the social and economic structures that existed.

2. What should jump out at you immediately is the division between North America, which was more fully industrialized, and Latin America, which was less industrialized. Industrialism had turned North American countries like the United States and Canada into nations with manufacturing economies that supplied a large middle-class consumer market both at home and abroad. In North America large fortunes were created, and the new industrial working class was exploited. But in your response you should note that even given those facts, industrialism provided wealth for all classes; by the early twentieth century the North American middle class was growing. In Latin America fully industrial economies were not created, though you could discuss Argentina having partially industrialized. Industrialism had turned these nations primarily into exporters of raw materials. To fund access to valuable raw materials, some Latin American countries allowed foreign investment, which often led to increased influence by foreigners in political and economic decision making. Supplying industrialized nations with raw materials did not create the middle class that industrialized countries developed, and economic benefits were gained by only a small portion of the nation.

21

AFRICA:
CIRCA 1900 TO THE PRESENT

KEY CONCEPTS

- During the first half of the twentieth century, much of Africa was under colonial rule by European powers, which resulted in the exploitation of labor, creation of cash crop systems, and extraction of raw materials for the benefit of colonial powers.
- Soldiers returning from fighting in World War II played a key role in demanding equality and an end to colonization.
- The era in which African nations gained political independence from European colonial powers spans from 1957 to 1991. The fight for freedom and independence became most violent in areas with large populations of white settlers unwilling to relinquish privileges or political control.
- During the Cold War, some African nations attempted to resist aligning with either superpower unless they could benefit from the superpower economically or politically.

KEY TERMS

- African National Congress (ANC)
- apartheid
- Bandung Conference
- colonialism
- El Alamein
- League of Nations
- mandate system
- proxy wars
- United Nations

Africa from 1900 to the present is discussed in *The Earth and Its Peoples,* fifth edition, Chapters 27, 28–33 and sixth edition, Chapters 25, 28, 30, 31, and 32.

WORLD WAR I

At first glance, the First World War seems to have little to do with the continent of Africa. However, a closer look reveals that while Africans themselves had little say in the events surrounding World War I, the destiny of Africans was intrinsically tied to the desires and aspirations of the European powers. By 1914, much of the African continent was under colonial rule by various European powers as a result of the 1884–1885 Berlin Conference. European powers, interested largely in African labor to extract resources for their industries, used various methods, such as the "Hut" tax or "Head" tax to force Africans into the colonial economies. In order to pay the taxes, Africans were forced to accept low-wage jobs—on plantations, in mines, on railroads, and the like—within the European colonial system.

Despite the agreements made at the Berlin Conference, the imperialistic ambitions of the European powers were not satiated, and they began competing for new territory and new resources to fuel industrialization within their own nations. The crumbling Ottoman Empire, which had outlying territories in North Africa, was at the center of this new scramble for territory and resources. In 1912, Italy conquered Libya, the Ottomans' last remaining territory in Africa. Imperialism proved a way to bolster both industrialization and nationalistic fervor, and nationalism offered the same reinforcement to colonization. So when the Great War began in 1914, Africans and their land were drawn into the conflict.

Only a few battles were fought on the African continent, but resources and manpower were greatly coveted. World War I exacerbated colonial hardships. The colonial powers forced Africans throughout the continent to grow export crops and sell them at low prices, imposed heavy taxes, and demanded foodstuffs in order to support European military forces. Over two million Africans served in colonial armies fighting side by side with Europeans. An even greater number of Africans was used as porters to carry military equipment. Many were badly fed and mistreated. African involvement in the war as well as the heavy demands and burdens placed on them provided an opportunity to demand equal rights, but even though Africans played a major role in the Allied victory, only a few demands for equality were met. At the beginning of the war, French and British forces attacked German ports in present-day Togo, Cameroon, and Tanzania. The Allied forces took over the German colony of Togo in West Africa. By 1915, they had conquered German Southwest Africa and German Cameroon. The British and the French were on their way to an even greater foothold on the continent than even they had expected.

THE INTERWAR PERIOD

The end of World War I brought little consolation for people throughout the African continent. Despite the idealistic and democratic rhetoric of self-determination, it became clear that none of these ideals were meant for the people of the colonies. Colonies previously run by Germany saw one colonizing force merely replaced by another. Tanganyika, a German colony in East Africa, for instance, became a British colony at the end of World War I. South Africa, a nation independent from Britain but run by a minority composed of Afrikaners and British settlers, replaced Germany as the new colonizers of Southwest Africa. According to the Treaty of Versailles, these former German colonies would be administered as class C mandates. Under the **mandate system**, the colonies were to be run by their new European rulers for "the material and moral well-being and social progress of the inhabitants." The rulers were also to be accountable to the newly formed **League of Nations**. But while the League of Nations was a world organization designed to foster world peace and cooperation, colonized people were excluded from decision making and all other forms of involvement. In that respect, the League was set up with a decided European and imperial bent. As such, autonomy for the colonies/mandates was a theoretical goal for some unspecified time in the future. Thus, like their counterparts in the Middle East and Asia, Africans yearned for still-elusive independence—equality as well as the promised material well-being.

Even after World War I, few Africans benefited from colonial rule. The colonial system was set up to benefit the European powers. Railroads and other forms of infrastructure were built merely to transport raw materials to the coast so that they might be shipped off to Europe for manufacturing. Colonial governments even stripped Africans of land to sell or lease to European companies or settlers. While colonial governments eagerly developed resources within the colonies, they refused to pay high wages to African workers. Sometimes their only means of acquiring workers was by forcing Africans to work for little or no pay, under harsh conditions. The French colonial government of Equatorial Africa, for example, forced 127,000 men to build a railroad from Brazzaville to the Atlantic coast during the 1920s; lacking food, clothing, and medicine, 20,000 workers—an average of sixty-four men per mile of track—died. Even hospitals and modern health care benefited few Africans. In fact, the colonial system often worsened public health. Diseases spread rapidly among migrant workers and soldiers; in Central Africa, sleeping sickness and smallpox ravaged entire villages. The need to pay colonial taxes forced many men into migrant work, causing severe problems for their wives, who were left in rural areas to farm and raise the children on their own. To feed so many migrant laborers, many colonial officials requisitioned food from rural areas, leaving people in rural areas undernourished and vulnerable to disease.

There were a few economic exceptions to the colonial rule. Cocoa farmers in Ghana and palm oil producers in Nigeria, for instance, profited from high prices. Coffee farmers in East Africa experienced similar benefits. In most of these cases, economic success was a result of colonial policies that divided land into small farms. Likewise,

African merchant women, allowed to continue as they had before **colonialism**, maintained a degree of economic independence at home as well as within society. But when the Depression hit in the 1930s, some Africans were severely affected—France and Great Britain forced their colonies to purchase their products. The economy in southern Africa, on the other hand, boomed during the Depression, as a result of the rising value of gold and the cheaper cost of mining copper in Rhodesia and the Belgian Congo as compared to Chile. But the wealth was enjoyed only by the small number of Europeans and white South Africans. While mining jobs and cash wages remained steady for many southern Africans, they gained little of the profits.

The most severe experiences of colonial rule occurred in the white settler colonies such as Algeria, Kenya, Rhodesia, and South Africa. While all cities built during the time of colonization had segregated housing, clubs, restaurants, and hospitals, racial discrimination was at its utmost in the settler colonies. Colonization also meant the spread of Christianity, especially in areas where European influences were the strongest. Mission schools were established across the continent as a way to encourage what was seen as a European religion. Few Europeans imagined that Africans would use Christianity in the fight to end colonization. Mission schools taught in colonial languages, thus helping Africans to work within the colonial economy. The schools created a new educated elite familiar with Western ways. Although only a few Africans gained a secondary education and even fewer were able to travel to Europe or the United States to attend a university, those few were exposed to liberal Western ideas that contradicted the racial prejudice and colonialism Africans faced every day. Many of the Western-educated elite returned home with a strong desire to work for freedom and equality. Senegalese Blaise Diagne, for example, fought for African political participation and equal treatment within the French army. Similarly, J. E. Casely Hayford struggled for African autonomy in British West Africa. In South Africa, Western-educated lawyers and journalists used the **African National Congress (ANC)**, established in 1909, as a means to fight for the rights of Africans. But Africans who received a university education overseas, seeing that people of African descent around the world were facing similar conditions, were drawn to Pan-Africanism. Popularized by the African-American W. E. B. Du Bois and the Jamaican Marcus Garvey, Pan-Africanism advocated the unity of all African peoples in the global struggle against white supremacy and colonialism. In many ways it combined European ideas of liberalism and nationalism neatly manipulated into a weapon against Western colonial powers.

AP Tip

While colonial hardships increased during World War I and World War II, the nature of colonialism within Africa remained constant. You should be able to compare Africans' experiences of colonialism with those of South and Southeast Asians. You should also be able to compare Africans' experiences of the world wars with those of Asians, Europeans, and people of the Americas.

World War II and Independence Movements

World War II had an even greater impact on the continent of Africa than the First World War. There were more Africans fighting, more battles within Africa, and more ramifications at the end of the war. For the continent of Africa, the Second World War perhaps began with the Italian conquest of Ethiopia in 1935, then one of only two independent African states. The invasion of Ethiopia was met by a very weak response from the European powers and the United States. The League of Nations protested but did little else to aid Ethiopia, one of its members. The international community failed to impose punishments, and it allowed Italian ships continued use of the Suez Canal. For many Africans, this showed a lack of respect for an independent African nation and symbolized European unwillingness to support African independence, despite the promises outlined during the post–World War I Paris Peace Conference.

The Italian invasion also emboldened Hitler, who concluded that German aggression would face little resistance. It was not until Italy joined forces with Germany as part of the Axis powers and Italian forces invaded British Somaliland in 1940 that the British offered support to exiled Ethiopian emperor Haile Selassie. In the meantime, Italian forces marched north and invaded Egypt. During 1941, British forces fought the Italians in Somaliland, and Haile Selassie led his troops into the Ethiopian capital, Addis Ababa, and reclaimed his title by ousting the Italians. During that same year the British also overtook the Italians in Libya, and at the end of 1942 defeated the Germans at **El Alamein**, Egypt.

For Africans, the effects of the Second World War were similar to those of the first but on a far broader scale. European colonial rulers increasingly forced Africans to labor in mines and on plantations. Raw materials were once again requisitioned, and as a result mining companies opened new mines and towns in Central Africa. Inflation afflicted most regions of the continent. As in World War I, millions of Africans served as soldiers and porters. Serving alongside Europeans in North Africa, Europe, and Asia, Africans became well aware of Allied propaganda lambasting Nazi aggression and racism and promoting European liberation efforts. They returned to their countries emboldened to demand liberty from the very colonizers with whom they fought against the Nazis.

Decolonization

The greatest impact of World War II was the impetus it gave anticolonial independence movements throughout Africa and Asia. For the people of Africa, India's independence in 1947 provided a model as well as extra motivation to demand independence for their respective nations. At the same time, support for colonialism was ebbing among the British, who were less willing to spend money to maintain colonial territories. The year of Indian independence was also the year of Kwame Nkrumah's return to the Gold Coast. Released from a British prison by public pressure, Nkrumah was appointed prime minister in 1951, but it took until 1957 for Ghana to gain full independence. Other British West African colonies soon became independent as well. The large and diverse nation of Nigeria gained independence in 1960. On the whole, French colonies were slower in gaining independence. But under the dynamic leadership of Sékou Touré, Guinea gained independence in 1958. Two years later in 1960, other French West African colonies followed.

Despite being severely weakened by the Second World War, European powers often struggled to hold on to their colonies. This frequently led to contentious and bloody fights, especially in areas with a large population of white settlers, who strongly resisted majority rule. The struggle for Algerian independence was just such a case. Not only was there a sizable French population within Algeria; the French economy was dependent on Algerian oil and gas fields. Even Algerian vineyards were the source of large quantities of French wine. The fight, therefore, was both bloody and brutal. French colonists considered Algeria rightfully a part of France and they swore to fight to the bitter end. Leading the independence movement was the Front de Liberation National (FLN), which received support from Egypt and other Arab and African countries. Algeria finally won independence in 1962, more than fifteen years after the end of World War II. At the end of the Algerian war for independence, many French colonists hastily returned to France. But their departure caused severe problems for the Algerian economy because few Algerians were trained for any of the technical and management positions. Economic problems also led many Algerians fleeing unemployment to seek opportunities in France. Nonetheless, despite the bloody war, France and Algeria managed to retain close, albeit shaky, ties.

The East African nation of Kenya faced a similar struggle to gain freedom. Though not as large as Algeria, it too had a white settler population that had gained wealth and influence as coffee planters in the colonial economy. Intent on retaining power in Kenya, the coffee planters characterized Kenyans as unequipped for self-government, referring to a Kikuyu protest movement as Mau Mau to suggest primitive savagery. The Kenyan rebels referred to themselves as Muingi, meaning "the movement," or the Kikuyu Central Association—the vast majority of the rebels belonged to the Kikuyu, an ethnic group that had been displaced by the settlers from the lush agricultural highlands. When violence between the settlers and the freedom fighters escalated in the early 1950s, British troops managed to capture the leaders and resettle them in fortified villages—essentially concentration camps—to prevent contact with other rebel fighters. The British then banned all political protest and activity, declared a state of emergency, and imprisoned Jomo Kenyatta and other nationalist leaders. Released in 1961 after eight years of imprisonment, Kenyatta negotiated with the British for independence and in 1964 was elected the first president of the Republic of Kenya.

No region had more white settlers than southern Africa, which made the fight for independence there longer and more intense. Throughout southern Africa the settlers defended white supremacy and white rule at all costs, provoking armed struggle. During the 1960s, an armed guerrilla struggle began against Portuguese rule in Angola and Mozambique. Ironically, war in the Portuguese colonies became increasingly unpopular in Portugal, causing the Portuguese army to overthrow the government of Portugal in 1974. In 1975, the new Portuguese government granted independence to both Angola and Mozambique. White settlers in Southern Rhodesia finally accepted African majority rule in 1980, after ten years of fighting. The new government changed the name of the nation to Zimbabwe, in honor of the ancient kingdom that predated European colonization.

The fight for independence proved hardest in South Africa and Namibia. In South Africa, the white minority-rule government was based on a system of racial separation and subjugation called **apartheid**. Though minority-ruled, South Africa had existed as an independent nation since 1910. Thus the struggle in South Africa was against apartheid, and the ANC was at the forefront of this anti-apartheid struggle. As in other regions with settler populations, armed struggle became inevitable. In 1960, South African police fired on hundreds of demonstrators in the town of Sharpeville. The government banned all forms of protest, and Nelson Mandela, the ANC leader, was captured and sentenced to life in prison in 1964. The ANC, banned in South Africa, was forced to operate armed resistance from neighboring countries, such as Mozambique and Tanzania, that had recently gained independence. The struggle against apartheid continued until 1990 when the government officially ended the practice.

THE COLD WAR

One cannot look at decolonization in Africa without looking at Cold War politics. Both the United States and the USSR were attempting to influence the newly independent states. As a result of this pressure and in hope of gaining allies in the fight against colonialism, various African leaders—among them Kwame Nkrumah and Egypt's Nasir—attended the **Bandung Conference** in 1955. The conference proclaimed the solidarity of all people fighting against colonial rule. Despite claiming to be nonaligned, African leaders were drawn, willingly or not, into the struggle of the two superpowers. African liberation movements often gained assistance from Cuba and the Soviets because no Western democracies supported African independence. The decision to accept aid from communist nations thrust them deep into the Cold War. In the Belgian Congo, competing political and ethnic groups received aid from Cuba and the Soviets on the one hand, while others received assistance from the West. Cold War struggles and the stubbornness of Belgian colonial authorities led to violence, property destruction, and heavy loss of life. In 1965, the first democratically elected prime minister, Patrice Lumumba, was assassinated after serving in office for only sixty-seven days. From the onset, Lumumba was surrounded by Cold War pressures. He received support from the Soviets, which angered United States president Eisenhower. Evidence has also revealed that the coup that removed Lumumba from office was CIA-sponsored.

In somewhat similar fashion, Ghanaian independence was also entrenched in Cold War politics. A year after Lumumba's assassination, Nkrumah was overthrown in a CIA-backed military coup while he was away on a state visit to Vietnam in 1966. Throughout the independence/anti-apartheid struggle, the South African government attempted to discredit the ANC by highlighting ties and support from Cuba and the Soviets. What is clear is that upon independence, African nations became prime battlegrounds for conflicts in which the United States and the USSR provoked, financed, and armed competing factions or parties. These **proxy wars**, as they were called, led to decades of violence and military struggle. They often resembled wars in which small newly independent nations were fighting at the bidding of the two superpowers, which were hoping to gain strategic advantages. Proxy wars also inflamed ethnic rivalries and hatreds that had been lying dormant during colonial rule. When the European colonial powers created artificial national boundaries during the Berlin Conference, they did so without regard to ethnic and religious makeup. The result was ethnic groups such as the Wolof, who were split among four different countries: Senegal, Gambia, Mali, and the Ivory Coast. Upon independence, feelings of ethno-nationalistic pride were stirred and encouraged by Africans and the superpowers alike.

AP Tip

Decolonization was a long and haphazard process in Africa. You should be able to identify the key factors that helped bring about independence and compare the nature of the independence struggle in various nations throughout Africa, as well as around the world.

THE POST–COLD WAR WORLD

The post–Cold War era has been stoked with both optimism and disappointment. Many viewed the fall of the Soviet Union as an opportunity for wealth and democracy to spread to the nations of Africa. Wealth and democracy, however, have been slow in coming. Military coups, often stemming from Cold War battles and frustrations, have been frequent in sub-Saharan Africa. Many leaders have also used their offices to limit the power of opponents and for personal enrichment. Conflicts over resources such as diamonds and other minerals have proliferated. The year 1994 witnessed a massive case of ethnic cleansing in the Central African nation of Rwanda. When political leaders incited the Hutu majority to massacre their Tutsi neighbors on claims of discrimination and favoritism stemming from the colonial period, the result was over 750,000 dead and millions of refugees flooding into the neighboring nations of Congo, Tanzania, and Burundi. As the international community was slow to respond, violence spilled over into Congo causing greater conflict and destabilization.

Nonetheless, post–Cold War Africa has witnessed many success stories, among them the ending of apartheid in South Africa and the 1994 election victory of former political prisoner Nelson Mandela and the African National Congress. The ANC victory marked the first time in which the black majority could participate equally. The 1990s also witnessed the election of Olusegun Obasanjo as president of Nigeria after years of military rule. Likewise, in 1992, the **United Nations**, with the help of various African nations, helped to end the civil war in Mozambique. For Angola, peace was not realized until 2002, and the civil war in Liberia did not end until 2003. Two years later, Liberians elected their first female head of state, Dr. Ellen Johnson-Sirleaf.

Peace and political stability, however, have not meant wealth. In fact, since 1945, the gap between rich nations and poor nations has only grown wider and has concentrated poverty in the former colonies of Africa, Asia, and Latin America. Many have struggled to diversify their economies from the cash crop systems established during the colonial period. Poverty in African nations has coincided with high mortality rates and low life-expectancy rates. And with the contemporary onset of AIDS, African nations are suffering some of the highest incidences around the world. In fact, 70 percent of the 40 million people infected with AIDS worldwide live in sub-Saharan Africa. Such drastic numbers are causing serious problems in food production and job staffing. The problem of AIDS, and its high mortality rate in Africa, is closely related to poverty. Hence, AIDS has become one of the greatest threats to contemporary Africa. Because treatment for AIDS is so expensive, recent global efforts have been made to provide drugs at lower costs. Poverty has also caused large-scale migrations. Numerous migrants from rural areas of Nigeria, for instance, have moved to the city of Lagos in order to find jobs. Migrations were not without reason. Urban residents throughout sub-Saharan Africa, for instance, are six times more likely to have potable water than their rural counterparts. Unfortunately, few nations have been able to expand basic services at the same rate as the rapid population growth. Many Africans have also sought better lives by emigrating to western Europe and the United States. A growing number of Moroccans and Algerians have found their way to Spain, France, and Belgium. A large population of Ghanaians and Nigerians have made new homes in Houston, Texas; Atlanta, Georgia; and Washington, D.C. Migration and emigration are fueled by exploding population growth that is far outpacing the rate in developed nations. Nonetheless, despite much progress since independence, the hope for national wealth has eluded most African nations, as well as their citizens.

Multiple-Choice Questions

1. All of the following statements about African involvement in World War I are true EXCEPT
   (A) Africans served in colonial armies fighting alongside Europeans.
   (B) Africans grew crops for Europeans and sold them at artificially low prices.
   (C) battles took place in West and East Africa.
   (D) treaties ending the war increased African political representation.

2. Which of the following statements is most accurate regarding the German colonies in Africa at the end of World War I?
   (A) The colonies were stripped from Germany and recolonized by the British, French, Italians, and South Africans.
   (B) The colonies gained independence and self-determination.
   (C) Germany maintained control of their African colonies.
   (D) The colonies were designated as Class A Mandates by the League of Nations, and thus allowed limited African control.

3. How did the Depression affect the economy in Southern Africa?
   (A) Because of the rising value of gold and copper, the economy boomed.
   (B) The region remained isolated from world affairs.
   (C) Local industries were stimulated by the reduction of imports.
   (D) The economy plummeted much as it did in other regions of the world that supplied raw materials.

4. How did the experience of Africans in the areas where large groups of Europeans settled differ from the experience of Africans in other areas of the continent?
   (A) They had less access to job opportunities.
   (B) They had greater access to educational institutions.
   (C) They had greater respect for the colonial regime and less desire for independence.
   (D) They faced greater and more rigid forms of racial discrimination.

5. Which of the following most accurately depicts the changes in the labor systems in African colonies during the early 1900s?
   (A) Africans migrated to different colonies in search of jobs.
   (B) Traditional African farming became more highly valued.
   (C) Africans worked in mines and on plantations for little pay.
   (D) Europeans exported African labor for the overseas slave markets.

6. How did the presence of African soldiers in World War II provide an opportunity for African independence?
   (A) African soldiers became aware of the Allied contradictions in fighting a war for freedom while colonizing African people.
   (B) African soldiers gained the technological skills to produce weapons to fight the European powers.
   (C) The organizational skills of African soldiers convinced the European powers that Africans were capable of self-rule.
   (D) African soldiers were able to bring weapons back to their country that they later used to wage guerrilla warfare.

7. Which of these allowed Ethiopia to regain independence in 1941?
   (A) Italy decided to retreat because its economy was being hurt.
   (B) Britain offered military support to Haile Selassie after Italy invaded the British colony of Somaliland.
   (C) France invaded Italy, thus forcing most Italians to return to defend the Italian peninsula.
   (D) Mussolini signed a treaty with Ethiopia that called for Italian withdrawal in exchange for Ethiopian cotton and tea.

8. Which of the following statements is an accurate comparison of Algerian and Kenyan independence?
    (A) Both were French colonies that were granted independence shortly after the end of World War II.
    (B) Both nations gained independence peacefully and saw a large number of Europeans arrive after independence.
    (C) Both were achieved by armed struggle as the European populations refused to give up control.
    (D) Neither had many economic resources and consequently gained independence rather easily.

9. African nations became prime battlegrounds for proxy wars because
    (A) they had little experience in self-rule and were thus unable to govern successfully.
    (B) the United States and USSR supported competing factions in order to gain influence within newly independent nations.
    (C) they were willing to sacrifice stability in exchange for the promise of profit from the two superpowers.
    (D) Soviet and American intention to colonize African nations forced many Africans to form armed resistance.

10. The 1994 election in South Africa was important for which of the following reasons?
    (A) It marked the end of civil war and the election of the first female head of state.
    (B) The military regime was finally deposed, and democratically elected officials were installed in the parliament.
    (C) Land and wealth was redistributed to the black South Africans as reparations for colonialism and apartheid.
    (D) It was the first time the black majority could participate equally.

11. Which of the following African countries had relatively large European populations in the first part of the 1900s?
    (A) Egypt and the Sudan
    (B) Algeria and Kenya
    (C) Nigeria and Ghana
    (D) Liberia and Ethiopia

12. What impact did European imperialism have on the health of Africans?
    (A) Health standards worsened because of war.
    (B) Health standards worsened since migration of people spread disease.
    (C) Health standards improved with broad access to European medical care.
    (D) Health standards improved because of new treatments for malaria.

13. How did French sub-Saharan African colonies differ from British sub-Saharan African colonies?
    (A) French colonies were more Christianized.
    (B) Independence movements in French colonies were more violent.
    (C) French colonial farmers were less dependent on cash crops.
    (D) Independence was achieved through a more gradual process in French colonies.

14. All of the following have been issues in sub-Saharan Africa in the late twentieth century EXCEPT
    (A) population decline.
    (B) ethnic cleansing.
    (C) regional trade associations.
    (D) global terrorism.

15. Which of the following represents a cultural shift that has occurred in Africa during the 1900s?
    (A) The rising popularity of monotheism.
    (B) The declining influence of socialism.
    (C) The declining role of international trade.
    (D) The declining significance of communicable diseases.

Free-Response Questions

1. Compare the struggle for independence in TWO of the following nations.
   ▪ Algeria
   ▪ Ghana
   ▪ Kenya
   ▪ South Africa

2. Focusing on ONE of the following factors, discuss the continuities and changes experienced in sub-Saharan Africa from circa 1900 to the present.
   ▪ social
   ▪ economic
   ▪ political

Answers

MULTIPLE-CHOICE QUESTIONS

1. **ANSWER: D.** More than four million Africans served in colonial armies during World War I as either soldiers or porters. Various battles were fought in West and East Africa in which the French and the British forces overtook the Germans and wrested control of the German colonies of Togo and Cameroon. But despite serving in Allied armies, Africans were not granted rights in the treaties that ended the war. In fact, in order to support the colonial

armies, Europeans forced Africans to grow export crops and sell them at low prices (*The Earth and Its Peoples,* 5th ed., p. 805/6th ed., p. 759).

2. ANSWER: **A.** The British and French defeated Germany and took control in both Togo and Cameroon. It was not until the end of the war that the Germans were defeated in Tanganyika. At the Paris Peace Conference the African colonies of Germany were officially divided among France, Great Britain, Italy, and South Africa (*The Earth and Its Peoples,* 5th ed., pp. 805, 808-809/6th ed., p. 768).

3. ANSWER: **A.** As prices dropped during the Depression, gold became more valuable. Similarly, the cost of mining copper in southern Africa was cheaper than in Chile. The result of both phenomena was an economic boom for southern Africa. However, only the small white minority benefited from this economic boom (*The Earth and Its Peoples,* 5th ed., p. 838/6th ed., p. 813).

4. ANSWER: **D.** Colonial cities throughout Africa reflected racial attitudes of colonialists, but patterns of racial discrimination were most rigid in the white-settler colonies of eastern and southern Africa (*The Earth and Its Peoples,* 5th ed., pp. 866-868, 870/6th ed., p. 801).

5. ANSWER: **C.** European rulers were most interested in African labor in order to develop and extract African resources. They often used police powers to force Africans to work in European-owned mines and plantations for little pay (*The Earth and Its Peoples,* 5th ed., pp. 866-867/6th ed., p. 800).

6. ANSWER: **A.** Millions of African soldiers fought alongside Europeans in North Africa, Europe, and Asia. They became acutely aware of the Allied propaganda calling for European liberation from Nazi racism and aggression. Meanwhile they wondered how such Nazi racism and aggression differed from Allied racism and aggression within Africa. Thus, having fought for Europeans, African soldiers returned home with an increased drive to fight for African liberation (*The Earth and Its Peoples,* 5th ed., pp. 870-871/6th ed., p. 802).

7. ANSWER: **B.** Despite initial appeals from Haile Selassie, the British refrained from helping Ethiopia until Italy invaded the British colony of Somaliland. While the Italians were occupied with the British counterattack, Selassie led his troops into the Ethiopian capital of Addis Ababa to reclaim his title of emperor (*The Earth and Its Peoples,* 5th ed., pp. 844-846/6th ed., p. 802).

8. ANSWER: **C.** The French controlled Algerian oil and gas fields as well as large tracts of arable land used as vineyards. Similarly, British settlers controlled the best lands in Kenyan highlands that were used for profitable coffee plantations. When peaceful attempts failed, organizations fighting for independence in Algeria and Kenya resorted to armed resistance. Independence was eventually gained only after years of violent struggle (*The Earth and Its Peoples,* 5th ed., pp. 896-897, 899/6th ed., p. 850–851).

9. ANSWER: **B.** Proxy wars were conflicts in which the rival super-powers financed and armed competing factions or parties in order to gain greater influence. As newly independent nations or those on the verge of independence, African countries were seen by the United States and USSR as being open to influence. Proxy wars occurred in Angola, Congo, Mozambique and other nations (*The Earth and Its Peoples,* 5th ed., pp. 899-900, 915-916/6th ed., p. 868).

10. ANSWER: **D.** The 1994 election marked the official end of white minority rule and the apartheid regime. Black South Africans were able to vote in national elections and overwhelmingly voted for the African National Congress (ANC), which had been at the forefront of the anti-apartheid struggle. Moreover, Nelson Mandela, the former political prisoner and anti-apartheid leader, became the nation's first democratically elected president (*The Earth and Its Peoples,* 5th ed., p. 954/6th ed., p. 906).

11. ANSWER: **B.** Only three African countries had significant European populations: Algeria with its French colonists, Kenya with its British colonists, and South Africa with its Dutch and British settlers. Other African colonies and countries had relatively few Europeans (*The Earth and Its Peoples,* 5th ed., p. 866/6th ed., p. 800).

12. ANSWER: **B.** Imperialism created a much more mobile population that traveled to new mining areas and cities. These migrants spread diseases like malaria, tuberculosis, syphilis, and gonorrhea. European medical care was not available to the overwhelming majority of Africans (*The Earth and Its Peoples,* 5th ed., pp. 866-867/6th ed., p. 800).

13. ANSWER: **D.** The French, with their policies of assimilation of colonial people, had colonies that wanted independence but in a more gradual manner. African leaders of these French colonies saw some advantages with maintaining connections to France (*The Earth and Its Peoples,* 5th ed., pp. 899-900/6th ed., p. 852).

14. ANSWER: **A.** The population of African countries has been rising sharply. Africans established two regional trade associations and ethnic cleansing in Rwanda and terrorist bombing in East Africa also occurred in the 1990s (*The Earth and Its Peoples,* 5th ed., pp. 925-926, 931, 951, 957, 961/6th ed., p. 878).

15. ANSWER: **A.** The religions of Islam and Christianity have significantly transformed African religious experience during the twentieth century. Large numbers of Africans have converted to these religions as the continent has transformed dramatically in economic and political ways. With decolonization and increasing majority rule in countries like South Africa, European elites have less influence than during the earlier period of imperialism. Many African countries adopted socialist governments after independence but still are economically very much at the whim of international trade. Diseases like AIDS and continuing problems with malaria have infected large numbers of Africans in recent years (*The Earth and Its Peoples,* 5th ed., pp. 717-718/6th ed., p. 801).

FREE-RESPONSE QUESTIONS

1. Five key factors explain the independence struggle throughout Africa—World War II, the role of Western-educated African elites, the independence of India, Pan-Africanism, and the weakening of Europe as a result of the two world wars. A good response should compare/contrast at least two of the factors. You must also be acutely aware of the role of white settler populations and their effect on the independence struggle. For example, both Kwame Nkrumah of Ghana and Jomo Kenyatta of Kenya studied abroad, in the United States and Great Britain respectively. There they witnessed the hypocrisy of Western democratic ideals while absorbing notions of black pride and Pan-Africanism. South Africa, Algeria, and Kenya were all areas with a significant population of white settlers. Whereas Africans in some places were eventually able to negotiate freedom after the success of Indian independence, the settlers fiercely resisted majority rule. Thus, Africans in Algeria, Kenya, and South Africa were forced to use armed struggle in order to gain independence.

2. A good response should begin with a thorough discussion of colonization. Politically, Africans were subject to laws imposed upon them by European nations. They were economically stripped of their resources for the benefit of the European colonizer. Socially, Africans were relegated to second-class citizenship in their own land. The struggle for independence marks a clear change as Africans in various nations began to organize resistance movements in order to fight for social, economic, and political power. During the 1940s and 1950s, Africans formed stronger bonds across national and continental boundaries in an effort to fight imperialism. The nonalignment movement that sprang out of the Bandung Conference was a key turning point in the Africans' struggle. When African nations gained political independence between the 1950s and the 1980s, they faced the daunting task of trying to define their own destiny despite being mired in the Cold War conflicts of the United States and the Soviet Union. The post–Cold War era has been marked by an effort to gain economic independence. Many foreign companies, especially those from the former colonial powers as well as the United States, maintain control of major industries within African nations. Nonetheless, drought, famine, and political instability have hampered efforts at reducing poverty. International organizations like the World Bank and IMF have offered aid, but often on condition that African countries cut subsidy and social programs. Poverty throughout sub-Saharan Africa, therefore, has led many people to migrate to western European nations as well as the United States. Colonization, Decolonization/Cold War, and the Post–Cold War era form a good framework for continuity and change over time in Africa.

22

THE MIDDLE EAST: CIRCA 1900 TO THE PRESENT

KEY CONCEPTS

- The mandate system divided German colonies and the Ottoman Empire among the victorious Allies of World War I—France, Great Britain, Italy, and Japan.
- Mandates were to be administered with the goal of their eventual independence, but in fact they experienced recolonization.
- Tension between Zionism and Arab nationalism remains a constant source of conflict in the Middle East today.
- Despite gaining independence from European powers in the 1950s, and despite the rise of oil wealth in the region, most Middle Easterners have remained poor, and no Middle Eastern nation has become a major industrial or geopolitical power.
- Islamic terrorist groups that emerged during the Cold War and the post–Cold War era have aimed much of their anger at the State of Israel and at the United States, the lone superpower wielding influence in the Middle East.

KEY TERMS

- al Qaeda
- Balfour Declaration
- El Alamein
- League of Nations
- mandate system
- militant Islam
- Organization of Petroleum Exporting Countries (OPEC)
- Palestinian Liberation Organization (PLO)
- terrorism
- United Nations
- Zionism

The Middle East during the twentieth century is discussed in *The Earth and Its Peoples,* fifth edition, Chapters 28, 29, 31, 32, and 33 and sixth edition, Chapters 27, 30, 31, and 32.

NATIONALISM AND THE DECLINE OF THE OTTOMAN EMPIRE

By the beginning of the twentieth century, the weakness of the Ottoman Empire had created a power vacuum in the Middle East. The rise of nationalism—the identification of people with a nation often centered on language or religion—had spread over much of Europe and by the turn of the century was affecting the Ottoman territories. The empire comprised dozens of ethnic, religious, and language groups, and officials were concerned about the impact of nationalistic sentiment. Would these minority groups remain loyal to the empire, or would they identify with others that proposed a new national identity?

The "sick man of Europe" began to receive its answer in the first decade of the twentieth century. In 1902 Macedonia rebelled and achieved independence a year later; in 1908 Austria-Hungary annexed the predominantly Muslim Bosnia. Italy conquered Libya in 1912, ending the Ottoman presence in North Africa. With the Balkan Wars (1912–1913), the Ottomans finally lost all control of Serbia, Bulgaria, and Romania. By 1913 all of the Ottoman European territories were either independent or under the control of a European power. Only Istanbul would remain within the empire.

Further demonstrating the weakening of the Ottoman Empire, European powers were meddling in various aspects of Ottoman affairs. To fund Ottoman modernization, loans from European nations were necessary, but these loans came at a price; European financiers had a controlling influence in tax collection, railroad construction, mine development, and public utilities. European nations also exerted their influence as they claimed to be protectors of different ethnic and religious minorities within the empire. In response to this outside control, the Young Turks, a nationalistic reform group, began to gain supporters. The Young Turks blamed Sultan Abdul Hamid for the empire's troubles and used their growing influence to have him replaced in 1909 by his brother Muhammad V Rashid (1909–1918). Reformers wanted to create a constitutional monarchy, and they helped reshape the bureaucracy, educational system, and law enforcement in an attempt to limit European influence. Because of the influence of nationalism, the empire increasingly saw itself as dominated by ethnic Turks, not as being multi-ethnic. With the support of the Young Turks, Ottoman officials began to crack down on ethnic minorities, such as Armenians and Greeks. These new reforms also came with a shift in European allies. The Young Turks, resenting French and British influence, began to align themselves more closely with Germany, which had been least involved in Ottoman internal affairs. As the world drifted towards World War I, this shift would lead the decaying Ottoman Empire to supporting the Central Powers during the war.

WORLD WAR I

The Middle East was central to the development of World War I. The vast majority of the region was under the control of the Ottoman Empire, which by the turn of the twentieth century had grown weak and was beginning to tear at the seams. Rebellions and loss of territory began in the provinces closest to Europe, such as Macedonia, Crete, and Albania. The internal problems of the Ottoman Empire provided a prime opportunity for the imperialistic-minded European powers to intervene and gain territory. It is at this particular time, long before the start of World War I, that alliances began taking shape. Each European power either coveted the territory of and/or sided with the ethnic minorities fighting for independence from the Turks. The Austro-Hungarian Empire, for example, sought the Slavic-populated regions of the Ottoman Empire, much to the chagrin of the Russians, who supported the Slavs. There was in essence both an internal and external tug of war.

The Ottoman Turks began to impose more restrictions on ethnic minorities, who were intent on pulling away and gaining independence. A group known as the Young Turks began a campaign for changes, among them the Turkification of ethnic minorities. This crackdown on minorities led to hundreds of thousands of Armenians being forcibly evacuated and massacred in what has recently become known as the Armenian holocaust. At the same time, Great Britain, Austria-Hungary, Russia, France, and Germany intervened as allies or rivals over Ottoman territory.

The spark for a world war came when the Archduke Franz Ferdinand of the Austro-Hungarian Empire was assassinated by ethnic Serbian nationalists angered by the presence of Austria-Hungary in the Balkans, which had recently gained independence from the Ottomans. The Russians supported the Slavic Serbians. The Germans supported the Austro-Hungarians. The British and French supported the Russians. The Ottoman Turks formed a secret alliance with Germany in hopes of gaining territory from the Russians. By the end of 1914, the Ottomans were heavily involved in the war; the following year the British unsuccessfully attempted to attack the Ottomans at Gallipoli, near Istanbul.

The British, however, did succeed in undermining the Ottomans by allying with disenchanted groups within the Ottoman Empire. In 1916 the British promised independence to Arabs who revolted against their Ottoman rulers. Hussein ibn Ali and his son Faisal led the Arab armies against the Turks, which contributed to the defeat of the Ottoman Empire. The British also made promises to Jewish minorities in eastern and central Europe who were calling for the creation of a Jewish state in the Jewish ancestral homeland of Palestine. This nationalist movement, known as **Zionism**, appealed to many European Jews as a solution to the problem of anti-Semitism in Europe. Just before the British armies gained control of Palestine in 1917, Foreign Secretary Sir Arthur Balfour wrote a statement, later known as the Balfour Declaration, which simultaneously gave sanction to Zionism while promising not to infringe on the rights of current Palestinian residents.

At the end of World War I, much to the dismay of many, independence did not come to the Middle East. Instead, the Allied

Powers claimed the former Ottoman territories as mandates. The mandate system, essentially a compromise made at the Paris Peace Conference, stipulated that the former German colonies and the Ottoman Empire would be divided among the Allied victors of World War I—namely, France, Great Britain, Italy, and Japan. All mandates were to be overseen by the **League of Nations**, and they were to be administered with the goal of eventual independence for the territory. In regard to the Middle East, the mandate system called for temporary British and French control. The British took control of Palestine, Iraq, and Trans-Jordan. The French took control of Syria and Lebanon.

AP Tip

You should be able to discuss the changes and continuities from colonialism under the Ottoman Empire to the mandate system under the British and French. You will have to draw upon some of your knowledge of the previous period when discussing the Ottoman Empire. However, you will be expected to detail changes and continuities regarding political leadership and power, as well as the economic and social impact on the people of the Middle East.

THE INTERWAR PERIOD

World War I proved the death knell for the once-powerful Ottoman Empire. But instead of independence, the people of the Middle East found themselves recolonized by the very group that claimed to fight for their freedom, the Allied Powers. Recolonization, which the Allied Powers accomplished by means of the mandate system, gave rise to various revolutionary nationalist movements throughout the region. One of the first nationalist uprisings erupted at the heart of the former Ottoman Empire. In 1919 Mustafa Kemal formed a nationalist government for Turkey, and by 1922 had regained the territory of Anatolia and Constantinople. Like the Young Turks who had preceded him, Kemal began to modernize Turkey, creating a secular state with a constitution modeled after those of the Western powers. He later took as his family name Atatürk—"father of the Turks."

A similar trend occurred in Persia when resentment toward British domination came to a head in 1921. The nationalist movement, led by army officer Reza Khan, overthrew the Qajar dynasty and kicked out the British. Once in control, Reza Khan became known as Reza Shah Pahlavi and Persia became known as Iran. Like Mustafa Kemal Atatürk of Turkey, Reza Shah proceeded to modernize Iran by creating a secular state based on Western ideals.

Most nationalist movements in the Middle East, however, did not find success. The French crushed nationalist uprisings in Lebanon and Syria, and while Iraq and Egypt were declared independent, Britain maintained economic and military control. There was one state, however, that managed to attain full independence. In 1932, Prince Ibn Saud united the many Arabian tribes and founded the Kingdom of

Saudi Arabia. When oil reserves were discovered in 1938, Saudi Arabia gained global importance.

Despite the lack of independence, massive changes occurred in the Middle East during the interwar period. Encouraged by Zionism and the **Balfour Declaration**, thousands of European Jews emigrated to Palestine in hopes of creating a Jewish state.

The British, however, attempted to limit immigration so as not to alienate the Arabs. In the end, both Arabs and Jews were angered by British rule. Jewish immigration was only one of many changes occurring in the region. Numerous people moved to the cities during the interwar years, causing many cities to double in size. While population in the Middle East doubled, nomads were becoming a dying breed, and Western ideals were becoming quite popular.

WORLD WAR II AND INDEPENDENCE MOVEMENTS

The Second World War would have tremendous consequences for the Middle East. Because much of the region was under the mandate of either France or Great Britain, its fate was inextricably tied to the Allied Powers. Unlike the First World War, fighting in the Second World War was widespread around the globe. As the imperial ambitions of Germany and Italy grew, fighting eventually spread to the Middle East and North Africa. Italy attacked Egypt from Somaliland in hopes of gaining territory, but British forces eventually overpowered the Italians, then proceeded to conquer the Italian colonies of Somaliland and Libya. Despite being tied up fighting the Soviets on the eastern front, Germany sent troops to help the Italians. With better intelligence in the region and a greater supply of matériel, the British eventually defeated the Germans at **El Alamein**, Egypt, and expelled the Nazis from North Africa. German losses on the eastern front in Stalingrad and in Egypt at El Alamein weakened the Nazis and precipitated the end of Nazi expansion and the eventual downfall of their regime. World War II also signaled the downfall of European colonial power, even in the form of the **mandate system**. The Middle East, however, would struggle to define independence in the wake of the emergence of the United States and the Soviet Union as the two global superpowers.

THE COLD WAR AND DECOLONIZATION

After World War II, Syria and Lebanon gained independence, and by the 1950s, Egypt, Iraq, and Jordan began removing British military presence and control. However, countries such as Jordan often depended on their former colonial ruler for financial assistance. Many leaders in the Middle East attempted both to break from colonial dependency and to extract money by playing the two superpowers against each other. This was most certainly the case in Egypt, as both Presidents Nasir and Sadat gained assistance from the superpowers. In order to increase its industrial potential, Nasir sought assistance from the United States to build a dam at Aswan; at the same time he courted the Soviet Union for weapons. This infuriated the United States, which then reneged on the dam project. In response, the Soviet

Union offered to complete the project. In many ways, Egypt exemplifies the Cold War in the Middle East. Both superpowers offered financial and military assistance in order to gain favor and influence in the region. However, regional leaders also attempted to gain power and assistance from the two superpowers by aligning sometimes with one, sometimes with the other.

While the Cold War did spill into the Middle East, affecting all areas of military and political life, the post–World War II Middle East was primarily dominated by two phenomena: the creation of Israel and the realization of Middle East oil capacity. After the fall of the Nazi regime in Germany, intense pressure grew to resettle more European Jewish refugees in Palestine. Tension between Palestinian Arabs and Jewish immigrants grew more intense as the **United Nations** deliberated on splitting Palestine into two nations: one Jewish and one Arab. In 1947, the United Nations voted in favor of partitioning Palestine into the two states. This attempt to solve a crisis created a larger one. Many Arabs believed the division of land was unfair, and they took up arms to fight the Jewish State of Israel, which declared its independence in May 1948. Over 700,000 Palestinian refugees fled to United Nations refugee camps in the neighboring countries of Jordan, Syria, Lebanon, and Egypt. Israel often had the assistance of two global powers, the United States and Great Britain, and thus usually prevailed. However, Israel constantly feared attack from neighboring Arab nations. In 1967, this fear resulted in Israel preemptively attacking Egyptian and Syrian air bases. The conflict, known as the Six-Day War, ended with Israel taking control of Arab territory in the West Bank, the Golan Heights, the Gaza Strip, and the Sinai Peninsula. Israel also won control of all of Jerusalem, which had previously been split with Jordan and Palestinians in the West Bank. The war produced an even greater number of Palestinian refugees and deeper conflicts over the Jewish and Muslim holy city of Jerusalem. The war also resulted in acts of **terrorism** against Israel and guerilla warfare by the **Palestinian Liberation Organization**, led by Yasir Arafat, and by Israeli attacks on Palestinians in Gaza and the West Bank. Fighting between Israelis and the Palestinians continues to this day.

The end of World War II coincided with the full realization of oil wealth in the Persian Gulf states. As the global demand for oil rose, the Persian Gulf states of Bahrain, Iran, Iraq, Kuwait, Saudi Arabia, Qatar, and United Arab Emirates joined other oil-producing nations in 1960 to form the **Organization of Petroleum Exporting Countries** (OPEC). The purpose of OPEC was to promote the collective interests of the oil producers, one of which was the support of the Palestinian Arabs in their struggle against Israel. Thus in 1973 OPEC placed an embargo on the United States and the Netherlands for their support of Israel. In 1974 OPEC vastly increased its oil prices. Oil became a weapon in the Cold War politics of the Middle East. It also allowed for nations in the Middle East to gain wealth and positions of power in global politics.

Oil clearly made the Middle East a region of interest for both the United States and the Soviet Union. Both superpowers became directly involved in military action within the region. In 1979, revolution erupted in Iran, at least in part because of covert American intervention to help the Shah of Iran retain his throne despite popular discontent. American backing of the corrupt and inefficient ruler led to his eventual overthrow. In the Shah's place, Ayatollah Khomeini, a Shi'ite cleric, rose to power. He established an anti-Western, conservative Islamic republic. Like other Middle Eastern nations moving away from Westernization, Iran scaled back many political and social gains and compelled women to wear modest Islamic dress. Iran vehemently opposed Israel and its perceived backer, the United States. Bordering the Soviet Union and with enormous oil reserves, Iran was of great strategic and economic importance to the United States. Thus, the Iranian revolution proved to be a black eye for the United States. The final blow to American prestige came when Iranian radicals held fifty-two American diplomats as hostages for over a year.

The Iranian revolution also led to war. Its neighbor, Iraq, invaded Iran in 1980 in hopes of toppling the Islamic regime. A secular nation based on Arab nationalism, Iraq was controlled by Saddam Hussein, a Sunni. Hussein feared that Iran's Shi'ite rulers would influence Iraq's Shi'ites, who formed a majority of the Iraqi population. By 1986 the United States was lending its support to Hussein. The Iraq-Iran conflict, lasting eight long years, featured covert American and Soviet action as well as weapons supplied by the superpowers.

AP Tip

You should be able to analyze the reasons for the rise of Islamic regimes and Islamic fundamentalism in the Middle East during the Cold War era. Be prepared to discuss poverty and the sense of global powerlessness as an impetus for social reform. You will also be expected to explain how religion was used as a unifying factor within Middle Eastern nations.

While the situation in Iran embarrassed the United States, Afghanistan was even more disastrous for the Soviet Union. Like Iran, Afghanistan bordered the Soviet Union. In 1979 the Soviets sent troops into Afghanistan to support a young communist regime that was fighting a small band of local guerillas. The guerrillas, backed by the United States, proved unbelievably resilient. The war was both costly and embarrassing for the Soviet Union, as fighting dragged on for more than ten years. In 1989, Soviet leaders withdrew their troops because the war in Afghanistan was causing domestic discontent in the Soviet Union.

THE POST–COLD WAR WORLD

The end of the Cold War did not bring peace to the Middle East. Nor did it bring stability. Despite the accumulation of oil wealth, many Middle Easterners remained poor. Moreover, conflicts that arose or existed at the end of World War II remained unsolved by the dawn of the new millennium. As in other parts of the world, some political groups in the Middle East used terrorism to proclaim and advance their political objectives. The premise of terrorism is that a government loses its legitimacy when it cannot protect its citizens from horrible acts of violence. Superpowers might have the technological ability to wage war with minimal casualties to themselves, but terrorism can be effective in the hands of those who are unable to match the might of stronger nations.

Because it is hard to combat, terrorism became a popular strategy by the end of the twentieth century. The most prominent groups using terrorist strategies were Palestinian groups angry at the existence of Israel. In 1968 Palestinian groups were involved in airplane hijackings; in 1972, their capture and murder of eleven Israeli athletes at the Munich Olympic Games generated global news coverage and struck fear around the world. Terrorist attacks on Israel and Israeli incursions into the West Bank and Gaza to kill suspected terrorists have become the pattern that continues to the present day. The controversy over the existence of Israel remains the paramount issue within the Middle East.

The first major post–Cold War conflict in the Middle East, however, was the Persian Gulf War of 1990–1991. Like most conflicts in the region, what began as a local problem quickly took on global implications. During the summer of 1990, Iraq invaded Kuwait in hopes of gaining control of Kuwaiti oil fields. Saddam Hussein was angered by the Kuwaitis' refusal to reduce Iraq's debt. Hussein believed that Iraq, being much larger and more powerful than Kuwait, would quickly and easily defeat the Kuwaitis. However, Saudi Arabia, another neighboring oil power, felt threatened by the actions of Iraq. Saudi Arabia appealed to the United States, its ally and the sole superpower, to intervene. The United States gathered a coalition of nations, amassed a large military force with sophisticated weapons, and had the approval of the United Nations, as well as various Islamic nations within the region. In early 1991, President George H. W. Bush ordered the attack on Iraq. The victory was quick and decisive, as the American-led forces drove Iraq out of Kuwait. The United States enforced a no-fly zone, which restricted Iraqi military movements, but it did not remain as occupiers, and Saddam Hussein was allowed to remain in power. Nonetheless, the coalition victory in the Persian Gulf War restored American military confidence after Vietnam and signaled to the world that the United States was the unrivaled global superpower.

Despite its efforts to "win the hearts and minds" of the people in the Middle East, the United States has often been viewed as an unwelcome intruder within the region. For instance, **al Qaeda**, the terrorist network formerly led by Usama bin Laden, has claimed responsibility for attacks on various American embassies and military targets throughout the Islamic world. Through al Qaeda, bin Laden used **militant Islam** as a rallying cry for Muslims around the world, which many desperate and disenchanted Muslims have heeded. This globalized terrorism has struck fear in the United States and other Western powers. Bin Laden has successfully united people beyond traditional nation-state boundaries and beyond Arab identity. In September 2001, terrorists sponsored by al Qaeda attacked within the United States. In response, American and NATO forces joined with Afghan opposition groups to overthrow the Islamic fundamentalist regime of the Taliban, which had been providing refuge for bin Laden in Afghanistan. This, the first effort in what President George W. Bush has called the war on terror, overthrew the Taliban but bin Laden eluded capture until 2011 when he was killed by U.S. forces in Pakistan.

The war on terror spilled into Iraq when the United States, claiming that Saddam Hussein was supporting terrorists and harboring weapons of mass destruction, invaded Iraq and overthrew Saddam Hussein in the spring of 2003. This attack on Iraq has become known as the Second Persian Gulf War. This time, however, American forces remained. Many Middle Easterners regard the Second Persian Gulf War as another example of American aggression in the region. Iraq remains an unstable nation with constant fighting and frequent attacks by Iraqi insurgents against both American forces and Iraqi civilians. Like Israel and oil, Iraq has become a central issue in the Middle East.

Multiple-Choice Questions

1. Before 1909, the Young Turks were
   (A) calling for the installation of Islamic law and increased cooperation with Egyptian Arabs.
   (B) advocating centralized rule and the establishment of a constitutional government by the sultan.
   (C) encouraging British and French involvement in Turkey and greater freedom for ethnic minorities within the Ottoman Empire.
   (D) encouraging modernization of Turkey and the adoption of Christianity as the state religion.

2. The Balfour Declaration
   (A) encouraged the creation of a Jewish state in Palestine.
   (B) denounced Zionism as a radical religious movement.
   (C) called for support of the Arab Revolt of 1916.
   (D) called for independence for Jews and Arabs living in Palestine.

3. Which of the following statements about the mandate system for territories in the former Ottoman Empire is true?
   (A) It was welcomed by the Arabs, who favored British rule.
   (B) It was promoted by Western oil and gas corporations.
   (C) It was established without the approval of the League of Nations.
   (D) It provoked protests in the Middle East, where it was viewed as another form of colonialism.

4. The creation of Israel in 1948 eventually resulted in which of the following?
   (A) More than half a million Palestinian refugees
   (B) Tension over the control of Jerusalem
   (C) A homeland for European Jews who had been displaced by anti-Semitism and the Holocaust
   (D) All of the above

5. The Turkish leader Mustafa Kemal Atatürk, a modernizer, did which of the following?
   (A) Expelled the British and reintroduced Islamic shari'a
   (B) Declared Turkey a secular republic and introduced European laws
   (C) Supported modernist architectural styles and imported American literature
   (D) Established Islamic schools throughout Turkey and redistributed money to the peasantry

6. What was the significance of the British victory at El Alamein?
   (A) It resulted in the expulsion of the German army from North Africa.
   (B) It ended Italian involvement in the Second World War.
   (C) It resulted in the independence of Libya and Egypt.
   (D) It resulted in the German army regaining control of Egypt.

7. British policy on Palestine between the world wars fluctuated between which of the following?
   (A) Encouraging the transfer of Arab refugees to Jordan and Egypt or halting the departure of refugees altogether
   (B) Support for Jewish Zionists or support for indigenous Palestinian Arabs
   (C) Seeking guidance from the United Nations or passing control of Palestine to the United States
   (D) Forcibly removing Arabs or demanding compensation from Jewish immigrants in order to support Arab residents

8. In 1960 the Organization of Petroleum Exporting Countries (OPEC) was formed in order to
   (A) promote the collective interests of oil-producing states in the wake of rising demand for oil.
   (B) compete against the economic and military power of NATO.
   (C) use oil wealth as a vehicle to spread the religion of Islam.
   (D) create a powerful political voice within the United Nations and force changes within the World Bank.

9. Saddam Hussein ordered the Iraqi attack of Kuwait
   (A) to gain international recognition so that Iraq could be recognized as a world power.
   (B) to provoke the Iranians, who were Shi'ite allies of the Kuwaitis, and force another war with Iran.
   (C) out of anger at the Kuwaiti royal family for their refusal to reduce Iraqi debt and to gain control of Kuwaiti oil fields.
   (D) out of jealousy that Kuwait and Saudi Arabia were favored by the Americans.

10. Which of the following statements is true about Osama bin Laden?
    (A) He openly opposed the nations of Saudi Arabia, Israel, and the United States.
    (B) He was the mastermind behind the network of terrorist organizations known as al Qaeda.
    (C) He took refuge in Afghanistan, where he had close ties with the Taliban.
    (D) All of the above are true.

11. "We do not acknowledge any right claimed by the French Government in any part whatever of our Syrian country and refuse that she should assist us or have a hand in our country under any circumstances and in any place."

   This quotation from the Memorandum of the General Syrian Congress, July 2, 1919, is in response to
   (A) the establishment of mandates in Arab lands.
   (B) the creation of the state of Israel.
   (C) the alliance of the Ottomans with Germany in World War I.
   (D) the invasion of Egypt by Napoleon Bonaparte.

12. What did the independence of Arab lands have in common with the creation of the state of Israel?
   (A) Both proclaimed independence from Ottoman Turks.
   (B) Both came as a result of agreements among Western powers.
   (C) Both emerged out of the nonaligned movement.
   (D) Both independence movements drew support from the USSR.

13. The economic situation of Middle Eastern states shifted the most after World War II as a result of
   (A) the aid provided by the Marshall Plan.
   (B) the reestablishment of overland caravan routes.
   (C) the building of the Suez Canal.
   (D) the increased demand for oil.

14. How did U.S. foreign policy toward Iran differ from Soviet policy in Afghanistan during the 1980s?
   (A) The United States used military force more than the Soviets.
   (B) The United States had more restraint than the Soviets.
   (C) The United States depended more on treaty agreements than the Soviets.
   (D) The United States used economic aid more than the Soviets.

15. All of the following were rationales for the U.S. invasion of Iraq in 2003 EXCEPT
   (A) to create democratic institutions in Iraq.
   (B) to destroy Iraq's weapons of mass destruction.
   (C) to punish Iraq for its anti-American alliance with Iran.
   (D) to prevent Iraq from supplying terrorist networks.

Free-Response Questions

1. Compare the causes and effects of the twentieth-century Islamic revolutions in Iran and Afghanistan.

2. Analyze the continuities and changes in the political structure of ONE of the following Middle Eastern nations during the twentieth century.
   ■ Egypt
   ■ Turkey
   ■ Palestine
   ■ Iraq

Answers

MULTIPLE-CHOICE QUESTIONS

1. **ANSWER: B.** The Young Turks blamed the sultan for the decline of the Ottoman Empire. They forced the sultan to institute various changes, including a new constitution and laws that forced greater assimilation on ethnic minorities (*The Earth and Its Peoples,* 5th ed., pp. 799–800/6th ed., p. 754).

2. **ANSWER: A.** British Foreign Secretary Sir Arthur Balfour announced in 1917 that a national home for Jewish people should be established in Palestine, suggesting that it would be brought to fruition once Britain gained control of the Ottoman territory of Palestine (*The Earth and Its Peoples,* 5th ed., pp. 805–806/6th ed., p. 760).

3. **ANSWER: D.** Arabs believed that the League of Nations had promised them independence. They were therefore angered by their lack of independence as British and French mandates (*The Earth and Its Peoples,* 5th ed., pp. 814–815/6th ed., p. 768).

4. **ANSWER: D.** In 1947, The United Nations voted in favor of partitioning Palestine into two states—one Jewish and one Arab. Instead of bringing peace, the creation of Israel, in 1948, increased tensions within the region (*The Earth and Its Peoples,* 5th ed., p. 907/6th ed., p. 841).

5. **ANSWER: B.** Mustafa Kemal Atatürk was among a growing number of leaders who were pushing to Westernize their nation in order to usher in a modern era and compete with the Western powers (*The Earth and Its Peoples,* 5th ed., pp. 815–817/6th ed., p. 769).

6. **ANSWER: A.** Great Britain's ability to break German codes and learn German military plans led to the decisive victory at El Alamein. The victory led to the expulsion of the Germans from North Africa in May 1943 (*The Earth and Its Peoples,* 5th ed., pp. 846–847/6th ed., p. 822).

7. **ANSWER: B.** The Balfour Declaration encouraged European Jewish immigration. However, far more immigrants arrived than anticipated, and the British attempted to limit immigration so that the Palestinian Arabs would not feel they were being pushed aside. In the end, both Jews and Arabs were unhappy with the British decision on the matter (*The Earth and Its Peoples,* 5th ed., pp. 815–819/6th ed., p. 773).

8. **ANSWER: A.** As global demand for oil increased, along with uncertainty about the supply, OPEC emerged to protect the interests of the oil-producing nations (*The Earth and Its Peoples,* 5th ed., pp. 907, 909/6th ed., p. 861).

9. **ANSWER: C.** Saddam Hussein had borrowed large amounts of money from the Kuwaiti royal family, and Iraq was in deep debt. When the royal family refused to reduce Iraq's debt, Hussein aimed at

their oil fields as a way to gain wealth for his nation (*The Earth and Its Peoples,* 5th ed., pp. 925–926/6th ed., pp. 878–879).

10. ANSWER: **D.** Osama bin Laden took refuge in Sudan, Afghanistan, and Pakistan after being expelled from Saudi Arabia. Bin Laden preached militant Islam and spoke against several nations, including Saudi Arabia, Israel, and the United States (*The Earth and Its Peoples,* 5th ed., pp. 954–955/6th ed., p. 906).

11. ANSWER: **A.** This quotation in the Diversity and Dominance special section shows the response of Syrians to the mandates set up after the war. According to the new League of Nations, France had responsibility over Syria and Lebanon (*The Earth and Its Peoples,* 5th ed., p. 817/6th ed., p. 771).

12. ANSWER: **B.** The independence of some Arab areas from Ottoman rule came as a result of the treaties that ended World War I. Britain and France still directly or indirectly controlled some of the region until the 1950s. Gradually they gave up control after World War II. Israel was created after the United Nations General Assembly voted for the partition of Palestine into two states (*The Earth and Its Peoples,* 5th ed., p. 907/6th ed., pp. 768–769).

13. ANSWER: **D.** The discovery of vast oil reserves in the Middle East after World War II led to the region becoming a major resource of fossil fuel for the economic development of the world. Demand for this oil boomed as the world economy became more complex (*The Earth and Its Peoples,* 5th ed., p. 907/6th ed., p. 861).

14. ANSWER: **B.** After the Iranian Revolution in 1979 and the hostage crisis, the U.S. pursued a lengthy process of restrained responses. The Soviets invaded Afghanistan (*The Earth and Its Peoples,* 5th ed., pp. 919–921/6th ed., p. 872).

15. ANSWER: **C.** After the terrorist attacks of September 11, 2001, the United States viewed Iraq as a danger because of its potential for violence on its own people and internationally through terrorists. Although weapons of mass destructions were not found in Iraq, the United States believed that they had WMDs and used this belief as a rationale for invasion. Iran was Iraq's enemy and did not have an alliance with Saddam Hussein (*The Earth and Its Peoples,* 5th ed., pp. 954–955/6th ed., p. 906).

FREE-RESPONSE QUESTIONS

1. A good response should discuss the Cold-War strategic importance of both nations—both were located on the border of the Soviet Union. Both the United States and the Soviet Union were attempting to gain influence and allies. Your response should also mention that Iran became an American war and Afghanistan a Soviet war. The United States resorted to covert involvement while the Soviets' involvement was more direct. In regard to effects, you should mention that both nations shunned Westernization for conservative Islam. You should also make clear that while the outcomes for both the United States and the Soviet Union would be considered failures, the Soviet Union suffered greater loss because of their greater sense of urgency and involvement.

2. A good response would include a discussion about colonization (and/or the mandate system), involvement in the Palestine/Israel situation, independence, rising oil wealth, and contemporary issues of terrorism. You should connect colonialism and imperialism to the push for the removal of foreign influence. Be sure to address the tension between modernization, Westernization, and conservative Islam. Continuities might include notions of rule by dictators and challenges with democracy.

23

ASIA:
CIRCA 1900 TO THE PRESENT

KEY CONCEPTS

- Despite many similarities in culture and civilization, Japan's and China's modern history took completely different paths; Japan quickly rose to become a modern industrial power, whereas China experienced foreign control and revolution.
- The Chinese revolution led to the fall of the Qing and the end of the dynastic system in 1911, but the country was unable to unite under a single national government as regional powers competed for control.
- The Nanjing massacre is often referred to as the "Hidden Holocaust" because of its similarities to the Holocaust in Europe.
- The surrender of Japan at the end of World War II thrust China into a civil war that had been brewing for decades. With greater popular support and seized Japanese weapons, the Communists overpowered the Guomindang. In 1949, Mao announced the founding of the People's Republic of China.
- Despite increased violence and partition into the two states of India and Pakistan, Indian independence in 1947 served as a model for other anticolonial movements around the world.
- While the Cold War caused massive deaths in Korea and Indochina, it also served as a catalyst in transforming numerous Asian economies.
- Japan, South Korea, Hong Kong, and Singapore all experienced rapid economic growth on the heels of the Cold War.

KEY TERMS

- Asian Tigers
- Bandung Conference
- Battle of Midway
- Boxer Rebellion
- Cultural Revolution
- Great Leap Forward
- Guomindang
- Indian National Congress
- Kashmir
- keiretsu
- Korean War
- Long March
- newly industrialized economies (NIEs)
- nonaligned nations
- Tiananmen Square
- Third World
- Twenty-One Demands
- Viet Cong
- Viet Minh
- Vietnam War

Asia during the twentieth century is covered in *The Earth and Its Peoples,* fifth edition, Chapters 28–32 and sixth edition, Chapters 25, 27–32.

THE COLLAPSE OF THE QING DYNASTY

For many, the **Boxer Rebellion** was final evidence of the need to get rid of the Qing dynasty and modernize their country. When Cixi died in 1908, a growing nationalist political movement, the Revolutionary Alliance, led by Sun Yat-sen, prepared to overthrow the Qing. Sun's thinking, combining nationalism, socialism, and traditional Confucian philosophy, appealed to many. But Sun also had to deal with the regional military warlords, who had modernized their armies and were not inclined to give up power to a new central government. In 1911 when one of these regional militias rebelled, the most powerful warlord, Yuan Shikai, refused to defend the Qing; the boy-emperor Puyi was forced to abdicate, finally ending the Qing dynasty. A revolutionary assembly elected Sun president of the new Chinese republic in 1911, but with no military force to defend his position, Sun stepped down in favor of Yuan, who became president. Sun's nationalist supporters formed the Guomindang (National People's Party), which Yuan, resistant to Western-style reform, repressed. The great dynastic system in China had come to an end, but as World War I approached, China remained a nation controlled by regional powers, both internal and external.

World War I

The twentieth century proved quite different for Japan and China. Japan became an industrialized power facing little intervention from the European imperial powers. China, on the other hand, began the new millennium militarily defeated by a coalition of various Western powers and Japan—all bent on staking claims on the Chinese mainland. This event, known as the Boxer Rebellion, caused many Chinese to demand revolutionary change, overthrow of the Qing dynasty, and modernization. In 1908 Sun Yat-sen formed the Revolutionary Alliance, or **Guomingdang**, which by 1911 had overthrown the last Qing ruler. To unify the country, Sun shared power with Yuan Shikai, a brilliant military leader and the most powerful regional general. But instead of peace, a struggle ensued between the military, led by Yuan, and the Guomindang, led by Sun.

The struggle in Japan was quite different. Industrialization programs implemented by the Meiji rulers were continued at the turn of the twentieth century. The Japanese economy, in fact, was growing faster than that of any of the Western powers. Sudden prosperity caused tensions within Japanese society. Many young urbanites who adopted Western ways and lifestyles clashed with traditionalists. Industrialization also caused tensions between the rising industrial conglomerates, which controlled most of Japan's industry and commerce, and poor farmers, who made up over half of the population. Nonetheless, Japan's prosperity largely depended on foreign trade, so like the Western powers, Japan depended on its ability to colonize resource-rich territories.

In that regard, World War I worked in Japan's favor. Having joined the war on the side of the Allies, Japan enjoyed rising demand for its products. More important, the war was an opportunity to gain territory. The Japanese quickly conquered the German colonies in the northern Pacific and on the coast of China. By 1915, Japan had extended its influence to the rest of China by imposing the **Twenty-One Demands**, which guaranteed Japanese control and access to resource-rich territories in China. In response, boycotts and anti-Japanese riots erupted throughout China.

India provides another example of the struggle against foreign influence in Asia. India had been under British colonial rule since 1857. By the turn of the century, many Indians had learned English and adopted British ideals and ways. Nonetheless, they confronted racial quotas and other methods used to bar Indians from jobs and even social clubs. Despite appeals from the Hindu-dominated Indian National Congress, founded in 1885, and the All-India Muslim League, founded in 1906, British colonial rule continued to favor British citizens. Nonetheless, Indians supported British efforts during World War I. Over a million Indians volunteered for the British Army, and millions of others contributed money and other resources. Still the British made only vague references to eventual independence of India.

THE INTERWAR PERIOD

China's hope for reclaiming its territory rested in the hands of the Allies, most of whom had played a part in forcing foreign influence on China at the turn of the twentieth century. But at the end of the war, it was decided at the Paris Peace Conference to give Japan continued control over the German holdings in northern parts of China. Protests led by students began in Beijing on May 4, 1919, then spread across China to become the May Fourth Movement. A new generation was no longer willing to tolerate foreign control and influence within their nation, and it was tired of the Chinese regional leadership. Perhaps sensing the growing disdain within Chinese society, Sun Yat-sen restructured the Guomindang along Leninist ideals. Sun was succeeded by Jiang Jieshi (Chiang Kai-shek) in 1925. A skilled military leader, Jiang crushed the regional lords and united the nation. Jiang's goal was modernization, but after crushing the Communist party and banning labor unions, his government was left with corrupt opportunists and incompetent administrators. As a result, modernization did not come to China.

China, because it was not dependent on imports, was not much affected by the Depression, but it did face numerous political challenges. In 1927 Jiang Jieshi's government began arresting and executing members of the Communist party and labor unions. Remaining Communists fled to the remote mountain region of Jiangxi to join Mao Zedong, a leader in the Chinese Communist party who had gained favor among peasants with his calls for social reform. The Chinese government, concerned about the growing popularity of Mao, pursued the Communists. In 1934, the Guomindang army surrounded the Communists, who escaped and began a one-year journey, the so-called **Long March**. At its end, in the remote northwest province of Shaanxi, only four thousand of the original one hundred thousand remained.

Dependent on exports to pay for food and fuel, Japan suffered greatly during the Depression. Hardest hit were farmers and fishermen, who saw their incomes steadily drop. The economic struggles created a reaction that in many ways mirrored that in Germany. Japanese ultranationalists believed that Japan could end its dependence on foreign trade by creating a colonial empire much like those of Great Britain and France. But much of Asia was already colonized by Europeans and Americans. Japan's colonial ambitions would inevitably conflict with the desires of its World War I partners. The colonial conquest of the entire resource-rich province of Manchuria, the first step in Japan's quest to dominate Asia, was condemned by the League of Nations; in response, Japan simply withdrew from the League. The conquest fortified the Japanese military, which began to encroach on the civilian-controlled government.

While the Guomindang fought the Communists, it tried to deal with external pressures. In 1937, Japanese troops attacked Beijing and within four months held Beijing, as well as Shanghai and other coastal cities. The fighting grew increasingly violent during the winter of 1937–1938 when the Japanese took over Nanjing, killing more than two hundred thousand Chinese civilians and prisoners, raping upward of twenty thousand Chinese women, and looting and burning much of the city. Both Jiang Jieshi's government troops and Mao's Communist troops had little success in fighting the Japanese. The government forces retreated to the central mountains of Sichuan. Jiang resorted to drafting men for the military and raising taxes despite a famine. In Shaanxi, Mao set up a Communist government and built up his military while the majority of China was under Japanese control. The Sino-Japanese War would last eight years, 1937–1945.

As the Chinese fought against the Japanese in Manchuria, Indians struggled against British colonial rule. In 1919, a British colonial officer ordered his troops to fire on a peaceful crowd of ten thousand demonstrators, killing 379 Indians and wounding 1,200. Demonstrations spread across the nation in response, but it was six months before the British appointed someone to investigate the massacre. In the years following the massacre, the British gradually and reluctantly admitted Indians to the Civil Service and the officer corps. The demands of the Indian National Congress and the Muslim League were finally coming to realization. Areas such as national education and public works were slowly placed under Indian control. Indians also fought for the right to erect tariff barriers to protect budding local industries, which in turn helped ward off the Depression. But it was Mohandas Gandhi who provided the moral leadership for independence. Gandhi's insistence on nonviolence and his affinity for the poor won him admirers worldwide. During the 1930s, Gandhi led numerous fasts and marches to protest colonial rule, and he was frequently arrested and jailed. Much to the dismay of the British, jailing Gandhi only made him more popular, both at home and abroad. Gandhi would eventually pass leadership to Jawaharlal Nehru, who is credited with leading India into independence and modernity.

WORLD WAR II AND INDEPENDENCE MOVEMENTS

On the eve of World War II, Indians still had little true power. Indeed, in 1939, the British viceroy declared war on behalf of India without consulting any Indians. A wave of protests ensued as Gandhi and other leaders demanded full independence immediately. The Indian National Congress opposed the war, and many of its members resigned from positions within the regional governments. A small number of Indians even joined the Japanese in order to fight against their colonizers. Still, as in World War I, Indians made an enormous contribution to the Allied war effort. Over 2 million Indians fought for the British, while large amounts of Indian raw materials were used to aid the Allied war machine. In the province of Bengal, over 2 million Indians starved to death in war-related famine.

At the end of the war, Britain began preparing India for independence. However, tensions between Hindus and Muslims were growing; Muslims feared that the Hindu-dominated **Indian National Congress** would not share power with the Muslim League. Despite Gandhi's appeals for tolerance, violent rioting broke out between Hindus and Muslims. In 1947, the Indian National Congress and the Muslim League agreed to partition the nation into two states: Hindu-dominated India and the Muslim nation of Pakistan. The split, however, came with continued violence between Hindus and Muslims. In protest, Gandhi refused to attend the independence day celebrations. The split also resulted in waves of refugees, as Hindus fled Muslim areas and Muslims fled Hindu areas. India did, however, annex the province of Kashmir, a resource-rich region in the north dominated by Muslims. While World War II helped usher in Indian independence, it came at a high cost in lives, violence, and sectarianism.

World War II provided Japan the opportunity to expand its colonial ambitions beyond China. While European nations were embroiled in conflict, Japan took aim at the European colonies in Southeast Asia. Like Britain, France, and the Netherlands, Japan coveted the rubber, oil, and other vital resources of Southeast Asia. When France fell in 1940, Japan moved in to occupy Indochina. Dismayed by Japan's increasing power, the United States and Great Britain responded by halting shipments of steel, iron, oil, and other products that Japan urgently needed. The Japanese chose to retaliate in December 1941 with a surprise attack on Pearl Harbor, an American naval base in Hawaii. They then proceeded to attack various European colonies in Southeast Asia. By March 1942, Japan occupied Thailand, the Philippines, Malaya, and all of the Dutch East Indies. While Asians initially viewed the Japanese as heroes who had liberated them from white colonialism, Japanese rule grew harsh, and Asians came to despise Japanese rule.

Japanese victories in Asia were geographically more extensive than those of the Nazis in Europe. But the United States joined Britain in battling the Japanese in Asia, and by the spring of 1942, the United States had bombed Tokyo and defeated the Japanese in the Coral Sea. Months later, in June, the Japanese suffered one of their largest defeats at the **Battle of Midway**. Allied bombing and submarine warfare cut Japan off from vital shipments of oil and other raw materials, severely damaging the economy and military. In August 1945, the United States dropped an atomic bomb on the Japanese city of Hiroshima. Three days later, a second bomb was dropped on Nagasaki. Over 200,000 Japanese civilians died as a result of the bombings. The massive civilian death toll convinced the Japanese emperor to surrender, signaling the official end of World War II.

Japanese surrender sparked a struggle for power in China. The Guomindang and the Communist forces began a civil war that would last four years. Although the Guomindang had more troops, weapons, and the support of the United States, it continued its harsh and corrupt practices. In certain regions the Guomindang looted, confiscated supplies, and taxed the Chinese people more heavily than the Japanese had. The Communists, on the other hand, worked for the support of the people—in Manchuria, for example, the Communists redistributed land to the peasants—and the widespread support of the citizenry proved far more valuable than the Guomingdang's superior weaponry. In 1947, Communist forces surrounded Nanjing, and by 1949 the Guomindang armies were collapsing and in full retreat. High-ranking members of the Guomindang fled to Taiwan, where they remained, protected by the U.S. Navy. On October 1, 1949, the Communist forces, led by Mao, announced the founding of the People's Republic of China.

THE COLD WAR AND DECOLONIZATION

Despite defeat in World War II, Japan served as an inspiration to many in Southeast Asia for the numerous, albeit temporary, defeats it inflicted on the British, French, and Dutch. Anticolonial movements gained plenty of steam after the war, leading to the independence of the Philippines in 1946, Burma and the Malay Federation in 1948, and Indonesia in 1949. However, many anticolonial leaders, attracted to communism, found themselves caught in the Cold War conflicts of the United States and the Soviet Union.

The end of World War II left the Soviet Union in control of the northern portion of Korea and the United States in control of the southern portion. No agreement could be made on nationwide elections, so in 1948 two nations were established: communist North Korea and capitalist South Korea. Two years later, North Korean troops invaded South Korea, sparking the **Korean War**. Almost immediately American troops came to the aid of South Korea, while North Korea received assistance from communist China. The struggle remained a deadlock after three years. Finally, a truce agreed on in 1953 fixed the boundary at the thirty-eighth parallel—the line established by the Americans and the Soviets in 1948. No one benefited from the war except, ironically, the Japanese, whose economy was stimulated by American military supply purchases and the purchases of American servicemen in Japan while on leave from Korea.

The Cold War also allowed Japan to concentrate on developing industry, trade, and new markets throughout Asia. The government gave assistance to the electrical, steel, and shipbuilding industries, all of which would help make Japan a global economic superpower by 1975.

The Cold War conflict in **Vietnam**, then part of French Indochina, proved far different from that of Korea. The struggle began at the end of World War II when the French refused to relinquish their colony. Led by Ho Chi Minh and helped by the Chinese, revolutionaries known as the **Viet Minh** eventually overthrew the French. The Viet Minh gained control in the north while a noncommunist government was in control of the south. The split led to a civil war. The United States, which had initially supported the French, gave support to the South Vietnamese government of Ngo Dinh Diem and, intent on stopping the spread of communism, increased its involvement in Vietnam. But the Viet Minh and the communist guerilla group in South

Vietnam, known as the **Viet Cong**, were unstoppable. In 1973, after massive casualties on both sides, the United States ended its military involvement in Vietnam. Two years later, Vietnam was united when South Vietnam was taken over by the communist forces of the Viet Cong and the Viet Minh government of the North.

While the Soviet Union was the global symbol and propagator of communism, China was the primary communist player in Asia, involved in both Vietnam and Korea. Indeed China received aid and support from the Soviet Union, even though it defined communism in a slightly different manner. While communism in China focused largely on the peasantry, communism in the Soviet Union ignored peasants and favored the urban working class. In 1958 Mao introduced his **Great Leap Forward**, an attempt to make China an industrial power by means of collectivizing agriculture and village-level industries. The Great Leap Forward, however, resulted not in industrialization but in more than 30 million deaths, mainly from famine. In 1966 Mao introduced the **Cultural Revolution** in an attempt to mobilize youth and rekindle revolutionary spirit, but this program led to factionalism, violence, incarcerations, and executions. By 1971, half a million Chinese had died as a result of the Cultural Revolution. Nonetheless, China continued on a path different from that of the Soviet Union, a path that led to reestablishing ties with the United States in 1971 and occupying a permanent seat in the United Nations Security Council.

While the conflict between capitalists and Communists ensnared most of Asia, partition and religious sectarianism afflicted South Asia. Even after independence, tensions between Hindus and Muslims in India and Pakistan resumed. Matters were made worse when the Hindu ruler of Kashmir chose to join India without consulting Kashmiri citizens, who were overwhelmingly Muslim. The annexation of Kashmir by India led to war with Pakistan, which also coveted the resource-rich territory. Over the years, tensions have flared in Kashmir, but an uneasy truce remains. Still, Pakistan, which defines itself by Islam, believes that it has a religious connection to the region of Kashmir. In 1971, however, the connection with its Bengali-speaking people of the east eroded. The region seceded from Pakistan and formed the independent nation of Bangladesh. India, meanwhile, formed a secular democracy based on socialism. Despite struggles, Indians have successfully managed to maintain unity in a nation of extreme linguistic diversity.

Despite Cold War politics, most Asians were primarily concerned with decolonization. In fact, most of the Cold War battles were intertwined with Asians' desires to rid themselves of colonial rule. Like other non-Europeans, they sought to define their own destinies. Both capitalism, pushed by the United States, and communism, pushed by the Soviets, looked too much like new forms of colonialism. In 1955, therefore, Indonesian President Achmed Sukarno called a meeting in Bandung, Indonesia, of twenty-nine Asian and African nations. The **Bandung Conference** produced an alliance of **nonaligned nations** that declared solidarity among non-European nations fighting colonialism. In direct reference to Cold War politics, these nations were often referred to as the **Third World**, representing countries that were not a part of either the capitalist bloc or the communist bloc. But despite the show of solidarity and their efforts at nonalignment, many of the nations were still sucked into the global conflicts of the Cold War.

AP Tip

India served as a model for other nations struggling to free themselves from European colonial rule. Indian independence in 1947 set off a wave of anticolonial momentum around the world. Be sure you can both compare various anticolonial efforts and explain how India changed over time during the twentieth century.

THE POST–COLD WAR WORLD

The Cold War helped propel Japan forward as a global economic superpower. During the 1970s and 1980s, Japan's economic growth was faster than that of any industrialized nation. By the 1990s, average income in Japan surpassed even that in the United States. Much of the economic success was a result of the industrial alliances, known as **keiretsu**, which received government assistance in the form of tariffs and import regulations, which protected them from foreign competition. Six major Japanese keiretsu formed. Alliances of banks, commerce, industry, and construction, the keiretsu developed some of the best manufactured goods in the world. As a result, Japan built up a huge trade surplus with other nations around the world. The United States and the European Community attempted to break the economic power of Japan by negotiating to force open Japan's markets.

This effort did not succeed, but Japan's economy was not as strong as it appeared. Japan's housing and stock markets became overvalued, and corruption and overspeculation took its toll on the Japanese economy. Still, other nations in Asia adopted the Japanese model. South Korea used keiretsu to spark rapid economic growth. In fact, the four giant Korean corporations—among them Hyundai, which produces a broad range of manufactured goods—account for nearly half of South Korea's gross domestic product. Taiwan, Hong Kong, and Singapore also modeled themselves after Japan, creating modern industrial and commercial economies. Along with South Korea, these **newly industrialized economies** (NIEs) were often referred to as the **Asian Tigers**. Certain characteristics help explain their rapid ascent: all invested in education, had high rates of personal savings, emphasized exports, used government sponsorship and protection, relied heavily on current technology, and had hard-working, disciplined labor forces. The Asian Tigers also share another feature: all of their economies were stimulated by American purchases of supplies during the Korean and Vietnam Wars. In this regard, the Cold War was central to the economic restructuring of East Asia.

China also experienced economic growth. After the death of Mao in 1976, the new leader, Deng Xiaoping, implemented numerous economic reforms. Limited private enterprise and foreign investment was allowed, and individuals were allowed to contract land for personal use. By 1993, China's per capita output had grown at a rate eight times faster than the global average. Despite the growth, China remained a poor nation, and economic reform did not translate into political reform. In 1989, Chinese students led a series of protests demanding democratic changes and an end to inflation and corruption. The protestors convened in **Tiananmen Square**, sparking a standoff that lasted for weeks. The Chinese government sent in tanks to crush the protest; hundreds of Chinese students were killed, thousands were arrested. Like other Asian nations, China's Communist government has struggled to balance rapid economic growth, population growth, inequality, unemployment, and large-scale migrations to the cities. Since Deng's death in 1997, China has allowed greater free expression.

Democracy is not a foregone conclusion in Asia. Whereas Indonesia moved from authoritarian rule to more open political institutions, India seemed to regress toward ethnic nationalism. In 1998, the Bharatiya Janata Party gained control through blatant appeals to Hindu nationalism. Violence against Muslims was often condoned, and social and economic progress by Untouchables was opposed. Likewise, the struggle between India and Pakistan over **Kashmir** grew more intense when both nations successfully tested nuclear bombs in 1998.

Despite the political swings throughout Asia, rapid economic growth has allowed many Asian nations to become transmitters, not just receivers, of culture. East Asian manufactured goods have become household names around the world. The Indian and Chinese film industries have carved an increasingly strong niche in the global film market. The growing global strength in Asia is unquestioned. In fact, by population alone, India and China are both superpowers. Those two nations currently account for one-third of the world's population. But it remains to be seen whether China or India can translate their dominance in population to the wealth and industrial muscle of a true global superpower.

Multiple-Choice Questions

1. Which of the following was an influence of World War I on Japan?
   (A) Japan gained territory in China.
   (B) Japan gained wealth by selling arms to both sides.
   (C) Japan remained neutral and was able to focus on domestic concerns.
   (D) Japan had numerous casualties provoking outrage within the country.

2. Which of the following statements is most accurate regarding the Indian Civil Service before World War II?
   (A) It consisted of British men who looked out for British imperial interests.
   (B) It consisted of British professionals who wanted to allow greater Indian autonomy.
   (C) It consisted of Indians who pushed fervently for radical change within colonial Indian society.
   (D) It consisted of Hindu and Muslim politicians who benefited from British rule.

3. By the 1920s, the demands of the Indian National Congress and the All-Indian Muslim League resulted in which of the following?
   (A) Higher tariffs to protect local industries and greater Indian control in education and public works
   (B) Independence and the expulsion of the British
   (C) The partitioning of India into three nations: India, Pakistan, and Bangladesh
   (D) The British viceroy to India answering to an Indian Civil Service under the control of Indians

4. What circumstances precipitated Mao Zedong's Long March?
   (A) Mao and the Communists, having gained control of southern China, set out to gain control of the North.
   (B) Mao and the Communists, pursued by the Japanese, were forced to flee from the Japanese.
   (C) Mao and the Communist forces needed food and shelter after a severe drought.
   (D) Mao and the Communists were nearly surrounded, forcing them to escape the Nationalist forces.

5. Which of the following accurately depicts events right after Indian independence?
   (A) Violence erupted between Hindus and Muslims resulting in the partition of the country.
   (B) The British remained in order to create a smooth transition from colonial status to independence.
   (C) A treaty united the Indian National Congress and the All-Indian Muslim League joined forces.
   (D) Gandhi became the first elected president of an independent India.

6. How did the start of World War II provide an opportunity for Japan to expand its colonial empire?
   (A) The European colonies in Southeast Asia were left vulnerable because Britain and France were engaged in fighting in Europe.
   (B) The United States, France, and Great Britain offered Asian colonies to Japan in order to enlist its support in the war.
   (C) Germany's hardships allowed Japan to take over Korea, China, Indochina, and Malaysia.
   (D) British surrender to Germany allowed Japan to take over Hong Kong, Burma, and Thailand.

7. How did Chinese communism differ from Soviet communism?
   (A) Chinese communism focused on the rural peasantry, whereas the Soviet version focused on the urban working class.
   (B) Chinese communism focused on creating a worldwide communist revolution, whereas Soviet communism concentrated on national affairs.
   (C) Chinese communism focused on the urban working class, whereas Soviet communism focused on the rural peasantry.
   (D) Chinese communism focused on large-scale industries, whereas Soviet communism focused on small, village-level industries.

8. What was the purpose of the Bandung Conference?
   (A) To extract money and support from the superpowers by playing both sides against each other
   (B) To ally with the United States and other Western powers
   (C) To bring former colonies together in order to gain more influence in the world
   (D) To incite a revolution uniting workers around the world

9. Which of the following accurately characterizes the nations known as the Asian Tigers?
   (A) They were previously Communist nations that gained rapid wealth when they converted to capitalism.
   (B) They had large investments from Western nations, democratic political institutions, and large workforces.
   (C) They had disciplined workforces, investments in education, and government protection of industries.
   (D) They had state-controlled economies, political repression, and emphasis on exports.

10. What reforms were implemented by Deng Xiaoping?
   (A) Collectivization of agriculture
   (B) Election of national governmental officials
   (C) The banning of multinational corporations
   (D) Limitations on foreign investment and private property

11. All of the following describe the demographics of China and India EXCEPT
   (A) both have falling population growth rates.
   (B) both have declining populations.
   (C) both have larger populations than any other country.
   (D) both had government efforts to limit population growth.

12. Which of the following describes how Pakistan's demographics differs from the demographics of South Korea?
   (A) Pakistan has more children as a percentage of the population than South Korea.
   (B) Pakistan has a more sharply declining labor pool than South Korea.
   (C) Pakistan has a more urban population than South Korea.
   (D) Pakistan has a more successful family planning system than South Korea.

13. All of the following describe Japanese social and economic conditions before World War II EXCEPT
   (A) Japan had limited land for agriculture.
   (B) Japan had few natural resources.
   (C) Japan had a limited industrial system.
   (D) Japan had rising population growth.

14. All of the following groups were active in China in the years following the collapse of the Qing dynasty EXCEPT
   (A) communists.
   (B) nationalists.
   (C) scholar-officials.
   (D) Japanese imperialists.

15. How did the Japanese policies change as a result of the Great Depression?
   (A) Japan became closer to the Soviet Union.
   (B) Japan industrialized.
   (C) Japan sought colonies abroad.
   (D) Japan relied more on international economic coordination.

Free-Response Questions

1. Compare the causes and effects of the Cold War struggle in TWO of the following areas.
   ■ Korea
   ■ Vietnam
   ■ China

2. Analyze the political continuities and changes experienced in ONE of the following nations between World War I and the present.
   ■ India
   ■ China
   ■ Japan

Answers

MULTIPLE-CHOICE QUESTIONS

1. ANSWER: A. Japan used World War I as an opportunity to advance its interests. It joined the Allies and witnessed an economic boom as demand for its products rose. It also was able to conquer the German colonies of northern China (*The Earth and Its Peoples,* 5th ed., pp. 813–814/6th ed., p. 765).

2. ANSWER: A. The Indian Civil Service originally consisted of British men drawn largely from the English gentry. They introduced technology to India, such as railroads and telegraph services, in order to increase foreign trade and strengthen British control. They also discouraged local industries that might compete with British

industries (*The Earth and Its Peoples,* 5th ed., pp. 861–862/6th ed., p. 791).

3. **ANSWER: A.** During the 1920s the British began to give in to the pressures of the Indian National Congress and the All-Indian Muslim League, gradually admitting Indians to the Civil Service and allowing them to control areas of education, economy, and public works. Indians then began to erect high tariff barriers to protect local industries from foreign, including British, imports (*The Earth and Its Peoples,* 5th ed., pp. 864–865/6th ed., p. 791).

4. **ANSWER: D.** The Guomindang army pursued Mao and his Communist forces into the mountains. The Communists responded with guerilla warfare until the Guomindang forces nearly surrounded them. Despite support from the peasants, Mao decided to lead his troops on an escape out of the mountains. The Long March began in 1934; after one year and six thousand miles, Mao and only 4000 of his original troops arrived in Shaanxi (*The Earth and Its Peoples,* 5th ed., pp. 841–842/6th ed., p. 817).

5. **ANSWER: A.** On the eve of independence, talks between the Indian National Congress and the All-Indian Muslim League broke down. Violent rioting broke out between Hindus and Muslims, despite Gandhi's protests and appeals. On August 15, 1947, India gained independence and was partitioned into two states: India and Pakistan. In protest, Gandhi refused to attend any independence day celebrations (*The Earth and Its Peoples,* 5th ed., pp. 864–866/6th ed., p. 796).

6. **ANSWER: A.** European colonies in Asia, and their vast resources of oil, rubber, and other materials, were left vulnerable because of fighting in Europe. France had already fallen, and Britain and the Soviet Union were battling Germany. Japan desperately sought the resources in their Asian colonies. In 1941, the French government allowed Japan to occupy Indochina. When the United States and Britain stopped shipments of resources to Japan in retaliation for occupying Indochina, the Japanese decided to widen the war and attack the United States (*The Earth and Its Peoples,* 5th ed., pp. 846–847/6th ed., p. 822).

7. **ANSWER: A.** Despite the fact that the Soviet Union remained a source of arms and support for China, when Mao Zedong took over and established the People's Republic of China, his form of communism diverged from that of the Soviets. Mao focused on the rural peasantry, with whom Chinese Communists had formed an intimate bond. The Soviets, intent on rapid industrialization, neglected the rural peasantry in favor of the urban working class (*The Earth and Its Peoples,* 5th ed., pp. 905–906/6th ed., p. 858).

8. **ANSWER: C.** At the Bandung Conference, twenty-nine African and Asian nations formed an alliance to fight colonial rule and gain influence as newly independent nations (*The Earth and Its Peoples,* 5th ed., pp. 904–905/6th ed., p. 856).

9. **ANSWER: C.** The newly industrialized economies of Asia, known as the Asian Tigers, all experienced rapid industrialization. Common

characteristics were disciplined workforces, high rates of personal savings, and emphasis on export strategies. The governments of these nations also protected and sponsored local industries (*The Earth and Its Peoples,* 5th ed., pp. 921–923/6th ed., p. 874).

10. ANSWER: **D.** After the death of Mao, Deng implemented various economic reforms that relaxed state control of the economy. Individual initiative was encouraged, and individuals were allowed to accumulate wealth. While Deng did not privatize land, he did allow individuals to lease land in order to consume or sell whatever they produced (*The Earth and Its Peoples,* 5th ed., pp. 922–924/6th ed., pp. 874–876).

11. ANSWER: **B.** The populations of both China and India have rising populations. The rate of growth for each, however, has been declining partly due to past government birth control efforts (*The Earth and Its Peoples,* 5th ed., pp. 930–932/6th ed., pp. 880–881).

12. ANSWER: **A.** Pakistan has a pyramid-shape age distribution with a large number of people at the younger ages and therefore has an increasing labor pool. Pakistan has a more rural population (*The Earth and Its Peoples,* 5th ed., pp. 929–932/6th ed., p. 883).

13. ANSWER: **C.** Japanese industry had been developing from the time of the Meiji Restoration, and the country had a relatively advanced system of factories (*The Earth and Its Peoples,* 5th ed., p. 813/6th ed., p. 740).

14. ANSWER: **C.** After the fall of the Qing dynasty in 1911, Confucian scholar-officials fell out of power. Conflicts emerged among communists, nationalists, military warlords, and the Japanese (*The Earth and Its Peoples,* 5th ed., pp. 813–814/6th ed., p. 767).

15. ANSWER: **C.** The world-wide economic crisis of the Great Depression caused Japan to seek stability through exploiting the resources of China and other Asian areas (*The Earth and Its Peoples,* 5th ed., p. 841/6th ed., pp. 766–767).

FREE-RESPONSE QUESTIONS

1. A good response should take up the involvement of the United States and the Soviet Union. It should make clear the ideological battle between capitalism and communism. However, resist the urge to place the desires of the United States and the Soviet Union as the primary factor. The various local interests, which shaped the beginnings and ends of each conflict, should be clearly explained.

2. All three nations had very different experiences during the twentieth century. Japan and China overlap and directly relate to each another. Nonetheless, all three regions faced various degrees of foreign involvement and colonization. A good response will illustrate this struggle, as well as the role played by the two world wars and the Cold War. It should also describe the economic growth that has positioned all three nations on the cusp of global power.

24

EUROPE: CIRCA 1900 TO THE PRESENT

KEY CONCEPTS

- European imperialism came to an end during the twentieth century, but not before Europeans had exploited nearly every corner of the globe.
- World Wars I and II, the Depression, and the Cold War not only resulted in the interaction of numerous nations; they ultimately led to the creation of technology such as the satellite and the Internet that would allow people around the world to communicate with one another in a matter of seconds.
- The United States and the Soviet Union arose as competing superpowers after World War II. For more than forty years they would attempt to influence other nations around the world to adopt capitalism or communism, respectively.

KEY TERMS

- Cold War
- European Union
- fascist
- globalization
- Great Depression
- Helsinki Accords
- Holocaust
- imperialism
- iron curtain
- Marshall Plan
- militarism
- multinational corporations
- nationalism

- ■ Nazis
- ■ nongovernmental organizations
- ■ North Atlantic Treaty Organization (NATO)
- ■ Treaty of Versailles
- ■ Warsaw Pact

Europe during the twentieth century is discussed in depth in *The Earth and Its Peoples,* fifth edition, Chapters 28–29 and 31–33 and sixth edition, Chapters 27–32.

WORLD WAR I

The industrialization of the late nineteenth century, which increased the power of Europeans and North Americans, resulted in a race to conquer or control other peoples and other lands. By the beginning of the twentieth century, young imperial powers such as the United States and Germany were on the rise. Technological superiority gave all of these powers great success in expanding their empires; however, that expansion led to a severe crisis when the imperial powers found themselves competing over the same territory. The decline of the Ottoman Empire meant that territory and resources would be up for grabs. As a consequence, the European powers began meddling in its affairs. **Imperialism** had clearly reached a boiling point.

The flames of imperialism, however, were also fueled by intense **nationalism**. Nationalism not only united nations under a common language and culture; it also engendered a deep hatred of those viewed as enemies. Moreover, in the name of nationalism, ethnic minorities attempted to break away from empires such as the Ottoman and the Austro-Hungarian.

To protect and expand their territories, European nations began to seek other nations as military allies. Two major systems of alliances developed: the Triple Alliance (Germany, Austria-Hungary, and Italy) and the Entente (Britain, France, and Russia). Such was the state of Europe when the Archduke Franz Ferdinand of the Austro-Hungarian Empire was assassinated by ethnic Serbian nationalists. Because of imperialistic desires, nationalistic fervor, military alliances, and maneuverings, this seemingly isolated incident blew into an enormous war that involved all of Europe and many colonies of the imperial powers. On July 28, 1914, Austria-Hungary declared war on Serbia, thus beginning the First World War.

World War I lasted for four years. It was the most destructive war in the history of the world up until that time, mainly because of technological advances that produced such deadly weapons as the machine gun and poison gas. At war's end, many of the traditional imperial powers, such as France and Britain, were weakened. The Austro-Hungarian and Ottoman Empires, meanwhile, were dissolved and divided into smaller, weak nations. World War I also caused the destruction of Russia's old regime and aristocracy and led to civil war, revolution, and the adoption of communism. Instead of creating a lasting peace, the League of Nations proved inefficient, serving primarily the interests of the victorious nations of France and Great Britain, both of which gained territory and colonies from Germany and the Ottoman Empire. Despite fighting alongside the Allies, Russia had no role in creating the **Treaty of Versailles**. Its exclusion would sow Russian bitterness. Moreover, the Treaty of Versailles humiliated Germany and laid the ground for the Second World War. The one nation that emerged unscathed was the United States, which became the wealthiest power in the world.

THE GREAT DEPRESSION AND THE RISE OF TOTALITARIANISM

While many people spoke of World War I as the "war to end all wars," imperialistic tendencies and the desire to attain national wealth did not abate. Indeed, the effects of World War I created greater problems than anyone could have anticipated. First and foremost, the astronomical cost of the war proved devastating to the economies of the European nations. Germany found it difficult to pay reparations to the Allies, so Great Britain and France were unable to repay their debts to the United States. The economic crisis in Europe became clear when banks began to fail and unemployment rose. France and Great Britain attempted to resolve the economic crisis by forcing their colonies to purchase their products. But as a whole, most European countries became insular in an attempt to protect domestic industries. Such protectionist efforts only crippled global trade and industry. Many governments thereupon intervened with social welfare and economic stimulus programs. All countries around the world were seeking radical answers to the economic crisis.

AP Tip

World War I and World War II caused a major shift in global power. They led to the decline of the European imperial powers, gave rise to independence movements throughout Africa and Asia, and set the stage for the emergence of the United States and the Soviet Union as the new superpowers. Be sure you can identify and analyze this change over time in global power.

Those nations that were young, had political institutions that lacked popular support, or were embittered by the results of World War I witnessed the rise of totalitarian regimes. Italy under Mussolini, Germany under Hitler, and Russia under Stalin—all experienced violent repression as the price for the reduction of unemployment and economic malaise. At the heart of these totalitarian regimes were the same long-term tendencies that led to World War I. Nationalist fervor was used to drum up support for taking over territories and dominating people and resources outside national boundaries. Germany blamed its economic depression directly on the Treaty of Versailles, which stripped it of colonial territories, restricted its access to resource-rich border lands, and handcuffed its ability to further industrialize. The anger fanned by Hitler caused Germans to scapegoat

German Jews and rebuild their military for the purpose of satisfying their imperial desires.

WORLD WAR II AND INDEPENDENCE MOVEMENTS

Japan's imperialistic successes in Asia during the early 1930s encouraged Nazi Germany in its hopes to expand German territory. Similarly, Mussolini's **fascist** regime in Italy was emboldened to invade Ethiopia. Both Germany and Italy supported the fascist regime of Francisco Franco in Spain. Despite the clear acts of **militarism** and the aggressive positioning of these authoritarian regimes, Britain and France, old imperial powers, attempted to avoid conflict and the prohibitive costs of war. By the end of the 1930s, however, Britain and France found themselves unable to avoid the conflicts for fear of German and Italian domination of Europe. As with the First World War, European nations began forming alliances to protect their own interests. Once again, Britain and France formed an alliance (the Allied powers) in competition with the rising authoritarian regimes of Germany and Italy (the Axis powers). Just before the start of the war, in 1939, the **Nazis** made a pact with the Soviets. Later, when the Germans broke that pact, the Soviets joined the side of the Allied powers. Japan, having common interests with Germany and Italy, would later join the Axis powers. Both the Allied and Axis alliances dragged numerous other nations into the conflict, which encompassed two-thirds of the entire planet and included sixty-one nations. As with World War I, the cost of World War II—estimated at 5 trillion dollars— was astronomical. So too was the human cost. Nazi Germany's crack- down on its minority populations, resulting in the genocide of 6 million Jews and millions of others considered inferior to the "Aryan" race, shocked the entire world. The **Holocaust**, as this extermination became known, was fashioned after the crackdown on minority populations in the Ottoman Empire at the time of World War I, in which Armenians and other minorities faced eradication.

The Axis powers seemed assured of victory until the United States entered the war in 1941 on the side of the Allies. This too had a hint of *déjà vu*. The United States, arguably the world's most powerful nation at the end of World War I, turned the tide in favor of the Allies. Allied victory in Europe came in 1945 following the suicide of Hitler. By the end of the war, 35 million people had lost their lives. The European imperial powers, with colonies around the world, finally lost their position of global dominance. People in the colonial territories who had fought and died on the side of the European powers began demanding independence, sparking decolonization throughout Africa and Asia. After two world wars, the European nations no longer had the means to maintain colonial territories. The mantle of global power shifted to two new superpowers, the United States and the Soviet Union. Even the Yalta and Potsdam Conferences of 1945 were dominated by the two new superpowers. And as was the case after World War I, peace proved only a façade.

380 ❖ Chapter 24

THE COLD WAR AND DECOLONIZATION

On the surface, the **Cold War** was a battle of West versus East, democracy versus communism. In reality, the Cold War was an attempt by the United States and the Soviet Union to influence other people and territories, promoting their economic ideologies of capitalism and communism respectively, all at a time when the downfall of the old imperial powers, crippled by the end of World War II, left a vacuum for the emergence of a new world order. Colonial territories throughout Africa and Asia broke free. Both the United States and the Soviet Union actively promoted their ideologies in these newly independent nations as well as throughout Europe.

The Western capitalist nations, led by the United States, created an international monetary system with prices determined by supply and demand. A system of exchange rates was also created. The Eastern Communist nations, led by the Soviet Union, constructed a system in which the state allocated goods and fixed prices. Both sides were suspicious of each other and perceived the success of one as the failure of the other. Nothing symbolized this suspicion more than Winston Churchill's reference to an **"iron curtain"** dividing Eastern and Western Europe. Western European nations recovered from the devastation of World War II with the aid of the United States's **Marshall Plan**. Eastern European nations also saw rapid—though only temporary—recovery with the aid of the Soviet Union.

On both sides of the iron curtain, the superpowers responded to each other both politically and militarily. When, for instance, the westerners established the **North Atlantic Treaty Organization (NATO)** as a military alliance, the easterners established the **Warsaw Pact**. Tensions along this east-west divide grew to enormous proportions, and many feared the onset of a third world war. Ironically, Germany proved the tensest battleground. During the post–World War II peace conferences, Germany, and its capital Berlin, were split into four parts. Berlin however, was located deep in the territory controlled by the Soviet Union. When the Soviets blockaded West Berlin in 1948, the United States airlifted supplies to West Berlin.

Incidents such as these filled the Cold War period, but the stakes were raised in 1949 when the Soviets successfully tested their first nuclear device. The whole of Europe seemed to watch as the two superpowers engaged in an arms race for nuclear supremacy. But rather than take part in the type of militarization that led to the world wars, the European nations, clearly exhausted from war, sought to ease tensions between the east and west. Take, for example, the **Helsinki Accords**, signed in 1975, which affirmed that boundaries within Europe were fixed and could not be altered by military force and called for increased contact and cooperation across the iron-curtain divide.

The fall of the Berlin Wall, in 1989, marks the end of the Cold War. During the 1980s, economic troubles caused social unrest in the eastern European nations. Despite many efforts to restructure the communist economies, citizens were demanding change. A flood of protest and rebellion swept through Poland, Hungary, Czechoslovakia, and Bulgaria. After the fall of the Berlin Wall, large numbers of East Germans began to cross into the western portion. These events in

Europe precipitated many changes in the Soviet Union and led eventually to its breakup in 1991, as Lithuania, Estonia, Latvia, and other small Soviet states declared their independence. After forty-six years, the United States emerged from the Cold War as the lone superpower.

AP Tip

After World War II, the United States and the Soviet Union arose as the world's two superpowers. Vying to fill the void left by the decline of the traditional imperial powers, each nation sought to influence countries around the world to adopt capitalism and communism respectively. Some wars and proxy wars developed, but not once did the two superpowers engage in direct conflict with each other. You must be able to compare the economic and political philosophies of the two Cold War superpowers, as well as their efforts to influence nations around the world.

THE POST–COLD WAR WORLD

The post–Cold War era is perhaps still without a true definition. But a New World Order that did not include a European superpower had clearly arisen by the early 1990s. Whether that new world order would finally bring about peace was still a matter of debate. And whether the United States as the lone superpower would impose and/or export its influence and create a true global community was also unclear.

Post–Cold War Europe was not free of conflict. Old tensions caused Yugoslavia to erupt into religious and ethnic factionalism. The struggle among Muslims, Catholics, Orthodox Christians, Serbs, Croats, and Albanians led to the disintegration of Yugoslavia and the creation, once again, of new nations. And once again, the world saw the rise of ethnic cleansing, as the Serbs of Bosnia, who are Orthodox Christians, attempted to rid the state of Muslims. Yugoslavia became a prime example of the failure of the nation-state and of a united global community.

However, the New World Order did bring about a new level of cooperation in Europe. In 1973, Great Britain joined the European Economic Community, which was established both to ensure economic cooperation and growth and to counteract the powerful economic influence of the United States. By the turn of the twenty-first century, most European nations had come together to form the **European Union** and had adopted a common currency, the Euro. Moreover, efforts to eliminate ethnic cleansing and other types of oppression and abuse led to the proliferation of **nongovernmental organizations** (NGOs). NGOs such as Amnesty International and Médecins Sans Frontières (Doctors Without Borders), in attempting to eliminate or at least reduce global suffering, were also effectively nullifying the traditional nation-state boundaries.

Nation-state boundaries were further eroded by **multinational corporations**—corporations with ownership and management teams from more than one nation. It was multinational corporations based in the United States that led the way, transmitting not only technological developments but also American culture around the world. McDonald's, CNN, and Coca-Cola became prime symbols of vehicles of American culture. Critics argued that powerful multinational corporations used sophisticated marketing techniques to promote consumption.

Despite the efforts to prevent American global dominance, most European nations joined the United States in efforts to stem terrorism and nuclear proliferation. Terrorism in the twenty-first century is largely associated with Islamic groups in the Middle East angered by the creation of Israel following World War II. Much of that anger is aimed at western European nations, which along with the United States are seen as staunch supporters of Israel.

Immigrant populations throughout Europe are growing rapidly, and fertility rates among immigrants are far outpacing those of native-born Europeans. As a result, many western European nations have implemented regulations to slow immigration. Thus **globalization** has not created a unified global culture. In fact, many social scientists marvel at the endurance of cultural diversity in the face of globalization. People around the world use technology such as the Internet and satellites to export and maintain their own ethnic and cultural values, even as the traditional nation-state weakens.

Multiple-Choice Questions

1. In which of the following ways did World War I affect Russia?
   (A) Russia gained stability and wealth through war reparations.
   (B) Russia split into independent republics.
   (C) Russia was devastated by revolution and civil war.
   (D) Russia created an expanded empire.

2. Which of the following statements is an accurate comparison of World War I and previous conflicts in Europe?
   (A) World War I left more dead and wounded than any previous war in Europe.
   (B) While World War I was fought over a larger area, there were fewer casualties because of advanced military strategies.
   (C) While more lives were lost, World War I resulted in fewer refugees.
   (D) Unlike the devastation of previous wars, World War I had little effect on the environment.

3. France and Great Britain escaped the worst of the Depression by
   (A) imposing authoritarian control over their society and economy.
   (B) consolidating private farms into collectives with government subsidies.
   (C) invading parts of Germany in order to extract resources.
   (D) making their colonial territories purchase their products rather than the products of other countries.

4. Compared with World War I, how did World War II impact European home fronts?
   (A) World War II witnessed fewer civilian casualties and less extensive destruction of urban and rural territories.
   (B) During World War II, military movements were slower and the area of fighting was larger.
   (C) Poison gas technology introduced in World War II resulted in more battlefield loss of life.
   (D) During World War II there was less distinction between military and civilian and civilians were more often targeted.

5. All of the following statements about the Holocaust is accurate EXCEPT
   (A) the Nazis especially targeted Jews.
   (B) Nazis killed the disabled, Gypsies, homosexuals, Jehovah's Witnesses, and Polish Catholics.
   (C) many German Jews were forcibly evacuated and sent to Israel.
   (D) ordinary citizens were involved in supporting the genocide.

6. Why did Western European nations and the United States form the North Atlantic Treaty Organization (NATO)?
   (A) To combat Soviet efforts to create a global communist revolution
   (B) To create a peacekeeping force made up of soldiers from nations around the world
   (C) To provide the funds and materials to rebuild Western Europe
   (D) To improve relations between the Soviet Union and Western nations

7. All of following are impacts of the fall of the Berlin Wall EXCEPT
   (A) East Germans crossed to West Germany in large numbers.
   (B) government services in East Berlin collapsed.
   (C) unemployment and budget deficits were drastically reduced.
   (D) Germany was soon reunified in 1990.

8. Which of the following statements about immigration in post–Cold War Europe is accurate?
   (A) Throughout Europe, immigrant populations are growing faster than the native-born population.
   (B) Immigrants have higher standards of living than the host population.
   (C) Many European nations increasingly promote immigration in order to solve labor shortage problems.
   (D) Immigrants to Europe have seamlessly assimilated into European cultural norms.

9. Which of the following is an example of a nongovernmental organization (NGO)?
   (A) The North Atlantic Treaty Organization, a military alliance aimed at protecting the interest of Western democracies.
   (B) Médecins Sans Frontières (Doctors Without Borders), which provides medical assistance in crises around the world.
   (C) McDonald's, whose fast-food restaurants are found throughout the world.
   (D) CNN, whose news footage is seen in numerous countries around the world.

10. The Kosovo crisis of 1999 is an example of which of the following?
    (A) The effects of cultural imperialism
    (B) The increase of nationalist ethnic cleansing
    (C) The power of multinational corporations
    (D) The influence of the World Bank and International Monetary Fund

11. Which of the following best describes the Bolshevik October Revolution in 1917?
    (A) It was led by hungry peasants.
    (B) It ended the bloodshed of the previous three years.
    (C) It instituted rapid industrialization.
    (D) It favored land distribution.

12. Which region of Europe had its territorial boundaries changed most dramatically as a result of the peace treaties that ended World War I?
    (A) Eastern Europe
    (B) Central Europe
    (C) Mediterranean Europe
    (D) Northern Europe

13. Which of the following describes the architectural "International Style" of the 1900s?
    (A) Ornamented surfaces
    (B) Exotic building materials
    (C) Simple designs
    (D) Bold colors

14. Which of the following best describes gender roles during World War II?
    (A) Soviet women dominated agricultural and industrial jobs.
    (B) British women served in combat units.
    (C) Axis countries used female labor more than Allied countries.
    (D) Gender roles in the military were transformed by air and naval warfare.

15. Which of the following economic policies did Western Europe follow in the years after World War II?
    (A) laissez-faire capitalism
    (B) government nationalization of major segments of the population
    (C) collectivization of agriculture
    (D) economically helping devastated Eastern Europe

Free-Response Questions

1. Compare the economic and political responses to the global depression of the 1930s for TWO of the following countries:
   ■ Great Britain
   ■ Germany
   ■ Italy
   ■ France

2. Discuss the continuities and changes in the political and economic structures of European nation-states during the second half of the twentieth century.

Answers

MULTIPLE-CHOICE QUESTIONS

1. ANSWER: **C.** On top of the enormous number of deaths, World War I was an unbelievably destructive force on Russian society, paving the way for both communism and industrialization (*The Earth and Its Peoples,* 5th ed., pp. 800–803/6th ed., p. 760).

2. ANSWER: **A.** World War I resulted in more deaths, war injuries, and physical destruction than any previous war in Europe. Moreover, millions of people were dislocated, creating a huge refugee problem throughout the continent (*The Earth and Its Peoples,* 5th ed., pp. 807–808/6th ed., pp. 761–762).

3. ANSWER: **D.** France and Great Britain could mitigate the severity of the global depression because they could exploit their colonial territories. Their experience led Germany and Japan to seek colonial territories as a response to the economic crisis plaguing their nations (*The Earth and Its Peoples,* 5th ed., pp. 836–837/6th ed., p. 811).

4. ANSWER: **D.** Advances in technology during the Second World War led to faster and more destructive military movements. Moreover, civilians were targeted as a strategy of war in order to demoralize the opponent (*The Earth and Its Peoples,* 5th ed., p. 850/6th ed., p. 826).

5. ANSWER: **C.** Along with 6 million Jews, the Nazis exterminated homosexuals, Jehovah's Witnesses, Gypsies, the disabled, and the mentally ill. They also killed 3 million Polish Catholics. The Holocaust resulted in torture, medical experimentation, and mass extermination, all in an effort to create a "pure race" (*The Earth and Its Peoples,* 5th ed., pp. 850–852/6th ed., pp. 827–828).

6. ANSWER: **A.** Western nations responded to the iron curtain and the growth of communism in China by creating the military alliance known as NATO in 1949. The leaders of these nations feared that the Soviets were encouraging a worldwide communist revolution. Their answer was the creation of an alliance capable of combating Soviet power and influence (*The Earth and its People,* 5th ed., p. 888/6th ed., p. 840).

7. ANSWER: **C.** Despite the euphoria, there were many problems that resulted from the reunification of Germany, among them high levels of unemployment and budget deficits (*The Earth and Its Peoples,* 5th ed., pp. 924–925/6th ed., p. 878).

8. ANSWER: **A.** While growing immigrant populations have resulted in cultural conflicts throughout Europe, they have also forced those

nations to redefine their conservative view of nationality (*The Earth and Its Peoples,* 5th ed., pp. 933–934/6th ed., p. 887).

9. **ANSWER: B.** Médecins Sans Frontières, founded in 1971, was awarded the Nobel Peace Prize in 1999 for its medical efforts throughout the world (*The Earth and Its Peoples,* 5th ed., p. 961/6th ed., p. 913).

10. **ANSWER: B.** Kosovo is another example of the ethnic struggles that plagued and forced the disintegration of Yugoslavia. This southern province of mostly Albanian-speaking Muslims faced discrimination and mistreatment from the larger Serbian population. Such mistreatment led to the direct involvement of NATO and, most especially, the United States (*The Earth and Its Peoples,* 5th ed., pp. 925–926/6th ed., p. 878).

11. **ANSWER: D.** The Bolshevik Revolution, which followed the Provisional Government, adopted the communist ideology of Marxism. Land was seized from wealthy landowners and distributed to farmers. Violent civil war resulted, and rapid industrialism came about more than ten years later (*The Earth and Its Peoples,* 5th ed., pp. 806–807/6th ed., p. 760).

12. **ANSWER: A.** New countries of Yugoslavia, Czechoslovakia, Poland, Lithuania, Latvia, and Estonia were all created in eastern Europe as a result of the treaties that ended World War I (*The Earth and Its Peoples,* 5th ed., pp. 809–810/6th ed., p. 762).

13. **ANSWER: C.** The International Style of LeCorbusier and Eero Saarinen stressed clean lines, simple design, and the idea that form should follow function (*The Earth and Its Peoples,* 5th ed., p. 822/6th ed., p. 788).

14. **ANSWER: A.** The Soviet Union mobilized 22 million men for the military. As a result women became dominant in nonmilitary production (*The Earth and Its Peoples,* 5th ed., p. 853/6th ed., pp. 812–813).

15. **ANSWER: B.** Britain, France, and other Western European countries nationalized major portions of their economy, such as coal, steel, and medical care following World War II (*The Earth and Its Peoples,* 5th ed., pp. 891–892/6th ed., p. 843).

FREE-RESPONSE QUESTIONS

1. A good response should include a comparison of the economic effects of the Depression as well as the political responses. Germany and Italy, for example, faced more devastating conditions during the Depression than England and France did. You should also discuss how nations with long traditions of representative government were better able to withstand the pressure to install an authoritarian regime as a response to the economic downfall. While the economic position and political responses were often intertwined, resist the urge to treat them as one. Instead, attempt to show how the economic conditions caused particular political responses. Likewise, be certain to discuss how each nation's political responses allowed them to weather the Depression.

2. A good response could begin with an explanation of the traditional European nation-state. You should then show how the Cold War created ideological blocks/alliances that were manifested within the United Nations, an organization that by its very nature is often asked to intrude in the affairs of sovereign nations. Nongovernmental organizations, multinational corporations, and the European Union have all chipped away at the role of the nation-state. Your job is to chart this increase in globalization to demonstrate how the nation-state is becoming more fluid and less bound by physical borders. Continuities could include the continuing use of transnational groups, such as alliances before World War I and groups like the League of Nations, the United Nations, and the European Union.

25

The Americas: Circa 1900 to the Present

Key Concepts

- Most nations in the Americas suffered from foreign economic control and a drastic degree of social inequality during the twentieth century.
- The United States became a wealthy global power after World War I and one of the two global superpowers following World War II.
- Throughout North and South America, the Depression caused unemployment, homelessness, and protectionist policies.
- Its foreign policy of containment during the Cold War led the United States to sponsor coups and proxy wars throughout Latin America.
- The emergence of the United States as the lone superpower at the end of the Cold War resulted in the globalization of culture, a more interconnected global economy, and the spread of democracy. It has also caused new conflicts in response to U.S. domination.

Key Terms

- Contras
- Dirty War
- import-substitution industrialization
- North American Free Trade Agreement (NAFTA)
- North Atlantic Treaty Organization (NATO)
- oligarquía
- Pearl Harbor
- proxy wars

388

- Sandinistas
- Truman Doctrine

The Americas during the twentieth century are discussed in *The Earth and Its Peoples,* fifth edition, Chapters 28–33 and sixth edition, Chapters 27–32.

WORLD WAR I

On the eve of World War I, most countries in the Americas could be defined by two common characteristics. First, most had sharp social divides between a small, very wealthy class and a large population of poor. Second, most were victims of foreign intervention or some sort of foreign economic control. Despite the success of the revolutions that rid them of colonial rule, Western Hemisphere nations had difficulty shrugging off the economic hold of European nations. The United States had proved one of the few exceptions to the second rule. It not only gained economic independence, but also became an imperial power itself, strategically positioned to exert economic influence over its neighbors in the Americas. Nonetheless, the social divide and foreign control caused simmering tensions in most American societies. In many cases, it was as if the revolutions of the nineteenth century were not yet complete.

Consider Mexico. Close to 1 percent of the population owned 85 percent of the land. These few wealthy families were mostly of direct Spanish origin and lived on huge estates. In contrast, the vast majority of the population consisted of poor peasants of Native American or mixed ancestry (commonly referred to as mestizos). Industry in Mexico was dominated by companies from the United States and Great Britain—both imperial and industrial powers—that controlled most of Mexico's railroads, mines, plantations, and other major industries. Wealthy Mexicans were often closely tied to the foreign companies, and together they forced the peasants to endure harsh working and living conditions. Thus, popular resentment was high, military coups were frequent, and revolutionary sentiment was rife. In southern Mexico, Emiliano Zapata led peasant revolts to wrest land from wealthy hacienda owners and return it to the Amerindian villages to which it had once belonged. Similarly, Pancho Villa organized peasant revolts in northern Mexico, where 95 percent of the people had no land at all. They also seized haciendas in an effort to redistribute wealth. Neither Zapata nor Villa was able to gain support outside their own locales, but their demands were heard. By 1920, a group of middle-class leaders known as the Constitutionalists had defeated all their adversaries, including Zapata and Villa, to gain control of Mexico. They did, however, restore communal lands to Amerindians and establish social programs for the poor. In an effort to chip away at foreign economic control, they also placed restrictions on foreign ownership of property.

Argentina and Brazil faced circumstances similar to those of Mexico. The governments of both nations represented the interests of a few wealthy landowners. In Argentina, this elite, known as the **oligarquía**, controlled vast tracts of farmland and made Argentina, like the United States, one of the world's largest producers of meat and wheat. As a result of its tremendous agricultural success, the oligarquía was quite content to let foreign companies control other industries such as public utilities and railroads. Likewise, Brazil's elite focused on coffee, cacao, and rubber exports, and let foreigners control industries. Railroads, harbors, public utilities, and other forms of infrastructure were controlled by Great Britain. While Argentina and Brazil exported agricultural goods, they imported almost all manufactured goods. During World War I, European nations slowed the importation of crops, which weakened the landowning classes in both Argentina and Brazil. The urban middle class was able to gain power during this time. However, little was done for the masses of poor, landless peasants, many of whom were of Native American and/or African ancestry.

World War I had a very different effect on the United States. A young yet growing industrial and imperial nation, the United States was catapulted into the position of a global power by the war. In the United States, as in other nations in the Americas, wealth was fairly restrictive, and much of it was secured for those of European descent. However, the United States had extensive and varied industries, a growing middle class, and a number of colonial territories from which to extract resources. At the start of World War I, the United States, seemingly content with its status, maintained an official position of neutrality. But the neutrality was only technical. While no military was involved in fighting, U.S. businesses were providing supplies to France and Great Britain. German submarines, therefore, began attacking all ships heading to Great Britain, resulting in numerous American civilian casualties. In 1917, President Woodrow Wilson asked Congress to declare war on Germany. That proved costly for the Central Powers. The arrival of fresh, healthy troops from the United States turned the tide in favor of the Allies. The Germans were soon in retreat. They signed an armistice to end the war in November 1918.

Most surprising, however, was the social and economic impact on the United States. To help the war effort, civilians were encouraged to invest in war bonds. As soldiers left their jobs and went off to war, employment opportunities opened up for women and African-Americans. Job openings in cities in the north led to large-scale migrations of African-Americans from the rural south. Social equality was by no means achieved, but the progress provided an impetus for groups that were discriminated against to fight for greater freedoms and opportunities. Businesses prospered too, especially if they were engaged in war production. All in all, the United States was the one nation that grew rich from the war.

AP Tip

The effect of World War I was drastically different on the United States than on other nations in the Americas. The United States thrived economically. Most nations in the Americas, however, suffered economically. You will need to be able to analyze the reasons for such differences.

THE INTERWAR PERIOD

The first event that symbolized U.S. ascendancy as a world power was the Paris Peace Conference. U.S. president Woodrow Wilson, along with British prime minister David Lloyd George and French premier Georges Clemenceau, laid out the framework for the Treaty of Versailles. In addition, Wilson proposed a League of Nations to help safeguard peace and foster international cooperation—ironically, the United States, in an effort to return to isolationism, refused to join. Many in the United States were comfortable with the newfound prosperity that the war had provided. A steady economic boom, the result of European nations borrowing American money and repaying wartime loans, brought an air of optimism to the United States in the 1920s. Many who had been marginalized increased their demands for equality and greater participation in American society—demand for social change seemed to accompany the economic growth. Having joined the labor force during the war, women pressed for the right to vote, which they got in 1920 with the Nineteenth Amendment. For most African-Americans, on the other hand, the right to vote was merely theoretical. Increasingly, organizations such as the National Association for the Advancement of Colored People (NAACP) and the United Negro Improvement Association (UNIA) pushed the nation to grant first-class citizenship to African-Americans.

South American countries also experienced growing prosperity during the 1920s. Trade with European nations, curtailed by the war, resumed, and agricultural exports once again commanded high prices. Both Argentina and Brazil used their profits to industrialize and improve their transportation and public utilities systems—a goal helped by Great Britain's need to sell many of its transportation holdings and industrial companies to Argentina and Brazil in order to pay its war debt. Still, with the introduction of new technologies, South American nations remained dependent on foreign companies. British, French, Germans, and Americans formed a cartel to control all radio communication in Latin America. The cartel set up a national radio company in each nation, held all the stock and received all the profits. European and American companies also controlled aviation technology in Latin America. Aeropostale and Pan American Airways introduced airmail services throughout the continent and were linked to cities in the United States and Europe.

Economic prosperity in Latin America also led to social changes. However, the more stratified societies of Argentina and Brazil witnessed various levels of turmoil as workers and middle-class professionals demanded social changes and a greater say in politics. Junior military officers in Brazil rose up to demand universal suffrage and freedom for labor unions, among other social reforms. In Argentina, demonstrations were crushed. However, they not only laid the groundwork for later change but also opened a space for the middle class to share power with the wealthy elite. Throughout both North and South America, the middle class was growing, but the growth was often at the expense of poor, landless peasants and urban workers. Social progress was perhaps greatest in Mexico, where the revolution ensured that representatives of rural communities, unionized workers, and public employees gained a greater voice in society. In 1928, President Plutarco Elías Calles established the National Revolutionary Party (PNR) to provide a forum in which businessmen, peasants, laborers, landowners, the military, and members of other interest groups could reach compromises for the good of the nation.

Throughout the Americas, prosperity and access to technology were spreading beyond the realms of the elite. In the United States, the economic boom gave rise to an overconfidence that foreshadowed the impending crisis. Few had anticipated the fall of the New York stock market, but sure enough, on October 24, 1929, the market plunged; the downward spiral would last for three years. Investors lost money, people lost their savings, and banks collapsed. The crisis grew circular, as consumers purchased less, so businesses produced less, so companies were forced to lay off workers, and laid-off workers could purchase less. In 1930, to protect U.S. businesses from foreign competition, Congress passed the Smoot-Hawley tariff, the highest import duty in U.S. history. Other nations around the world retaliated by raising their tariffs. World trade was crippled, dropping by 62 percent. Three years after the stock market crash, the U.S. economy was cut in half, and unemployment had reached a record high of 25 percent of the workforce.

The Depression devastated Latin America as well. Most Latin American countries depended on exports and were thus hit hard, as most industrial nations imposed high tariffs and reduced their imports. Sugar exports from the Caribbean fell. Coffee exports from Brazil and Colombia dropped, as did tin exports from Bolivia and beef exports from Argentina. Exports from Latin America fell by two-thirds from 1929 to 1932. Again, the devastation was circular. Nations could no longer import manufactured goods. Industrialization efforts within nations were set back. Unemployment and homelessness increased dramatically.

In many nations, military officers seized power, and governments began imposing authoritarian rule. Getulio Vargas of Brazil, one such authoritarian ruler, staged a coup and came to power in 1930. He initially made some socially progressive changes—for example, broadening the franchise, allowing labor unions, and installing pension plans—but his reforms were largely geared to urban workers. He did little to help the millions of landless peasants for fear of provoking the ire of the powerful landowners. Vargas was, however, successful in helping Brazil recover from the Depression. His policy of **import-substitution industrialization**, which aimed at building the nation's industry by restricting foreign trade, became a model emulated by other Latin American nations. By 1938, however, Vargas had abolished his own constitution, banned political parties, and jailed opposition leaders. Argentina followed a path similar to Brazil's. In 1930, General José Uriburu overthrew the popularly elected President Hipólito Irigoyen. The new government protected the interests of the oligarquía and big business. Tension among the poor and the working class continued to build.

Mexico, however, proved different from the others. The revitalized revolution saw Lázaro Cárdenas come to power, renaming the PNR the Mexican Revolutionary Party (PRM). Cárdenas removed generals from government positions and redistributed more than 44 million acres of land to peasant communes. In an effort to break the foreign economic stranglehold, Cárdenas nationalized railroads and foreign-owned oil companies. The revitalized revolution under Cárdenas brought some of the most widespread changes of any nation in the Americas, but Mexico remained stubbornly poor, with little industrialization. Like Mexico, the United States did not fall to an authoritarian regime, and had to use dramatic intervention to overcome the Depression. When Franklin D. Roosevelt became president in 1932, he implemented his New Deal program to stimulate and revitalize the economy. Despite the many critics who complained that the New Deal resembled socialism and communism, it was extremely successful. But it would take the Second World War to fully push the United States out of the Depression.

WORLD WAR II

When war erupted in Europe and Asia during the latter half of the 1930s, the United States once again adopted an official policy of isolationism. But as in the First World War, it began profiting from the war by making loans and selling supplies to France and Great Britain. The guise of neutrality remained thin when the United States, along with Britain, stopped shipments of steel, oil, and other materials that the Japanese needed for their war and industrial efforts. That action led the Japanese to attack the United States by bombing **Pearl Harbor** in 1941. The bombing of the naval base put an end to the nation's isolationist stance, as the United States joined Britain, the Soviet Union, and other nations in an alliance commonly known as the Allies. Once again, U.S. involvement in the war was crucial in turning the tide in favor of the Allies. The Americans played an essential role in forcing Italy to surrender and in storming the Normandy Coast, which pushed the Germans into retreat. In May 1945, Germany surrendered. Turning its attention to Japan, the United States dropped atomic bombs on Hiroshima and Nagasaki in August. Japan surrendered a week later.

World War II clearly helped the United States escape from the Depression. The economy flourished during the war. The United States alone produced more weapons and supplies than all of the Axis Powers combined. Such demand and production capacity led to plentiful jobs and opportunities. The war effort was boosted by the sale of bonds and rationing, which resulted in a tremendous growth in personal savings. Like the First World War, the Second built up national and individual wealth. And it once again gave strength to the efforts of minorities and women in fighting for democracy and equality. As job opportunities opened up during the war, employers hired women, African-Americans, Latinos, and other minorities. The many minorities who fought and died on the battlefield alongside white Americans, in a war billed as a fight for freedom and democracy, returned home demanding the same freedom and democracy in the United States. The demand of soldiers and laborers was a huge impetus for the impending Civil Rights movement.

Despite turning Brazil into a fascist state, Vargas's regime allied itself with the United States during World War II. Argentina, on the other hand, remained officially neutral. However, the military rulers of Argentina were clearly inspired by Nazi Germany. In 1943, under the leadership of Colonel Juan Péron, Argentina hoped to conquer South America just as the Nazis were conquering Europe. But as the Nazis began losing ground, the popularity of Argentina's military officers began to wane as well. In an effort to regain the trust of the populace, Péron departed from his previous military stance. He and his charismatic wife, Eva Duarte Péron, began appealing to urban workers, pushing for social benefits for women, children, and the poor. With his wife's help, Juan Péron become a popular leader and won the presidency in 1946. Under him, Argentina was essentially a populist dictatorship, much like Brazil under Vargas. Like Brazil, Argentina also industrialized rapidly. But industrialization only masked internal social and economic problems. When Eva Péron died in 1952, her husband lost his popular appeal and was overthrown in a military coup later that year.

THE COLD WAR

Devastation throughout Europe at the end of World War II, combined with the tremendous wealth amassed by the United States during the war, resulted in the further ascendancy of the United States as a world superpower. The Soviet Union also emerged from the war a global superpower as it too had witnessed stunning industrial growth. But the United States distrusted the USSR and its communist economic system, which ran counter to American capitalism. Suspicion grew between both new superpowers. In 1947, the United States issued the **Truman Doctrine**, which promised military aid to any nation that was fighting communist or socialist insurrections. In 1949, the United States and various Western European nations established the **North Atlantic Treaty Organization** (NATO), a military alliance. In response, the Soviet Union and Eastern European countries formed the Warsaw Pact. Measures meant to quell the tensions only exacerbated them. Even the United Nations, which had been established to maintain world peace, became just another arena in which the Cold War would be played out.

Early Cold War conflicts all took place on the back of post–World War II settlements. When the Soviets blockaded Berlin, Germany, in 1948, the United States orchestrated an airlift to get supplies to the people of West Berlin. In Asia during that same year, Korea split into a communist North Korea and a capitalist South Korea. When North Korea invaded South Korea in 1950, the United States came to the aid of the South Koreans, while communist China sent troops to assist the North Koreans. Fighting lasted for three years before a truce was signed that fixed the border at its original post–World War II line, the thirty-eighth parallel. The Korean War convinced many Americans that the USSR was fomenting communist revolutions worldwide. Fear of communism even spilled onto the domestic scene when the government, as well as private individuals, began blacklisting, harassing, and discriminating against people thought to be members of the Communist Party in the United States. Thousands of Americans lost their jobs, many as a result of the vaguest unsubstantiated accusations.

In the same vein, the government adopted a foreign policy, known as containment, that communism should be stopped at all costs anywhere in the world. When the Cold War reached Vietnam, the containment policy took on greater urgency. Some Americans began to cite the domino theory—that if Vietnam became communist, the rest of Southeast Asia, nation by nation, would fall to communism. The United States supported the noncommunist government of South Vietnam against North Vietnam and the Viet Cong, the communist rebels in the south. The United States supported South Vietnam despite the fact that the government was corrupt, unpopular, and undemocratic. Nonetheless, the United States was so committed to containment that it spent more than a decade fighting a war to defeat the Viet Cong and the North Vietnamese. The United States finally withdrew in 1973. The Vietnam War had profound domestic consequences. A huge antiwar movement developed during the war that questioned not only the handling of the war but also its validity. At times the antiwar movement meshed with the civil rights movement, which highlighted the contradiction of fighting a war overseas in the name of freedom and democracy when those were not realities at home. Nonetheless, the obsession with fighting communism worldwide continued to affect both foreign and domestic policy.

The U.S. desire to contain communism often came into direct conflict with the ideals of the people and nations of Latin America. In seeking economic freedom, Latin Americans were essentially challenging the supremacy of the United States. Even after World War II, U.S. corporations controlled large portions of industry there—communication networks throughout Latin America, sugar in Cuba, coffee in Colombia, bananas in Guatemala, and copper in Chile. Efforts by Latin Americans to rid their nations of foreign control were often perceived by the United States as communist insurrections, financed and fueled by its arch-nemesis, the Soviet Union. In fact, Soviet involvement was minimal. Latin American nations had been attempting to reclaim their economic power for over a century. Even their attraction to communist ideals was less about the Soviet Union and more about efforts to address the vast economic and social disparities within their own nations. Nonetheless, Latin American nations were effectively dragged into the middle of the Cold War. During the 1950s, Guatemalan president Jacobo Arbenz Guzmán attempted to nationalize various industries, including the U.S.-controlled United Fruit Company. Perceiving this as a move toward communism, the U.S. Central Intelligence Agency (CIA) sponsored a military coup that resulted in the removal of Arbenz from power and decades of civil war and instability in Guatemala.

In Cuba, however, the CIA did not experience the same success. U.S. economic control in Cuba was even more extensive and over-whelming than in Guatemala. Public utilities, banking, transportation, and sugar, Cuba's most important industry, were all controlled by U.S. companies. Wealth was held by foreigners and the small Cuban elite. Moreover, President Fulgencio Batista's regime was undemocratic, corrupt, and repressive. Still, the United States gave Batista wide support. In 1959, Fidel Castro led a popular rebellion that forced Batista from power. The Cuban Revolution under Castro was a huge blow to U.S. power in Cuba. Castro redistributed land, lowered urban rents, raised wages, and nationalized foreign-controlled corporations. Within a year, Castro had effectively transferred 15 percent of the national income from the rich to the poor. In response to the Revolution, the CIA hoped to overthrow Castro, just as it had overthrown Arbenz in Guatemala. However, the CIA-sponsored Bay of Pigs invasion failed. His reputation bolstered, Castro asked the Soviet Union for assistance to help prevent a U.S. takeover. The Soviets were more than willing to oblige by placing nuclear missiles in Cuba—U.S. missiles were already deployed in Turkey. A crisis ensued. Eventually, Soviet president Nikita Khrushchev backed down and withdrew the missiles from Cuba. The 1962 Cuban missile crisis was perhaps the closest that the United States and the USSR came to direct military confrontation. However, Castro had proved that U.S. economic domination could be challenged and that economic and social reform could be achieved. Cuba would serve as a model for revolutionary change even in the post–Cold War era.

A conservative response to the Cuban Revolution erupted in Brazil as military officers, claiming that civilian leaders could not protect the nation from communist rebellion, staged a coup. The constitution was suspended, and paramilitary organizations known as death squads were sanctioned by the government in order to eliminate opposition leaders. Thousands of civilians were detained, tortured, and executed. Brazil's mix of military dictatorship, violent repression, and industrialization through import-substitution, known as the Brazilian solution, was adopted by other Latin American nations. In 1973, Chile's democratically elected president Salvador Allende was overthrown in a CIA-backed coup as he attempted to nationalize U.S.-owned copper mines. Coup leader Augusto Pinochet took control of the nation and, with the backing of the United States, implemented various aspects of the Brazilian solution. Civilians were imprisoned, tortured, and executed. Socialist reforms in Argentina also resulted in the rise of military dictatorship. Between 1976 and 1983, Argentineans would experience what was known as the **Dirty War**, in which thousands of civilians were tortured and executed.

Revolutionary movements in Central America found a bit more success than those in South America. In 1979, revolutionaries known as the **Sandinistas** overthrew the U.S.-backed Nicaraguan dictator, Anastasio Somoza. With support from Cuba, they then fought off the **Contras**, rebels supported by the United States. In El Salvador, the United States intervened to prevent Salvadoran revolutionaries from overthrowing the U.S.-allied military dictatorship. As a result, a decade-long civil war ensued.

AP Tip

The quest for economic independence in Latin America often ran counter to the Cold War ambitions of the United States. As such, proxy wars erupted throughout the Americas. Be sure you can analyze U.S. involvement in various Latin American nations and compare the causes and effects of these interventions.

THE POST–COLD WAR WORLD

In many ways, the Cold War contributed to the transformation of Latin America into a region of revolution, counterrevolution, violence, and repression. In search of economic independence and social equality, nations unwittingly became arenas for **proxy wars**, in which the United States and the Soviet Union armed and financed the warring parties. However, U.S. military interventions in Grenada and Panama, in 1983 and 1989 respectively, sent a powerful message that the United States was to be the dominant force in the region. The 1990s, therefore, ushered in a new era throughout the Americas. The military dictatorships of Brazil, Chile, and Argentina all came to an end after being undermined by reports of corruption, torture, and violence. Civil war came to an end in Nicaragua as the Sandinistas called for free elections in 1990; the election of a moderate coalition led by Violeta Chamorro clearly signified that Nicaraguans were tired of decades of violence and civil war. The end to civil war in neighboring El Salvador was also negotiated during the 1990s.

Economically, Latin American nations found themselves in debt at the end of the Cold War. Many nations had borrowed heavily during the Cold War era, and the rise of oil prices during the 1980s forced many nations to build up greater debt. This escalation of Latin American debt, along with the collapse of the Soviet Union, provided even greater opportunity for the United States to gain more influence in the area. Latin American nations introduced economic reforms that were advocated by the United States. Industries that had earlier been nationalized were sold to foreign-owned companies, and free-market policies that reduced protectionism were implemented. By 1994, the **North American Free Trade Agreement** (NAFTA), which eliminated tariffs among the United States, Canada, and Mexico, governed the largest free trade zone in the world. With the United States leading the way, free market capitalism was taking hold and connecting economies around the world. Although democracy has become almost universal in Latin America, poverty has continued. The people of the Americas, like those elsewhere, are still primarily driven by the hope of economic stability.

Technological advances were also helping to spread U.S. culture around the world. American organizations like CNN ensured the airing of television programs and viewpoints from the United States.

In 2001, a group known as Al Qaeda successfully organized attacks on the World Trade Center in New York City and on the Pentagon in Washington, D.C. In response, the United States began a global war against terror.

Multiple-Choice Questions

1. What effect did the United States' entry have on the outcome of World War I?
    (A) The entrance of U.S. troops and equipment turned the tide in favor of the Allies.
    (B) U.S. troop involvement encouraged Japan to attack the United States.
    (C) Though effective at first, U.S. troops lost effectiveness as the war dragged on.
    (D) U.S. troops prolonged the war by adding another dimension to the fighting.

2. What effect did World War I have on the economies of Brazil and Argentina?
    (A) It caused increased wealth as the demand for raw materials from Europe increased.
    (B) It resulted in widespread poverty and homelessness as agricultural exports slowed to a halt.
    (C) It resulted in the decrease of agricultural exports, thus weakening the landowning class.
    (D) Native Americans and those of African descent gained entry into the workforce.

3. Which of the following statements about the United States and the League of Nations is accurate?
    (A) Americans embraced the League of Nations as a global effort to prevent terrorism.
    (B) The League of Nations provided a forum for African-Americans to address inequality.
    (C) Woodrow Wilson proposed the establishment of the organization as a way to foster peace.
    (D) Congress supported U.S. membership in the League of Nations in order to maintain links with European nations.

4. How did the global Depression affect nations in Latin America?
    (A) Revolutions spread throughout the continent as the poor demanded a redistribution of wealth.
    (B) Democracy spread and citizens demanded a greater voice in government.
    (C) Exports fell, and unemployment and homelessness increased.
    (D) The cost of goods dropped dramatically, giving consumers a higher standard of living.

5. How did World War II affect the civilian population in the United States after the beginning of U.S. involvement?
    (A) It opened up job opportunities for African-Americans, Latinos, and women.
    (B) It corresponded with major civil rights legislation and the legal integration of public facilities.
    (C) It impoverished large segments of the nation since jobs and money were scarce.
    (D) It started an aggressive antiwar movement that called for the withdrawal of troops from Europe.

6. How did Eva Péron influence politics in Argentina?
   (A) She took over as president after the death of her husband.
   (B) She persuaded her husband to provide social benefits for women, children, and the poor.
   (C) She pushed for protection of the elite and encouraged foreign investment.
   (D) She called for a Marxist redistribution of wealth and nationalization of major industries.

7. What was the result of the 1961 Bay of Pigs invasion in Cuba?
   (A) Fidel Castro was successfully overthrown by the CIA-sponsored coup, and communism was contained in Cuba.
   (B) The invasion failed, therefore boosting Castro's reputation.
   (C) The invasion ended in a stalemate, and Cuba was split between communists in the north and noncommunists in the south.
   (D) The invasion caused Latin American nations to boycott products from Cuba.

8. How did the United States respond to the economic reform policies of Guatemalan president Jacobo Arbenz Guzmán?
   (A) It supported Arbenz because he was democratically elected.
   (B) It implemented a trade embargo, forcing Arbenz to alter his policies.
   (C) It viewed him as a communist, and sponsored a coup to remove him from power.
   (D) It encouraged American businesses to leave Guatemala.

9. Which of the following is an accurate comparison of the dictatorships of Brazil, Chile, and Argentina during the 1970s and 1980s?
   (A) They were supported by the Soviet Union.
   (B) They promoted policies of corruption, torture, and violence.
   (C) Their economies flourished under military rule.
   (D) All expelled foreign-owned companies and implemented state control over the economy.

10. Which of the following statements is true regarding the North American Free Trade Agreement (NAFTA)?
    (A) It violated international monetary rules and was shut down.
    (B) It created a free trade zone by eliminating tariffs among the United States, Canada, and Mexico.
    (C) It allowed consumers to transport products anywhere within the United States, Canada, and Mexico.
    (D) It served as a model for the European Union and NATO.

11. How did the Mexican Revolution of 1910 compare to the independence movement in India?
    (A) For both, the greatest changes were achieved nonviolently.
    (B) For both, religious diversity created divisions.
    (C) For both, freedom from European imperialism motivated change.
    (D) Mexican revolutionaries had a more fragmented set of goals and leadership.

12. All of the following resulted from reforms that the Mexican Revolutionary Party of Lázaro Cárdenas instituted EXCEPT
(A) confiscation of property of foreign oil companies.
(B) redistribution of land to poor peasants.
(C) reduction of Catholic Church influence in education.
(D) decentralization of politics in the provinces.

13. Which of the following is correct about the Cuban Revolution of 1959?
(A) The Cuban Revolution was led by workers and students.
(B) The Cuban Revolution overthrew a democratically elected government.
(C) The Cuban Revolution had the support of major business interests.
(D) The Cuban Revolution was undermined by a successful counter-revolution.

14. Which of the following conflicts in the Americas during and after the Cold War had the most influence on politics throughout the Americas?
(A) Chile and Argentina
(B) Haiti and the Dominican Republic
(C) Cuba and the United States
(D) The United States and Mexico

15. In which of the following aspects are the Americas most unified when compared to Asia, Africa, and Europe?
(A) Ethnic identity
(B) Socio-economic status
(C) Religion
(D) Gender roles

Free-Response Questions

1. Compare the nature of the Mexican Revolution in the early twentieth century with that of the Cuban Revolution in the 1950s and 1960s.

2. Analyze the political continuities and changes experienced in ONE of the following nations from World War I to the end of World War II.
   ■ Argentina
   ■ Brazil
   ■ Mexico

Answers

MULTIPLE-CHOICE QUESTIONS

1. ANSWER: A. For the first three years of the war, the United States remained neutral. When it finally entered the war, the Allies and

the Central Powers were in a stalemate, and their soldiers were fatigued and demoralized. U.S. soldiers were fresh and invigorated, and it was their presence that turned the tide in favor of the Allies (*The Earth and Its Peoples*, 5th ed., pp. 807–808/6th ed., p. 759).

2. ANSWER: **C.** The outbreak of war in 1914 caused European nations to halt their imports in order to focus on war production. However, Brazil and Argentina depended on the export of crops. The disruption of this trade so drastically affected their economies that it weakened the landowning class, who lost money and power from the lack of exports. The middle class in both Argentina and Brazil used this opportunity to push for voting rights and a greater say within society (*The Earth and Its Peoples*, 5th ed., pp. 874–875/6th ed., p. 797).

3. ANSWER: **C.** Woodrow Wilson proposed the establishment of a League of Nations, a global organization of nations around the world that would maintain peace and foster international cooperation. Although the League was established, the Senate refused to let the United States join (*The Earth and Its Peoples*, 5th ed., pp. 808–809/6th ed., p. 762).

4. ANSWER: **C.** Most Latin American nations depended on exports. Sugar was the main export from Cuba, coffee from Brazil and Colombia, tin from Bolivia, and beef from Argentina. The Depression caused the industrial nations to curb imports. Latin Americans were thus hit hard. In many cases the Depression prompted military coups and takeovers (*The Earth and Its Peoples*, 5th ed., pp. 838–839/6th ed., p. 798).

5. ANSWER: **A.** The war loosened racial and gender constraints as employers, needing workers, were more willing to hire minorities and women. It also caused increased demand by these groups for full equality and justice within society (*The Earth and Its Peoples*, 5th ed., pp. 852–854/6th ed., p. 828).

6. ANSWER: **B.** A charismatic actress, Eva Duarte Péron was adored by many Argentineans. She attracted the support of many commoners and inspired her husband, Juan Péron, to appeal to urban workers and to establish social reforms for women, children, and the poor (*The Earth and Its Peoples*, 5th ed., pp. 876–877/6th ed., p. 799).

7. ANSWER: **B.** The Bay of Pigs was the CIA's attempt to emulate its earlier success in Guatemala. More than fifteen hundred Cuban exiles, trained and armed by the CIA, were defeated by the Cuban army. The failed invasion not only tarnished the reputation of the United States but also bolstered Castro's image. To prevent another invasion, Castro invited the Soviet Union to install missiles in Cuba, which precipitated the Cuban missile crisis (*The Earth and Its Peoples*, 5th ed., p. 904/6th ed., p. 856).

8. ANSWER: **C.** When Arbenz came to power, he confronted the powerful United Fruit Company, an American corporation that controlled much of Guatemala's infrastructure. He attempted land

reform that would have transferred the company's uncultivated land to the rural poor. The United States feared that Arbenz was turning to communism. Thus the CIA sponsored a military coup in 1954 that removed Arbenz from power, one of the CIA's first major overseas operations (*The Earth and Its Peoples,* 5th ed., pp. 900–901/6th ed., p. 853).

9. ANSWER: **B.** Brazil, Chile, and Argentina had military dictatorships that promoted industrialization while implementing methods of violent repression of its citizenry. All three dictatorships came to an end between 1983 and 1990, undermined by credible reports of kidnappings, tortures and corruption (*The Earth and Its Peoples,* 5th ed., pp. 918–919/6th ed., p. 868–869).

10. ANSWER: **B.** NAFTA was established in 1994 to promote economic growth in the neighboring countries of Canada, Mexico, and the United States. It basically eliminated tariffs among these nations so as to encourage trade. While it was modeled after the European Union (EU), it created the world's largest free trade zone (*The Earth and Its Peoples,* 5th ed., pp. 948–950/6th ed., p. 889).

11. ANSWER: **D.** The Mexican Revolution against the conservative and elite Mexican government was primarily a social movement, not a movement of independence. Many leaders emerged with different agendas in Mexico, but most of the issues were related to the huge social divisions that fragmented Mexican society (*The Earth and Its Peoples,* 5th ed., p. 817/6th ed., p. 712).

12. ANSWER: **D.** The Mexican Revolutionary Party pursued many of the goals that the original Mexican Revolution of 1934 desired. It reduced the influence of the Catholic Church, landowners, and both foreign and domestic companies (*The Earth and Its Peoples,* 5th ed., pp. 872–873/6th ed., p. 797).

13. ANSWER: **A.** Fidel Castro and other Cuban revolutionaries drew their support from a number of groups that opposed the corruption and elitism of the previous government. Most important was the support from students and workers (*The Earth and Its Peoples,* 5th ed., p. 901/6th ed., p. 839).

14. ANSWER: **C.** The Cold War tension resulting from U.S. policies after the Cuban Revolution had wide-ranging influences in other Latin American countries. Conservative, anti-Communist governments throughout the region could expect support from the United States (*The Earth and Its Peoples,* 5th ed., pp. 915–917/6th ed., p. 848).

15. ANSWER: **C.** The majority religion of every country in the Western Hemisphere is Christianity. Although many other religious faiths are worshiped in the Americas, Asia, Africa, and Europe are much more religiously diverse (*The Earth and Its Peoples,* 5th ed., p. 960/6th ed., p. 912).

FREE-RESPONSE QUESTIONS

1. Despite the difference in time period, both revolutions were responses to two fundamental issues that plagued nations in the Americas during the twentieth century: foreign economic

domination and social inequality. Mexicans were dismayed by the fact that the largest industries in Mexico, such as oil, mining, and transportation, were controlled by companies from the United States and other foreign nations. Similarly, Cuba's largest industries, sugar production, banking, and transportation, were controlled by Americans. Thus in both Mexico and Cuba, wealth was being accumulated and held by foreigners and the small domestic elite. The vast majority of people in both Mexico and Cuba were poor. The Mexican Revolution was more gradual and experienced a period of very moderate progress. In Cuba, on the other hand, Fidel Castro succeeded in transferring 15 percent of the national income from the rich to the poor in the first year. While both nations witnessed drastic social transformations, Cuba faced harsh and consistent pressure from the United States to alter the effects of the Revolution.

2. All three nations began the twentieth century as politically independent states that were economically influenced by the industrialized nations of Europe and North America. The Depression caused all three nations to turn to state intervention and import-substitution industrialization. However, Mexico accomplished wide-ranging social changes that allowed more people to participate in politics, gain free education, earn higher wages, and even gain land through the program of land redistribution to peasants. Argentina and Brazil fell under military rule that largely maintained the interests of wealthy landowners and thus did not alter the social inequalities within their nations.

Part III

Practice Tests

Practice Test 1
AP WORLD HISTORY EXAMINATION
Section I: Multiple-Choice Questions
Time—55 minutes
Number of questions—70

DIRECTIONS Each of the questions or incomplete statements below is followed by four suggested answers or completions. For each question, select the best response.

NOTE This examination uses the chronological designations B.C.E. (before the Common Era) and C.E. (Common Era). These correspond to B.C. (before Christ) and A.D. (anno Domini), which are used in some world history textbooks.

1. The successful construction of large-scale monuments in early civilizations such as the Nile or the Indus River Valley civilizations can best be attributed to
    (A) superior metal tools that facilitated such construction.
    (B) a large labor force directly controlled by the ruler made possible because of increased agricultural efficiency.
    (C) rapid advancements in building technology and machines by knowledgeable engineers.
    (D) assimilation of earlier building techniques that were far more advanced.

2. Which of the following statements best compares the nature of early societies in the Eastern Hemisphere with those of the Western Hemisphere?
    (A) The shift from foraging to agriculture did not occur in the Western Hemisphere until Europeans introduced technological advancements such as the wheel and the plow.
    (B) Different geographical circumstances of the two hemispheres resulted in distinct patterns of development in each, although political and social similarities did exist.
    (C) Early societies in the Americas lacked clear political structure and specialization of labor because, unlike their counterparts in the Eastern Hemisphere, they did not domesticate animals.

(D) Societies in the two hemispheres had similar technological advancements and agricultural techniques because the Western Hemisphere was populated by migrants from Asia.

3. The Neolithic age is characterized by
    (A) the origins of agriculture.
    (B) the development of pastoralism.
    (C) the use of fire to prepare food.
    (D) the use of clay pots.

4. What was the impact of the rise of civilization in Egypt and Mesopotamia?
    (A) Outsiders adopted the language, religion, and lifestyle of each civilization, thus helping to sustain them.
    (B) Women in Egypt and Mesopotamia earned a higher degree of respect and equality.
    (C) Population increased in Egypt and Mesopotamia, which strained the food supply and forced people back into hunting and gathering.
    (D) Technological advancements enabled Egyptians and Mesopotamians to control and harness the flood patterns of their rivers and overcome nature completely.

GO ON TO NEXT PAGE

5. The Olmec society of Mesoamerica and the Chavín civilization of the Andes are similar in that they both
   (A) dominated their neighbors with their strong militaries and subjected conquered people to oppressive rule.
   (B) declined because of violent wars with rivals and the subsequent political and economic disruption.
   (C) influenced their neighbors and subsequent societies of the Americas in terms of their cultural and economic characteristics.
   (D) competed with each other for control of strategic resources.

6. Which of the following explains why the Roman Republic failed?
   (A) Landless farmers switched their allegiance from army commanders to the state, thus eroding the strength of the military.
   (B) The republic outlawed slave labor, which dramatically slowed construction and development.
   (C) The number of peasant farmers declined, causing a shortage of men who owned the necessary property required for military service.
   (D) Large estates were divided among peasants, which decreased the overall wealth of Rome and undermined incentive and entrepreneurship.

7. The collapse of both the Roman Empire and the Han dynasty can be attributed to
   (A) a combination of external pressures and internal conflict.
   (B) economic ruin brought on by environmental factors, including drought.
   (C) political instability caused by the rise in popularity of rival groups within society.
   (D) the expansion of the Mongols from their homeland in Central Asia.

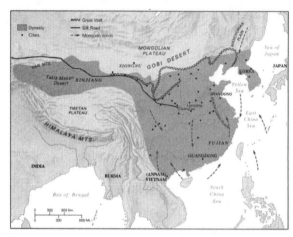

Cengage Learning

8. Which Chinese dynasty is represented in the map above?
   (A) Shang
   (B) Qin
   (C) Han
   (D) Song

9. Which of the following is a characteristic of the Mandate of Heaven?
   (A) The monarch was considered the "Son of God."
   (B) Failure to abide by Confucian tenets legitimized changes in monarchs.
   (C) Corruption, violence, and arrogance were viewed as signs of divine pleasure.
   (D) Rulers were expected to govern as wise and principled guardians of the people.

10. Which of the following is true of the relationship between the Greek city-states of Athens and Sparta?
    (A) Athens and Sparta battled each other for survival during the Peloponnesian War.
    (B) Both Athenian and Spartan foreign policies were cautious and isolationist, and they tried to maintain peace through a system of alliances with their neighbors.
    (C) Both Athens and Sparta implemented limited democracies in which the upper classes participated in an assembly.
    (D) Both the Athenian and Spartan armies were constantly ready and superior to all others in the region.

11. The society of the Persian Empire
    (A) lacked a clear social structure.
    (B) was patriarchal in nature.
    (C) placed little value on warriors and the military.
    (D) was centralized and homogenous.

12. In the sixteenth century, which region of the world experienced the greatest amount of demographic and environmental change?
    (A) The Middle East
    (B) West Africa
    (C) North America
    (D) The Caribbean

Archaeology has uncovered traces of copper mining in the Sahara from the early first millennium B.C.E. Copper appears in the Niger Valley somewhat later and in the Central African copper belt after 400 C.E. Most important of all, iron smelting began in northern sub-Saharan Africa in the early first millennium C.E. and spread southward from there. (Bulliet et al., 6th ed., p. 236)

13. The most readily available and versatile metal in West Africa from 600 to 1450 was
    (A) bronze.
    (B) silver.
    (C) copper.
    (D) iron.

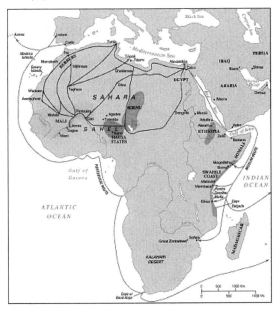

Cengage Learning

Use the map above to answer questions 14 and 15

14. The map above shows that between 600 and 1450, trade networks primarily linked sub-Saharan Africa with
    (A) the Islamic world.
    (B) Mesoamerica.
    (C) the Ming Empire.
    (D) the Tokugawa Shogunate.

15. Which of the following languages is a direct result of the interactions of the peoples of the Indian Ocean trade network?
    (A) Swahili
    (B) Persian
    (C) Hindi
    (D) Arabic

16. Which statement best describes the economic and political conditions in the early Middle East of circa 1000 B.C.E.?
    (A) Strong diplomatic and commercial relations between states resulted in the flow of goods and ideas.
    (B) Economic contacts were strained because of constant warfare among the states in the region.
    (C) The region benefited from the relative peace within the long-lasting Assyrian Empire, and goods and ideas flowed freely.
    (D) There was little economic interaction among the wandering hunter-gatherers of the region.

17. In comparison to developing civilizations in the Western Hemisphere, the challenging environment of the Americas most uniquely impacted pre-Columbian civilizations in the following way:
    (A) purposefully restricting long-distance trade and requiring all pre-Columbian civilizations to be entirely self-sufficient.
    (B) requiring the development of unique labor systems such as slavery that allowed for all the hard work required to meet basic needs in challenging environments.
    (C) requiring the movement of water for irrigation through dikes and canals.
    (D) requiring the development of agricultural techniques that could withstand both tropical weather and dry seasons.

GO ON TO NEXT PAGE

18. The collapse of which of the following empires led to the economic dominance of the Indian Ocean trade network in the thirteenth century?
    (A) Mali
    (B) Delhi Sultanate
    (C) Mongol
    (D) Ming

I forbade the infliction of any severe punishment on the Hindus in general, but I destroyed their idol temples, and instead thereof raised mosques. ("The Deeds of Sultan Firuz Shah." Overfield, 7th ed. p., 247)

19. The Delhi Sultanate had a tense relationship with most people of India because
    (A) the Delhi Sultanate was ethnically tied to the Mongol Empire, which was already a threat to Indian sovereignty.
    (B) the Baghdad caliph refused to acknowledge the Delhi Sultanate as an official Muslim state.
    (C) the Delhi Sultanate successfully conquered the Hindu princes of southern India, and the sultanate was resented for that.
    (D) the rulers of the Delhi Sultanate were not indigenous to the region and were Muslim rather than Hindu.

20. Which of the following is a characteristic of the Tang Empire?
    (A) The banning of Buddhism as a popular religion
    (B) The rejection of trade along the Silk Road
    (C) The creation of a strong tributary system within the greater region
    (D) The rejection of Central Asian cultural practices

21. Which of the following was a major reason for the initial spread of Islam in East Africa and Asia?
    (A) Missionary efforts by merchants and traders
    (B) Forced intermarriage between local women and Muslim men who traveled the trade routes
    (C) Forced conversion that required subject peoples to adopt Islam immediately
    (D) The strict social hierarchies of Islam

22. The mamluks were originally Turkic slaves who
    (A) were put in power by the Ottoman Empire after they defeated the Abbasid Caliphate.
    (B) ruled in Egypt until they were decapitated en masse by the Mongols.
    (C) came to power in Egypt and Syria after working as mercenaries under the Abbasid Caliphate.
    (D) were forced to work for the Byzantine Empire until their defeat by the Ottomans.

23. Which of the following is a similarity between Christianity and Buddhism?
    (A) Early practitioners of both religions placed importance on the existence of a god.
    (B) Followers of both religions predominantly came from the privileged classes.
    (C) Both are based on a set of actions and rituals that include feasting.
    (D) Both were founded by an individual and based on his teachings.

24. During the period 1000–1200, western Europe experienced an economic revival as a result of
    (A) population decline caused by plague outbreaks, which opened up more job opportunities.
    (B) increased political unity under the pope, which allowed for safer flow of long-distance trade.
    (C) new technologies and an increase in autonomous cities that focused on maritime trade.
    (D) the destruction of the Byzantine Empire, which increased the economic strength of western Europe.

25. Which of the following statements is an accurate comparison of Christian women and Islamic women during the early medieval period, circa 1000 C.E.?
(A) Both Islamic women and Christian women could own land.
(B) Both Islamic women and Christian women could choose their husbands.
(C) Islamic women could travel freely and engage in business, while Christian women could not.
(D) Christian women never wore the veil, while Muslim women always did.

He, who has dominion in the kingdom of humanity and who will give it to whom He might wish, has transferred the empire of Constantinople from the proud to the humble, from the disobedient to the obedient, from schismatics to Catholics, namely from the Greeks to the Latins. (Pope Innocent III, Letters to the Crusaders. Overfield, 7th ed., p. 334)

26. According to the passage above, the Eastern and Western Churches of Europe competed
(A) for the loyalty of the kings and dukes of western Europe.
(B) for political and religious influence over Jerusalem, Antioch, and other Christian centers.
(C) over the right of the Byzantine emperor to control the pope.
(D) to convert Slavic peoples such as the Russians and Poles.

27. The Aztec and Mongol Empires were similar because both empires
(A) relied on tribute to provide a substantial portion of daily food.
(B) were of similar size.
(C) were defeated by Europeans.
(D) originated with peoples who were nomadic.

28. The Ottoman Empire's most significant, long-standing rival for power in Central Asia was
(A) the Byzantine Empire.
(B) the Mongol Il-khanate.
(C) the Mughal Empire.
(D) Russia.

29. What was one important impact of European contact on the economy of West Africa between 1450 and 1750?
(A) It brought about a shift to large-scale plantation-style farming.
(B) It destroyed the indigenous production of textiles and metalwork.
(C) It brought Africa out of its former isolation from long-distance trading networks.
(D) It allowed some indigenous African merchants to gain great wealth from trade.

30. In the period 1450–1750, the Islamic world's African slave trade was most similar to Europe's African slave trade in that both
(A) preferred male slaves to female slaves.
(B) avoided taking slaves who had not reached adulthood.
(C) needed slaves mainly for agricultural labor.
(D) had no significant religious prohibitions against trading or owning slaves.

31. The Ottoman Empire was formed primarily through
(A) conquests by a military that combined tradition with innovation and new technology.
(B) Timur's capture of the key trading center of Constantinople.
(C) its leaders' understanding of the importance of establishing a large and powerful naval presence in the Atlantic and Indian Oceans.
(D) the use of serf labor to cultivate lucrative cash crops for export.

GO ON TO NEXT PAGE

32. Religion in Amerindian society provided continuity despite major changes that resulted from the Columbian Exchange in that it
    (A) continued to represent the earliest forms of monotheism.
    (B) the entire hemisphere worshiped the same deities which tied the culture of the region so closely that Christianity had a hard time finding converts.
    (C) continued to focus exclusively on animal sacrifice to atone for human sins.
    (D) continued in helping rulers cement political authority and was a communal activity.

Akbar was the most illustrious sultan of the Mughal Empire in India. He expanded the empire and pursued a policy of conciliation with Hindus. (Bulliet, et al., 6th ed., p. 536)

33. Which of the following is true of the Mughal ruler Akbar?
    (A) He built the Taj Mahal.
    (B) He banned the sale of Indian textiles to Europe.
    (C) He ended the forced conversion of Hindu prisoners to Islam.
    (D) He formed the powerful trade alliance with the Ottomans and Hindus known as the Silk Road.

34. What was one factor in the reduction in European birthrates in the sixteenth and seventeenth centuries?
    (A) New Protestant churches allowed the practice of birth-control techniques.
    (B) Large numbers of young European women were migrating to the Americas during this period.
    (C) Young males often delayed marriage in order to save money or complete their education.
    (D) The Little Ice Age led to widespread famine, which caused decreased fertility among young adults.

It is said the Indians are being worked to death cultivating fields for their caciques and principales and enriching these lords, but those who say this are mistaken. Neither drunkenness nor their well-organized communal labor is killing them off. The cause is their labor on Spanish public works and their personal service to the Spaniards, which they fulfill in a manner contrary to their own ways and tempo of work. (Zorita, Overfield, 7th ed., p. 103)

35. As stated above, under the encomienda system
    (A) South American lands were taken from indigenous leaders and combined into large plantations.
    (B) Amerindian peoples were forced to provide Spanish settlers with labor, food, or other goods.
    (C) peasants from Europe were provided passage to the Americas in exchange for several years of unpaid agricultural labor.
    (D) the Spanish king appointed viceroys and other high officials to administer New World territories.

36. Which of the following characteristics was shared by the New World colonial empires of Spain, Portugal, France, and England?
    (A) The enslavement of Amerindian peoples
    (B) Involvement in the commercial activities of the Atlantic
    (C) The isolation of plants and animals from the Eastern Hemisphere
    (D) The establishment of religious and cultural uniformity

Cengage Learning

37. This 1641 Dutch world map would have been MOST offensive to
(A) the Chinese, who viewed China as being at the center of the world.
(B) the Ottomans, whose land holdings were omitted because of Dutch imperial rivalry.
(C) the North American colonists, because their various territories were not demarcated.
(D) the Japanese, who would want Japan more prominently depicted to increase their trade with Europe.

38. From 1450 to 1750, both Africa and the Middle East were influenced by
(A) a colonial takeover by European powers.
(B) migration of peoples from the Americas.
(C) growing European dominance of the global trade network.
(D) conversion to Christianity by a large percentage of their populations.

39. Which of the following comparisons between the Spanish Empire and the Qing Empire is true?
(A) Both were strongly impacted by the spread of Christianity.
(B) Each was governed by a form of monarchy.

(C) Both became strong land-based empires.
(D) Each transformed itself from a land-based to a sea-based empire.

40. Why was the period between 1450 and 1550 such a turning point in European history?
(A) The collapse of the Byzantine Empire led to the division of the Christian church.
(B) European explorers established the first regular contact among the world's continents.
(C) The English defeat of the Spanish Armada signaled the rise of a new imperial power.
(D) The early Enlightenment initiated an era of important political reform in Europe.

41. The Zulu Empire emerged in the early nineteenth century out of a conflict over
(A) water rights in western Africa.
(B) grazing and farming land in southern Africa.
(C) access to trading port cities in eastern Africa.
(D) prisoners of war and the slave trade.

GO ON TO NEXT PAGE

42. What was the most significant difference between the Ming and Qing Empires in China?
    (A) The Ming economy was far more prosperous because of the rapid introduction of New World crops.
    (B) Qing officials' adoption of Christianity displaced the Ming Empire's Neo-Confucian values.
    (C) The Qing economy plunged into depression when the flow of silver from the Americas declined.
    (D) The Ming Empire's indigenous rule was succeeded by a foreign imperial government.

43. In the nineteenth century certain women in China were able to wield political power in
    (A) peasant communities as local officials.
    (B) imperial positions in the civil service.
    (C) aristocratic alliances as powerful leaders.
    (D) urban reform movements allied with Westerners.

And one of the ways of their government is the building of their sovereignty upon three things: the people's persons, their honor, and their possessions; and whomsoever they wish to kill or exile or violate his honor or devour his wealth they do so in pursuit of their lusts, without any right in the *Sharia*. (Usman Dan Fodio, Overfield, 7th ed., p. 220)

44. The most widespread religious reform movement in West Africa during the late eighteenth and nineteenth centuries was based on
    (A) Christianity.
    (B) Islam.
    (C) animism.
    (D) Hinduism.

Use the following excerpt to answer questions 45 and 46.

The continuous counterattacks from the West, the discontent and insurrections in the muslim world, as well as the dissensions between the various elements which this policy had artificially brought together within certain limits, had the ultimate result of burying the Ottoman Empire, in the same way as many others, under the pall of history. (Mustafa Kemal, Overfield, 7th ed., p. 434)

After the Crimean war, the Ottoman Empire increased its involvement with European commerce. Sweeping changes in the 1850's expedited the creation of banks, insurance companies, and legal firms throughout the empire. (Bulliet et al., 6th ed., p. 640)

45. At the end of the nineteenth century, the Ottoman Empire could best be described as
    (A) militarily and economically expanding into North Africa and Arabia.
    (B) technologically innovating and economically modernizing.
    (C) economically in debt and territorially contracting.
    (D) technologically stagnant, but increasingly democratic.

46. In the Ottoman Empire, the most significant demographic shift during the mid- to late nineteenth century was
    (A) the migration of European merchants and diplomats into the Empire.
    (B) the movement of people from rural areas into large cities.
    (C) the movement of people from large cities to rural areas.
    (D) the migration of people out of the empire to the Americas.

Your England is not the only nation trading at Guangzhou. If other nations following your bad example, wrongfully importune my ear with further impossible requests, how will it be possible for me to treat them with easy indulgence? (Zianlong Emperor on trade with England, Overfield, 7th ed., p. 237)

47. In the early nineteenth century, the Chinese viewed Western nations as
    (A) remote and providing few real benefits.
    (B) strong allies in the battle to defeat Japan.
    (C) competitors for imperial possessions in Southeast Asia.
    (D) valued sources of needed technical assistance.

48. The most significant effect of the Franco-Prussian War was
    (A) the division of the Austro-Hungarian Empire.
    (B) the formation of the modern German nation.
    (C) the rise of nationalism in the Ottoman territories.
    (D) the growth of the French Empire.

49. Which of the following is a reason that the environment in the Americas was dramatically altered in the nineteenth century?
    (A) The declining importance of mining
    (B) The acceleration of rural settlements
    (C) The growing use of horses
    (D) The intensification of agriculture

50. Which of the following technological innovations allowed international shipping companies direct communication among Europe, Africa, Asia, and the Americas at the end of the nineteenth century?
    (A) Telephones
    (B) Coal-powered steam ships
    (C) Electrical power lines
    (D) Submarine telegraph cables

Cengage Learning

51. This late nineteenth-century photo is an example of which of the following?
    (A) Chinese interest in European technology
    (B) European interest in Chinese military strategy
    (C) China's alliance with Great Britain
    (D) Ineffectiveness of European technology in Chinese conflicts

It is found that the [proposed literacy test] will bear most heavily upon the Italians, Russians, Poles, Hungarians, Greeks, and Asiatics, and very lightly, or not at all, upon English-speaking emigrants or Germans, Scandinavians, and French. (Henry Cabot Lodge, Speech to the US senate, Overfield, 7th ed., p. 275)

52. Immigrants to the Americas in the mid- and late nineteenth century came primarily from
    (A) East Asia and southern and eastern Europe.
    (B) Southeast Asia and West Africa.
    (C) East Africa and East Asia.
    (D) southern Africa and Southeast Asia.

53. Migratory labor in colonial southern Africa
    (A) damaged family life and depleted rural areas, as men left to work in cities.
    (B) resulted in increased wealth and knowledge for African families.
    (C) improved public health, as more Africans had access to modern health care.
    (D) caused Africans to abandon the cities in order to produce food for the nation and their families.

54. The most influential political idea in nineteenth-century Europe was
    (A) utopian socialism.
    (B) Social Darwinism.
    (C) nationalism.
    (D) democracy.

GO ON TO NEXT PAGE

55. Which of the following is an example of unification based on the growing concept of nationalism in the nineteenth century?
    (A) France
    (B) Italy
    (C) Great Britain
    (D) The Ottoman Empire

56. The growth of cities in the nineteenth century can be directly attributed to
    (A) the increase in tourism and pilgrimage.
    (B) large-scale migration to North and South America.
    (C) land erosion in rural communities.
    (D) the increase in railroad links.

57. Which of the following statements are true about multinational organizations such as the Organization of Petroleum Exporting Countries (OPEC)?
    (A) They were developed to promote the collective economic interests of nations who exported a common commodity such as oil.
    (B) They resulted in a massive transfer of wealth to nations that produced specific commodities.
    C) In general they were organized as an economic response to NATO and the Warsaw Pact.
    (D) The massive concentration of wealth resulting from these multinational organizations resulted in a new economic power.

Passive resistance is a method of securing rights by personal suffering; it is the reverse of resistance by arms. When I refuse to do a thing that is repugnant to my conscience, I use soul-force. (Mohandas Ghandi, Indian Home Rule, Overfield, 7th ed., p. 446)

58. Which of the following reflects Mohandas Gandhi's political philosophy?
    (A) It was based on nonviolence and was adopted from Dr. Martin Luther King, Jr.
    (B) It excluded the lower castes and the Untouchables.
    (C) It often called for nationwide fasting that led to numerous deaths.
    (D) It combined Hindu and Christian concepts of nonviolence.

59. Which of the following statements are true about terrorism during the latter half of the twentieth century?
    (A) It was not easy to combat, and thus generated fear.
    (B) The bombings in the British Isles by the Irish Republican Army and the release of nerve gas in the Tokyo subway system were terrorist efforts used to advance political means.
    (C) Terrorism became a globally popular way of deploying violence for political ends.
    (D) It was a weapon used exclusively by Arab extremists dedicated to the destruction of Israel.

European Economic Community: An organization promoting economic unity in Europe, formed in 1957 by consolidation of earlier, more limited, agreements. (Bulliet et al., 6th ed., p. 843)

60. In what ways did the economic roles of western European nations change after World War II?
(A) Governments established cooperative economic policies that encouraged the movement of goods and capital across national borders.
(B) Laissez-faire policies that reduced government involvement in various economic arenas were adopted.
(C) Nations established command economies in hope of emulating the success of Soviet industries.
(D) Western European nations agreed to submit to U.S. economic demands and be incorporated within the American market.

61. Which of the following best describes the contribution of technology to the process of global interaction in late twentieth and early twenty-first centuries?
(A) It has stagnated the process of interaction because few people outside of the United States and western Europe have been able to afford technological innovations.
(B) It has displaced local culture, crushed cultural diversity, and created a world based on the United States.
(C) As technology has become more widespread, distant cultural influences and ideas have spread rapidly and become integrated with local traditions.
(D) U.S. films have spread around the world, but international films have not had an influence in the United States.

62. Which of the following statements is true regarding the Universal Declaration of Human Rights passed in 1948?
(A) It was an agreement established by the Allied victors of World War II and was forced upon unwilling nations around the world.
(B) Passed by the United Nations General Assembly in 1948, it reflected a growing acceptance of the importance of social and economic equality.
(C) It has gone unchallenged and serves as an example of universal consensus.
(D) Its ideas have been followed more by Asian countries than western European countries.

63. The most important struggle in Latin America during the first half of the twentieth century can best be described as
(A) a battle over capitalism versus communism.
(B) a debate over whether to colonize the nations in the Pacific.
(C) an effort to become global powers similar to western European nations and the United States.
(D) a quest for economic independence from European and U.S. control.

64. Which of the following statements best describes the situation in the Belgian Congo upon independence?
(A) Belgium and all other foreign powers refrained from intervening in order to allow the Congolese to determine their own future.
(B) The Belgian Congo united with the French Congo to form the United Republic of Congo and made French the official language.
(C) Civil war erupted as the Congo became a proxy war during the Cold War.
(D) The Congo became a communist nation, and all major industries were immediately nationalized.

GO ON TO NEXT PAGE

65. Which of the following represented an action pursued by the Ottoman Turks during World War I?
    (A) The Ottomans closed the Dardanelles Straits, hoping to frustrate their German adversaries.
    (B) The Ottomans joined the British in attacking Germany and the Austro-Hungarian Empire.
    (C) The Ottomans formed a secret alliance with Germany, hoping to gain land at Russia's expense.
    (D) The Ottomans hired a British general to help modernize their troops.

Enormous changes taking place in our society make it both possible and urgently necessary to advance the unfinished revolution of women toward true equality now. (National Organization for Women Statement of Purpose, 1966. Overfield, 7th ed., p. 500)

In 1979 the United Nations General Assembly adopted the Convention on the Elimination of All Forms of Discrimination Against Women, and in 1985, the first international conference on the status of women was held in Nairobi, Kenya. (Bulliet et. al., 6th ed., p. 915)

66. From the excerpts above, it is evident that one of the purposes for the first international conference on women's rights was
    (A) to push men to view women as equal partners in shaping societies, and to recognize that different societies cannot always agree on what eliminating discrimination might entail.
    (B) to pressure governments to grant women reproductive rights.
    (C) to fight for equal access to education.
    (D) to demonstrate for voting rights.

67. Economic growth in Japan during the 1970s and 1980s was largely related to which of the following?
    (A) An expansion of the military, which gave Japan the ability to colonize new territories and gain valuable resources.
    (B) An industrial economy in which major companies received government assistance in the form of tariffs and import regulations that inhibited foreign competition.
    (C) A free market economy with few trade barriers, which allowed full economic competition.
    (D) Recall of post–World War II loans given to Western European nations, including Great Britain, France, and Germany.

It is sometimes asked whether it is not possible to slow down the tempo a bit, to put a check on the movement. No, comrades, it is not possible! The tempo must not be reduced! On the contrary, we must increase it as much as is within our powers and possibilities. This is dictated to us by our obligations to the workers and peasants of the U.S.S.R. This is dictated to us by our obligations to the working class of the whole world. (Joseph Stalin, 1931 speech delivered to a conference of industrial managers. Overfield, 7th ed., p. 396)

68. How did the Soviet Union change under Stalin?
    (A) It witnessed rapid industrialization, but many people suffered under Stalin's brutal methods.
    (B) The nation failed to industrialize and so remained poor and destitute.
    (C) It reverted to pre–World War I conditions, with widespread serfdom and leadership under the tsar.
    (D) Civil war expanded, and the nation eventually split into two countries.

69. Which of the following statements is an accurate comparison of Brazil and Argentina during the twentieth-century interwar years?
    (A) Both Brazil and Argentina failed to industrialize because the elite refused to allow the involvement of foreign companies in their nations, thus remaining isolated economically.
    (B) The Depression hardly affected Brazil and Argentina because both imposed high import duties to protect their infant industries from foreign competition.
    (C) Both Brazil and Argentina were semi-industrial but dependent on the technology of European and U.S. companies; thus, both were dramatically affected by the global depression.
    (D) Both Argentina and Brazil veered toward authoritarian regimes that imposed strict economic policies that favored the USSR, thus creating a resilient economy.

70. In the twentieth century, women's rights activists complained that
    (A) women were locked out of the workforce.
    (B) women were given menial jobs.
    (C) women were treated disrespectfully.
    (D) women were paid poorly for the work they performed.

**STOP
END OF SECTION I**

IF YOU FINISH BEFORE TIME IS CALLED, YOU MAY CHECK YOUR WORK ON THIS SECTION. DO NOT GO ON TO SECTION II UNTIL YOU ARE TOLD TO DO SO.

Section II: Free-Response Essays

NOTE This exam uses the chronological designations B.C.E. (before the Common Era) and C.E. (Common Era). These labels correspond to B.C. (before Christ) and A.D. (anno Domini), which are used in some world history textbooks.

Part A: Document-Based Question (DBQ)
Suggested writing time—40 minutes
Percent of Section II score—33⅓

DIRECTIONS The following question is based on the accompanying Documents 1–7. The documents have been edited for the purpose of this exercise. Write your answer on the lined pages of the Section II free-response booklet.

This question is designed to test your ability to work with and understand historical documents.

Write an essay that

- Has a relevant thesis and supports that thesis with evidence from the documents.

- Uses all of the documents.

- Analyzes the documents by grouping them in as many appropriate ways as possible. Does not simply summarize the documents individually.

- Takes into account the sources of the documents and analyzes the authors' points of view.

- Identifies and explains the need for at least one additional type of document.

You may refer to relevant historical information not mentioned in the documents.

1. Using the following documents, analyze the roles of class and gender in China before 1450 C.E.

Historical Background: Although many different dynasties controlled China during this time, Confucianism, Daoism and Buddhism provided cultural unity.

Document 1

Source: Liu Hsiang, "Biographies of Admirable Women," account of the life of the mother of Confucian philosopher Mencius written three centuries after she lived, 33 B.C.E.   ◦

A woman's duties are to cook the five grains, heat the wine, look after her parents-in-law, make clothes, and that is all! She has no ambition to manage affairs outside the house. She must follow the "three submissions." When she is young, she must submit to her parents. After her marriage, she must submit to her husband. When she is widowed, she must submit to her son.

Document 2

Source: stone rubbing of a horse-drawn carriage, first century B.C.E.

Cengage Learning

Document 3

Source: Ban Zhao, female Chinese scholar, advisor on state matters to Empress Deng, and imperial historian, 106 C.E.

On the third day after the birth of a girl the ancients observed three customs: first to place the baby below the bed; second to give her a potsherd with which to play; third to announce her birth to her ancestors by an offering. Now to lay the baby below the bed plainly indicated that she is lowly and weak, and should regard it as her primary duty to humble herself before others. To give her potsherds with which to play indubitably signified that she should practice labor and consider it her primary duty to be industrious. To announce her birth before her ancestors clearly means that she ought to esteem as her primary duty the continuation of the observance of worship in the home.

Document 4

Source: Shi Baochang, Lives of the Nuns, a biography of a Buddhist nun, 516 C.E.

Xu Chong returned home and permitted his daughter to become a nun. Lingshou thereupon cut off her hair, discarded secular ornaments, and received the rules of monastic life from Fotudeng and nun Jingjian. She established Foundling of Wisdom Convent, and Fotudeng presented her with a cut-flower embroidered vestment, a seven-strip monastic robe, and an elephant-trunk-shaped water ewer. In the religious communities of that time there was no one who did not honor her. The Emperor honored her and promoted her father to the official court position of undersecretary of the Yellow Gate and administrator of the Qinghe Commandery.

GO ON TO NEXT PAGE

Document 5

Source: Chinese legal code, seventh century.

The king occupies the most honorable position and receives Heaven's precious decrees. Like Heaven and Earth, he acts to shelter and support, thus serving as the father and mother of the masses. As his children, as his subjects, they must be loyal and filial. Should they dare to cherish wickedness and have rebellious hearts, however, they will run counter to Heaven's constancy and violate human principle. Therefore, this is called plotting rebellion.

Document 6

Source: Extract from a scholar's account of the day-to-day realities of country life, late eighth century.

When a farmer falls on bad times, he has to sell his field and his hut. If it is a good year, he might be able to pay his debts by selling out. But no sooner will the harvest be in than his storage bins will be empty again, and he will have to try and contract a new debt promising his labor for the next year. Each time he indentures himself he incurs higher interest rates, and soon will be destitute again.

If it is a bad year, and there is a famine, then the situation is hopeless. Families break up, parents separate, and all try to sell themselves into slavery. But in a bad year nobody will buy them....

The gentry however, live off their rents, with no troubles and no cares. Wealth and poverty are very clearly divided.

Document 7

Source: Odoric of Pordenone, a Roman Catholic missionary working in China, report of travels, 1330.

When the lord Khan is seated on his imperial throne, the empress resides on his left, and one step below sit two of the other wives whom he keeps. At the bottom of the stairs are all the other women of his family. All of the women who are married have on their heads something shaped like a human foot, which is a good forearm and a half long. On the lower portion of the so-called foot are crane's feathers fashioned into a peak, and the entire "foot" is ornamented with great pearls. Whatever large and beautiful pearls there are in the world, they are to be found on the decorations of those ladies.

End of Part A

Part B: Continuity and Change over Time Essay
Suggested planning and writing time—40 minutes
Percent of Section II score—33 ⅓

DIRECTIONS You are to answer the following question. You should spend 5 minutes organizing or outlining your essay.

Write an essay that

- ▨ has a relevant thesis and supports that thesis with appropriate historical evidence.
- ▨ addresses all parts of the question.
- ▨ uses world historical context to show continuities and changes over time.
- ▨ analyzes the process of continuity and change over time.

2. Analyze the continuities and changes in the Islamic world between 622 and 1750.

End of Part B

GO ON TO NEXT PAGE

Part C: Comparative Essay
Suggested planning and writing time—40 minutes
Percent of Section II score—33 ⅓

DIRECTIONS You are to answer the following question. You should spend 5 minutes organizing or outlining your essay.

Write an essay that:

- ▥ has a relevant thesis and supports that thesis with appropriate historical evidence.
- ▥ addresses all parts of the question.
- ▥ makes direct, relevant comparisons.
- ▥ analyzes relevant reasons for similarities and differences.

3. Compare the causes and effects of the French Revolution with one of the following:
   - ▥ Haitian Revolution (1791–1804)
   - ▥ Mexican Movement for Independence (1811–1821)

ANSWERS FOR SECTION I

ANSWER KEY FOR MULTIPLE-CHOICE QUESTIONS

1. B	15. A	29. D	43. C	57. A
2. B	16. A	30. D	44. B	58. D
3. A	17. D	31. A	45. C	59. B
4. A	18. C	32. D	46. B	60. A
5. C	19. D	33. C	47. B	61. C
6. C	20. C	34. C	48. B	62. B
7. A	21. A	35. B	49. D	63. D
8. C	22. C	36. B	50. D	64. C
9. D	23. D	37. A	51. A	65. C
10. A	24. C	38. C	52. A	66. A
11. B	25. A	39. B	53. A	67. B
12. D	26. B	40. B	54. C	68. A
13. D	27. D	41. B	55. B	69. C
14. A	28. D	42. D	56. D	70. D

SCORING   The multiple-choice section counts for 50 percent of your examination grade.

EXPLANATIONS FOR THE MULTIPLE-CHOICE ANSWERS

1. **ANSWER: B.** Monumental architecture in early civilizations was built with stone tools and simple machines like levers, pulleys, and rollers. The success of these projects can be attributed to the large number of people forced into service—probably when no agricultural work could be completed and when the civilization relied on stored grains from the previous harvest (HTS: Comparison, periodization. *The Earth and Its Peoples*, 5th ed., pp. 42–43/6th ed., p. 36).

2. **ANSWER: B.** The geographic characteristics of each hemisphere influenced the nature of early civilizations, though societies in both regions demonstrated political structure, social stratification, specialization of labor, urbanization, monumental building, and technological and artistic development (HTS: Comparison, causation. *The Earth and Its Peoples,* 5th ed., pp. 2–3/6th ed., p. 3).

3. **ANSWER: A.** The Neolithic Age is the New Stone Age and is characterized by the development of agriculture. The Neolithic Revolution is synonymous with the Agricultural Revolution, which describes the domestication of plants and animals and marks a dramatic change in world history (HTS: Periodization, contextualization. *The Earth and Its Peoples*, 5th ed., pp. 19–20/6th ed., p. 8).

4. **ANSWER: A.** Despite great diversity in each civilization, Egypt and Mesopotamia achieved a sense of cultural continuity as outsiders

assimilated to the indigenous society (HTS: Periodization, comparison. *The Earth and Its Peoples*, 5th ed., pp. 53–54/6th ed., p. 29).

5. **ANSWER: C.** Both the Olmec and Chavín exercised cultural influence over a wide area, and their political and social traits would be adopted by their successors (HTS: Comparison, changes and continuity over time. *The Earth and Its Peoples*, 5th ed., pp. 85–87/6th ed., p. 192).

6. **ANSWER: C.** When peasant farmers were away from home on military service, their land was often taken over by investors and consolidated into large estates. As a result fewer men owned the minimum amount of property that was required for military service. In time, these landless peasants switched their allegiance to local army commanders, who promised them land in return for their service (HTS: Changes and continuity over time, periodization. *The Earth and Its Peoples*, 5th ed., pp. 174–175, 176–177/6th ed., pp. 142–143).

7. **ANSWER: A.** Each empire faced the economic and logistical challenges associated with managing a vast territory. Additionally, external pressures by groups on their frontier highlighted the inability to manage the borders (HTS: Comparison, causation. *The Earth and Its Peoples*, 5th ed., p. 201/6th ed., p. 160).

8. **ANSWER: C.** The map shows the farthest extent of the Han dynasty. Its control extended to all of eastern China and many western territories. Walls on the north and northwest frontier were joined together to prevent nomadic people of the steppes from coming into Han China (HTS: Synthesis, argumentation. *The Earth and Its Peoples*, 5th ed., p. 186/6th ed., p. 154).

9. **ANSWER: D.** Legitimacy came from ruling in a just manner and earning the blessing of the chief deity rather than from a reliance on Confucianism (HTS: Contextualization. *The Earth and Its Peoples*, 5th ed., p. 71/6th ed., p. 78).

10. **ANSWER: A.** Sparta and Athens were involved in a long period of war known as the Peloponnesian wars (HTS: Comparison, contextualization. *The Earth and Its Peoples*, 5th ed., p. 149/6th ed., pp. 120–121).

11. **ANSWER: B.** Like most other early civilizations and empires, the Persian Empire was patriarchal. Men led the household and had nearly absolute power over family members (HTS: Periodization, contextualization. *The Earth and Its Peoples*, 5th ed., p. 133/6th ed., p. 108).

12. **ANSWER: D.** The European introduction of plantation farming, along with animals, plants, and peoples from the Eastern Hemisphere, brought drastic changes to the West Indies. Soil exhaustion, deforestation, and extinction of indigenous species (including Amerindian peoples) followed soon after the Europeans' initial contact with the region (HTS: Periodization. *The Earth and Its Peoples*, 5th ed., pp. 522–524/6th ed., p. 465).

13. **ANSWER: D.** Iron was the most available metal and was used in a variety of ways, from weaponry to agricultural tools; gold and copper were the most valuable for trade (HTS: Synthesis, interpretation. *The Earth and Its Peoples*, 5th ed., pp. 377–378/6th ed., p. 240).

14. ANSWER: **A.** The majority of sub-Saharan Africa's trading relationships were along routes such as the trans-Saharan and the Indian Ocean trading network, which were populated with Muslims from various ethnic backgrounds (HTS: Synthesis, interpretation. *The Earth and Its Peoples*, 5th ed., p. 379/6th ed., p. 236).

15. ANSWER: **A.** Swahili has many words taken from the Persian and Arabic traders who came to the east coast of Africa; the word Swahili was the name used by these visitors to describe the people with whom they came into contact. Swahili is an example of the permanent social and cultural influences that trade brought to the region (HTS: Synthesis, causation. *The Earth and Its Peoples*, 5th ed., pp. 366–367/6th ed., p. 385).

16. ANSWER: **A.** From 1700 to 1100 B.C.E., the Middle East experienced a cosmopolitan era during which cultures shared characteristics because of extensive diplomatic and economic contacts (HTS: Periodization. *The Earth and Its Peoples*, 5th ed., pp. 93–94/6th ed., p. 42).

17. ANSWER: **D.** It is actually the opposite; the challenging environment required many societies to exchange goods and resources because they could not provide for all of their needs within one ecological environment (HTS: Contextualization. *The Earth and Its Peoples*, 5th ed., p. 331/6th ed., p. 196).

18. ANSWER: **C.** The collapse of the Mongol Empire ended the smooth flow of the Silk Road and other overland trade routes in Central Asia, allowing the Indian Ocean trade network to become a more significant artery of communication and trade for the peoples of Eurasia and Africa (HTS: Causation, periodization. *The Earth and Its Peoples*, 5th ed., pp. 462–465/6th ed., p. 284).

19. ANSWER: **D.** Turks established the Delhi Sultanate. They did not successfully conquer the south but were recognized as a Muslim state by the Baghdad caliph. The source of tension was rooted in religious difference—India was majority Hindu, while the sultanate was Muslim (HTS: Synthesis, contextualization. *The Earth and Its Peoples*, 5th ed., pp. 382–385/6th ed., p. 375).

20. ANSWER: **C.** The Tang developed a strong tributary system (HTS: periodization, contextualization. *The Earth and Its Peoples*, 5th ed., p. 269/6th ed., p. 298).

21. ANSWER: **A.** Islam spread well along the Indian Ocean trade routes because many of the merchants and missionaries who traveled in the Indian Ocean actively promoted their faith and married locally (HTS: Causation, periodization. *The Earth and Its Peoples*, 5th ed., pp. 392–393/6th ed., pp. 384–385).

22. ANSWER: **C.** The mamluks became a powerful group in the Middle East as the Abbasid Caliphate lost power and broke up into different caliphates and kingdoms. The mamluks ruled in both Egypt and Syria (HTS: Periodization, patterns of continuity and change. *The Earth and Its Peoples*, 5th ed., pp. 234–236/6th ed., p. 380).

23. ANSWER: **D.** Both Buddhism and Christianity were based on the exemplary lives of specific individuals (HTS: Comparison, contextualization. *The Earth and Its Peoples*, 5th ed., pp. 180–182, 212–213/6th ed., p. 282).

24. ANSWER: **C.** After experiencing centuries of stagnation, the economy of western Europe began to grow, thanks to new technologies, and cities in Italy and Flanders that focused on trade (HTS: Periodization. *The Earth and Its Peoples*, 5th ed., pp. 272–273/6th ed., pp. 287–288).

25. ANSWER: **A.** Islamic women had more rights under the law than Christian women, but as was the custom in the Byzantine and Sassanid Empires, Islamic women—urban women in particular—tended to be secluded and were veiled in public. In both societies, women did not have much say in whom they married, but they could own land (HTS: Comparison, contextualization, periodization. *The Earth and Its People*, 5th ed., pp. 241–242, 261–263/6th ed., pp. 260–261, 273–274).

26. ANSWER: **B.** The Eastern and Western churches were divided because of a number of doctrinal disagreements. Western Christians invaded Byzantium during the fourth Crusade, destroying many Eastern Churches and vying for doctrinal and political power (HTS: Synthesis, argumentation. *The Earth and Its Peoples*, 5th ed., pp. 277–278/6th ed., p. 272).

27. ANSWER: **D.** Both the Mongols and the Aztecs were initially nomadic groups that established sophisticated empires based on conquest and complex relationships with subject peoples (HTS: Comparison. *The Earth and Its Peoples*, 5th ed., pp. 316–317/6th ed., pp. 321, 391).

28. ANSWER: **D.** During the reign of Tsar Ivan IV in the mid-sixteenth century, Russian Cossacks steadily gained presence and power in Central Asia, and established Russia as the Ottoman Empire's main rival in the region—a rivalry that would continue into the following period as Russian leaders continued their quest for a warm-water port on the Black Sea (HTS: Periodizaton, causation. *The Earth and Its Peoples*, 5th ed., pp. 590–591/6th ed., p. 538).

29. ANSWER: **D.** Although Europeans gained much more wealth from their trade with Africa, numerous African merchants profited from trading consumer goods and slaves during this period (HTS: Causation, periodization. *The Earth and Its Peoples*, 5th ed., pp. 538–539/6th ed., pp. 509–510).

30. ANSWER: **D.** European traders took primarily young adult males to work on New World plantations, while Muslim traders took more female slaves to work in various capacities, as well as boys who would work as harem guards following their conversion to eunuchs. Neither Christians nor Muslims of the era, however, had any moral reservations regarding the capture, trade, and use of slaves. Although Islam forbade the enslavement of Muslims, Muslim rulers in Bornu, Hausaland, and elsewhere were not strict observers of that rule (HTS: Comparison, periodization. *The Earth and Its Peoples*, 5th ed., pp. 538–539, 582–583/6th ed., p. 518).

31. ANSWER: **A.** Following Osman's establishment of the Ottoman Empire in the 1300s and Mehmed II's capture of Constantinople from the Byzantine Empire in 1453, the Ottoman Empire continued to grow through the territorial conquests of its well-trained, innovative military (HTS: Periodization, causation. *The Earth and Its Peoples*, 5th ed., pp. 581–582/6th ed., pp. 524–526).

32. ANSWER: **D.** There are numerous examples of the role of religion in political rule. Not only did priests have considerable social power, but the kings of Amerindian societies used religious ritual to show their link to the gods. It was important that these be performed in front of subject peoples to show the authority and power of the ruler. Once Europeans arrived, new religious rituals served similar functions (HTS: Change and continuity over time. *The Earth and Its Peoples*, 5th ed., p. 331/6th ed., pp. 471–472).

33. ANSWER: **C.** Akbar was known as the greatest of all Mughal emperors; his reign, a period of political, economic, and social stability and progress, included significant efforts intended to reduce tension between Hindus and Muslims in India (HTS: Synthesis, argumentation. *The Earth and Its Peoples*, 5th ed., pp. 561–562/6th ed., p. 537).

34. ANSWER: **C.** As Europe's economy was transformed through this period, many social changes occurred as well. In the expanding bourgeois class, more young men completed more education than before, while members of the lower classes often served prolonged apprenticeships to learn a trade. Marriage thus occurred at a later age in Europe than in other regions, which in turn led to a lower birthrate (HTS: Causation, contextualization, periodization. *The Earth and Its Peoples*, 5th ed., p. 472/6th ed., p. 449).

35. ANSWER: **B.** The encomienda system, in which Spanish colonists compelled Amerindians to work, remained in place until the mid-1500s, at which time the deaths of many indigenous peoples from epidemics or overwork helped to end the system. Meanwhile, slaves from Africa began replacing the Amerindian peoples in growing numbers (HTS: Synthesis, argumentation. *The Earth and Its Peoples*, 5th ed., p. 498/6th ed., p. 472).

36. ANSWER: **B.** All colonial empires became an integral part of the Atlantic network, trading between Europe, America, and Africa (HTS: Periodization, contextualization. *The Earth and Its Peoples*, 5th ed., p. 513/6th ed., p. 488).

37. ANSWER: **A.** Like Europeans, the Chinese viewed themselves as being at the center of the world, but thanks to the explorers of the fifteenth and sixteenth centuries, European mapmakers such as Mercator were able to depict the world more completely and accurately than ever before. Distortions still occurred—Mercator's projection exaggerated the size of lands distant from the equator, and it presented the world from a Eurocentric perspective (HTS: Synthesis. *The Earth and Its Peoples*, 5th ed., p. 470/6th ed., p. 447).

38. ANSWER: **C.** Choices A, B, and D are not true for this time period, although some changes like those would soon be precipitated by the rise of the powerful new sea-based empires of Europe (HTS: Patterns of change

and continuity over time, periodization. *The Earth and Its Peoples*, 5th ed., pp. 456–457/6th ed., pp. 512–513).

39. ANSWER: **B.** China made enormous territorial gains during the Manchu rule of the Qing Empire, but they resulted in the expansion of the borders of China itself, not the creation of an overseas Chinese empire. Both empires were ruled by monarchs (HTS: Comparison, contextualization. *The Earth and Its Peoples*, 5th ed., p. 581/6th ed., pp. 562–563).

40. ANSWER: **B.** In a mere hundred years, European explorers opened new trade routes across the Atlantic, Indian, and Pacific Oceans and brought about permanent contact among all the world's continents for the first time (HTS: Contextualization, periodization. *The Earth and Its Peoples*, 5th ed., p. 449/6th ed., p. 431).

41. ANSWER: **B.** Because of a severe drought in the early part of the nineteenth century, there was conflict over the remaining grazing lands, which led to the formation of the Zulu Empire in southern Africa (HTS: Synthesis, interpretation. *The Earth and Its Peoples,* 5th ed., pp. 713–714/6th ed., p. 694).

42. ANSWER: **D.** Although a very small minority, the Manchu leaders of the Qing Empire established a nonnative dynasty (China's last) that would retain power for more than two centuries, until the revolution that began in the early twentieth century (HTS: Comparison, contextualization. *The Earth and Its Peoples*, 5th ed., pp. 181–182/6th ed., p. 563).

43. ANSWER: **C.** Qing emperors became less powerful toward the end of the nineteenth century. In a decentralized China, a coalition of aristocrats stepped forward to attempt reform. One of the leaders of this new coalition was Cixi, also known as the Empress Dowager. After the 1880s, Cixi turned away from reform, but she still played a powerful leadership role in Chinese imperial politics (HTS: Periodization, contextualization. *The Earth and Its Peoples,* 5th ed., pp. 707–708/6th ed., p. 746).

44. ANSWER: **B.** Islamic reform movements in West Africa became important early in the nineteenth century as religious reformers attacked both rural peasants, who followed traditional African religious practices, and city dwellers, whom they considered too casual in their practice of Islam. The Sokoto Caliphate used this reform spirit to advance its political and legal systems, which were based on Islamic principles (HTS: Synthesis, contextualization. *The Earth and Its Peoples,* 5th ed., pp. 714–715/6th ed., p. 697).

45. ANSWER: **C.** By the nineteenth century, the Ottoman Empire had fallen behind the powers of Europe and found itself in debt. Its attempts to modernize were unsuccessful, and it continued to lose territory (HTS: Periodization, contextualization. *The Earth and Its Peoples* 5th ed., p. 694/6th ed., pp. 693–694).

46. ANSWER: **B.** As the Ottoman Tanzimat officials attempted to modernize after the Crimean War, their reform increasingly brought more rural peasants into the urban areas looking for jobs (HTS: Synthesis,

contextualization. *The Earth and Its Peoples,* 5th ed., p. 694/6th ed., p. 754).

47. ANSWER: **B.** In the early nineteenth century, the Qing leadership had little interest in trade with Europeans and was unaware of the large fortunes that trading empires were accumulating. Because of this lack of interest, the Qing also ignored new technological innovations that were giving Europeans and the United States a military and economic advantage (HTS: Synthesis, interpretation. *The Earth and Its Peoples,* 5th ed., pp. 699–700/6th ed., p. 554).

48. ANSWER: **B.** The German defeat of France, in 1870, created the modern boundaries of the German nation. Hostility between Germany and France would continue throughout the coming decades, eventually leading to armed conflict in World War I (HTS: Contextualization, causation. *The Earth and Its Peoples,* 5th ed., pp. 577–578/6th ed., p. 738).

49. ANSWER: **D.** The improvement of agricultural technology dramatically changed the natural environment in the Americas during the late nineteenth century (HTS: Periodization, contextualization. *The Earth and Its Peoples,* 5th ed., p. 680/6th ed., p. 682).

50. ANSWER: **D.** As global trade increased, shipping companies supported the use of submarine telegraph cables that made instant communication between vast distances a reality. By 1886, this new technology connected Africa, the Americas, Asia, and Europe (HTS: Periodization, contextualization. *The Earth and Its Peoples,* 5th ed., pp. 744–745/6th ed., pp. 724–725).

51. ANSWER: **A.** By the end of the nineteenth century, Qing officials had become more interested in European technology, particularly military technology (HTS: Contextualization, argumentation. *The Earth and Its Peoples,* 5th ed., pp. 705–707/6th ed., p. 746).

52. ANSWER: **A.** Millions of immigrants from East Asia and southern and eastern Europe came to the Americas in the second half of the nineteenth and early twentieth centuries. Poverty, the creation of new transportation links into rural areas of Europe, and employment opportunities in the Americas all drove this large demographic change (HTS: Synthesis, argumentation. *The Earth and Its Peoples,* 5th ed., pp. 672–673/6th ed., p. 673).

53. ANSWER: **A.** When colonial governments recruited men to work as migrant laborers, they depleted rural areas of farmers, which had a devastating effect on food production. Moreover, men were away from their families for extended periods of time, damaging family life (HTS: Contextualization. *The Earth and Its Peoples,* 5th ed., pp. 866–869/6th ed., p. 717).

54. ANSWER: **C.** In the nineteenth century, nationalism reshaped people's view of their relationship to their government. Shared language and culture created new nations—as well as new tensions between countries that claimed to represent people not living within their borders (HTS: Periodization, contextualization. *The Earth and Its Peoples,* 5th ed., p. 756/6th ed., p. 736).

55. ANSWER: B. The unification of Italy, based on a shared language and culture, was completed in 1870 and is an example of nationalism. People who viewed themselves as a nation increasingly challenged the legitimacy of multinational unions like the Austro-Hungarian and Ottoman Empires (HTS: Periodization, contextualization. *The Earth and Its Peoples,* 5th ed., p. 756/6th ed., p. 736).

56. ANSWER: D. As more people began to accept jobs created by industrialism, urban areas were able to grow because new railroad lines connected the old walking cities to the countryside (HTS: Causation, patterns of changes and continuity over time. *The Earth and Its Peoples,* 5th ed., p. 748/6th ed., p. 729).

57. ANSWER: A. Multinational organizations were formed to promote specific products of a region. OPEC was formed to promote the interests of the oil-producing nations in the face of tremendous demand for oil. While OPEC did actively advance political measures such as placing an embargo on oil shipments to the United States and the Netherlands for their support of Israel, it was not a response to NATO or the Warsaw Pact. Nor did the multinationals always produce a more powerful region, or lead to economic advancement (HTS: Contextualization, crafting historical evidence. *The Earth and Its Peoples*, 5th ed., p. 907/6th ed., pp. 860–861).

58. ANSWER: D. Gandhi abhorred power, struggle, and combat. He was inspired by both Hindu and Christian concepts, and the values that he preached were *ahimsa,* or nonviolence, and *satyagraha,* or the search for truth (HTS: Synthesis, argumentation. *The Earth and Its Peoples*, 5th ed., pp. 862–863/6th ed., p. 793).

59. ANSWER: B. Political groups and individuals around the world have employed terrorist tactics. The 1995 Oklahoma City bombings, Irish Republican Army bombings in the British Isles, and the Tokyo subway nerve gas attacks are examples of terrorist efforts used for very different political purposes (HTS: Contextualization, periodization. *The Earth and Its Peoples,* 5th ed., p. 957/6th ed., pp. 908–909).

60. ANSWER: A. After World War II, Western European nations began to establish cooperative economic policies at variance with the ideals of the traditional nation-state. In 1957, six nations signed a treaty forming the European Community, also known as the common market, which lowered tariffs and encouraged the movement of goods and capital (HTS: Synthesis, argumentation. *The Earth and Its Peoples*, 5th ed., pp. 891–892/6th ed., p. 843).

61. ANSWER: C. Electronic communications such as the radio, TV, and the Internet are now widespread and not limited only to elites. Thus cultural influences have spread rapidly around the world, often meshing with local cultures (HTS: Contextualization, periodization. *The Earth and Its Peoples*, 5th ed., p. 964/6th ed., p. 888).

62. ANSWER: B. Shortly after the end of World War II, the United Nations secured an agreement on labor standards, the rules of war, and the rights of refugees. The Universal Declaration of Human Rights, passed by the General Assembly in 1948, condemned slavery, torture, cruel and inhuman punishment, arbitrary arrest, detention, and exile, among

other things. Thus it clearly exhibited a growing acceptance of the importance of social and economic equality. However, some critics have challenged the universality of the declaration, arguing that its principles are clearly based on Western standards (HTS: Causation, periodization, patterns of changes and continuity over time. *The Earth and Its Peoples*, 5th ed., pp. 957, 961/6th ed., p. 840).

63. **ANSWER: D.** Latin American nations had gained political independence from European nations during the early part of the nineteenth century. Still, by the mid-twentieth century, they continued to be dominated economically by companies from the United States and Europe. Political leaders throughout Latin America set out to break the economic dependency (HTS: Contextualization, periodization. *The Earth and Its Peoples*, 5th ed., pp. 900–901/6th ed., p. 673).

64. **ANSWER: C.** Independence in the Belgian Congo was at best chaotic. Various political and ethnic groups vied for power and allied with competing capitalist and communist world powers. The result was civil war that essentially became part of the Cold War. It included foreign mercenaries and led to large-scale loss of life (HTS: Patterns of changes and continuity over time, periodization. *The Earth and Its Peoples*, 5th ed., pp. 899–900/6th ed., p. 852).

65. **ANSWER: C.** The Ottomans were long adversaries of the British, who had actively fostered unrest in Ottoman territories. For that reason the Ottomans actually formed a secret alliance with Germany in hopes of gaining Russian territory, and were thus an active part of the Central Powers (HTS: Periodization, contextualization. *The Earth and Its Peoples*, 5th ed., pp. 805–806/6th ed., p. 759).

66. **ANSWER: A.** Seventeen thousand women from around the world attended the conference, which focused on equal access to education and jobs and on matters of sexual control and exploitation; it became clear that there were a great variety in the views concerning what constituted women's rights (HTS: Synthesis, argumentation. *The Earth and Its Peoples*, 5th ed., p. 963/6th ed., p. 915).

67. **ANSWER: B.** Japan experienced a faster rate of economic growth in the 1970s and 1980s than any other major industrial nation. Its growth was centered around major industrial conglomerates. The government ensured the growth of these companies by setting high tariffs and import regulations that prevented foreign competition (HTS: Periodization, contextualization. *The Earth and Its Peoples*, 5th ed., p. 922/6th ed., p. 920).

68. **ANSWER: A.** Joseph Stalin helped transform the USSR into a great industrial and military power. His goal was largely to prevent the nation from suffering humiliating defeats like those of World War I. The Soviet Union experienced rapid industrialization. However, it came with massive social costs. Stalin used terror and brutal methods to ensure not only labor production, but also allegiance to the state (HTS: Synthesis, argumentation. *The Earth and Its Peoples*, 5th ed., pp. 831–834/6th ed., p. 808).

69. **ANSWER: C.** The elites of Argentina and Brazil controlled the land and agricultural production. However, most major industries outside of

agriculture were controlled by foreign companies, mainly U.S. and British. Government leaders during the interwar periods set out to increase industrialization, as well as to break the domination of foreign companies (HTS: Contextualization, periodization. *The Earth and Its Peoples*, 5th ed. pp. 873–876/6th ed., pp. 798–799).

70. **ANSWER: D.** Women were exploited because they were paid little for the work they did (HTS: Synthesis, argumentation. *The Earth and Its Peoples*, 5th ed., pp. 20–21/6th ed., p. 916).

ANSWER FOR SECTION II, PART A:
DOCUMENT-BASED QUESTION (DBQ)

THE DOCUMENTS

Below are short analyses of the documents. The italicized words suggest what your margin notes might include:

DOCUMENT 1 *Duty is based on gender.* Women are to tend to the home and submit to prominent males in their lives. This document seems to transcend class and speak about women in general. Doing one's duty is important

DOCUMENT 2 Wealthy people are traveling by horse-drawn carriage while another tends to the horse. All look happy—even the horse, for that matter—conveying the message that *there is a benefit in doing one's duty.*

DOCUMENT 3 *Duty is based on gender.* Women are to be submissive, industrious in household chores, and are to be the spiritual keepers of the house. The author of this document is clearly upper-class, but doing one's duty transcends class, and perhaps even these prescribed gender prescriptions since Ban seems to have power well beyond those normally associated with Han dynasty women.

DOCUMENT 4 *If the father permits it, women can become nuns and escape the prescribed duties of a woman.* All parties are rewarded for the way they executed their duty.

DOCUMENT 5 *According to the law code, the king is to be a paternal leader, and—important for the king—citizens are to be loyal followers.* Balance is achieved when everyone does their duty for the benefit of all.

DOCUMENT 6 *Difficulties for the farmers in escaping the cycle of poverty, while the gentry benefits from the system.* In this document, duty is class-based. The document might imply that while the peasant submits to his duty, the gentry seem not to embrace theirs since they do not care about the peasants.

DOCUMENT 7 *Women in the royal household have an honored place and are dressed quite ornately.* According to this, court life does not seem significantly different from what would be described in Europe, other than the presence of multiple wives.

YOUR ESSAY FOR THE DOCUMENT-BASED QUESTION

A potential thesis for this DBQ would argue that before 1450, social structure in China was a rigid system in which one's position and lifestyle were dictated by gender and class, as well as a moral duty to fulfill one's appointed role as understood through Confucian principles. Your thesis does not have to sound like this word for word, but it should communicate these basic ideas. You need to be sure your thesis makes an argument that clearly answers the prompt and addresses all parts of the question.

You are then ready to prove your thesis, using the documents one by one to address the question and provide evidence in the context of your groupings. In the thesis above, the groups would include class, gender, and duty. This grouping is just one way to group the documents; you can incorporate other groupings as well.

Remember that your essay needs to cover a lot of bases in addition to addressing the question—document analysis, the use of evidence, your suggested additional documents and reasons for why you need them, and point of view!

Thinking about point of view, two of the documents are especially useful. Written by a Han Confucian scholar, Mengzi (Mencius), Document 1 describes his mother's life. Mengzi is upholding the Confucian social system and the traditional ideals to which he has dedicated his life. As a published Confucian scholar, he would want to spread values that support the strict social and gender structure of Han society. His gender and class also matter; as an upper-class male, he was part of the social class that propagated the ideas about gender roles, particularly for the upper-class females with whom upper-class males would come into contact. Document 5, the excerpt from the Tang law code, imposes expectations of good citizenship and loyalty on Chinese subjects. Those in power would want to encourage such behavior so as to maintain their position of authority.

To decide on additional documents that would be helpful, look at the sources that are provided and the sources that are missing. The ideal is to have as broad an array of sources as possible. One additional document that would represent a voice you do not have would be a journal entry from a working-class woman showing how class impacted gender expectations and roles. Here, all of the documents about women pertain to upper-class women; a document from a less-affluent woman could be insightful.

Remember, you must take up the point of view in two of the documents and propose one additional document, with an explanation of why it would be helpful, in order to get all of the basic core points on the DBQ!

SCORING 1 point for thesis in the opening line, 1 point for understanding the basic meaning of all documents, 2 points for using all of the documents as evidence that supported the thesis, 1 point for analyzing the point of view in two documents, 1 point for groupings, and 1 point for an explanation of possible additional documents. If the essay earns basic core, it can earn 2 expanded core points for having relevant outside historical content, for persuasively using the documents as evidence, and for proposing—in addition to the one extra document required for basic core—a second extra document.

The DBQ essay counts for one-third of the free-response grade, one-sixth of the examination grade.

ANSWER FOR SECTION II, PART B:
CONTINUITY AND CHANGE OVER TIME QUESTION

This essay asks you to address major changes and continuities in connection with the spread of Islam. The question purposely does not give you a specific region; there are many areas of the world that felt the impact of Islam.

Beginning with your thesis, you need to be sure you address both changes and continuity. Your essay should take the reader through the entire period, citing specific pieces of evidence of change and continuity and providing thorough analysis. To get the analysis point, you should be discussing how and why Islam made changes as well as how and why certain continuities remained.

What kinds of information should you be discussing? Beginning you might point out that Islam had a political aspect from the very beginning in that Mohammad was both a religious and political leader for the umma. Discuss the rise of the caliphates and the political organization that took place in order to manage the large territories of the Middle East, North Africa, and Spain that Muslims quickly conquered. Discuss how the various caliphates ruled and acknowledge the changes brought about as more and more non-Arabs converted to Islam. The way that the Turks and Persians came to power in their respective areas could be discussed as well. You can then discuss the rise of new Islamic states in Northern Africa, West Africa, and East Africa, as well as in India. Your strongest examples of specific evidence here would be the Mali Empire and the Delhi Sultanate, the wealthiest and largest Islamic states by 1500. Another major change in the Islamic world that you should address is the birth of the Ottoman Empire through the defeat of the Byzantine Empire, and the nature of initial Ottoman rule. By the end of the period, the Safavid and Mughal Empires were two other land-based Muslim empires that existed along with the Ottoman Empire. An important political continuity throughout the period is the use of Islamic law and courts to promote justice and safety, which allowed for economic prosperity.

You might also discuss economic changes and continuities brought about by Islam. You should be sure to analyze the role of trade as an important continuity throughout the entire period. Mohammad himself was a merchant, and the urban nature of various Islamic empires fostered trade and commerce, as people came to the cities to learn about what it meant to be a Muslim. The role of cities is an important piece of analysis in terms of the economic impact of Islam. Islam also spread by economic interactions along the trade routes of the Silk Road and later the Indian Ocean trade network. Other important evidence of change can be the types of goods that Islamic merchants introduced to various regions, as well as the impact Islamic knowledge had on learning and industry.

Again, be sure to discuss both change and continuity. Use specific evidence—there is a wealth of information for this topic—and back up your argument with good analysis to get a high score on this essay.

SCORING 1 point for a thesis in the opening line that addresses the whole time period, 2 points for fully addressing the question in terms of both change and continuity, 2 points for appropriate evidence to support the thesis, 1 point for the global context, and 1 point for analysis of change and continuity. If the essay earns basic core, it can earn 2 expanded core points for addressing all parts of the questions evenly and providing good evidence rooted in a solid understanding of the global events that brought about change.

The continuity and change over time essay counts for one-third of the free-response grade, one-sixth of the examination grade.

ANSWER FOR SECTION II, PART C:
COMPARATIVE QUESTION

This essay asks you to address two out of three political revolutions in the eighteenth and nineteenth centuries, comparing their causes and effects. You need to be sure to address the causes and effects of the French and one of the other revolutions, and be sure that your thesis includes similarities and differences in order to get the full points for addressing the question and thesis.

One of the key issues in addressing political revolutions is motive. The motives of the French were very different from those of the Haitians and the Mexicans. Haiti and Mexico were similar in that they were both under colonial rule, the Haitians by France and the Mexicans by Spain. The French Revolution was different because it began not because of colonial rule but because of internal unrest over the structure of the French government. Despite this key difference, all three societies were similar in having groups who felt disenfranchised and discriminated against, and the complexity of social structure in all three places is an important aspect to talk about. Showing your specific comparative knowledge of social hierarchies in France and either Haiti or Mexico will help secure your points for evidence. In Haiti and Mexico, similarities are discrimination justified by ethnic racism and economic inequality; a contrast is that in France, discrimination was based on class and one's position in the estate system. Both Mexicans and Haitians wanted independence from their colonial masters, while the French wanted to bring about internal political change.

The French Revolution was a source of inspiration for both the Haitian and Mexican Revolutions. The French Revolution came before the Mexican and Haitian Revolutions, which began when Napoleon was in power in Europe; his control of both France and Spain, and subsequently their colonies, was a cause for both revolutions and should be discussed. Another similarity might be a comparison of the goals of the leaders of two of the revolutions: L'Ouverture in Haiti and Hidalgo and Morelos in Mexico.

In terms of effects, you can analyze the successes and failures of the revolutions in terms of what were their original goals. Haiti and Mexico were similar in succeeding in breaking away from colonial rule, and all three revolutions were violent; you might analyze why that was the case. The impact that these three revolutions had on the region of Latin America and the Caribbean is another similarity. You could argue that the French Revolution spurred other revolutions, in particular in Haiti. For a contrast, an analysis of the results of the French Revolution for France itself shows that it was not as successful as was initially hoped.

Again, be sure to discuss similarities and differences, and take the time to analyze why you are claiming certain similarities and differences. With good evidence to support your comparisons, you should be able to get a high score!

SCORING 1 point for the thesis in the opening line, 2 points for addressing both similarities and differences, 2 points for using accurate evidence that supports the main ideas presented in the thesis, 1 point for making a number of specific direct comparisons, and 1 point for analysis. If the essay earns basic core, with consistent use of both evidence and direct comparison it can earn 2 points for expanded core.

The continuity and change over time essay counts for one-third of the total free-response grade, one-sixth of the total examination grade.

CALCULATING YOUR SCORE

The following is based on the 2011 AP World History Examination, which is the only released examination at this time.

SCORING THE MULTIPLE-CHOICE SECTION

Use the following formula to calculate your raw score on the multiple-choice section of the exam:

_____ × 0.8571 = _____
number   weighted Section I score
correct
(out of 70)

[Note: The guessing penalty has been eliminated for all AP exams starting with the 2011 exam.]

SCORING THE FREE-RESPONSE SECTION

Use the following formula to calculate your raw score on the free-response section of the exam:

Part A _____ × 2.2222 = _____
        (out of 9)   (do not round)

Part B _____ × 2.2222 = _____
        (out of 9)   (do not round)

Part C _____ × 2.2222 = _____
        (out of 9)   (do not round)

Sum = _____
weighted Section II score
(do not round)

YOUR COMPOSITE SCORE

_____ + _____ = _____
weighted   weighted   composite score
Section I   Section II   (round to nearest whole number)
score   score

Once you have calculated your composite score, see where it falls in the Composite Score Range below. *Remember that your composite score is only an estimate of your performance on the College Board exam.*

AP GRADES BY SCORE RANGE

Composite Score Range	AP Grade
78–120	5
62–77	4
43–61	3
27–42	2
0–26	1

Practice Test 2
AP WORLD HISTORY EXAMINATION
Section I: Multiple-Choice Questions
Time—55 minutes
Number of questions—70

DIRECTIONS Each of the questions or incomplete statements below is followed by four suggested answers or completions. For each question, select the best response.

NOTE This examination uses the chronological designations B.C.E. (before the Common Era) and C.E. (Common Era). These correspond to B.C. (before Christ) and A.D. (anno Domini), which are used in some world history textbooks.

"If a man has destroyed the eye of another free man, his own eye shall be destroyed... If he has destroyed the eye of a peasant he shall pay one mina (three ounces) of silver. If he has destroyed the eye of a slave,... he shall pay half his value..." (Excerpt from Hammurabi's code. Overfield, *The Human Record,* 7th ed., p. 16)

1. According to the excerpt above, which social change came about with the development of agriculture-based societies?
   (A) Overall population increased dramatically and became stratified with a more stable food supply.
   (B) People lived longer because of the decrease in the amount of violence in settled communities.
   (C) Women gained in status and power as they assumed new roles in society.
   (D) Farmers battled constantly over access to and control over land.

2. Which of the following made the early Israelites unique among early civilizations?
   (A) They had a set of basic tenets that established proper conduct and provided guidance.
   (B) They inhabited a territory that was poor in natural resources yet established a viable economy.
   (C) They believed in the idea of a god and the possibility of an afterlife.
   (D) They maintained a strong sense of culture and religious unity despite being dispersed.

3. River valley civilizations such as Egypt and ancient Mesopotamia were similar in that both

(A) used coined money extensively as witnessed by the variety of coins found in elite tombs.
(B) lacked a system of writing.
(C) used a system of slavery, usually made up of captured individuals.
(D) had multiple sparsely populated urban centers.

Robert Fisher

4. The sculpture (above) would most likely be found in which region of the world?
   (A) East Asia
   (B) South Asia
   (C) West Africa
   (D) Mesoamerica

GO ON TO NEXT PAGE

Overlaps in rock art imply that camel riders in desert costume constitute the latest Saharan population… The first mention of camels in North Africa comes in a Latin text of 46 BCE. (Bulliet et al., *The Earth and Its Peoples,* 6th ed., p. 231)

5. Which of the following would best describe camel domestication's significance in the first millennium B.C.E.?
   (A) It would allow desert dwellers to establish a reliable means of trade between the Mediterranean and sub-Saharan Africa.
   (B) It would have led to the Roman discovery of salt mines in North Africa.
   (C) It would have given desert dwellers a source of meat and milk.
   (D) It would have facilitated the spread of Islam to the previously isolated desert regions.

Caravans traveling the Silk Road took more than four months to trek across the mostly unsettled deserts, mountains, and grasslands of Inner Asia… carrying with them agricultural goods, manufactured products, and ideas. Musicians and dancing girls traveled too, as did camel pullers, merchants, monks, and pilgrims. (Bulliet, et al., *The Earth and Its Peoples,* 6th ed., p. 223)

Iranian whirling girl, Iranian whirling girl,

Her heart answers to the strings,

Her hands answer to the drum…

In vain did you labor to come east more than ten thousand tricents.

For in the central plains there were already some who could do the Iranian whirl…

(Bulliet et al., *The Earth and Its Peoples,* 6th ed., p. 223)

6. From the quotes above, it is evident that the Silk Road
   (A) allowed missionaries to spread various religions.
   (B) helped the stirrup spread from northern Afghanistan to Europe and Asia.
   (C) facilitated economic contact between the Roman and Han Empires.

(D) facilitated a complex social system between far-flung civilizations.

7. The spread of the Roman Empire throughout Europe and the Mediterranean was accompanied by
   (A) mass deportations and slavery.
   (B) the spread of Christianity.
   (C) the spread of Latin and the Roman way of life.
   (D) a decrease in economic activity and travel.

Excavation of Andean graves reveal that superior-quality textiles as well as gold crowns, breastplates, and jewelry distinguished rulers from commoners. (Bulliet et al., *The Earth and Its Peoples,* 6th ed., p. 196)

8. Which of the following lasting contributions to the societies of the Americas was made by the Chavín?
   (A) The wheel
   (B) A writing system
   (C) Metallurgy
   (D) Stone carving

9. Which is true of both Christianity's impact on the Roman Empire and Buddhism's impact on Han China?
   (A) Christianity's adherence to monotheism did not mesh well with existing pagan beliefs, while Buddhism fit more easily with traditional Chinese values.
   (B) Christianity had little impact on the Roman Empire, while Buddhism transformed the government and culture of Han China.
   (C) Both Christianity and Buddhism had little impact on the government of each empire because their messages appealed most to the poor and disenfranchised.
   (D) Christianity's role in the Roman Empire ended with the rise of emperor Constantine, as did Buddhism's influence when Shi Huangdi came to power.

10. The Persian model of using provinces governed by satraps for administering their vast empire is most similar to that of which other empire?
   (A) Assyrian
   (B) Roman
   (C) Mauryan
   (D) Qin

11. Powerful civilizations appeared centuries later in the Western Hemisphere than in the Eastern Hemisphere because
   (A) more species of plants in the Western Hemisphere could be used in agricultural communities.
   (B) the orientation of the land masses in the West allowed for the rapid spread of ideas along the north/south axis.
   (C) the Western Hemisphere had fewer species of animals that were well suited for domestication.
   (D) climactic changes caused domestication of plants to take longer.

12. Although little is known about the Olmec, there are indications that
   (A) they practiced a limited democracy in which all adult males could participate.
   (B) they were ruled by a king, who combined religious and secular roles.
   (C) their government was decentralized and lacked the power to direct its citizens.
   (D) women played an influential role in government and were equal to men.

13. Between 600 and 1450, Andean and Mesoamerican civilizations differed because
   (A) Mesoamerica was ethnically homogeneous, while the peoples of the Andes were diverse.
   (B) Andean civilizations did not create urban centers, while Mesoamerican civilizations did.
   (C) Andean civilizations relied on reciprocal labor obligations like the mit'a, while Mesoamerican civilizations did not.
   (D) Mesoamerican civilizations did not practice any form of sacrifice as a part of religious ritual, while Andean civilizations regularly did.

14. There is evidence that North American cultures were influenced by Mesoamerican culture in
   (A) the construction of similar temples such as pyramids.
   (B) the production of similar agricultural products like the potato and tobacco.
   (C) the playing of similar ritual ball games.
   (D) the adaptation of similar agricultural technology.

15. The city-states of tropical Africa and Asia were similar to the nation-states of fourteeth-century Europe in that
   (A) both relied on agriculture in order to achieve economic prosperity.
   (B) both lacked access to maritime trading opportunities.
   (C) the growth of stronger political entities enabled religious learning in both places.
   (D) both were conquered by Muslims.

16. By 1100, Islam had failed to spread to
   (A) northern Africa.
   (B) sub-Saharan Africa.
   (C) Spain.
   (D) Central Asia.

17. How does imperial rule in Japan compare to Chinese imperial rule?
   (A) As in China, the powerful Japanese emperor justified his rule through the Confucian Mandate of Heaven.
   (B) Unlike in China, Japanese emperors were constantly fighting to maintain their positions of power.
   (C) Unlike in China, Japanese women could rule as empresses.
   (D) The Japanese imperial dynasty was one continual lineage, and the emperor was more of a figurehead whereas in China the emperor had absolute power.

GO ON TO NEXT PAGE

18. Which of the following statements was true about the early spread of Christianity into Africa?
    (A) Christianity was seen as a direct competitor to Islam and thus never took hold in Africa.
    (B) Christianity spread into eastern Africa through trade from the Mediterranean region.
    (C) Christianity was forced upon the Africans when Arabs invaded.
    (D) Christianity was controlled by Rome and thus never became an authentic African religion.

19. Which of the following statements best describes the process of early conversion to Islam?
    (A) Arabs immediately sought to convert the people who were incorporated into the new Umayyad Caliphate.
    (B) Conversion was forced on subject peoples during the conquest period in the seventh and eighth centuries.
    (C) Arabs were initially a ruling Muslim minority, and in the ninth century, conversion of non-Arabs began to increase.
    (D) The majority of Muslims were Arab, and that was still true at the end of the ninth century.

20. Which of the following describes the significance of the migration of the Bantu and Aryans?
    (A) As they moved, both imposed a rigid social structure that oppressed lower classes.
    (B) The rapidity of both migrations forced other people to move, thus disrupting regional stability.
    (C) Each spread language and cultural components that transformed the societies they encountered.
    (D) The Bantu and Aryan migrations resulted in the spread of Islam and Hinduism respectively.

21. For the Europeans of the twelfth century, the Crusades resulted in
    (A) gradual exposure to Muslim ideas, goods, and intellectual accomplishments.
    (B) the permanent and successful conquest of Jerusalem for Christendom.

    (C) the fall of the Holy Roman Empire at the hands of the Turks.
    (D) the end of trading relationships between Europeans and Muslims.

22. One important similarity between the Tang dynasty in China and the Delhi Sultanate in India was
    (A) that Hinduism was the dominant religion.
    (B) state-sponsored education.
    (C) government-sponsored hydrologic control systems.
    (D) mandatory military service.

23. Swahili is a language that developed because of which trade network?
    (A) The trans-Saharan trade network
    (B) The Central Asian overland trade routes
    (C) The Mediterranean trade routes
    (D) The Indian Ocean trade network

24. Which statement best describes Mongol rule in Russia?
    (A) Russian princes submitted to Mongol authority in name only, allowing them to rule under official Mongol oversight.
    (B) The Mongols destroyed the Orthodox Church in order to eliminate potential threats.
    (C) The Mongols ruled primarily from afar and rewarded Russian princes who submitted to their authority.
    (D) Mongol rule brought many benefits to Russia, particularly in terms of economic gains.

25. In comparison with the Western Roman Empire, which of the following is true of the Byzantine Empire in 600 C.E.?
    (A) It had lost important territory in the Middle East.
    (B) It barely survived the migrations that ruined the western portion of the Roman Empire.
    (C) Economic prosperity and political stability enabled it to continue the legacy of the Greeks and Romans.
    (D) It remained in Rome's political and cultural shadow because of the growing power of the pope.

26. In late-medieval Europe, the role of knights in the feudal system was most undermined by
    (A) advances in maritime technology, which encouraged exploration.
    (B) advances in military technology, in particular armor.
    (C) the Black Death in the fourteenth century.
    (D) advances in military technology, in particular the crossbow and firearms.

27. Intellectual pursuits in the late fourteenth century in Europe were characterized by which of the following?
    (A) The founding of Christian universities which sought to confer divinity degrees to many
    (B) The teaching of curricula in Latin to ensure common understanding
    (C) Increasing Christian religious influence on curriculum and literature
    (D) Use of printing, which helped to spread ideas

One of the best things in these parts is, the regard they pay to justice; for, in this respect, the Sultan regards neither little nor much. The safety, too, is very great; so that a traveller may proceed alone among them, without the least fear of a thief or robber...Another is, their insisting on the Koran's being committed to memory: for if a man finds his son defective in this, he will confine him till he is quite perfect, nor will he allow him his liberty until he is so.

–ibn Battuta, 1353

28. The quote above describes which of the following states/empires?
    (A) The Yuan Empire
    (B) The Holy Roman Empire
    (C) The Mali Empire
    (D) The Byzantine Empire

29. In response to the collapse of the Mongol Empire in China, Korea and the Ming
    (A) established new non-Mongol dynasties that emphasized indigenous ethnicity.
    (B) rejected all Mongol contributions from the period of the Yuan Empire.

    (C) rejected Confucianism and embraced Buddhism as their new state religion.
    (D) went to war against each other, a conflict that ended after the Ming collapsed.

Cengage Learning

30. The carved ivory saltcellar shown above, depicting a Portuguese ship supported by Portuguese nobles, provides evidence of which new influence brought to West Africa by the Europeans?
    (A) The addition of salt to food as a preservative
    (B) The concepts of monarchy and nobility
    (C) The promotion of the Christian religion
    (D) The production of goods for trade

GO ON TO NEXT PAGE

31. How did contact with the Islamic world affect Africa between 1450 and 1750?
    (A) The trans-Saharan slave trade benefited Africa's economy, while Islamic customs shaped legal and political activity in many urban areas of the African continent.
    (B) The spread of Islam into Africa spurred European interest in the continent, provoking new religious crusades and a European takeover of much of sub-Saharan Africa's territory.
    (C) The trade of female African slaves to the Islamic world led to a significant decline in the population of sub-Saharan Africa.
    (D) The demand for African timber in the Middle East created an environmental crisis of deforestation, agricultural neglect, and famine in sub-Saharan Africa.

The Anatolian port of Izmir transformed itself from a small town into a multi-ethnic, multi-religious, multi-linguistic entrepôt because of the Ottoman government's inability to control trade and the slowly growing dominance of European traders in the Indian Ocean. (Bulliet et al., *The Earth and Its Peoples*, 6th ed., p. 565)

32. According to the passage above, one important cause of the Ottoman Empire's struggle to retain its influence and cohesion after the late sixteenth century was
    (A) internal rivalries between Sunni and Shi'ite Muslim factions.
    (B) frequent rebellions among the empire's Christian subjects.
    (C) the rise of the Atlantic and Indian Ocean trade networks and the decline of the Silk Road.
    (D) near-constant warfare on the Ottomans' western border with the rising Austro-Hungarian Empire.

33. Which of the following was a problem shared by the Ottoman and Safavid Empires?
    (A) The cost of maintaining a large naval force
    (B) A seventeenth-century environmental crisis of prolonged drought leading to famine
    (C) The reluctance among certain military personnel to switch from bows to firearms
    (D) Domestic overproduction of silver currency, which caused severe inflation in the seventeenth century

34. How did the structure of the Aztec Empire compare with the Inca ayllus?
    (A) The Aztec economic system allowed for a much more equitable distribution of wealth.
    (B) Unlike the Aztec political system, the Inca ayllus participated in a form of representative government.
    (C) Both the Aztec society and the Inca ayllus valued farmers for sustaining their citizens and placed them near the top of the social pyramid.
    (D) While the Aztecs demanded tribute victims from conquered territories mainly for religious sacrifice, the Inca ayllus regularly provided the empire with temporary warriors, builders, and other workers.

35. Which characterization of the Atlantic System in the sixteenth century is most accurate?
    (A) It was an interactive, intercontinental economic system.
    (B) It led to the domination of native plants and peoples in the Americas.
    (C) It was mostly constructive and only a little destructive.
    (D) It replaced Islamic influence in Africa with European influence.

36. Which of the following was the most significant revolution experienced by Europe in the period 1450–1750?
    (A) Financial: the rise of communism
    (B) Scientific: the rise of quantum physics
    (C) Political: the rejection of absolute monarchy in leading powers of western and Central Europe
    (D) Religious: the Protestant Reformation

Patterns of French settlement more closely resembled those of Spain and Portugal than of England. The French were committed to missionary activity among Amerindian peoples and emphasized the extraction of natural resources. (Bulliet et al., *The Earth and Its Peoples*, 6th ed., p. 483)

37. Using your knowledge of history and the information from the passage above, what was the driving force behind French settlement in North America?
    (A) The European market for beaver and other types of fur
    (B) The disruption of the French economy by the Thirty Years War
    (C) French Protestants' fear of the Catholic Church's Inquisition
    (D) The discovery of Canadian silver mines that promised to surpass the output of Potosí in Bolivia

"Since there are many who promote to officer rank their relatives and friends—young men who do no know the fundamentals of soldiering, not having served the lower ranks—and since even those who serve do so for a few weeks or months only, as a formality; therefore...Henceforth there shall be no promotion of men of noble extraction or of any others who have not first served as privates in the guard." (Peter the Great, Decree on Promotion to Officer's Rank 1714. Overfield et al., 7th ed., p. 152)

38. One of Russia's greatest challenges from the sixteenth through eighteenth centuries was
    (A) maintaining administrative control of its vast empire.
    (B) fending off repeated attacks of the Golden Horde.

(C) battling China for access to the North American fur trade.
(D) balancing the power of the Duma (parliament) and the tsar.

39. Between 1450 and 1750, which of the following regions was LEAST transformed by the increasing globalization of world trade?
    (A) East Asia
    (B) Western Europe
    (C) West Africa
    (D) Southeast Asia

40. Which of the following characterizations of the African slave trade is true?
    (A) The slave trade's volume soon virtually eliminated other economic activity in West Africa.
    (B) European interest in the African slave trade built upon previously established trading practices and patterns.
    (C) African merchants generally demanded—and received—specific goods of high quality in exchange for slaves.
    (D) African leaders forced European traders to follow African trading customs, and they profited from rivalries among the European powers.

41. Immediately after independence, which groups represented the strongest force in newly independent governments in Latin America?
    (A) Peasants and indigenous people
    (B) The church and military
    (C) Local political leaders and merchants
    (D) Western-educated elites and advisers

42. The actions of nations in South and North America toward Amerindians in the nineteenth century is best characterized by the fact that Amerindians
    (A) received increased legal rights and citizenship.
    (B) were imprisoned and deported.
    (C) were militarily defeated and their tribal identities were attacked.
    (D) were given autonomous zones and political independence.

GO ON TO NEXT PAGE

43. The primary goal of British expansion in South Asia and Southeast Asia during the late eighteenth and nineteenth centuries was the
    (A) provision of raw materials for Indian manufacturing centers.
    (B) expansion of democracy and humanitarian reform.
    (C) provision of aid and assistance to modernize the region.
    (D) creation of trading posts to expand free trade in the region.

44. Responses of African societies to European invasion in the late nineteenth century included
    (A) fighting invaders and forcing them back to Europe.
    (B) managing the growing colonial presence by creating enclaves for the foreigners and trying to continue to live as before.
    (C) signing alliances with competing European powers to maintain independence.
    (D) modernizing armed forces to defend against European military intrusion.

45. As a result of the end of the transatlantic slave trade
    (A) slavery ended in the Americas.
    (B) slave traders found it difficult to continue trading large numbers of slaves.
    (C) slavery became less prominent in North Africa and the Middle East.
    (D) slave traders shifted to southern and eastern Africa.

"When he was setting out with the Sultan in a campaign against them, to raise from his household servants a troop of 200 horsemen and arm them with firearms as they would cause much alarm... But they had not completed half the journey when their guns began to get out of order. Every day some essential part of their weapons was lost or broken, and it was not often that armorers could be found capable of repairing them. So, a large part of the firearms having been rendered unserviceable, the men took a dislike to the weapons..." (Ghiselin de Busbecq, Flemish nobleman, impression of the Turks in 1555; Overfield, *The Human Record,* p. 49)

46. According to the Flemish envoy, Turks did not like modern technology because of
    (A) the limitation of the weapon's range.
    (B) the difficulty in using firearms around horses.
    (C) the restriction in wearing loose trousers.
    (D) the unreliability of firearms over the long run.

Cengage Learning

47. The expansion of British and Spanish territory and the reduction of French territory in North America, illustrated in the maps above, was a result of what event?
(A) Proclamation of 1763
(B) Treaty of Tordesillas
(C) American Revolution
(D) French and Indian War (Seven Years War)

48. Nineteenth-century imperialism differed from earlier imperialism in which of the following ways?
(A) All political control was taken from local populations.
(B) Large numbers of citizens were educated and economies modernized.
(C) Imperial control over local raw materials became increasingly important.
(D) Most regions welcomed colonial changes and industrialism.

49. The British defeated the Qing dynasty in the Opium War because
(A) although the Qing had a strong navy it was gunned by British warships.
(B) the Qing did not take the threat of opium seriously.
(C) the limited number of modern weapons used by the Qing military.
(D) the insufficient number of Qing troops to defend coastal cities.

GO ON TO NEXT PAGE

The Japanese invasion devastated Korea, and China suffered even more dire consequences. The battles in Manchuria weakened the Chinese garrison there, permitting Manchu opposition to consolidate. (Bulliet et al., *The Earth and Its Peoples*, 6th ed., p. 557)

50. How did the attempted invasion of the Asian mainland by the Japanese warlord Hideyoshi affect China?
    (A) It disrupted trade with Europe, plunging China into economic depression.
    (B) It resulted in the Japanese annexation of the Chinese island of Hong Kong.
    (C) It led to the consolidation of Manchu forces, which went on to conquer China.
    (D) It forced the Chinese to modernize their military and begin purchasing firearms from the Europeans.

51. What late nineteenth-century intellectual and political movement arose from the combination of Enlightenment ideas and the effects of industrialism?
    (A) Laissez-faire capitalism
    (B) Colonialism
    (C) Socialism
    (D) Fascism

52. The most significant shift in the lives of working-class women in Europe during the nineteenth century was that they
    (A) increasingly worked outside the home in factories and domestic service.
    (B) began entering a wide variety of professions such as teaching, law, and medicine.
    (C) married early and removed themselves from the working world.
    (D) increased their membership in trade unions and women's rights organizations.

53. By 1750, South Asia and Latin America were MOST similar in that
    (A) the majority of indigenous peoples had adopted Christianity.
    (B) native efforts to overthrow European imperialism had led to ongoing military conflict.

    (C) they had contributed new crops, livestock, and diseases to the Columbian Exchange.
    (D) their economic systems were being transformed by the era's global-trade network.

54. Which of the following was MOST similar to China at the time of the Ming and Qing Empires?
    (A) France
    (B) The Safavid Empire
    (C) Spain
    (D) England

Accordingly we made use of all circumstances only from one point of view, which consisted therein: to raise the nation on to that step on which it is justified in standing in the civilized world, to stabilize the Turkish Republic more and more on steadfast foundations... and in addition to destroy the spirit of despotism for ever. (Mustafa Kemal, Overfield, *The Human Record,* 7th ed., p. 436)

55. In the early twentieth century, the Ottoman Young Turks used nationalist ideas to press for
    (A) the expansion of the Ottoman Empire into Russia.
    (B) Turkification of ethnic minorities.
    (C) strengthening the powers of the sultan.
    (D) acceptance of ethnic and religious minorities.

56. Which of the following was a challenge to nation-building during the era of decolonization of the 1950s and 1960s?
    (A) An overabundance of skilled workers
    (B) Maintenance of advanced infrastructure
    (C) Language and ethnic divisions
    (D) Diversified cash crop economies

57. Like Mohandas Ghandi, most early leaders of the Indian nationalist movement shared which of the following characteristics?
    (A) They came from lower castes.
    (B) They worked for the British raj.
    (C) They were Western-educated.
    (D) They rejected Hinduism and traditional Indian values.

"Firm Measures must be taken against any student who creates trouble at Tiananmen Square… In the beginning, we mainly used persuasion… But if any of them disturb public order or violate the law, they must be dealt with unhesitatingly." (Remarks made by Chinese Premier Deng Xiaping in December 1986. HR after 1500, 7th ed., p. 514)

58. Which of the following statements accurately illustrates the situation of Tiananmen Square in 1989?
    (A) Chinese officials convened a high-level meeting to discuss the economic and political future of the nation.
    (B) A small number of protestors surrounded the square and demanded that the Chinese government address environmental problems within the nation.
    (C) Thousands of Chinese protestors gathered to demand the expulsion of all foreign companies and the annulment of the Open Door Treaty.
    (D) Chinese students and intellectuals led a series of protests calling for more democracy and an end to inflation and corruption.

"Perestroika means priority development of the social sphere aimed at ever better satisfaction of the Soviet people's requirements for good living and working conditions, for good rest and recreation, education, and health care." (Mikhail Gorbachev, 1987, Overfield, *The Human Record,* 7th ed., p. 517)

59. Mikhail Gorbachev's policy of *Perestroika* was
    (A) a political initiative permitting criticism of the government and the communist party.
    (B) an economic attempt to further nationalize all major industries in an effort to create a stronger communist state.
    (C) an effort to create an international trade partnership of all communist nations around the world.
    (D) an effort to address economic problems by moving toward a more modern and open economic system.

The British attempted to control the Middle East after World War I with a mixture of bribery and intimidation. They made Faisal, leader of the Arab Revolt, king of Iraq and used bombers to quell rural insurrections. In 1931 they reached an agreement with King Faisal's government: official independence for Iraq in exchange for… a military alliance. (Bulliet, et al., *The Earth and Its Peoples,* 6th ed., p. 772)

60. According to the passage above, the British agreement with King Faisal of Iraq in 1931 included which of the following?
    (A) Official independence for Iraq in exchange for the denunciation of Zionist efforts to create a Jewish state.
    (B) Official independence in exchange for continued bombing raids to quell revolts.
    (C) British military protection in exchange for purchase of Iraqi oil.
    (D) Official independence for Iraq in exchange for the right to keep two airbases and access to petroleum.

61. The Persian Gulf War of 1990–1991 and the Iraqi war of 2003 were similar because
    (A) American troops invaded Iraq both times.
    (B) American troops were defeated and suffered large numbers of casualties.
    (C) although American troops quickly made it to Baghdad both times, they failed to quell sectarian violence.
    (D) the United States helped plant the seeds of democracy in the Arab region.

62. Which of the following is an apt comparison of the African National Congress and the Indian National Congress?
    (A) Both were founded by veterans of World War II.
    (B) Both were small organizations with limited influence.
    (C) Both fought for the freedom of people in India.
    (D) Both were founded by English-speaking or Western-educated professionals.

GO ON TO NEXT PAGE

Helsinki Accords: Political and human rights agreement signed in Helsinki, Finland, by the Soviet Union and Western European countries. (Bulliet, et al., *The Earth and Its Peoples,* 6th ed., p. 848)

63. Which of the following statements is accurate regarding the 1975 Helsinki Accords?
    (A) It paved the way for dialogue by calling for economic, social, and governmental contacts across the iron curtain.
    (B) It was a compromise that secured the boundaries between North and South Korea.
    (C) It created a nuclear nonproliferation agreement between the United States and the Soviet Union.
    (D) It punished communist countries for human rights abuses.

Employment opportunities created by the [Great] War played a major role in the migration of African-Americans from the rural south to the cities of the north.

64. Using the statement above and your knowledge of history, which of the following statements accurately reflects the economic effect of World War I on the United States?
    (A) Millions of Americans died, causing massive labor shortages.
    (B) The United States, economically drained from fighting the war, was suddenly plunged into a depression.
    (C) Employers were unable to fill jobs because all capable workers were sent to the front lines to fight.
    (D) The U.S. government and businesses grew rich from war production and loans.

65. Which of the following statements accurately reflects the environmental concerns in the post–World War II world?
    (A) Environmental concerns were limited to nonindustrial societies because they did not have the technology to deal with industrial waste.
    (B) New technologies required increased resources, led to increased consumption, and put a strain on the environment.
    (C) Environmental activism was less of a concern after World War II as nations began joining together to improve the environment.
    (D) Transnational corporations led the way in fighting against pollution and other environmental problems.

66. Economically, World War II affected people throughout Africa by
    (A) increasing the wealth of African people as the sale of raw materials increased exponentially.
    (B) increasing production and a small-scale industrial revolution that produced war materials for Western nations.
    (C) causing inflation, requisitions of raw materials, and increasing amounts of forced labor.
    (D) resulting in political freedom for African nations and individuals.

67. In what way did the Korean War benefit Japan?
    (A) Japan was able to gain wealth by producing and selling weapons.
    (B) It weakened North Korea and South Korea, which allowed Japan the opportunity to conquer both nations.
    (C) The Japanese economy was stimulated through large-scale purchases of supplies by the U.S. military and spending by American servicemen on leave in Japan.
    (D) It gave Japan the opportunity to serve as a global mediator and regain international trust.

"I know that in your minds there are questions like these; you are saying, 'Woman Suffrage is sure to come; the emancipation of humanity is an evolutionary process, and how is it that some women, instead of trusting to that evolution, instead of educating the masses of people of their country, instead of educating their own sex to prepare them for citizenship, how is it that these militant women are using violence and upsetting the business arrangements of the country in their undue impatience to attain their end?'" (Emmeline Pankhurst, Overfield, et al., 7th ed., p. 285)

68. At the beginning of the twentieth century, leaders of women's rights organizations such as Emmeline Pankhurst most forcefully demanded which of the following?
    (A) An end of male domination in educational institutions
    (B) The right to vote in national and local elections
    (C) A socialist political system that would create gender equity
    (D) A ban on the sale of alcohol

69. What political effect did the Great Depression have on Latin America?
    (A) Proliferation of military rule and authoritarian governments
    (B) Increased freedoms of speech, press, and assembly
    (C) Increased democratization across the continent
    (D) Large-scale growth in the sale of raw materials

70. Which of the following statements is an accurate comparison of the goals of Ho Chi Minh of Vietnam and Cuba's Fidel Castro?
    (A) Castro sought to establish communism in Cuba, while Ho Chi Minh was a nationalist revolutionary with a strong belief in capitalism.
    (B) Both sought primarily to rid their nations of foreign influence and adopted communism as a way to create greater equality in their respective nations.
    (C) Castro always had pro-Soviet tendencies, whereas Ho Chi Minh, weary of Soviet support, sought support from the French.
    (D) Neither Castro nor Ho Chi Minh found success in defeating the more powerful US military.

STOP
END OF SECTION I

IF YOU FINISH BEFORE TIME IS CALLED, YOU MAY CHECK YOUR WORK ON THIS SECTION. DO NOT GO ON TO SECTION II UNTIL YOU ARE TOLD TO DO SO.

Section II: Free-Response Essays

NOTE This exam uses the chronological designations B.C.E. (before the Common Era) and C.E. (Common Era). These labels correspond to B.C. (before Christ) and A.D. (anno Domini), which are used in some world history textbooks.

Part A: Document-Based Question (DBQ)
Suggested writing time—40 minutes
Percent of Section II score—33⅓

DIRECTIONS The following question is based on the accompanying Documents 1–8. The documents have been edited for the purpose of this exercise. Write your answer on the lined pages of the Section II free-response booklet.

This question is designed to test your ability to work with and understand historical documents.

Write an essay that

- has a relevant thesis and supports that thesis with evidence from the documents.

- uses all of the documents.

- analyzes the documents by grouping them in as many appropriate ways as possible. Does not simply summarize the documents individually.

- takes into account the sources of the documents and analyzes the authors' points of view.

- identifies and explains the need for at least one additional type of document.

You may refer to relevant historical information not mentioned in the documents.

1. Using the documents, analyze the roles of women in twentieth-century political movements.

HISTORICAL BACKGROUND: Women's rights played a significant role in the history of western Europe and North America in the late nineteenth and early twentieth centuries. Communist leaders considered women, at least legally, to be equal to men.

Document 1

Source: Petition by Ellen Leeuw and 122 South African black women to the Mayor of Johannesburg, 1910.

It is well known that our husbands are getting low wages and cannot afford to discharge their liabilities unless they get our assistance. All classes of work formerly performed by women are now in the hands of men, such as kitchen or general servants work, washing and ironing, eating houses for natives, nursing in native hospitals.

Document 2

Source: H. N. Brailsford, British socialist, from his book *Rebel India,* describing Indian women's efforts to keep shoppers from buying British goods during the boycott, 1931.

In ones and twos women were resting themselves on chairs at the doors of certain shops....If anyone attempted to enter, the lady joined her hands in supplication; she pleaded, she reasoned, and if all else failed, she would throw herself across the threshold and dared him to walk over her body.

Document 3

Source: Josie Mpama, commenting on a law that further restricted the mobility of South African black women, 1937.

We women can no longer remain in the background or concern ourselves only with domestic and sports affairs. The time has arrived for women to enter the political field and stand shoulder to shoulder with their men in the struggle.

Document 4

Source: Draft Constitution for the African National Congress, a group founded to promote the rights of South African blacks, 1945.

In the Congress women members shall enjoy the same status as men, and shall be entitled to elect and be elected to any position including the highest office. Notwithstanding this fact, however, and without in any way diminishing the rights of women members, the Congress may, recognizing the special disabilities and differences to which African women are subjected and because of the peculiar problems facing them, and in order to arouse their interest and facilitate their organization, create a Women's Section within its machinery, to be known as the ANC Women's Section.

GO ON TO NEXT PAGE

Document 5

Source: Jawaharlal Nehru, from his book *The Discovery of India* published one year before he became the first prime minister of India, 1946.

Most of us menfolk were in prison. And then a remarkable thing happened. Our women came to the front and took charge of the struggle. Women had always been there, of course, but now there was an avalanche of them, which took not only the British government but their own menfolk by surprise. Here were these women, women of the upper middle classes, leading sheltered lives in their homes, peasant women, working class women, rich women, poor women, pouring out in their tens of thousands in defiance of government order and police lathi.*

*lathi means sticks.

Document 6

Source: Photograph of Haydee Santamaria and Celia Sanchez, female guerrilla rebel leaders, with Fidel Castro, the leader of the Cuban Revolution, 1950s.

Cengage Learning

Document 7

Source: Photograph of Argentinian president Juan Perón and his wife Eva Perón riding in a procession in Buenos Aires, 1952.

Bettman/Corbis

GO ON TO NEXT PAGE

Document 8

Source: Women's Charter, adopted at the founding conference of the Federation of South African Women, 1954.

Preamble: We, the women of South Africa, wives and mothers, working women and housewives, African, Indians, European and Coloured, hereby declare our aim of striving for the removal of all laws, regulations, conventions and customs that discriminate against us as women, and that deprive us in any way of our inherent right to the advantages, responsibilities and opportunities that society offers to any one section of the population.

Women's Lot: We women share with our menfolk the cares and anxieties imposed by poverty and its evils. As wives and mothers, it falls upon us to make small wages stretch a long way. It is we who feel the cries of our children when they are hungry and sick. It is our lot to keep and care for the homes that are too small, broken and dirty to be kept clean. We know the burden of looking after children and land when our husbands are away in the mines, on the farms, and in the towns earning our daily bread.

End of Part A

SECTION II, Part B: Continuity and Change Over Time Essay
Suggested planning and writing time—40 minutes
Percent of Section II score—33 ⅓

DIRECTIONS You are to answer the following question. You should spend 5 minutes organizing or outlining your essay.

Write an essay that

- ▓ has a relevant thesis and supports that thesis with appropriate historical evidence.
- ▓ addresses all parts of the question.
- ▓ uses world historical context to show continuities and changes over time.
- ▓ analyzes the process of continuity and change over time.

2. Analyze the continuities and changes in the relationship between political authority and religion in China from 600 to 1450.

End of Part B

SECTION II, Part C: Comparative Essay
Suggested planning and writing time—40 minutes
Percent of Section II score—33 ⅓

DIRECTIONS You are to answer the following question. You should spend 5 minutes organizing or outlining your essay.

Write an essay that

■ has a relevant thesis and supports that thesis with appropriate historical evidence.
■ addresses all parts of the question.
■ makes direct, relevant comparisons.
■ analyzes relevant reasons for similarities and differences.

3. Compare China's response to the West (Europe and the United States) from 1600–1800 to the response of ONE of the following countries to the interaction with the West from 1600 to 1800.
    ■ Russia
    ■ Japan

ANSWERS FOR SECTION I

ANSWER KEY FOR MULTIPLE-CHOICE QUESTIONS

1. A	15. C	29. A	43. D	57. C
2. D	16. B	30. C	44. D	58. D
3. C	17. D	31. A	45. D	59. D
4. B	18. B	32. C	46. D	60. D
5. A	19. C	33. C	47. D	61. A
6. D	20. C	34. D	48. C	62. D
7. C	21. A	35. D	49. C	63. A
8. C	22. C	36. D	50. C	64. B
9. D	23. D	37. A	51. C	65. B
10. C	24. C	38. A	52. A	66. C
11. C	25. C	39. A	53. A	67. C
12. B	26. B	40. A	54. C	68. B
13. C	27. B	41. B	55. B	69. A
14. D	28. C	42. C	56. C	70. B

SCORING The multiple-choice section counts for 50 percent of your examination grade.

EXPLANATIONS FOR THE MULTIPLE-CHOICE ANSWERS

1. ANSWER: A. The adoption of food production transformed societies and supported gradual population increase and stratification of society because there was a more reliable food supply (HTS: Causation, historical Interpretation. *The Earth and Its Peoples*, 5th ed., p. 23/6th ed., p. 18).

2. ANSWER: D. In the face of dispersion, known as the Diaspora, Jews maintained a strong sense of culture and unity even though they were spread over great distances. This was facilitated by institutions like the synagogue, which physically brings Jews together and serves as the center of religion and education (HTS: Patterns of changes and continuity over time, contextualization. *The Earth and Its Peoples*, 5th ed., p. 117/6th ed., p. 59).

3. ANSWER: C. Neither Egypt nor Mesopotamia used coinage. Both had a complex writing system and several densely populated urban centers. Both also relied on slaves captured in battles (HTS: Comparison, contextualization. *The Earth and Its Peoples*, 5th ed., p. 39/6th ed., p. 19).

4. ANSWER: B. This image of Buddha from the second or third century C.E. is from northwest India (HTS: Synthesis. *The Earth and Its Peoples*, 5th ed., p. 212/6th ed., p. 171).

5. ANSWER: **A.** The domestication of the camel made it easier for people to roam the desert and trade goods across the Sahara (HTS: Historical argumentation. *The Earth and Its Peoples*, 5th ed., p. 212/6th ed., p. 234).

6. ANSWER: **D.** The Silk Road spanned Asia and thus connected the Mediterranean with East Asia. Although the quotes indicate an economic connection, they emphasize the social connection that the roads facilitated (HTS: Synthesis, historical argumentation. *The Earth and Its Peoples*, 5th ed., p. 200/6th ed., pp. 226–227).

7. ANSWER: **C.** Among the most lasting consequences of the rise of the Roman Empire was the spread of Latin and the Roman lifestyle. This Romanization was most dramatic in the western portion of the empire (HTS: Periodization, causation. *The Earth and Its Peoples*, 5th ed., pp. 179–180/6th ed., p. 95).

8. ANSWER: **C.** Metallurgy in the Americas developed in the Andean region, and the gold and silver artifacts from the Chavín show clear advances in the technology (HTS: Synthesis, argumentation. *The Earth and Its Peoples*, 5th ed., p. 86/6th ed., p. 196).

9. ANSWER: **A.** Monotheism, as prescribed by Christianity, undermined the authority of the Roman emperors, who wished to be viewed as divine, and the religion conflicted with the existing pantheon of gods. On the other hand, Buddhism came to China during Han rule and flourished in the post-Han era in part because it was more easily incorporated with existing values and beliefs (HTS: Comparison, contextualization. *The Earth and Its Peoples*, 5th ed., p. 201/6th ed., p. 147).

10. ANSWER: **B.** Both the Persian and Roman Empires developed a system that included some level of local autonomy and control. The Roman Empire was also administered through a series of networks and towns (HTS: Comparison, contextualization. *The Earth and Its Peoples*, 5th ed., pp. 135, 178–179/6th ed., pp. 109, 160).

11. ANSWER: **C.** Continental axis, lack of domesticatable animals, and fewer agriculturally productive crops resulted in Western Hemisphere civilizations such as the Chavín and the Moche developing later than similar types of civilizations in the Eastern Hemisphere (HTS: Comparison, synthesis, contextualization, periodization. *The Earth and Its Peoples*, 5th ed., p. 61/6th ed., p. 192).

12. ANSWER: **B.** A kingship emerged as urban centers arose. Kings also oversaw religious rituals that were used to control the society (HTS: Interpretation, synthesis. *The Earth and Its Peoples*, 5th ed., pp. 84–85/6th ed., p. 192).

13. ANSWER: **C.** An important economic and cultural continuity for the Andean civilizations between 600 and 1450 was the use of labor systems like the ayllu and mit'a, which required clans to work together to care for the herds and fields as well as work on larger public works projects (HTS: Comparison, periodization. *The Earth and Its Peoples*, 5th ed., p. 324/6th ed., p. 208).

14. ANSWER: **D.** There is evidence that certain North American societies were influenced by Mesoamerican agriculture, technology, and culture, but

many of the buildings and dwellings constructed in North America were unique to the needs of the particular region (HTS: Causation. *The Earth and Its Peoples*, 5th ed., pp. 319–322/6th ed., p. 207).

15. **ANSWER: C.** With the rise of new empires and cities in both places, the city-states of tropical Africa and Asia and the nation-states of late-medieval Europe were able to facilitate religious learning—Islam in the former and Christianity in the latter (HTS: Comparison, periodization. *The Earth and Its Peoples*, 5th ed. p. 422/6th ed., pp. 247–248).

16. **ANSWER: B.** Islam would not spread to sub-Saharan Africa until circa 1200, and some of the greatest Muslim states would be established there (HTS: Periodization. *The Earth and Its Peoples*, 5th ed., p. 234/6th ed., p. 252).

17. **ANSWER: D.** There was no concept of the Mandate of Heaven in Japan. Because there was only one imperial dynasty, warfare over the imperial seat was limited. The emperor was more of a figurehead, and real power was in the hands of others (HTS: Comparison. *The Earth and Its Peoples*, 5th ed., pp. 301–302/6th ed., p. 312).

18. **ANSWER: B.** Early Christianity spread quite naturally through trade within the Mediterranean region. Areas of North Africa such as Egypt and areas of eastern Africa such as Ethiopia had strong Christian traditions (HTS: Causation. *The Earth and Its Peoples*, 5th ed., pp. 867–870/6th ed., p. 275).

19. **ANSWER: C.** Even though Muslims controlled a huge territory, they did not require immediate conversion, and initially most Muslims were Arab. However, by the ninth century, more and more non-Arabs began to convert (HTS: Causation, periodization. *The Earth and Its Peoples*, 5th ed., p. 234/6th ed., p. 253).

20. **ANSWER: C.** The Bantu migration in Africa and the Arya (Indo-European) migration into South Asia brought linguistic and cultural changes. The Arya migration into India established the varna system, the foundation for the caste system, while the Bantu displaced the hunting and gathering lifestyle (HTS: Comparison. *The Earth and Its Peoples*, 5th ed., pp. 209–210, 254–255/6th ed., pp. 167, 221).

21. **ANSWER: A.** In many ways the Crusades increased the flow of intellectual ideas and goods to western Europe, which would be critical for European revival and the Renaissance. Exposure to the sophisticated Muslim world showed Europeans how much their own societies were missing (HTS: Causation, patterns of change and continuity over time. *The Earth and Its Peoples*, 5th ed., pp. 275–277/6th ed., p. 289).

22. **ANSWER: C.** Controlling water and moving it to where it was needed was crucial for sustaining life in both the Tang dynasty and the Delhi Sultanate (HTS: Comparison, contextualization. *The Earth and Its Peoples*, 5th ed., pp. 375–376/6th ed., pp. 298, 375).

23. **ANSWER: D.** The Indian Ocean trade network brought merchants from Arabic-speaking lands to the east coast of Africa, where their vocabulary was incorporated into the Swahili language. The word Swahili comes from an Arabic term meaning "shores of the blacks"

(HTS: Contextualization. *The Earth and Its Peoples*, 5th ed., p. 387/6th ed., p. 388).

24. ANSWER: **C.** The Mongols had a huge impact on the Russian economy through heavy taxation as well as their domination of trade. Russian princes who submitted to Mongol authority benefited politically and economically (HTS: Contextualization, patterns of change and continuity. *The Earth and Its Peoples*, 5th ed., pp. 353–354/6th ed., pp. 332–333).

25. ANSWER: **C.** The eastern portion of the Roman Empire survived the migration of Germanic tribes that decimated the western portion. It became known as the Byzantine Empire, and its vitality contrasted greatly with the stagnation of western Europe (HTS: Periodization, patterns of change and continuity. *The Earth and Its Peoples*, 5th ed., pp. 156–157/6th ed., pp. 151–152).

26. ANSWER: **D.** New abilities with weaponry—in particular, the use of fire-arms and armor-piercing bows—meant that knights were no longer effective soldiers for kings to employ through the vassal system. This change was exemplified in the Hundred Years War (HTS: Periodization, causation. *The Earth and Its Peoples*, 5th ed., pp. 419–420/6th ed., pp. 367–369).

27. ANSWER: **B.** All university classes were taught in Latin, so students and instructors could communicate no matter where they were from. This allowed students and professors to travel to study at the universities that focused on the discipline they wanted (HTS: Periodization. *The Earth and Its Peoples*, 5th ed., pp. 412–413/6th ed., p. 363).

28. ANSWER: **C.** Ibn Battuta visited Mali in 1353, during the reign of Mansa Suleiman. He commented on much that he saw there, particularly the influence of Islam on society. Mali is the only Islamic state/empire of the choices given (HTS: Periodization, interpretation, synthesis. *The Earth and Its Peoples*, 5th ed., pp. 385–386/6th ed., p. 385).

29. ANSWER: **A.** Both Korea and the Ming Empire wanted to establish indigenous authority after years of control by foreigners, and Confucianism gained strength in the Ming Empire in particular. Mongol contributions were long-lasting, however (HTS: Causation, periodization. *The Earth and Its Peoples*, 5th ed., pp. 358–359, 364/6th ed., pp. 332, 341).

30. ANSWER: **C.** The cross displayed prominently around the noble's neck reflects the Portuguese determination to spread Christianity as they explored the world. In West Africa, the Christian religion was virtually unknown before the arrival of the Europeans in the late fifteenth century (HTS: Synthesis. *The Earth and Its Peoples*, 5th ed., pp. 440–441/6th ed., p. 415).

31. ANSWER: **A.** North Africa had long since become a part of the Islamic world, and traders had helped to spread Islam—and its practices and influences—over land and sea to trading centers in sub-Saharan Africa (HTS: Periodization, patterns of change and continuity. *The Earth and Its Peoples*, 5th ed., p. 537/6th ed., p. 392).

32. ANSWER: **C.** During this period, the global economy was transformed dramatically by the rise of the sea-based empires of western Europe. As European maritime exploration and trade expanded, the relative significance of the Silk Road trade began to decrease, leading to economic and political instability within the Ottoman Empire (HTS: Synthesis, historical argumentation. *The Earth and Its Peoples*, 5th ed., p. 555/6th ed., p. 408).

33. ANSWER: **C.** In an era of rapidly changing military technology and tactics, both the Ottoman Empire cavalry and nomadic Safavid warriors resisted giving up their traditional bows for guns. Leaders in both empires responded by creating a new corps of soldiers made up of slaves equipped with firearms (HTS: Comparison, periodization. *The Earth and Its Peoples*, 5th ed., p. 560/6th ed., p. 527).

34. ANSWER: **D.** The peoples conquered by the Aztecs were occasionally called upon to provide labor for large-scale engineering projects, but were primarily used to produce tribute items of food, cloth, military equipment—and as victims for religious sacrifice. In contrast, the Inca ayllus maintained the mit'a system, which provided one-seventh of its adult males to serve the empire in various temporary, rotating capacities (HTS: Comparison. *The Earth and Its Peoples*, 5th ed., pp. 318–319/6th ed., pp. 214–215).

35. ANSWER: **D.** The Atlantic System had mostly negative effects, economic and otherwise on Latin America and Africa but did not transform Africa the way it transformed the Americas. The African continent remained under indigenous control, and Africa's cultural and political links with the Islamic world remained stronger (for the time being) than their connections with Europe (HTS: Periodization, causation. *The Earth and Its Peoples*, 5th ed., pp. 538–539/6th ed., p. 424).

36. ANSWER: **D.** Although economic and scientific changes were important, neither specific example was correct. It was not until after 1750 that the Enlightenment eventually brought great political change in Europe and the Americas, thus making the political change incorrect as well. The only plausible revolution was the protestant revolution which wrought numerous changes to Europe (HTS: Periodization, contextualization. *The Earth and Its Peoples*, 5th ed., pp. 475, 476–478, 483/6th ed., pp. 435–436).

37. ANSWER: **A.** The waterways and forests of North America provided an ideal habitat for beaver and other animals whose pelts were in high demand by consumers in chilly European climates. French settlers in Canada and Louisiana cultivated mutually beneficial trade relationships with knowledgeable Amerindians to expand the profitable fur market (HTS: Synthesis, contextualization. *The Earth and Its Peoples*, 5th ed., pp. 508–509/6th ed., p. 483).

38. ANSWER: **A.** By 1750, Russia had emerged from Mongol domination and assembled the world's largest land empire. The task of administering such a huge, diverse land-based empire would be difficult under any circumstances, but it was particularly so in an era marked by the European sea-based empires' dominance of the global economy (HTS: Synthesis, historic argumentation. *The Earth and Its Peoples*, 5th ed., p. 592/6th ed., pp. 539–540).

39. ANSWER: **A.** Western Europe led the globalization of world trade, and soon had linked West Africa and the Americas in the transfer of raw materials, manufactured goods, and peoples known as the Atlantic System; also, in the sixteenth and seventeenth centuries, many European nations took colonial possessions in Southeast Asia (such as the Spanish conquest of the Philippines in 1570). In East Asia, however, China and Japan rigorously defended their economic autonomy and political sovereignty against the pressures of a rapidly changing world economy (HTS: Argumentation, synthesis. *The Earth and Its Peoples,* 5th ed., p. 565/6th ed., p. 568).

40. ANSWER: **A.** Although slaves became the most valuable West African export during this period, other goods such as gold, ivory, and timber continued to make up a significant percentage of the region's total trade volume (HTS: Periodization, causation. *The Earth and Its Peoples,* 5th ed., p. 534/6th ed., p. 508).

41. ANSWER: **B.** Determining the role of the Catholic Church and the amount of power for the military were two of the major issues for newly independent Latin American nations. As these nations attempted to create democratic institutions, charismatic military leaders often stepped in and assumed dictatorial powers, limiting the development of these young democracies (HTS: Contextualization, comparison. *The Earth and Its Peoples,* 5th ed., pp. 663–664/6th ed., p. 665).

42. ANSWER: **C.** By the end of the nineteenth century, Amerindian groups in the Americas had been militarily defeated, and many nations actively worked to break apart their tribal ties (HTS: Contextualization, periodization. *The Earth and Its Peoples,* 5th ed., pp. 669–670/6th ed., pp. 671–672).

43. ANSWER: **D.** Britain would end up with a huge imperial empire by the end of the nineteenth century, but its chief goal was the creation of trading posts in an effort to expand free trade throughout the world (HTS: Contextualization, periodization. *The Earth and Its Peoples,* 5th ed., pp. 729, 731/6th ed., p. 703).

44. ANSWER: **D.** Africans had a wide variety of responses to European colonial invasion, but some were able to modernize equipment to fight off European invaders (HTS: Causation, contextualization. *The Earth and Its Peoples,* 5th ed., pp. 780–781/6th ed., pp. 700–701).

45. ANSWER: **D.** The British were able to finally stop the transatlantic slave trade in 1867, but that did not end the demand for slaves. Slave traders moved to both southern and eastern Africa and continued supplying slave markets in Brazil and the Middle East (HTS: Causation, periodization. *The Earth and Its Peoples,* 5th ed., pp. 719–720/6th ed., p. 695).

46. ANSWER: **D.** The reforming Ottoman military leader quickly found out that Eurpoan firearms had the reputation of falling apart in the harsh desert environments in which the Turks fought (HTS: Synthesis, argumentation. *The Earth and Its Peoples,* 5th ed., p. 692/6th ed., p. 527).

47. ANSWER: **D.** The French and Indian War, known as the Seven Years War in Europe, pushed France off the mainland of North America when it

was forced to cede New France to Spain and Great Britain. According to the terms of the 1763 Treaty of Paris, France would retain only its colonial possessions in the Caribbean (HTS: Interpretation, periodization. *The Earth and Its Peoples,* 5th ed., pp. 510–511/6th ed., p. 606).

48. ANSWER: C.   Unlike earlier forms of colonialism, the Industrial Revolution led to the growing importance for imperial powers to control raw materials. As large regions of Asia and Africa were taken over, European colonial powers tapped local natural resources to support their own industrial development (HTS: Patterns of change and continuity over time. *The Earth and Its Peoples,* 5th ed., pp. 791, 793/6th ed., p. 711).

49. ANSWER: C. Although the Qing understood the threat posed by opium and had had a sufficient number of troops to fight in the war, their premodern army and nonexistent navy was easily defeated by Britain (HTS: Causation, periodization. *The Earth and Its Peoples,* 5th ed., pp. 700–701/6th ed., p. 645).

50. ANSWER: C.   When Hideyoshi and his army invaded the Chinese province of Manchuria, they significantly weakened the Ming Empire's military presence there. Manchu forces were thus allowed to build their resistance, and eventually aid Chinese rebels in toppling the Ming Empire and proclaiming their own rule in China (HTS: Causation, synthesis. *The Earth and Its Peoples,* 5th ed., pp. 574–575/6th ed., p. 747).

51. ANSWER: C. The harsh effects that industrialism had on the working class, coupled with Enlightenment ideas of equality, gave rise to socialism in the nineteenth century (HTS: Causation, contextualization. *The Earth and Its Peoples,* 5th ed., pp. 751, 753/6th ed., p. 596).

52. ANSWER: A.   The nineteenth century ushered in the age of industrialism. During this period, working-class women left the home and took jobs in factories and domestic service (HTS: Periodization, patterns of change and continuity over time. *The Earth and Its Peoples,* 5th ed., pp. 751, 753/6th ed., p. 595).

53. ANSWER: D. While Spanish explorers initiated the first links between Europe and the Americas at the start of the sixteenth century, the Portuguese were beginning to take control of vital trading ports in the Indian Ocean. Soon both Latin America and South Asia were enmeshed in the developing global trade network (HTS: Comparison, periodization. *The Earth and Its Peoples,* 5th ed., p. 427/6th ed., p. 411).

54. ANSWER: C. The Safavid Empire was a land-based empire—like Ming- and Qing-era China—in a period when wealth and power were shifting to sea-based empires, such as Spain, England, and France (HTS: Comparison, contextualization. *The Earth and Its Peoples,* 5th ed., p. 592/6th ed., pp. 532–533).

55. ANSWER: B.   Ethnic minorities were expected to embrace the Turkification of the empire as a way to show their allegiance to the state (HTS: Synthesis, conceptualization. *The Earth and Its Peoples,* 5th ed., pp. 799–800/6th ed., p. 754).

56. **ANSWER: C.** Newly independent nations faced numerous problems, most especially the ethnic and language divisions that emanated from artificially created political entities (HTS: Synthesis, causation. *The Earth and Its Peoples,* 5th ed., pp. 895–896/6th ed., p. 848).

57. **ANSWER: C.** Most early Indian nationalist leaders had been educated in Europe (HTS: Comparison, contextualization, periodization. *The Earth and Its Peoples,* 5th ed., pp. 727–728/6th ed., p. 791).

58. **ANSWER: D.** During the late 1980s, a movement, led largely by students and intellectuals, spread in China, calling for more democracy and an end to corruption as well as inflation. In 1989, hundreds were killed in Tiananmen Square in Beijing when government tanks moved into the square where hundreds of thousands were protesting (HTS: Synthesis, contextualization. *The Earth and Its Peoples,* 5th ed., pp. 923–924/6th ed., p. 876).

59. **ANSWER: D.** When Soviet leader Mikhail Gorbachev came to power in 1985, he implemented a number of major reforms. *Glasnost,* his policy of political openness, allowed criticism of the government and communist party. *Perestroika* was his effort to address economic problems and move the nation away from planning by the state to a more open economic system (HTS: Historical interpretation. *The Earth and Its Peoples,* 5th ed., pp. 924–925/6th ed., p. 877).

60. **ANSWER: D.** British efforts to control the Middle East were quite transparent. They used both bribery and intimidation. After the British propped up the leader of the Arab Revolt, Faisal, as the King of Iraq, they came to an agreement with Faisal's government. Official independence for Iraq would be granted in exchange for Great Britain's right to maintain two air bases in Iraq, as well as a military alliance. Moreover, Great Britain was guaranteed a continued flow of petroleum (HTS: Patterns of change and continuity over time, causation. *The Earth and Its Peoples,* 5th ed., p. 819/6th ed., p. 859).

61. **ANSWER: A.** The similarity between the two conflicts is that the United States invaded Iraq both times. U.S. military superiority was clearly obvious both times, although the United States decided against pushing into Baghdad during the Gulf War. While the United States would have liked to use Iraq as an example of democracy and thus plant the seeds for political change in other countries within the region, there is no evidence to connect the events to the recent Arab Spring (HTS: Comparison, change and continuity over time. *The Earth and Its Peoples,* 5th ed., pp. 925–926, 954–955/6th ed., pp. 879, 906–907).

62. **ANSWER: D.** The Indian National Congress was established in 1885 by a small group of English-speaking Hindu professionals for the purpose of fighting for the political rights of Indians. Similarly, the African National Congress was a political organization established by English-speaking, Western-educated South Africans in 1909 (HTS: Comparison, contextualization. *The Earth and Its Peoples,* 5th ed., pp. 861–862, 870/6th ed., pp. 791, 802).

63. **ANSWER: A.** Close to forty nations, including the Soviet Union and the United States, signed the Helsinki Accords in 1975. The agreement

called for the assurance that boundaries within Europe would not be changed by military force. It also called for economic, political, and social contacts across the iron curtain (HTS: Historic interpretation, synthesis. *The Earth and Its Peoples*, 5th ed., pp. 895–896/6th ed., p. 848).

64. **ANSWER: D.** When the United States abandoned its neutral policy in 1917 and joined the war, the government, as well as businesses, made huge profits from war production. The war also played a major role in expanding employment opportunities for women and African-Americans (HTS: Synthesis, causation. *The Earth and Its Peoples*, 5th ed., pp. 805–806/6th ed., p. 759).

65. **ANSWER: B.** While new technologies increased productivity and resulted in increased wealth for industrialized nations, they also had negative effects on the environment. Factories sprang up and threatened the environment. Rain forests were depleted, pollution increased, and the erosion of soil became a constant problem (HTS: Periodization, contextualization. *The Earth and Its Peoples*, 5th ed., p. 935/6th ed., p. 888).

66. **ANSWER: C.** World War II resulted in increased hardships for people throughout Africa, and thus further incited the various independence movements. The war caused inflation, as well as the increase in forced labor. Moreover, raw materials were requisitioned by the colonial governments in order to fuel the war effort (HTS: Periodization, contextualization. *The Earth and Its Peoples*, 5th ed., pp. 866–867/6th ed., pp. 850–851).

67. **ANSWER: C.** Despite the many restrictions placed on Japan by the Allied Powers after World War II, the Japanese economy bounced back in many ways, thanks to the Korean War. The war in Korea stimulated the Japanese economy much as the Marshall Plan had for Western Europe. Because of Japan's proximity to Korea, massive supplies were purchased from Japan by the U.S. military. Moreover, U.S. servicemen on leave spent money in Japan, which also served as a stimulus for growth (HTS: Periodization. *The Earth and Its Peoples*, 5th ed., p. 893/6th ed., p. 873).

68. **ANSWER: B.** Women's rights groups worked for many different goals during the early twentieth century, but the most important of these was the struggle to achieve suffrage, voting rights for women (HTS: Synthesis, argumentation. *The Earth and Its Peoples*, 5th ed., pp. 751, 753/6th ed., p. 785).

69. **ANSWER: A.** The Depression caused massive unemployment, homelessness, and instability throughout Latin America. In response, military officers seized power in many countries. They imposed authoritarian control, often imitating the European dictatorships in hopes of stimulating their economies (HTS: Periodization, causation. *The Earth and Its Peoples*, 5th ed., p. 838/6th ed., pp. 798–799).

70. **ANSWER: B.** While Cuba gained political independence well before Vietnam, both were still dominated economically by the United States. The popular rebellion led by Castro was in protest of foreign economic domination, political repression, and corruption under the Batista

regime. Vietnam was still a French colony during the Cold War, and suffered under the brutality of its French occupiers. Like Castro, Ho Chi Minh led a movement to free Vietnam from colonial rule. Ho Chi Minh turned to communism after his appeal for independence was rejected at the Treaty of Versailles. While Castro gained support from the USSR, evidence suggests that his efforts were aimed mainly at ending foreign power in Cuba and creating a dramatic social transformation (HTS: Comparison. *The Earth and Its Peoples,* 5th ed., pp. 893, 901/6th ed., pp. 846, 847).

ANSWER FOR SECTION II, PART A: DOCUMENT-BASED QUESTION (DBQ)

THE DOCUMENTS

Below are short analyses of the documents. The italicized words suggest what your margin notes might include:

DOCUMENT 1 This document shows some of the issues women are facing in terms of working and supporting their families. *This document also shows women carrying out political roles by petitioning the government.*

DOCUMENT 2 *This document shows the lengths Indian women went to in order to fight against British colonial rule in India. This boycott tactic was a powerful strategy that would be used by other groups in history.*

DOCUMENT 3 This is *a call for women to act and to be involved politically with what is happening to women and in the larger struggle for equal treatment.*

DOCUMENT 4 This document shows the African National Congress responding to women's call for equal political representation in one of the key organizations fighting for African rights in southern Africa. *This document is an example of women's goals of having equal status while at the same time acknowledging women's particular concerns.*

DOCUMENT 5 *The document gives insight into women's active participation in the Indian independence movement.*

DOCUMENT 6 Both women are noted revolutionary leaders in the Cuban Revolution. You see them both armed here and in that way *they are carrying out roles that are stereotypically thought of as men's roles in revolution.*

DOCUMENT 7 *This image shows Perón with her husband in what might seem like an expected role for a woman.* Yet Eva Perón had a powerful influence on the politics of Argentina in the mid-twentieth century, and she was a hero of the working class.

DOCUMENT 8 This document is similar to Document 3 in that it *describes the ongoing struggles of both men and women living under an oppressive regime in South Africa. It calls for particular rights for women as well as the general fight against poverty. This is another example of women organizing politically.*

There are several ways to group the documents; you could group by location—Africa, Latin America, and India—by time, by the types of roles, or by the types of goals you see addressed in the documents.

YOUR ESSAY FOR THE DOCUMENT-BASED QUESTION

For this DBQ, you need to be sure your thesis makes an analytical argument for the differing roles women played as described in the documents. The documents can be grouped in a few ways, and the key will be to analyze those groups in light of the prompt. There are some good opportunities for point of view as well—in particular, notice Nehru's tone in Document 5. The tone in Document 2 could work well for point of view, and if you address point of view with reference to several of the other documents, you can get expanded core points.

For your analysis, it is important to remember the historical context. A discussion of what was happening in India, South Africa, and Latin America at the time is an important component of your essay. Both India and South Africa were experiencing the inequalities of imperial rule firsthand, and women suffered in particular ways because of those inequalities. Latin America was not experiencing direct colonial rule; the Cuban Revolution was affected by global conflict, while Argentina was facing similar internal political struggles with political leadership.

The documents give good insight into the global issues. You should also devote some attention to an analysis of the many issues faced by women as caregivers and political activists. What are women's roles at home? What are women's roles in the nation?

SCORING 1 point for thesis in the opening line, 1 point for understanding the basic meaning of all documents, 2 points for using all of the documents as evidence that supported the thesis, 1 point for analyzing the point of view in two documents, 1 point for two groupings, and 1 point for an explanation of possible additional documents. If the essay earns basic core, it can also earn 2 expanded core points for having relevant outside historical content, for persuasively using the documents as evidence, and for proposing—in addition to the one extra document required for basic core—a second extra document.

The DBQ essay counts for one-third of the free-response grade, one-sixth of the examination grade.

ANSWER FOR SECTION II, PART B:
CONTINUITY AND CHANGE OVER TIME QUESTION

This essay asks you to address major changes and continuities in the role of religion or a belief system in supporting and justifying political authority from 600 to 1450. Let's say you chose China, and thus Confucianism. Be sure you address both change and continuity and have an analytical statement evaluating Confucianism's significance in supporting and justifying political authority.

A good place to start is with an overview of key Confucian principles that are prominent in the beginning of the period. Confucianism was the foundation for China's political and social structure by the time of the Han dynasty, and would be a continuity throughout the period. The importance of family roles, patriarchal order, education, and ethical conduct was woven into the ethos of Chinese life from the emperor to the smallest child. The Confucian concept of the Mandate of Heaven was also an important political continuity in the period, and you should elaborate on that. Another important political continuity is the impact of Confucian thought and ideas on the political structure of countries in the region, including Korea and Japan. These countries had some political similarities but also some key differences. Still, Confucianism had an impact.

As other influences come into East Asia, including Buddhism and outside rulers like the Mongols, we see changes regarding the incorporation of Confucian ideas, as well as the principles of Confucian thought. Neo-Confucianism in the Song period is an important example of change that you should discuss. Another change would be the Yuan Empire and the political changes that the Mongols brought in while keeping some of the Confucian traditions. The Ming Empire ends the period your essay is to cover with a resurgence of Confucian thought that brought back the civil service exams. This would be a good place to analyze why the Ming revived the exams in terms of asserting their political authority.

Be sure to discuss both changes and continuities and provide specific evidence for your claims. That, along with good analysis, should get a high score on this essay.

SCORING 1 point for a thesis in the opening line that addresses the whole time period, 2 points for fully addressing the question in terms of both change and continuity, 2 points for appropriate evidence to support the thesis, 1 point for the global context, and 1 point for analysis of change and continuity. If basic core is earned, 2 expanded core points can be earned for addressing all parts of the questions evenly and providing good evidence rooted in a solid understanding of the global events that brought about change.

The continuity and change over time essay counts for one-third of the free-response grade, one-sixth of the examination grade.

ANSWER FOR SECTION II, PART C: COMPARATIVE QUESTION

This essay asks you to compare the policy of China to one out of two countries in terms of their interaction with the West from the sixteenth through the eighteenth centuries. Be sure to include both similarities and differences in order to get the full points for addressing the question.

Of the three, Russia was unique in that it made some radical changes in an effort to embrace Western ideals under the leadership of autocrats like Peter the Great. China took a more cautious approach, limiting trade using the Canton system in order to keep careful control over economic interactions with foreigners; one specific example of this might be the failure of the British Macartney mission in the late eighteenth century, which did not succeed in getting China to increase foreign trade. Japan took an even stronger approach, severely limiting interaction through trade and basically cutting off interaction with the West under the Tokugawa Shogunate, which lasted until 1868. Here you should analyze why each country made its particular choice regarding interaction with the West, comparing and contrasting their reasons. All three regions were protective of their domestic traditions and cultural identities. Remember, you must compare China to either Russia OR Japan.

Again, be sure to discuss similarities and differences, and take the time to analyze why you are claiming certain similarities and differences. Use good evidence to support your comparisons so you can get a high score.

SCORING 1 point for the thesis in the opening line, 2 points for addressing both similarities and differences, 2 points for using accurate evidence that supports the main ideas presented in the thesis, 1 point for making a number of specific direct comparisons, and 1 point for analysis. If the essay earns basic core, consistent use of both evidence and direct comparison will earn another 2 points for expanded core.

The comparative essay counts for one-third of the free-response grade, one-sixth of the examination grade.

CALCULATING YOUR SCORE

The following is based on the 2011 AP World History Examination, which is the only released examination at this time.

SCORING THE MULTIPLE-CHOICE SECTION

Use the following formula to calculate your raw score on the multiple-choice section of the exam:

_____ × 0.8571 = _____
 number   weighted Section I score
 correct
 (out of 70)

[Note: The guessing penalty has been eliminated for all AP exams starting with the 2011 exam.]

SCORING THE FREE-RESPONSE SECTION

Use the following formula to calculate your raw score on the free-response section of the exam:

Part A _____ × 2.2222 = _____
       (out of 9)   (do not round)

Part B _____ × 2.2222 = _____
       (out of 9)   (do not round)

Part C _____ × 2.2222 = _____
       (out of 9)   (do not round)

              Sum = _____
                    weighted Section II score
                    (do not round)

YOUR COMPOSITE SCORE

_____ + _____ = _____
weighted   weighted   composite score
Section I   Section II   (round to nearest whole number)
score   score

Once you have calculated your composite score, see where it falls in the Composite Score Range below. *Remember that your composite score is only an estimate of your performance on the College Board exam.*

AP GRADES BY SCORE RANGE

Composite Score Range	AP Grade
78–120	5
62–77	4
43–61	3
27–42	2
0–26	1